THE EARLY POEMS OF
JOHN CLARE
1804–1822

Volume I

For the first time all Clare's early poems are brought together with all known variants, and with Clare's characteristic vocabulary, grammar, spelling, and punctuation presented. The poems range from juvenilia to the published poems that first established Clare's reputation with *Poems Descriptive of Rural Life and Scenery* and *The Village Minstrel*; but the reader will appreciate how many more poems Clare composed in these early years that have not previously seen the light of day. Strenuous efforts have been made to recover poems obliterated in some of Clare's first manuscripts, and the complete text of *The Parish*, his major satirical poem, is included. A glossary is provided for both volumes, together with extensive annotation. Clare's own dating of his first poems is employed and every attempt has been made to establish a dependable chronology.

This edition provides the first reliable basis for a new assessment of Clare's poetic growth. The reader will be able to trace his growing assurance as a poet writing in a characteristic idiom of his own, and may be surprised to find how early Clare's individuality as a poet emerges.

ERIC ROBINSON is Professor of Modern History at the University of Massachusetts at Boston.

DAVID POWELL is the retired Technical Services Librarian of Nene College, Northampton.

MARGARET GRAINGER is Senior Lecturer at the West Sussex Institute of Higher Education.

THE EARLY POEMS OF
JOHN CLARE

1804–1822

Volume I

General editor
ERIC ROBINSON

Edited by
ERIC ROBINSON and DAVID POWELL

Associate editor
MARGARET GRAINGER

CLARENDON PRESS · OXFORD
1989

Oxford University Press, Walton Street, Oxford OX2 6DP
Oxford New York Toronto
Delhi Bombay Calcutta Madras Karachi
Petaling Jaya Singapore Hong Kong Tokyo
Nairobi Dar es Salaam Cape Town
Melbourne Auckland
and associated companies in
Berlin Ibadan

Oxford is a trade mark of Oxford University Press

Published in the United States
by Oxford University Press, New York

British Library Cataloguing in Publication Data
Clare, John, 1793–1864
The early poems of John Clare, 1804–1822.
(Oxford English texts). Vol. I
I. Title II. Robinson, Eric, 1924– III. Powell, David, 1925–
IV. Grainger, Margaret, 1936–
821'.7   PR4453.C6
ISBN 0–19–812314–0

Library of Congress Cataloging in Publication Data
Clare, John, 1793–1864.
The early poems of John Clare, 1804–1822.
Includes indexes.
I. Robinson, Eric, 1924– . II. Powell, David,
1925– . III. Grainger, Margaret, 1936–
IV. Title.
PR4453.C6A6 1989b 821'.7 87–31416
ISBN 0–19–812314–0

Set by Hope Services, Abingdon
Printed in Great Britain
at the University Printing House, Oxford
by David Stanford
Printer to the University

*To the John Clare Society and to
all friends of John Clare*

CONTENTS

VOLUME I

Poems from the following manuscripts are included in these volumes in the order in which they appear in the manuscripts, except where a note is included reserving them for treatment in another volume because the poems were printed in a volume published in Clare's lifetime or were copied by Clare into 'The Midsummer Cushion' volume. The copy-text, however, may not be the manuscript in which the poem first appears in our list here.

VOLUME II

INTRODUCTION

It is a miracle that John Clare ever became a poet. Everything was against him: an illiterate mother and barely literate father, agricultural poverty in a small village on the fringes of Northamptonshire, a strictly hierarchical society made more rigid by the tyranny of parish officials, and schooling limited to a dame-school and a nearby parish class-room, an education sporadic and incomplete. The story has often been told and has always excited wonder. It has a Dick Whittington style about it, though it was surely easier for a poor boy to succeed in commerce and by making a good marriage than it was for Clare to become a poet. It is sometimes said that there were precedents— Ann Yearsley, Stephen Duck, Thomas Chatterton, and Robert Bloomfield—but even Bloomfield, the best of these, is but a poor parallel to Clare. Who would dream of claiming for Bloomfield a place among the great poets of his age, as we demand for Clare? There is a majesty even in the length of Clare's life and in his persistent adherence to his poetic vocation. It is an education in the marvels of the human will to work among Clare's MSS, preserved for posterity by the burgesses of Peterborough and Northampton, who recognized, much earlier than the learned world, that they had a genius amongst them in the person of this village farm-boy. In one thing alone Clare has been fortunate. Throughout his life and through the generations after his death there have always been a few who have believed in him and in his creative genius. The MSS themselves are a testimony to his intoxication with his art, to the sharpness of his vision, and to the fecundity of his muse, but their tattered scraps of reused paper (letters, advertisements, and bills), their clumsily sewn gatherings, their smudges of goodness-knows-what, their home-made and corrosive ink, their quality as palimpsests, also tell of a poverty that few of us can imagine. Nevertheless it is not his poverty nor his difficulties that we wish to stress here, and in this at least we follow the poet's own desires. He wrote to Mrs Eliza Emmerson:

. . . all I wish now is to stand upon my own bottom as a poet without any apology as to want of education or any thing else & I say it not in the feeling of either ambition or vanity but in the spirit of common sense—[1]

[1] Clare to Mrs Emmerson, 13 Nov. 1832, in M. Storey (ed.), *Letters of John Clare*

It is in the spirit of common sense that we claim recognition for John Clare as one of England's greatest poets. For that claim to be asserted, let alone justified, it is necessary for readers to know what Clare has written, as they know the extent of other great poets' writings. Until now, editors of Clare have been Little Jack Horners—they have put in a thumb, into the pie of Clare's writings, and pulled out a plum and said, 'What a good boy am I!' We do not except ourselves from this criticism. But now the world must see John Clare whole, or as whole as a quarter-century of study can make him.

We have already published in two volumes of the Oxford English Texts as many poems as we could find of Clare's later years, starting with the last because more work had been done upon those poems and because there were fewer variant readings. The variants were fewer because most of the poems exist only in copies by an amanuensis and perhaps because Clare, neglected, forgotten, and insane, no longer reworked his poems as extensively as he had done in his earlier years. Now we turn to Clare's earliest poems, to the young tangled coppice and brush from which emerged his first published volumes, *Poems Descriptive of Rural Life and Scenery* and *The Village Minstrel*. The years of publication of these two volumes, 1820 and 1821, were the years in which Clare's publisher, John Taylor, had the greatest control over which of Clare's poems were to be read by the public at large. As will be seen, Taylor was heavily selective, for a variety of reasons. Commercially it would have been quite impossible to publish all the poems, or even a majority of the poems, that Clare had then written. Proper literary discrimination required also that the young poet should be presented in the best light possible and only his best work seen. Discretion necessitated that poems offensive to contemporary political opinions among the reading class or to the moral standards of Evangelicalism be kept as far as possible away from Taylor's customers. Sensitivity to the predicament of Clare's new wife, well advanced in pregnancy before her marriage, required that she should not be exposed to public shame, confronted by Clare's doubts about her fidelity, nor angered by the depth and constancy of her husband's love for his first sweetheart, Mary Joyce, nor by his philanderings with other village girls, even a village whore. Contemporary taste, especially Taylor's, suggested that poems in dialect, especially poems dealing with marriage and courtship in a down-to-earth way, were not

(Oxford, 1985), p. 604. This volume is hereafter referred to as *Letters*, and is the best text available for Clare's correspondence.

acceptable to the middling class but should be confined to the halfpenny sheets of itinerant ballad-vendors. It also seems that the tale in verse was not popular in the eighteen-twenties and that the gap between provincial and London tastes was very large both in subject-matter and in style. All these ifs and buts, not to be lightly dismissed as sheer prejudice, limited the number of Clare's poems that could be published. Beyond that, there were the important limitations being imposed by increasingly standardized rules of grammar and lexicography, which made Taylor repunctuate and reword much of Clare's writing, a task which he found more and more tiresome and time-consuming. If a poem was too unorthodox in its sentiments, its language, or its punctuation and grammar, its chances of survival into print were very limited. Taylor, moreover, set his face against Clare publishing his poems as songs, on broadsheets, or in newspapers, though he could not always prevent this practice. There was, therefore, little in the way of alternative outlet for Clare's poems. In our volumes, therefore, will be found some hundreds of poems never before published.

Clare himself, like most writers, did not want all his work published. He wrote in late 1819 to Edward Drury, the Stamford bookseller and John Taylor's cousin:

To E. Drury
As I expect the words of the dead are venerably noticed which they le[a]ve behind let me hope then from you (if my survi[v]er) that my wishes may be complied with in publishing no poems which are against my inclination in any improvd form what ever but to utterly condemn them to oblivion   M.S.S. excepted [X]   if I knew such things I dissaprove of shoud appear in print after my death it woud be the greatest torture possible   therefore all you find in these books mark wi a cross are of the above description   this is the only thing I wanted to look the books over for & this is a thing which as a friend I hope one day or other you will see acted according to my wishes

John Clare[2]

Since Clare was contemplating suicide in 1819, this message has even greater force than usual. Nevertheless we have gone against Clare's explicit wishes. Why? Because neither Clare nor we can know how tastes will change over time and we owe it to posterity to let it make its

---

[2] *Letters*, p. 14. Clare is intending to indicate that poems marked X are to be excepted from his strictures.

own choices. Because the private embarrassments of Clare's life can no longer affect him or his descendants. In any event most of Clare's peccadilloes have long ago been revealed by his biographers. Because we believe that, on the whole, Clare's fame will benefit rather than suffer from fuller knowledge of his work. Because Clare's reservation was addressed to a particular person and a particular MS and ought to be judged in a total context. Because, as editors, we owe allegiance to historical truth and not to the imperfect foresight of any individual writer. Because we want others to share the fascination that we have enjoyed in our years of research. Because, finally, there is plenty of evidence that publication avoids more completely the loss resulting from the destruction or theft of a manuscript.[3] To those who, like Geoffrey Grigson, disagree, we only say that we have come to this decision in the light of two separate lifetimes dedicated to the honour of Clare's work.

To turn to more specific characteristics of Clare's poetry published in these volumes, the second instalment of an enterprise which aims to publish all Clare's known poems, let us consider the dialect-poetry represented here. In most of Clare's poems already published he is not a dialect-poet and does not intend to be one. Odd words or phrases from his Helpston vocabulary are glossed in his early published volumes, rusticisms of grammar occasionally evade John Taylor's eye, and later editors or biographers have occasionally referred to a true dialect-poem, but, in general, Clare's dialect-poetry is still unknown. The omission of it creates a very misleading picture of Clare—a picture as misleading as Hilton's portrait of him in the National Portrait Gallery: all refinement and no vulgarity, the farm-boy decked out in party clothes. (It is symbolic, perhaps, that the silk cravat shown in Hilton's portrait, and to this day preserved in Stamford Museum, was a purchase made by Clare during his first visit to London and to the *literati* of Taylor's acquaintance.) 'My Mary', which is not a dialect-poem but reeks of the farmyard, was published in the first edition of *Poems Descriptive of Rural Life and Scenery* but was later omitted. Poems such as 'Impromtu Suggested While Viewing an Infant Grave', 'Upon the Plain: a ballad', 'On Seeing a lost Greyhound in winter lying upon the Snow', 'Address to an Insignificant Flower obscurely blooming in a Lonely Wild', and others with equally emotive titles get into the first volume, but 'The Crafty Maid', 'Song: Ere

[3] E. Robinson (ed.), *Birds Nesting: John Clare's Lost Manuscript* (Market Drayton, 1987).

Meggy left hur mam an' dad', 'Love Epistles between Richard and Kate', 'O thrice lucky town', and many more were set aside. 'A Familiar Epistle to a Friend' got in, presumably because it was addressed to Sir Walter Scott's friend, Captain Sherwill, but 'Dolly's Mistake' had a hard time of it, in and out like a waitress through a kitchen half-door. It would be unfair to suggest that John Taylor gave no place to Clare's commoner muse and had no interest in Clare's country matters, but they are certainly underrepresented in *Poems Descriptive*. Yet these poems provide an important counter-statement to the poems written in the cult of the sentimental. They reveal Clare as hard-headed, reeking of the farm, well-acquainted with village morals or the lack of them, and capable of self-ridicule. Without them, or without a sufficient number of them, Clare's muse appears a little mawkish. Similar remarks apply to *The Village Minstrel*. Poems like 'Another' contrast severely with 'Mary the day of loves pleasure has been' but only the latter was published. 'There was a time when love's young flowers' and 'Damon and Collin' got into the published volumes but 'Ballad: Ere the church bell i the morning had tung four' and 'Ballad: & Ralph ye have leard a fine language to woo me' are omitted, so that on the whole we are left with a picture of this gentle, lovelorn, rustic, full of ideals and sentiment, but scarcely in touch with reality when it comes to affairs of the heart. Those 'boarding-school misses' of which Clare made such fun could have read his first publications with hardly a blush or a titter, but what would they have done on his knee?

It is true, of course, that poems of deep feeling addressed to Mary Joyce did appear, but many more, where the specifics of their relationship and their social differences were more clearly expressed, are omitted, for whatever reason. Certainly Taylor felt that too many love-poems to Mary were no compliment to Martha and in limiting them he may have rendered a service to Clare's family life, but it is clear from several unpublished poems that Martha (Patty) was not always the rose-bud that she first seemed to Clare and that his love for Mary continued to be the dominant part of his emotional life. To omit some of Clare's early poems to Mary is to lose some of his best early poems, written with something more than sentiment and bringing the ballad tradition to some of its finest exposition. Because of their simplicity such poems as 'Warm passions of love first the maidens heart heaving' become poignant rather than sentimental, and whenever Mary is actually named, in a poem such as 'Lonely oer the heaths to ramble' or 'Ive often had hours to be meeting the lasses', the temperature rises and we are aware that we are dealing with more than convention. Clare was well aware of his tendency to idealize the ladies but equally aware of his susceptibility:

. . . youll have very few more love things from me & that youll not regret for Im weary of whining over eyes of sunbeams lips of rubies & rosey cheeks & liley bosoms with this hopeless sickening clog at ones foot & a proof of its faded reallitys at ones elbow [*Patty?*]—but this is weakness & vanity for there are faces in existance that might make me a liar before this letter im now scribbling is finished[.][4]

Clare was in fact a writer of love poems almost to the end of his days. The Tibbles thought that many girls to whom he addressed his poems were figments of his imagination. On the contrary, most were real enough to pinch.[5] But Clare is a poet to read in quantity. To survey the whole range of his poetry about Woman is to encounter a many-faceted, exhilarating, and erotic sensibility.

The most important thing to understand about Clare as a poet, despite his debts to Cowper, Thomson, Milton, and the Cavalier Poets, is that he grows out of popular culture—a popular culture not narrowly defined by the professional folklorist but reflective of the wide gamut of popular taste in his period. Ballad and broadsheet, vaudeville and pantomime, poster and woodcut, jig and sailors' hornpipe, neck-verse and bawdy, sermon and moral tale, spelling-book and fairy story, sailor's lies and fairground prattle, all are close to his heart and are reflected in his poetry. The ballad-singer, the ploughman, the quack, the ranting minister, the milkmaid, the foddering boy, the parish clerk, and many others all occur in his cast of characters. Clare creates an all-encompassing world in which one's imagination may journey endlessly, but above all it is a world of the people. The more confident he becomes in his own culture and his own creative resources, the more he dispenses with literary fashions, with the trappings of mythology, and with the airs of the modish writer, but in these early poems, though there are anticipations of Clare at his best, he has not yet thrown off the literary world and its customary models. If one looks at 'Sketches in the Life of John Clare written by himself', the creative influences in his life appear in the following order:

    [4] Clare to Taylor, 11 Aug. 1821, *Letters*, p. 207.
    [5] See E. Robinson and G. Summerfield, 'John Clare: An Interpretation of Certain Asylum Letters', *Review of English Studies*, NS, 13 (1962), 135–46.

(a)   'my father coud read a little in a bible or testament'
(b)   '& was very fond of the supersti[ti]ous tales that are hawked
      about a sheet for a penny, such as old Nixons Prophesies,
      Mother Bunches Fairey Tales, & Mother Shiptons Legacy, &c'
(c)   'he was likewise fond of Ballads . . . he coud sing or recite above
      a hundred'[6]
(d)   '. . . the old womens memorys never faild of tales to smoothen
      our labour, for as every day came, new Jiants, Hobgobblins, &
      faireys was ready to pass it away'[7]
(e)   'Dame school and parish school'[8]
(f)   'the bible & Prayer Book, the prophetical parts of the former,
      with the fine hebrew Poem of Job, & the prayers and simple
      translation of the Psalms in the latter'[9]
(g)   'the Sixpenny Romances of 'Cinderella', 'Little Red Riding
      hood', 'Jack & the bean Stalk', 'Zig Zag', 'Prince Cherry',
      &c'[10]
(h)   'Books of mathematics'[11]
(i)   'Thomsons Seasons'[12]
(j)   'Wesley's hymns'[13]
(k)   'Collins' poems'[14]
(l)   'Pomfret's poems'[15]
(m)   'Pilgrim's Progress'[16]
(n)   'Milton's Paradise Lost, Joe Miller's Jest Book, a Collection of
      hymns'[17]
(o)   'Newspapers, Old Moore's Alamanac'[18]

Of course this list could be greatly amplified from other sources but it
is clear that, apart from the Bible, Clare's earliest introduction to
creativity was through popular songs and tales, and it was these which
first engendered in him the desire to become a writer. The more
obvious literary models come later. In his early attempts at rhyme it
was more likely to be a poem casually encountered in a newspaper or
periodical that started him off than a book of poems. Thus it seems
likely that a few lines from Samuel Bamford's 'The Weaver Boy'
quoted in *Drakard's Stamford News* for 20 August 1819 may have

[6] E. Robinson (ed.), *John Clare's Autobiographical Writings* (Oxford, 1983), 2. This
volume is hereafter referred to as *Autobiographical Writings*.
[7] Ibid. 3.   [8] Ibid. 4–5.   [9] Ibid. 5.   [10] Ibid. 5.
[11] Ibid. 7.   [12] Ibid. 9.   [13] Ibid. 9.   [14] Ibid. 9.
[15] Ibid. 12–13, but see also, 45–6, 48, 83, 101, 102, 124, 130.
[16] Ibid. 13.   [17] Ibid. 14.   [18] Ibid. 15.

helped to spark off Clare's poem, 'Solitude', while a poem entitled 'The Eve before the Battle' from Miss Holford's 'Wallace, or the Fight of Falkirk' in *The Enquirer* for 1811, may have inspired 'Pause before Battle', and I.B.'s 'The Forgathering of Twa Unco Thick Auld Neebors On a Winter's Murky Ee'nin', in the same volume of *The Enquirer*, may have been the starting-point for Clare's 'Letter to Sherwill' and similar poems. Bamford's poem appealed to him because it was the work of a poor boy like himself, and the latter two poems because they were about Scots, Clare himself being one-quarter Scottish. Clare's fine poem, 'What is Life?', is very similar to a poem entitled 'Life's Likenesses' by an anonymous author in the *Stamford Mercury* for 26 June 1818. This last could conceivably be by Clare and we have printed the two together in this edition. Taylor's selection of poems for the first published volumes allows some of these popular influences to shine through, but it is when we study Clare's poetry as a whole that their predominance is clearly demonstrated.

Patriotic songs about Nelson and Wellington, ballads of lovers parted by the war, invocations to the king to right the wrongs of the people, poems about battles and shipwrecks abound. They are about as good as such things usually are, and some would pass if set to music. The influence of Dibden is strong here. We cannot claim that Clare is at his best in this genre but probably a tune was ringing in his head as he composed them. Epigrams, such as 'A Maiden-haid', 'Written in Wesleys Philosophy', and 'A Simile', fables by Aesop re-versified, and snappy verses rebuking a schoolmaster, a parson, or an innkeeper's wife—all figures of authority to a villager—form other genres. A very strong category is the tale in verse, usually about murder, suicide, robbery, or rape, Clare complained bitterly about the bowdlerization of 'Dolly's Mistake' and 'My Mary', telling Hessey that they were 'by the multitude reckoned the two best in the book—I have lost my tail—by it, but never mind.'[19] To cut him off from the multitude was indeed to castrate him. A little earlier he had written to Octavius Gilchrist:

I am now Ryhming some of my Mother's 'old Stories' as she calls 'em   they are Local Legends Perhaps only known in these Places As my enquiry [h]as never gained any hints of 'em elsewhere   'The Lodge House' is one & nearly finished . . .[20]

'The Lodge House' is a masterpiece of verse story-telling, superior to

---

[19] Clare to Hessey 10? July 1820, *Letters*, p. 84.
[20] Clare to Gilchrist [late Dec. 1819], *Letters*, p. 24.

'The Cross Roads', 'Valentine's Eve', 'The Fate of Amy', and other stories that found their way to publication in Clare's lifetime. What blindness stopped his publishers from recognizing its excellence? Verse-tales about the cart-horse, Dobbin, and the unfortunate encounters of villagers with witches and hobgoblins, true or imagined, resemble the tales that frightened many of us when we were children. Country life without these stories is almost unimaginable by ordinary folk, but only Clare has raised them to an art-form. He has a marked ability to characterize the story-teller and to get into the texture of village life and speech. His later versifications of the Psalms and parts of the Prophets are anticipated in the early 'Imitation of the 148th Psalm'. It was intended for publication in the *Stamford Mercury*[21] and is a fluent piece of writing. It is perhaps surprising that Clare tried his hand so seldom at hymns or songs of praise, though there are a few.

But it was in secular song and ballad that he first found his *métier*. Clare tells us how the process began:

my father woud sometimes be huming over a song, a wretched composition of those halfpenny ball[a]ds, & my boast was that I thought I coud beat it; in a few days afterwards, I used to read my composition for his judgment to decide, but their frequent critisisms & laughable remarks drove me to use a process of cunning in the business some time after, for they damp'd me a long time from proceeding. My method on resuming the matter again was to say I had written it out of a borrowd book & that it was not my own[.][22]

And again:

I cannot say what led me to dabble in Ryh[me or] at what age I began to write it but my first r[ude attempts took the form of] imitations of my fathers Songs[.][23]

It is clear that Parker Clare's repertoire included not only traditional ballads but also the new ballads and songs contemporaneously composed.[24] Some of Clare's early poems are memories or versions of traditional ballads and date from at least as early as 1819. 'I saw the girl just to my mind' is such a traditional ballad[25] and anticipates

---

[21] Clare to Drury [Apr. 1819], *Letters*, p. 9.
[22] *Autobiographical Writings*, p. 12.
[23] Ibid. 82–3.
[24] The outstanding contribution made by George Deacon in his *John Clare and the Folk Tradition* (London, 1983) to the study of this subject has placed all lovers of Clare in his debt.
[25] This particular ballad, for a very good reason, was missed by George Deacon. See below, pp. xxiii–xxiv.

similar ballads in Peterborough MS A37, not dated by Dr Grainger in her catalogue but possibly emanating from the mid-1820s. Other songs and ballads, such as 'Since Flora disdains me—her once loving swain', 'Her hair bound in tortoise or else loosley flowing', 'Guardian Angels O protect me', 'When lingering suns in sumer sets', 'When Chloe's gone then fancy lays', are all typical of eighteenth-century and early nineteenth-century taste. Some of Clare's songs in this style might have come straight out of *The Beggar's Opera*—a work of which he was very fond—or some other ballad-opera. 'Brittania cease—For Nelsons doom' is a patriotic song; 'Young Jemmy the pride of the Hamlett and mill' is a bawdy song such as might be found on many a broadsheet, and parallels such a song, in its ruder versions, as 'Coming through the Rye', which also appears heavily obliterated in a later Clare MS. Naturally, the bawdy songs do not appear in the published volumes and Clare himself probably scored out 'Young Jemmy' so that it should not be seen by eyes prying into his MSS. Though George Deacon has made some valuable suggestions about later ballads it is almost impossible to name the airs which may have been ringing in his head when Clare wrote most of these songs. There is no doubt, however, that he did associate them with music since he describes his first attempts at poetry as 'reading imatations of some popular song floating among the vulgar at the markets and fairs',[26] and was himself a collector of tunes. The wife of his friend, Octavius Gilchrist, had a good voice and she was very interested in Clare's songs. Among those Clare sent to her were 'I love thee my Mary but love thee in fear', 'Now that the even is hanging so glooming', 'The Jewell of all', and 'O let me love thee Mary'.[27] Clare also wrote a group of songs for Edward Drury, a great encourager of Clare's taste for ballads, to be set to music by F. W. Crouch. Crouch visited Drury in Stamford, performed at the theatre there,[28] and met Clare. The songs were: 'What's Beauty's Love',[29] 'Mary, Mary',[30] 'Of all the days in Memory's list',[31] 'While Birdies with their notes so sweet',[32] 'Anna's Absence',[33] and 'Give me

---

[26] *Autobiographical Writings*, p. 82. [27] *Letters*, p. 23.
[28] *Drakard's Stamford News*, 31 Dec. 1819. Crouch appeared with Haydn Corri at a concert.
[29] C1–9a. Where MSS are cited with a letter before the number they are to be found in the collection at Peterborough Museum. The second number is the page or folio number. Where MSS are cited with a number not preceded by a letter they are to be found in the Local History Collection of Northampton Public Library.
[30] B2–131, B4–R92. [31] A5–62, C2–48a. [32] Unidentified.
[33] Possibly C3–325, though unlikely, since this is a late MS.

Life's ease'.[34] We have been unable to trace the music for any of these songs. There is, however, still in existence a setting by F. W. Crouch of 'Sweet the Merry Bells Ring Round'.[35] If only we knew the music that sounded in Clare's head when he wrote his songs a new dimension would be given to them. As it is, we should never forget that they are written by a purchaser of street-ballads, a fiddler at public houses, a lover of gypsies and gypsy music, and a frequenter of concerts and the vaudeville. Clare's song-writing was born in music; in the scrape of the fiddle and in the voices of his mother and father singing in that small cottage in Helpston.

What is most striking about Clare's early verse when it is assembled together is its variety. He experimented in many genres and in many metric forms, sometimes measuring the beat against the thrum of his mother's spinning-wheel. Occasionally he stumbles but his ear is remarkably true. Even when he comes to the rhyming couplet, that most demanding of verse-forms, or to the Spenserian stanza, he writes verse with fluency and control. Of all his earliest poems, perhaps the most ambitious was *The Parish*, only recently published in its entirety.[36] We have recently discovered that a section from it was published as a eulogy to Lord Fitzwilliam in *Drakard's Stamford News* shortly after it was composed,[37] but the nature of the material as a whole, strongly critical of parochial officialdom, made it unacceptable to a London reading public during Clare's lifetime. One section of it Clare produced as a separate poem, 'The Vicar', because it was eulogistic, but in the complete poem the vicar is an exception to the tyranny exercised by parish officials over the poor. In order to save space in these volumes we have chosen to publish 'The Vicar' as part and parcel of 'The Parish' rather than to print it as a separate poem. 'The Parish' is unique as an indictment of petty bureaucracy written by a poor labourer. Crabbe wrote of similar things in 'The Borough' but, as Clare said, 'Crabbe writes about the peasantry as much like the Magistrate as the Poet'.[38] Certainly some of Clare's descriptions of farmers and their kin-folk are unforgettable.

Clare's other early long poem is 'The Village Minstrel' which headed the original volume of that name. Taylor chose to delete 249 lines and make many other alterations. Now for the first time the

[34] A40–46, A54–307.   [35] British Library G806a (45).
[36] See *John Clare: The Parish* (Harmondsworth, 1985).
[37] See 'The Parish', in Vol. 2 of this edition, pp. 697–779.
[38] Clare to Allan Cunningham, 9 Sept. 1824, *Letters*, p. 302.

reader has the poem just as Clare originally wrote it, and a remarkable poem it proves to be. Its realism, its sustained beauties, its social comment, its humour, its autobiographical undertones, its intimacy, its compassion without sentimentality, its wide-ranging picture of country life, its handling of rhythm and language, all are signs of a growing confidence and a sense of direction. Clare, on reading Beattie's *The Minstrel* in May 1820, feared that he might be accused of plagiarism,[39] but the poem owes little more than its stanza form to the earlier work, rejecting its artificiality and rhetoric. Mark Storey suggests that 'The Village Minstrel' 'has a substance and firmness of purpose that hint at the strengths' of 'The Shepherd's Calendar'.[40]

Despite the number of poems published in these two volumes, we know that they do not represent all the poems Clare wrote from about the age of 14 to the age of 28. Clare tells us how his illiterate mother took some of his poems merely for handwriting exercises and used them in the kitchen for kettle-holders and fire-lighters.[41] He also tells us that he himself burnt many of his very earliest poems, among them perhaps 'The Morning Walk', described by Clare as the first thing he committed to paper, and its sequel 'The Evening Walk'.[42] From lists in Clare's hand in Peterborough MS A2 and St Ives Norris SAVNM CL/1, we know that there were poems not yet traced:

'To a sprig of Barley;
'Letter to a friend' (unless this is the letter to Sherwill);
'She knows every sorrow that absence awakens';
'Ryce Wood'.

In his letters we find references to 'Travels of the Book', 'Nutting', 'What can poor Peggy do?', 'The Promised Day', 'Love lost her tether', 'Cautious Nancy', 'Hibernias Song', 'Burghely Park', 'Days gone bye', 'Loves Soliloquy', and 'Labour & Luxury'. Like 'While Birdies with their notes so sweet', mentioned above among the songs set by Crouch, none of these has been traced. It is unlikely that their discovery would change substantially our knowledge of Clare's early talent. He also speaks of destroying many of the poems written for *The Village Minstrel*.[43] If we find any early poems subsequent to the publication of this volume, we shall publish them in the last volume of the series.

[39] Clare to Chauncey Townsend, 6 May 1820, *Letters*, p. 63.
[40] Mark Storey, *The Poetry of John Clare* (London, 1974), p. 50.
[41] *Autobiographical Writings*, pp. 13 and 82.   [42] Ibid. 10.   [43] Ibid. 106.

Clare was so prolific in his writing throughout his life, but more especially between 1819 and 1822, that it is not surprising that some poems have gone astray. And he was prolific despite continuing his work as a farm-labourer and, after the publication of his first book, constant interruptions by the curious:

... they will not let me keep quiet as I usd to be—they send for me twice & 3 times a day out of the fields & I am still the strangers poppet Show   what can their fancys create to be so anxious & so obstinate of being satisfied   I am but a man (& a little one too) like others   still as they will come I will still sit in my corner in readiness for them & ryhme & jingle in the teeth of trouble & scrat away on my 'Cremona' striving to make the best use of the world while I am in it[.][44]

Clearly he worked in frightening spurts of daemonic energy which kept him from both sleep and food, though not, alas, from drink. He wrote to Taylor in February 1822: 'I fear I shall get nothing ready for you this month   at least I fear so now   but may have 50 subjects ready to morrow   the Muse is a fickle Hussey with me'.[45]

On another occasion he wrote: 'when I am in the fit I write as much in one week as woud knock ye up a fair size Vol',[46] and sometimes listed as many as a dozen poems completed or in composition at the same time.[47] He wrote and wrote until Drury began to fear for his health and his sanity:

It is to be greatly feared that the man will be afflicted with insanity if his talent continues to be forced as it has been these 4 months past; he has no other mode of easing the fever that oppresses him after a tremendous fit of rhyming except by getting tipsy.[48]

His corrections came as he wrote, for the most part:

I always wrote my poems in great haste & generaly finishd them at once wether long or short for if I did not they generaly were left unfinishd   what corrections I made I always made them while writing the poem & never coud do any thing with them after wards.[49]

This observation, however, is not strictly accurate since the MSS

[44] 32–27. Clare to Taylor, 31 Aug. 1820, *Letters*, p. 89.
[45] Clare to Taylor, 8 Feb. 1822, *Letters*, p. 230.
[46] Clare to Taylor, 20 May 1820, *Letters*, p. 70.
[47] Clare to Holland [Oct.? 1819], *Letters*, p. 16.
[48] Drury to Taylor, 2 Jan. 1820, *Letters*, p. 70 n. 3.
[49] *Autobiographical Writings*, p. 86.

clearly show different versions written on several separate occasions, sometimes with substantial differences.

We now turn to the problem of presenting Clare's grammar, spelling, and punctuation, though this must be less severe in an edition of this sort than in a popular edition lacking any complicated critical apparatus. Clare's schooling was limited and he has himself described his beginnings as a writer:

> . . . I became a scribbler from down right pleasure in giving vent to my feelings & long & pleasing painful was my struggles to acquire a sufficient knowledge of the written language of england before I could put down my ideas on paper even so far as to understand them myself—but I mastered it in time sufficiently to be understood by others & then I became an author by accident & felt astonished that the critics should notice me at all & when they please others whose taste is better than mine the pinnacle of my ambition is attained—& I am so astonished that I can hardly believe I am myself for no body believed I could do any thing here & & [*sic*] I never believed that I could myself—I pursued pleasure in many paths & never found her so happily as when I sung imaganery songs to the woodland solitudes & winds of autumn[.][50]

But besides his limited schooling, we should take into account that the culture from which he stemmed was more old-fashioned than that of his London editors and friends. Just as his tastes in reading were not primarily in Wordsworth, Coleridge, or Keats but in Thomson, Cowper, and Byron, so his freedom in spelling, including the spelling of proper names, and the laxity of his punctuation and grammar were more common in the eighteenth century than in the nineteenth, as the diaries of several eighteenth-century notables will testify. The standardization of literacy was less advanced in Peterborough than in London, though, of course, it was being reinforced by sixpenny pamphlets and newspapers:

> . . . although I never saw a book on grammar before I was 20 or knew any thing what ever of the proper construction of sentences—yet I was so far benefited from reading in old newspapers now & then as to write pretty correctly & never any other wise than to be intelligible although before this I could not scarcly write a common letter so as to understand it my self.[51]

Taylor and most subsequent editors have not hesitated to tidy up Clare's writings and even to rewrite his lines when they thought fit, but we have tried as far as possible to present Clare as he wrote. It is sometimes possible, for example, to detect in an MS with reasonable

---

[50] B7–82, 85.   [51] B5–90/1.

certainty where Taylor has changed the punctuation. In such instances
we have restored Clare's original intentions or have made it clear in the
textual notes that we suspect Taylor's emendation. As Clare matured
and became more confident he tended to reduce punctuation to a
minimum both in prose and verse. In some of his early poems, in the
versions submitted to Drury, however, he fell into the opposite
extreme, probably in response to suggestions coming from several
quarters that he ought to be more 'correct'. When he did this the
punctuation became so excessive that it seriously interfered with the
reader's enjoyment of the poetry. We have therefore removed the
punctuation when it was clearly wrong but have provided the evidence
of exactly what we have done. The reader may therefore easily restore
Clare's original punctuation if he so wishes in the few poems that we
have dealt with in this way. An editor today exists in a time capsule no
more than Taylor and Hessey or the Tibbles did. We know from
experience that a little practice in reading Clare will soon remove
problems created by misspellings, mistakes in grammar, and mispunc-
tuation, especially as Clare is fairly consistent in his errors.

In some instances it is clear that Clare's spellings are deliberate. For
example, when he writes 'chancd', 'drownd', or 'glancd', he intends
these words to be pronounced as monosyllables, but when he writes
such words as 'chanced', 'drowned', and 'glanced' the words are
almost invariably intended to be pronounced as two syllables. This
only accounts, however, for a small minority of misspellings. Others
are more nearly related to Clare's method of pronouncing certain
words, and this can clearly be established when a misspelling occurs in
a word used in the rhyme-scheme.

Where we have to ask for greater indulgence from our readers is in
the imperfection of our readings from Peterborough MSS A1 and A2.
These two small leather-backed notebooks contain some of Clare's
earliest verses and date from 1819. Poems were written in them in
pencil and then erased, presumably so that the notebooks could be
reused. Clare often suffered from a shortage of writing-paper. Until
now these MSS have been regarded as almost totally unreadable. As a
result of many months of turning the pages to different angles of
sunlight, it has become possible to venture plausible readings of a good
deal of their contents. Ultraviolet and infra-red light have also been
used to very little effect with these notebooks. The British Library's
videospectral comparator Mark II was little help since the span of
words that it could handle was too limited. Peterborough Museum has

refused to allow any test by police forensic methods requiring particles of graphite. Photography also produced no solutions. Therefore, until more sophisticated methods of investigation can be employed, this is the best that can be done. We believe that about 80 per cent of our readings from A1 and A2 can be relied upon but it would be an impossible task to specify those occasions when we are positive, half-sure, and very uncertain. Where we have been able to verify the text by reference to another Clare MS or to a transcript by an amanuensis we have found this helpful and have done so, and we have also discovered that our readings were not entirely reliable where the poem had been heavily erased. For a short period of time Professor Robinson was able to use a former operating-theatre with a glass roof at the top of the Peterborough Musuem for reading these books and that was a great help, but most of the time he has been obliged to work in rooms ill-lit by natural light. Our observations here on A1 and A2 apply to a much lesser extent to other MSS in several other libraries. It needs to be pointed out that Clare sometimes wrote poems in ink over the top of poems in pencil and vice versa, that his MSS are often heavily discoloured by use and by age, that they are often badly sewn together, frayed at the edges, with heavy crossings-out that even ultraviolet light cannot resolve. It is unlikely that the MSS of any other major poet are in a comparable condition and that must be one of our excuses for taking so long about our task. The principal reason for delay, of course, is the extent and variety of Clare's MSS and the imperfections and scantiness of previous editorial work. Editors exist in a tradition and our safest claim is that we will have contributed something to the tradition of editing John Clare.

NOTE

It was discovered, after page-proofs had been corrected, that Peterborough manuscript A31, pp. 211–13, contains a deleted revision of ll. 1630–759 of *The Parish* which had been omitted in our collation. Fortunately the only significant variants are:

1724 restore] to hire

1752/3 [These sacred claims was deemed to be forgot]

The complete variants will appear, with any other omissions, in the final volume of the series.

EDITORIAL CONVENTIONS AND ABBREVIATIONS

For reasons of space no attempt is made here to give a full physical description of all the MSS and other sources used in the preparation of these two volumes. We reserve such full descriptions for the last volume in the series. In the mean time, we suggest that the reader consult the catalogues of the two major collections, namely, D. Powell, *Catalogue of the John Clare Collection in the Northampton Public Library* (Northampton, 1964) and M. Grainger, *A Descriptive Catalogue of the John Clare Collection in Peterborough Museum and Art Gallery* (Peterborough, 1973). Miss Barbara Rosenbaum's Clare section in the second volume of the *Index of English Literary Manuscripts* (London, 1982) is also a mine of information. The notes that follow are supplementary to these works.

MS 1: The longest section of our *RL* volume consists of poems that are to be found in MS 1, a 252-page 'book of blank Paper', which Clare bought in 1814 when he was 21 from J. B. Henson, the Market Deeping bookseller. He gave eight shillings, the equivalent of a week's wages, and copied into it all those poems to date which he thought worthy of preservation. He also included the prose passage 'The Woodman or the Beauties of a winter Forrest', Northampton MS 1, pp. 128–30 (see *Natural History Prose Writings*, pp. 1–9).

There are three categories of content: (*a*) poems in elegant penmanship, with often excessive punctuation which seems to have been added by Clare subsequently and in darker ink; (*b*) poems in margins and spare pages in ink; (*c*) poems in margins and spare pages in pencil. It is tempting to conclude that categories (*b*) and (*c*) were composed at a later date, but this is not necessarily so although some may have been copied later. Thus 'The Woodman' appears in category (*a*) although Grainger dates it in, or just prior to, 1820. The MS contains poems that were composed over a long period of time, between perhaps 1808 and 1819 with the occasional one possibly a year or two earlier.

MS B2/MS 3: These two MSS were at one time one and the same—a large quarto volume of neatly copied poems by Clare, and the most important single MS in our *VM* volume. There are pencilled emendations throughout which are only doubtfully Clare's. The last five poems are not in Clare's hand. Clare writes in a letter to Sherwill dated 9 February 1820 that he has been preparing this volume 'for the press this Winter'[1] and it seems likely that almost all the poems it contains were written during the twelvemonth June 1819 to May 1820.

Pierpont Morgan Library, New York, MA 1320: This has the following inscribed title-page: 'Village Scenes / and / Subjects on rural / Occupations / By John Clare / the Northamptonshire / Peasant Author of / "Poems on life & Senery" & "Rural Poems & Songs" / Helpstone / August 21 1820'. This 115-page quarto MS contains sixteen neatly copied poems.

MS A1/MS A2/MS 2: MS A1 and MS A2 are two octavo notebooks which Clare was using 1819–20. MS A2 has the following inscribed title-page: 'Pastoral Sketches / Poems / Songs / Ballads / & Sonnets / By John Clare / the Northamptonshire / Pheasant / London / Printed by Taylor & Hessey / & Edward Drury Stamford / 1819'. MSS A1 and A2 seem to have been used in conjunction with MS 2, a shorter octavo notebook inscribed, on p. 1, 'John Clare' (e.g. 'The Woodman' is distributed between all three). They are all written in pencil and most of the writing is rubbed out. Ours is the first (though at times tentative) attempt to recover their contents.

MS A3: A foolscap volume of poems which Clare was using in 1819, interesting because of the comments and instructions in Clare's hand to his publisher Taylor and because Clare has dated retrospectively many of the poems written earlier.

MS 11: This is a 447-page quarto cypher-book which Clare was using from the age of 10. Inside the front cover is inscribed 'Steal not this book for fear of Shame / For here doth Stand the owners Name / John Clare / 1806' and 'John Clare His / Book Helpston / Northamptonshire 1803', and on p. 37 'J. Merrishaw / 1803'. The verse in this MS is probably the earliest Clare ever wrote.

Houghton Library, Harvard University: Here there is what appears to be an author's proof copy of *RL* minus preliminaries, glossary, publisher's advertisements, and 'Crazy Nell'. There are occasional corrections, but probably not in Clare's hand, which are incorporated in our collations. There is a half-title 'POEMS' and the following title page: 'POEMS, / SONGS, AND SONNETS.' / BY / JOHN CLARE. / A

---

[1] *Letters*, p. 31.

NORTHAMPTONSHIRE PEASANT. / O rural life! what charms thy meanness hide; / What sweet descriptions bards disdain to sing, / What loves, what graces on thy plains abide: / Oh, could I soar me on the Muse's wing, / What rifled charms should my researches bring! / Pleas'd would I wander where these charms reside; / Of rural sports and beauties would I sing; / These beauties, Wealth, which you in vain deride, / Beauties of richest bloom, superior to your pride. / LONDON: / FOR TAYLOR AND HESSEY, FLEET STREET. / 1819.' The spine has a written label: 'Clare / Poems / 1819'.

Stratfield Saye: Sir Gyles Isham in a brief article 'Some Clare Manuscripts at Stratfield Saye', *Northamptonshire Past and Present*, III (1964), 199–200, refers to five poems, probably all in transcript among the MSS of the Duke of Wellington at Stratfield Saye. The poems are: 'In Helpstone Church Yard', 'O native scenes, nought to my breast clings nearer', 'Written on a birthday—20th year' (this poem is printed in the article), 'Sorrows for a Favorite Cat', 'O Sweet is Love. A Song'. Unfortunately they no longer appear to be in the Duke of Wellington's possession and so we have been unable to consult them.

ARRANGEMENT OF MATERIAL

The starting-points of our present two volumes are respectively *Poems Descriptive of Rural Life and Scenery*, published 16 January 1820, and *The Village Minstrel, and other Poems*, published March 1821, but we have also included a huge mass of material that was excluded from the original books. Owing to the impossibility of precisely dating a large amount of Clare's poetry we have felt it more sensible in these and later volumes in the Oxford English Text series to group poems of similar date round established titles rather than to attempt the hopeless task of fitting poems into separate volumes bearing inclusive dates on their title-pages. This policy means that some poems that were written earlier will not appear until later if they were first published in *SC* or *RM*, or were copied into 'The Midsummer Cushion' volume (Peterborough MS A54).

We have taken MSS 1, B2/3, and MA 1320 as the three key MSS of our two volumes. MS 1 forms the basis of *RL*, and B2/3 and MA 1320 of *VM*. 'Jewel of all' appears in MSS 1 and B2 and is printed in our *VM* volume, but otherwise no poem appears in more than one of these MSS. MS 1 comes first in our *RL* volume and the poems follow as closely as possible in the same order. Poems are collated with versions that appear in a wide variety of other MSS and so on through the two volumes.

In *RL* we have taken our second layer of MSS to be MSS A1–A6, with 'The Meeting' which appears in MS A8 (the contents of which are otherwise in our *VM* volume) and was a late inclusion for the original *RL*, and also MSS D1–D4. Many of the poems in these MSS will have been collated already with MS 1.

Later sections in *RL*, our third layer, consist of early poems that do not appear in either MSS 1, A1–A6, or D1–D4, and derive from a variety of sources. These include the only poems in the volume of which there is no known Clare autograph—'Morning Walk', in MS 4, a transcript; 'Emma', in MS 5, a transcript; 'To a Cold Beauty, Insensible of Love', in *RL*, and the only poem in the volume for which we have neither a Clare autograph nor a transcript; 'On Youth', 'The First of May', 'Approach of Spring', 'Summer', in *RL* and MS B1, a transcript; and 'Address to a Sluggard', in MS B1, a transcript.

A similar arrangement procedure has been adopted in dealing with the poems in *VM*. The second layer this time becomes MSS A5 ('Of all the days in memorys list' only), A7–A16, A18, and A21–A25. Our third layer consists of miscellaneous poems of similar date that have so far not been included. Among these are two poems for which we have no Clare autograph—'Absence', in *VM* and MS C1 and Berg, transcripts, and 'Thou lovely bud, with many weeds surrounded', in *VM* only. Then follows MS 1320, our third key MS. We conclude the volume with 'The Parish', parts of which are scattered among no less than twenty-two autograph MSS and two transcripts.

HEADNOTES

The headnotes for each poem have up to four sections:

(1) AUTOGRAPHS Here we list all MSS in Clare's hand, giving page- or folio-references for each line of the poem. If the poem is in pencil as opposed to ink we say so, and if it has been subsequently rubbed out we denote this by 'erased pencil'. The word 'deleted' usually means that a line has been drawn through the poem. When a poem is described as 'o.p.' or overpunctuated turn to pp. 557–64 (pp. 780–2 in Vol. 2) for a full collation.

(2) TRANSCRIPTS Here we list (with page references) all MSS not in Clare's hand. They normally have no textual authenticity and have

not been collated in the Textual Notes unless: (*a*) they contain corrections in Clare's hand as in MSS C1 and C2; (*b*) they assume importance because of lack of Clare autographs; (*c*) they are of interest for some specific reason.

(3) When a poem was printed in *RL* the page-reference is given for the first edition. If the complete poem was omitted or changed its relative position in a later edition we say so here. We also note when a poem was printed in contemporary periodicals and newspapers and occasionally later publications. In all cases any line omissions are given.

(4) Here we supply the date of each poem as precisely as the evidence allows. The source of the evidence is briefly quoted. If a date is given in inverted commas, it means that the date was supplied by Clare himself. For further information the reader is sometimes referred to the Explanatory Notes at the end of the volume.

COPY-TEXT

The copy-text may be any of the listed sources for a particular poem but is always denoted by being listed first in the Headnotes. Where the Headnotes show that lines are absent in the copy-text, the text followed is given at the appropriate line in the Textual Notes. Titles of poems have been regularized.

[   ]   = words or letters missing in copy-text and supplied by the editors. A glance at the Textual Notes will often show that many missing words are to be found in one or more alternative source.

⟨   ⟩   = indecipherable, used notably in MSS A1 and A2 where the Headnotes indicate erased pencil. When words or letters are supplied within the angled brackets such readings must be regarded as doubtful. Occasionally used as in Textual Notes but a note will make this clear.

TEXTUAL NOTES

These follow each individual poem and list departures, if any, from the copy-text, all variants in other autograph MSS (occasional variants in transcripts as described above under Headnotes (2)), and all substantive variants in printed sources (i.e. disregarding punctuation, capitalization, and most spelling), including alterations between editions in the case of *RL*.

When a contemporary printed version states that it is reprinted from another printed source the reader may normally assume no variants between them, but on the rare occasions when this is not so we do give them, though they are presumably misprints. When a contemporary printed version does not state that it is reprinted from another printed source (though of course it may be) we quote both throughout the collation.

Words taken from our source materials, whether MS or printed, are given in Roman, while our own observations are given in *Italic*.

In presenting the line notes in the *apparatus criticus* we have tried to be economical of space without, we hope, sacrificing clarity (for example, we have not repeated the copy-text word in the notes when the reference is obvious). We follow primarily the sequence of words in the line and not the sequence of MSS in the headnote. The latter comes into play only as we examine each word in its order in the line. It is the attempt to show how Clare altered his spelling, choice of words, and grammatical structure from one MS to another that has persuaded us to follow this procedure. The reader who wishes to reconstruct the readings of a particular MS will find our method a little less convenient, but a choice has to be made, since both objectives cannot be attained with equal clarity.

[   ]   = cancelled, but not used when the Headnotes indicate that the whole of the passage has been deleted. We have distinguished between *through*, *over*, and *below* in describing less complex emendations. Thus *over* and *below* refer to relative vertical positions, but *through* means actually superimposed upon the original phrase, word, or letter. In the case of more complex emendations where Clare has changed his mind several times we have abandoned this method and tried to disentangle the sequence of emendations by adopting the following formula: *successively* (*a*) [   ]; (*b*) [   ]; (*c*) [   ].

⟨   ⟩ = smudged, torn, blot, faded, lost in binding, covered by seal, hiatus, uncertain, illegible. The reason for the problem usually follows the sign, but in MSS described in the Headnotes as 'erased pencil' the reader can assume illegibility.

∧   = mark of punctuation missing, usually in a variant text. This applies to punctuation before or after a word but not within it.

]   introduces variant in another text.

:   is used for separating variants in the same line in the same text.

p.e.   = pencil emendation, in a text written in ink.

?   indicates an uncertain reading, e.g. And *through ?* As, a *over* [*?* may]. If we had been unable to make a suggestion these would have appeared as And *through indecipherable* and a *over indecipherable*.

124/5   introduces material which falls between lines 124 and 125.

EXPLANATORY NOTES

These have a threefold purpose: (1) to provide the evidence for the dating of poems; (2) to describe the provenance of poems; (3) to comment on anything in the text that seems to require further information or explanation.

We have preferred whenever possible to use Clare's own words and those of his friends and we have made frequent quotations from and references to *Autobiographical Writings*, *Letters*, and, to a lesser extent, *Natural History Prose Writings*. The reader can therefore follow up the context of such passages if he so wishes. In each case we have looked again at the original MS and have silently corrected the·occasional error. We have provided MS references for passages that are not easily available in print. When we have failed to solve a query we have said so in the hope that someone else may do better.

In the interest of space, we have made no attempt to give a day-to-day account of Taylor's editing of Clare. We plan to do this for both *RL* and *VM* in two periodical articles. In the mean time *Letters* is the best help available.

ABBREVIATIONS

RL	*Poems Descriptive of Rural Life and Scenery* (1820)
VM	*The Village Minstrel* (1821)
SC	*The Shepherd's Calendar* (1827)

RM	*The Rural Muse* (1835)
LM	*London Magazine*
Autobiographical Writings	*John Clare's Autobiographical Writings*, ed. Eric Robinson (Oxford, 1983)
Deacon	George Deacon, *John Clare and the Folk Tradition* (London, 1983)
Later Poems	*The Later Poems of John Clare*, ed. Eric Robinson and David Powell (Oxford, 1984)
Letters	*The Letters of John Clare*, ed. Mark Storey (Oxford, 1985)
Martin	Frederick Martin, *The Life of John Clare* (London, 1865)
Natural History Prose Writings	*The Natural History Prose Writings of John Clare*, ed. Margaret Grainger (Oxford, 1983)

ACKNOWLEDGMENTS

Our debt to librarians and curators everywhere is immense, as it must be for anyone involved in an enterprise of this complexity, continuing in two continents for a quarter of a century. We hope that we shall be forgiven for not naming persons who have helped us in their professional capacity for it would be invidious to make distinctions between such loyal servants of the public. We have also been helped, however, by a number of persons who were in no way obligated to assist us and yet did so with a generosity and kindness that have been overwhelming. Both of us wish to thank George and Mary Dixon for their friendship, their encouragement, and their hospitality over periods of several months at a time. Without their help these volumes might have been delayed for years. Professor Robinson also wishes to thank Daphne and Godfrey Faux, who first made it possible for him to live in the village of Helpston and get his bearings there. In addition they have housed his books, his clothes, and his old MG, so that they were available during his frequent visits from the USA. He is also indebted to Margaret Powell for putting him up and putting up with him in Northampton, as well as undertaking valuable research at the Northamptonshire Record Office. In earlier years, Mr Bruce Bailey was also his generous host in Northampton and Mr Saner-Norton in Stratton Audley. He has spent several happy weeks at the home of Mrs Gillian Richardson in Brixworth. Professor and Mrs Basil Mitchell know well how he values their friendship and how many times he has stayed with them while working at the Bodleian. The late Ian Bowman always responded promptly to enquiries about Clare's Scottish connections and wrote the best appreciation in Lallans of Clare. Dr and Mrs Pattison not only accommodated Professor Robinson in New Haven while he worked at the Beinecke Library but supplied him with thrillers as diversion. Professor Kelsey Thornton, Chairman of the John Clare Society, and Mr Mark Storey, editor of Clare's letters, have freely supplied information and, when asked for it, advice, from their own extensive knowledge of Clare's work. Professor Robinson also wishes to thank those of his colleagues at the University of Massachusetts at Boston who contributed to his securing two awards for distinguished scholarship and for thus endorsing scholarly work not limited to history, pure and simple. Special thanks are due to

Provost Robert Greene of the University of Massachusetts at Boston. Most of the typing for these volumes has been done by David Powell, but we are also grateful to Miss Margaret Dixon of Peterborough and Miss Victoria Donahue of West Newbury, Massachusetts, for typing drafts and articles connected with this edition. Many years ago Professor Robinson received a small grant from the Leverhulme Trust to study Clare MSS in New York and New Haven. That award was the first received in support of this edition.

David Powell wishes to acknowledge generous research grants, from the Leverhulme Trust and from the British Academy, which have enabled him to meet basic travel and subsistence expenses in England and to undertake a six-week visit to the USA to visit libraries in New York, New Haven, and Cambridge. He is also grateful for a smaller award from East Midlands Arts.

We thank Northampton Public Library and Peterborough Museum and Art Gallery, the two major collections of Clare MSS, and also the following institutions, for permission to publish material in their possession:

Berg Collection, New York Public Library
Bodleian Library, Oxford
British Library, London
Fitzwilliam Museum, Cambridge
Houghton Library, Harvard University
Norris Museum, St Ives, Huntingdon
Northumberland Record Office, Newcastle upon Tyne
Oundle School
Carl and Lily Pforzheimer Foundation Inc., New York
Pierpont Morgan Library, New York
Wisbech and Fenland Museum
Yale University (Beinecke Rare Book and Manuscript Library)

Mr. John Chandler, the one private MS-owner, was no less quick to give his permission, and was helpful in other ways, for which we are grateful.

Finally, we owe special thanks to the John Clare Society (Membership Secretary, George Dixon, 8 Priory Road, Peterborough, PE3 6EB) for sympathetic encouragement.

Poems Descriptive of Rural Life and Scenery
and other poems

Poems Descriptive of Rural Life and Scenery

Title page of Nor. MS 1:*

A RUSTIC'S PASTIME, IN LEISURE HOURS;

——————

J* CLARE.

——————

Some like to laugh their time away,
To dance while pipes or fiddles play,
And have nae sense of ony want
As lang as they can drink or rant.
The rattling drum or trumpets tout
Delight young swankies that are stout;
May i be happy in my lays,
*   *   *   *   *
Is all my wish; well pleas'd to sing
Beneath a tree, or by a spring.

RAMSAY.

——————

HELPSTON;

1814.

———

* The lines are from 'Address To the Right Hon. William Earl of Dalhousie' which is included in Allan Ramsay, *Poems on Several Occasions* (1793), item 341 in Clare's library.

A Collection of Trifles
In verse

By John Clare
of Helpstone

Some like to laugh their time away,
To dance while pipes & fiddles play,
And have nae sence of ony want
As lang as they can drink & rant.
The rattling Drum & trumpets tout
Delight youn Swankies that are stout:
May I be happy in my lays.
And win a Lasting Wreath of Bays!
Is a' my wish well pleasd to sing
Beneath a tree or by a Spring.

Ramsay

(In pen, written later:)

These leaves of scribbling that only deserve & certanly woud have been obliterated by the flames had not frendships warm atachments interposed to retrieve them from so just a fate are left to E. Drury as desired.

John Clare

Helpstone July 1820

(In pencil, written later:)

As the ensuing Trifles are nothing but the simple production of an Unlettered Rustic their faults & Imperfections will undoubtedly be nothing more than what might be expected—as correct composition & Gramatical accuracy can never be lookd for from one whose mental facculties (such as they were) being continually oerburthend & depressd by hard labour which fate ordained to be his constant employment—It is hoped the unnoticd Imitation should any occur (being* unknown to the author will not be deem'd as Plagarisms as the†

* being *through* tho   † the *through* his

humble station of life in which providence has placed him has ever debarred him from Reaping that advantage of extending his knowledge by reading of Books the small catalogue he has seen might easily be enumerated a Thompson & a Milton when a school boy was the constant companions of his leisure hours—The first of which still continues to be his favourite author—

> whos mildly pleasing song
> he hums in rapture as he strolls along

the imitations if any he may be proud of as boasting thou[g]hts similar to those of his superiors therefore resting in the humble hopes [*MS ends abruptly*]

AUTOGRAPH: Nor. MS 1, p. 1 (ll. 13–30, 35–6, 41–6, 85–92, 187–92, 195–6, deleted), p. 2 (ll. 67–84, deleted), p. 9 (ll. 193–4, pencil), p. 16 (ll. 123–30), p. 95 (ll. 95–102, deleted), p. 96 (ll. 1–8, 55–60, 65–6, deleted), p. 111 (ll. 103–20, 131–40, deleted), p. 112 (ll. 141–58, deleted), p. 249 (ll. 9–12 deleted, 49–54, 61–4, 159–70, 173–4), p. R252 (ll. 177–82): Pet. MS A1, f.1ᵛ (erased pencil, deleted, fragment).
TRANSCRIPT: Pet. MS B1, pp. 48–53.
Printed in *RL*, pp. 130–9 (ll. 29–30, 117–40, omitted).
Dated: 1817–19 (*RL* Introduction, p. xxii 'In the last two years').

SUMMER EVENING

> The sinken sun is takin leave
> & sweetly gilds the edge of eve
> While purple [clouds] of deepening dye
> Huddling hang the western skye
> Crows crowd quaking oever head   5
> Hastening to the woods to bed
> Cooing sits the lonly dove
> Calling home her abscent love
> Kirchip Kirchip mong the wheat
> Partridge distant partridge greet   10

SUMMER EVENING   *Title:* Summer Evening *RL, wanting MS 1*   *ll. 29–30 and 33–4, 139–40 and 141–2, 193–4 and 195–6 are alternative lines*   3 While huddling clouds of purple dye *RL*   4 Huddling] Gloomy *RL*   5 quaking] croaking *RL*   9 With 'Kirchip! kirchip!': wheats *RL*   10 greets *RL*

Beckening call to those that roam
Guiding the squandering covey home
Swallows check their rambling flight
& twittering on the chimney light
Round the pond the martins flirt   15
Their snowy breasts bedawbd in dirt
While the mason neath the slates
Each morter bearing bird awaits
Untaught by art each labouring spouse
Curious daubs his hanging house   20
Bats flit by in hood & cowl
Thro the barn hole pops the owl
From the hedge the beetles boom
Heedless buz & drousy hum
Haunting every bushy place   25
Flopping in the labourers face
Now the snail has made his ring
& the moth with snowy wing
Fluttering plays from bent [to bent]
Bending down with dews besprent   30
Circles round in winding whirls,
Through sweet evening's sprinkled pearls,
On each nodding rush besprent;
Dancing on from bent to bent:
Then on resting branches hing   35
Stren[g]th to ferry oer the spring
Playful still his hours to keep,
Till his time has come to sleep;
In tall grass, by fountain head,
Weary then he drops to bed.   40
From the hay cocks moistend heaps
Frogs now take their Vaunting leaps

11 call] hints *RL*   12 Guiding the squandering] That guide the squander'd *RL*
13 rambling] winding *RL*   16 in] with *RL*   19 By art untaught *RL*
23 the beetles boom] in drowsy hum *RL*   24 Heedless buzzing beetles bum *RL*
27 hath *RL*   31–4 *Copy-text: RL*
35–6
                              Now to downy grasses clung,
                              Resting for a while he's hung;
                              Then, to ferry o'er the stream,
                              Vanishing as flies a dream;   *RL*

37–40 *Copy-text: RL*   42 Frogs now take their] Startled frogs take *RL*

& along the shaven mead
Quickly travelling the[y] proceed
Flying from their speckled sides   45
Dewdrops bounce as grass divides
Now the blue fog creeps along,
And the bird's forgot his song:
Flowrets sleeps within their hoods
Daisys button into buds   50
From soiling dew the butter cup
Shuts his golden jewels up
& the Rose & wood bine they
Wait again the smiles of day
Neath the willows wavy boughs   55
Nelly singing milks her cows
While the streamlet bubling bye
Joins in murmuring melody

Now the hedger hides his bill
& with his faggot climbs the hill   60
Driver Giles wi rumbling joll
& blind ball jostles home the roll
Whilom Ralph for doll to wait
Lolls him oer the pasture gate
Swains to fold their sheep begin   65
Dogs bark loud to drive em in
Plough men from their furrowy seams
Loose the weary fainting team

44 Quickly travelling] Jumping travellers *RL*
45–6
                     Quick the dewy grass divides,
                     Moistening sweet their speckled sides;
                     From the grass or flowret's cup,
                     Quick the dew-drop bounces up. *RL*

45 Flying *through* Jump in the *MS 1*   46 bounes *MS 1*   47–8 *Copy-text: RL*
49 Flowrets] Flowers now *RL*   56 Nelly]Dolly *RL*   57 streamlet] brook, as *RL*
59 Hedgers now along the road *RL*   60 the *repeated MS 1*   Homeward bend
beneath their load *RL*   61 Dick and Dob, with jostling joll *RL*   62 Homeward
drag the rumbling roll *RL*   66 bark loud to] loud barking *RL*
67–8 Ploughmen loose their unweary teams / Leaveing by halves the unfinishd seams
MS 1 variant   And from the long furrow'd seams, / Ploughmen loose their weary
teams: *RL*   68 *MS 1 variant followed by:* Dob so loath tos work to com[e] / Well as
best now blunders home / x x x / Tugging at the load of hay / As passing Gileso hugs
away

Ball wi cirging lashes weald
Still so slow to drive afield   70
Eager blundering from the plough
Wants no wip to drive him now
At the stable door he stands
Looking round for friendly hands
To loose the door its fastening pin   75
Ungear him now & let him in
Round the Yard a thousand ways
The beest in expectation gaze
Tugging at the loads of hay
As passing fotherers hugs away   80
& hogs wi grumbling deafening noise
Bother round the server boys
& all around a motly troop
Anxious claim their suppering up
From the rest a blest release   85
Gabbling goes the fighting geese
Waddling homward to their bed
In their warm straw litterd shed
Nighted by unseen delay
Poking hens tha[t] loose their way   90
Now within the hovel flies
Slumbering there [the foxes prize]
Now the cat has ta'en her seat,
With her tail curl'd round her feet;
Patiently she sits to watch   95
Sparrows fighting on the thatch
Dogs lick their lips & wag their tails
When doll brings in the milking pails

69 cirging] urging *RL*   74 looking *MS 1*   75 To *through* The *MS 1*
76 And let him with his corn begin *RL*   78 The *through* watering *MS 1*   The
beest] Beasts *RL*   79 Tugging *through* Bellowing *MS 1*] Catching *RL*
80 Passing fodd'rers tug away *RL*   aways *MS 1*   81 & hogs] Hogs *RL*
83 all around] far and near: a motly troop] the motley group *RL*   86 Gabbling
through Waddling *MS 1*   goes] home: fighting] quarreling *RL*   87–8 *Transposed*
RL   87 And, waddling, prate away to bed *RL*   88 In] Seek *RL*
90 hens *through* capons *MS 1*   91 On the hovel's rafters rise *RL*
93–4 *Copy-text: RL*   95 Patiently she sits] Crafty cats now sit *MS 1*
97–8 *Tranposed RL*   97 Dogs . . . &] And dogs begin to *RL*   98 Now Doll
brings th' expected pails *RL*

With stroaks & pats their welcomd in
& they with looking thanks begin   100
She dips the milk pail brimming oer
& hides the dish behind the door

Prone to mischief boys are met
Gen the heaves the ladders set
Sly they climb & softly tread   105
To catch the sparrow on his bed
& kill em O in cruel pride
Knocking gen the ladderside
Cursd barbarions pass me by
Come not turks my cottage nigh   110
Sure my sparrows are my own
Let ye then my birds alone
Sparrows come from foes severe
Fearless come yere welcome here
My heart yearns for fates like thine   115
A sparrows lifes as sweet as mine
To my cottage then resort
Much I love your chirping note
Wi my own hands to form a nest
Ill gi ye shelter peace & rest   120
Oh quick desert each pilfering boy
Ere they your little life destroy
O woud they meet some mysery
Some foe as bad as they're to thee
Shoud rogues disturb their waking dream   125
How hard how cruel woud it seem
Forcd from theer beds their rest resign
& take their lives as they do thine
What pains woud rack those hearts forlorn
That now'd be laughing them to scorn   130

---

100 thanks] wants *RL*   101 She dips] Slove in *RL*   102 & hides the]
She pops their *RL*   104 Gen] 'Neath *RL*   105 & softly] in softest *RL*
107 Massacred, O cruel pride *RL*   108 Knocking gen] Dash'd against: ladder's
side *RL*   112 thy *MS 1*   113 Sparrows come] Come, poor birds *RL*
114 you're *RL*   115 for fates] at fate: yours *RL*   116 ours *RL*
121–2 *Copy-text: MS B1*   124/5 Was they to meet like misery / Some foes as bad
as they to thee *MS 1*

Trifling are the deed[s] ye do
Grait the pains ye undergo
Cruel man woud Justice serve
Their crueltys as they deserve
& justest punishment pursue   135
& do as they to others do
Ye mourning chirpers fluttering here
They woud no doubt be less severe
Tho ye pluck the farmer[s] wheat
Hunger forces all to eat   140
Foolhardy clown neer grudg[e] the wheat
Which hunger forces them to eat
Your blinded eyes worst foes to you
Neer see th[e] good which sparrows do
Did not the sparrows watching round   145
Pick up the inscet from your grounds
Did not they tend your rising grain
You then might sow—to reap in vain
Thus providence when understood
Her end & aim is doing good   150
Sends nothing here without its use
Which Ign'rance loads with its abuse
Thus fools despise the blessing sent
& mocks the givers good intent
O god let me the best pursue   155
As Id have other[s] do to me
Let me the same to others do
& learn at least Humanity

Dark & darker glooms the sky
Sleep gins close the labourers eye   160

---

138 doubt *through* less *MS 1*   141 Hardy clowns! grudge not the wheat *RL*
142 them] birds *RL*   143 worst *over* are *MS 1*   144 Neer]
Can't *RL*   145 the sparrows] poor birds with *RL*   146 insects *RL*
147 they not *RL*   148 then *through* vain *MS 1*   149 when] right *RL*
150 Her] Whose *RL*   152 Which] Though: with its] it with *RL*   153 Thus]
And *RL*   the blessing sent [despise] *MS 1*   154 mock *RL*   155 the best]
what's good *RL*   156–7 *Tranposed RL*

Dobson on his greensward seat
Where neighbours often neighbour meet
Of c[r]ops to talk & work in hand
& battle News from foreign land
His last wift hes puffing out   165
& Judie putting to the rout
Who gossiping takes great delight
To shool her nitting out at night
Jingling newsing bout the town
Spite o dobs disliking frown   170
And many a thing, her evil eye
Can see they don't come honest by.
Chattering at her neighbours door
The summons warns her to give oer
Prepar'd to start, she soodles home,   175
Her knitting twirling o'er her thumb,
Leaveing th'unfinishd tale in pain
Soon as evening comes again
Wi Apron folded oeer her arms
The tale so fraught wi lieings charms   180
So loath to leave afraid to stay
She bawls her story all the way

161 ff.

Neighbours no will neigh greet
& by each door on bench or seat
Gospps fond of news & chat
Leave houshold concerns & that
Listening at each neighbour door   *MS 1, p. 19 variant* 5

161 on] leaves *RL*   162 Neighbours where they neighbours meet *RL*   163 Of
... talk] Crops to praise *RL*   164 battle News] battles tell *RL*   165 While
his pipe is puffing out *RL*   166 & Judie] Sue he's *RL*   167 Gossiping, who
takes delight *RL*   169 Jingling newsing] And back-bite neighbours *RL*
170 Who's got new caps, and who a gown *RL*   171–2 *Copy-text: RL*
173 her] a: door] house *RL*   174 She hears call out her frowning spouse *RL*
175–6 *Copy-text: RL*
177–82

As, loth to leave, afraid to stay,
She bawls her story all the way:
The tale so fraught with 'ticing charms,
Her apron folded o'er her arms,
She leaves the unfinished tale, in pain,   5
To end as evening comes again;   *RL*

And in the cottage gangs with dread,
To meet old Dobson's timely frown,
Who grumbling sits, prepar'd for bed,   185
While she stands chelping 'bout the town.

Night winds now on sutty wings
In the cotters chimney sings
Sweet I raise my drowsy head
Thoughtful stretching on my bed   190
Listning to their ushering charms
That shakes the Elm trees mossy arms
Yet still I love my lonley watch to keep
While all the drowsy world are lost in sleep
In soft Slumbers till they stronger creep   195
Then rockd by winds I fall to sleep

183–6 *Copy-text: RL*   187 The night-wind now, with sooty wings *RL*
189–90 *Tranposed RL*   189 Sweet] Soft *RL*   190 Now, as stretching o'er
the bed *RL*   191 their] the *RL*   192 shake *RL*   193 Till sweet
slumbers stronger creep *RL*   194 Deeper darkness stealing round *RL*
195 In *through* all *MS 1*   Then, as rock'd, I sink to sleep *RL*   196 'Mid the
wild wind's lulling sound *RL*   *The following lines in MS A1, f. 1ᶜ may be connected with this
poem:*

            Curling round in winding weeds
            Thro sweet evenings speckld heads
            Darting oer the ⟨awthorns⟩ bush
            Dancing round the nodding rush
            In playful sports its hours to keep   5
            Till its time is come to sleep

            Now dogs threatning barks are done
            & wounds no more the murdering gun

(l.2 speckld *through* speckling; l. 3 Darting *through* Darkening; l. 8 no] now)

AUTOGRAPHS: Pet. MS A4, pp. 5–6: Nor. MS 1, p. R3 (ll. 1–28, 41–3 only).
TRANSCRIPT: Pet. MS B1, pp. 115–16.
Dated: '1819' (MS A4, p. 5).

SOMTHING NEW

How varying is the taste of man
Still eager to pursue
That ever pleasing novelty
In meeting somthing new

In infancy the rage begins   5
(So tempting is the view)
Babes throw aside their once lov'd things
To sigh for somthing new

The hoop to day which boys are seen
So eager to pursue   10
To morrow lies a toy despis'd
Exchang'd for somthing new

Young miss's (if not catch'd in time)
—Be lovers ere so true
Grow fickle tires & turns 'em off   15
To seek for somthing new

Old maids whom every hope forsakes
The self same end pursue
& put their wrinkl'd mouths in form
To look for somthing new   20

SOMTHING NEW   *Title:* Somthing New *MS A4, wanting MS 1*   2 egear
MS 1   3 That] The *MS 1*   pleasing *underlined and line then deleted MS A4*
4 something *MS 1*   5 In *through* En *MS 1*   rage *underlined and line then deleted*
MS A4   6 is *through* its *MS A4*   (So powerful to subdue *MS 1*   7 [& b]
Babes *MS A4*   will thro: lovd *MS 1*   aside *over* [bye] *MS A4*]   by *MS 1*
8 To] & *MS 1*   9 The hoop the boy to day is seen *MS 1*   11 Thrown by to
morrow theyr forgot *MS 1*   12 Exchand *MS 1*   13 The maiden if not taen
in time *MS 1*   14 ‸ Be: eer *MS 1*   15 Grows: tire: turn em *MS 1*
16 something *MS 1*   17 hop *MS 1*   18 Save one remaining true *MS 1*
19 &] Will: rinkld: mouths] face *MS 1*   20 something *MS 1*

E'en wives—but hasty muse for bear
(Tho wives shou'd have their due)
Will often harbour evil thoughts
& wish for somthing new

Lawers & doctors each in turn   25
One common aim pursue
When one good job is finish'd they
Look out for somthing new

Poor victim poets vainly priz'd
By the diserning few   30
Still ryhme in hopes o' better days
& dwell on somthing new

—Ah shatter'd coat & wanted groat
When wil't be mine to view?
Thee thrown aside? & pockets lin'd   35
With hopefull somthing new

—Booksellers often miss the chance
Their customers pursue
When throwing usless books about
They search for somthing new   40

Tho fashions change with every day
Their votaries will pursue
Come as they will or fast or slow
They cry is 'somthing new'

So Gentlemen & ladies here   45
(In hopes to meet his due)
A humble clown exerts his skill
To offer somthing new

21 E'en wives] Nay wive *MS 1*   22 ∧ Tho: shoud: due ∧ *MS 1*   24 &] To
MS 1   25 Each *MS 1*   26 1 comon end pursue *MS 1*   27 & when 1
job is finishd they *MS 1*   28 somethin *MS 1*   29 victim *underlined*
MS A4   30 few *underlined MS A4*   33 wanted *underlined MS A4*
36 hopefull *underlined MS A4*   40/1 [Frail fashions change but every day / &
bells & beaus pursue] *MS A4*   41 Tho] The: changes: with *omitted MS 1*
42 Which bells & beaus pursue *MS 1*

He wishes every taste to please
& hopes to find it true 50
So good or bad or what they will
This "Trifles'" somthing new

AUTOGRAPH: Nor. MS 1, p. 5 (reverse of title-page, pencil).
Dated: 1808–19 (MS 1).

No hailing curry favouring tothers
Muses gins my story
Blunt—as when ones wrongd by another
I fling my case before ye
& curse the hour ye weigling Witches 5
Your weiglings ere got round me
& wish I had been dead ye bitches
Ere ye a Jingling found me
That evil day I came your laky
& laugh stock for a century 10
When vain subscriptions fussd poor Jacky
To 'pear among the gentry
When thrown aside my spade & pickers
Wi vain aspiring spirit
I left my mates wopstraws & diggers 15
& fancied I had merit
But yourns the fault ye blinking bitches
(The Lord a'mighty bless us)
To fancy one that dug in ditches
Might work on mount parnassus 20
Thus as twas you that wispering said it
& well enough you knew it
I might come in for fame & credit
If Id stick up for poet
I was contented wit while earning 25
A shilling mong my neighbours
Unknown to books unknown to learning
& peace then crownd my labours

NO HAILING CURRY FAVOURING TOTHERS *Title: wanting* 1 No
through If   5 *First* i *through* g *in* weigling   24 id

AUTOGRAPH: Nor. MS 1, p. 6.
TRANSCRIPTS: Nor. MS 4, p. 1: Pet. MS C2, p. 27.
Dated: 1808–19 (MS 1).

ON MR — LOCKING UP THE PUBLIC PUMP

To lock up Water—must undoubted stand
Among the Customs of a Christian land
An Action quite Uncommon and unknown
Or only practic'd in this place alone
A Thing unheard of yet in Prose or Rhyme 5
And only witness'd at this present time
—But some there is—a stain to Christian Blood
That cannot bear to do a Neighbour good
—No!—to be kind and use another well
With them's a torment ten times worse then hell 10

Such Fiends as these whose charity wornt give
The begging Wretch a single chance to live
—Who to nor Cats nor Dogs one crumb bestows
Who even grut[c]h the droppings of their Nose
—Its my Opinion of such Marngrel curs 15
Whom Nature scorns to own and Man abhors
That could they find a f—t of any use
They'd even burst before they'd set it loose!

ON MR — LOCKING UP THE PUBLIC PUMP   *Title:* On Mr — locking up the
Public Pump *MS 4 MS C2, wanting MS 1   Pencil emendations in MS 1 are probably
Taylor's*   1 Water *to* water (*p.e.*) *MS 1*   2 Customs *to* customs (*p.e.*):
Christian *to* christian (*p.e.*) *MS 1*   3 Action *to* action (*p.e.*) *MS 1*   4 practic'd
to practis'd (*p.e.*) *MS 1*   7 is *to* are (*p.e.*): Christian *to* christian (*p.e.*): Blood *to*
blood (*p.e.*) *MS 1*   11 wornt *to* won't (*p.e.*) *MS 1*   12 a *over* [one] *MS 1*
17 *fart*

AUTOGRAPHS: Nor. MS 1, p. 10 (o.p.): Pet. MS A6, p. 15.
TRANSCRIPTS: Nor. MS 4, pp. 1–2: Pet. MS C2, pp. 27–27a.
Date: 1808–19 (MS 1).

LINES WRITTEN WHILE VIEWING SOME REMAINS
OF AN HUMAN BODY IN LOLHAM LANE

    Sure t'was the murderers hand that laid thee low
    And with the ponderous club or dredful knife
        Or such like weapon struck the deadley blow
        And rob'd thy body of its precious life
            Nay it might not be so:—   5
            Perhaps these mangled bones
        When they was blest with life tho long ago
        Hath trac'd sweet musick thro her highest tones
        Perhaps a genious powerful and strong
        Well skill'd in all the majesty of song   10
    Dwelt in this dust—and this his wish to have
    His bone inter'd in this sequester'd spot—
    Vain roving thought—what this a poets grave
    And not one record left—but all forgot
            What such reward?   15
            If thou had eloquence
            What thou a bard?
            And this thy recompence

    Sure this cant be—howe're as nothing's shown
    All these congecterings are but idly vain   20
    Thy fate thy fame a like to me unknown
    And all my searching fruitless to obtain

LINES WRITTEN WHILE VIEWING SOME REMAINS OF AN HUMAN
BODY IN LOLHAM LANE *Title*: Lines, written while viewing some Remains, of
an / Human, Body; in Lolham Lane. *MS 1*, Lines occasioned by viewing some remains
of an human / Body in Lolham lane *MS A6*   *Pencil emendations in MS C2 are Clare's*
1 the *to* thee (*p.e.*) *MS 1*] the *MS A6*   2 dredful *to* dreadful (*p.e.*) *MS 1*] dreadful
MS A6   3 likie: deadley] dreadful *MS A6*   7 was *to* were (*p.e.*) *MS C2*
8 Have *MS A6*] Hath *to* Have (*p.e.*) *MS C2*   tracd *MS A6*   10 *Second* l *through* d
in skill'd *MS 1*] skilld *MS A6*   11 *Second* this *to* twas (*p.e.*) *MS C2*
12 bones: sequestered *MS A6*   15 reward? [if thou] *MS A6*   16 had *to*
hadst (*p.e.*) *MS C2*   17 bard? [and] *MS A6*   19 howe'ere: nothings *MS A6*
21 alike *MS A6*   22 all *inserted MS 1*   fruitless *MS A6*

Yet he that governs all
And earth and air and sky
He knew thy death and end—he saw thy fall   25
And when and where for he is ever nigh
And if some impious ruffian laid the[e] low
If he or they it was that gave the blow
They will appear on that tremenduos day
When the redeemer comes to judge the land   30
Then will they all their guilty crimes display
Without disguise—and first that bloody hand
Then is their fate prepar'd
For this their vile offence
Then will they get their just reward   35
And thou thy recompence

AUTOGRAPH: Nor. MS 1, p. 10 (o.p.).
TRANSCRIPTS: Nor. MS 4, p. 2: Pet. MS C2, p. 27a.
Dated: 1808–19 (MS 1).

LINES TO BATH

Ye waters fam'd the ills of life to heal
Know what a son does for a Father feel.
He near worn out with the rumatic pain
Oft sought relief alas but sought in vain
Is now repairing to your healing wave   5
In hopes that it may be the means to save.
    If so as now you do that charge retain
If so as now he's safe upon thy shore
    If so as now thou cannot ease his pain
Send him save back—and I desire no more.   10

25 Death *MS A6*   27 the *MS A6*   29 tremendous *MS A6*   30 *Second*
the] this *MS A6*   33 prepard *MS A6*   35 get] meet *MS A6*
    LINES TO BATH   *Title:* Lines; / To Bath. *MS 1*

AUTOGRAPH: Nor. MS 1, p. 11 (o.p.).
TRANSCRIPTS: Nor. MS 4, pp. 2–3: Pet. MS C2, pp. 27a–28.
Dated: 1808–19 (MS 1).

THE FLOWER POTT

or Morrality and Reflection

On a fine sunday morning the house swep so clean
    And a flower pot for ornament plac'd
Compos'd of oak branches so spreading and green
    Intermingled with blue-bells the window-board grac'd.

To view their gay colors I rather inclin'd   5
    While resting myself near the wall
Which soon brought morality into my mind
    And thus I had model'd their fall.

'Tho your charms seem so tempting ye gay blooming flowers
    'As to make every stranger look on   10
'Yet if I stay here three or four passing hours
    'I shall see you all whither'd and gone!'

But afterwards thinking on what I had said
    Reflection soon made me to sigh
And once more reviewing their sweet smelling shade   15
    I suppos'd from the flowers this reply.

'Vain unthinking mortal how ready thou'rt prone
    'To condemn the short date of our flowers
'But stop with thy morals—turn the case to thine own!
    'And thou'l find it a deal worse than our's.'   20

'For go where thou pluck't us next year o'er the ground
    'There thou'lt find us as gay as before!
'But when once moralizer thy spring's gone its round
    'It never will blossom no more!'

THE FLOWER POTT OR MORRALITY AND REFLECTION   *Title:* The
Flower Pott; / Or Morrality, and Reflection. *MS 1*   5 *First* o *in* colours
inserted MS 1   17 Vain unthinking *to* Unthinking vain *(p.e., Clare) MS C2*

AUTOGRAPH: Nor. MS 1, p. 11 (o.p.)
TRANSCRIPTS: Nor. MS 4, pp. 3–4: Pet. MS C2, pp. 28–28a.
Dated: 1808–19 (MS 1).

FAREWELL TO A THICKETT

Dear blooming wild your shades and all
    Are so Familliar grown
That in my rapture I do call
    Your lonley scenes my own
Wildness I love—and loath to part   5
    From shades so wild as you
To leave lies heavy at my heart
    But I must bid adieu.

Nor can thy bower's romantic twine
    As if by faireys wove   10
My melancholly breast incline
    To settle in your grove
For know ye shades tis love that calls
    Tis love that does subdue
'Tis love which now my heart enthralls   15
    And makes me bid adieu.

But couldst thou boast within thy bower
    Of shrubs so rudely drest
One single twining branch or flower
    By my dear So[ph]y prest   20
O! then it would such thoughts convey
    Of love erewhile so true
That I could sit from day to day
    And never bid adieu!

FAREWELL TO A THICKETT *Title:* Farewell, to A Thickett. *MS 1*
20 So—y *MS 1*

AUTOGRAPHS: Nor. MS 1, pp. 12–15 (o.p.): Pet. MS A6, pp. 26–31 (ll. 1–136 only).
TRANSCRIPTS: Nor. MS 4, pp. 4–11: Pet. MS C2, pp. 28a–32.
Dated: 1808–19 (MS 1).

ROBIN AND SUKE
or *The Midnight Quarrel*

A Ballad

It thunder'd loud—the clock struck nine
  And pitchy darkness come
Poor frighted suke began to whine
  For Robin worn't got home

No friendly moon to lend her light   5
  He's all in darknes crost
Then who could think in such a night
  But what he would be lost

She rocks her chair and sobs and cries
  In a despairing plight   10
The dying fire neglected lies
  A mellancholy sight

And oft she ventures in the street
  Amid the dark profound
And often thinks she hears his feet   15
  Along the unseen ground

But ah! these fancied thoughts were vain
  No robin yet was nigh
She shuts the hated door again
  And heaves a mournful sigh   20

ROBIN AND SUKE *Title:* Robin, and Suke; or the Midnight Quarrel; / A Ballad.
MS 1, Robin and Suke / or / the midnight Quarrel *MS A6* *Stanzas 1–32 numbered in MS A6* *Pencil emendations in MS C2 are Clare's* 1 It thunder'd loud—] The white owl skream'd *MS A6* 3 began *altered to* begun: wine *MS A6* 4 robin *MS A6* wor'nt *MS A6*] worn't *to* not *(p.e.) MS C2* 8 what *to* that *(p.e.) MS C2* they *MS A6* 12 Melanclly *MS A6* 17 But ah that fancy'd thought was vain *MS A6*

'He's surely lost or else I think
'He would'n't stop thus late
'Unless the nasty vaporing drink
'Has settled in his pate'

'If so I hope he's sence enough   25
'To shun that lonley park
'The footpads are so wildley rough
'And more so in the dark'

'Besides them fishponds black and deep
'Lie just beside the road   30
'O! if the precious moon could peep
'It would be well bestow'd'

Such are the might be doubts and fears
That haunt the troubl'd breast
And his past conduct fresh appears   35
Which makes her more distrest

But hope that name which all invokes
Brought notions much more free
'Perhaps' she cries 'theres other folks
'About as well as he'   40

Thus consolated from despair
By hopes assistance blest
She sits down in her old low chair
To make herself at rest

21 'Hes: think' *MS A6*   22 wou'dn't: late' *MS A6*   23 drink' *MS A6*
25 sense enough' *MS A6*   26 park' *MS A6*   27 foot pads: wildly rough'
MS A6   29 ∧ Besides: fish ponds *MS A6*   30 ∧ Lie *MS A6*   31 ∧ O!:
could *through* woud *MS A6*   32 ∧ It: bestow'd ∧ *MS A6*   33 Might: &
MS A6   34 That *through* Which: the] her *MS A6*   37 all *inserted MS 1*
39 she cries] say she: 'theirs: folks' *MS A6*   44 And makes her self at rest (e *in*
self *inserted) MS A6*

But when a mind is once distres't   45
   What trifles will renew
A dreadful owl when all at rest
   Near to her window flew

It shriek't how horrid was the tone
   Especially to her   50
She sigh'd and cried 'by this I'm shown
   'That worse things will occur'

Again what hopeles doubts and fears
   Disturb her troubl'd breast
Again that dreaded park appears   55
   In horrors mantle drest

In the dark wood she see's him stand
   Prest with contending strife
Distinct she hears the rogues demand
   'Your money or your life'   60

Frighted to death with thoughts like these
   All hopes away she threw
Vain as they where nought could appease
   Now she believ'd them true

The fire gone out and tinder damp   65
   She mourn'd her troubles sore
But ere she struck a rough-hew'd stamp
   Spoke something near the door

45–8 *Replaced in MS A6 by*   The glasses mounted on her nose
                            All ready to begin
                            She fetches out the worsted hoes
                            And sticks the needle in

                            But ere she pul'd the worsted threw 5
                            O piercing was the smart
                            A Shriek owl near the window flew
                            It chill'd her very heart

49 shriek't] scream'd *MS A6*   51 & cry'd: shown' *MS A6*   53 what *through* the: & *MS A6*   55 that] the *MS A6*   58 Prest with] In fierce *MS A6* 61 death! *MS A6*   62 All hopes] Her work *MS A6*   64 em *MS A6* 65 and] the *MS A6*   67 [h]ere: struck— *MS A6*

She listn'd strict it stamp't anew
   And then began to cough   70
By this last sighn full well she knew
   The lost man worn't far off

Yet 'stead of joy as one would think
   The blood boild in her veins
For still the 'fishponds' and the 'drink'   75
   Perplex'd her crazy brains

'I'll warrant him I'll learn him how
   'To stop again thus late
'And surely if he fronts me now
   'He'll get a broken pate'   80

Her muttering's stopt—the door went clench
   He's com'd in sight almost
No sooner in but—'well my wench
   'Didn't ya think me lost'

So soft so greeting was the tone   85
   So civil who could blame
Yet his old nasty forked joan
   Could not return the same

'Think ya lost not I indeed
   'There's no such luck as that   90
'Would it where so I should be free'd
   '—But I must bear my lot'

He heard (besure) yet hadn't caught
   To where they did refer
For poor old boy he little thought   95
   How matters stood with her

69 strict!: anew! *MS A6*   72 Poor robin wor'n't far off *MS A6*   74 boil'd *MS A6*   vains *MS 1*   75 'fish ponds' *MS A6*   76 cazy *MS A6*   77 i'll *MS 1 MS A6*   how' *MS A6*   78 late' *MS A6*   79 now' *MS A6*   80 ∧ He'll: pate ∧ *MS A6*   81 mutterings stop't: whent *MS A6*   83 wench' *MS A6*   84 yah *MS A6*   86 civil—: blame? *MS A6*   87 his] the: jone *MS A6*   89 yah lost—: i indeed' *MS A6*   90 that' *MS A6*   91 Wou'd: freed' *MS A6*   92 '—' But *MS A6*   93 hard *MS A6*

'"Luck to be lost" 'bless us' thinks he
   'This must be something odd
'And "bear my lot" what can it be?
   'That knocks agen her nodd'   100

Thus thought he to himself why not
   Yet still he was to seek
'Luck to be lost' and 'bear my lot'
   To him appeard as greek

The case stood thus—(which soon will show   105
   That cottering suke thought wrong)
T'was clipping time and then you know
   A shepherds in full throng

His own sheep left—for he was loth
   To loose this lov'd employ   110
And as he could not do 'em both
   He fors't to hire a boy

But still he took a great delight
   About his flock to con
And always whent that way at night   115
   To see how they got on

So as he whent his usual round
   On this unlucky night
Suprising change when near the ground
   No flock appear'd in sight   120

Vext to the quick he went away
   Nor stood awhile to doubt
But quickly call'd to poor old trey
   'Boy we must find em out'

97 lost'—*MS A6*   99 'Bear: be $_\wedge$ *MS A6*   100 again: Nodd $_\wedge$ *MS A6*
101 him self *MS A6*   104 appear'd *MS A6*   107 time—*MS A6*
108 Shepherd's *MS A6*   111 doe *MS 1*   em *MS A6*   112 forst *MS A6*
113 still] yet *MS A6*   114 his *to* his own *(p.e.) MS C2*   115 whent that way]
wander'd round *MS A6*   119 change!: when *through indecipherable MS A6*
121 Vex'd *MS A6*   122 awile *MS A6*   123 poor old] faithful *MS A6*

Oer hill and dale they went that night   125
   Thro many a neighbouring ground
At last a shepherd set them right
   And pointed to the pound

At hearing this good story oer
   Joy glow'd within his breast   130
His fears and doubts was then no more
   All troubl'd thoughts had rest

The boy still lost—but this you see
   Could not fresh griefs begin
For 'bout such idle rouge's as he   135
   He never car'd a pin

And now the cause which made him late
   Is plump and plainly shown
We'el turn the tale to Robins fate
   And visit noisey joan   140

Who murmur'd much and shook her head
   But as a Fox more sly
He patiently heard all she said
   And never made reply

T'was droll to see the old boy sit   145
   His nose straight looking down
With broad brim'd hat turnd up to fitt
   That scarce could boast a Crown

He seemd a dad of ancient taste
   In such a antique barge   150
With great coat belted round his waist
   And buckles monstrous large

But in describing coat and hat
   We still loose sight of home
For in a ballad rightly pat   155
   Digressions ne'er should come

125 O'er *MS A6*   126 Thro' *MS A6*   128 pounde *MS A6*
132 troubled *MS A6*   135 rogues *MS A6*

Therefore with these descriptive things
   In future we'l be dumb
But turn where scolding musick rings
   With never ceasing hum   160

Suke when she did forsee with all
   Her scolding to affright
That Bob who never spoke a't'all
   Would gain the Vic'try quite

Turn'd to a more majestic tone   165
   With railings not to seek
That might torment a very stone
   Or urge the dumb to speak

'Ah! thou poor degected sight
   'Disgraceful quite to men   170
'Do what I would to keep the[e] tight
   'My labour provd in vain'

'But yah may mend yar rags ya sen
   'For Ive no more to do
'And where ya have been go agen   175
   'With all yar trumpery too'

'That coat I bought the rogue one fair
   'No other was so stout
'Tis but nine year since I declare
   'And now its quite wore out'   180

'Its all in vain—hes such a stroy
   'Buy hose or what I will
'Just like a young and ramping boy
   'Hes always wanting still'

'Ah!—(and shook her head) thou ragged ruff   185
   'Thy conduct grieves me sore
'But I'm determin'd thats enough
   'To rap and rend no more'

164 the] ℅ *MS 1*   168 spake *MS 1*   169 thou *to* thou'rt a *(p.e.) MS C2*
174 ive *MS 1*   184 His *MS 1*

Thus she whent on in railing wad
  Which provd succesful too   190
For Robin grew so wonderous mad
  He knew not what to do

Wether to speak or still keep mute
  He knew not which to try
But buying 'coats' would never suit   195
  That forc'd him to reply

'Ya poor old silly prating fool
  'Ya make me call ya so
'Whor I a boy that went to school
  'More power ya cou'dn't show'   200

'Thou buy me coats and this and that
  'Why thou'rt a funny duke
'That love's to hear thy ownself chat
  'Who finds the Money suke?'

'There lies the point—is't ya or I?   205
  'Say that or else give oer
'If ya'r the finder then beguy
  'I'll never work no more'

This struck so deep—no more she said
  But striving to get o'er   210
Wang went the platter at his head
  The candle on the floor

One was to mark him if she could
  The other was to blind
For sure she thought he never would   215
  His way thro darkness find

But he deciev'd a second time
  For nimbly as the lark
He did the old rough ladder climb
  Nor car'd about the dark   220

185 ['Ah!'] *(p.e.) MS C2*   193 spake *MS 1*   206 oer *to* in *(p.e.) MS C2*
208 no more *to* again *(p.e.) MS C2*   215–16 *Through two indecipherable lines MS 1*

Soon as he gaind the wellknown spot
    Where he had often lain
He triumph'd oer the vic'try got
    And sung the 'point' again

'There judie where thy proud stiff joint   225
    'Of self conceit gave way
'And still I say the "points" the "point"
    'And money rules the day'

'Think as ya will suke I dont care
    'But I'm determind quite   230
'After ya'r good behaviour there
    'To be ya'r match this night'

'I am not drunk if so I think
    'It very strange must be
'But as for talking 'bout the drink   235
    'That matters not to thee'

'If I like to get drunk I will
    'For all such fools as suke
'I said so once and own it still
    'That ya'r a funny duke'   240

'The "points" the "point" ah! thats the song
    'I love so dear to play
'Old suke shall hear it all night long
    'While morning brings the day'

Theres mighty words in triumph led   245
    All overpowering quite
Muse bind thy laurels round his head
    As Victor in the fight

225 There judie where *to* Stay Suke below till *(p.e.) MS C2*   226 gave *to* give
(p.e.) MS C2   229 i *MS 1*   232 To be yar match] *successively (a)* [Here ye
shall stay] *(b)* Ye shall remain *(p.e.) MS C2*   237 i *(second word) MS 1*
246 All *through* He *MS 1*

AUTOGRAPHS: Nor. MS 1, p. 16 (o.p.): Pet. MS A6, pp. 16–17 (ll. 1–48, 61–6 only).
TRANSCRIPTS: Nor. MS 4, pp. 11–13: Pet. MS C2, pp. 32–32a.
Dated: 1808–19 (MS 1).

THE INVOCATION

How mournful glides this purling streem
Ye oaks how lonley do ye seem
   The thickett and the grove
From whence the cause?—this strikes me near
I need not ask 't'is B[etse]y dear   5
   Her whom I truly love

She loves the wispers of your trees
She loves the evenings cooling breeze
   She loves to walk the grove
But now she's absent while I stray   10
Then O! what can these sighs convey
   And truly tell my love

Can you ye breeze's oak's or streem
Can you in thought in form or dream
   A lovers herald prove?   15
They wisper 'yes' O! precious scenes
I love your shades of various greens
   Go truly tell my love

And first this flower shall be addrest
Perhaps the first by B[etse]y prest   20
   When hither she does rove
O! charming flower if ever she
Should press the velvet leaves like me
   Ne'er fail to tell my love

THE INVOCATION   *Title:* The Invocation *MS 1,* The Frantic Lovers Exclamation *MS A6*   1 stream *MS A6*   2 seem [that] *MS 1*   3 thicket *MS A6*
5 tis *MS A6*   B——y MS 1 *MS A6*   12 And] To *MS A6*   13 breezes oaks and stream *MS A6*   14 thoughts *MS A6*   15 Lovers: prove ∧ *MS A6*
16 'yes': scenes *through indecipherable MS A6*   20 B——y *MS 1*] be—y *MS A6*
22 O!] Then: if] when *MS A6*   23 Should] Does: the]thy *MS A6*
24 Ne'er fail] Fail not *MS A6*

But in a softer sweeter strain   25
From thy perfuming sweets complain
   As ever yet could move
For know she's fickle as shes fair
Then charming flower dont dally there
   But quickly tell my love   30

And you ye breezes bland and cool
That bend the reed along the pool
   And shake the aspin grove
My wailings waft where B[etse]y lies
Hide nothing tending to suprise   35
   But truly tell my love

And O! ye shadowey clouds that flie
Beneath the blue ethereal skie
   And in due order move
When ere ye fall in showers of rain   40
Beat in her ear a pensive strain
   And truly tell my love

Thou night which so at ease can wear
Each visionary form—be there
   And oer her pillow move   45
Wrapt in my shade with streeming eye
Mourn forth her name then heave a sigh
   And truly tell my love

And still within this mazy round
Is there aught else that can be found   50
   Succesfully to prove?
This brook might take—but then alas!
She might be absent when they pass
   And never hear my love

25 sweeter] seeming *MS A6*   26 perfumings *MS 1*   29 charming] lovley:
don't *MS A6*   32 bend *through* shade *MS 1*   34 B——y *MS 1*] betsey
MS A6   36 truley *MS A6*   39 move] rove *MS A6*   42 truley *MS A6*
43 wair *MS A6*   44 form.— *MS A6*   46 streaming *MS A6*   48 truley
MS A6   49 *Through* Is there aught else that can be found *MS 1*

But O! yon bird might easy gain   55
Reception for my abscent pain
  Then haste thee gentle dove
Coo in her ear my lonley fate
As soft as to thy own dear mate
  And truly tell my love   60

And thou blest fancy deign to lend
Thy kind assistance to a friend
  Which might so usful prove
Go haunt her by each pebly stream
In pensive mood or soothing dream   65
  Most truly tell my love

Then this is all I ask ye powers
Enough the breezes birds and showers
  With flowrets of the grove
O! when my charmer comes this way   70
Each one this only charge convey
  To truly tell my love

AUTOGRAPH: Nor. MS 1, p. 16 (margin).
Dated: 1808–19 (MS 1).

      I dreamd & even think I see him now
      As I sat milking our old pedy cow
      Came up & made my heart jump up for fear
      & rapt me oer the arm & calld me dear
      My dear he said you need not be afraid   5

61–4 *Through a draft of the first three lines of the next verse MS 1*   62 Thy] Some
MS A6   63 Which[It: useful *MS A6*   64 pebley *MS A6*   66 truley
MS A6   72 *Followed in MS 1, p. 17 by* Sonnet, on Home *which is published in our
volume for 'The Village Minstrel'*

  I DREAMD & EVEN THINK I SEE HIM NOW   *Title: wanting*   5 i *through*
d *in* said

AUTOGRAPHS: Nor. MS 1, p. 17 (o.p., deleted in pencil): Pet. MS A3, p. 73.
TRANSCRIPTS: Pet. MS B1, p. 124: Nor. MS 5, p. 126.
Printed in *RL*, p. 191.
Dated: 1807–10 (*AW*, p. 103 'when I was 14 or 15'; MS A3, p. 73 'Old 8 or 10 ago'; *RL* Introduction, p. xxii 'before he was seventeen').

THE GIPSIES EVENING BLAZE

To me how wildly pleasing is that scene
    Which does present in evenings dusky hour
A Group of Gipsies center'd on the green
    In some warm nook where Boreas has no power
Where sudden starts the quivering blaze behind   5
    Short shrubby bushes nibbl'd by the sheep
    That alway on these shortsward pastures keep
Now lost now shines now bending with the wind
And now the swarthy sybil [k]neels reclin'd
    With proggling stick she still renews the blaze   10
    Forcing bright sparks to twinkle from the flaze
When this I view the all attentive mind
    Will oft exclaim (so strong the scene prevades)
    'Grant me this life, thou spirit of the shades!'

THE GIPSIES EVENING BLAZE *Title:* Gipsies Blaze, at Eve. *MS 1*, The Gipsies Evening Blaze a Sonnet *MS A3*, The Gipsy's Evening Blaze *RL*   1 me, *MS A3*   2 doth *RL*   evenings *inserted MS 1*   3 Group *to* group *(p.e.):* Gipsies, *to* gipsies, *(p.e.):* Green *to* green *(p.e.) MS A3*   4 (In *to* In *(p.e.):* nook,: power) *to* power *(p.e.) MS A3*   soom *MS 1*] soom *to* some *(p.e.) MS A3*   5 suden *to* sudden *(p.e.):* Quivering *to* quivering *(p.e.) MS A3*   6 shruby *to* shrubby *(p.e.) MS A3*   7 alway] mostly *MS A3 RL*   short-sward: keep— *MS A3*   8 shines *through* seen *and* shines *written over in pencil MS A3*] seen *RL*   9 kneels *MS A3*   11 from *through* in *MS 1*   flaze *to* haze *(p.e.) MS A3*   12 allattentive *MS 1*] alattentive *to* all attentive *(p.e.) MS A3*   13 (so *to* so *(p.e.):* prevades) *to* prevades *(p.e.) MS A3*   scenes *MS 1*   14 Life∧ *to* life∧ *(p.e.) MS A3*   *Followed in MS 1,* p. 17 by Poverty *which is published in our volume for* 'The Village Minstrel'

AUTOGRAPHS: Pet. MS A3, p. 73: Nor. MS 1, p. 18 (deleted in pencil).
TRANSCRIPT: Pet. MS B1, p. 124 (deleted in pencil).
Dated: 'old' (MS A3, p. 73).

EPIGRAM ON ROME

Occasioned by Reading Mr Rolts Translation
of Sannazarios (Famous!) Epigram on Venice

Sannazar'o makes Neptune to exclaim
'That men built Rome, but Gods did venice frame!'
Here he must flatter—for if thats the odds
Rome shows that men had better skill then Gods

AUTOGRAPHS: Nor. MS 1, p. 18 (o.p.): Pet. MS A6, p. 20 (ll. 21–4
omitted).
TRANSCRIPTS: Nor. MS 4, pp. 14–15: Pet. MS C2, pp. 33–33a.
Dated: 1808 or later (*Cottage Poems* 1808).

TO MRS ANNA ADCOCK AUTHOR OF 'COTTAGE POEMS'

Sweet rural Songstres of the Rustic grove
How dear to me thy sympithizing strain
Thy faults I trifles deem thy lays I love
Nor shall those trifles strive to please in vain

EPIGRAM ON ROME *Title:* Epigram on Rome / Occasioned by Reading Mr
Rolts Translation / of Sannazarios (Famous!) Epigram on Venice *MS A3*, Epigram, on
Rome. / Occasioned, by Reading, Mr Rolts Translation, of / Sannazario's (Famous!)
Epigram, on Venice. *MS 1*   1 Sannazar: makes] supposes, *MS 1*   2 Men:
but] and: Gods,: Venice frame'. *MS 1*   3 But, stop vain Boaster: —for if thats
the odds, *MS 1*   4 that men] her Men,: than Gods!!. *MS 1*

TO MRS ANNA ADCOCK AUTHOR OF 'COTTAGE POEMS' *Title:* To Mrs
Anna Adcock, Author, of, / 'Cottage Poems.' *MS 1*, To Mrs Anna Adcock Author of
'Cottage Poems' *MS A6*   1 songstress: rustic *MS A6*   3 I trifles deem] as
Trifles deem'd—: lays] songs *MS A6*   4 those trifles] thy verses *MS A6*

But O! Enthusiastic natures child   5
    When ere I roam thro lone Eves moistning dew
Thy 'Poems' charm me in the dreary wild
    While added lustre brings their scenes to view

There when I see the 'Wild briers straggling rose'
    Thy wildness brings me to Simplicity   10
For lo the sting which slighted Friendship knows
    Throbs thro my bosom as it did with thee

And know sweet Songstres:—(tho I cant impart
    High learned lays to court what Witts bestow)
I store within this breast a feeling heart   15
    That melts with pity oer anothers woe

Thy fate I mourn alas! but thats in vain
    Tho its no more than every Poets doom
And this to ease they seek the Muses train
    On Parnas hill where joys for ever bloom   20

There Thompson sought for charms to ease his grief
    And there those charms by Thompsons lyre was gaind
There poor lost Goldsmith crav'd and got relief
    Which he by Labour otherwise maintain'd

Then keep thy Epithet 'Meek natures Child'   25
    From her gay stores another Garland weave
Resing the beauties of each blooming wild
    And like thy kindred ever cease to grieve

5 Natures Child *MS A6*   6 eve's *MS A6*   7 Thy . . . me] I read
thy Volumne *MS A6*   8 thy *MS A6*   9 see] view: ∧wild: stragling rose∧
MS A6   10 I own thy wildness in simplicity *MS A6*   11 I feel the sting wich
slited friendship know (feer *altered to* feel) *MS A6*   12 And all those troubles that
encompass thee *MS A6*   13 And]For: songstres:— ∧tho *MS A6*   14 wits
bestow∧ *MS A6*   15 I . . . breast] Within this breast I hold *MS A6*   16 oer]
for *MS A6*   17 I mourn thy fate alas!—: that's *MS A6*   18 (Tho: poets
doom) *MS A6*   19 And to ease which they seek some tender strain *MS A6*
20 That brings them quickly to a welcome tomb *MS A6*   22 g *through* f *in*
gaind *MS 1*   25 epithet 'meek Natures Child∧ *MS A6*   28 And . . . kindred]
—And may dire evils *MS A6*

AUTOGRAPH: Nor. MS 1, p. 19 (o.p.).
TRANSCRIPTS: Nor. MS 4, p. 15: Pet. MS C2, p. 33a.
Dated: 1808–19 (MS 1).

SUN-RISING IN SEPTEMBER

How delightfuly pleasant when the cool chilling air
   By september is thrown oer the globe
When each morning both hedges and bushes do wear
   Instead of their green—a grey robe.

To see the sun rise thro the skirts of the wood   5
   In his mantle so lovley and red
It cheers up my spirits and does me much good
   As thro the cold stubbles I tred.

Tho not that his beams more advances the scene
   Or adds to the Landscape a charm   10
But all that delights me by him may be seen
   That the ensuing hours will be warm.

And this with the poet as yet in the world
   In a parrarel sence will comply
For when he does view the gay scenes there unfurl'd   15
   Tis only to light him on high.

AUTOGRAPH: Nor. MS 1, p. 19 (o.p.)
TRANSCRIPTS: Nor. MS 4, p. 16: Pet. MS C2, pp. 33a–34.
Dated: 1808–19 (MS 1).

SONG

Since Flora disdains me—her once loving swain
   Forever I'le cease to adore
And leave the[e] my Tray with this crook on the plain
   In quest of some pleasenter shore.

SUN-RISING IN SEPTEMBER   *Title:* Sun-rising, in September. *MS 1*
8 tred∧ *MS 1*   11 is—by (*Clare seems to have changed his mind here*) *MS 1*
SONG   *Title:* Song. *MS 1*

Lo! the vales once so charming no more appear gay   5
    Since she does my prescence despise
For if she but sees me oer the hill far-away
    Quik down in the valley she flies.

To withstand this contempt in a maiden so cruel
    Resolution itself is in vain   10
And her once seeming kindness returns with fresh fuel
    That serves to rekindle my pain.

What must be the reason—to me is unknown
    Not a fortnight can tell of the change
Since she us'd to call 'the fond shepherd her own'   15
    And wherever I pleasd she would range.

T'was then when the best smelling flowrets so fair
    That grew in the meadow or grove
I culled—and wove in fresh wreaths for her hair
    Which she falsely repaid me with love.   20

But these past illusions are never to ease
    Nor serve me my folly to blind
So I'le seek for soft pleasures ne'er failing to please
    And erase the false maid from my mind.

AUTOGRAPH: Nor. MS 1, p. 22 (margin).
Dated: 1808–19 (MS 1).

ON HOPE

    Vain flattering hope while woes distress me
    Thy flattery I desire again
    Still still I beg on thee to bless me
    & thou art nurser of my pain

8 flies∧ *MS 1*   24 *Followed in MS 1, pp. 20–2 by* Narrative Verses, Written after / An Excursion, from Helpston, to Burghley Park *which is published in our volume for 'The Village Minstrel'*

ON HOPE   *Title:* On hope (*Vain flattering of first line through* On hope)
2 I again

When dissapointments vex & fetter   5
& tells me hope thy cordials vain
Still must I rest on thee for better
Still live—& be decievd again

I cant but listen to thy p[r]attle
I still must hug thee to my breast   10
& like a child thats lost its Rattle
Without my toy I cannot rest

AUTOGRAPH: Nor. MS 1, p. 22.
TRANSCRIPTS: Nor. MS 4, p. 20: Pet. MS C2, p. 36.
Dated: 1808–19 (MS 1).

A MAIDEN-HAID

A maiden head the virgins trouble
Is well compared to a bubble
On a navigable river
—Soon as touch'd 't'is gone for ever

AUTOGRAPH: Nor. MS 1, p. 23.
Dated: 1808–19 (MS 1).

Hail England old England my Country & home
Thou pride of thy Sons & thou dread of the world

Hail England old England my country & home
Now thy colours in libertys cause are unfurl'd
I Glory to hear how thy brave heroes roam   5
The pride of their country and dread of the world

8 diecievd
   A MAIDEN-HAID   *Title:* A Maiden-haid *(i through d in* Maiden*) MS 1*
1 i *through* d *in* maiden *MS 1*   4 touch'd *through* prickd *MS 1*
   HAIL ENGLAND OLD ENGLAND MY COUNTRY & HOME   *Title: wanting*
2/3 *Row of asterisks in a space enough for seven lines*   4 thy *repeated*

Then hail to thy flowers with their cannons & Guns
That to guard thee are always in motion
And the same to the sea all around thee it runs
All hail to thy waves guardian Ocean   10

AUTOGRAPH: Nor. MS 1, p. 23.
Dated: 1808–19 (MS 1).

WONDER!!! IF A WOMAN KEEPS
A SECRET

'O what charming ringlets' cries Chloe amazd
   To a Lady a Maid of three score
'Are these false curls of yours Maum the heavens be praisd
   'If I ere saw such beauties before'

'False curls Maum' affronted belinda replied   5
   'Tho you're to such trumpry prone
'For my part I cannot your set-offs abide
   'Be as fine as they will they're my own'

'Yours'!! 'Yes' Cries her Maid like a blobing out Jay
   'That they are Maum I know't to be true   10
'For I my self Bought them of shavers to day
   'And gave him a Crown for 'em too!!

AUTOGRAPH: Nor. MS 1, p. 24.
Dated: 1808–19 (MS 1).

   Behind the far woods lowly sunk was the sun
   Scarce a streak could be seen in the west
   All the horison round was encircl'd wi' dun
   And Owls ere and there with their hoopings begun

10 *Followed by a double row of asterisks in a space enough for another eight lines*

WONDER!!! IF A WOMAN KEEPS A SECRET   *Title:* Wonder!!! If a Woman
keeps / A Secret.

BEHIND THE FAR WOODS LOWLY SUNK WAS THE SUN   *Title: wanting*

And Crows where all flocking to rest   5
When Ra[l]ph on the road from the fair once again
Had seven long miles for to go
And now these sad omens appeard but too plain
And this way & that way he turnd & again
He hopd that it couldnt be so   10

AUTOGRAPHS: Nor. MS 1, p. 24a (o.p.): Pet. MS A3, p. 99.
TRANSCRIPTS: Pet. MS B1, p. 159: Nor. MS 5, p. 47.
Printed in *RL*, p. 194.
Dated: 'Old' (MS A3, p. 99).

THE PISMIRE

Thou little insect infinitely small
What curious texture marks thy minute frame
How seeming large thy foresight and withall
Thy labouring tallents not unworthy fame
To raise such monstrous hills along the plain   5
Largher than mountains when compar'd with thee
To drag the crumb dropt by the village swain
Thrice bigger than thy self—is strange indeed to me
But that great instinct which foretells the cold
And bids 'em gard 'gainst winters wasteful power   10
Endues this mite with cheerfulnes to hold
Her toiling labours thro the sultry hour
So that same soothing power of Misery
Cheers the poor Pilghrim to Eternity!

9 And *through* ? As

THE PISMIRE   *Title:* Sonnet, on the Pismire. *MS 1*, The Pismire *MS A3*, The
Ant *RL*   *Stanza divisions after ll. 4, 8, 12 MS 1 MS A3*   1 Inscet *MS A3*
3 & with all *MS A3*   6 Larger then mountains! *MS A3*   8 Thrice . . . —]
Hughe size! to thine—*MS A3*, Hugh size to thine, *RL*   me—*MS A3*   9 Instinct
MS A3   10 &: guard: wastefull *MS A3*   'em] to *RL*   11 chearfulness
MS A3   12 Her] Its *MS A3 RL*   13 —So: misery *MS A3*   of] in *RL*
14 pilgrim *MS A3*

AUTOGRAPH: Nor. MS 1, p. 24a (o.p.).
TRANSCRIPTS: Nor. MS 4, p. 74: Pet. MS C2, pp. 62–62a.
Dated: 1808–19 (MS 1).

SONG

Fast by a Brook beneath a bending willow
    Where shrubs surounding in a roomy glade
While yellow king cups form'd a golden pillow
    Seeming retirement! blest with cooling shade.

To shun the heat fair Florimella came   5
    Nor thought what harm such lonley shades might bring
But carlesly lay down—and soon her flame
    Was lulld to slumber by the purling spring.

Without the bower her crook neglected lay
    While favorite Rover tended it so true   10
These where the only things that did betray
    For Collin saw them and away he flew!

Void of all fear he sought her snowey charms
    Where a loose robe display'd her panting breast
Eager he claspt her in his clownish arms   15
    And soon his longing wickedness had rest.

She tho unconscious of her undone fate
    Startled suppris'd from feelings new begun
Alas! poor girl her slumbers broke too late
    Since virgin sweetnes Beautys all was gone!   20

Be this a Caution then to all fair maids
    That still can boast their maidenheads so pure
Nor trust like florimel to sleep in shades
    However seeming lonley or secure!

SONG   *Title*: Song. *MS 1*   24 *Followed in MS 1, p. 25 by* To the Violet *which is
published in our volume for 'The Village Minstrel'*

AUTOGRAPH: Nor. MS 1, p. 25 (margin).
Dated: 1808–19 (MS 1).

    Souls so distrest no comfort never knows
    But hopes despairing hatches keener woes
    Who now as prisoner sits prepard to flye
    On each wingd groan & heavy rending sigh
    Rent is the heart with dark dessending fate   5
    Views all around it in a kindred state
    Each object now seems witness—to her cost
    & hints that Innocence neglect had lost
    The things that once coud pleas now pleas no more
    & as their im[a]ge bygone scenes explore   10
    Memerys rank poison festers still more deep
    & what was once gives fresh[er] cause to weap
    Ah coud I see the Cheat I now can see
    A[s] I was then the sigh I *now* might be
    Ill fated girl—the days still come & go   15
    But marys settld grief no Change can know
    Bent on her end the fate known [best]
    & night invites to sleep—but not to rest.

AUTOGRAPH: Nor. MS 1, p. 27 (o.p.).
TRANSCRIPTS: Nor. MS 4, p. 75: Pet. MS C2, p. 63.
Dated: 1808–19 (MS 1).

SONG

    'If Kittys rosy presence now
      'Should chance to bless my sight
    'Again the oft repeated vow
      'She'd witness with delight

SOULS SO DISTREST NO COMFORT NEVER KNOWS *Title: wanting
Preceded by:* The soul oer gloomd in sure impending fate / Views every object in a
kindred state   10 explore *through* restore   12/13 [Ah could I see the cheat
that now is seen]   16 C *through* g *in* Change   18 *Followed in MS 1, pp. 25–6
by* Helpston Green *which is published in our volume for 'The Village Minstrel'*
SONG   *Title:* Song. *MS 1*

'Again the church again the spire   5
'Would promt her bosom with desire
'But O sweet kitt spurn not delay
'Time will bring the promis'd day.'

Thus sung the poor enarmourd swain
    As labouring along   10
Echo viebrating catch'd the strain
    And brought him back the song
        Again the rocks again the plains
        In mellower sound repeat the strains
        Till all in chorus roundelay   15
        Join and sing the 'promisd day.'

AUTOGRAPH: Nor. MS 1, pp. 27–31 (o.p.).
TRANSCRIPTS: Nor. MS 4, pp. 76–81: Pet. MS C2, pp. 63–6.
Dated: 1808–19 (MS 1; *Letters*, p. 131 'earlyish I think about 15' (i.e. 1808–9)
but this seems unlikely as Hurn's *Rural Rhymes* (l. 52) appeared in 1813).

THE WISH

If wishes could be gaind and I might have
What ere of worldly things I lik'd to crave
Such as would free me from all labouring strife
And make me happy to the end of life,
In doing this I'de take the surest plan   5
To bind contentment with the future man;
And first if wishing could such pleasure give,
I'de chuse a descent house wherein to live.
The spot should be beneath a neighbouring hill
Fronting the south close to a winding rill;   10
As other cots the plan both wide and long
With walls made roughly durable and strong,
One outward door might all my needs suffice
Tho' in such trifles I should not be nice.

11 viebriating *MS 1*   15 Will *altered to* Till *MS 1*
    THE WISH   *Title:* The Wish. *MS 1*   7 wishing *inserted MS 1*

Of british oak the roofing should be made   15
And best of slate should be upon them lade,
I would chuse slate tho thatch is my desire
Because slate roofs will not so easy fire,
Then when the outside wall and roof where lade
Inside convenience should be nicely made,   20
First room for a small cellar should be found
Wholesome and cool but not made under ground;
They serve to loose the fabrics weighty load
And proves a harbour for the nuisom toad,
Therefore it should be level with the rest   25
Well stor'd with ale the oldest and the best
On whose good cheering strength I might depend
When making welcome with a trusty friend
For lifes a drone where friendship has not part
A utter stranger to the feeling heart.   30
And next a pantry suitable indeed
To store that nourishment we mostly need;
With dairy joining where the brimming pale
Demands a situation very swale,
For this a window northward should be made   35
With clumps of elder closley set to shade.
Methinks thus far the things are so compleat
They promise fair a comfortable seat.
A noice small parlour too I should desire
So well convinient for a winter fire   40
For in that season larger rooms are cold
Small ones are snuger as the less they hold,
Hung round with little pictures it should be
For these are trifles which I love to see,
Near the fireside close fitted in the wall   45
I'de have a nice made cubboard not too small
Each shelf in breadth so uniformly pland
That books in eightvo size or more might stand
For this one use I'd have the cubboard made
Where none but choisest authors should be laid,   50

19 made *altered to* lade *MS 1*   20 convienience *MS 1*   26 with *repeated*
MS 1   30 the *inserted MS 1*   39 noise *altered to* noice *MS 1*
42 Smallones *MS 1*

Such as Dermody Scott Macniel and Burn
With rural Bloomfield Templeman and Hurn
These are the authors that can boast the power
Of giving raptures in a leisure hour,
And tho I read some of them every night   55
Their songs near fail of adding fresh delight.
A descent Bed too here would surley prove
A neat appendage for a winter stove
Where daily living in't would make the air
More warm and dry then emty chambers are;   60
Now this would be compleat—but then I doubt
A little kitchen can't be done without,
Then this I'de have with coppers neatly hung,
Likewise a oven closley arch'd and strong
With other things nescesity would plan   65
As shelves for dishes or a wellscour'd pan,
But these are trifles which might soon be got,
Two chambers now would just compleat my cot,
In chusing these I'de ask no more than two
They would be plenty quite and nicely do,   70
The one wherein thro summer I might sleep
The other should my orchards produce keep
Yet both sho[u]ld boast a bed as one might be
Useful for those that came to visit me,
Of this there should be very little shown   75
Tho friends and nearest kin I'd never cease to own
But as my self they both alike should fare,
And while it lasted might be welcome there.
My chamber window should oer look the east
That in delicious views my eyes might feast   80
There girt with crimson see the morning sun
Thro distant trees his journey just begun
Still mounting every moment stages higher
And as his height increases so the fire
At other times succeeds the vapouring mist   85
Hiding each object quite from east to west.
While other mornings shine with pearly dews
Then is the time to look for distant views.

77 share *altered to* fare *MS 1*   86 quuite *MS 1*

The Tree the Wood the Cot and distant Spire
I would search after with a fond desire.   90
In this said window too I would peruse
Each sweet production of the rural muse
While sparrows from the eves in chirping throng
Should never fail to welcome with their song.
And now the house is fram'd beyond excuse   95
Wanting naught else but household goods for use:
They should preserve one order all along
Made roughly descent durable and strong
For like to Pomfret I could n'er endure
The needles pomp of gaudy furniture.   100
What I should want few words may soon explain
All that was useful nesessary plain
These and no more would bound my ample choise
And decorate my cot extreemly nice.
And now a garden pland with nicest care   105
Should be my next attention to prepare;
For this I'd search the soil of different grounds
Nor small nor great should mark its homley bounds:
Between these two extreems the plan should be
Compleat throughout and large enough for me;   110
A strong brick wall should bound the outward fence
Where by the suns allcheering influence
Walltrees should flourish in a spreading row
And Peach and Pear in ruddy lustre glow.
A five foot bed should follow from the wall   115
To look compleat or save the trees withall
On which small seeds for sallading I'd sow
While curl-leaf Parsley should for edges grow.
My Garden in four quarters I'd divide
To show good taste and not a gaudy pride;   120
In this the middle walk should be the best
Being more to sight exposed than the rest,
At whose southend a harbour should be made
So well belov'd in summer for its shade:
For this the rose would do or jessamine   125
With virginbower or the sweet woodbine,

Each one of these would form exactly well
A compleat harbour both for shade or smell.
Here would I sit when leisure did agree
To view the pride of summer scenery   130
See the productions promis'd from my spade
While blest with liberty and cooling shade.
But now a spot should be reserv'd for flowers
That would amuse me in those vacant hours
When books and study cease their charms to bring   135
And Fancy sits to prune her shatterd wing,
Then is the time I'd view the flowrets eye
And all loose stragglers with scotch-mattin tye;
The borders too I'd clean with nicest care
And not one smothering weed should harbour there: 140
In trifling thus I should such pleasure know
As nothing but such trifles could bestow.
This charming spot should boast a charming place
Southwardly plan'd my cottage front to grace.
There a nice gras plat should attract the eye   145
Mow'd every week more level then the dye.
Ah! think how this would decorate the scene
So fine a level and a finer green.
My borders they should lie a little flue
And rear the finest flowers that sip the dew   150
The roses blush the lilies vying snow
Should uniform their namles beauties show,
With fine ranuncullus and jonquil fair
That sweet perfumer of the evening air
The scabious too so jocolatley dusk   155
Should there be seen with tufts of smelling musk
The woodbine tree should all her sweets unfurl
Close to my door in many a wanton curl.
Aside my wall the vine should find a place
While damask roses did my window grace: 160
And now a walk as was the plan before
Exactly coresponding with the door
Should lead my footsteps to another bower
Whenever leisure gave the pleasent hour.

131 productions promis'd *(first* o *in* productions *inserted) through two indecipherable words* MS *1*   160 s *in* damask *inserted MS 1*   161 a *inserted MS 1*

But once again the greens delightful spot   165
Should wear a ornament I quite forgot;
A little pond within a circle laid
It would look nice and might be useful made:
The side with freestone should be walled round
And steps the same to bevel with the ground.   170
There sweet Nymphea lover of the tide
Should deck my mimic pool with spangling pride.
Oft would I seek the steps in midday hour
When sol mounts high in full meredian power
To see its leaves that on the surface lie   175
Prove Boats of Pleasure to the dragon flye.
Ah scenes so happy void of all controul
Your seeming prospects heightens up my soul;
E'en now so bright the fairy vision flies,
I mark its flight as with possesing eyes   180
But thats in vain—to hope the wish was gave
It clogs the mind and binds the heart a slave.
Tis nothing but a wish one vents at will
Still vainly wishing and be wanting still
For when a wishing mind enjoys the view   185
He dont expect it ever will come true,
Yet when he cherishes the pleasing thought
He still keeps wishing till he wants for nought,
And so will I—My eyes shall wander oer
A Pleasent prospect, Acres just threescore,   190
And this the measure of my whole domains
Should be divided into woods and plains,
O'er the fair plains should roam a single cow
For not one foot should ever want the plough
This would be toiling so I'd never crave   195
One single thing where labour makes a slave.
Tho health from exercise is said to spring
Foolhardy toil that health will never bring.
But 'stead of health—dire ills a numerous train
Will shed their torments with afflictive pain.   200
Be as it will I hold in spite of strife
That health ne'er rises from a labouring life;

176 boats *altered to* Boats: the *inserted MS 1*   185 For *through* Nay! *MS 1*
191 the *inserted MS 1*   195 toiiling *MS 1*   198 never *inserted MS 1*

Therefore the busines that such labour gave
When I could do without I'd never have:
All I would do should be to view my grounds 205
And every morning take my daily rounds
To see that all was right and keep secure the bounds:
With trifling in the garden now and then
Which finds employment for the greatest men
Each coming day the labour should renew 210
And this is all the labour I would do,
The other hours I'd spend in letterd ease
To read or study just as that might please,
This is the way my plan of life should be
Unmaried Happy in Contentment free. 215
For he that's pester'd with a noisey wife
Can neer enjoy that quietnes of life
That does to life belong—Therefore I'd ne'er
Let Hymen's torch within my cot appear.
For all domestic needs that did require 220
Womans assistance—I'd a servant hire
She should be mistres of the whole conscern
And what she could'n't do she soon might learn
But this should be the character I'd seek
Well made not proud her looks entirley meek 225
Not fond—but witty nor unknown to books
With mind entirley modest as her looks.
That charming she that was adorn'd with these
Could never fail in quietnes to please.
And now my income which I have not made 230
Should touch at living desent yearly paid,
This would suffice me—for I'd never stride
O'er scenes of descency to follow pride.
A little over plus I might expend
T' relieve a Beggar or to treat a friend 235
For while I'd money left or bread to spare
The Beggar always should be welcome there.
Tho' this was all in wishing I would have
Posses'd of these I nothing more should crave,

205–7 *Bracketed together because of triple rhyme MS 1*　　216 For he that's *through three indecipherable words MS 1*　　231 touch . . . desent *through four indecipherable words MS 1*

Save when the worn out numbers of fourscore 240
Had fix'd their standard on my grey grown shore
Then one more wish should be the last I'd crave
A Painless Exit to a welcome grave.

AUTOGRAPH: Nor. MS 1, p. 31 (margin).
Dated: 1808–19 (MS 1).

How welcome & sweet is springs infant dawning
The Elder as witness puts out her broad leaves
The Robin sweet tutles his hymn to the morning
& sparrows are chirping their joy in the eaves

O sweet shines the sun on the wakening morning 5
O rich the young landscip his lustre displays
& sweet his first smile on the crocus flower dawning
Whose borrowd pride shines dizend out in his rays

AUTOGRAPH: Nor. MS 1, pp. 31–2 (o.p.).
TRANSCRIPTS: Nor. MS 4, p. 82: Pet. MS C2, pp. 66–66a.
Dated: 1808–19 (MS 1).

EDWARD'S GRAVE

When others, fearful of the Gloom,
　Their homeward path pursue,
Fond sally seeks for Edwards tomb
　Her sorrows to renew.

Where prayers of tenderness and love 5
　By pilgrims often heard
Does court the angelic realms above
　Her lover to reward.

HOW WELCOME & SWEET IS SPRINGS INFANT DAWNING *Title:*
wanting 3 Robin *through* sparow
EDWARD'S GRAVE *Title:* Edward's Grave *MS 1*

Nor wizzards jump, nor gobblin tale,
   Nor mimic elfin sprite,   10
Nor moping gost, nor spectre pale,
   Nay the most dismal night

When hollow winds does wisstle thro
   The mournful cypress shade,
When bent in howling rage the Yew—   15
   Can never fright the maid.

No, no, her ever sorrowing mind
   Attach'd to grief so strong
Does never listen to the wind,
   Nor heed the gobblin throng.   20

Her sighs are urgh'd in heartfelt grief
   For Edwards haples fate,
She seeks but cannot find relief
   All sorrow is too late.

Alas! poor maid, thy Edwards dead   25
   And far beyond thy power;
In vain thy low reclining head
   Bends down the sickly flower;

He cannot hear, he cannot see,
   Pent low beneath the sod.   30
Then rise, chear up from misery
   And leave his fate to God.

24 sorrow is *through* is too late *MS 1*

AUTOGRAPHS: Nor. MS 1, p. 32 (o.p.): Pet. MS A3, pp. 101–2.
TRANSCRIPT: Pet. MS B1, pp. 160–1.
Printed in *RL*, pp. 166–9.
Dated: 'Old' (MS A3, p. 101).

MY LAST SHILLING

O dismal disaster! O troublesome lot!
What a heart rending theme for my musing Ive got
Then pray whats the matter? O friend I'm not willing
   The thought grieves me sore
   Now I'm drove to the shore   5
And must I then spend the last shilling the shilling
   And must I then spend the last shilling

O painful reflection thou whole of my store
That for these three months in my breeches I've wore
To spend thee, to spend thee, that thought turns me chilling   10
   O must I in spight
   Of all reason this night
A Farwell bid to my last shilling my shilling
   A Farwell bid to my last shilling

How oft in my corner I've troubl'd my pate   15
First mournd at my shilling and then at my fate
To think the gay world all a sporting and billing
   While I must endure
   The sad pain past a cure
Of being drain'd to my very last shilling my shilling   20
   Of Being draind to my very last shilling

MY LAST SHILLING   *Title:* My last Shilling. *MS 1 RL*, My Last Shilling *MS A3*
1 lot,! *MS A3*   2 ive *MS A3*   3 —Then *MS A3*   5 Im *MS A3*   drove
to the] driven to *RL*   6 & *MS A3*   *First* the] my: *second* the] last *MS A3 RL*
7 &: the] my *MS A3*   8 reflection, *MS A3*   9 I've *through* m *MS A3*] I *RL*
10 thee∧—*(third word) MS A3*   that] the *MS A3 RL*   11 spite *MS A3*
12 all *through* my *MS 1*   13 farewell *MS A3*   *Second* my] last *MS A3 RL*
14 fare well *MS A3*   too *MS 1*   15 Ive *MS A3*   troubl'd] botherd *MS A3,*
bother'd *RL*   16 mourn'd *through* mourned: & *MS A3*   17 To think
the worlds riches—thought painfull & killing *MS A3 RL* (thought] though *RL*)   a
sporting *through* sport *MS 1*   18 must] here *MS A3 RL*   20 *Second* my] last
MS A3 RL   Shilling *(last word) MS A3*   21 being *MS A3*

O coudst thou but answer dear whole of my store
I'd ask thee a Question:—thus friendles and poor
Whether thou would to leave me be willing
  Or wether it still   25
  Would be more to thy will
To stay and be call'd my last shilling my shilling
  To stay and be call'd my last sh[i]lling

Thou scourse of reflection my friend and my all
For now Im left friendles thou sticks to thy stall   30
And thro each vexing trouble seems cheary and willing
  Thee to keep I'll contrive
  Or Im sure I sha'n't thrive
If ever I spend such a shilling a shilling
  If ever I spend such a shilling   35

Then my only companion stick true to the breeches
And wear this old pockett thread bare to the stiches
For ever to keep thee Im certainly willing
  For who knows but what thou
  Tho' Im drove to shore now   40
May turn out a lucky last shilling last shilling
  May turn out a lu[c]ky last shilling

22 Answer *MS A3*   23 friendless & *MS A3*   24 Wether: leave & forsake me *MS A3*   'Tis whether: leave] forsake *RL*   wouldst *MS A3 RL*   27 &: calld *MS A3*   *Second* my] last *MS A3 RL*   28 &: calld: shilling *MS A3* 29 source: reflection—: & *MS A3*   30 now] tho': stick'st *RL*   friendless *MS A3*   31 & *twice MS A3*   seem'st *RL*   33 Or] For *RL*   shant *MS A3* 34 Shilling *twice MS A3*   35 Shilling *MS A3*   36 Then my only] So still old *MS A3 RL*   my *inserted MS 1*   Companion *MS A3*   37 &: pocket *MS A3*   the] its *MS A3 RL*   sticthes *MS 1*   38 Forever *MS A3*   Im certainly] I really am *MS A3 RL*   39 For] & *MS A3*, And *RL*   knows ? *MS A3* 40 (Tho I'm: now) *MS A3*   drove to shore] hard ashore *RL*   42 lucky *MS A3*

AUTOGRAPH: Nor. MS 1, p. 32 (margin).
Dated: 1808–19 (MS 1).

How lovly the thorn in the newly laid hedges
Shades wi deepening blushes a delicate green
Where linnets preparing for loves tender pledges
Cannot shelter their newly built cot from being seen

Point sharper your thorns soon unfold your gay branches   5
& keep out the schoolboy from prolling among

AUTOGRAPH: Nor. MS 1, p. 33 (o.p.).
TRANSCRIPTS: Nor. MS 4, pp. 82–3: Pet. MS C2, p. 66a.
Dated: Early 1819 (Explanatory Notes).

LINES ON WELLINGTON

Brittannia cease—For Nelsons doom
    From such bewailing cries
Since he has order'd from his tomb
    A Wellington to rise.
        O rather than his fate bewail   5
    Praise his unerring choise
        And this thy present heroe hail
    With bold triumphing voice,
He fights thy cause and will mantain
Thy power triumphant on the main,   10
    Whoever dare to crave
On Land or Sea where e'er he roves,
    Each Element a heroe proves,
        As skilful and as brave.

HOW LOVLY THE THORN IN THE NEWLY LAID HEDGES   *Title: wanting*
LINES ON WELLINGTON   *Title*: Lines on Wellington. (Welllinton *altered to* Wellingon) *MS 1*

When Nelson dy'd—France blest the same,   15
   But never thought no more
That other Nelsons—(Gallant Name)
   Whou'd terrify their shore.
     Poor Nap thinking to end the fight
   Rejoic'd in what was done   20
     And little thought that Nelsons night
   Could bring a Morning Sun.
For had he knew that Englands shore
Could boast one Gallant heroe more
   He'd surely curs'd that day   25
That sent a Nelson to the skies
   And bid a Wellington arise
     From Nelson's pregnant Clay.

AUTOGRAPH: Nor. MS 1, pp. 34–5 (o.p.).
TRANSCRIPTS: Nor. MS 4, pp. 83–6: Pet. MS C1, pp. 11a–13.
Dated: ?c.1816–19 (Explanatory Notes).

TO THE MEMORY OF
JAMES MERRISHAW
A VILLAGE SCHOOLMASTER

Remem'brance paints the scene of backward days
Prompting my Mem'ry to begin the lays;
But ah! a pause—the subject makes me grieve
And sorrowing sadness bid my bosom heave.
—Methinks the Muse in angry tone replys,   5
'Clown, with thyself no more apologize,
'Go search the churchyard were thy master lies,
'There seek the friendless grave without a stone,
'There find his mouldering dust that lies alone

4 Wellinton *altered to* Wellington *MS 1*   23 For *through* So! *MS 1*
28 [Remov'd], from: pregnant *inserted MS 1*   *Followed in MS 1, p. 33 by* Sonnet   Once
musing oer an old effaced stone *which is published in our volume for 'The Village Minstrel'*
TO THE MEMORY OF JAMES MERRISHAW A VILLAGE SCHOOLMASTER
Title: To the Memory, of / James Merrishaw; / A Village Schoolmaster. *MS 1   Pencil
emendations in MS C1 are Clare's*   5–7 *Bracketed together because of triple rhyme MS 1*

'Near where a bending walnut fans the grave
'With sweeping branches "idly bid to wave"
'There press the sod and muse upon the spot
'That once had kindred now by all forgot,
That once had learning worthy highest fame
'Yet still liv'd friendless and to die the same   15
'Think on all this—and tho more cold than clay
''T'will surley warm the[e] to begin the lay.'
—The Muse is right—I feel the kindling fire
Of indignation and a fond desire;
Ah! injur'd shade, this bosom felt for thee   20
Tho it was absent in thy misery.
I've often sought thy grave without a stone,
I've often strove to make thy memory known,
But all in vain—the spot was still unknown,
The simple lay no sooner made than flown,   25
My weak attempts seem'd all in vain to try;
Declining weakness—all was born to die.
But now I will attempt the promis'd lay,
And tho rough language points the vulgar way
It still shall boast this honorable part   30
Of having its origin from the heart.
Flattry shall never tempt my homley lays,
I neither want reward nor yet the praise,
Can only one succeed then alls repaid;
—To snatch thy memory from oblivions shade,   35
If in this single point my muse succeeds
'T'will be the whole reward her labour needs.
Ah! tho thy injur'd grave's without a stone
And nothing left to make thy memory know[n]
Tho no neglecting muse to force the tear   40
Mourn'd one soft strain oer thy unnotic'd bier
With me thy precious worth shall never die
While life remains to aid the feeling sigh.
O! then dear shade accept this rural lay
A Pupil brings thy kindnes to repay.   45
Tho weak his genious which would fain attone
To make thy memory and thy virtues known,

10 l *through* n *in* walnut *MS 1*   32 *Through* Can only thee succeed then alls
repaid *MS 1*   33 *Through* To snatch thy memory from *MS 1*   34 one
through this *MS 1*

Tho mean the lay to what thy worth requires,
'Yet naught is vain which gratitude inspires;'
Tis she that bids my artless muse pursue   50
Her lowley flight and give the tribute due,
Due to thy worth thy memory and thy grave,
For thou it was dear injur'd man that gave
This little learning which I now enjoy;
A Gift so dear that nothing can destroy.   55
Twas thou that taught my infant years to scan
The various evils that encompas man,
Thou Also taught my eager breast to shun
Those vain pursuits where thousands are undone.
And if such choise Examples I decline,   60
Then shame belongs to me—the praise is thine.
All this he's done for me—then ris[e] my soul
Above the littlenes of lifes controul;
Mind not what Booklearnt men or critics say,
Thine is the debt and be it thine to pay   65
Then muse arise—but first repeat the tone,
'A friendless grave that lies without a stone.'
Here sons of Learning candidates for fame
Whose Labouring toils a deathles merit claim;
Here see the wreck that poverty regards   70
A son of Learning yet theres no rewards.
He who pursue'd that ardorous task to rear
Young tender shoots to blossom and to bear
And in that labour did so strictly rule
As provd the man sufficient for a school   75
He who so skilld in arts would yield to none
And Science own'd him for her darling son
On Music's farthest shore he'd safley land
Touching her magic notes with powerful hand.
Thro Mathematics hidden depths he'd pry,   80
Trace all her windings with a skilful eye.
And in Geometry his searching view
Could draw a figure admirably true.
Figures or symbols either at his will
Would fetch the answer with uncommon skill.   85

56 thou *inserted MS 1*   60 Example[s] *(p.e.) MS C1*   67 less *in* friendless
inserted MS 1   70 theres no *to* without *(p.e.) MS C1*   76 so skilled *to* had
skill *(p.e.) MS C1*

Either to sing or plan or write or read
In each his powerful genius would succeed
Now he where all this ellegance was shown
'Lies mouldring in the grave without a stone.'
Ah! think on this ye sons to learning dear   90
And on his fate bestow a single tear.
Had he been rich possesing wealthy power
Ah! then the scene as changeful as the hour
Would turn another way—the flatt'rers verse
Must sing his praises and his worth rehearse.   95
His death would find the elegiac reed,
And 'Lines' and 'odes' would numberles succeed.
Granduer must now their once fine man reliefe
A Herse to carry and a Coach to grieve.
Next oer his grave the marbles taught to shine   100
Exact in features animatley fine:
And now the polishd muse must fondly give
Her last adieu and bid his memory live.
The verse must flourish round the collumns base
Enrich'd with each good deed and namless grace,   105
Such as perhaps he never did possess
(For splendid basenes never fails address)
Had he been rich this surley would be shown,
But he was poor and poverty his own
Which nipt his Genius on the learned stage   110
And held his labours from a thankles age
'Ah! think on this ye sons to learning dear'
'And on his fate bestow a single tear'
When press'd with poverty you muse alone,
'Think on the friendles Grave without a stone.'   115

87 ful *in* powerful *inserted MS 1*   88 Now ... all *through indecipherable MS 1*
94 the] a *inserted in pencil MS C1*   95 and ... rehearse *through indecipherable MS 1*
97 And 'Lines' and *through indecipherable MS 1*   104 The *through* This *MS 1*
110 nipt *to* kept *(p.e.):* on *to* from *(p.e.) MS C1*   111 And *to* With *(p.e.) MS C1*

AUTOGRAPHS: Nor. MS 1, p. 35 (o.p.): Pet. MS A3, p. 139.
TRANSCRIPT: Pet. MS B1, p. 9.
Printed in *RL*, p. 103.
Dated: 1808–19 (MS 1).

BEAUTY

Beauty how changhing and how frail
As skies in April showers
Or as the summers minute gales
Or as the morning flowers.

As April skies so Beauty shades   5
As Summer gales so Beauty flies
As Morning flowers at Evening fades
So Beautys tender Blossom dies!

AUTOGRAPH: Nor. MS 1, p. 36 (o.p.).
TRANSCRIPTS: Nor. MS 4, pp. 86–7: Pet. MS C1, p. 13.
Dated: 1808–19 (MS 1).

A CHARACTER

Her hair bound in tortoise or else loosley flowing
    (Lo each is a beautiful show)
More blacker than jet the fine ringlets seem glowing
    Nay they rival the Micaelmas sloe.

Her face cloth'd in blushes like the east in a morning   5
    Sheds a lustre so healthful and gay
And O! her sweet neck is with Cupids adorning
    More whiter than blossoms of May.

BEAUTY   *Title:* Beauty. *MS 1*, on Beauty *MS A3*, On Beauty *RL*   1 Beaty: changing & *MS A3*   2 april *MS A3*   4 flowers∧ — *MS A3*   5 april: beauty *underlined MS A3*   6 summer: beauty *MS A3*   7 morning: evening *underlined MS A3*   flowers, *MS A3*] flower *RL*   8 beautys: blossom *MS A3*

A CHARACTER   *Title:* A, Character. (ha *through* ar) *MS 1*

Her beautiful bosom with love sweetly swelling
   Whould make e'en a Hermit to long   10
And O! of her eyes and her lips theres no telling
   They'r out o' the reach of my song.

Her height with the rest in exactest propotion
   Nought defective throughout can be seen
And her fine limbs conceal'd will oft show their sweet motion   15
   When met by the wind on the green.

Tho her form is so charmingly fine tall and slender
   It does not outrival her mind,
She's equaly Modest Obliging and Tender
   That she seems for an angel designd.   20

She also is Witty and quick in descerning,
   Nor a stranger to Helicon's spring,
She's an able proficient in all sorts of Learning,
   To Draw or to Write or to sing.

O! Cupid since thou with thy Bow fast pursuing   25
   Made an Arrow flie twang thro my heart
Give me but this Maid I'll ne'er mourn the subduing,
   But bless the good aim of thy dart.

AUTOGRAPH: Nor. MS 1, p. 36 (o.p.).
TRANSCRIPTS: Nor. MS 4, p. 87: Pet. MS C1, p. 13a.
Dated: 1808–19 (MS 1).

THE POWERFUL SMILE

Dead lies poor Collin murder'd by a frown
   Shot from the strong arm'd tower of Chloe's eye,
The cruel dart did all his hopes uncrown,
   Pierc'd thro his heart—and made him seem to die.

27 subduing *through* pursuing *MS 1*
  THE POWERFUL SMILE   *Title:* The Powerful Smile. *MS 1*   3 crue⟨l
d⟩art *blot MS 1*   4 Pierc'⟨d t⟩hro *blot MS 1*

Yet spight of this—if oer his half-shut eyes   5
   Sweet Chloe deigns a magic smile to fling
Instant emerging in a wild suprise
   From death to life fond Lazarus will spring.

AUTOGRAPH: Nor. MS 1, p. 37 (o.p.).
TRANSCRIPTS: Nor. MS 4, pp. 87–8: Pet. MS C1, p. 13a.
Dated: 1808–19 (MS 1).

TO HOPE

O Muse bestow—nor think it vain
(While praise rebounds in just excess)
To a weak clown one single strain,
Fit and becoming hopes address,
   For O in every grief we find   5
   Her ready aid to cheer the mind.

Hail soothing hope recruiting power
In penitence and haples fate;
Assistant proof in latest hour
E'en thro the prisons gloomy grate   10
   Where Culprits almost hopeless grieve
   Thy form will glimmer to reprieve.

Thro life thus far—(so cloth'd in stains
Of Motley troubles as it is)
Me thou hast chear'd and still remains   15
To point to shores of endless bliss,
Tho doom'd perhaps another way
Sweet hope endears the wisht essay.

Thou balmy bland enlivner hail
Or false or true to the distrest   20
Thy form will dart in sorrows vale
A thwarting joy on troubles breast.

5 ⟨—⟩ *blot MS 1*
   TO HOPE   *Title:* To Hope, / A Fragment *MS 1*

AUTOGRAPH: Nor. MS 1, p. 37 (o.p.).
Dated: ?c.October 1819 (Explanatory Notes).

AUTUMN

Lo! Autumn's come—wheres now the woodlands green?
    The charming Landscape? and the flowrey plain?
All all are fled and left this motly scene
    Of fading yellow tingh'd with russet stain

Tho these seem desolatley wild and drear   5
    Yet these are spring to what we still shall find
Yon trees must all in nakednes appear
    'Reft of their folige by the blustry wind

Just so 't'will fare with me in Autumns life
    Just so I'd wish—but may the trunk and all   10
Die with the leaves—nor taste that wintry strife
    Where Sorrows urge,—but still impede the fall.

AUTOGRAPHS: Nor. MS 1, pp. 37–8 (ll. 4, 51–2 omitted): Norris Museum
SAVNM CL/14 (ll. 33–8 omitted).
Dated: 1808–19 (MS 1).

O who can paint the anguish of the heart
Or who the souls Ideas can impart
At that dread moment the self murderer stands
To fall   x   x   x   x   x
In that dread moment when the frantic heart   5
From Life the world & all prepares to start
To somewhere still unknown without a name
Or heavens bliss or hells eternall shame

AUTUMN   *Title*: Autumn

O WHO CAN PAINT THE ANGUISH OF THE HEART   *Title: wanting MS 1*
Norris   2 ideas *Norris*   4 *Copy-text: Norris*   *Line space MS 1*   6 Life,:
World, *Norris*   7 somwhere: Name *Norris*   8 eternal *Norris*

The Victims anguish here the heart conceals
& none can tell but [only] them that [feels]   10
When at the ponds steep verge she trembling stood
& gazd in horror on the whelming flood
That gent[l]y crimpld on its breezy wave
Soon to be ruffld with her watry grave
In musing anguish for awhile she stands   15
Holding her bosom with her clasping hands
Then Looks around in pains too deep to tell
& bids to all around a last farewell
& o that anguish more then death severe
That villians wrongs in dying doubly dear   20
In silent prayer her eyes are fixt on heaven
Her prayers are his that he may be forgiven
Herself forgot her prayers are all for him
& fear & fondness shivers every limb
Then firm resolvd to end her every woe   25
She takes a headlong plunge & dives below
The water splashes in convulsive sound
& foaming Eddies curdle all around
To the pond side the dashing billows gush
& starts the blackbird from the hanging bush   30
The wreathing chasm ebbs a weaker wave
Forever closes on her watry grave
& starting bubles in disorder rise
Where struggling fate beneath in horror dies
Then puft by breezes out then rise again   35
More small & small the leesening drops remain

10 only: them] *successively (a)* [them] *(b)* [thou] *(c)* he: feels *Norris*   13 genty *Norris*
14 with] as: Grave— *Norris*   16 with] in *through* with *Norris*   17 Looking
around in pain too sad to tell *Norris*   18 farwell *Norris*   19 O *Norris*
20 The wretch that wrong'd her 'een undying dear ('een *over* [now]) *Norris*
21 silent prayer] stedfast gaze *Norris*   22 Her . . . his] Prays [in tears] in her tears
(Prays *through* & prays: in *through* with): forgiven.— *Norris*   23 prayers] thought:
for] on *Norris*   24 shivers *to* shiver *(p.e., Taylor) Norris*   25 Till in a firm
resolve to end her woe *Norris*   [pain] woe *MS 1*   26 head long: dives] sinks
Norris   27 The soft flood takes her in a splashing sound (soft *through* flood)
Norris   First v *through* f *in* convulsive *MS 1*   29 ponds: dashing] foaming
through clos *Norris*   30 scares *over* starts *(Taylor)*: black bird: hanging] driping
Norris   31 wreathing] ebbing *through indecipherable*: ebbs] winds *Norris*
32 Forever] & ever *Norris*   36 remain[s] *MS 1*

Diminishing at last they all retire
& in a little train of froth expire
Ring within ring as faint they reach the side
Widening & weakening gradually subside   40
The dashing sound & Eddying wreaths are oer
& gentle calms ensue as heretofore
The breezes sweet crimps the curdling plain
The blackbird seeks her nest & sings again
The sun smiles happy on the neighbouring scene   45
& all seems now as tho there nought had been
The pond as usual meets each Gazers Eye
Gazers as usual peeps & hurrys bye
& as they mark the breezes curling wreath
They little think of her that lyes beneath   50
& little thinks as swells each harmless wave
That it is rolling over marys grave

AUTOGRAPH: Nor. MS 1, pp. 38–9
TRANSCRIPTS: Nor. MS 4, pp. 88–90: Pet. MS C1, pp. 13a–15.
Dated: 1808–19 (MS 1).

LOVE EPISTLES BETWEEN RICHARD AND KATE

Epistle 1st from Richard

Dear kate
    Since I no longer can
Go on in such a mopeing plan
I send these lines with ham and hum
To let the[e] 'no' I mean to cūm'

37 retire *through* expire *MS 1*   41 eddying *Norris*   43 breeze: as wont the:
⟨ plain⟩ *torn Norris*   [?lee unmolested] sweet *MS 1*   44 blackbirds *MS 1*]
black bird *Norris*   45 ⟨scene⟩ *torn Norris*   46 b⟨een⟩ *torn Norris*
47 each] the *Norris*   G *through* g *in* Gazers *MS 1*   48 peeps] look: hurry
Norris   50 lyes] sleeps *Norris*   51–2 *Copy-text: Norris*   51 swells
through indecipherable *Norris*   52 it is *over* [they are] *Norris*

LOVE EPISTLES BETWEEN RICHARD AND KATE *Title:* Love Epistles
between; / Richard and Kate. (i *in* Epistles *inserted) through* Epistles from Richard a
Cuntry Clown; / To Kitty the Milkmaid *MS 1*

Sūm' time or ūther you to see   5
W'en things ar' fitting to agree
For ever since you jog'd from here
The day to me do's seem a year
I can't endur't so 'tis no use
I love you wel' without excuse   10
Therefore as now I plainly show't
I only wish for you to 'now't
And w'en the let'er you do get
Let it suffice you how I fret
For e'rēy night I gang to bed   15
Nou'ht but kit runs in my he'd
The boys they all keep clit'er clat'er
Wondering w'at can be the mat'er
W'y I look dul'.—and w'ats befel'
They on'y wish I wou'd but tel'   20
But I'm determind not to do't
They'l' on'y call me foolish fo' 't
Yet not as I shou'd car' for that
'T' wou'd on'y then be tit for tat
But if I bro'ght thy name I 'no'   25
Up 'mong such chaps as Jim and Jo
(Tho Jim if he 'ad on'y sensē)
(To tel' mi'te be of conseq'ence)
For he can reēd an' never spel'
(An' 'rite a let'er mons'orous wel')   30
Was thou to heār't as likly mi''te
'Twou'd presen'ly to'n luv' to spite
An' wou'd so much a terify'd thee
As you ne'er after cou'd abide me
This is the reēson kit (don't dou't it)   35
That I ne'er tel' the boys about it
For I'll sweet kit the thing is tru'
Do ōny thing to pleasur' you
And w'ōt you do'n't like sh'u'd be
Shal' be the last thing dūn by me   40
For ere I 'rit this scraūling let'er
(I wish I cou'd ha' 'rit a bet'er)

12 only *altered to* ony *MS 1*   14 i *MS 1*   21 i'm *MS 1*   25 i *twice MS 1*

Fe'ēring sūm peeping chaps mi"te 'no'
I 'new not 'ardly w'ere to go
Yet anx"us stil' to send you one   45
I at last contriv'd an' pitch'd upon
Our bushy clos' agen the link
'Twas ther' I went wi' pen an' ink
The ink I stole from Jīmys box
For that he 'ardly ever lo'ks   50
(And if I'm 'ang'd for doing so
It wil' be you that caus'd the wo')
The paper at the shop I got
And lu'ky pitch'd upon this spot
Wher' skīlarks wis'l'd oer my head   55
And morning shun so bri"tē an' red
The dū on e'rēy bush did hing
An' bōds of al' so'tes did so sing
That cou'd I sing like farmer's Jo'
(For shep'āds all can sing you 'no')   60
I'd surely sung this very morn
An' made a song in bushy laūn
But thats all now't I can'ot sing
Nor 'bout this lawn nor 'bout the spring
En'ūf for me cans't thou but read   65
This baddy stuf quite bad indeed
An' w'at made worser on't you see
Was writing on't upon my 'nee
But w'y su'h 'pologin odrotit
The stufs for you an' we'n you've got it   70
Excuse the whol' an' never wonder
That 'tis in all a worthles' blunder
But kitty think nor think in vain
My daily toȳls my ni'tēly pa'nē
O if thy "art can tender be   75
'Twil' neyer fa'lē to pity me
I must konclude ther'fore ad"u
My "art an' so'lē's for' ever tru'

51 i'm *MS 1*   61 this *through* that *MS 1*   64 the *altered to* this *MS 1*

Answer 1st from Kate

Richard
   You sent your letter right
It came 'an' pat' on friday night   80
Brought by Farmers servant 'Hobbs'
Who always does the Market jobs
As luck wou'd have it he came by
Our Lee close where the cows all lye
He soon see me tho getting late   85
And rode plump up before the gate
His comeing thus supprisd me quite
And set my very hair upright
I'd lik'd to faint; til he cry'd out
'Hoi dont be frighted I'm no scout'   90
'Ive sūmmōt here ya'l not refuse'
'Fūr if I'm right its goodēr news'
Well more good news I says the better
Whi' that he pulled out a Letter
Is't mine 'ah to be sur'' he said   95
And whats the seal then Black or red
This I ask'd quickly, tho' unwilling
The very thoughts o' 't turn'd me chilling
For if the seal had not been red
I shou'd have thought some friend were dead   100
But soon the fancying terror fled
When I look'd on't and see it red
'Hoi hoi' Hobs says 'Ya needn't squint'
'Ther's nothing but good lūving in't'
'It cūm's̄ from sūm' fine chap or ūther'   105
Well never mind 'bout this or t'ot[h]er
Whats in't I says is nought to you
So I paid post and bid him go

88 v *through* f *in* very *MS 1*   92 i'm *MS 1*   106 or *inserted MS 1*
108 [his] post *MS 1*

AUTOGRAPH: Nor. MS 1, p. 40.
TRANSCRIPTS: Nor. MS 4, p. 91: Pet. MS C1, p. 15.
Dated: 1808–19 (MS 1).

AN ANSWER TO M.L.A.

I love thee Lucy love thee well
    But love to such excess
That how I love I cannot tell
    Untill I love thee less
And that I'm sure will never be   5
    To doubts then bid adieu
On Time relye and you shall see
    What Collin says is true

AUTOGRAPH: Nor. MS 1, p. 40.
TRANSCRIPTS: Nor. MS 4, p. 91: Pet. MS C1, pp. 15–15a.
Dated: 1808–19 (MS 1).

AN ACROUSTIC

Matchless the maid whom I so highly prize
In whom my evry hope encenter'd lies
She seems to me the fairest of the fair
She's more to me then hurds to mizards are
But O alas my love can't meet return   5
Eternally in secresy I burn
Taught by those friends to Silence.—Fear & shame
Secret I sigh for what I durst not name
Yet when that form appears which all excells
Nature my love by conscious blushes tells   10
E'en when her lovly face from sight retires
Wish after wish in fruitles hopes expires

AN ANSWER TO M.L.A.   *Title:* An Answer to M.L.A. *MS 1*
AN ACROUSTIC   *Title:* An Acroustic *MS 1*

But now I will (tho fearfull) tell my mind
O then sweet maiden tender prove & kind
Nor treat my humble suit with slight disdain   15
A smart most piercing to a love-sick swain
So lovly maid if you will tender prove
Hear him who fond (tho truley) tells his love
Trust swains no more who oft in outward shew
On lies depend to gain the point in view   20
No turn from these to him that loves thee true

AUTOGRAPH: Nor. MS 1, p. 41.
TRANSCRIPTS: Nor. MS 4, p. 71: Nor. MS 4, p. 92 (deleted): Pet. MS C2,
pp. 60a–61.
Dated: 1808–19 (MS 1).

SONG

Guardian Angels O protect me
  Help me all the powers above
In my troubles dont neglect me
  Now I'm cross'd in hopeles love

Love by you was first created   5
  To make every creature blest
O then let my pains abated
  Give my heart a little rest

Of proud Betsey I'm complaining
  She the fairest of the fair   10
Kills me with her proud disdaining
  Kills me with her scornful air

Tho so oft I've pray'd and pleaded
  Told the pains which I endur'd
Not a single prayer was heeded   15
  Not a single wound was cur'd

19–21 *Bracketed together because of triple rhyme MS 1*   20 the *through* p *MS 1*
SONG   *Title:* Song *MS 1*   8 a] al *MS 1*   11 her *through* so *MS 1*

Guardian Angels O protect me
Help me all ye powers above
In my troubles dont neglect me
Now I'm cross'd in hopeles love   20

Love by you was first created
To make every creature blest
O then let my pains abated
Give my heart a little rest

AUTOGRAPH: Nor. MS 1, pp. 42–9.
TRANSCRIPTS: Nor. MS 4, pp. 92–9: Pet. MS C1, pp. 15a–19.
Dated: 1808–19 (MS 1).

A HUNT FOR DOBIN OR THE FORCE OF LOVE
A Tale
A Hunt for Rambling Dobin
by which we Mean to Prove
how Cupid on Rough Robin
Inflicts the Force of Love

Just oer the trees and uplands swelling height
The rising sun most beautifully bright
Apearing shone and shot a slanting ray
Upon the teded swaths and wither'd shocks of hay
Now farmer Gubbins leaves his restles bed   5
And to the chamber window walks in dread
For fear it should be rain.—but when he sees
The sun shine clear above his willow trees

21/2 [To make every] *MS 1*

   A HUNT FOR DOBIN OR THE FORCE OF LOVE   *Title:* A Hunt for Dobin or
the force of Love/ A Tale *MS 1*

                    A hunt for rambling dobin
                       By which we mean to prove
                    How Cupid on rough Robin
                       Inflicts the force of Love *MS 1*

6 in *through* out *MS 1*

'Thank god' he cries and 'mid his boundles joys
He shuffles off to call the servant boys   10
'Come; up Boys up' re echos round about
'T'is a fine morning and the sun looks out'
The unwellcome voice they hear through out the lodge
And first of all a jobs laid out for Hodge
'Boy fetch the horses but before yah go   15
'Make haste I charge yah—now tis fine yah know
'Them shocks want carreying—and that tedded hay
'Some how or other must be made to day
'Then boy make hast and let us see from this
'How fast yah can go' Hodge he answer'd 'Yes'   20
But wisper'd to him self contrary 'No
'Not a Mite faster then I us'd to go
'Yah want my bones an' all but that sha'n't be
'What benefit is making ha[s]te to me?'
So soodl'd off with alter by his side   25
To put on dobin whom he us'd to ride
But when he came to where they lay at night
No nag-horse Dobbin ne'er appear'd in sight
And what was worse—tho two was left behind
Old Trip that night got lame! and Rose was blind!   30
'Well heres a stud!' cries Hodge 'the L—d be prais'd!
'When witler knows he'll certainly go crais'd
'Last week it rain'd and now a fair day's come
'We've got no horse's that can 'cart hay home
'What should one do' ——— ————   35
At last by weighing matters round about
He thought it better to go back without
And soon the boys who saw him come with none
Forboded what misfortune had been done
'Aye Hodge what now' the wondering servants cries   40
'What now Indeed' young nettle'd hodge replies
'Wy dobins gone and were the theif got out
'I cannot find for I've look'd all about
'Well wheres the rest' the next Enquirey rose
'Why' Hodge replies 'old trip as I supose   45

42 dobons *altered to* dobins *MS 1*   43 for *through* tho *MS 1*

'By blundering a'ter dobin tumbl'd oer
'Some stump or dyke that lam't him very sore—
'Or else he went near rose and got a cuff
'Hows 'miver he's got lame so thats enough
'And very lame indeed—for when I wur   50
'Nigh him as I am you he'd hardley stir
'Nay when I forc'd him up in such a pother
'He scarce could set one leg before the other
'Well well' Says I 'if thats to be yahr pace
'Yahr little use to us so keep yahr place   55
'And now I realey wish with all my heart
'That our Old nacker he would bring his cart
'(It would be charity—and clear the grounds)
'To take such trammel to m' Lords foxhounds
'For well or not I'm sure 't's a shame to lay   60
'A pair of gears on such poor things as they
Hodge stopt—and twas so humerous a stile
That surley Robin could'n't help but smile
While none found falt but said he reason'd well
And off they went the gauling news to tell   65
To there old master—seated in his chair
Who when he heard—burst out—in deep despair
'Well—sure no man alive is plagu'd like me
'Ill Luck for ever's 'lotted out I see
'Theres some misfortune coming every day   70
'And now to hinder—dobins stroll'd away
'Curse his old carcass where could he get out
'This sweetful day will all be lost I doubt
'I'm certain sure (but g–d forbid I shou'd)
'Tho its enough to make me if I wou'd   75
'Do what one shou'dn't do—for right along
'Something or other dailey turns out wrong
'But this makes things no better thats the deuce
'Old dobins lost and murmuring's no use
'So as we cannot help it our best plan   80
'Is to contrive and do the best we can
'Therefore I think that you robin wou'd be
'More fit then hodge to take a [s]troll and see

54 'Says I' *MS 1*

'What you can do—for tho he's got a tongue
'He wi' n't make use on't as he goes along   85
'Theres naught like asking—so enquire about
'He's our teams stay and cant be done without
'So spare no pains but go from pound to pound
'Stint not for time thats nothing till he's found
'For tho the days so fine and hay quite fit   90
'We without dobbin cannot cart a bit
'So Robin do your best; I pray you do
'Strive all you can and mind not where you go'
Bob to reply look'd craftily behind him
'If hes above ground Master why I'll find him'   95
'I'll trust you bob so speed you on your way
'And them there boys may go to turn the hay'
No sooner said but off they tumble out
Quite tir'd and sham'd at lingering about
And proud to do as matters are agreed   100
Bob too lobs off with far more haste than speed
For swell'd with pride at Gubbins confidence
He stiles himself a man of consequence
And thinks as such he's authoris'd to fling
His arms in motion with a manley swing   105
So with his stockings shaumbling down at heel
His shuffles alterd to a rolling reel
Which does he fancies certainley oer top
The jack ass shoutings of the Strut-bub fop
His cloaths likewise by being smeer'd with dirt   110
And hung on carles seem the better for 't
Which they for certain do to make compleat
A thorough sloven down from head to feet
Lo his old hilos stiff and hard as horns
Resisting fence 'gainst stones and sharpest thorns 115
Went sluthering all unlac'd from day to day
While their brown barkles color provd that they
Of oil ne'er tasted not a single drop
Nor new a k[n]ife since taken from the shop
And as his knee buttons was never done   120
His hoes fell down for garters he had none

103 consequence] confidence *MS 1*   120 as *inserted MS 1*   121 none] done *MS 1*

His braceles breeks down too performing scarce
Their office meant—as shelter for his a—se
While like a clout his dangling shirt behind
Turns its uncleaness to the exposive wind.—   125
Tho to ape fashion hunks could neer abide
Yet still he's not quite destitute of pride
But self consieted as a manley taste
His smockfrock's belted round about his waste
While bacon greese does seem his favourite boast   130
For in such stuff its quite entireley lost
His neck'loth too bound with a single tuck
Displays another beautious scene of Muck
Lo! there in open view his bosom shines
Where coats of muck for weeks and months combines   135
To challenge Ethiopia's son's to vie
With its new tinge of scarce conscieved dye
Tho in the language of his fellow swains
Dandey-go-russet is the name it gains
Nor can his face by natures laws expos'd   140
Be scarsely seen so thick with much inclos'd
Which gives his features such a comic air
That fellow chaps who Master of him are
(For none but such dare say their souls their own)
Will laugh and tell him in a jeering tone   145
That was they him on such a pair of cheeks
They would for certain sow a bed of Leeks
For sure say they it is a shame to see
Such deep rich ground from year to year lye lee
Yet he regardles of their jeirs and stares   150
About his face nor their advice near cares
But still the soil which dailey gathers more
He keeps unculter'd as he did before.—
Nor is his crap unfitting for his face
But as an equal well becomes its place   155
Napless and bare a weather beaten brown
Bereft of brinks and open at the crown
Through which his hair more stubbern the[n] the swines
In upright tufts and bristley bunshes shines.

137 its *through* their *MS 1*   142 feautures *MS 1*   144 say *through* call *MS 1*
146 on *through* with *MS 1*   150 stares] slares *MS 1*   154 is *through* his *MS 1*

Such is the Hero of our simple song 160
And if we grant twill not be granted wrong
Him the same title oer the sloven tribe
Which we have just attempted to describe
But the attempt imperfectly and low
Falls far beneath the picture it would show 165
For to describe and give a perfect sketch
Of the original is out of reach
And far beyond the great descriptive strain
Of magic moulding fancy to attain
So lets pursue and let his person slip 170
As he's unmatch'd in point of rivalship
Fair was the morn and Summer in its prime
For whats more lovlier than hay-making time
When sweet perfumes from every flower arise
And sweeter still from swaths that withering lyes 175
When work-folks stript appear in every ground
And thronging waggons ever rattling round
And Cows and Sheep as full as they can snive
In grounds made clear—where shepherds all alive
In merry dittys tune their oaten strains 180
And waken Echo in the distant plains
All Chaps but robin in a morn like this
Would never surely take such jobs amis
But rather love to wander wide about
And deem it luck at Dobbins getting out 185
Especially the swain who loves to see
The distant steeple cottage brook & tree
Who loves at times to walk in solitude
Oer desart heaths and woody thickets rude
Who loves at times to court domestic plains 190
And join the gambols of his fellow swains
But who more dearly loves alone to prye
In Natures gambols—Wild Variety
To such a one (and many such abounds
In the low path which poverty surrounds) 195
And tho by want and poverty opprest
Full many a Genius rich tho roughly drest

168 ri *through* r *in* descriptive *MS 1*   184–5 *Inserted MS 1*   192 But; *MS 1*
195 surrounds∧ *MS 1*

In spite of all unaided by the muse
By easy flights his rural strain pursues
While other gems uncultivated towers   200
Beyond the reach of Cultivated powers
While some o'erpowerd in Labours moiling vale
(Akin to him who sings this simple tale)
Who when their needful labour they pursue
(Struck with the beauties wich they daily view)   205
Atempt to sing them but atempt in vain
What the heart feels the tongue cannot explain
The bursts of thought with which it is perplex'd
Are bred one moment and are gone the next
Yet still the heart will kindling sparks retain   210
And thoughts will rise and fancy strive again
Till by succesles sallies wearied quite
The memory fails and fancy takes her flight
The wicket nipt within its socket dies
Borne down and smotherd with a thousand sighs   215
Yet still they mark the varied scenery
And turns their beauties to Obscurity
To such as these such journeys would be dear
Their curious eye would pry in every where
Pleas'd would they carless look and list around   220
On every rural sight and rural sound
The old deep pond where the coy morehen lyes
Where on whose side the turfy hillocks rise
Where the broad flag and fuzy bulrush grows
Curving adown to the least wind that blows   225
And where surrounding bushes form a shade
As wild as ever was by nature made
The oaken folliage shaken by the wind
The dark green ivy round their trunks entwind
With all the mingling many shaded greens   230
That decorate the woodlands mixing scenes
These are the haunts & these the scenes so wild
Which are so dear to Natures every child
To sport in wildness nature dearly loves
And all her Children of her taste approves   235

214 scoket *MS 1*   220 they *inserted MS 1*   228 a *through* g *in* folliage *MS 1*

And many more their fancy would select
Nor would they 'ere their Masters work neglect
But all their Errands they would justley do
And in a ready puntual manner too
And O! poor Dobbin happy wouldst thou be   240
Was such a one a hunting now for thee
What oaths would 'scape thee—& oh! blows beside
That falls like thunder on thy poor old hide
Which scarcely bloodless bruise full many a wound
Which thou must have as soon as thou art found.—   245
These blest wi' sence & wi' a reasoning mind
Would know thou only acted to thy kind.
But surley bob thy gauling enemy
Has got no sence to feel nor yet to see

The woodbine courts his eye but courts in vain   250
His tastless soul such beauties would disdain
Great sheets of dasies too about was strowd
And clumps of Clover deckt the waggon road
Whose ruddy collord heads so short and sweet
Tempted poor Dobbin on his way to eat   255
Ah thoughtless Dob hadst thou but had more wit
And never stopt to touch a single bit
But gone straight forward on the gravel road
The treacherous dew thy footsteps neer had show'd
But—Halt—consider—had he miss'd the grass   260
Why then our tale had never came to pass
So let him still be right while we pursue
Rough robins journey every inch on't through
Who now enrag'd & fierce just like a hound
That keener grows when he the scent has found   265
So he on knowing dobbins limping strides
Curse follow'd Curse and what he'd do besides

So he bump'd down beneath the hazel shade
Fingering his breeks wi many a brusing blade
The lonesome place made him the more distrest   270
And thus tormented he his woes expres'd

249/50 *A row of twelve asterisks MS 1*   259 h *in* treacherous *inserted MS 1*
267/8 *A row of twelve asterisks MS 1*

—Have I the impudence in such a plight
To ever think o' ventering in her sight
Can I believe the door as open thrown
Or if she knew me she would ever own   275
I'm certain sure she'd be ashamd to see
Such mucky slovens in her house as me
'Sides the old Dame takeing my visit base
Would bid me go and hide my brazen face

Go to some mucky strumpet ugley swine   280
And never think to wrong a child of mine
Thus the vex'd dame would let her vengance flye
And if the maiden said so I should dye!
For hopes would all be lost I'm sure they would
So now I think on't (while my shoes are good)   285
I'll travel home again as no one knows
And wait awhile till I get better cloaths

AUTOGRAPHS: Pet. MS A4, pp. 13–15: Nor. MS 1, pp. 50–4 (three
attempts: (1) ll. 1–24, 61–96, (1a) ll. 1–20, 25–8, 37–44, (1b) ll. 1–96).
TRANSCRIPT: Pet. MS B1, pp. 153–5: Nor. MS 5, pp. 58–62 (deleted).
Printed in *RL*, pp. 82–8.
Dated 1818 (MS A4, p. 13 '1818 finished'; *RL* Introduction, p. xxii 'In the
last two years').

MY MARY

Who lives where Beggars rarley speed?
& leads a humdrum life indeed
As none beside herself would lead
          My Mary

275 ever *inserted MS 1*   279/80 *A single asterisk MS 1*   284 i'm *MS 1*
287 *Followed by two rows of ten and nine asterisks respectively MS 1*

   MY MARY   *Title:* My Mary *All versions*   My Mary altered *MSS 1a 1b*   1 beggars
MSS 1a 1b   rarely *MS 1*] rearely *MS 1a*   speed∧ *MSS 1 1a 1b*   2 And *MSS 1*
1a 1b   leads] lives *MSS 1a 1b*   humdrum *underlined MS A4*] hum-drum *MSS 1*
1a 1b   3 E'en as the Devil would't lead *MS 1*] Such as the devil wou'd'nt lead *MS*
1a, As no one but herself would lead *through* Such as the devil wou'dn't lead *MS 1b*

Who lives where noises never cease?   5
& what wi' hogs & ducks & geese
Can never have a minutes peace
       My Mary

Who nearly battl'd to her chin
Bangs down the yard thro thick & thin?   10
Nor picks a road nor cares a pin
       My Mary

Who (save in sunday bib & tuck)
Goes daily (waddling like a duck)
Oer head & ears in grease & muck   15
       My Mary

Unus'd to pattins or to clogs
Who takes the swill to serve the hogs?
And steals the milk for cats and dogs
       My Mary   20

Who frost & Snow as hard as nails
Stands out o' doors & never fails
To wash up things & scour the pails
       My Mary

Who bussles night & day in short   25
At all catch jobs of every sort
& gains her mistress' favor for't
       My Mary

5 cease∧ *MSS 1 1a 1b*   6 And *MSS 1 1a 1b*   hogs] turkeys *MS 1a*   and (*fifth word*) *MSS 1 1b*] omitted *MS 1a*   Ducks *MS 1*   Geese *MSS 1 1b*] Gease *MS 1a*
7 Peace *MS 1*   10 Yard through *MS 1*   thin∧ *MSS 1 1a 1b*   11 *First* a] her *RL*   Pin *MS 1*   13 ∧ save: and *MS 1*   Sunday *MSS 1 1a 1b*] Sunday's *RL*
Bib *MSS 1a 1b*   tuck∧ *MS 1*] Tuck *MS 1a*   14 Duck *MS 1b*   15 and *twice* MS 1] an' *twice MS 1b*   Muck *MS 1*   hears *MS 1a*   Grease *MSS 1 1a*
17 Pattins: Clogs *MSS 1 1b*   18 Hogs∧ *MS 1*] hogs∧ *MSS 1a 1b*   19 Milk: and Dogs *MSS 1 1b*   Cats *MS 1*   21 Frost *MS 1*   and: Nails *MSS 1 1b*
snow *MS 1b*   22 out o' doors] in the yard: and *MSS 1 1b*   23 wash up things *and* pails *underlined MS A4*   and: the] her *MSS 1 1b*   Pales *MS 1*
25 buffles (*old-fashioned 'ss'*) *MS A4 MSS 1a 1b*   and Day *MS 1b*   26 catch jobs *underlined MS A4*   27 And: Mistress favour *MS 1b*   fort *to* for't (*p.e.*) *MS A4,* (Tho look'd on near the better for't) *MS 1a*

& who is oft repaid wi praise?
In doing what her mistress says   30
& yielding to her wimmy ways
                    My Mary

For theres none apter I believe
At 'creeping up a Mistress' sleve'
Then this low kindred stump of Eve   35
                    My Mary

Who when the baby's all besh–t
To please its mamma kisses it?
And vows no Rose on earths so sweet
                    My Mary   40

But when her Mistress is'n't nigh
Who swears & wishes it would die
& pinches it to make it cry
                    My Mary

O rank deceit! what soul could think—   45
But gently there revealing ink
—At faults of thine this friend must wink
                    My Mary

Who (not without a 'spark o' pride'
Tho strong as Grunters bristly hide)   50
Does keep her hair in papers ty'd?
                    My Mary

---

29 And: wi' praise∧ *MS 1b*   30 Mistres *MS 1b*   31 And Yielding: wimmey
MS 1b   34 ∧creeping: sleve∧ *MS 1b*   35 Eve *underlined MS A4*
37 babeys *MS 1a*   bes—t *MS 1a*] —— *RL*, unfit *RL 2nd edn.*   38 please *inserted*
MS 1a   mamma, *MS 1a*] Mamma *MS 1b*   it∧ *MS 1a 1b*   39 And: vows]
swears: rose *MSS 1a 1b*   earth *MS 1a*] Earth's *MS 1b*   41 her *through* its *MS
A4*] its *MSS 1a 1b*   Mistress] mamma *MS 1a*, Mamma *MS 1b*   is not *RL*   nigh]
night *MS 1b*   42 and *MSS 1a 1b*   43 And *MSS 1a 1b*   pinches it] gripes its
ar—e *MS 1b*   to make] and makes *RL*   45 O *MS 1b*   47 ∧At
MS 1b   this] the *MS 1b*, thy *RL*   49 ∧not: ∧spark o pride∧ *MS 1b*
50 (Tho: brissl'y *MS 1b*   Grunters bristly hide *underlined MS A4*   51 Doth
RL   tied∧ *MS 1b*

& mimicking the Gentry's way
Who strives to speak as fine as they?
& minds but every word they say   55
        My Mary

& who (tho's well bid blind to see
As her to tell ye A from B)
Thinks herself none o' low degree?
        My Mary   60

Who prates & runs oer silly stuff?
& 'mong the boys makes sport enough
—So ugly, silly droll & ruff
        My Mary

Ugly! Muse fo' shame o' thee   65
What faults art thou a going to see?
In one thats lotted out to be
        My Mary

But heedless sayings meaneth nought
Done Innocent without a thought   70
We humbly ask thy pardon for't
        My Mary

Who low in Stature thick & fat
Turns brown from going without a hat?
Tho not a pin the worse for that   75
        My Mary

---

53 And *MS 1b*   54 they∧ *MS 1b*   55 And *MS 1b*   57 And: tho as
MS 1b   58 (As: you *MS 1b*   59 her self: of: degree∧ *MS 1b*
61 Who takes all jobs both smooth and rough *MS 1*   stuff∧ *MS 1b*   62 And
suits her mistress well enough *MS 1*   And mong *MS 1b*   63 By being so ugly
hard and tough *MS 1*] By being so Ugly, Droll, and ruff *MS 1b*   65 Muse—
MS 1   for *MSS 1 1b*   66 falts *MS 1b*   are we *MS 1*
MS 1   that's *MS 1b*   lotted out *underlined MS A4*   67 one] her
MS 1   67 one] her
70 innocent *MSS 1 1b*   73 stature *MSS 1 1b*   74 wi'out *MS 1b*   hat∧
MSS 1 1b   75 Tho] But *MS 1*, And *MS 1b*

Who's laugh'd at too by every whelp
For failings which they cannot help?
But silly fools will laugh & chelp
     My Mary   80

For tho in stature mighty small
& near as thick as thou art tall
That hand made thee that made us all
     My Mary

& tho thy nose hooks down too much   85
& prophecies thy chin to touch
I'm not so nice to look at such
     My Mary

No no about thy nose & chin
Its hooking out or bending in   90
I never heed nor care a pin
     My Mary

& tho thy skin is brown & ruff
& form'd by nature hard & tuff
All suiteth me! so thats enough   95
     My Mary

---

78 she *RL*   help∧ *MSS 1 1a*   79 And was I near I'd stop their chelp *MS 1*
82 And *MSS 1 1b*   83 that *(fifth word)*] which *MSS 1 1b*   85 And *MSS 1 1b*
86 tuch *MS 1*   89 and *MSS 1 1b*   89–90 [I never heed nor care a Pin]
MS 1b   90 Its] There *MS 1*   hooking[s] out *underlined MS A4*] hookings out
MSS 1 1b   bending in *underlined MS A4*   bendings *MS 1b*   91 or *RL*   pin.m
MS 1   93–6 *Follow l. 84 in MS 1*   93 & *through* A *MS A4*] And *MSS 1 1b*
and rough *MS 1*   94 And *MSS 1 1b*   Nature *MS 1b*   and *MS 1*   cuff *altered*
to tuff *MS A4*] tough *MS 1*   95 All] It: so] and *MS 1*   me∧ *MSS 1 1b*
enough, *MS 1b*

AUTOGRAPH: Nor. MS 1, p. 55.
TRANSCRIPTS: Nor. MS 4, p. 100: Pet. MS C1, p. 19.
Dated: 1808–19 (MS 1).

SPRING (a)

Welcome gentle breathing Spring
Now the birds are heard to sing
And the budding tree is seen
Putting forth her tender green
O delightful season hail   5
May my footsteps never fail
When time permits to visit thee
And view thy new born scenery

AUTOGRAPH: Nor. MS 1, p. 55.
TRANSCRIPTS: Nor. MS 4, p. 100: Pet. MS C1, p. 19a.
Dated: 1808–19 (MS 1).

SPRING (b)

Welcome gentle breathing spring
Now the birds begin to sing
Now the Swelling shade is seen
Putting forth its tender green
While the Suns extended way   5
Sweetly shows the lengthend day
O delightful Season hail
May my footsteps never fail
When I've time to trample where
All thy beauties reappear   10

SPRING   *Title:* Spring *MS 1*   3 the *squeezed in MS 1*   8 view *through*
all *MS 1*

SPRING   *Title:* Spring *MS 1*   3 [bir] Swelling *MS 1*

AUTOGRAPHS: Nor. MS 1, p. 55: Pet. MS A3, p. 72.
TRANSCRIPT: Pet. MS B1, p. 124 (deleted).
Dated: 'Old' (MS A3, p. 72).

ON A LOVER OF BOOKS

When a Book Phil. can borrow he'll sure enough do't
And love it most dear never doubt him
But when without buying he cannot come to't
Why then—Phil. he cares nought about 'em

AUTOGRAPH: Nor. MS 1, p. 56 (ll. 1–32), pp. 61–6 (ll. 33–234).
TRANSCRIPTS: Nor. MS 4, pp. 100–1 (ll. 1–58 only): Pet. MS C1, pp.
19a–20 (ll. 1–58 only).
Dated: 1808–19 (MS 1).

THE DEATH OF DOBBIN

Old Dobbin dead I sing a mournful theme
The noted horse of many a former team
Who in the Glory of his youthfull days
Near fail'd to reap his drivers daily praise
Who too the hero of each story prov'd   5
Of weights he carried & of loads he mov'd
But ah the praises of the world abide
Long as a buble on a floating tide
Poor worn-out Dobbin good as he had provd
In spite of all the loads he bore & mov'd   10
And spite of all his worthy labours past
Fell like the rest a cumber ground at last
Ah poor old injur'd Dobbin well might we
Be warn'd to know the worlds deciet from thee
Thou an Example both to horse & man   15
Shows how we're serv'd when we've done all we can

ON A LOVER OF BOOKS   *Title:* On a Lover of Books *MS 1 MS A3*
1 book *MS A3*   2 &: him] it *MS A3*   4 Phil$_\wedge$: 'em] it *MS A3*
   THE DEATH OF DOBBIN   *Title:* The Death of Dobbin. *MS 1*   10 woads
altered to loads *MS 1*

But tho thy lot old Dobbin-boy was hard
For such real merit to meet such reward
Tho by thy master used so unkind
The rural Muse is glad at heart to find   20
'Mong thy old friends thy memory still survive
Where worthy deeds are sure to keep alive
Those old companions of thy former time
That knew thee well & knew thee in thy prime
When thou outmatch'd by none to none would yield   25
That often geard thee in their team to field
Those old Companions of thy former prime
That yok'd thee out to field full many a time
And many a day and many a weary morn
That have with thee the lengthning furrow drawn   30
And through each timley season as they roll'd
The summers heat & winters cutting cold
Have stood with the[e]; with the[e] as partners shar'd
The toiling slaves to those that better far'd
These where thy friends & these thy friends well knew   35
A horses worth that might be trusted too
And this they every day could prove & see
The value dobbin of a horse like thee
They by expirience taught knew how to prize
That worth which unexpirienc'd fools despise   40
And treat thy Memory with that due respect
Which thy self loving master does neglect
Never through him by hardy work's attain'd
And lasts no longer then his ends are gain'd
Sway'd by self interest—when thy best was o'er   45
As he could profit by thy strength no more
When courage left thee & old age came on
And all the hopes of an amendment gone
When willing still weak efforts provd too true
That thou hadst done the utmost thou cou'dst do   50
Then merits past and praises all adieu
His profits vanishd and his praises too
On merits past he could'n't tent to call
Nor spare a praise where merits past was all

18 real *through* lik *MS 1*   23 b *through* p *before* old *suggesting that a first version read* bold   33 far'd *altered to* shar'd *MS 1*

But turnd the[e] out in yon bare grounds to feed   55
To pine or die as future fate decreed
And happy future fate did so ordain
To see thy sufferance and to ease thy pain
The Death of Dobbin rural Muse rehearse
Recount his Merits in thy lowly verse   60
Low as it is if thou thy Verse denies
Poor dobbins merit with his carcass dies
Poets would near (but shame to hint their aid
In things so mean and where no gains are staid)
For well well we now what dobbins left behind   65
Will neer tempt fulsome flattery to be kind
The task is thine for theres no gains in view
So tune thy reed & Dobbins song pursue
Where grass at stand still all the year is found
Winter & summer scarce above the ground   70
Where Rushes (usless in most places seen)
Are all devoured (hungers bites so keen)
Where spite of all the spears their leaves contain
Sharp prickly thistles strive to rise in vain
There with a motley drove of sheep & cows   75
(That on the green all summer daily brouze)
His latter days poor dobbin ended there
When helpless age requird the tenderest care
There painful wanderd up & down the plain
And sought unceasing for a bite in vain   80
Tho sheep & cows & other horses too
Whent all the day as dobbin usd to do
Tho they expeirencd ere the day was gone
The painful pangs of hunger coming on
Yet doubly blest & happily they fard   85
When this their lot to Dobbins was compard
Tho daily pind the punishment was small
All day they hungerd & the day was all
When twelve long hours or seeming long was past
The welcome evening brought their wisht repast   90
Joyful they saw the swains & Maidens come
And heard the signal to prepare for home

61 t *through* n *in* thou: V *through* v *in* Verse *MS 1*

There to regale oer upheapd cribs of hay
Their sorrows closing with the closing day
But Dobbin luckless horse of Misery   95
No hopes had he of upheapd cribs to see
Usless to him approachd each close of day
There he was turn'd & there he was to stay
No pleasure he from closing day could find
But the sad pleasure of being left behind   100
To him alike the morn & evening came
Each found him pind & left him still the same
There left alone he pind the night away
And blest had he been left alone by day
For had these pilferers on his wretched fare   105
Ceas'd their intruding daily visits there
He might have joy'd to see the grass encrease
And passd away his latter days in peace
But luck like this for dobbin wor'n't reservd
Twas his misfortune to be pind & starvd   110
There to remain & patiently to bear
His days & nights in restless hunger there
To search unceasing all in vain for food
And dye by Inches till he died for good
And doubly blest that hour & doubly dear   115
That showd poor dobin that his end was near.
No happier moment in his life e'er past
Then that sweet moment when he breathd his last
No dearer night since he first drew his breath
Then that dear night which clos'd his eyes in death   120
Joys was the pains to those he felt before
Pains (happy prospect) he would feel no more
His pains & hunger all for ever flew
When the last groan bid weary life adieu.
Ah poor old dobin badly was't thou serv'd   125
To what thy merits & thy worth deserv'd
And could thy fellow kind have sence to see
Well might they prove the worlds deciet from thee
From thy Example plainly might be guest
How they'll be thought of when they've done their best   130

For still theres many a Dobbin left b[e]hind
That to their sorrow will thy treatment find
That spite of all their worthy merits past
Will fall like thee meer Cumber ground's at last.
No merits nothing—or in Lifes decline   135
This usage dobbin would have neer been thine
For better horse could not be harnesd out
Then Dobbin was when he was young & stout
For well we know and ploughmen all agree
That none for working could be match with thee   140
For well twas known by ploughman in his prime
Who to their joy hath provd it many a time
When he was young by nature formed stout
A Better horse could not be harnesd out
His heart was willing & too good to yield   145
Alike the same at home or in the field
True to his trust (a faithful servant provd)
If aught set fast could possible be movd
If down a craggy road or mirey fore
A load had helted f[e]lley deep or more   150
(For Drivers all for Dobbins help applied)
In courage noble and as nobly tried
No sooner yokd and the fond drivers pride
Had clapt his praises on the heroes side
Then he with all his might his strength decreed   155
Fell too as willing as he went to feed
Pull after pull he'd take without a word
Wind & repeat it of his own accord
Repeated trials urg'd in vain to flinch
What ere he gaind he never lost an inch   160
And soon (if equal to his strength it provd)
The joyful driver saw his doubts removd
(Ah! then old Dobin well might be envy raise
Your fellow horses to deserve the praise
Which the pleas'd rustic in his raptures paid   165
For thy past efforts so deserving made)
And if repeated pulls did plainly prove
The deep sunk load beyond his power to move

141 his *through* thy *MS 1*   143 he *through* thou *MS 1*   145 His *through* Thy
MS 1   147 his *through* thy *MS 1*   164 Your *through* .By *MS 1*

Tho worn fatigued his heart undaunted still
Always obedient to his drivers will   170
And if still left beyond his power to try
Upon his knees the worthy beast would lye
And there his fruitles efforts still mentain
There lye & pull & rise & fall again
And had his drivers faild to interfere   175
And let him still keep pulling as he were
So true the courage he so often showd
He'd broke his heart & fell beneath his load.
Nor was his worth alone confined here
In drawing well or heavy Lifts to clear   180
At other labour he was still the same
The best in being & the first in fame
At lighter jobs that gentler ways require
He still performd them to his guides desire
For tho so turbulent when strength's requird   185
A gentler creature could not be desird
Mild as a lamb a very child might guide
And walk undanger'd by his gentle side
E'en from each Maiden Dob did praise recieve
That to his Masters yearly came to live   190
Could they (a favour from rough will or john)
But once get Dobbin to ride Market on
His fames foundation then was surely laid
To be aughmented all the time they staid
For tho he was (as carters mostly prove)   195
But slow of foot (tho never hard to move)
Tho he requird of time a greater share
And on his journey neer had much to spare
His worth & safety did his fame secure
His ways all gentle & his slowness sure   200
—At Ploughing too he still reservd his fame
His willing heart & Courage still the same
He'd draw a furrow straight without a bend
Clear out the plough & turn it round the end
Without a Leader & without a guide   205
Ploughmen in Dob with Leader was suplied

169 fantigued *MS 1*   199 secure *through* ensure *MS 1*

Use made him perfect & his heart was good
He took all gamly be what jobs they wou'd
Threatnings were useles either fresh or tir'd
Good words where all the notice he requir'd   210
No wipcord lashes never markd a Limb
Whipcord & whips were usless all to him
In short (his worth being well & often provd)
At every job his prescence was belovd
The ploughmans only wish & only pride   215
Was but to be with Dobbins aid supplyd
To have him in their team—for well they knew
That Dobbins merits could be trusted too
But ah resemblance of a flattering Dream
What Boots it Dobbin to have your esteem   220
—Vain world we know thee—well thy ways can tell
Worth may gain praise when intrest bears the bell
But when thats gone then praises all adieu
Our worth is vanishd & our praises too
The Cobweb praises of the world abide   225
Long as a Bubble on a floating tide
Poor worn-out Dobbin good as thou had provd
In spite of all the Loads thou bore & movd
In spite of all thy worthy Labours past
To fall (sad fate) a Cumber ground at last   230
A poor old injurd Dobbin well might we
Be warnd to shun the worlds deciet from thee
Thou an example both to horse & man
Shows how we're servd when weve done all we can

225–34 *Cf. ll. 7–16*

AUTOGRAPHS: Nor. MS 1, pp. 57–9: Nor. MS 1, p. 60 (ll. 21–4, 53–76 only).
Dated: 1808–19 (MS 1).

THE WOUNDED SOLDIER

O cruel War when will thy horrors cease
And all thy slaughtering of poor men give oer
O sheath O sheath thy bloody blade in peace
Nor stain thy hand with human blood no more

See at yon door were round the children swarm   5
The piteous object of thy rage appears
Thou'st left him nothing but a single arm
Both legs are gone & he is old in years

O shatter'd man did ever eyes behold
A more distressing form of misery   10
Sure no good Christian heart will ere withold
His worthy deeds of Charity from thee

I'll sit me down and hear his woful tale
And here he comes & noising at his heels
The Laughing boys too—O can Laughs prevail   15
But they are young and know not what he feels

Poor shatter'd fragment how he stumps the streets
And how contentedly he seems to be
He tells his woful tale to all he meets
And now he'll tell his woful tale to me   20

'O christian friend do pity & relieve
'A poor and pitious object in distress
'Say not I mean your goodness to decieve
'Look at these stumps they'll soon the truth confes'

THE WOUNDED SOLDIER   *Title:* The Wounded Sailor *(preceded by* [O friens]*)*
MS 1, p. 60; wanting MS 1   *The number* 11 *written in pencil at the head of the poem
on p. 57*   21–4 *Quotation marks omitted MS 1, p. 60*   21 O friends and
neighbours pity & relieve *MS 1, p. 60*   22 A Poor old wounded sailor in distress
MS 1, p. 60   23 Say not] Nor think *MS 1, p. 60*   24 These wooden stumps
will soon the truth confess *MS 1, p. 60*

Thus far proceeded—ah poor soul I cried   25
The truth too true with grief at heart I see
And tho thy wants can be but ill suplied
Yet what I have I'll gladly share with thee

He plac'd his crutch & rais'd his silver'd head
Which seem'd at this to wear a joyful cast   30
'Here take my hand my only hand he said
'And let me greet a brother found at last'

'O what I owe the tender feeling poor
'Since I've been brought to this sad state you see
'Ne'er have I left their lowly welcome Door   35
'Without some token of their Charity'

'But O in vain (it grieves me to relate)
'These wooden stumps & this poor armless side
'Attracts the pity of the rich & great
'They deem my sorrows far beneath their pride'   40

'Yon house that shows its owners wealth & power
'Lur'd me to ask relief but ask'd in vain
'A scornful proudling drove me from the door
'To crave a morsel from the needy swain'

'But ah ye Rich as rich as you may be   45
'You—tho You fancy you can't want no more
'May by misfortune be reduc'd like me
'And glad to beg a crust from door to door'

But stay thy rage my heart & let them rest
And to this tender friend thy woes reveal   50
Thou'rt provd all hardships the[e]ve been ever blest
And neer experiencd what it is to feel

---

29 i *in* silver'd *inserted MS 1*

Alternative stanza to ll. 45–8:

> But ah ye proud as rich as you may be
> You cannot tell what may hang oer your head
> Rich as you are you may perhaps like me
> Some time be glad to beg a crust of bread

These sixty years & heavens knows it true
I've fought my countrys freedom to mentain
And spite of all the dangers Ive gone through   55
It was my fortune to come home again

But little thought I Land I dearly prize
That I should stump thy plains without a leg
And O my parents (here he wipd his eyes)
But little thought friend I was born to beg   60

But ah none knows what they are doom'd to see
Riches my friend that boasts to want no more
May by his fortunes be brought down like me
And glad to beg a crust from door to door

For you must know my bringing up was good   65
My friends liv'd well and brought me up at school
And now might I h' been happy if I wou'd
But fate ordain'd that I should play the fool

The school I hated playing was my joy
And soldier playing was my dearest game   70
When—tho an age that scarce compleats the boy
At twelve years old a soldier I became

My youthful heart with vain ambition fir'd
And with the hopes of future glory stird
I fled my home and ere the day expir'd   75
I stood a private in the sixty third

A unexpeirenc'd youth & unadvis'd
Those golden fancies which delighted thee
Now must they all be provd & reallizd
And soon by fate it was ordaind to be   80

53–84 *No stanza divisions MS 1*   53 (&: true) *MS 1, p. 60*   54 Countrys
MS 1, p. 60   55 I've *MS 1, p. 60*   59 And my old mother—here he wip'd
his eyes (— *through* he) *MS 1, p. 60*   60 friend] too *MS 1, p. 60*
61–4 *Cf. ll. 45–9*   61 Yet still the rich that fareth sumpsously *MS 1, p. 60*
62 Riches . . . that] And in their consience *MS 1, p. 60*   63 May by his fortune be
deciev'd like me *MS 1, p. 60*   67 h' *omitted MS 1, p. 60*   I'd *MS 1*   68 play
the] be a *MS 1, p. 60*   71 compleates *MS 1, p. 60*   72 A twelve years old
through A Soldier I became: Soldier *MS 1, p. 60*   75 and ere the] & here that
MS 1, p. 60   76 63rd, *MS 1, p. 60*   78 Those *through* N *MS 1*

For little better than a week was spent
From the commencement of our new career
Before ou[r] serjant had his orders sent
That we should march & mar[c]h I knew not where

AUTOGRAPHS: Pet. MS A3, p. 139: Nor. MS 1, p. 61 (deleted).
TRANSCRIPTS: Pet. MS B1, p. 10: Nor. MS 5, p. 130.
Printed in *RL*, pp. 104–5.
Dated: 1808–19 (MS 1).

IMPROMTU SUGGESTED WHILE VIEWING AN INFANT GRAVE

Beneath the Sod where smiling creeps
The daisy into view
The Ashes of an Infant sleeps
Whose soul's as smiling too
—Ah doubly happy—doubly blest—   5
Had I so happy been
Recall'd to heavens eternal rest
Ere it knew how to sin

Thrice happy Infant great the bliss
Alone reserv'd for thee   10
Such joy—twas my sad fate to miss
& thy good luck to see

IMPROMTU SUGGESTED WHILE VIEWING AN INFANT GRAVE   *Title:*
Impromtu / Suggested while / Viewing an Infant Grave *MS A3,* An Infants Grave *MS 1,*
On an Infant's Grave *RL   No stanza division MS 1   Preceded in pencil in MS A3 by:*

As mortal as the leaves I sing
As subject to decay
To morrow may our summons bring
Then lets prepare to day

1 the] this: sod: smileing *MS 1*   creeps *through* peeps *MS A3*] peeps *MS 1,*
creep *RL*   2 dasie *MS 1*] daisies *RL*   3 A *through* a *in* Ashes *MS A3*] ashes
MS 1   Infant[s] *MS A3*   sleep *RL*   4 Sou'ls: smileing *MS 1*   5 ∧Ah:
happy∧: blest∧ *MS 1*   6 happy] blest ha' *MS 1*   7 [Snatch] Recall'd *MS
A3*] Snatchd up *MS 1*   9 Thrice] Ah *MS 1*   10 reservd: thee] the *MS 1*
11 joys∧ *MS 1*   12 And: luck *through* fate *MS 1*

For Oh when all must rise again
To have their sentence gave
What crowds will wish with me in vain   15
They'd fill'd an Infants Grave

AUTOGRAPH: Nor. MS 1, p. 67.
TRANSCRIPTS: Nor. MS 4, p. 102: Pet. MS C1, pp. 20–20a.
Dated: 1808–19 (MS 1).

THE SNOWDROP

How beautiful the snowdrop shines
    In purest white array'd
Just as when Innoscence combines
    To form the virtuous maid

Fair emblemn of meek innoscence   5
    Sweet modest flower with thee
My Chloe's matchles excellence
    Exactly does agree

And o how charming is her face
    Just like the snowdrop flower   10
It gives to every downcast grace
    In love,—A double power

Tho every way she darts her eye
    Does kindling flames inspire
But, when her downcast glances flye   15
    They set my soul on fire

13 For *through* And: O *MS 1*   14 And sentence then shall have *RL*
16 grave *MS 1*

THE SNOWDROP   *Title:* The Snowdrop *MS 1*   13 darts *through* turns *MS 1*

AUTOGRAPH: Nor. MS 1, p. 67.
TRANSCRIPTS: Nor. MS 4, p. 102: Pet. MS C1, p. 20a.
Dated: 1808–19 (MS 1).

ON A WITHER'D CROWFLOWER

Poor wither'd harbinger of spring
   In thee reflection seems to dawn
For from the simplest trifling thing
   Instructive morals may be drawn

Thy golden dress tempted—so gay   5
   Some swain to stoop as passing by
But when he smelt it—ah then away
   Thy gold he threw to fade and dye

Alas just so does female charms
   That yields in youths unguarded hour   10
To trust the Coxcombs treacherous arms
   Fall wretched like this scentles flower

AUTOGRAPH: Nor. MS 1, p. 67.
TRANSCRIPTS: Nor. MS 4, p. 102: Pet. MS C1, p. 20a.
Dated: 1808–19 (MS 1).

A REPLY TO THE ENQUIREY 'WHAT AILS YOU?'

Was I to tell you what I ail within
About the wounds you would'n't care a pin
Sooner I fear you would be adding new
By telling me 'I need not think of you!'

ON A WITHER'D CROWFLOWER   *Title:* On a wither'd Crowflower *MS 1*
3 from *through* in *MS 1*

A REPLY TO THE ENQUIREY 'WHAT AILS YOU?'   *Title:* A Reply to the
Enquirey / 'What ails you?' *MS 1*   4 you!ᴧ *MS 1*   *Followed in MS 1,*
pp. 68–70 by Damon and Collin *which is published in our volume for 'The Village Minstrel'*

AUTOGRAPH: Nor. MS 1, p. 71.
TRANSCRIPTS: Nor. MS 4, p. 71: Pet. MS C2, p. 61.
Dated: 1808–19 (MS 1).

SONG

The Harebell decks the woods in blue
    The daise trims the plain
The Cowslips to the Meadows true
    Adorn's the banks again
And is my lovly blossom true   5
    Does Kitty truly prove
Will she her smiles on me renew
    And bless me wi' her love

O gentle Birds that finds a mate
    In every bush & tree   10
Go sing your tender songs to Kate
    And tender sing o' me
O mind her of her lowley swain
    And how she ought to prove
How charm me wi' her smiles again   15
    And bless me wi' her love

AUTOGRAPH: Nor. MS 1, pp. 71–2.
TRANSCRIPTS: Nor. MS 4, p. 72: Pet. MS C2, pp. 61–61a.
Dated: 1808–19 (MS 1).

SONG

When lingering suns in sumer sets
    North westly oer the lee
When winds too in that quarter gets
    How Dear they are to me

SONG   *Title:* Song *MS 1*
SONG   *Title:* Song *MS 1*   4 they *through* are *MS 1*

For there my lovely B[etse]y dwells   5
 Whose charms in charms appear
Fair flowers clear brooks all wears & tells
 The 'semblance of my Dear

There's not a wind thats blowing west
 Or westernly inclind   10
There's not a Sun sinks there to rest
 But leaves her in my Mind
Nor yet a Beauty wearing flower
 Nor brookie wimpering clear
But holds the same enchanting power   15
 To mind me o' my Dear

AUTOGRAPHS: Nor. MS 1, p. 72: Pet. MS A3, p. 98.
TRANSCRIPTS: Pet. MS B1, p. 158: Nor. MS 5, p. 112.
Printed in *RL*, pp. 167–8.
Dated: Old (MS A3).

SONG

Sad was the day when my willie did leave me
 Sad was the moments that wing'd him away
And Oh most distressing & most it did grieve me
 To witness his looks when I press'd him to stay
It hurt him to think that in vain was my crying   5
 Which I couldnt help tho I knew it [so] too
The Trumpets all sounding the Colours all flying
 A Soldier my wilie he couldnt but go

8 *B——y MS 1*

 SONG *Title:* Song *MS 1 MS A3*, Sad was the Day *RL* 1 Willie *MS A3*
2 were *RL* 3 & oh *MS A3* 4 when] while *MS A3 RL* *First* s *through* e
in press'd *MS 1*] beg'd *MS A3*, begg'd *RL* 5 my] I *MS A3 RL* 6 cou'd'n't
MS A3 so *MS A3 RL* 7 trumpets: colours *MS A3* 8 wilie . . . but]
Willy—my Willy must *MS A3 RL*

The youths never heeding tomorrow & danger
   Where laughing & toasting their girls oer their beer   10
But O my poor Willie just like a lost stranger
   Stood speechles among them half dead as it where
He kiss'd me—twas all—not a word when he started
   And oh in his silence too much I could see
He knew for a truth & he knew broken hearted   15
   That kiss was the last he should ever gie me

AUTOGRAPHS: Nor. MS 1, p. 73 (ll. 1–60 only): Pet. MS A3, pp. 30–1:
Pforzheimer Library, Misc. MS 197 (Clare's corrections of ll. 47–50).
TRANSCRIPTS: Pet. MS B1, pp. 94, 167 (ll. 61–6 deleted): Nor. MS 5,
pp. 101–4 (ll. 61–6 deleted).
Printed in *RL*, pp. 12–15 (ll. 1–60 only).
Dated: 1815 (MS A3, p. 30 '4 years').

ADRESS TO A LARK SINGING IN WINTER

Aye—little Larkie whats the reason
Singing thus in winter season
Nothing surely can be pleasing
   To make the[e] sing
For I see nought but cold and freezing   5
   And feel it sting

Perhaps (all done wi' silent mourning)
Thou thinks that summer is returning
And this the last cold frosty morning
   To chill thy breast   10
If so I pity thy discerning
   And so I've guest

9 to morrow *MS A3*   10 Where] Kept *MS A3 RL*   11 Oh: Willy *MS A3*
12 speechless: were *MS A3*   13 —He: 't'was *MS A3*   14 & *MS A3*
16 Kiss: shou'd *MS A3*   give *RL*

ADRESS TO A LARK SINGING IN WINTER *Title:* Adress to a Lark Singing /
in Winter *MS 1*, Address to a Lark singing / in Winter *MS A3*, Corrections in the /
'Address to a Lark' *Pfz*   1 Aye!—Little Larkey: reason? *MS A3*   3 surlly
altered to surely *MS A3*   4 thee *MS A3*   5 & *MS A3*   6 & *MS
A3* its *MS A3 RL*   8 thinkst *MS A3*] think'st *RL*   9 & *MS A3*
11 diserning *to* discerning *(p.e.) MS A3*   12 & *MS A3* i've *MS 1*] Ive *MS A3*

Poor little songster vainly cheated
Stay leave thy singing uncompleated
Drop were thou was beforehand seated   15
   In thy warm nest
Nor let vain wishes be repeated
   But sit at rest

Tis winter let the cold content thee
Wish after nothing till its sent thee   20
For dissapointments will torment thee
   Which will be thine
I know it well for Ive had plenty
   Misfortunes mine

Advice sweet warbler dont despise it   25
None knows whats what but them that tries it
And then they well know how to prise it
   And so do I
Thy case with mine I sympathise it
   With many a sigh   30

Weak hope—of thee Ive had my portion
Mere flimzy cobweb—Changing ocean
That flits the scene at every motion
   And still egs on
With sweeter view & stronger notion   35
   To dwell upon

Yes Ive dwelt long on idle fancies
Strange & uncommon as romances

---

14 Stay, *through* Go *MS A3*   15 where *MS A3*   was *to* wast *(p.e.) MS A3*]
wast *RL*   21 disapointments *MS A3*   23 I've *MS A3*   25 dont *to* don't
(p.e.) MS A3   26 them] he *RL*   trys *to* tries *(p.e.) MS A3*   27 &: prize
MS A3   he: knows *RL*   28 & *MS A3*   29 wi' *MS A3*   symphathise
(second s *through* z*) MS 1*] sympathize *MS A3*   30 with *MS 1*   31 Weak]
Vain *MS A3 RL*   I've *MS A3*   32 flimzy: changing *MS A3*   34 &: egs *to*
eggs *(p.e.) MS A3*   *Clare's note MS A3, p. 32:* 'egs on' in the 'address to the Lark'
wether provincial or what I cannot tell but it is common with the vulgar (I am of that
class) & heartily desire no word of mine to be altered   35 Wi' *MS A3*
37 I've *MS A3*

On future luck my noddle dances
    What I should be   40
But ah when future time advances
    Alls Blank to me

Now twenty years Ive packt behind me
Since hopes deluding tongue inclind me
To fuss myself—But warbler minde me   45
    Its all a sham
& twenty more's as like to find me
    Poor as I am

Im poor enough theres plenty knows it
Obscure & dull my scribling shows it   50
Then sure twas madness to suppose it
    What I was at
To gain preferment! There Ili close it
    So mum for that

Let mine sweet bird then be a warning   55
Advice in season do'n't be scorning
But wait till springs first days are dawning
    To glad & cheer thee
& then sweet Minstrel of the morning
    I'll wish to hear thee   60

These restless early warning dasies
Whose forward bloom the morning freezes
Last evenings sun (delusion pleases)
    Left their despair
When doing well—Content cant please us   65
    What fools we are

39 future *below* [future]: [*? to and indecipherable*] my *MS A3*   40 would
MS A3 RL   42 blank *MS A3*   43 I've *MS A3*   44 inclin'd *MS A3*
45 mind *MS A3*   47–8 *(See Clare's letter to Drury ?Apr. 1819, Pfz MS 197:*
Corrections in the 'Address to a Lark'[:] Instead of these Lines   '& Twenty more the
same may find me / 'Just as I am' Print these[:] & Twenty more's as like to find me /
Poor as I am *(Letters, p. 10))*   47 Twenty *Pfz*   more's . . . to *Pfz*] more the same
will *MS 1*, more the same may *MS A3*   48 Poor *Pfz*] Just *MS 1 MS A3 RL*
49 I'm *MS A3*   50 Obscure & dull *Pfz*] Obscure—how dull *MS 1 MS A3*,
Obscure; how dull *RL*   scribling *to* scribbling *(p.e.) MS A3*] scribbling *Pfz*   shews
RL 2nd edn.   51 supose *to* suppose *(p.e.) MS A3*   53 there I'll *MS A3*
56 dont *MS A3*   57 springs *to* Springs *(p.e.) MS A3*   59 minstrell *to*
minstrel *(p.e.) MS A3*   60 Ill *MS A3*] I'd *RL*   61–6 *Copy-text: MS A3*
61 Thus *through* These *through* Thy *MS A3*

AUTOGRAPH: Nor. MS 1, p. 74: Nor. MS 2, p. R47 (fragment, erased pencil, deleted).
TRANSCRIPTS: Nor. MS 4, p. 106: Pet. MS C1, pp. 22–22a.
Dated: 1808–19 (MS 1).

TO THE WELLAND

Hail Welland to thy reedy stream
Unthought of long in poets dream
And no more honner'd now I deem
   By this my artless verse
Yet still by this thou well may'st know   5
What (if the Muses would bestow
A gift to sing) I'd fainly show
   And willingly rehearse

What streams where sung whilst thou lay lost
But now thy fame increases most   10
Since thou as well as them can boast
   A Poet of thy own
And now the Muses shall essay
To chase oblivions clouds away
And make by their aspiring lay   15
   Thee with thy poet known

E'en I the meanest of the train
While now I hum this simple strain
Along thy banks.—cannot refrain
   My praises to reveal   20
For when his charming page I turn
Nay at the very name of Hurn
My heart and soul with raptures burn
   And quite inspir'd I feel

TO THE WELLAND   *Title:* To the Welland *MS 1*   17 e *through* n *in* E'en
MS 1   24 p *through* ir *in* inspir'd *MS 1*

Then roll thy waves his fame to spread   25
While village maids by shepherds led
Shall gather garlands for his head
    And weave a rural Crown
And swains more fit his praise shall tell
While Spalding—Honington as well   30
Alike—(not caring to excell)
    Shall gain the same renown

AUTOGRAPH: Nor. MS 1, p. 75.
TRANSCRIPTS: Nor. MS 4, pp. 106–7: Pet. MS C1, pp. 22a–23.
Dated: 1808–19 (MS 1).

LINES TO CHLOE

Tho Chloe from her Collin strays
    And many miles between us lye
Behind her lovely image stays
    Beaming bright in memorys eye

Nor shall that mornings interview   5
    When Chloe nodded from her cot
Sweetly smileing 'how d'ye do'
    Ever be by me forgot

And still I'll love that Elder bower
    Where thou reveal'd thy mind so free   10
From which you also pluck'd a flower
    O precious gift—and gave it me

The following fragment in MS 2, p. R47 may be connected with 'To the Welland':

[No more shall I wander by well lands stream]
O welland no more by the side of thy stream
⟨   ⟩ shall I wander to gaze
The Joys of my youth ⟨have   ⟩
That moment tho wretched more wretched to leave 5

LINES TO CHLOE   *Title:* Lines to Chloe *MS 1*   12 i *through* a *in* gift *MS 1*

Thrice happy hours thrice happy state
  So lately join'd so soon to part
Tho Abscence never did create   15
  One single pang to wound my heart

And dearest maiden could I find
  That you as usual would be true
I should be happy in my mind
  Yes happy now I write.—   20
               Adieu

AUTOGRAPH: Nor. MS 1, p. 75.
TRANSCRIPTS: Nor. MS 4, p. 107: Pet. MS C1, p. 23.
Dated: 1808–19 (MS 1).

TO MR J. TURNILL

T[urni]ll (lov'd name) a clown would fainley send
  To thee some token that thou mightest know
How he esteems thee as a real friend
  For favours past which he must ever owe
Yet anxious far as lies within his power   5
  To make acknowledgement for all thy pains
Thou took to learn him every leisure hour
He humbly greets thee with these simple strains
  Simple indeed!—yet simple as they are
O best and dearest friend could they but show   10
  That this warm praise is utter'd from the heart
That without flattery friendship makes me glow
  O could they but to thee these truths impart
Ah then my hopes are Crown'd beyond compare

TO MR J. TURNILL   *Title:* To Mr J. T—n–ll *MS 1*   1 T——ll *MS 1*

AUTOGRAPHS: Nor. MS 1, p. 76: Pet. MS A4, pp. 15–16: Pet. MS A40,
p. 36a (deleted).
TRANSCRIPTS: Pet. MS B1, pp. 155–6: Nor. MS 5, pp. 79–81.
Dated: 1808–19 (MS 1).

THE DISSAPOINTED MILKMAID

Along the road as goes the tale
A Cuntrey girl with milking pale
Thus profits from her ware to sell
E're she got there began to tell
'This milk will bring me at a Clash   5
'Tenpence or more in ready cash
'And then that tenpence will effegs
'Buy me at least a dozen eggs
'Then from them eggs—lets see—if set
'Beneath a hen—why—I shall get   10
'We'll say ten chickens—them when grown
'Will clear a pig to be my own
'That pretty pig when fat I vow
'Will make me Mistriss of a Cow!
'Then from the dairey in a souse   15
'I get enough to buy a house—
'Theres for y' then—(with land to plough!)
'What I'm come to by saving now!

THE DISSAPOINTED MILKMAID   *Title:* The dissapointed Milkmaid *MS 1 MS
A4,* The Dissapointed Milkmaid *MS A40   Clare's note in MS A4:* The prose from
which this was versified may be seen in Le Strangers Esop tho with that difference that it
may be justly called nothing more then an Imitation   2 Country *MS A4*] country
MS A40   wi' *MS A4*   pail *MS A4*   3 Thus] Of *MS A40*   4 Ere *MS A4
MS A40*   tell— *MS A4*   5–20 *Quotation marks omitted MS A40*   5 Clash
underlined MS A4] clash *MS A40*   7 & *MS A4*   then *through* that *MS 1*   effegs
underlined MS A4] i' feggs *MS A40*   9 them] the: *first—through* le *MS A40*
10 —why—] [soft] why— (— *through I) MS A4,* —why *MS A40*   11 Well *MS
A40*   say—: Chickens— *MS A4*   them] they *MS A4 MS A40*   12 Pig *MS A4*
13 Pretty *MS A4*   14 mistress *MS A4 MS A40*   cow∧ *MS A40*   15 dairy:
souse *underlined MS A4*   16 house∧ *MS A40*   17 There's: wi' *MS A4*
ye: plough∧ *MS A4 MS A40*   *Brackets omitted MS A40*   18 Im: now∧ *MS A40*
too *MS 1 MS A4*   saving— *MS A4*

'Well now I've naught to do but hurd
'And then a sweetheart!'—at that word   20
She jump'd for joy—but thought no more
Of what she'd on her head before
Till down it squashd upon the ground
And laid the dusty road around
So there whent milk—and thats not all   25
For in that sad dissasterous fall
Her Eggs, her poultrey, piggs, and Cow,
With dairy, House, and land to plough—
But O of accidents the worst
Misfortune urghing to be curst   30
That sweetheart worse than all desir'd
In this too shocking fall expir'd!
Then let us take warning that we may'n't be catch'd
But keep the old proverb in view
'Not to crack of our chickings before they are hatch'd'   35
As 'Golden dreams seldom come true'

19 Ive *MS A40*   nought *MS A4 MS A40*   then *through*
there *MS 1*] then *through* there[s] *MS A4,* theres *MS A40*   a] the *MS A4*   sweetheart!
underlined MS A4] sweetheart∧∧—*MS A40*   21 jumpt *MS A4 MS A40*   —but]
& *MS A40*   nomore *MS A4*   22 ⟨O⟩f *torn MS A4*   shed *MS A40*
23 ⟨Ti⟩ll *torn:* squash'd *MS A4*   24 ⟨&⟩ *torn MS A4*] & *MS A40*
25 went *MS A4 MS A40*   milk∧ *MS A40*   & *MS A40*] but *MS A4*
26 dissast'rous *MS A4*] disasterous *MS A40*   27 Eggs∧ *MS A4*] eggs∧ *MS A40*
poultry∧: cow∧ *MS A4 MS A40*   piggs∧ & *MS A4*] & her *MS A40*   28 With]
Her: house∧ &: plough∧ *MS A4 MS A40*   dairy∧ *MS A4*] dairey *MS A40*
29 But] &: Oh *MS A4*   30 urghing *through* ready *MS 1*] urging *MS A4 MS A40*
31 sweetheart *underlined:* worse] more *MS A4*   worse . . . desir'd *through* wanted more
then all *MS 1*   then: desired *MS A40*   32 Together wi' the rest expir'd *MS A4*]
Together with the rest expired *MS A40*   *Through* ? Tumbl'd too the shocking fall!
MS 1   33 lets us *MS 1*   mayn't *MS A4*] maynt *MS A40*   catched *MS A40*
34 But keep *through* But *MS 1*   Proverb *MS A4*   35 ∧Not: hatchd∧ *MS A40*
chickens *MS A4 MS A40*   36 ∧golden: true∧ *MS A40*

AUTOGRAPH: Nor. MS 1, pp. 77–9.
TRANSCRIPTS: Nor. MS 4, pp. 107–10: Pet. MS C1, pp. 23–4.
Dated: 1808–19 (MS 1).

MY ROVER

Who nightly in his den does lye
That slumbers only with one eye
And barks if any thing stirs nigh
        My Rover

Who without Cocks (disturbing rest)   5
Can tell when morning comes the best
And leaves his bed first ready drest
        My Rover

Who finds me out both far and near
Tracing my footsteps every where   10
And when I wistle's sure to hear
        My Rover

Who will himself from day to day
Tend sheep so well when I'm away
As not to let one go astray   15
        My Rover

And who tho batter'd out compleat
Anxious to rest his masters feet
Oer the rough fallow clods will beat
        My Rover   20

Who stands upon his under legs
And wistful on his master glegs
To show me how genteel he begs
        My Rover

MY ROVER   *Title:* My Rover *MS 1*   *Pencil emendations in MS C1 are Clare's*

And who when I at dinner sit   25
In silence seems to beg a bit
Then wags his tail in thanks for it
                    My Rover

Who oer me such a watch will keep
As flies themselves dare hardley creep   30
To bit me when I fall asleep
                    My Rover

And who to please me with a trick
Will carry in his mouth a stick
Or any thing thats not too thick   35
                    My Rover

Who when the sun in Summer grows
So hot will lye upon my cloathes
And start as jealous of the Crows
                    My Rover   40

Nay I need not no further go
For every thing in short that you
Can please me with thoult freeley do
                    My Rover

Then shall I like the world at last   45
Forgetful of thy goodness past
Bid thee seek shelter in the blast
                    My Rover

No when old age has made thee weak
And plough'd a furrow down thy cheek   50
Thou shalt not have a friend to seek
                    My Rover

33 trick *through* stick *MS 1*   41 [Nay] *(p.e.)*: no *to* any *(p.e.) MS C1*   42 you
to thou *(p.e.) MS C1*   44 R *through* r *in* Rover *MS 1*   50 cheeck *MS 1*

For I should have a heart more hard
Than Adamant—not to regard
One who once toild for me so hard 55
        My Rover

Compassion on thy age I'll show
And turkish like I'll never go
To hang thee up as others do
        My Rover 60

But thou by the fire side shalt lye
And oft I'll think when sitting by
How times whent once with you and I
        My Rover

When you in youth—ere sense took place 65
Would after Hares or Rabits race
Spending whole hours in fruitles chase
        My Rover

But now thou by experience taught
When leizure minnutes may be caught 70
Will lye thee down and think of naught
        My Rover

And could I but lye down with thee
From trouble so entirely free
How happy surely should I be 75
        My Rover

Tho thats deny'd—and wishing vain
Then lye thee down and sleep again
And I'll no more of that complain
        My Rover 80

But stop—that Lark see—leaves the sky
And wistling Lab'rers homeward hie
Then sure tis time for you and I
        My Rover

63 you *to* thou *(p.e.) MS C1*   65 you *to* thou *(p.e.) MS C1*   83 you *to* thou
(p.e.) MS C1

So lets go home as well as they   85
For morning brings another day
When we as usual must away
                    My Rover

And first we'll sup and then thy den
Shall be a Bed till morn agen   90
And so I'll sing no more till then
                    My Rover

AUTOGRAPH: Nor. MS 1, p. 79.
TRANSCRIPTS: Nor. MS 4, p. 110: Pet. MS C1, pp. 24–24a.
Dated: 1808–19 (MS 1).

A MOMENTS RAPTURE WHILE BEARING THE LOVLEY WEIGHT OF A. S--R--S

Unequal'd raptures happiest happiness
   For sure no raptures can compare with thee
Now lovley Anna in her sunday dress
   In softest pressure sits upon my knee.—
For O to see the snowey bosom heave   5
And feel those robes to me so softley cleave
Robes which half show what modesty consceals
   While round her slender wa[i]ste I fling my arms
   And while her eye what's wanting yet reveals
To me apears such (more than heavenly) charms   10
That might I wish—and could I be so blest
   To have it granted—O I'd wish to be
For ever of this matchles maid posses'd
   To bear her weight through all Eternity

A MOMENTS RAPTURE WHILE BEARING THE LOVLEY WEIGHT OF
A. S—R—S   *Title:* A moments rapture while bearing the lovley weight of A. S—r—s
MS 1   13 ever *inserted MS 1*   14 *Followed in MS 1, pp. 80–1 by* The
wood-cutters night Song *which is published in our volume for 'The Village Minstrel'*

AUTOGRAPH: Nor. MS 1, pp. 81–2.
TRANSCRIPTS: Nor. MS 4, pp. 110–11: Pet. MS C1, pp. 24a–25.
Dated: 1808–19 (MS 1).

CHUBS REPLY

Nature unequal modelizes all
Some she makes great and others mighty small
Of this last fairey sort tho jiant proud
One market day amid the gaping crowd
A three foot nothing did a horse bestride   5
'Pareing as well as when on bullocks hide
A shouting jackdaws seen to sit alone
Just so this monster on the saddle shone
And as for pride no jiant no goliah
Could of his mighty person think no higher   10
For all who look'd (and many was affraid)
Nay if a stranger stopping only made
A wrinkled brow as ready for a stare
He in a passion would begin to swear.
—But spite of this young chub in close review   15
Just like a pointer fairley stard him thro'
For having often heard the story told
About tom thumkin and his acts so bold
He really took this mighty man to be
Tom Thumkins person in reallity   20
So on he stard with all the eyes he had
Till his suppos'd tom thumb grown wond'rous mad
In thundering vengance made this question known
Demanding answer in magestic tone
'Thou sensles dog, why thus my views impede?   25
'Thou two leg'd bastard of the swinish breed
'What makes you stare so mungrel of a whore?
'Did you ne'er see base dog—a man before?
Chub vex'd at such foul names soon turnd awry
His mouth in posture ready to reply   30

CHUBS REPLY   *Title:* Chubs Reply *MS 1*   5 three *through* ?four *through*
?two *MS 1*   16 s *through* t *in* Just *MS 1*   17 often *inserted MS 1*
28 base *through ?* wise *MS 1*

'Why theres no doubt of that—(then fleer'd and gave
His beaver a cock up)—'but what I have
'But I should be d—nd cunning could I see
'E'en the worst sort in such Tom-thumbs as thee!'
'Thumb' struck with this he little thought to hear   35
From such a fool as chubby did appear
Sneak'd off asham'd and still as ere he could
For fear the crowd that gaping round 'em stood
Should catch the sharp reply and run him down
By joining chorus with the gauling clown   40
Warn'd by this caution for the time to come
To keep his questions and affront at home
For Madam Wit no chuser of her place
Is often cloath'd in rags as well as lace

AUTOGRAPHS: Nor. MS 1, p. 82: Pet. MS A3, p. 70.
TRANSCRIPTS: Pet. MS B1, p. 122: Nor. MS 5, p. 144.
Printed in *RL*, pp. 169–70. In 2nd edn. moved from fifth to second poem in
'Songs and Ballads' section. Omitted in 4th edn.
Dated: 'Old' (MS A3, p. 70).

FRIEND LUBIN

Friend Lubin loves his saturdays
    That brings him resting sundays
But witler loves contrary ways
    And wishes all were Mondays
The Labourer doats on welcome night   5
    To rest his weary limbs
And Misses in the day delight
    To show their dressy whims

FRIEND LUBIN   *Title*: Song. *MS 1*, Song *MS A3*, Friend Lubin *RL*
1 Saturdays *MS A3*   2 bring: resting] rest on *RL*   3 [But] While *MS A3*
4 And *through* He *MS 1*] & *MS A3*   where mondays *MS A3*   5 labourer *MS A3*
7 & *MS A3*

But O the night and day to me
  The saturday & monday 10
I care not wich-a-way they be
  On work' i' day or Sunday
O no I care not what they be
  Tho night I most approve
But o the day is dear to me 15
  That brings me to my love

AUTOGRAPHS: Pet. MS A40, pp. 35a–36 (deleted): Nor. MS 1, p. 83: Pet. MS D4, p. 8.
TRANSCRIPTS: Pet. MS B1, pp. 23–4: Nor. MS 5, pp. 173–4.
Dated: 'Old' (MS D4, p. 8).

A BEGGING ORPHANS ADDRESS TO A LADY

Good lady stay pity a poor begging orphan
Who's got neither parents or friends
O hear my true ditty too oft made a laugh on
O pity & make me amends
My mam woudnt let once the cold wind blow on me 5
Little thinking what I shoud come to
My dad proved as tender till death took him from me
O pity me good Lady do

9 & MS A3   day and night RL   10 The through B MS 1   &] or MS A3 RL
11 wich a way (way below indecipherable) MS A3   12 On] Or MS A3 RL   Worki[n]'
MS A3   15 But through & MS A3] And MS 1   O through o MS A3   day' is
through days MS 1

   A BEGGING ORPHANS ADDRESS TO A LADY   Title: A Beggings Orphans
Address to a Lady MS A40, The begging Orphan MS 1, Begging Orphans / Address to
a Lady MS D4   1 Lady; MS 1] Lady— (— through stay) MS D4   Orphan
MS D4   2 Who's] I've MS 1   nor MS 1 MS D4   3 too] so MS 1
4 O pity &] Then I hope you will MS 1   5 Mam' MS 1] Mam. MS
D4   wou'd'n't MS 1] wou'dn't MS D4   6 should: too MS 1 MS D4
7 My . . . as] And my Dad was: 'em MS 1   dad. prov'd MS D4   8 O] Then
MS 1

O if my dear parents knew how I am used
Coud they from high heaven but see   10
How by that sad tyrant their orphans abused
Theyd sadly be troubled for me
Soon as rich or poor see me they cry in a passion
'Begone sir weve nothing for you'
Nor my rags nor misfortunes can crave their compassion   15
O pity me good lady do

When I hold up my fingers so blistered & perished
By making my bed on the snow
They cry 'O you scoundrel they soon woud be cherished
'They only want somthing to do'   20
Dont you think tender lady such folks are hard hearted
I am sure by your tears that you do
Tho Ive been so ill used since my parents departed
I never need fear it from you

O Im to have victuals to keep me from starving   25
O heavens & cloathed to be
Such uncommon goodness may I be deserving
Ill strive far as life lies in me
God bless you good lady now freed from all tyrants
Ill near miss my mother in you   30
For what youll do for me is more then my parents
If they were both living coud do

9 O . . . dear] And oh if my *MS 1*   10 Could *MS 1 MS D4*   11 that] the:
tyrants: orphan's *MS 1*   12 They'd: troubl'd *MS 1 MS D4*   sadly] soreley be
through be soreley *MS 1*   sadly [sad]: be *through* ly: me— *MS D4*   14 'Be off sir
we've *(first* e *through* h *in* we've) *MS 1]* 'Begone—we have *MS D4*   15 compasion
MS D4   16 O] Then *MS 1*   Lady *MS 1 MS D4*   17 hold up] show
them: so blistered &] by winter quite *MS 1*   blister'd *MS D4*   perish'd *MS 1*
MS D4   18 By] From *MS 1*   19 you scoundrel they] by jingos them *MS 1*
scoundrell *MS D4*   wou'd *MS 1 MS D4*   cherish'd *MS 1]* cherishd *MS D4*
20 whant *(n through t)* : something *MS 1*   do∧ *MS A40*   21 Lady *MS 1*
22 I am] Yes I'm *MS 1*, I'm *MS D4*   23 I've: us'd *MS 1 MS D4*   24 never
need] hope not to *MS 1*   25 −'O: Victuals!: starving— *MS D4*   I'm *MS 1*
MS D4   26 & . . . be] and cloathes all from thee! *MS 1*   be! *MS D4*
27 Such] Of such *MS D4*   Then to be of such uncommon goodnes deserving *MS 1*
28 I'll *MS 1]* —I will *MS D4*   Life lyes *MS 1*   29 God] O God: good
omitted: Lady: free *MS 1*   30 Ill] I shall *MS 1 MS D4*   ne'er *MS 1]* neer
MS D4   31 For] Nay: you'll *MS 1 MS D4*   than *MS 1*   32 where: both]
now: could *MS 1 MS D4*   do. *MS 1*

AUTOGRAPHS: Pet. MS A3, p. 61: Pet. MS A3, p. 64 (ll. 1–8 deleted): Nor. MS 1, p. 84 (ll. 17–24 omitted).
TRANSCRIPTS: Pet. MS B1, p. 113: Nor. MS 5, p. 145.
Printed in *RL*, p. 163–5. Omitted 2nd edn.
Dated: 'Old' (MS A3, p. 61).

THE COUNTRY GIRL

O dear what fine thinkings beset me
Sin' the young Farmer yesterday met me
To tell me for truth he wou'd get me
   Some service more fitting in town
For he said 'twas a shame & he swore too   5
That I should be serv'd so & more too
& that he was vex'd oer & oer too
   To see me so sadly run down

When to thank him—for curtsy'ng I dropt me
He said twas all foolish & stopt me—   10
& into his arms Oh he popt me!
   And crumpl'd my bonnet awry
The tray sav'd the fall till he mov'd it
& this way & that way he shov'd it
Good behaviour he said how he lov'd it   15
   When maids wa'n't so foolish & shy

O dear what fine thinkings beset me
Since the young Farmer promis'd & met me

THE COUNTRY GIRL   *Title:* The Country Girl *MS A3 RL*, The Cuntry Girl.
MS 1   2 Since *MS 1*   farmer *MS A3, p. 64 MS 1*   3 To tell] And told *MS A3, p. 64,* When he told *MS 1*   would *MS 1*   4 town *underlined MS A3*
5 twas *MS A3, p. 64 MS 1*   and *MS 1*   6 shou'd: servd *MS A3, p. 64*
so serv'd and *MS 1*   7 And: and *MS 1*   vexd *MS A3, p. 64*   *MS 1*
9 When To (When *inserted*) *MS A3*   And when to make curtsey I dropt me *MS 1*
10 To thank him—he ran'd up and stopt me *(and through to) MS 1*   11 And: o:
me∧ *MS 1*   12 awry *over* [peak down] *MS 1*   13 tray *underlined MS A3*
But I ne'er took pet when he shov'd me *MS 1*   14 So just as he wanted he mov'd
me *MS 1*   15 And said for that reason he lov'd me *MS 1*   16 wa'n't so] were
not *RL*   And swore he would buy me a gown *MS 1*

Of what he would do & would get me
How my heart pittapatters about   20
Tho Fear—none but fools make a trade on
—He swore when he saw what I play'd on
'My word is my bond pretty maiden'
Then why need I harbour a doubt

Tho the tell clacking grass's foul staining   25
In my holiday clothes is remaining
I ne'er shall go make no complaining
  I've promise o' better in Town
So Chub needn't come no more croaking
To maul one about so provoking   30
I know what is what—wi'out Joking
  Theres nought got by pleasing a Clown

20 pittapatters *underlined MS A3*   22 see *MS A3*
25–32
                    Then Chub need'n't come no more croaking
                    To maul me about so provokeing
                    Since his honor tells me without jokeing
                        Theres nought got by pleasing a clown
                    And rot this drab tho the grass staint it   5
                    I ne'er shall go make no complaint wi't
                    Since he (tho at last he ne'er nam'd it)
                        Has promis'd to buy me a Gown!   *MS 1*

(l. 6 ne'er shall *through* shall neer)

25 tell]tale— *RL*   27 no] a *RL*   29 no more] again *RL*   *In margin in*
MS 1:
                    From falling I hardly could save me
                    Unnumberd the kisses he gave me
                    So well he said I did behave me
                    No Girl was so charming as I.

(l. 2 *Second* n *through* d *in* Unnumberd)

AUTOGRAPH: Nor MS 1, p. 84.
Dated: 1808–19 (MS 1).

A REPLY TO – – OF – ON STYLEING
HIS HUMBLE SERVNT A FOOL

He that has witt from Nature for a fool
   Is deem'd by Wisdom as a ready thing
Which proves a handle fit for every tool
   To please a beggar or instruct a King

So you for once have honour'd me too much   5
   By styleing me a Member of that Class
My witt & brains like yours I fear is such
   They're scarce sufficient to Improve an Ass!

AUTOGRAPH: Nor. MS 1, p. 85.
TRANSCRIPTS: Nor. MS 4, pp. 111–12: Pet. MS C1, p. 25.
Dated: 1808–19 (MS 1).

SONG

Since Edward departed and lef me behind
   My heart is for ever in fear
But if a short hope in his abscence I find
   Tis in Summer the prime of the year
When the wind with the Zephers can scarce intervene   5
   A Curse on the billows to form
When the Sky's Cloudless aspect so clear and serene
   Puts me out of doubt of a storm
Then a Moments Composure I catch from the breeze
And fancy my Edward as safe on the seas   10

A REPLY TO – – OF – ON STYLEING HIS HUMBLE SERVNT A
FOOL   *Title:* A Reply to – – of – on styleing his humble Ser^vnt, A Fool   8 There
altered to They're: Ass!!!.

SONG   *Title:* Song *MS 1*

But O when in Autumn I shrink at the thought
  The Hurricanes terribly rise
With such force as to meet with resistance from naught
  And toss the ships up to the skies
& o to experience the lightnings red flash   15
  Which darts thro' my window at night
When instant the thunder rolls off with a Clash
  That stuns me to death with affright
And when it is over my heart know's no ease
From thinking what Edward endures on the seas   20

O then thou almighty that rides on the wind
  And makes the dread thunder to roar
To a poor timid maiden in pity be kind
  And Bid it to thunder no more
Make the wind all his strength so oerbearing resign   25
  Or let him have no other power
Then the Zephers so harmles:—with them let him join
  To dance in the Leaves of my Bower
Then a daily composure I'll catch from the Breeze
And for ever think Edward as safe on the sea's   30

AUTOGRAPH: Nor. MS 1, p. 87.
TRANSCRIPTS: Nor. MS 4, p. 114: Pet. MS C2, pp. 66a–67.
Dated: 1808–19 (MS 1).

IMPROMTU

Ah woodbine shade the very sight of thee
Has spoilt my silence and tranquility
When just before I had thy wild shade caught
I wander'd happy blest without a thought
But now alas thy image does restore   5
False chloes woodbine round her cottage door

13 with *over* [no] *MS 1*   23–4 *Through two indecipherable lines MS 1*
30 *Followed in MS 1, pp. 86–7 by* To the Butterflye *which is published in our volume for*
'The Village Minstrel'
  IMPROMTU   *Title:* Impromtu *MS 1*   2 silence [n] *MS 1*

That door which now to me access denies
Yet still my heart its wishing fondness sighs
'Did chloe know where collin is this hour
'How he thinks of her by the woodbine flower'   10
—O! cease fond heart and let me call thee mine
Leave that false bosom which will neer be thine
How canst thou fancy without gains or aught
False love will flatter for a simple thought?

AUTOGRAPH: Nor. MS 1, pp. 88–9 (ll. 61–8 added later, o.p.).
TRANSCRIPTS: Nor. MS 4, pp. 115–16 (ll. 61–8 omitted): Pet. MS C2,
pp. 67–67a.
Dated: 1808–19 (MS 1).

ELEGY

*Humbly attempted (from the overflowing effusions
of a feeling heart) to pay a small tribute of
esteem and gratitude to the memory of my
dear friend companion and schoolfellow
R[ichard] T[urnill] who was suddenly cut
off in his youthful days by the fatal
depredations of the Tipus Fever*

Ah cruel death to Friendship such a foe
  What fiend malicious could enforce thy power
Thus in an instant to impede the blow
  Of budding hopes that rapt the finest flower.

Did envy wrankling with her hollow eye   5
  Point to thy victim as above her clan
Or did the angellic band from realms on high
  Deem him more fit an Angel then a man.

14 thought?! *MS 1*

  ELEGY *Title:* Elegy. *MS 1*   Humbly attempted, (from the overflowing effusions,
/ of a feeling heart;) to pay a small tribute, of / esteem, and gratitude, to the memory, of
my / dear friend, companion, and schoolfellow, / R T who was suddenly cut / off in his
youthful days, by the fatal / depredations of the Tipus Fever. *MS 1*   3 l *through* o
in blow *MS 1*

But what's enquirey now? that must be vain
   Since his dear form (heartrending thought) is fled,   10
Since he's demanded from his native plain
   To sleep unnotic'd with the silent dead.

O tortering to[r]ments like a flood ye swell
   Oerbounding anguish and afflictive pain
To think of him who so untimley fell   15
   Daily encreasing 'cause I mourn in vain.

No couple sure throughout the world beside
   In friendship so familliar could be found,
Friendship begun in childhoods earliest pride
   Endearing more as Reason gained ground.   20

Ah childish scenes which manhood has declin'd,
   Ah trifling sports alike for ever fled
How your remembrance often brings to mind
   My dear companion sleeping with the dead.

The village close and green for play renown'd,   25
   The hedgerow bank where oft in searching ken
We both have crawl'd along the mossy ground
   To hunt the snailhorn in his secret den.

The thymy seated hill, the hoof plod ground
   Whose batterd surface ownd the marble ring,   30
The straggling bush where many a nest was found,
   The shelterd hovel and the bathing spring.

The uncooth name employment once for life
   Which still yon bridge within its arch retains,
Mishapen rudley by his artless knife   35
   The only relic of his dear remains.

(Oer whose unpolishd dints at eventide
   (Pure seeming scene of emblematic woe)
The suns departing rays will faintly glide
   'And oer the whole a mournful lustre throw.')   40

23 often *inserted MS 1*   37 h *in* unpolishd *inserted MS 1*   39 glide *through*
throw *MS 1*

These are the scenes which grieve me to behold;
   Anon the wheat-field where the blue-cap grew,
With crimson corn-flowers and the yellow gould,
   All which our youth would eagerly pursue.

These tell of other days with strength combind   45
   Of all our sports so innoscently rude,
Which only serve to load my troubl'd mind
   With added griefs on others still renew'd.

Then cease remembrance since it's all in vain
   To dwell on themes which nothing can restore   50
These days are past my collin's left the plain
   And friends and kindred to return no more.

And O his loss to kindred was severe
   'For in that heavn'ly youth for ever ends'
(What rarley does in riper age appear)   55
   'The best of sons, of brothers, and of friends.'

Adieu all goodnes centr'd in one piece
   Adieu dear friend—and thee to find again
My hopes on that shall dwell and never cease
   Till death reveals my endless joys or pain.   60

But the dear ties which love & Nature binds
   And fond affection's heart adhereth too
These cruel death undissapointed finds
   And these his hand is readiest to undo.

Farewell companion of my early days   65
   & while thy grave a brothers tears bedew
I'll not forget my tributary praise
   To friendship sacred & to memory due.

52 more∧ *MS 1*   55 rarley *over* [never]: does *through* did: riper *over* [equal] *MS 1*
56 friends∧' *MS 1*   61 & *through* off *MS 1*   62 heart *through* else *MS 1*
64 undo∧ *MS 1*   68 due∧ *MS 1*

AUTOGRAPH: Nor. MS 1, p. 90.
TRANSCRIPTS: Nor. MS 4, pp. 116–17: Pet. MS C2, p. 68.
Dated: 1808–19 (MS 1).

SONG

When Chloe's gone then fancy lays
Her cunning schemes a thousand ways
   And what I might have done
And (only charm for absent pain)
When ere she comes this way again   5
   How Chloe may be won

But when alas the maiden's nigh
The languid look the half-sown sigh
   Is all that finds a way
For plans and schemes are all destroy'd   10
While fancy flies an hopeles void
   And leaves me naught to say

AUTOGRAPH: Nor. MS 1, pp. 90–1.
TRANSCRIPTS: Nor. MS 4, pp. 117–18: Pet. MS C2, pp. 68–68a.
Dated: 1808–19 (MS 1).

COLLIN'S COMPLAINT

When lovers to each other true
   In every virtuous wish agree
How pleasing is the interview
   Alas! but how unknown to me

For Chloe timid as the fawn   5
   Nor yet less timid then she's proud
Call's 'virtue' to resist the lawn
   And 'pr[i]de' to shun me in a crowd

SONG   *Title:* Song. *MS 1*   7 m *through* M *in* maiden's *MS 1*
8 half-sowln *MS 1*   9 away *MS 1*   12 say! *MS 1*
COLLIN'S COMPLAINT   *Title:* Collin's Complaint *MS 1*

Thus with her virtues blushing grace
    (Tho more disdainful pride I fear)   10
She hates the private-public place
    And leaves me absent every where

While Damon with his Fillis roves
    Freely possesing every charm
Thro level meeds and shady groves   15
    They wander sweetly 'arm in arm'

O! what can equal love like this
    When both with equal fondness burn
Yielding—he gives a rapturous kiss
    Which she as freely does return   20

But cease to praise—unconsious heart
    As Fillis is her Damons care
He soon may take a jealous part
    And think that collin longs to share

And if fair Chloe once should hear   25
    Soon soon excuse's would be crost
Disdain now hid would then appear
    And hopes to gain entirley lost

Then cease—and tho thy love seems naught
    But fancied hope in distant dreams   30
And in a reality of thought
    Is nothing else but what it seems

Yet hope and dwell on fond delay
    That time-to-come may better prove
Make Chloe kind—and that I may   35
    In virtues bounds posess her love

AUTOGRAPHS: Nor. MS 1, p. 91: Pet. MS A3, p. 74.
TRANSCRIPTS: Pet. MS B1, pp. 125–6: Nor. MS 5, pp. 121–2.
Printed in *RL*, pp. 42–4.
Dated: 1808–10 (MS A3, p. 74 'Old 8 or 10 years ago', *RL* Introduction, p. xxii
'before he was seventeen').

THE ROBIN

Now the snow hides the ground little birds leave the wood
And flie to the cottage to beg for their food
While the domestic robin more tame then the rest
(With its wings drooping down and rough feathers undrest)
Comes close to our windows as much as to say   5
'I would venture in if I could find a way
'I'm starv'd and I want to get out of the cold
'O! make me a passage and think me not bold'
Ah poor little creature thy visits reveal
Compla[i]nts such as these to the heart that can feel   10
Nor shall such complainings be urged in vain
I'll make thee a hole if I take out a pane
Come in and a welcome reception thou'lt find
I keep no grimalkins to murder inclin'd
—But O! little robin be careful to shun   15
That house where the peasant makes use of a gun
For if thou but taste of the seed he has strew'd
Thy life as a ransom must pay for thy food
His aim is unerring his heart is as hard
And thy race tho so harmles he'll never regard   20
Distinction with him boy is nothing at all
Both the wren and the robin with sparrows must fall

THE ROBIN *Title:* The Robin *MS 1 RL*, The Ro[b]bin *MS A3*   2 flye
MS A3   3 Domestic Robin *MS A3*] Robin, domestic *RL*   4 & *MS
A3*   rough] its *MS A3 RL*   5 Windows *MS A3*   6 away *MS 1 MS A3*
7 & *MS A3*   8 'Oh∧: & *MS A3*   10 Complaints *MS A3*   12 thee]
the *MS A3*   13 &: resception *MS A3*   14 Grimalkin *MS A3*] grimalkin
RL   inclind— *MS A3*   15 ∧But oh∧: Robin *MS A3*   16 pheasent *MS 1*]
pheasant *MS A3*   18 the *through* thy *MS A3*] the *RL*   20 &: harmless
MS A3   21 Boy *MS A3*   22 Wren: &: Robin: Sparrows *MS A3*

POEMS DESCRIPTIVE   125

For his soul (tho he outwardly looks like a man)
Is in nature like wolves of the appenine clan
Like them his whole study is bent on his prey   25
Like them he devours what e'er comes in his way
Then be careful and shun what is meant to betray
And flie from these men-masked wolves far away
Come come to my cottage and thou shalt be free
To perch on my finger or sit on my knee   30
Thou shalt eat of the crumbles of bread to thy fill
And have leisure to clean both thy feathers and bill
Then come little robin and never believe
Such warm Invitations are meant to decieve
In duty I'm bound to show mercy on thee   35
While God dont deny it to sinners like me!

AUTOGRAPHS: Nor. MS 1, pp. 92–3 (o.p.): Pet. MS A3, pp. 83–4.
TRANSCRIPTS: Pet. MS B1, pp. 138–9 (deleted): Nor. MS 5, pp. 98–100.
Dated: 1808–19 (MS 1).

THE DISABLED SOLDIER

or British Loyalty

'Neighbours and country men for once relieve
    A poor disabl'd soldier in distress
Suspect no lie the truth ye may believe
    These stumps will soon my noble trade confess

24 like wolves] a Wolf *MS A3*, a wolf *RL*   26 [his wholes] he: what ere *MS A3*
27 & *MS A3*   28 flye: men masked Wolves *MS A3*   29 & *MS A3*
30 or] & *MS A3*, and *RL*   32 and] & *MS A3*   33 Robin & *MS A3*
36 While] Since *MS A3 RL*   me!— *MS A3*

THE DISABLED SOLDIER   *Title:* The disabled Soldier, / or british Loyality; / A
Petitional Ballad.— (Sollder *altered to* Soldier) *MS 1*, The disabl'd Soldier / or british
Loyality / [a petional ballad] *MS A3*   *Quotation marks omitted throughout MS A3*
1 & countrymen *MS A3*   4 stumps will soon] wooden stumps *MS A3*

'These sixty years as true as here I stand   5
    I've fought my countrys freedom to mentain
Forty whereof Ive spent upon the land
    The rest Ive brav'd with Nelson on the main

'And from the field of Battle now Ive came
    Where Britons dauntless as the lion stood   10
Nor would they flie—for this their only aim
    Was Death or Victory spite of human blood

'Lo I myself as dauntles and as brave
    As any Briton which does boast that name
To many a Limb a ready lopping gave   15
    And now in turn you see I'm serv'd the same

'Which may to some as a Misfortune shine
    To own these pegles stumps—this armles side
But its not so with this old heart of mine
    No, no, I view them with uncommon pride   20

'Nor did their loss my courage e'er abate
    Firm as it was this fragment still remains
Yes just as firm and fierce as when of late
    I shouted Victory on Egyption plains

'And should my country ever stand in need   25
    Of men again their freedom to mentain
Away I'd hop with more than willing speed
    To take the field or brave the watry main

'There as a mark for the insulting foe
    I'd fix my standard, in the formost file,   30
That they might see for once and plainly know
    What stumps of Valour come from Albion's isle

5 sixty] twenty *over* [20] *MS A3*   6 Ive: maintain *MS A3*   7 Forty]
Fifteen: I *MS A3*   8 The ... brav'd] & brav'd the rest *MS A3*   9 &: battle
MS A3   11 flie] yield *MS A3*   12 death *MS A3*   13 Lo] While: my
self: dauntless & *MS A3*   14 any *inserted MS 1*   briton: which ... that] that can
boast the *MS A3*   15 limb *MS A3*   16 &: In *MS A3*   17 misfortune
MS A3   18 pegles stumps] peg less: arm less *MS A3*   19 this *repeated MS 1*
23 firm and fierce] bold m' boys *MS A3*   24 victory: Egyptian *MS A3*
25 & shou'd *MS A3*   26 her: maintain *MS A3*   27 wi' *MS A3*
30 standerd,: file ∧ *MS A3*   31 & let proud french men to their terror know
MS A3   32 valour's: come from] bred in: albions *MS A3*

'With equal rage as tho I limbs posses'd
  I'd deal around the missle shafts of death
And at my glorious exit fall confess'd   35
  A True Blue Britton in the arms of death

'For did no harm belong in chusing death
  So as my soul here after might be free
In Battles Field I'd chuse to loose my breath
  Amid the shouts of 'England's Victory'   40

'All this is from my heart—then pray 'releive
  'A poor disabl'd soldier in distress
'Suspect no lie the truth ye may believe
  'These stumps will soon my Noble trade confess'

AUTOGRAPH: Nor. MS 1, pp. 93–4 (o.p.).
TRANSCRIPTS: Nor. MS 4, pp. 118–20: Pet. MS C2, pp. 68a–69.
Dated: 1808–19 (MS 1).

THE DEATH OF MYRTILLA

or The latter catch of a pathetic Tale In Imitation of H . . . B . . .

Dark was the night, in woeful plight
  Myrtilla mourn'd alone!
No kind relief to ease her grief,
  Myrtilla's sorrow's own!

The rude blasts roar the hugh trees oer,   5
  Myrtillas sorrow's own!
While wispering nigh the foliage sigh,
  Myrtilla's early grave!

33 Bold as the rest (my loss of limbs is all) *MS A3*   34 I'd point my gun & bayonet
unsheath *MS A3*   35 & when by abler frenchman doom'd to fall *(*abler *underlined)*
MS A3   36 A . . . Britton] Smile a True briton *MS A3*   38 hereafter *MS A3*
39 battles field *MS A3*   40 Amidst: ∧England's victory∧ *MS A3*   41 relieve
MS A3   43 lye *MS A3*   44 stumps will soon] wooden stumps: noble *MS A3*

    THE DEATH OF MYRTILLA   *Title:* The Death of Myrtilla.—or The latter catch
of a pathetic Tale / In Imitation of H . . . B . . . *(*The Death of *through* The Death:
pathetic *inserted) MS 1*   3 t to *MS 1*

The faries near all strive to chear
   Myrtilla's frighted mind,   10
Each to her brought a hopeful thought,
   Myrtilla hears the wind.

Loudly crying 'fear not dying,
   'Myrtilla never fear,
'Soon the morning will be dawning   15
   'Myrtilla's soul to chear!'

But soon the rain revers'd the strain,
   'Myrtilla—tilla lie!'
And cruel fate had fix'd his hate,
   'Myrtilla—tilla die!'   20

Far oer the plain the loving swain
   Myrtilla's voice did hear!
And in the rain he call'd amain
   'Myrtilla—tilla dear.'

The swelling floods and hollow woods   25
   Myrtilla's name resound,
The faries hear and wisper near
   Myrtilla will be found!

But ah the lad so thinly clad
   Myrtilla must forgoe!   30
Like fate the wind on him designd
   'Myrtilla—tilla O!'

When this was said, he droop'd his head:—
   Myrtilla on the wind
In dying sounds no more resounds,   35
   Myrtilla's left behind.

Ah wretched sight, if collins plight
   Myrtillas eyes could see,
O hopeles view, 'twould thrice renew
   Myrtillas misery!   40

12 wind∧ *MS 1*   22 near *altered to* hear *MS 1*

'A tender form, unus'd to storms,'
   Myrtillas breaking heart
On this relied, and often crie'd
   Myrtilla's friends are tart.'

She softly sigh'd, and faintly cried,   45
   'Myrtilla thus distrest
'Might but her woe for Collin's floe,
   'Myrtilla then could rest!'

'For if he's nigh he'll quickly flie,
   'Myrtilla's griefs to share   50
O fate be kind! blow soft the wind!
   'Myrtilla's Collin spare!'

' 'T'is all I crave, then welcome Grave!'
   Myrtilla said no more,
Death stopt her grief and blest releif,   55
   Myrtilla's griefs are oer!

Ah friends severe that would'n't hear
   Myrtillas Innocense,
Ah cruel love that would'n't prove
   Myrtilla's Recompence.   60

Now both are dead and both are fled,
   Myrtilla and her dear,
To other isles where morning smiles,
   'Myrtilla's soul to chear!'

Beyond the grave may Collin have   65
   Myrtilla for his due,
While nightley here the fays revere
   Myrtilla's love so true!

AUTOGRAPHS: Nor. MS 1, p. 94: Pet. MS A3, p. 109.
Dated: 1808–19 (MS 1).

WRITTEN IN WESLEYS PHILOSOPHY

Bacon unveil'd philosophy
And fancied that enough
Till Wesley daring genius came
And stript her into Buff.

AUTOGRAPH: Nor. MS 1, p. 95.
TRANSCRIPTS: Nor. MS 4, pp. 120–1: Pet. MS C2, p. 69a.
Dated: 1808–19 (MS 1).

THE ROSE

Or a Wish for Transformation To E.N.

How highly esteem'd is the sweet smelling rose
    Tis reckon'd the 'finest of Flowers'
Unrival'd in flower-pots and posies it glows
    Nay the Queen of Parnassuse's Bowers

And was I like Proteus so powerful indew'd   5
    With that uncommon magical power
My form should this instant be chang'd and renew'd
    Yes turn'd to this beautiful flower

Tho this strange Metamorphus by me so excited
    'T'is not for my love of the flowers   10
Nor is it the title with which I'm delighted
    To be 'Queen of parnassion bowers'

WRITTEN IN WESLEYS PHILOSOPHY   *Title:* Written in Wesleys Philosophy
MS 1 MS A3   1 Philosophy *MS A3*   3 genius! *MS A3*   4 &: in to
buff. *MS A3*

    THE ROSE   *Title:* The Rose, / Or a wish for Transformation; to, E.N.—*MS 1*

No no thats a trifle not worth the possesing
  Far beneath the fond wish of a swain
In the way that I crave it—'t'would—O a blessing!   15
  A blessing not call'd so in vain

My wish for the change—is to win Chloe's bosom
  Those two swelling mountains of snow
Where so nice in the Valley—each side to repose—on!
  I could see them both heave too and fro   20

There posses'd of my Love a rose-life (or a day)
  I would kiss all its heaving alarms
And when doom'd to wither I'd secretly stray
  To die in the midst of her charms

This is why I wish for't:—my Chloe my dear   25
  Believe the fond truth that I show
Tho you cannot expect the strange scene to appear
  Yet my Uncommon Love you may know!

AUTOGRAPHS: Nor. MS 1, p. 95: Pet. MS A3, p. 108.
TRANSCRIPTS: Pet. MS B1, p. 173: Nor. MS 5, p. 124.
Dated: 'Old' (MS A3, p. 108).

A WINTER WISH

My wish now's to sit in a cottage made snug
  By a fire burning roozy and bright
With a Friend to make shorter short days by a Jug
  And some Books for amusement at night

And could I enjoy such a peaceable lot   5
  I'd ne'er cast on Fortune a frown
Nor would I possesing my Friend, Books, and Cott
  Exchange 'em away for a—Crown!

28 know!. MS 1

A WINTER WISH   *Title:* A Winter Wish *MS 1 MS A3*   1 Cottage *MS A3*
2 & *MS A3*   3 friend: a Jug] jug *MS A3*   4 &: books *MS A3*
5 & coud *MS A3*   6 fortune: Frown *MS A3*   7 wou'd: & *MS A3*
8 Crown∧ *MS A3*

AUTOGRAPH: Nor. MS 1, pp. 96–7.
TRANSCRIPTS: Nor. MS 4, pp. 121–3: Pet. MS C2, pp. 69a–71.
Dated: 1808–19 (MS 1).

THE EAGLE AND THE CROW

A Fable

How aggravating 't'is to hear
A Four-foot-nothing o'er his beer
Crack and brag what he can do
And what he has done years ago
How when he was but boyish quite   5
(And not much better now in hight)
Could shoulder sacks of corn—alone
Run like a Top with massy stone
Top every gate he came but nigh
And jump the locks where none durst try   10
In climbing trees he'd yield to none
Beat every one to walk or run
Pelt o'er the steeple twice as high
As any one he'd testify
While chocking hole & marble ring   15
Always own'd him for their king
To boxing too he could aspire
And minded not the best Goliah
At wrestling:—he'd such notions in it
To wang their heels up in a minnute   20
Howe'er in short this monstrous man
Pretends to king of every clan
So strong to bear so lythe to run
So vers'd in jokes for sport and fun
So skill'd so powerful in his youth   25
So fond of every thing—but truth!
For this the boaster does abhor
Yet thinks hes nought to answer for

THE EAGLE AND THE CROW   *Title:* The Eagle and the Crow / A Fable. *MS 1*
2 nothing *repeated MS 1*   19 he's *altered to* he'd *MS 1*

When he's been cracking swearing lying
He never fears the least of dying   30
He goes to church as others do
And thinks him self as righteous too
—But his religion! what of that?
'T'is not the thing I pointed at
His swaggering boasts and cracking stuff   35
Is all I mean (and thats enough)
Yes quite enough (in terms hydrolic)
To kill his hearers with the cholic
And what is worse this silly elf
Will let none chatter but himself   40
—To such concieted sons of pride
I have a Fable near allie'd
Which shows their easy over match'd
And sometimes in a tether catch'd

An Eagle once both stout and able   45
(No matter where—tis but a fable)
Struck at a little playful lamb
While sporting near its frighted dam
Pounc'd it and took it all together
Easier than linnets do a feather   50
A crow hard by from neighbouring wood
Who near the scene of action stood
Saw all:—But never blest her eyes
No[r] deem'd it matter of supprise
'Cant I' she cries 'as well [as] yon   55
'Fine poltry Eagle just now gone
'Strike at a lamb and bear't away?
'Yes yes I can and will to day
'Altho her tallons are more long
'Mine are as sharp if not so strong   60
'And tho my bodys not all out
'So big so frightful and so stout
'Yet that in pouncing has no part
'I know I've got a bolder heart!'

34 the *repeated MS 1*   38 *Second* r *through* s *in* hearers *MS 1*   50 feather.
MS 1

So saying from the tree she springs   65
And in a Lamb her tallons flings
But ah poor crow she soon found out
'T'was harder than she talk'd about
Soon she began to peck and pull
To free her tallons from the wool   70
But alls no use she's tangled still
In vain the tallons wings or bill
The more she tries to get unbound
The more the nasty wool laps round
Till quite worn out:—she waits to die   75
And murmurs this reproving sigh
'Had I ne'er like a boasting elf
'With such vain exploits fuss'd my self
'I ne'er had lit of this mishap
'Nor ventur'd headlong in a trap   80
'Oh could I but enjoy once more
'That Liberty I had before
'I'd never dream nor think I saw
'A tallon on my silly claw!'
But 'mid this trouble so severe   85
A shepherd who was listning near
H[e]ard the sad cause of her mishap
And took her from her wooly trap
But not for Liberty? no never!
This griev'd poor crowey worse than ever   90
He clipt her wing and took her home
To make some sport for little tom
Who soon began with eager brawl
'These dont destroy the lambs an' all?
'No certainly howe'er put to't   95
'I think such mortals could'n't do't!'
'Child' cries the shepherd 'you cant tell
'How high concieted minds will swell
'—'T'is no great while—if I can guess
'About a couple hours or less   100
'Since that concieted silly beagle
'Fancy'd herself to be an eagle

---

67 ah *inserted MS 1*   97 shepherd[s] *MS 1*   98 How *through* High *MS 1*

'But now I think the lambkins hide
'Has dampt a little of her pride
'And surley too she's learnt to know 105
'Her name was nothing but a Crow!'

AUTOGRAPHS: Norris Museum SAVNM CL/13: Pforzheimer Library, Misc. MS 197: Pet. MS A52, p. 1 (ll. 1–16 only, deleted): Nor. MS 1, p. 97 (ll. 1–16 margin), p. 135 (ll. 17–24 margin): Pet. MS D2, p. 9 (ll. 1–8 only, deleted).
TRANSCRIPT: Pet. MS B1, p. 37 (ll. 13–16 deleted).
Printed in *RL*, pp. 120–1.
Dated: April 1819 (Pfz. '1819').

TO AN APRIL DAISY

Welcome old Maytey peeping once again
    Our meeting minds me of a pleasent hour
Springs pencil pinks thy cheek that blushy stain
    & Summer glistens in thy tinty flower

Hail Beautys gem disdaining time nor place 5
    Carlessly creeping on the dunghills side
Demeanour softens in thy crimpled face
    & Decks thee with a charm unknown to pride

106 Crow!' *MS 1*

TO AN APRIL DAISY *Title:* To An April Daisy *Norris*, To an April Daisy *Pfz MS A52 RL*, To an April daisy *MS 1*, To An April Daisey *MS D2*   1 Welcome old Maytey] Hail early Maytey (Maytey *underlined*) *MS A52*, Hail early blossoms *MS 1* matey *Pfz*] maytey *underlined MS D2*, comrade *RL*   2 Our meeting minds] Thou meets to mind *MS A52*, To meet & mind *MS 1*   pleasent] better *MS A52*, pleasing *MS 1*   3 Spri⟨ngs p⟩encil *torn MS D2*   pinks *underlined MS D2*   thy cheek that] thee in that *Pfz RL*, thy cheek in *MS D2*   flushy *Pfz*   4 summer *Pfz MS A52 MS 1*   glistnens *Pfz*   tinty *underlined MS A52 MS D2*   5 H⟨a⟩il *torn*: Gem *MS D2*   beautys *Pfz MS A52 MS D2*] beauties *MS 1*   6 Carelessly *MS D2* 7 Demeanors *MS 1*] Demeanours *Pfz MS A52 RL*   softness *Pfz MS A52 MS 1 RL* crimpld *MS 1*] crimpled *underlined MS D2*   8 Decks thee in beautys unataind by pride *Pfz*] Decks thee in beautys unatain'd by pride *MS A52*, Decks thee in beautys unataind by pride (Decks *through* Visits) *MS 1*, & decks thee in a charm unknown to pride *MS D2*, Decks thee in beauties unattain'd by pride *RL*

Hail 'venturer once again—that fearless here
  Encampeth on the hoar hills sunny side   10
Springs early messenger thourt doubly dear
  & Winters loss by thee is well suply'd

Now winters storms shall cease their pelting rage
  Nor need I mention Winters woes to thee
Far better luck thy visits well presage   15
  & be it thine & mine that luck to see

Ah may thy smiles confirm the hopes they tell—
  To see thee frost bit I'd be griev'd at heart
I meet thee happy & I wish thee well
  Till ripening summer summons us to part   20

Then like old friends or mates thats neighbours been
  Well part in hopes to meet another year
& at thy exit from this changing scene
  Well mix our wishes in a tokening tear

9 venturer *MS 1*   again∧ *Pfz MS 1*   11 Spring *MS 1*   mesenger *MS A52*
12 winters *Pfz*   loss] frost *RL*   by] in *Pfz MS A52 MS 1*   suplyd *MS 1*
13 *Preceded in Norris by*: [Thy hopes bids Winter cease his pelting rage]   Winters *MS
A52*   Now . . . shall] The storms of Winter *MS 1*   storms] frowns *Pfz MS 1 RL*
13/14 [& winters woes to thee I need not tell] *(& through* But*) Norris*   14 But
winters woes I need not tell to thee *Pfz*] But Winters woes to thee I need not tell *MS A52
MS 1*, But winter's woes I need not tell to thee *RL*   14/15 [In thy comission
better things presage] *MS A52*   15 [Thy] Far *MS A52*] As *MS 1*   Visits *MS 1*
16 Springs thy Comission & I wish thee well *MS A52*] Thats thy comission & I wish
thee well *MS 1*   17 tell∧ *Pfz MS 1*   18 Id *MS 1*   grievd *Pfz MS 1*
19 *First* thee] the *MS 1*   20 sumer sumons *MS 1*   21 friends] mates *Pfz
RL*   mates] two *Pfz MS 1 RL*   thats] who've *RL*   22 We'll *Pfz*   another] as
rolls the *MS 1*   23 at *over* [wi] *Norris*] oer *Pfz MS 1*, o'er *RL*   23/4 [Our
hopes shall mingle in a tokening tear] *Norris*   24 We'll *Pfz*   a tokening tear]
betokening tears *MS 1*

AUTOGRAPH: Nor. MS 1, pp. 98–9.
TRANSCRIPT: Pet. MS C1, pp. 7a–8.
Dated: 1808–19 (MS 1).

LOBIN CLOUTS SATIRICAL SOLLILOUQUY ON THE TIMES

A Lab'rour journeying to his work betimes
Thus reak'd his vengance on the awkard times
'O cou'd I think as I wos doom'd to see
Sich shoking times as these ar' got to be
Poor men hod now be batter nokt o' t' head   5
Thon ha' to wok fo' nothin' else but bred
Ney ar' old ma'stur nosty fleerin' to'k
Say's I've no time for 'atins wen I wok
D—n his old c–r–s (g–d forgive my s–l)
How I shud like a bruzzer at his joul   10
But tak' my wod he wil be f[i]tted fo't
When wonce the d–v–l hes his carcos got
No all his fleerin's oer all wul be dun
When he hes got his w–d–n j–k–t on
When swarms of m–g–ts at his h–m–r s–k   15
And turn thot p–dg–y s–ll–ng t–b to muk
Then whon he sees th' place he must be in
He'll wont to pray fur all his wiked sin
But he'all wont whot never must be had
His crimes will be so meny an' so bad   20
An' then he'll cos I wonty fo't the day
He ever chet poor labourers o' their pay
Ah he'all wish he'd pey'd um fo' their wok
An' never plag'd um wi' sich fleering tauk
So I mun wait an' I shal' see him sarv'd   25
Just os I wish'd an' just os he d[e]sarv'd

LOBIN CLOUTS SATIRICAL SOLLILOUQUY ON THE TIMES *Title:*
Lobin Clouts satirical sollilouquy on the times *MS 1*   5 men *inserted MS 1*
6 h *through* w *in* ha' *MS 1*   8 i've: time for *inserted MS 1*   9 *Damn: carcos:*
god: soul   12 *devil*   14 *wooden jacket*   15 *maggots: humour: suk*
16 *podgey swilling tub*   18 to *inserted: prey MS 1*   21 *curse: warrant ye*

But his mak gamlely touk meks me so mad
And if I leave him uthers ar' os bad
Aye Aye they'r all a like poor–pekt–up hogs
They treat the poor os if they wo' but dogs   30
An' if ther' is sum better on's fo' sooth
That wou'd hear reason when we spok' th' truth
Sich d m–d deep r–g–s os ar old be–g–r is
Soon smells it out on tutors em a mis
For like a scab'd a–sd–ship on rogue's enouf   35
To foul a very nation throf an' throf
Then if are goes to then an wines about
(Tho they'd be sorry ot their hart no doubt)
Yet 'fear o'fruntin' th' d–m–d r–g–sh set
They'll em anaye an that is all yah'll get   40
Be os it will they'r sure to mek excuse
So beggin' prayin' nothink's a' no use

AUTOGRAPHS: Nor. MS 1, p. 99 (ll. 1–44 only): Pet. MS A3, pp. 59–60.
TRANSCRIPT: Pet. MS B1, pp. 112–13.
Printed in *RL*, pp. 159–62.
Dated: 'old' (MS A3, p. 59).

UPON THE PLAIN

A Ballad

Upon the plain there livd a swain
A Flock his whole employ
Unknown loves cares & all its snares
To damp his humble joy

33 *damned*: *rogues*: *beggar*   35 –a–sd–ship: enough *altered to* enouf *MS 1*
38 *damned roguish*   40 ani' aye *MS 1*   42 preyin' *MS 1*

UPON THE PLAIN   *Title:* A Ballad *MS 1 MS A3*, Upon the Plain. A Ballad *RL*
1 liv'd: Swain *MS A3*   2 —A *MS A3*

Industry toils whil Fortune smiles   5
To bles him with increase
Contentment made his humble trade
A Scene of Health & Peace
But Cupid sly whose jealous eye
Envied his happines   10
With pointed darts & subtle arts
Resolvd on his distress
Tho first in vain he Workd his brain
But practisd in deceit
Fresh schemes & plans where nigh at hand   15
& some was sure to hit
In fatal hour he provd his power
A Shepherds form he tain
With hook & song he hums along
& thus acosts the swain   20
Go friend he cried to yonder side
The hedge that bounds the plain
For there a lamb has lost his dam
& calls for help in vain
He instant starts his tender heart   25
Oerlooks the subtle snare
The swains beguild pleasd Cupid smild
Fair florimel was there
The Rosys red her cheeks bespred
Her bosom lily white   30
To view her charms each bosom warms
Enrapturd at the sight

---

5 while fortune *MS A3*   6 bles] bess *MS A3*   7 *Second* e *through* a *in*
Contentment *MS A3*   8 health: peace *MS A3*   9 slye *MS A3*
10 happiness *MS A3*   13 Tho *through* A *MS 1*] —Tho *MS A3*   work'd *MS A3*
14 But] Yet *RL*   desceit *MS A3*   15 at] his: hands *RL*   16 & *MS A3*
were *RL*   17 power *altered to* hower *(third word) MS 1*   prov'd *MS A3*
18 —A *MS A3*   he's taen *RL*   19 hook] crook *MS A3 RL*   Song *MS A3*
20 And: accosts *MS A3*   21 'Go friend': 'to *MS A3*   r *in* friend *inserted MS 1*
22 'The *MS A3*   23 'For ther *MS A3*   his] its *MS A3 RL*   24 'And: vain'
MS A3   calls] bleats *MS A3 RL*   25—He *MS A3*   He instant starts] Intent to
start *RL*   26 Oer looks *MS A3*   27 pleas'd *MS A3*   28—Fair *MS A3*
29 Roseys: Cheeks bespread *MS A3*   30 her *MS 1*   bosom's *RL*
31 Charms *MS A3*   32 Enraptur'd *MS A3*

Her heaving breast her slender waist
Her shape genteel & tall
Her charms divine Unrivald shine   35
Alike confest by all
Beneath the shade the lovly maid
Was shelterd from the sun
O luckles swain go fly the plain
Or stay & be undone   40
For ah twas provd by them that lovd
She had a scornful eye
Her pride was vain no way to gain
He[r] pity but to dye
—Stretchd on the Green—her beauty seen   45
To all advantage there
To meet the breeze that fand the trees
Her snowy breast was bare
She meets his view Sweet Peace adieu
And Pleasures kno[w]n before   50
He sighs—Approves—Admires & loves
—His heart's his own no more

AUTOGRAPH: Nor. MS 1, p. 100.
Dated: 1808–19 (MS 1).

O Charming bird thy melody so sweet
    Makes even hodge that vulgar foe to song
In wistful tone to imitate repeat
    Thy 'Sweet Jug' Music as he plods along

33 her *MS 1*   37 lovley *MS A3*   38 Was] Lay *MS A3 RL*   shelter'd: Sun
MS A3   39 —O luckless: Go flye *MS A3*   40 Stay *MS A3*   41 prov'd:
lov'd *MS A3*   42 had] own'd *MS A3 RL*   scornfull *MS A3*   43 vain—
MS A3   no] the *MS A3 RL*   44 he *MS 1*] Her *MS A3*   pity—: Dye
MS A3   but] was *MS A3 RL*   45–52 *Copy-text: MS A3*   45 beauty's *RL*
48 breast] neck *RL*
    O CHARMING BIRD THY MELODY SO SWEET   *Title: wanting*

AUTOGRAPH: Nor. MS 1, p. 100.
Dated: 1808–19 (MS 1).

ON LABOUR

That nessesary tool of Wealth & pride
—The humble ploughman in his daily rounds
Where natures beauties lavishly abounds
Will feel delighted when he turns his eye
To witness prospects of the earth or sky   5
& oft will make a pause & stand to see
The passing clouds the cottage brook or tree
—The king cup courts his eye with gayest p[r]ide
& modest cowslaps tremble by his side
& type of Innoscence without disguise   10
The Vilet creeps to meet his vulgar eyes
While on the sunny bank the daisys seem
With smiling charms to court the clowns esteem
Nor do they spread their smiling charms in vain
His bosom warms enrapturd at the sight   15
With secret pleasure & unknown delight
His swelling soul to memorys treasure flies
& strives to speak—but Ignorance denies

AUTOGRAPH: Nor. MS 1, p. 100.
Dated: 1808–19 (MS 1).

So gay in summer as thy boughs where drest
So soft so cool as then thy leaves did wave
I knew thee well & knowing am distrest
& like as friendship leaning oer the grave
Loving ye all ye trees & bushes dear   5
I wander where ye stood & drop my bosom tear

ON LABOUR   *Title:* On labour   4 will   5 to   15 his   17 his
SO GAY IN SUMMER AS THY BOUGHS WHERE DREST   *Title: wanting*

AUTOGRAPHS: Pet. MS A3, pp. 117—20: Norris Library SAVNM CL/8.
Includes cancelled draft of a letter to Drury: 'This piece is sent for Insertion in
the "trifles"—& in the Authors opinion crowns the whole— . . .': British
Library, Eg. MS 2245, f. 9ᵛ (pencil, ll. 31–48, 55–66 only). A letter to
Clare from J. B. Henson, Deeping, 21 December 1818: Nor. MS 1, p. 100
(pencil beneath ink, ll. 31–48 only).
TRANSCRIPT: Pet. MS B1, pp. 179–82.
Printed in *RL*, pp. 92–8 (ll. 61–78 omitted).
Dated: '1819' (MS A3, p. 117).

A FAMILLIAR EPISTLE TO A FRIEND

'Friendship peculiar boon of heaven
'The noblest minds delight & pride
'To men & angels only given
'To all the lower world deny'd
'Thy gentle flows of guiltless joys
'On fools & villians ne'er descend
'In vain for thee the tyrant sighs
'& hugs a flatterer for a friend'.

Sam. Johnson

This morning just as I awoken
A black cloud hung the south—unbroken
Thinks I just now we have it soaking
    —I rightly guest
Feth glad wer' I to see the token   5
    I wanted rest

& fex a pepsing day theres been on't
But caution'd right wi' what I'd seen on't

A FAMILLIAR EPISTLE TO A FRIEND   *Title:* A Familliar Epistle / To a Friend
MS A3, Epistle to a Friend *Norris,* Familiar Epistle, to a Friend *RL*   *(a)* Friendship,
Norris   *(f)* neer *Norris   Pencil emendations in Norris are Taylor's*   3 we'l
pencilled below we *Norris*] we'll *RL*   soken *Norris*   4 ∧I *Norris*   5 was
pencilled below wer' *Norris*] were *RL*   7 pepsing] pepp'ring *RL*   ont *Norris   In*
pencil in margin in Norris, not Clare's: Theres like to be a pouring day on't   8 But]
&: cautiond: ont *Norris   In pencil in margin in Norris, not Clare's:* I'm caution'd by
what now I see on't

Keeping at home has kept me clean on't
    Ye know my creed   10
Fool hardy work—I neer wer' keen on't
    But lets proceed

I write to keep from mischief meerly
Fire side & comforts 'joying cheerly
& brother·chip I love ye dearly   15
    Poor as ye be
Wi' honest heart & soul sincerely
    There all to me

This scrawl—mark thou the applicaton
(Tho hardly worth thy observation)   20
Meaneth a humble Invitation
    On some days end
O' all 'rag'd muffins' i' the nation
    Thou art the friend—

Ive long been agravated shocking   25
To see our gentry folks so cocking
But sorrows often catch'd by mocking
    The truth I've seen
Their pride may want a shoe & stocking
    For like has been   30

---

9 has] is: ont *Norris   In pencil in margin in Norris, not Clare's*: To 'vide at home and
sever me from 't ('vide *over* [keep]*)   10 *Through* But lets proceed *Norris
In pencil in margin in Norris, not Clare's*: Ye'll now pr   11 work_∧ *to* work! _∧ *(p.e.)*:
out *to* out, *(p.e.) Norris*   neer wer' *over* [Im not so] *MS A3*] Im not so *Norris*   was *RL*
12 But *through* So *MS A3*] So *through* But *Norris*, So *MS D1 correction*, So *altered to* But
Harvard proof copy, But *RL   In pencil in margin in Norris, not Clare's*: and sae keep out on't
13 write] wish: meerly *to* meerly, *(p.e.) Norris*   14 My *before* Fireside *(p.e.)*:
cheerly *to* cheerly, *(p.e.) Norris*   & *omitted Norris RL*   15 brother-chip *Norris*
16 be *to* be; *(p.e.) Norris*   17 The *pencilled below* Wi' *Norris*   Wi'...soul *through
the same words written again MS A3*   18 Thou'rt *pencilled below* There *Norris*]
They're *RL*   19 scrawl *through* scrat *Norris*   21 an *RL*   hearty *pencilled
over* humble: Invitation [on some days] *Norris*   22 end *to* end. *(p.e.) Norris*
23 poets *pencilled below* muffins *Norris*   24 Thou art *to* I am *(p.e.) Norris*
27 sorrows often *to* sorrow's often's *(p.e.) Norris*   28 ive *Norris*   29 There
MS A3   Shoe *Norris*   &] or *RL*   30 For the like *through* Such things *and* th'
pencilled below the *Norris*

Prides power's not worth a roasted Onion
I'ds leave be prison mouse wi' Bunyan
As I'd be king o' our dominion
    Or any other
When shoffl'd through—its my opinion   35
    One's good as tother

Nor wou'd I gi' from off my cuff
A single pin for no such stuff
Riches besh—t a pinch o' Snuff
    Woud dearly buy ye   40
Whos got ye keeps ye—thats enough
    I dont envy ye

If fates so kind to lets be doing
Thats, just keep cart o' wheels fo' going
Oer my half pint I can be crowing   45
    As wells another
But when theres this & that stan's owing
    O curse the bother

For had I money like a many
I'd balance even to a penny—   50
Want, thy confinement make[s] me scrany
    That spirits mine
I'd sooner gi' then take from any
    But worth cant shine

31 Prides power's] For pride's *Norris*, Power thourt *BL*, Wealths *MS 1*   onion *Norris*
MS 1   32 Ids: wi *MS 1*   lief *RL*   bunyan *BL MS 1*   33 Ide: o *MS 1*
dominion [or any other] *Norris*   35 shoffl'd through—] both are past *BL*
MS 1   s *through* b *in* shoffl'd: thro'∧ *Norris*   its *through* is *MS A3*   36 Ones
BL MS 1   'to'ther *Norris*   37 Nor wou'd I] I woudnt *MS 1*   woud *BL*   gie
Norris BL] gie *inserted MS 1*   38 A] One: fo' *Norris BL*   no] all *RL*   sich
BL   A pin for no such silly stuff *MS 1*   39 bes—t– *BL*] be hangd *through*
besh–t *(Taylor's alteration) Norris*, bes—t∧ *MS 1*, rubbish! *RL*   o *BL MS 1*   snuff
Norris BL MS 1   40 Wou'd *Norris*] woud *MS 1*   bye *Norris MS 1*] by *BL*   em
MS 1   41 Who's *Norris*] Whose *BL*   em: em∧ *MS 1*   enough *to* enough,
(p.e.) Norris   42 ye *to* ye. *(p.e.) Norris*] em *MS 1*   43 kind— *MS 1*   to . . .
doing] just keeps me going *BL*, lets me be doing *MS 1*   44 Thats∧: 'keep: weels'
Norris   Thats, just keep] That is keeps *BL*   Thats just keepe cart o weels & going
MS 1   Explain this *written in margin in pencil Norris*   o'] on: fo' a *RL*   46 as
MS 1   well's another— *Norris*   47 when] where *BL*   stand *BL*] stans
MS 1   owing *to* owing! *(p.e.) Norris*   48 o' *MS 1*   bother *to* bother! *(p.e.)*
Norris   50 I woudnt owe one single penny *Norris*   51 Want, *underlined*
MS A3] Want∧ *underlined Norris*   makes: obscure *pencilled over* scrany *Norris*
52 That *through* ? Thou *Norris*   53 Id: gie *Norris*

O independence oft I bait thee 55
How blest I'd been to call ye Matey
—Ye fawning flattering slaves I hate ye
    —Mad harum-scarum
If rags & tatters underrate me
    Free still I'll wear 'em 60

What sc——d—ls honours light infesteth
Which her few votaries detesteth
Which honesty as vain arresteth
    She cant be heard
In reasons proof she vain protesteth 65
    Worth's no reward

By why these politicks & pluther
The muse ill knows such usless bluther
She turns old friend to greet a brother
    & brags to name it 70
Just as one beggar owns another
    Like wants they claim it

& soon as ere a change o' weather
Frees us from labours cramping tether
(Sorrow thrown by heart lights a feather) 75
    Mind what I tell ye
A jovial crush we'll have to gether
    —Ye plainly spell me

55 ye *BL RL*   56 Id *BL*   be *RL*   matey—*underlined Norris*] matey *BL*
57 ∧Ye *Norris*   slaves] crowd: ye—*BL*   58 *Underlined MS A3 Norris*   ∧Mad
harum ∧skarum *BL*   59 under rate *Norris BL*   60 Free *underlined MS A3*]
Free—*underlined Norris*   Ill *Norris*   em *Norris BL*   61 *scoundrels   In pencil at
end of line in Norris*: obscure   Sh— is what the wise detesteth *(what through* wheth:
the *inserted*: detested *altered to* detesteth*) BL*   62 [vain] detesteth *MS A3*] Vain
detesteth *Norris*   What pilates swindling rogues infesteth *BL*   63 [requesteth]
arresteth *MS A3*] requesteth *Norris*   Vainly poor honesty requesteth *BL*   64 e *in*
heard *inserted Norris*] hard [her humble clame] *BL*   66 Worths *Norris BL*
67 politcks *Norris*   71 another *through indeciperable Norris*   72 they] my
Norris   73 ere *through indecipherable Norris*   74 cramping *over* [cursed] *MS
A3*] cursed *Norris*   teather *Norris*   75 light's *Norris*   77 A] As
MS A3   day *pencilled over* crush: have *to* ha *(p.e.)*: together *Norris*

P–x take all Sorrows now I'll bilk em
Whats past may go so—time that shall come   80
Or's bad or worse or how it will come
   I'll neer despair
Poor as I am friends shall be welcome
   As rich on's are

So from my heart old friend I'll greet ye   85
No out side brags shall never cheat ye
Wi' what I have wi' such I treat ye
   Ye may believe me
I'll shake ye're Rags when ere I meet ye
   If ye decieve me   90

So mind ye friend 'whats what' I send it
My letters plain & plain I'll end it
Bads bad enough but worse wornt mend it
   So I be happy
& while I've sixpence left I'll spend it   95
   In cheering nappy

A hearty health shall crown my story
Dear native England I adore thee
—Britons—may ye wi friends before ye
   Neer want a quart   100
To drink your king & countrys glory
   Wi upright heart

79 P–x take] But hang *RL*   Deuce take whats past, the time that shall come *(*past *to* past, *p.e.) Norris*   80 may] shall *RL*   Or's bad or worse or how it will come *Norris* 81 Or's] Or *RL*, As *RL 2nd edn.*   Plauge take all sorrows, now I'll bilk em, *(*sorrows *to* sorrows, *p.e.*: em *to* em, *p.e.) Norris*   82 Nor more despair; *(*despair *to* despair; *p.e.) Norris*   83 am *to* am, *(p.e.)* : friends shall be] my friends are *Norris*   84 on's] men's *RL*   are *to* are. *(p.e.) Norris*   85 old … greet *over* [I now entreat] *MS A3*   Wi hearty welcome I intreat ye; *(*ye *to* ye; *p.e.) Norris*   86 outside: ye *to* ye; *p.e.) Norris*   ever *pencilled over* never *Norris*] ever *RL*   87 I'll *RL* 88 beleive: me *to* me; *(p.e.) Norris*   89 yo'r *Norris*] your *RL*   rags *Norris* 90 yed: me *to* me. *(p.e.) Norris*   91 it *to* it; *(p.e.) Norris*   92 it *to* it; *(p.e.) Norris* 93 enough *to* enough, *(p.e.)* : worse] wores: it *to* it *(p.e.) Norris*   won't *RL*   94 Ill *Norris*] I'll *RL*   happy *to* happy. *(p.e.) Norris*   95 Ive: left *to* left, *(p.e.) Norris* 96 Nappy *Norris*   97 story *to* story; *(p.e.) Norris*   98 — Dear *Norris*   ye— *Norris*] ye *RL*   99 ∧Britons,—: wi friends] neer want *Norris*   100 Neer … quart] A brimming Quart, *(*Quart *to* Quart, *p.e.) Norris*   101 Countrys Glory, *(*Glory *to* Glory, *p.e.) Norris*   102 heart. *Norris*

Postscript

Ive oft meant tramping oer to see ye
But d–d old fortune g–d forgi' me
She's so cross grain'd & forked wi' me   105
    Be ere so willing
Spite o' my jingling powers—'ti'n't i' me
    To scheme a shilling

& poverty her cursed rigour
Spite o' Industry's utmost vigour   110
Dizens me out i' such a figure
    I'm sham'd being seen
'Sides my old shoon—poor muse ye twig her
    Waits roads being clean

Then here wind bound till fates confer'd on't   115
I wait ye friend—& take my word on't
I'll (spite o' fate) scheme such a hurd on't
    As we wi'n't lack
So no excuses shall be heard on't
    —Yours random Jack.   120

102/3 Postscript *through* Poscript *MS A3*   103 I've: traming: you *Norris*
104 pray *pencilled over* g–d *Norris*   106 'ere: willing, *Norris*   107 Spite
o'] With all *RL*   jingling powers∧ *to* jingling-powers,∧ *(p.e.)*: ti'n't *Norris*
108 Shilling *Norris*   109 her] with *RL*   110 Industrys: vigour *to* vigour,
(p.e.) Norris   111 s *through* e *in* Dizens: in *Norris*   112 seen *to* seen; *(p.e.)*
Norris   113 muse *to* (muse *(p.e.)*: her *to* her) *(p.e.) Norris*   115 Then
through So *MS A3*   decree'd *pencilled over* confer'd *Norris*   117 sich *altered*
to such *MS A3*   hoard *RL*   118 won't *RL*   119 Excuses *Norris*
120 Yours *to* By *(p.e.)* / Luckless *pencilled before* 'Random Jack' *Norris*

AUTOGRAPH: Nor. MS 1, pp. 101–3.
TRANSCRIPT: Pet. MS C1, pp. 4a–5a.
Dated: 1808–19 (MS 1).

TO JANE —— OF —— IN THE MANNER O' BURNS

O with thy looks & feeling heart
   I am so highly tain
That well or ill I must impart
   My love to bonny Jane
Tho words pretend to tell my love   5
   But weakly they explain
What if I had a chance to prove
   I'd do for thee my Jane

In all that Language can declare
   In every joy and pain   10
To please to comfort or to share
   I'd do it for my Jane
The dangers were more dangers shine
   My help should near detain
Well pleas'd to risk my life for thine   15
   I'd fly to save my Jane

If winters cold & driving snows
   Thy tender breast shou'd pain
I'd naked go wi'out my cloa'hs
   To shelter the[e] my Jane   20
And if Misfortunes storms o' care
   More apt should gie thee pain
Tho' griev'd I'd even joy to share
   The sorrows o' my Jane

O if I had a world in worth   25
   I shou'd be rich in vain
Without the richest gem on Earth
   My sweet unrival'd Jane

TO JANE —— OF —— IN THE MANNER O' BURNS   *Title:* To Jane — of — in the manner o' Burns *MS 1*

The barest Desart I could rove
    Which Grasses e'en disdain   30
More then a Paradise wou'd prove
    With thee my Charming Jane

O wer' I highest o' renown
    As King o' Kings to reign
The topmost honour o' my crown   35
    Should be unrival'd Jane
An' if i' prides rebelling eye
    My choise should prove a stain
I'd instant lay my King-ship by
    To equal lowley Jane   40

And o more dear then Crowns to me
    Cou'd I that honour gain
What I so daily wish to be
    A Part'ner o' my Jane
To doat for ever on her charms   45
    And night and day detain
The sweetest Angel in my arms
    My bonny charming Jane

And O I'd live and love so true
    And would so true remain   50
That death it self should not subdue
    My Love for Charming Jane
And tho ere Death could us remove
    Her sighs might cause a pain
Yet mine the sweetest Death would prove   55
    To think I dy'd wi' Jane

Then O my Charmer now be kind
    To thy adoreing swain
Nor let me to my sorrow find
    Ill nature in my Jane   60
On you and you alone depends
    My Endless Joy or pain
Tis truth the lovers heart befriends
    O hear me Gentle Jane

53 the *altered to* tho *MS 1*   60 Ill *through* In *MS 1*   64 G *through* g *in* Gentle
MS 1

AUTOGRAPHS: Nor. MS 1, p. 103: Pet. MS A3, p. 57: Pet. MS A3, p. 108
(ll. 7, 13–14 omitted, deleted).
TRANSCRIPTS: Pet. MS B1, p. 111: Nor. MS 5, p. 116.
Proposals For Publishing (P): the *Stamford Mercury*, 12 November 1819 (*SM*):
RL, p. 187: the *London Magazine*, January 1820, p. 10 (*LM*): *Drakard's
Stamford News*, 7 January 1819 (reprinted from *LM*): *The Englishmans Fire-side*,
February 1820, p. 32 (*EF*).
Dated: 1807–15 (Explanatory Notes).

THE SETTING SUN

This scene how beautious to the musing mind
That now swift slides from my enchanted view
The sun sweet setting yon far hills behind
In other worlds his visits to renew
What spangling glories all around him shine   5
What nameless colours cloudless & serene
Rich heavenly colours brightest in decline
Atend his exit from this lovley scene
So sets the Christians sun in glories clear
So shines his soul at his departure here   10
No clouding doubts nor misty fears arise
To dim hopes golden rays of being forgiven
His sun sweet setting in the clearest skies
In safe assurance wings the soul to heaven

THE SETTING SUN   *Title:* Sun-set *MS 1*, The Setting Sun / A Sonnet *MS A3 P*,
The Setting Sun *MS A3, p. 108 RL LM EF*, Lines on the Setting Sun *SM*   1 the]
a *RL*   2 slides] glides *EF*   enchanting *MS A3 P SM RL (1st edn. only)*
3 Sun *MS A3 MS A3, p. 108* hill *LM EF*   4 Visits *over* [Glories] *MS A3*] visit
SM LM EF   5 spangled *RL*   [beauties] Glories *MS A3, p. 108*   6 namless
MS A3, p. 108   cloudles *MS A3*   7 *(A* heavnly prospect brightest in decline*)*
MS A3 P SM RL LM EF   8 Attend *MS A3*] Attends *LM EF*   lovly scene—
MS A3   9 —So *MS A3 MS A3, p. 108*   christians *MS A3*   Glories *MS A3,*
p. 108   10 Soul: its Departure *MS A3, p. 108*   11 cloudy *SM LM EF*
12 Rays *MS A3, p. 108*   13 His *in all versions, but Clare has a note on this line MS A3,*
p. 132: It should be—Faiths sun &c skyes *MS A3 MS A3, p. 108*   14 safe] Faith's
RL 2nd edn., meek *LM EF*   heaven— *MS A3*

AUTOGRAPH: Nor. MS 1, pp. 104–7.
TRANSCRIPT: Pet. MS Cī, pp. 6–7a.
Dated: 1808–19 (MS 1).

THE DISSAPOINTMENT

Young peggy the milking maid lusty and neat
   Met her old sweetheart jo at the fair
But being so modest and very discreet
   She hated to talk with him there

Yet botherd to dead with his sorrowful whine   5
   Of 'pray'r a do peggy go wi'd—us'
She promis'd that if the next sunday was fine
   She'd walk with him down in the meadows

Tho in one dissapointed he bless'd his good luck
   And in a pleas'd caper cut off   10
And often would wisper 'the good natur'd duck'
   Then shrug up his shoulders and laugh

Till just reccolecting the maid was ill serv'd
   His carelesness nettled him sore
To be so forgetful of what she deserv'd   15
   He dash'd his thick head oer and oer

For surely he thought if the wench had been bad
   As the proud stuck up mortals are all
He cou'd'n't have serv'd her more worse then he had
   To offer her nothing at all   20

So he brush'd away back and desird her to take
   (While his former ill manners he chid)
A fareing to keep while she liv'd for his sake
   As sweethearts in generaley did

THE DISSAPOINTMENT   *Title:* The Dissapointment *MS 1*   4 walk
altered to talk *MS 1*   5 Yet *through* So *MS 1*   6 us∧ *MS 1*   8 a *in*
meadows *inserted MS 1*   14 n *through* g *in* nettled *MS 1*   19 m *through* w *in*
more *MS 1*

O dear about that jo soon cried the good creature   25
    You need not be troubl'd however
And with a sweet smile that bespoke her good nature
    Refus'd all he offer'd to give her

Yet assur'd him for certain she'd still meet him there
    Then made her self ready to start   30
While jo halloo'd carles of folks in the fair
    This farewell salute from his heart

'Well god b[l]ess you goodby if you wornt then I'll go
    But I love you as s' true as I'm born
And peg but not quite so familiar as jo   35
    Nodding smileingly wishd him good morn

Pleas'd as punsh by himself all the rest of the day
    He struted about very proud
And when ever peg happen'd to fall in his way
    He slipt unobserv'd in the crowd   40

For as things where agreed on where they was to go
    If he met her he'd nothing to say
So he thought (as he cou'd'n't abide to do so)
    'T'was the best to keep out of her way

And when safe at home from the squabble and show   45
    Fix'd at his old job the plow tail
Tho he fancied the days pass'd away very slow
    He sung like the sweet Nightingale

At length sunday morn so much wishd for arose
    While before hand on saturday night   50
Jo brightn'd his hilo's and brush'd up his cloaths
    To make his apperance look tight

But alas to his sorrow the morning rose dull
    And thro his old window half slatted
The dykes in the streets all appeared chock full   55
    While big drops 'gainst the glass light still patted

26 neednot *MS 1*   34 i'm *MS 1*   35 jo *through* that *MS 1*
40 r *through* v *in* unobserv'd: r *in* crowd *inserted MS 1*
MS 1

To be so much balk'd how tormented was he
    Yet he swore if the day turn'd out so .
As the roads could get stiffen'd he'd still go & see
    To be sure if she met him or no   60

All the morning impatient on peggy and love
    He often look'd out at the door
However at last the noon happen'd to prove
    Just as he had wish'd heretofore

O promising prospects no joys could surpass   65
    The feelings which they did beget
In the garden he bustl'd to feel if the grass
    Was any way free'd from the wet

In this he sucseded and never gave out
    That the short sooner dry'd than the long   70
But to get himself ready he scamper'd about
    As to stay past the time would be wrong

In his best now adorned he slove to the glass
    And glanc'd at himself oer and oer
While to set off his face for engageing the lass   75
    He parted his hair down before

Then he cock'd up his hat on his nob newly shorn
    As neat and as trim as the day
And took up his hand stick a neatly trim'd thorn
    And bang'd thro the village away   80

And with the best pace he could put on for fear
    His old Comrades should see him alone
For he knew very well if they did they'd enquire
    About matters not meant to be known

And soon by his swiftness the meadow the spot   85
    Where they was to meet came in sight
And tho doubting wether she'd be there or not
    The place fill'd his heart with delight

60 besure *MS 1*   65 surpass *through* beget *MS 1*   70 *First* the *inserted MS 1*

He made many stops ere he came to the spot
   And oft thought he saw something stir   90
Looking earnestly round and the nearer he got
   Hope wisper'd 'more speed yonders her'

But joys soon abated.—hopes wispers was o'er
   When he came up so nigh to the place
As fancys false visions could cheat him no more   95
   When every thing wore its own dress

For alas to his sorrow sad sorrow when there
   No Peg could be found high nor low
An old touch-wood tree of both bark and leaves bare
   Was the object that cheated him so   100

AUTOGRAPH: Nor. MS 1, pp. 107–8.
Dated: 1808–19 (MS 1).

      A Uglier mortal ne'er has been
         Than N—. upon the plain
      A Sweeter angel ne'er was seen
         Than B[etse]y down the Lane

      Yet N—. in spite of all her faults   5
         So ugly & uncommon
      Fair B[etse]ys every charm asaults
         And deems her worse than woman

      'Was I' the brawny mortal cries
         But half as plain as Bess   10
      My face for ever Id despise
         And neer pretend to dress'

91 hearnestly *MS 1*   93 wispers war o'er *through* wisperd no more *MS 1*
95 cheat *inserted MS 1*   100 *Followed in MS 1 by a double row of asterisks*

  A UGLIER MORTAL NE'ER HAS BEEN   *Title: wanting*   1 U *through* hu *in*
Uglier   3 e *through* n *in* angel   4 B——y   7 B——ys

AUTOGRAPH: Nor. MS 1, p. 108.
Dated: 1808–19 (MS 1).

Friend take my advise would you do yourself good
& get your house Custom & peace
Take down from that door post the billet of Wood
& hang up your Wife in its place

AUTOGRAPHS: Nor. MS 1, p. 108: Pet. MS A4, p. 16.
TRANSCRIPT: Pet. MS B1, p. 156.
Dated: 1808–19 (MS 1).

A SIMILE

A Mushroom its Goodness but Shortly Endures
Decaying as soon as its Peeping
—Woman much like them—for'ts known very Well
That they Seldom Get better by Keeping

FRIEND TAKE MY ADVISE WOULD YOU DO YOURSELF GOOD   *Title:
wanting*

A SIMILE   *Title:* A Simile *MS 1 MS A4*   1 Mushroom—: goodness: shortly
endures *MS A4*   2 peeping *MS A4*   3 —Women's: 'em—: for'ts] 't'is: well
MS A4   4 seldom get: keeping *MS A4*

AUTOGRAPHS: Pet. MS A3, pp. 25–9: Nor. MS 1, p. 108 (ll. 163–6,
175–8, pencil), p. 154 (ll. 167–74, 179–86, pencil), p. 225 (ll. 1–8, 47–8,
145–54, 157–62, pencil, deleted except ll. 1–8), p. 240 (ll. 85–94, 125–40,
deleted), p. 241 (ll. 95–7, 105–8, 111–14, deleted), p. 251 (ll. 117–22,
deleted), p. 237 (variants of ll. 1–4, 159–62, deleted).
TRANSCRIPTS: Pet. MS B1, pp. 93, 97–8, 166–5 (ll. 11–16, 33–42,
153–8, 179–86 deleted): Nor. MS 5, pp. 17–25 (ll. 23–46 omitted, 11–16,
153–8, 179–86 deleted).
Printed in *RL*, pp. 3–11 (ll. 11–16, 33–42, 153–8, 179–86, and in 4th edn.
ll. 125–34 omitted): *The Englishman's Fire-side*, June 1820, pp. 191–3
(ll. 1–10, 17–32, 43–94), July 1820, pp. 231–3 (ll. 95–152, 159–78).
Dated: 1809–13 (MS A3, p. 25 '9 or 10 years ago', *RL* Introduction, p. xxii
'before he was seventeen').

HELPSTONE

Hail humble Helpstone where thy valies spread
& thy mean Village lifts its lowly head
Unknown to grandeur & unknown to fame
No minstrel boasting to advance thy name
Unletterd spot unheard in poets song   5
Where bustling labour drives the hours along
Where dawning genius never met the day
Where usless ign'rance slumbers life away
Unknown nor heeded where low genius trys
Above the vulgar & the vain to rise   10
Whose low opinions rising thoughts subdues
Whose railing envy damps each humble view
Oh where can friendships cheering smiles abode
To guide young wanderers on a doubtful road

HELPSTONE   *Title:* Helpstone *MS A3 RL EF, wanting MS 1   Pencil emendations
in MS A3 are Taylor's*   1 humble] lowly: spred *MS 1, p. 237*   h *through* e *in*
where *MS 1*] were *MS 1, p. 237*   helpstone *MS 1*]helpston *MS 1, p. 237*   Vallies
MS 1   2 &] Where *MS 1, p. 237*   Village *to* village *(p.e.) MS A3*] vilage *MS 1,
p. 237*   lowly *over* [humble] *MS A3*] humble *MS 1 MS 1, p. 237*   3 Grandeur
MS 1   4 thy] the *MS 1*   Thourt dear to me I love thy very name *MS 1, p. 237*
5 Unletter'd *MS 1*   6 hours *over* [days] *MS A3*   7 genius...day] Genius
never sprung to light *MS 1*   8 usless *to* useless *(p.e.) MS A3*   Where ignorance
slumbers one continued night *MS 1*   11 vow *altered to* low: sub-dues *to* sub-due
(p.e.) MS A3

The trembling hand to lead, the steps to guide   15
& each vain wish (as reason proves) to chide—
Mysterious fate who can on thee depend
Thou opes the hour but hides its doubtful end
In fancys view the joys have long appear'd
Where the glad heart by laughing plentys cheer'd   20
& fancys eyes as oft as vainly fill
At first but doubtful & as doubtful still

So little birds in winters frost & snow
Doom'd (like to me) wants keener frost to know
Searching for food & 'better life' in vain   25
(Each hopeful track the yielding snows retain)
First on the ground each fairy dream pursues
Tho sought in vain—yet bent on higher views
Still chirps & hopes & wipes each glossy bill
Nor undiscourag'd nor dishartn'd still   30
Hops on the snow cloth'd bough & chirps again
Heedless of naked shade & f[r]ozen plain
With fruitles hopes each little bosom warms
Springs budding promise—summers plentious charms
A universal hope the whole prevades   35
& chirping plaudits fill the chilling shades

---

17 [Ah] Mysterious *MS A3*   18 Thou opes the hour] *successively (a)* [The present
hopes] *(b)* Thou hopes [the day] *(c)* Thou hopes the hour *MS A3*   19 views
EF   the *through* thy: joys have long *below* [happy scenes] *MS A3*   20 plentys *to*
plenty's *(p.e.) MS A3*   21–2 [& still I hope those happy days to see / Which still
endears & cheers my poverty] *MS A3, p. 32, instruction to delete*
22/3

            [Ah was it mine those happy days to see
            So hopes (tho doubtful) cheers my poverty
            & still I hope those happy days to see
            Which still endears & cheers my poverty] *MS A3*

23 So *through* & *MS A3*   24 *First to omitted EF*   27 pursues *to* pursue *(p.e.)*
MS A3] pursue *RL EF*   28 yet *over* [still] *MS A3*   views *to* view *(p.e.) MS A3*]
view *RL EF*   29 chirps *to* chirp *(p.e.) MS A3*] chirp *RL EF*   hopes *to* hope *(p.e.)*
MS A3] hope *RL EF*   wipes *to* wipe *(p.e.) over* [smooths] *MS A3*] wipe *RL EF*
30 dishartn'd *to* disheartn'd *(p.e.) MS A3*   And undiscourag'd, undisheartn'd still
RL EF   31 Hops *to* Hop *(p.e.) MS A3*] Hop *RL EF*   chirps *to* chirp *(p.e.) MS A3*]
chirp *RL EF*   33–42 *Note in MS B1:* I am sorry to omit these Lines, but they are
evidently unfit for the public Eye—   35 A *through* One *MS A3*

Till warm'd at once the vain deluded flies
& twitatwit their visions as they rise
Visions like mine that vanish as they flye
In each keen blast that fills the higher skye   40
Who find like me along their weary way
Each prospect lessen & each hope decay
& like to me these victims of the blast
(Each foolish fruitless wish resign'd at last)
Are glad to seek the place from whence they went   45
& put up with distress & be content—

Hail scenes obscure so near & dear to me
The church the brook the cottage & the tree
Still shall obscurity reherse the song
& hum your beauties as I stroll along   50
Dear native spot which length of time endears
The sweet retreat of twenty lingering years
& oh those years of infancy the scene
Those dear delights where once they all have been
Those golden days long vanish'd from the plain   55
Those sports those pastimes now belovd in vain
When happy youth in pleasures circle ran
Nor thought what pains awaited future man
No other thought employing or employ'd
But how to add to happiness enjoy'd   60
Each morning wak'd with hopes before unknown
& eve possesing made each wish their own
The day gone bye left no pursuit undone
Nor one vain wish save that they went too soon
Each sport each pastime ready at their call   65
As soon as wanted they posses'd em all
These joys all known in happy infancy
& all I ever knew where spent on thee

---

38 twitatwit *underlined MS A3*   *Note in MS A3, p. 32:* The word 'twitatwit' ([if a word]
if a word it may be calld) you will undoubtedly smile at but I wish you to print it as it is for
it is the Language of Nature & that can never be disgusting   43 &] Till *RL EF*
[damned] like: to *inserted MS A3*   44 resign *EF*   45 from[e] *MS A3*
49 reherse *to* rehearse *(p.e.) MS A3*   57 youths *RL*   64 it *RL EF*
68 on] in *RL EF*

& who but loves to view where these where past
& who that views but loves em to the last   70
Feels his heart warm to view his native place
A fondness still those past delights to trace
The vanish'd green to mourn the spot to see
Where flourish'd many a bush & many a tree
Where once the brook (for now the brook is gone)   75
Oer pebbles dimpling sweet went wimpering on
Oft on whose oaken plank I've wondering stood
(That led a pathway o'er its gentle flood)
To see the beetles their wild mazes run
With getty jackets glittering in the sun   80
So apt & ready at their reels they seem
So true the dance is figur'd on the stream
Such justness such correctness they impart
They seem as ready as if taught by art
In those past days (for then I lov'd the shade)   85
How oft I've sighd at alterations made
To see the woodmans cruel axe employ'd
A tree beheaded or a bush destroy'd
Nay e'en a post (old standards) or a stone
Moss'd o'er by age & branded as her own   90
Would in my mind a strong attachment gain
A fond desire that there they might remain
& ah old favourites fond taste approves
Griev'd me at heart to witness their remove[s]

Thou far fled pasture long evanish'd scene   95
Where nature's freedom spread the flowry green

69 where *to* were *(p.e.) MS A3*   70 em *to* them *(p.e.) MS A3*   72 past
through dre *MS A3*   75 (for *to* for *(p.e.)*: gone) *to* gone *(p.e.) MS A3*
76 dimpling sweet; went whimpering on *(wimpering to* whimpering, *p.e.) below*
[wimpering sweet when dimp] *MS A3*   80 getty *to* jetty *(p.e.) MS A3*   84 by]
be *MS A3*   85 those past] those lovd *pencilled over* [infant]: lovd *MS 1*   (for *to*
for *(p.e.)*: shade) *to* shade *(p.e.) MS A3 MS 1*   86 Ive often *to* How oft Ive
(p.e.): as *to* at *(p.e.) MS 1*   87 wood mans *MS A3*   axe' *MS A3*] ax
MS 1   employd *MS 1*   88 Tree: destroyd *MS 1*   89 e'[v]en: *first* a
inserted: Post *MS 1*   (old *to* old *(p.e.) MS A3*   standards) *to* standards *(p.e.) MS A3*]
standard *RL EF*   90 Mosd oer *MS 1*   brandend *to* branded *(p.e.) MS A3*
91 my] y *MS 1*   attactchment *MS A3*   92 ther *MS 1*   93 ah *to* all *(p.e.) MS*
A3] all *EF*   favoutes *MS 1*   94 Grievd: witnes: remove *MS 1*   95 pastur:
evanishd *MS 1*   96 natures *MS 1*   flowry *over* [daysied] *MS A3*

Where golden kingcups open'd in to view
Where silver dazies charm'd the 'raptur'd view
& tottering hid amidst those brighter gems
Where silver grasses bent their tiny stems　　　　100
Where the pale lilac mean & lowly grew
Courting in vain each gazer[s] heedless view
While Cows laps sweetest flowers upon the plain
Seeminly bow'd to shun the hand in vain
Where lowing oxen roamd to feed at large　　　　105
& bleeting there the shepherds woolly charge
Whose constant calls thy echoing vallies cheer'd
Thy scenes adornd & rural life endeard
No calls of hunger pitys feelings wound
Twas wanton plenty rais'd the joyful sound　　　　110
Thy grass in plenty gave the wish'd supply
Ere sultry sun's had wak'd the troubling flye
Then blest retiring by thy bounty fed
They sought thy shades & found an easy bed

But now alas those scenes exist no more　　　　115
The pride of Life with thee (like mine) is oer
Thy pleasing spots to which fond memory clings
Sweet cooling shades & soft refreshing springs
& tho fates pleas'd to lay their beauties bye
In a dark corner of obscurity　　　　120

---

97 opend into *MS 1*　　　98 Where *through* & *MS A3*　　Where silver daisies in profusion grew *RL EF*　　99 tottering *through* trem *MS A3*　　100 Where *through* The: silver grasses *underlined MS A3*　　silver] silken *RL EF*　　102 gazer *to* gazer's *(p.e.) MS A3*　　103 Cows laps *to* cows laps *(p.e.) MS A3*　　104 Seeminly *to* Seeminly *(p.e.) MS A3*　　98–104 *Replaced in MS 1 by:* Where cowslips trembld & the daisy grew / & where low peeping neath the lowly thorn / The humble vi'let met the dewy morn　　105 lowing *over* [horned]: roamd *over* [went]: *to inserted MS 1* 106 bleeting *to* bleating *(p.e.)*: shepherds *to* shepherd's *(p.e.) MS A3*　　wooly *MS 1* 107 thy] the: valey cheerd *MS 1*　　　108 Adornd thy scenes: rural *below* [vilage] *MS 1*　　adornd [thy scenes adorn'd] *(p.e.) MS A3*　　109 pitys *to* Pity's *(p.e.) MS A3* 110 plenty *to* Plenty *(p.e.) MS A3*　　　111 gras in plentious: wisht suply *MS 1* 112 sun's *to* sun *(p.e.) MS A3*] suns *MS 1*　　flye *to* fly *(p.e.) MS A3*] fly *MS 1* troubld *MS 1*　　　116 Life *to* life *(p.e.) MS A3*　　　117 spots . . . clings *below* [prospects thy delightful glades] *MS A3*　　Thy plasing prospects thy delightful glades *MS 1*　　　118 shades] springs: springs] shade *MS 1*　　　119 & *omitted*: pleasd: beautys *MS 1*　　tho *to* though *(p.e.) MS A3*] Tho *MS 1*　　fates *to* fate's *(p.e.) MS A3*] fate is *MS 1*　　bye *to* by *(p.e.) MS A3*] by *MS 1*　　120 Obscurity *MS 1*

As fair & sweet they blo[o]m'd thy plains among
As blooms those Edens by the poets sung
Now all laid waste by desolations hand
Whose cursed weapons levels half the land
Oh who could see my dear green willows fall   125
What feeling heart but dropt a tear for all
Accursed wealth oer bounding human laws
Of every evil thou remains the cause
Victims of want those wretches such as me
Too truly lay their wretchedness to thee   130
Thou art the bar that keeps from being fed
& thine our loss of labour & of bread
Thou art the cause that levels every tree
& woods bow down to clear a way for thee

Sweet rest & peace ye dear departed Charms   135
Which once Industry cherish'd in her arms
When peace & plenty known but now to few
Where known to all & labour had his due
When mirth & toil companions thro' the day
Made labour light & pass'd the hours away   140
When nature made the fields so dear to me
Thin scattering many a bush & many a tree
Where the wood minstrels sweetly join'd among
& cheer'd my needy toilings with a song

---

121 &] as: bloom *MS 1*   122 bloom *RL EF*   edens *MS 1*   123 all's *RL
4th edn.*   124 weapons *to* weapon *(p.e.) MS A3*] weapon *RL EF*   125 Oh]
&: can *MS 1*   126 drops *MS 1*   127 oer *to* o'er *(p.e.) MS A3*   Accursed
wealth first in ambitions train *MS 1*   128 remains *to* remainst *(p.e.) MS A3*]
remain'st *RL EF*   the cause remain *MS 1*   129 The poor whom want & toil
untimly end *MS 1*   130 Where lifes but misery—death their only friend *MS 1*
131 When nature droops for want of being fed *MS 1*   132 loss;: labour, *MS A3*
To truly murmurs thine—their los of bread *MS 1*   133 Thou . . . cause] The
weapon thine *MS 1*   134 a] the *MS 1*   135 Sweet] O *MS 1*   Charms *to*
charms *(p.e.) (Charms through days) MS A3*] days *MS 1*   136 Industry *to* industry
(p.e.) MS A3   industry once *RL EF*   Which thro sad change a fresh remembrance
raise *MS 1*   137 peace *to* Peace *(p.e.) MS A3*] ease *RL*   plenty *to* Plenty *(p.e.)
MS A3*] plenty— *MS 1*   138 Where *to* Were *(p.e.) MS A3*] its *RL EF*
139 toul: thro *MS 1*   140 pasd *MS 1*   143 wood minstrel *RL*]
Wood-minstrel *EF*

Ye perishd spots adieu ye ruind scenes   145
Ye well known pastures oft frequented greens
Tho now no more—fond memory's pleasing pains
Within her breast your every scene retains
Scarce did a bush spread its romantic bower
To shield the lazy shepherd from the shower   150
Scarce did a tree befriend the chattering pye
By lifting up its head so proud & high
(Whose nest stuck on the topmost bough sublime
Mocking the efforts of each boy to climb
Oft as they've fill'd my vain desiring eye   155
As oft in vain my skill essay'd to try)
Nor bush nor tree within thy vallies grew
When a mischevious boy but what I knew
No not a secret spot did then remain
Through out each spreading wood & winding plain   160
But in those days my presence once posest
The snail horn searching or the mossy nest

Oh happy Eden of those golden years
Which memory cherishes & use endears
Thou dear beloved spot may it be thine   165
To add a comfort to my life[s] decline
When this vain world & I have nearly done
& times drain'd glass has little left to run

145 ruind *to* ruin'd *(p.e.) MS A3*   Yet spots well known ye oft frequented scenes *MS 1*
146 well known *to* well=known *(p.e.) MS A3*   Ye pleasing pastures & delightful
greens *MS 1*   147 Tho *to* Though *(p.e.) MS A3*   fond] yet: memorys *MS 1*
148 scenes *EF*   149 Scarce did] There's scarce *(scarce over* not]*) MS 1*   a *in*
spread *inserted MS A3*] spreads *over* [with] *MS 1*   150 To . . . lazy] That shields
the idle *MS 1*   151 Scarce did] Theres scarce: befriends *MS 1*   152 That
lifts its head so lofty & so high *MS 1*   153 ∧Whos *MS 1*   sublime *underlined*
MS A3   154 Mocking the] Mocks the vain *MS 1*   155 [These] Oft (O
through o) *MS A3*   157 within *through* that: valleys *MS 1*   158 boy— *MS 1*
159 No] Where: did then remain] unknown remains *MS 1, p. 237*   seeret *altered to*
secret *MS A3*] sceret *MS 1 MS 1, p. 237*   did] could *MS 1*   160 Throughout
thy spreading wood & winding plain *MS 1*] Throught thy spreadin woods & winding
plains *MS 1, p. 237*   161 days] rays: prescence *MS 1, p. 237*   posest *to* possest
(p.e.) MS A3] posses'd *MS 1*, confest *MS 1, p. 237*   162 snailhorn: mosy *MS 1*
MS 1, p. 237   163 O then thou eden of youths golden years *MS 1*
164 memory *to* mem'ry *(p.e.) MS A3*   166 life *to* life's *(p.e.) MS A3*] lifes *MS 1*
167 world *below* [strife] *MS A3*   So when vain life with me has nearly done *MS 1*
168 times *to* Time's *(p.e.) MS A3*

When all the hopes that charm'd me once are oer
To warm my soul in extacys no more   170
By dissapointments prov'd a foolish cheat
Each ending bitter & beginning sweet
When weary age the grave a r[e]scue seeks
& prints its image on my wrinkl'd cheeks
Those charms of youth that I again may see   175
May it be mine to meet my end in thee
& as reward for all my troubles past
Find one hope true to die at home at last

So when the Traveller uncertain roams
On lost roads leading every where but home   180
Each vain desire that leaves his heart in pain
Each fruitless hope to cherish it in vain
Each hated track so slowly left behind
Makes for the home which night denies to find
& every wish that leaves the aching breast   185
Flies to the spot where all its wishes rest

---

169 charmd *MS 1*   170 warm *below* [leave] *MS A3*] warm *through* leave
MS 1   extacys *to* extacy *(p.e.) MS A3*] extacy *MS 1 RL EF*   171 provd *MS 1*
172 That a leaves the bitter there takes the sweet *(t through w in there) MS 1*
173 weary *over* [painful]: Grave: rescue *MS 1*   174 on *through* in *MS A3*   And
marks its outlines on my furrowd cheeks *MS 1*   175 Those] To *MS 1*
177 & as *through* As a: my *over* [those] *MS 1*   178 Find *through* Prove *MS 1*
179 Traveller *to* traveller *(p.e.) MS A3*   When doubtful Travellers unscertain roam
MS 1   180 Lost *MS 1*   181 What vain desires leave their hearts in pain
MS 1   182 Each fruitless hope] & fruitless hopes *MS 1*   183 To shun
the hated track they leave behind *MS 1*   184 Makes for] To gain *MS 1*
185 &] The *MS 1*   [his] the *MS A3*] their *MS 1*   186 Flies *through*
Swells: were: their *MS 1*

AUTOGRAPHS: Pforzheimer Library, Misc. MS 197: Nor. MS 1, p. 161
(ll. 77–98, pencil), p. 109 (ll. 98–141, pencil), pp. 191–2 (ll. 142–66, 177–
87, 189, 191 twice, 193 twice), p. 234 (ll. 168–74, pencil): Nor. MS 7–41
(pencil, ll. 202–5 only).
TRANSCRIPT: Pet. MS B1, pp. 12–17 (marked in pencil 'Wisht to be
withdrawn').
Dated: 'Old' (Pfz).

THE QUACK & THE COBLER

In country town,—as story goes,
   There liv'd a snob,
  In shop of stud & mud
Who got by cobbling up old shoes
    & some new jobs   5
A descent livlihood

& such a one was he to laugh & joke
   & drink & smoke
That folks would fill his shop at night
Merely for sake O' sport to hear the fun   10
But this is natural to all the craft
   Those sons of wax & tallow
Plow tail mechanics took a great delight
& always joind him soon as jobs where done
For they was mighty pleas'd to see the fun   15
   & hear the jokes
& thought him wondorous wise to other folks
For true enough he was a funny fellow
   & roard out chorus'd laughs as loud as thunder
    This pleasd the cobler well—but thats no wonder   20
For all men love most dearly to be prais'd
& so did he & while the laugh was rais'd
   To keep it up—& oer & oer he told it
   Good boys & hold it!

THE QUACK & THE COBLER   *Title:* The Quack & the Cobler *Pfz, wanting*
MS 1   6 d *through* h *in* livlihood *Pfz*   11 is *inserted Pfz*   15 see *through*
hear *Pfz*   18 For *through* & *Pfz*   24 *Underlined Pfz*

Cobbling old shoes & cutting scraps o' leather 25
  & erst the while his hammer loudly knocking
He would repeat it twenty times together
  & wonderous to tell—& faith twas shocking
To see poor John-o-nokes in corner sitting
(Care taken o' the swill tub & the trough) 30
    So thunder struck at what the cobler sed
    & had he shut his eyes they'd thought him dead
      As hedging mitting
    But faith such wonderous talk
    No fierce grimmalkin stuck upon a fork 35
Ere stared half so much as did the oaf
His sparrow mouth the while out's outmost stretch
  Lud what a sight! The snob him self declard to't
That tailors yard band length ont woudnt reach
    Horse collar!—twas a mousehole when compard tot 40
    A quartern loaf
    Or bigger thing!
Chockd at the hole wi' but a carless swing
  In compas faith I tell it
  Woud slipped down as easy as a pellet 45
    Down Eldern gun
& Nokes neer known the least o' what was done
Such wonderous things his every story crownd
In every joke such fun there did abound
  Not only louts that nightly came 50
  But distant hamlets heard our coblers fame
Upon a certain day (so fate ordaind)
  The common fate of all
The utmost zenith of his glory gaind
  Our snob fell sick & forcd to leave his stall 55
    Took to his bed
& soon his custom gan to take alarm
  The new struck dread
His business stopping seemd a public harm
Their want o' shoes wer' bad as want o' bread 60

---

29 poor *through* young *Pfz*   41 quartain *altered to* quartern *Pfz*   52 (so fate ordaind) *through* So *and two indecipherable words Pfz*   55 d *through* t *in* forcd *Pfz*

Moreover coblers all the towns around
Near turn'd work out o' hand so staunch & sound
 Such leather cut & knock'd em up so stout
No slippery Jobs from him was never found
  They'd wear the year about   65
   & when In merry glee
& random shot discourse he oft exclaim
'No man in England can a Village name
'That boasts a work man to compare wi' me!'—
 Great was his fame—a useful man no doubt 70
  & greatly feared was the coming evil
  Deaths visit (as suppos'd) was deemd unsivil
   So neighbours thought
  To leave so many worthless fellows out
   Quite good for nought   75
  & put our useful cobler to the rout
A doctor no[w] was evidently thought
 A nessesary man—so friends agreed
& with all possible dispatch & speed
His doctorship was sought   80
But here the cobler harbourd different views
 He knew full well—that doctors did
Profess to coble life—he cobld shoes
 & tho by different methods well he knew
Docters & snobs one common aim pursues 85
 Say what they will or do what ere they do
 To him the secret was by no means hid
 Money made coblers work—& doctors too
  He thought em useless quite
 & never cou'd be made in all his life   90
 (Like Jealous cuckold by his wife)
  To think they acted right

72–6 *These appear for insertion at the end of the poem. Clare's note:* See the Asteric in the Tale I forgot 2 Lines & was forcd to cramb them in between the others afterwards Print them thus See the mark in 'Tale' 77 now *MS 1* thought [a nessesary man] *Pfz* 78 *Second* e *through* a *in* nessesary *Pfz*] nessary *MS 1* so *through* his *MS 1* 80 His] Instant his *MS 1* 81 difft Views *MS 1* 83 cobbld *MS 1* 84 diferent: methods] starts: well] full *MS 1* 85 Doctors: one] on: aim] end *MS 1* 88 makes: work‸ *MS 1* 89 usless *MS 1* 90 coud *MS 1* 91 jealous: his] a *MS 1*

But what he said or did was no avail
He coudnt help himself—so friends prevail
   A doctors sent for & a doctor comes   95
      They point the way
      He hams & hums
    & mounts the scaffold where the cobler lay
& thus accosts in authorative tone
(They will stick up for gentlemen—its known)   100
    'How have you been today
    'Indeed' & shook his head
'You[r] pulse gives fearfull signs—I needs must own'
    Snob stard him in the face & bluntly sed
    'Let me alone'—   105
'Poh poh man that wornt do' the doctor cries
Shaking his head & seeming wonderous wise
   One hand the phisick holding pills in tother
   & now his fees—the money filld his head
Lo! bent in hopefull posture oer his bed   110
Began proceed about the pills & draught
& tell the snob his patient as he thought
    The pills &c how he was to take 'em
   & 'first' says he & taking out a pill
'You may have this directly if you will   115
    'One in the morning—one again at night
   'Each time between—a spoonful of the mixture N° 1
      'Then N° 2
    '& then youll quickly do
    '& man dont spare Ive more when these are gone   120
     'So take as orderd & before you take em
     'Just take the bottles up & shake em'

97–8 *Transposed MS 1, p. 161*   98 & . . . where] Up stairs he goes to were *MS 1, p. 109*, Up stairs he wonderd where *MS 1, p. 161*   100 gentlmen∧ tis *MS 1*
101 Well man how have u been to day *MS 1*   101/2 [I want to feel your puls & can u rise] *MS 1*   102 Well man & shook his head *MS 1*   103 'Your puls: gives fearfull signs—] is very bad *MS 1*   own *through* say *Pfz*   105 ∧Let: alone∧∧ *MS 1*   106 ∧Poh: do∧ *MS 1*   cries' *Pfz*   107 Shaking] & shook: wondrous *MS 1*   108 the] his: holdin *MS 1*   109 *First* his *through* fees *Pfz*   fees∧: mony fild *MS 1*   110 Lo∧: hopeful *MS 1*   111 pills, *Pfz*
113 &c . . . 'em] the mixturs &c how he shoud tak em *MS 1*   114–65 *Quotation marks omitted MS 1*   115 have] take *MS 1*   116 morning∧ *MS 1*
117 between∧: mixtur: No 1 *underlined MS 1*   118 no *MS 1*   119 *Inserted MS 1*   120 these are] that is *MS 1*   121 em [e] *MS 1*   122 em *MS 1*

Take 'em yourself—thinks snob
 But nothing sed
 The powderd Quack—still bending oer his bed   125
 Rather surprisd ats patients being so still
 & wearied quite of holding draught & pill
To see if he was in a dose or sleep
 He gave a peep
  & then began again—'I think' says he   130
  'By paying no attention unto me
'It seems as if you woudnt take my stuff'
& feth thinks coblers you think right enough
  'Indeed I shant
  'You cant   135
'Perhaps you think—you never try
 'How ist you wornt?
'If youve got any reason speak it
 'Or do you wish to dye?'—
 'No Sir I dont   140
  '& thats the very reason I wornt take it
'So friend I wish you'd leave me if you please
'A little sleep would give a little ease
 '& at this moment do a deal of good'—
  —My p[h]isick wou'd'   145
'Your phisic my be d—nd says enragd snob
For being in hopes that hed done teazing there
 Spite of his doctor ship & powderd nob
The dissapointment made him mad to sware
'But if' continues he 'you want a job   150

123 em your self∧: snob—for ill have none *MS 1*   124 said *MS 1*
125 quack∧ *MS 1* 126 suprisd *MS 1* 127 draugh *MS 1*
130 think∧ *Pfz* 131 your paying: unto] uto *MS 1* 132 as *through* if: would
not: stuf∧ *MS 1* 133 thinks *through* says *Pfz*] says *MS 1* cobler *MS 1*
134 Indeed] For I indeed *MS 1* 137 wornt∧ *MS 1* 138 got any *over*
[a]: spake *MS 1* reason[s] *Pfz* 139 dye∧∧ *MS 1* 140 sir *MS 1*
142 friend] sir: youd *MS 1* 143 litle *twice MS 1* i *through* a *in* give *Pfz*
144 good∧ *MS 1* 145 —My Phisick woud— *MS 1* 146 Your Phisic:
damnd *MS 1* 147 hed one: teasing *MS 1* 149 disappointment: swear
MS 1 e *through* l *in* made *Pfz* 150 —But *MS 1*

'Your actions looks as if you did I think
'Next door to me's a devil-of-a-wife
'Youd use her well to dose her with a drink
'The hen peckd husband weary of his life
    'To see her finish'd daily begs & prays   155
'Your phisick is a thing thats wanted there
  'As somethings wanted that woud end her days
  'Twou'd fit him to a hair
    'Therefore I pray thee leave me here to rest
    'Take drugs & go   160
  'I know your presence woud be welcome there
    '& what will suit you best
  'He'll gie ye double fees for what ye do
'With him efex the killing is no crime
'But I dont wish to dye before my time!'   165
  Who coud stand this—
  The doctor stampt & swore
  For nothing agravates a doctor more
  Urging enough no doubt
To hear folks talk so lightly of his trade   170
  & of his phisic bear no more consceit
  (No hopefull fees display'd)
Then think em useless articles in trade
  That might be done without
    Such usefull things egad   175
Call phisic poison! sure the man was mad.
The quack turnd round & swore but that was all
  He neer so much as stopt to make a[s]say
But instant put up drugs & whent away
  Hed often start before   180

151 acting: you] youd *MS 1*   152 Next door to me there livs a scolding wife *MS 1*   153 So use her well (she wants a drink) *MS 1*   154 The hen peckd] But her poor *MS 1*   155 To see the end ont hourly begs & prays (h *through* d *in* hourly) *MS 1*   157 As he wants somthing that woud end his days *MS 1* 158 twoud *MS 1*   159 thee] the *MS 1*   160 Tak drgs *MS 1*   161 woud *through* there: welcom *MS 1*   163 hell *MS 1*   164 k *through* b *in* killing *Pfz* 165 wish] chuse: die: time∧ *MS 1*   166 could stan this∧ *MS 1*   168 (For: Doctor *MS 1*   169 doubt) *MS 1*   170 To hear folks] When people *MS 1* 172 hopful *MS 1*   173 Than: usless: in] of *MS 1*   174 with out *MS 1* 176 poisoin *Pfz*   177 quack turnd round] doctor stampt: swore) *MS 1* 178 Struk dum—he never stopt to mak a say *MS 1*   a say *Pfz*   179 But instant went away *MS 1*   180 Hed often] He oft would *MS 1*

But hopeful half a crown
   Fors journey made,
   & Something more for pill
   To make a Bill
   The way of trade   185
If he could force one down
Made him in lingering mood to tarry still
   But now efex his hopes to speed was oer
   He stopt no more
Poison! efeth the cobler usd his aul   190
   No clenching nail was ever tighter hit
No leather pincerd closer on his stall
   Then nipping quack in hopes to bite—was bit
The friends & neighbours lookd at one another
   'How is he sir?'—we thought him very bad'   195
Small use to him was their enquiring bother
   'How is he' frowns the doctor 'why hes mad!'
Without the door stood ty'd his sorry hack
   & instant mounting on his back
With hopeful smack he jossteld thro the muck   200
In quest O' prey & hopes O' better luck
& soon to's friends suprise snob did revive
Tho feth his 'scaping death wer' fine's a hair
& Louts well pleas'd to see the sport survive
Right merry hearted to his shop repair   205
& fun & laughing keeps the game alive
& oft new tales the cobler will contrive
& oft he jokes upon the droll affair

---

181 Half: Crown *MS 1*   crown [fors journey] *Pfz*   182 made$_\wedge$ *MS 1*
183 somthing *MS 1*   184 Bill *underlined MS 1*   185 the *MS 1*
187 lingerin: tary *MS 1*   189 But now he never stopt no more *MS 1*
191 No no efex the nail was rightly hit *MS 1, p. 191 first version*] . . . it *MS 1, p. 191
second version*   193 & the biter he who thought o biting bit *MS 1, p. 191 first
version*] & [he the] biter in his hops of bitin bit *MS 1, p. 191 second version*   nip *through*
?fret *in* nipping *Pfz*   200 smack *or* shack *through ?* plan *Pfz*   201 *Successively*
(a) [In quest O' better prey & better luck] *(b)* [In quest O' prey & hope better luck] (hope
inserted) *(c)* In quest O' prey & hopes O' better luck *Pfz*   202 *New page headed in*
Pfz: Continuation of 'Quack & Cobler'   soon to's] *?* to his *MS 7*   re *through* su *in*
revive *and* revive *written again in margin Pfz*   203 was *MS 7*   204 & louts
right glad to find the game alive *MS 7*   205 Righ *MS 7*   208 affair *to* affair.
(p.e.) Pfz

AUTOGRAPH: Nor. MS 1, p. 110.
TRANSCRIPTS: Nor. MS 4, pp. 123–4: Pet. MS C2, pp. 71–71a.
Dated: 1808–19 (MS 1).

THE 'RUINS OF DESPAIR'

Yon mouldering wall compos'd of nought but mud
(Which has for ages in that manner stood)
Is rightly stil'd the 'Ruins of Despair'
For nought but wretchedness assembles there
All son[s] of grief and daughters of despair   5
Within that hut;—but how can life live there?
Thats strange indeed,—while these old walls of mud
('Which has for ages in that manner stood')
Keeps daily mouldering in a lost decay
Leaning on props that want themselves a stay!   10
Well may those wrankling nettles thrive and grow
So duley water'd with the tears of woe
—Lo on the floor with gulling holes oerspread
Their wretched feet betray a shooles tread:—
The 'Ruins' covering nought but loose-laid straw   15
Which winds blow off and leave a frequent flaw
There snows drive in upon the wretches head
There hasty rains a threatn'd deluge shed
Thrice wretched wretched 'Ruins of despair'
What griefs are thine.—O 'how can life live there?'   20
—A rag-stuft hole,—where bits of Lead remain
Proof of what was,—but now without a pane
A roof unceal'd displays the rafters bare
Here dangling straws and cobwebs dropping there
No white-wash'd walls to pictur'd taste incline   25
Instead of pictures threatn'd carvings shine
The dismal harth is nothing but a hole
To wood a stranger and the same to coal
Light straw and rubbish make their sorry fires
Kindl'd no quicker than the flame expires   30

THE 'RUINS OF DESPAIR'   *Title:* The 'Ruins of Despair'. *MS 1*   16 *First* e
through a *in* frequent *MS 1*

Instead of chairs great stones bedeck the ground
(Rough seats indeed!)—and closley raing'd around
On these the wretched tribe spend half their days
Dythering and weeping oer the dying blaze
A blaze that does more paint than heat supply   35
Tingeing their faces with a smoaky dye.—
No shelves no Cubboards no convieneience there
'T'was plan'd in grief and finish'd with despair
They make their shelves and cubboards on the floor
In a dark hole behind the broken door   40
There an old pitcher broke beyond excuse
(For wants consceald by them is little use)
Stands with the filthy shadow of a pan
Filthy and nausious,—O!—what being—can
Endure!—Grief searching muse give oer   45
On such a dismal scene essay no more
Stay thy too curious search,—forbear,—forbear,
No more describe the 'Ruins of Despair!'

AUTOGRAPH: Nor. MS 1, pp. 111–16.
TRANSCRIPTS: Nor. MS 4, pp. 125–30: Pet. MS C2, pp. 71a–74
(ll. 1–180 only).
Dated: 1808–19 (MS 1).

DOBSON AND JUDIE

or *The Cottage*

Behold yon Cottage on the green
    Where Fortunes riches never went
Yet tis the pallace of a Queen
    A Queen by shepherds call'd content

32 i *through* n *in* raing'd *MS 1*   42 use. *MS 1*   48 Despair!. *MS 1*

DOBSON AND JUDIE   *Title:* Dobson and Judie / or the Cottage *(a through g in*
Cottage*) MS 1*

Securley seated wharm and low 5
   Shelter'd round with willow trees
Where capons in a morning crow
   And dogs sallute the evening breeze

Lo! this secluded small estate
   Lonely retire from village throng 10
Belongs to Dobson and his mate
   The heroes of my simple song

This honest couple had no doubt
   Experienc'd what belong'd to life
And so it seems they search'd about 15
   To find some corner free from strife

They pitch'd on this and surely found
   Their every whant and wish supply'd
For envy there ne'er me[e]ts the ground
   Nor follys warp them into pride 20

Both at their ease enjoy content
   Who as a daughter dwells among
She leads old judies oer the bent
   And smiles at Dobsons merry song

For what few lands they have to till 25
   Old dobson hires his neighbours plough
And judie not against her will
   Both night and morning milks a cow

And like an ussiff dairy wife
   With pleasure will the work engage 30
As being brought up to't all her life
   She looks for't still in spight of age

He too will sometimes find employ
   To potter in the sunny air
His garden is his only joy 35
   Potatoes greens and leeks to rear

16 some *inserted MS 1*

Where spring recloathes the yellow moor
   Then dobson seeks his grassy seat
Built close beside the southern door
   Where woodbines bloom so nice and sweet   40

There judie too will oft repair
   To smoke a wiff while dobson sings
Thrice happy couple happy pair
   Your hut might tempt the greatest kings!

Alltho my dim descriptive song   45
   Nought but a misty view can bring
A misty view presented wrong
   Yet Memory cannot cease to sing

For what I've heard and what I've seen
   In this;—and other scenes as well   50
When leisure moments intervene
   My artles mind delights to tell

Delights to tell the harmles ways
   Which occupy their every hour
And show the picture that displays   55
   The cot, the tree, and garden flower

More close than burs these pictures cling
   Impresive to their gazers view
Raptures without a muse they bring
   —So right or wrong I will pursue   60

O happy couple happy pair
   Your curious cottage fills mine eye
With every thing convinient there
   From wind and rain both snug and dry

Granduer (its stubble roof) excells   65
   Adorned with the house-leek flower
Which holds (as superstion tells)
   A Charm to quell the lightnings power

With its low windows diamond glass
  In vain may polish'd crown compare   70
Nor can the Bowe's new mould surpass
  The homley old inventions there

For when the sun emits a ray
  It brings a clock as well as light
And both can tell the time of day   75
  Exactly by the shadows height

The rooms more comfortable made
  Than courts or pallaces can be
Tho all the ornament display'd
  Was furnish'd from necessity   80

Save Ballads, songs, and Cutts, that hide
  Both window-shutters, wall, and door,
Which tell of many-a-murder'd bride
  And desperate Battles daubed oer

'Keep within compass' courts the eye   85
  To read and learn a morral truth
With 'Golden Maxims' paste'd nigh
  And 'Pious counsils' plan'd for youth

There too on poltry paper wrought
  Disgrac'd with songs upon the screen   90
(Of some poor penny hawker bought)
  King Charles's 'Golden Rules' are seen

These with hundreds more beside
  In every hole and corner shine
Displaying forth in cottage pride   95
  An Exebition simply fine

Oh happy scenes what joys abound
  Not only which thy walls posess
For every foot of Dobsons ground
  Claims the sweet name of Happiness!   100

80   c *through* s *in* necessity *MS 1*

The hedge that bounds the pastur'd plains
    Was so beloved for its shade
That all the shepherds and the swains
    Their hutts beneath its shelter made

And hinds:—but what I would pursue   105
    Lengthens too much my simple ryhme
—The broad-old-oak now meets my view
    Where dobson sits in summer-time

O for a poets pen to show
    (When birds infest the rip'ning corn)   110
How dobson hopples too and fro
    With brushing pole, or bell, or horn

And simple ways and trifling things
    Which still his aged mind can please
That every day successive springs   115
    As well from labour as from ease

Lo! when he toils the bending grain
    Beats in his face her promis'd store
And when he rests this little plain
    Reminds him of the crowded door   120

In fancys eye the rustling sheaves
    Appear to treasuring ripness grown
And his glad heart more rapturous heaves
    Because these treasures are his own!

How e'er in short:—this happy pair   125
    So lonley in the valleys hid
Enjoys more pleasure free from care
    Then e'er their Father Adam did!

Spring's sprouting blade and swelling bud
    Summer's blown-flower and clefted-ground   130
And Autumns yellow fading wood
    Brings joy in one continued round

111 How *repeated MS 1*

Winter wrapt in her dismal forms
   Cannot their happiness annoy
Cold days, black nights, and snowy storms   135
   Inspire them with reflective joy

Old dob when sitting by the fire
   Will often bid old judie 'hark
'I fear the wind is rising higher
   'And o the night is dismal dark'   140

'Ah think' he cries, (while judie smoaks)
   'In this most dismal wintry night
'How many poor tir'd travelling folks
   'Now meets the storm in woeful plight!'

'Perhaps now at this very hour   145
   'Some poor lost soul lays—down his head
'Beneath a tree which turns no shower
   'And cannot find a better bed'

'For cloth'd with snow instead of dew
   'No longer they a shelter yield   150
'More worse I know 'twill winnow thro
   'Then standing in the open field'

'O heavens now the wind gets higher
   'It grieves me;—yet I'm pleas'd to think
'How we are blest with house and fire   155
   'A good warm bed, and meat, and drink,'

'And if the lost:—(I hope as well)
   'Should ever find their homes again
That true old-saying then will tell
   'How sweet the pleasure after pain!'   160

'Then will they sit like you and I
   'And tell how Darkness led astray.—
'O God with thy all-seeing eye
   'Guide the lone wanderer on his way'

149 with *through* in MS 1   151 threw MS 1

Thus Dobson often does reflect   165
   When winters horrid tempests blow
For he not blinded by neglect
   Can quickly feel anothers woe

Nor does his fond reflections dwell
   On human self-like souls alone   170
To the dumb Animals as well
   His feeling tendernes is shown

He knows how cold the winters night
   Would be if he himself where there
He feels for dogs—and takes delight   175
   In letting them his cottage share

There soon as darkness speads the eve
   Tray takes his lodging near the door
While purring puss with granted leave
   Prefers a Cushion to the floor   180

Sometimes judie knits and sews
   While o'er the sutty hearth so snug
He's often busied with the news
   Accompyni'd with bonny jug

O happy couple happy pair   185
   Your little cottage fills mine eye
With longing wishes to be there
   From wind and rain so snugly dry

But other scenes suround thy spot
   Scenes in childhood vallued dear   190
Nor shall they ever be forgot
   While life remains—or hope can cheer

---

175 dogs. *MS 1*   180 *Note inside back cover in MS C2:* Old Dobson finishes with
13 more Verses, in which the tale is carried on completely and in an uniform manner.
192 remains. *MS 1*

Yon garden fancy still retains
   Seated so warmly in the nook
Of noted green-ends flowry plains   195
   Where closley flows the bubling brook

There shepherd-lads and milking-maids
   Oft gather'd on its rushy brink
Or in the willows cooler shades
   To rendevouze with sugar-drink   200

But custom did these sports dispel
   Long ere old dob or judie where
Yet still posterity can tell
   And still the tale they love to hear

While some tho lov'd by shepherds long   205
   Dropt on a sudden like the wind
Or lik'er still (as will) my song
   They dropt to leave no wreck behind

The awthorn hedge that fences round
   Dob clips with all a gard'ners skill   210
And shows his master-ship profound
   Instead of shears to use a bill

There 'tat'es and leeks and cabbage grow
   With greens and lettuce's profuse
There too the sweet carnations glow   215
   As well for pleasure as for use

And there with rural sweetness made
   'In natures simplest habit clad'
The elder bower displays its shade
   Low bending o'er the grassy pad   220

Thrice lovly shades;—this elder bower
   Old tasteful judie loves to see
And loves to view each new-blown flower
   The bursting bud; or blossom'd tree

215 l *through* r *in* glow *MS 1*

—Now I must leave your shades so dear   225
Tho dearer still as yet remain
O! would some Bloomfield wander near
To give such scenes an equal strain

Adieu then lovly spot adieu
Thou fountain of Felicity   230
Fancy shall never loose her view
Nor Silence cease to muse on thee

AUTOGRAPH: Nor. MS 1, pp. 116–17 (heavily erased throughout all that is left visible being little more than the tops and tails of ascenders and descenders).
Dated: 1808–19 (MS 1).

SONG

Young Jemmy the pride of the Hamlett and mill
The pride of the ⟨border⟩ the vally and Hill
Once the pride of the lasses—well—so he is still
Altho hes undone the poor maid of the mill
   Still he lives in the vally   5
   With maidens to dally
Altho hes undone the poor maid of the mill

When the Hamlett and mill are all sleeping quite still
And night slowly creeping hides vally and Hill
He oft kisses the maiden in secret by the mill   10
To see the coy maiden that liv'd at the mill
   Who few in the vally
   Tho dozens woulds dally
So coy was the maiden that liv'd at the mill

But one night (and he deems its Sunday night still)   15
Then he used the maid for what we all do well on the Hill

228 scenes *through* strain *MS 1*
   SONG   *Title:* Song   3 r *in* pride *inserted*

'Come, come' 'But ——' 'O' never mind that if you will'
'I'll for ever love sally—the maid of the mill
   He still cooing and billing
   At last she was willing   20
'Oh my lovley sweet sally, the maid of the mill

Think then of the 'slanders and dally here still'
'Or Judgment you'll ⟨soon⟩ find is shame for the Maid of the Hill
'Come, come' 'Yes' 'But' 'O' never mind that if you will
'Ill for ever love sally the maid of the mill   25
   Now his heart was all wooing
   O he long'd to be doing
'O how I love sally the maid of the Hill

'Now now never mind ⟨dearie⟩ O' my charmer sit still
'Well well to be sure on these ⟨ ⟩ ⟨ ⟩ meadow rill   30
'Coud Jem now be so fond ⟨of doing⟩ your will?
'If you ever lov'd Jemmy dearest maid of the mill
   O the billing and cooing
   He so long'd to be doing
'If you ever lov'd Jemmy ⟨dearest⟩ maid of the mill   35

'—Well, well,—but I says, then we never need wait'—
'If you'll ⟨swear to⟩ marry me & then Say I, [will]'
Now Jemmys soon busy ⟨ ⟩ when I will
For he could not speak plain to the maid of the mill
   As the poor maiden sigh'd   40
   Jemmy still half reply'd
For he could not speak plain to the maid of the mill

'Now Jemmy (O dearest) since you've just had your will
'I hope you'll be loving and marry me still'
'Ah the church Jemmy pleads we cannot wait till'   45
'Till when?' asketh sadly the lovley sweet maid of the mill
   'Come never talk of parting
   ''Tis time we were starting—'
'—Till when?' 'Ah tis done—so return to [the] mill'.

37 *Clare has a dash for 'will'*   49 *Followed in MS 1, p. 117 by* Sonnet Ye brown
old oaks that spread the silent wood *which is published in our volume for 'The Village
Minstrel'*

AUTOGRAPHS: Nor. MS 1, p. 117: Pet. MS A3, p. 58.
TRANSCRIPTS: Pet. MS B1, p. 111: Nor. MS 5, p. 5.
Printed in the *Stamford Mercury*, 12 November 1819 (*SM*): *RL* p. 188: the
London Magazine, January 1820, p. 10 (*LM*): *Drakard's Stamford News*,
7 January 1820 (reprinted from *LM*): *Gentleman's Magazine*, March 1820,
p. 258 (reprinted from *RL*): *The Englishman's Fire-side*, April 1820, p. 113 (*EF*).
Dated: 1807–17 (Explanatory Notes).

THE PRIMROSE

Welcome pale primrose starting up between
Dead matted leaves of ash and oak that strew
The every lawn the wood and spinney through
Mid creeping moss and Ivys darker green
How much thy presence beautifies the ground   5
How bright thy modest unaffected pride
Glows on the sunny bank and woodland side
And where thy fairy flowers in groups are found
The school-boy roams enchantedly along
Plucking the fairest with a rude delight   10
And the meek shepherd stops his simple song
To gaze a moment on the pleasing sight
Oerjoy'd to see the flowers that truley bring
The welcome News of soft returning spring

THE PRIMROSE   *Title:* The Primrose *MS 1 RL*, The Primose / A Sonnet *MS A3*,
To a Primrose *SM LM*, Sonnet to the Primrose *EF*   1 Primrose *MS A3*
2 oak, and ash *SM LM EF*   3 & spinny *MS A3*   4 & *MS A3*
5 prescence: Ground *MS A3*   u *in* beautifies *inserted MS 1*   6 bright] sweet
MS A3 SM RL LM EF   7 & *MS A3*   woodland] woods warm *MS A3*, wood's
warm *SM RL LM EF*   9 school boy *MS A3*   11 And] While *MS A3 SM RL
LM EF*   12 [on] a *MS A3*   13 Oer joy'd: truly *MS A3*   14 soft] sweet
MS A3 SM RL LM EF   Returning Spring—*MS A3*

AUTOGRAPH: Nor. MS 1, p. 118 (heavily erased throughout).
Dated: 1808–19 (MS 1).

SONG

When mountain billows roar amain
  And death looks in each sailors eye
Vex'd Jemmy in oerpowring strain
  'Cries Susan tis for thee I die'
    Mid swelling sighs   5
    Still jumps and cries
  'Proud susan tis for thee I die'

When lightning lacerates the cloud
  And waves increasing foams more high
His rage more urgent calls aloud   10
  'Curs'd Susan tis for thee I die'
    Hem'd in with waves
    Still jumps and raves
  'Curs'd Susan tis for thee I die'

But when the billows cease to rise   15
  And when their former calmness give
Fond Jemmy soon recanting cries
  'Sweet Susan tis for thee I live'
    In jovial flings
    Still drinks and sings   20
  'Sweet Susan tis for thee I live'

SONG   *Title*: Song

AUTOGRAPH: Nor. MS 1, p. 118.
TRANSCRIPTS: Nor. MS 4, p. 131: Pet. MS C1, p. 26a.
Dated: 1808–19 (MS 1).

CRAZY JANE

A Fragment

Hark what shrill mournful strains
Sounds from yon lonely plains
Where the low-bending willow
Drips thro the mimic billow
Rais'd by the adverse winds that curl the stream   5
How mournfully and plain
Their dying langour on the breezes seem
Say from what throat
Or is this note?
The song of Crazy Jane!—   10

Ye swains from whence and where?
Comes this sad grief so drear?
It must be,—(O' so grieveing)
Some loss thats past reprieving
Or hope forlorn that never will return   15
—They'r dumb;—Enquirey's vain
Then lead me on ye sounds and let's descern
And further know
If all this woe
Come's from poor Crazy Jane.   20

CRAZY JANE   *Title:* Crazy Jane, A Fragment *MS 1*   20 *Followed in MS 1, pp. 119, 121–2 by* The Jewel of all *and pp. 119–20* To Health *which are published in our volume for 'The Village Minstrel'*

AUTOGRAPHS: Pforzheimer Library, Misc. MS 197: Nor. MS 1, p. 120
(margin): Norris Museum SAVNM CL/14.
TRANSCRIPT: Pet. MS B1, p. 39 (deleted).
Printed in *RL*, p. 198.
Dated: '1819' (Pfz).

TO THE WINDS

Hail gentle winds I love your murmuring sounds
The willows charm me wavering too & fro
& oft I stretch me on the dasied ground
To see you crimp the wrinkling flood below
Delighted more as brisker gusts succeed   5
& give the landscape around a sweeter grace
Sweeping in shaded waves the rip'ning mead
Puffing their rifl'd fragrance in my face
Pictures of nature ye are doubly dear
Her childern dearly love your wispering charms   10
Ah ye have murmurd sweet to many an ear
That now lies dormant in deaths Icy arms

TO THE WINDS   *Title:* Sonnet to the Winds *Pfz*, To the Winds *Norris RL, wanting
MS 1*   1 Ye gentle Gales How sweet your murmurings sound *Norris*   your
murmuring sounds *through* to hear ye *MS 1*   murmuring *below* [pleasing] *Pfz*   sound *RL*
2 & sweet ye wave the Willows two & fro *Norris*   Willows *MS 1*   to *MS 1 RL*
3 oft] pleas'd: me *inserted Norris*   & pleasd I often stretch me on the ground *MS 1*
3/4 [To mark you wrinkle the crimpt flood below] *Pfz*   4 To mark thy wrinkles in
the floods below *MS 1*] To see your Wrinkles in the brook below *(in over* [on]: brook *over*
[floods]*) Norris*   5 suceed *MS 1 Norris*   6 & give] & gives *MS 1*, To give *Norris*
Landsape *Norris*] the scenes *MS 1*   round *Norris RL*   7 In shaded waves swift
sweeps the grassy mead *MS 1*] In shaded waves now sweeps the Grassy mead *Norris*
ripening *RL*   8 Puffing] & puffs: rifeld *MS 1 Norris*   their] its: Face *Norris*
8–9
Blow on ye winds—[& ye shall gently wave]
        to natures childern dear
Still the long grass—& still the waters wave

Pictures of Nature ye are doubly dear
Your meanest trifles cannot fail to please   5
& ah I sigh in thanks While wandering here   *MS 1*

(l. 6 in thanks *through* to mark it)

9 Pictures] Painters *RL*   nature *altered to* Nature *Harvard proof copy*   Blow on ye
winds—to nature chilerd dear *MS 1*] Blow on ye Winds—to Natures childern dear *Norris*
10 children *RL*   loves *Pfz*   In whose wild Eye your meanest trifle charms *MS 1*] . . .
Trifle charms *Norris*   11 Ah] Oh *MS 1*   murmur'd *Norris*   Ear *MS 1 Norris*
12 now lies *through* nows *MS 1*   icy *MS 1 Norris*

& at this moment many a weed ye wave
That hide[s] the bard in his forgotten Grave

AUTOGRAPH: Nor. MS 1, pp. 121–6.
TRANSCRIPT: Pet. MS C1, pp. 2–4a.
Dated: 1808–19 (MS 1).

THE WELCOME STRANGER

'Come suke begin to blow the fire
  '—The storm beats high—I hope no harm
'And now we're up its my desire
  'To get this dithering stranger warm'

'But stay—poor soul he wants some cloaths   5
  'Then fetch him down my best supply
'Altho but very mean god knows
  'They're comfortable clean and dry'

'Thus robin spoke before he knew
  Or ask'd his guest the cause that brought,—   10
But where real goodnes does pursue
  To save!—demands their every thought

He heard a noise! and up he got
  Pierc'd deep with sorrows not his own
And to recieve a friend or not   15
  Instant his door was open thrown

Aloud he cries 'you're welcome here!'
  His bowels did with pity yearn
The unseen stranger trampl'd near
  And lowly thank'd him in return   20

13 Moment: Weed *Norris*   14 hides: Bard *MS 1 Norris*   *Followed in MS 1,*
pp. 120–1 by May-day *which is published in our volume for 'The Village Minstrel'*

    THE WELCOME STRANGER   *Title:* The Welcome Stranger *MS 1*   3 now
inserted: w[h]'ere *MS 1*

And O such epithets so mild
   On the lost man they both bestow'd
'Poor dear lost soul' and 'wandering child'
   In the dark cottage sweetly flowd

But when the kindling fire was litt   25
   And show'd a man most nobly drest
Their soothings fled and sorley frit
   Poor robin thus excuses prest

'Sir, I beg pardon for I'm sure
   'I never thought of such a man.—   30
'God knows my heart altho I'm poor
   'I feel for other sir I can'

'But still I own I was to[o] free
   'So muzzling in the darkness hid
'I talk'd too fast ere I could see   35
   'And now I'm vex'd because I did'

'We live almost unknown to all
   'No gentleman came here before
'None but poor-men who some times call
   'To crave a morsel at the door'   40

'So sir you see my wife and I
   'Took you to be as one of them.—
'But still the worst on't is be-gu'y
   'We've nothing fit for gentlemen!'

'For what few sorry things we've got   45
   'Are trifling and will ne'er amount.—
'But tho I shou'd'n't grudge my lot
   'I'm sorry sir on your account'

'To see a gentleman so wet
   'In hopes 'while-back to find relief   50
'And to be disappointed yet
   'I'm sure sir yourn's the worst of grief'

2 your's *altered to* yourn's *MS 1*

'I'm vex'd.—but ere the stranger rose
   And interrupted with a smile
'Old Man forbear no wants disclose   55
   'Peace peace and be at ease awhile'

'If so you think you think amiss
   'Whats here I little thought to see
'Your "worst of grief" to me is bliss
   'Old man I mean humanity!'   60

I find it here,—my lost distress
   'And seeming grief you share a part
'Nor is it outwardly to bless
   'No thou art honest from the heart!'

'Thou didst recieve me good or bad   65
   'Thou gave me instantly relief
'With thy own clothes I may be clad
   'Then is there any room for grief?'

'No!—this old hut believe me brings
   'More solid comforts to my mind   70
'Then all the luxury of kings
   'Or richest pallaces can find!'

'Man has not where to lay his head'
   '—When lost—on this—I wish'd and sigh'd
'But now (bless god) all doubts are fled   75
   'And every wish is well supply'd'

'My luck was great to wander here
   'I love the poor mans social glee
'Then pray resume your former cheer
   'T'will be more happines to me'   80

Here he was stopt for robins heart
   Of warmest praises got so full
That Bold or not he must impart
   In spite of Judies twitch and pull!

78 sosicaι *MS 1*   84 of *inserted*: twicth *MS 1*

'God bless you sir your very ways   85
   'Shows a great gentleman I'm sure
'For our proud bug-struts now-a-days
   'Will not bear talking to the poor.'

'When one's wi' them why there I stand
   'At every word I'm forc'd to bow   90
'My grey head bare and Hat in hand
   'For age makes nothing wi' 'em now!'

'Then it's not fashion—no that drops
   'As soon as ever they begin
'For scorning to level with such fops   95
   'Men like your honor gives it in'

'So deuce take these concieted cre'tur's
   'They cause such altering 'mong 'em all
'That when one gets before ones betters
   'We can't tell how to do a't 'all'   100

Here sukie gave a shake and squint
   He saw—and criticiz'd no more
Full well he knew the silent hint
   Was meant in manners to give oer

The stranger now from top to toe   105
   Equip'd in robins Best so tight
Made him begin again to show
   What if conceal'd would not be right

'Them things' quoth robin 'one by one
   'Are sweet and clean sir every way   110
'So never fear to keep 'em on
   'You'll catch no harm I'll 'bound to say'

---

105 *In margin:* 27 *MS 1*   108 conceal'd *through* reveal'd *MS 1*   110 e *through*
a *in* clean *MS 1*

'I'm free again—but now the plan
  ' 'Bout that is alter'd—since I find
'Your honor such a gentleman   115
  'To talk a little I dont mind'

'So let me tell you sir my cot
  'Is at your service while you stay
'And to the little all we've got
  'You're welcome as the flowers in may!'   120

'You're tir'd likwise and sleep must need
  'And tho we've gott'n but one bed
'We should be happier sir indeed
  'Would you but take it in our stead'

'No—since night's short' the stranger cried   125
  'I'd rather sit up here than go—
'Well sir' the cottagers replied
  'Just as you like we'd have yo' do'

Then she reach'd out her homley fare
  With every look of real good will   130
And robin must again repair
  To bid his stranger welcome still

He still kept pressing 'take some more'
  And 'Sir we're sorry tis our best'
The stranger thank'd him oer and oer   135
  With nod and smile to tell the rest

And though no dainties set to please
  Nor viands grac'd his lowly board
A hard brown loaf and harder cheese
  Being all his cottage would afford   140

The stranger was well satisfy'd
  With this one step 'bove poverty
For wise good men cannot abide
  The rant of noisey Luxury

121 tir'd *inserted MS 1*   140 a *in* cottage *inserted MS 1*

And now the things being set aside   145
    Old sukie she retir'd to rest
While robin did more sticks provide
    To cheer and warm his welcome guest

Whose tale (not bid) he wish'd to hear
    Of all the dangers he'd been in   150
Howe'er at last (tho much in fear)
    Enquirey forc'd him to begin

'I hope sir what I ask you'll grant?
    'Yet thats unmanner'dly I trow
'But you'll excuse me for I can't   155
    'Do things no better than I know'

'I want to hear how you this night
    'Was so unlucky to be lost
'And how your honour came to light
    'Of our old hut that's hid a'most'   160

'Well well old man to pleasure you
    'I'll tell it then without excuse
The stranger cried—'exactley true
    'And first of all my name is Bruce'

'From stamford town this night I've came   165
    'But how I cannot find it out
'For which I own I'm much to blame
    'Tho 't'was not late when I set out'

'But what I thought was getting oer
    '(As seeming likely to abate)   170
'Turn'd to rain harder than before
    'And that allur'd me to my fate'

'For had it rain'd when I was there
    'I never should have come away
'But as it look'd so nice and fair   175
    'I thought I'd better go then stay'

160 i *through* e *in* hid *MS 1*

'While darkness soon at earlier hour
  'Hid every house and every tree
'Then to find roads I had no power
  'For every road was strange to me'   180

'And o when ones benighted so
  'What fancies darkness will beget
'What dismal seeming pits below
  'Lie gapeing every foot we set'

'Some times I hardly dar'd to move   185
  'When I so very lost had got
'Before I prog'd my stick to prove
  'The road as wether sound or not'

'Nay all the while I was in fear
  'And always had a scene to dred   190
'For thoughts of unseen dangers near
  'For ever serv'd to fill my head'

'At length by drenching rain half drown'd
  'I at your Cottage did advance
'At which you wonder how I found   195
  'Indeed old man twas all by chance'

'And when I saw the ponds so blea
  And heard the trees so hoarsley sound
I realey took the place to be
  Some ancient Castle moated round'   200

'I fancied (far beneath a man)
  'Those fables which the weak believe
'Of dire Enchantments Spectres wan
  'And all Romances can concieve'

And oft I wander'd round thy shed   205
  'And listn'd at thy window near
'And oft I tapt thy door with dread
  'But nothing stird as I could hear'

---

190 *Through indecipherable line ending in* my head *MS 1*   197 ∧And: blea *through*
bee *MS 1*   207 oft *inserted MS 1*

'Yet as the well known proverb says
  'Force never puts us to no choise'   210
'For spite of all such timid ways
  'I forc'd at last with loudest voice'

'To call for shelter hit or miss
  'And when good soul thou didst appear
'Soon to my unexpecting bliss   215
  'I found that I was welcome here'

AUTOGRAPH: Nor. MS 1, p. 130.
TRANSCRIPT: Pet. MS C1, p. 10.
Dated: 1808–19 (MS 1).

EPITAPH ON A WOU'D-HAVE-BEEN-CHARITABLE-MAN

But For Certain Reasons Which He So Wisley Explain'd

O what a blessing is the gift
To him that has a good foresight
x   x   x   x
x   x   x

Here lies a man of reason rare
  Who had a foresight best of any
Who had enough and much to spare
  Yet never gave a single penny

His reasons was the people say   5
  As he was mortal like to others
He knew he soon shou'd drop away
  From his poor starving friends and brothers

210 never *inserted MS 1*   212 at last *through* to call *MS 1*   214 disdst *(second
d through* t) *MS 1*

EPITAPH ON A WOU'D-HAVE-BEEN-CHARITABLE-MAN   *Title:* Epitaph
on a Wou'd-have-been-charitable-man / But for certain Reasons which he so wisley
explain'd *MS 1*

And so if he unstrung his purse
  He knew the missing o' him wou'd   10
Fret 'em and hurt 'em ten times worse
  Then all his gifts wou'd do 'em good

O reasoning soul may he for this
  He did foresee and plan so well
That th' poor his gifts should never miss   15
  Near miss the devils gift o' h—ll

AUTOGRAPHS: Nor. MS 1, p. 131: Pet. MS A3, p. 33: Pet. MS A40, p. 31 (deleted).
TRANSCRIPTS: Pet. MS B1, pp. 167–8: Nor. MS 5, pp. 96–7 (ll. 17–24 omitted).
Dated: 1811–12 (MS A3, p. 33 '7 years ago').

THE CRAFTY MAID

What dangerful rascals the fellows all are
  Like wolves ever prowling for prey
And many poor maidens are catchd in the snare
  But I'll be as crafty as they
For if ever to peggy they dare to come near   5
  And run oer their impudence so
I'll soon send 'em off with a flea in their ear
  And ne'er let em ruin me so

Young ra[l]ph 'tother day as we sat by the brook
  A poor nasty rogue if he could   10

THE CRAFTY MAID *Title:* The Crafty Maid *MS 1*, The Crafty maid *MS A3*, The Crafty Maid a Ballad *MS A40*   2 pree *to* prey *(p.e.) MS A3*   3 & *MS A3 MS A40*   catch'd *MS A3*] caught *MS A40*   4 Ill *MS A40*   5 peggy *to* Peggy *(p.e.) MS A3*] Peggy *MS A40*   near] nigh *MS A3 MS A40*   6 (I'm no fool—that I'll let 'em to know) *over* [& run oer their impudence so] *MS A3*] ∧Im: fool∧: Ill: 'em: known *MS A40*   7 I'll] But I'll *through* I'll *MS A3*, But Ill *MS A40* soon[e] *MS A3*   em *MS A3*] them *MS A40*   8 & *MS A3 MS A40*   ne'er] near: 'em *MS A40*   9 raph *to* Ralph *(p.e.) MS A3*] Ralph *MS A40*   'to'ther *MS A3*] tother *MS A40*   *Second* o *in* brook *inserted MS A3*   10 poor nasty] wild naughty *MS A40*   cou'd *to* could *(p.e.) MS A3*] coud *MS A40*

By pretending he wanted a shaft for his crook
   Would have weagl'd me into the wood
But says I 'Go along wi' y'r lyes y' proud elf
   Or if ye want shafts pr'ythee go
Away 'bout y'r busn'ess and get 'em y'rself   15
   And near think to ruin me so

And last night too Jocky as bad as the rest
   Came smileing up 'How d' ye do'
But guessing his meaning as sharp as the best
   I answer'd 'No better for you'   20
For he knowing master and mistres was safe
   Thought I with [him] sawning would go
But I bid him 'Off' as I did nasty ra[l]ph
   And ne'er hope to ruin me so

And so I'll serve all—be as fine as they please   25
   Unless they keep fairley in bounds
Which I can soon tell, Aye wi' just as much ease
   As I can a crack't pot by the sound[s]
But there's many maids not so crafty as I
   Who hears it and yet does'n't know   30
To these they will daily whine wimper and sigh
   But Laugh when they've ruin'd 'em so

11 By] Wi' *MS A3*   he wanted] to get me *MS A3 MS A40*   his crook] my hook
through his crook *MS A3*, my hook *MS A40*   12 Woud: veigled *MS A40*
13 'go: with your lyes ye *MS A40*   lies *MS A3*   14 Or] & *MS A40*   ye want
shafts] y' will get me shafts *(me through a) MS A3*, ye'll get shafts *MS A40*   prythee *MS*
A3] prithee *MS A40*   15 your: yourself *MS A40*   bus'ness *MS A3*] business
MS A40   & *MS A3 MS A40*   16 & *MS A3 MS A40*   neer *MS A3*
17 & *MS A3 MS A40*   jocky *to* Jocky *(p.e.) MS A3*] Jockey *MS A40*   rest *through*
best *MS A3*] best *MS A40*   18 smiling *MS A3 MS A40*   'how do ye do' *MS A40*
19 But *through* & *MS A3*   20 answered *MS A40*   'no *MS A3 MS A40*
21 & *MS A3 MS A40*   mis'ess *MS A3*] mistress *MS A40*   22 him *MS A3*
MS A40   wou'd *MS A3*] woud *MS A40*   23 'off' *MS A3*] ∧off∧ *MS A40*
nasty] master *MS A3 MS A40*   raph *MS A3*] Ralph *MS A40*   24 & neer *MS A3*
MS A40   25 & *MS A3 MS A40*   Ill: all∧ *MS A40*   26 fairly *MS A3*
MS A40   27 I'm up to their deepness wi' just as much ease *MS A3*] Im: with *MS A40*
28 can] tell: crackt: by the sound] when it sounds *MS A3 MS A40*   29 theres *MS*
A3 MS A40   30 hears] see's *MS A3*, sees *MS A40*   & *MS A3 MS A40*   yet]
then *MS A3*   does not *MS A40*   31 whimper *MS A40*   & *MS A3 MS A40*
32 laugh *MS A3 MS A40*   theyve ruined them *MS A40*

AUTOGRAPH: Nor. MS 1, pp. 132–3.
TRANSCRIPT: Pet. MS C1, pp. 10–10a.
Dated: 1808–19 (MS 1).

JOHN BUMKINS LUCY

Well stop bill wi' dogging me so oer an' oer
I've told yah hur name—what and now summot more?
Gosh boy but thats hardish to tell yah wi out—hur
Hur looks an hur tallnes an all things about—hur
—La' us see whot is like to tha straitness of hur   5
Theres summot cums near to't d' yah see yender fur
Well then do yah mind me she's straiter then that
An' hur eye's an' hur hair is az blak az my hat
  O' my pritty deer Lucy az I am a sinnur
Hite op wi' old byard go on   10
    I'll zartinly do all I can for to win hur
    Ha az shure az my crisn'd name's jon

Hur face is not like to yahr kitts i' the town
Nor fine coking jinny's so roozy an' brown
No if yah did kno hur yah'd think em a site   15
Its so wite an' red sumhow I cant tell yah rite
But I think if tha rosey an' may grow'd togither
'Tw'd be summot like-it but not so fine nither
How-so-miver she beets all the wenches I kno
An' hur big-roundy bosom is witer then sno   20
  O' my pritty deer lucy az I am a sinnur
Hite op wi old byard go on
    I'll zartinly do all I can for to win hur
    Ha az shure az my crisn'd name's jon

JOHN BUMKINS LUCY   *Title:* John Bumkins Lucy *MS 1*   1 an'[d] *MS 1*
2 name, *MS 1*   3 without *altered to* wi out *MS 1*   6 a *through* e *in* yah *MS 1*
8 z *through* s *in* az *twice MS 1*   9 z *through* s *in* az: sinner *altered to* sinnur *MS 1*
12 z *through* s *in* az *twice MS 1*   20 bossom *MS 1*   21 z *through* s *in* az *MS 1*
24 z *through* s *in* az *twice MS 1*

Now Ive told yah about hur az much az I can   25
How to get hur bill-boy is the next thing to plan
Well that I can deel wi' an' soon yah shal see
Jon Bumkin a shentleman fine oz can be
An' now then to tell yah a bit o' my pride
This greezey old smokfrok I'll fost thro aside   30
Nex I'll change this old crap for a fine beaver hat
Drest about wi a blak ribbin bo' an' all that
   Then so wastly fine bill-boy az I am a sinnur
Hite op wi' old byard go on
      'T'will zartinly be a good shilling to win hur   35
      Ha oz shure oz my crisn'd name's jon

Then there'll be the waiscot an' briches an' cote
An' lite shoo's an stokin's wi' all tha' best sote
Then old women will chatter an' say 'he looks neet
'From tha crown of his hed to tha sole of his feet'   40
But I shal think more wen they cum to be mine
That better then neetnes they'll look very fine
How-so-miver it sing-i-fys nothink to me
If the[e] will but noistish an' do but agree
   Wi' my pritty deer Lucy—for az I am a sinnur   45
Hite op wi' old byard go on
      I'll zartinly do all I can for to win hur
      Ha az shure oz my crisn'd name's jon

AUTOGRAPH: Nor. MS 1, pp. 133–4.
Dated: 1808–19 (MS 1).

LINES ON THE DEATH OF MRS BULLIMORE

For fellow-creatures which we long have known
Familliar fondness must be surley shown

25 z *through* s *in az twice MS 1*   28 z *through* s *in oz MS 1*   33 z *through* s *in az MS 1*   40 a *through* e *in* tha *(second word) MS 1*   45 z *through* s *in az MS 1*
48 z *through* s *in az MS 1*

LINES ON THE DEATH OF MRS BULLIMORE   *Title:* Lines on the death of
Mrs B———

And when the sollemn bell with chilling toll
Speaks the departure of a self-like soul
Their exit to be seen on earth no more   5
The feeling heart will naturally deplore
But when to these the ever active thought
Adds a good action which they once have wraught
On him who sighs.—ah then the bosom bleeds
And fond regret in sympathy suceeds   10
Tis thus for her whom now but few regard
Sleeping unconsious in the cold-church-yard
My soul for past good-deeds does now design
To tell its warmth which nothing can confine
For in my earliest-days I us'd to be   15
Left in her care to con my A,B,C,
And in her well-known yard 'mong play-mates gay
I've often loiter'd with a fond delay

Beneath her ruling rod tho' not severe
I rellish'd learning and I lov'd to hear   20
Those pleasing tales which she would often tell
How Johnny Armstrong fought and how he fell
How the fair Rosamond by poison dy'd
And Jane shore suffer'd for unlawful pride
These where her tales and these so powerful where   25
So mildly pleasing to the infant ear
That every day we long'd to have them told
And oft-repeating never made 'em old
We always lov'd them and she would comply
Then should this goodness so familiar die   30
Because 'twas only employ'd to rear
The simple child entrusted to her care?
Whose learned all—not studiously bent
Extended only to the testament!
Is memory useless when it leaves to fame   35
No other record than a virtuous name?
Should theirs be lost who willingly would shew
To them that needed any thing they knew?

Who gave instructions where they whould recieve
As far as lay with in their power to give?   40

—No surely not—the first impressions made
On the young plant its tender shoot to aid
Must give the promise of a statley tree
And the first cause of its perfections be
In the same sence of her it may be said   45
Who's guiding hand my infant foot-steps led
To learning path—that her impressing plan
First laid the basis of the future man
And by imbibing what she simply taught
My taste for reading there was surely caught   50
However if it was or not fullfil'd
(In philosophic arguments not skill'd)
Its naught to me—her memory can impart
Familiar fondness to a feeling heart
And when the neighbours shook their heads to sigh   55
'Poor Mrs B[ul]l[imor]e will surely die'
My youthful breast with sighing wishes swell'd
I hop'd—I shudder'd—at the truth they tell'd
But when the passing bell began to knoll
All hopes where lost it chill'd my very soul   60
The truth to[o] true it mournful seem'd to say
'Her flitting soul has left its house of clay'

Then farwell tutor of the infant mind
Now thou art gone and left thy flock behind
Free from all trouble callumney and scorn   65
'Slow through the church-yard-path I saw thee born'
I saw thy grave remembering with a sigh
That I my self in such a one must lie
And often since I've stood to view thy stone
By kindred gave to make thy memory known   70
Whose uncooth ryhmes imperfectly apply'd
Without the aid of sculptures gaudy pride
From neighbourings friends and kindred passing by
Near fails to raise the heart-affecting sigh

56 B—l——e   74 *Followed by a row of asterisks*

AUTOGRAPHS: Nor. MS 1, p. 134 (deleted): Pet. MS A3, p. 136.
TRANSCRIPTS: Pet. MS B1, p. 9: Nor. MS 5, p. 105.
Printed in *RL*, p. 197.
Dated: '1815' (MS A3, p. 136, Clare first wrote 'Old' and then deleted it).

EVENING

Now glareing daylight's usher'd to a Close
And nursing eve her soothing care renews
To welcome weary Labour to repose
And cherish nature with reviveing dews
Hail cooling sweets that breathe so sweetly here   5
Hail lovly eve who's hours so lovly prove
Thy silent calm to solitude so dear
And O this darkness dearer still to love
Now the fond lover seeks thy silent plains
And with his charmer in fond dalliance strays   10
Vowing his love & telling jealous pains
Which fearful fancy in their abscence raise
Ah tho such pleasures center not in me
I love to wander & converse with thee

EVENING   *Title:* Evening. *MS 1,* Evening *MS A3 RL*   1 day light's: close
MS A3   3 Repose *MS A3*   4 reviving *MS A3*   5 —Hail: breath:
sweatly *MS A3*   6 Eve whose Hours *MS A3*   7 Silent: Solitude *MS A3*
8 Darkness: love.— *MS A3*   dearer *altered to* dearest *altered to* dearer *Harvard proof
copy*   10 & *MS A3*   11 love— *MS A3*   12 fearful] doubtful *MS A3*
Fancies *MS A3*] fancies *RL*   Abscence Raise— *MS A3*   13 Pleasures *MS A3*
14 thee. *MS 1*

AUTOGRAPH: Nor. MS 1, pp. 135–6.
TRANSCRIPT: Pet. MS C1, p. 11.
Dated: 1808–19 (MS 1).

THE WOOD NIMPH'S PETITION

Unthinking Gunner O forbear
  To pull thy murdering Gun
These little Birds in pity spare
  For they no harm have done

Oer corn of thine they never range   5
  My wood they only claim
Judge rightly ere you take revenge
  And not the harmles blame

Lo here thou dost not judge a right
  Thou undeserning Clown   10
For Wood larks are unable quite
  To get a kirnell down

Their little throats are far too small
  Altho they come so near
Tis only for the sun thats all   15
  Which shineth warmer here

For here they love to sit and pick
  Their coats of finest brown
And bask—and wipe their little beaks
  And stroak their feathers down   20

Then mind and for the time to come
  Hurt not the innoscent
And of all crimes before-hand done
  I hope you will repent

THE WOOD NIMPH'S PETITION *Title:* The Wood Nimph's Petition to a
Gunner on the point / Of shooting at a flock of Wood larks seated in the hedge by / the
Side of his Corn *MS 1*   12 r *through* n *in* kirnell *MS 1*

Go talk with reason to be wise   25
   And know what should be done
She'll soon with justice you advise
   To lay aside your Gun

Not only wood-larks spare but all
   From sparrows to the wren   30
For birds and all both great and small
   Are sent for use to men

Altho some times by hunger led
   They nibble at an Ear
For faults so small their blood to shed   35
   Is cruel and severe

For the few corns from you they take
   Their Songs do thrice repay
Then spare them all for Musicks sake
   And let 'em fly away   40

AUTOGRAPHS: Nor. MS 1, pp. 136–7: Pet. MS A3, pp. 71–2.
TRANSCRIPTS: Pet. MS B1, pp. 122–3: Nor. MS 5, pp. 138–40.
Printed in *RL*, pp. 37–40.
Dated: 'Old' (MS A3, p. 71).

ON SEEING A LOST GREYHOUND IN WINTER LYING UPON THE SNOW IN THE FIELDS

Ah thou poor neglected hound
   Now thou'rt done wi' catching hares
Thou mayst lye upon the ground
   Lost for what thy master cares

33 t *through* o *in* Altho *MS 1*
   ON SEEING A LOST GREYHOUND IN WINTER LYING UPON THE
SNOW IN THE FIELDS   *Title:* On seeing a Lost Greyhound in winter lying / upon
the snow in the fields (upon *through* on) *MS 1*, Efusions of Pity / On seeing a lost
Grewhound lying on the / Snow— *MS A3*, On a lost Greyhound on the Snow *RL*
1 c *through* t *in* neglected *MS 1*   2 thou'st *RL*

To see thee lye it makes me sigh   5
   A proud hard hearted man
But men we know like dogs may go
   When they've done all they can

And thus from witnesing thy fate
   Thoughtfull reflection wakes   10
Tho thou'rt a dog (with grief I say't)
   Poor men thy fare partakes
Like thee lost whelp the poor mans help
   Ere while so much desir'd
Now harvests got is wanted not   15
   Or little is requir'd

So now the over plus will be
   As useles negros all
Turn'd in the bitter blast like thee
   Meer cumber grounds to fall   20
But this reward for toil so hard
   Is sure to meet return
From him whose ear is always near
   When the oppressed mourn

For dogs as men are equally   25
   A link in natures chain
Form'd by the hand that formed me
   Which formeth naught in vain
All life contains as't were by chains
   From him still perfect are   30
Nor does he think the meanest link
   Unworthy of his Care

9 & *MS A3*   n *through a second* t *in* witnesing *MS 1*] witnessing *MS A3*   11 Tho]
To: wi': e *through* f *in* grief *MS A3*   13 welp *MS A3*   15 harvest's *MS A3*
16 required *altered to* requir'd *MS A3*   18 useless negro's *MS A3*
23 r *through* t *in* near *MS 1*   24 opperesed *MS A3*   26 in] of *MS A3 RL*
27 the *through* that *MS 1*] that *MS A3 RL*   formed] fomed *MS A3*   28 nought
MS A3   29 'twere *RL*   by *through* my *MS 1*   32 care *MS A3*

So let us both on him relye
   And he'll for us provide
Find us a shelter warm and drye   35
   With every thing beside
And while fools void of sense deride
   My tenderness to thee
I'll take thee home from whence I've come
   So rise and gang wi' me   40

Poor patient thing he seems to hear
   And know what I have said
He wags his tale and ventures near
   And bows his mournful head
Thou'rt welcome—come and tho' thou'rt dumb   45
   Thy silence tells thy pains
So wi' me start to share a part
   While I have aught remains

AUTOGRAPH: Nor. MS 1, pp. 138–9 (ll. 1–56), p. 222 (ll. 57–64).
Dated: 1808–19 (MS 1).

WILLIAM AND SALLEY

A Tale

Beneath a sheltering covert's shade
   Where many a tree expands
Their branches oer the neighbouring brook
   A lowley cottage stands

Meek salley child of innosence   5
   As dew wash'd lilley fair
Her widow'd mothers only hope
   Once dwelt contented there

33 lelye *MS 1*] lely *MS A3*   34 & *MS A3*   35 & dry *MS A3*   36 With]
& [With]: thing *omitted MS A3*   37 & *MS A3*   39 thee] the *MS A3*
40 & *MS A3*   42 & *MS A3*   43 tail & *MS A3*   44 & *MS A3*
45 Thourt: —come—& *MS A3*   46 t *through* s *in* tells *MS 1*] speaks *MS A3 RL*
   WILLIAM AND SALLEY   *Title:* William and Salley / A Tale.   2 expands
through oerhangs   7 wi *through* ag *in* widow'd

No tenderer Mother to a child
   Throughout the world could be   10
And in return no daughter prov'd
   More dutiful than she

For when by palsey and by age
   She was quite helpless brought
To do for her the best she could   15
   E[m]ploy'd her every thought

Alike of sorrow and of joy
   She claim'd an equal share
In short the aged helples dame
   Was salleys onley care   20

But beauteys strong resistles power
   Which oft so fatal proves
Doom'd her to feel the hopeles pain
   Of an unequal love

Young william he a youth genteel   25
   As hunting in the wood
One day pass'd by the lonley spot
   Where salleys cottage stood

O had he turnd another way
   Thrice fortunatley he   30
But fate and fortune did ordain
   It otherwise to be

Tho little thinking such a maid
   Liv'd in so mean a shed
At first to view the muddy walls   35
   He scarcely turn'd his head

18 claim'd *through* took   35 mud—dy

But when the maid approach'd his sight
    O agravating pain
He sigh'd—he felt—he knew not how—
    And look'd and look'd again   40

Frantic with love he stopt his horse
    And gaz'd with fond desire
Which act so seeming rudely done
    Set salleys face on fire

The soft rose left its station for   45
    The headache's crimson flower
Which sooner then abate his love
    Arm'd it with double power

For where real virtues jealous eye
    At trifles takes alarm   50
Such innocense triumphs repleat
    With every winning charm

Meeknes the female softnes suits
    And when they both combine
Beyond the reach of beautys boast   55
    Far sweeter graces shine

The fairest flowers that deck the wild
    The most endeangerd stand
Sure to be seen and fall a prize
    To some destroying hand   60

And well the hand that plucks their sweets
    This truth may prove and show
That plainess triumphs still secure
    While Beauty proves a foe

42 gas'd   43 seeming[ly]   53 *First* e *through* a *in* female   56 *Followed*
by two rows of asterisks   57 *Headed:* William & Sally Continued:

AUTOGRAPH: Nor. MS 1, p. 140.
TRANSCRIPTS: Nor. MS 4, pp. 59–60: Pet. MS C2, p. 55.
Dated: 1808–19 (MS 1).

SONG

Ere Meggy left hur mam an' dad
   For Lunnun in a swither
O lud whot happy deys we had
   A'tentin she'p togither
But now these happy days are oer   5
   And happy as they were
They on'y make me fret the more
   Fo' looseing o' my dear

And now w'en I am forc'd to see
   What she had us'd to like   10
That poor-old-oak her pritty tree
   And thender runnin' dyke
It makes me mope and wine an' sigh
   And feel so very quere
That then I'm aulaus' fit to die   15
   Wi misin' o' my dear

And now ye ba-lam's hold yo'r tong'es
   Go lie ye down to sleep
Ye thrushes too gie oer yo'r songs
   Or out o' hearin keep   20
For Meggy lov'd you as my sen'
   But meggy is'n't here
And now you mek me fret agen
   Wi' thinkin o' my dear

An' o ye flowers o' Meggy's choise   25
   Ye cows laps hung wi' dew
That tell how meggy wou'd rejoice
   If she could be wi' you

SONG   *Title:* Song *MS 1*   1 peggy *altered to* Meggy *MS 1*   7 f *through* g
in fret *MS 1*   11 That *through* The *MS 1*   12 thender runnin *to* yonder
running *(p.e., Clare) MS C2*   19 too *inserted MS 1*

Now alaus keep below the gres
An' never more appear   30
You on'y h'i'ten my Distress
To mind me o' my Dear

AUTOGRAPHS: Nor. MS 1, pp. 141–3 (ll. 1–84 only): Pet. MS A4,
pp. 19–20 (ll. 1–64 only): Pforzheimer Library, Misc. MS 197 (ll. 65–86
only).
TRANSCRIPT: Pet. MS B1, pp. 10–12.
Dated: ? 1815 (the date of Waterloo).

WATERLOO

Ye tip-top Southeys first in fame
Ye poets worthy of the name
Arise arise great Bards arise
And sound your harps beyond the skies
Ye finest songsters of the plains   5
Ye Bloomfields sing your sweetest strains
Touch your top notes and highest strings
While England round with musick rings
To Britton's sons the praise is due
Her Sons who faught at Waterloo   10

Ye lowliest of the lowly plain
Ye meanest of the tunefull train
With me (your lowly brother) play
A tune to cellebrate the day
The lucky day when Brittons sons   15
Had chance to prove with swords and Guns

31 You] Your *MS 1*

WATERLOO *Title:* Waterloo *MS 1*, Wild Effusions after reading an / account of
the dreadful battle (& Glorious Victory) of / Waterloo (& Glorious Victory *inserted and
pencil note:* Just after the event) *MS A4*   *Stanzas numbered 1–6 in MS A4*   2 Poets
MS A4   3 bards *MS A4*   4 &: skyes *MS A4*   7 & *MS A4*
8 music *MS A4*   9 britons *MS A4*   son's *MS 1*   10 sons: fought *through*
faught *MS A4*   12 tuneful *MS A4*   14 celebrate *MS A4*   15 B *through*
b *in* Brittons *MS 1*] britons *MS A4*   16 swords *through* sords: & guns *MS A4*

Their british courage british breed
How they could fight how they could bleed
For their own right and others too
So Nobly prov'd at Waterloo 20

Then all ye brother britons round
Still left behind on british ground
Who love to hear your Countreys fame
The glorious victorey proclaim
Let steeples bear the streaming blue 25
As Emblemn of her sons so true
While the bonfires blaze away
And the Guns and Cannons they
In thunders volly forth their praise
'Mid bursting cheers of loud Huzza's 30
Their fame demands all ye can do
To crown her sons at Waterloo

I from my labour will away
And twirl my beaver to Huzza
Now triumphing victories voice 35
Bids me for her sons rejoice
True bred sons of Britons isle
Boastfull thought creates a smile
Now it comes adieu to toil
And my rural strains awhile 40
Englands Victory now prevails
Over loves unfinish'd tales
Yes yes my bosom's fir'd from you
Ye British flowers at Waterloo

18 *First* they *inserted MS 1*   19–20 *Through* & t'was a noble stance for you / Ye
British plowmen of Waterloo *MS 1*   19 own *inserted MS 1*   & *MS A4*
20 nobly: waterloo *MS A4*   21 Then britons to your country dear *MS A4*
22 Whose pride is her success to hear *MS A4*   23 Whose glory is your countrys
fame (Who glory in *altered to* Whose glory is) *MS A4*   24 victorey] victory now
MS A4   26 As *through* An: Emblem *MS A4*   28 & *twice*: guns: cannons
MS A4   29 that *through* thy *MS 1*   30 huzza's *MS A4*   32 W *through*
w *in* Waterloo *MS 1*] waterloo *MS A4*   34 &: huzza *MS A4*   35 When *to*
Now *(p.e.) MS 1*   triumphings *MS A4*   36 regoice *MS A4*   37 son o'
britons *MS A4*   38 Boastful *MS A4*   39 When *to* Now *(p.e.) MS 1*   its
come *MS A4*   40 & *MS A4*   41 Victory *through indecipherable MS 1*] victory
MS A4   43 bosoms *MS A4*   44 british: waterloo *MS A4*

The Cannons roar in fancys ear   45
And long extended lines appear
All in motion! all in arms!
Drums still beating to alarms
Guns their vollies pour again
Smoak decends to hide the slain   50
Britons wounded—glorious sight!
With redoubl'd fury fight
Prolong it fancy—let me view
How Britons faught at Waterloo

Whats Commanded now the cry   55
'Charge like Britons' rend the sky
O! the savage blade is drawn
Now the bloody work comes on
Off they start Huzza's the noise
O! your Courage british boys   60
Now the soldier's valour's try'd
Soldiers flail on Englands side
Fancy rest—the trumpet blew
Victorys gain'd at Waterloo

Now my Country's glory come   65
Sheath your swords and march for home
Welcome to your native Isle
Here in triumph from your toil
March near deaf'n'd with Huzza's
Which we for your valour raise   70
For your valours glorious deeds
Englands Highest hope exceeds
All her boast and all her pride
True-blue britons prov'd and try'd
Come away your foes have flew   75
Thunder struck from Waterloo

45 cannons *MS A4*   46 & *MS A4*   47 motion∧: arms∧ *MS A4*
50 ascends *to* decends *(p.e.) MS 1*] descends *MS A4*   51 sight∧ *MS A4*
54 brittons: waterloo *MS A4*   55 comanded *MS A4*   56 britons' *MS A4*
59 'Huzza's' *MS A4*   60 courage *MS A4*   61 soldiers valours *MS A4*
62 flail] hail *MS A4*   63 trumpets *MS A4*   65 Countrys *Pfz*   66 & *Pfz*
67 isle *Pfz*   69 ne'er deafen'd: huzzas *Pfz*   72 England highest hopes *Pfz*
73 & *Pfz*   74 provd & *Pfz*   76 Thunder-struck: waterloo *Pfz*

Hero's all alike in Fame
None more worthy of the name
By his fellow none out brav'd
All as one in fight behav'd   80
British courage bold & true
Fir'd the noble army through
Gen'rals Privates all as one
Each at heart a Wellin[g]ton
Heroes hail—accept your due   85
Glory—fame,—& Waterloo

AUTOGRAPHS: Pforzheimer Library, Misc. MS 197: Nor. MS 1, p. 143.
TRANSCRIPT: Pet. MS B1, p. 17.
Dated: 1808–19 (MS 1).

A PLOUGHMANS SKILL AT CLASSIFICATION
AFTER THE LINEIAN ARRANGEMENT

'Go wipe your shoes' says mistress shrew
To Hodge who up for's dinner drew
' 'Tis'n't fitting that such hogs as you
'Shou'd come into a house'
'Why not' says hodge—'if thats the case   5
'I cant come in a better place
'For surely there is no disgrace
  For *hogs* to herd wi' *Sows*

77 fame *Pfz*   79 By *through* Al *MS 1*   82 Fird *Pfz*   83 privates *Pfz*
84 Wellington *Pfz*   *Followed by a row of asterisks MS 1*   85–6 *Copy-text: Pfz*
A PLOUGHMANS SKILL AT CLASSIFICATION AFTER THE LINEIAN
ARRANGEMENT *Title:* A Ploughmans Skill / at Classification / after the Lineian
Arrangement *Pfz, wanting MS 1   All quotation marks omitted MS 1*   1 Mistres
MS 1   2 s *through* r in for's *Pfz*] 'for's *MS 1*   3 'T'isn't: that *through* for
MS 1   4 Should *MS 1*   5 Why . . . of] O yes says Hodge if *MS 1*
8 hogs *and* Sows *not underlined:* herd] be: wi *MS 1*

AUTOGRAPH: Nor. MS 1, p. 146.
Dated: 1808–19 (MS 1).

TO THE WINDS

Ye hollow Winds that thro the Woodlands Rave
Pleasd do I view you Wreath their leafy Grains
& Roll in Waves the Grassy Bented Plains
& Verge the Silver Pool in Cooling Waves
Pierst as I am with never ceasing pains   5
Vext as I am with hopes decietful strains

AUTOGRAPHS: Nor. MS 1, p. 146: Pet. MS A3, p. 106.
TRANSCRIPT: Pet. MS B1, p. 171.
Dated: 'Old' (MS A3, p. 106).

A SCHOOL BOYS WIT

Go Silly Brains the Master said
To one who'd misd a Letter
A Dunces Cap shall fit your head
If you dont do no better
'Boy instant upward cast his eye   5
On's masters nodle winking
The Master ask'd the Reason why
Why sir says he Im thinking

TO THE WINDS   *Title:* To the Winds   *Preceded by:*

   Ye Hollow Wind that Wave along the Woods
   Pleasd do I view you Reath their leafy Grains
   & Rolling Wave the Grass along the plains
   & Curling Verge along the silver floods

1 thro *through* wave

A SCHOOL BOYS WIT   *Title: wanting MS 1,* A School Boys wit *MS A3*
1 'Go silly Brains': master *MS A3* 2 miss'd *MS A3* 3 'A: cap *MS A3*
4 'If: do] learn: better' *MS A3* 5 Boy Instant *MS A3* 6 noddle *MS A3*
7 master: reason why? *MS A3* 8 'Why' says the boy 'Im thinking' *MS A3*

As yours & my head seem o' kin
To save ye farther trouble   10
It would when once your hand is in
Be best to make a couple

AUTOGRAPH: Nor. MS 1, p. 147 (pencil).
Dated: 1808–19 (MS 1).

For her my youth in fruitles hopes decay
For her black sadnes turns the day to night
Awd by her frown my chill soul shrank away
& life it self grows hateful to my sight

AUTOGRAPH: Nor. MS 1, p. 147.
Dated: 1808–19 (MS 1).

O worst of anguish in that aching heart
When fate not choise ordains true love to part
While truest love with strongest ties does bind
With natures choice & coresponding mind

9 'As *MS A3*   10 'To *MS A3*   11 'It wou'd *MS A3*   12 'Be: Couple'
MS A3
FOR HER MY YOUTH IN FRUITLES HOPES DECAY   *Title: wanting*
O WORST OF ANGUISH   *Title: wanting*

AUTOGRAPH: Nor. MS 1, pp. 148–9 (ll. 21–6 pencil).
Dated: 1808–19 (MS 1).

THE NOSEGAY

Sweet Philis as fair as the hedge Rosey seems
& while the maids Envy the charms she displays
The swains to gain favour are planning their schemes
& daily to please her try all winning ways
Their nosegays all charm her—I knew what she lovd   5
T'other day I took courage to try for the Maid
I hopd—& I sought for the flowers she approvd
& presented the gift as she sat in the shade
O the magic of Beauty—the power of her eyes
How I trembld approaching her near   10
She turnd a look to'ard me of carles suprise
O my heart how it flutterd for fear
As soon as she saw me she rose from her seat
I approochd her—stood silent—Made a bow & admir'd
& the Nosegay I gatherd—laid it down at her feet   15
She than[k]d me & pickd out the best & Retird
But shepherd take courage when on[c]e you begin
Let trifles neer daunt—nor by fears be subdud
Fair maids are too fickle for faint hearts to win
I still trusted hope—dispeld fears——& pursud   20

THE NOSEGAY   *Title:* The Nosegay   *On p. 147:*

> For Phillis's nosgay I yesterday rovd
> & to come at the prize how I wanderd the plains
> I knew the fair flowers which the charmer approvd
> & to try for her favour I spared no pains

*(*l. 1 yesterday *over* [painfully])
5 & *over* —
12/13

> [But shepherds take courage when once you begin
> Let trifles neer scare you as ive often done
> Fair maids are too fickle for faint hearts to win
> I relyd upon hopes—dispeld fears—& went on]

(l. 3 faint hearts *over* [fair maids])

She fled but her swiftnes neer seemd like retreat
Oft turning behind her the meaning I gesst
She waited to hear me I was not to seek
While I begd that a kis for my pains mite be spard
She smild her consent—wipt the curls from her cheek   25
& the sweets of those Roseys provd double reward

AUTOGRAPH: Nor. MS 1, p. 149.
Dated: 1808–19 (MS 1).

Thrice welcome to thy slumbering peace o Grave
Tho when as yet thou art I know it not
Thee I address as death the stroke had gave
& laid me happy in thy silent spot
O could I lay me down with thee in peace   5
Would Death but be my friend I should be blest
With thee the wicked from their troubling cease
With thee the weary lie & are at rest

AUTOGRAPH: Nor. MS 1, p. 150 (pencil).
Dated: 1808–19 (MS 1).

O should these humble artles strains
Sweet myras bosom move
To pity the sad Shepherds pains
I then may hope to love

SHE FLED BUT HER SWIFTNES NEER SEEMD LIKE RETREAT   *Title:*
wanting   3 *Over* [The meaning I instantly guest] *followed by a space for two*
lines

THRICE WELCOME TO THY SLUMBERING PEACE O GRAVE   *Title:*
wanting   5 downw   8 & *through* a

O SHOULD THESE HUMBLE ARTLES STRAINS   *Title: wanting*

—Sweet Angel pity & pursue   5
O Shun the scornful maid
& in the slighted Henry view
Your collins self pourtrayd

Ah could his anguish be reveald
—What hoples days hes lovd   10
Which shame for ever keeps conceald
Your bosom might be movd

Go aching heart & meet her eye
Your only cure to find
Compasion cannot but comply   15
Your pain will make her kind

Go mournful tale to Myra go
Inscribd with collins name
Go let her read sad Henrys woe
& wisper thine the same   20

AUTOGRAPHS: Pet. MS A4, pp. 17–18: Nor. MS 1, pp. 151–2.
TRANSCRIPTS: Pet. MS B1, pp. 140–1: Nor. MS 5, pp. 67–8.
Printed in *RL*, pp. 62–4 (ll. 13–16 omitted).
Dated: 'old' (MS A4, p. 17).

ADDRESS
TO AN INSIGNIFICANT FLOWER OBSCURELY
BLOOMING IN A LONELY WILD

And tho thou seemst a weedling wild
    Wild & neglected like to me
Thou still art dear to natures child
    & I will stoop to notice thee

5 & pursue *over* [while you view]   13 & . . . eye *over* [before her eye]
ADDRESS TO AN INSIGNIFICANT FLOWER OBSCURELY BLOOMING
IN A LONELY WILD   *Title*: Address / To an Insignificant Flower obscurely
blooming / in a lonely wild *MS A3 RL*, To an Insignificant Flower obscurely growing /
in a lonely Wild *MS 1*   2 and *MS 1*   4 And *MS 1*

For oft like thee, in wild retreat   5
   Aray'd in humble garb like thee
Theres many a seeming weed proves sweet
   As sweet as garden flowers can be

& like to thee, each seeming weed
   Flowers unregarded like to thee   10
Without improvement—runs to seed
   Wild & neglected like to me

Like unto thee, so mean & low
   Nothing boasting like to thee
No flattering dresses tempting show   15
   Can tempt a friend to notice me

& like to thee, when beautys cloath'd
   In lowly raiment like to thee
Disdaining pride (by beauty loath'd)
   No beauties there can never see   20

For like to thee, my Emma blows
   Flowers like to thee I dearly prize
& like to thee, her humble cloaths
   Hides every charm from prouder eyes

5 thee∧: hurld *altered to* wild *MS 1*   8 sweet *through* sour *MS A4*   9 &]
But: thee∧: each] these: weeds *MS 1*   10 For want of culture like to thee *MS 1*
11 Without *through* Wanting *MS A4*   Can never live to raise their seed *MS 1*
12 Kill'd by the scorn that murders me *MS 1*   13–16 *Replaced in MS 1 by:*

    And like to thee for want of friends
     All wild and friendless like to thee
    They drop forgot without amends
     The Certain fate that waiteth me

    For like to the I've naught to show   5
     And as ive nothing:—like to thee
    No flattering bard will never go
     To force a tear to flatter me

(l. 5 I've *through* as)

13 unto to *MS A4*   17 And: thee∧: beauties cloth'd *MS 1*   19 Disdainful *RL*
20 u *through* w *in* beauties *MS A4*] Beauties *MS 1*   there] then *MS 1*   ever *RL*
21 For like to thee my Hellen blows *to* For like thee the humble beauty blows *(p.e.) MS 1*
22 Flowers like to] A flower like *RL*   And like to thee her sweets I prize *MS 1*
23 But lucky thing *to* & like to thee *(p.e.) MS 1*   24 Hide *RL*   every charm] her
sweets *MS 1*

Altho like thee, a lowly flower   25
 If fancied by a polish'd eye
It soon would bloom beyond my power
 The finest flower beneath the sky

& like to thee, lives many a swain
 With Genius blest—but like to thee   30
So humble, lowly, mean & plain
 No one will notice them nor—me

So like to thee, they live unknown
 Wild weeds obscure—& like to thee
Their sweets are sweet to them alone   35
 —The only pleasure known to me

Yet when I'm dead lets hope I have
 Some friend in store as I'm to thee
That will find out my lowly grave
 & heave a sight to notice me   40

AUTOGRAPH: Nor. MS 1, p. 153.
TRANSCRIPTS: Nor. MS 4, p. 65: Pet. MS C2, p. 58.
Dated: 1808–19 (MS 1).

THE LUCKLESS JOURNEY

Tho' fine prov'd the morning O sad prov'd the ramble
 Adown by the Willows adown by the lee
Adown by the cottage where Hedge rows of bramble
 Hides it from all strangers but unlucky me

25 For tho *to* Alltho *(p.e.) MS 1*] But though *RL*   thee ∧ *MS 1*   27 She
RL   would *through* should: bloom *through* climb *MS A4*   e *in* beyond *inserted MS 1*
28 skye *MS 1*   28/9 [& like to thee, lives many a swain / With many a beauty like
to thee] *MS A4*   29 And: thee ∧: lives many] there lives *MS 1*   30 Would
sing as sweet as sweets from thee *MS 1*   31 But like to thee so mean so plain *MS 1*
32 or *RL*   No finer men will look on me *MS 1*   33 thee ∧: they] I *MS 1*
34 Wild weeds] A weed: obscure ∧ and *MS 1*   35 My: sweet] sweets: to me
alone *through three indecipherable words MS 1*   are *through* & *MS A4*   36 ∧ The:
known *through ?* shown *MS 1*   37 [I] hope *MS A4*   39 will *through ?* shall
MS A4   lowley Grave *MS 1*   40 And: heave a sigh] shed a tear *MS 1*
    THE LUCKLESS JOURNEY   *Title:* The Luckless Journey *MS 1*

For there I espied and admir'd a young rosie   5
   I lov'd and had hopes in possesing the flower
Till Cupid flew laughing away with the posie
   And left me the thorns which I feel at this hour

O Willows and brambles—what deamon beset me
   To make me to go where your cottage arose   10
Yet still was you all I could hope to forget ye
   But o there's no hopes in forgetting the rose
The wounds are not lightly that abscence should ease 'em
   No no they'r so deep twill but poison the pain
Tho lifes sober autumn may wisely appease 'em   15
   A pang sad Remembrance will ever retain

AUTOGRAPH: Nor. MS 1, pp. 155–7 (ll. 1–90), p. 170 (ll. 91–8), p. 172
(ll. 99–118).
Dated: 1808–19 (MS 1).

     By lonesom Woods & Unfrequented Streams
     How oft I stretch me in the Silent Shade
     Hopefully Wishing in some pleasing dreams
     To Catch a 'zemblance of the lovley Maid
     But ah I lay me on the Ground in vain   5
     Waking or Sleeping—be it as It will
     Distressing Scenes disturb my Frantic Brain
     & Grief & Anguish my Companions still
     Nay even when my Flimsy hope prevails
     & I to Clasp her stretch my arms in vain   10
     In that Fond Moment the False Vision fails
     & Waking leaves me to severer pain
     O Wheres the Man that lives to mourn like me
     & in vain Sighs to Waste his lingering Breath
     When easy Ways are known to set him free   15
     & make him happy in the arms of Death

had *inserted MS 1*

BY LONESOM WOODS & UNFREQUENTED STREAMS   *Title: wanting*
strecth   6 I will *altered to* It will   14 e *in* Breath *inserted*

These 8 long years have I for Myra sigh'd
So long the Angel which I only prizd
These 8 long years have I endurd her pride
So long a Lover & so long despis'd   20
But ah deluding hope is always near
To Wisper Joys that serve to Sweeten Life
With better times she fills my greedy ear
& still that Myra lives her Damons Wife
Deluded hopes & more deluded Man   25
Oh still how canst thou dally with thy pain
When Reason plain detecting every plan
Shows every Wish & every hope is vain
Hear lovley Girl & hearing O be kind
For once let pity that dear bosom melt   30
Tis no pert fop to Flattery inclind
That Mocks & tells the Pains he never felt
No tis thy Damon in whose choise so free
Myra alone the fairest Angel seems
Of all the World who fancies none but thee   35
The only Girl his aching heart esteems
Tis him who sighs his love in Myras ear
Tis him who sues for Pity at her feet
Tis him reveals—& O reveals in fear
But still in hopes—a kind return to meet   40
Say lovley Maid—for thou alone canst tell
May Damon hope—or hopes his heart in vain
May he still Wish that all may yet be Well
Myra prove kind & he releasd from pain
Or is he doomd in Misery to live   45
& drag this hated Life unto a Close
Unnoticd still & she no promise give
To ease this heart of her oerburdend Woes
Speak lovley Girl to What I here enjoin
Is sorrow ended now or not begun   50
For still this Weak this foolish heart of mine
Relies on hopes till the last Moments gone
A Hopeful Captive while I'm doomd to be

42 Damon *inserted*   47 s *through* y *in* she   52 till *inserted*

Still must I live to hug these gauling chains
Which Cupid de[i]gns thy Slave should wear for thee   55
Till the last Ray of Glimmering hope remains
Yes lovley Girl (tho Weary now of Life)
Still will I linger on with hopes in store

Till then sweet Girl (tho weary now of Life)
I'll linger on in hopes as here to fore   60
But when I Myra find anothers Wife
Then Hopes Adieu—thy Lubin lives no more
I once flushd with hopes catchd from Myra a smile
& venturd to sue for a kiss
O heavens thought I [h]eres an end to my toil   65
& this the beginning of Bliss
Myra once flushd my hopes with a smile
& I venturd to sue for a kiss
O I deemd it an end of my toil
& the safe promisd era of Bliss   70
But ah my Congectures were vain
Some trifles were still incompleat
Some doubts still creating a pain
To mingle the bitter & sweet
I prest her dear hand—plain my love might be spelt   75
With the fondest impatience I burnd
But O who can tell what a coldness I felt
When I found not the token returnd

I thought I Read love in her eyes
But when her soft Bosom I prest   80
It alarmd me with jealous suprise
To find that her heart was at Rest
Ah alas to my self then I sighd
Now I hopd that my sorrows were done
But the nearer she comes to be tryd   85
Plainer proves that they'r only begun
Sad tokens too plainly they prove
Tho this silly heart will not see
That she but disembles her love
& has not the least Value for me   90

65 an] and   67–70 *Alternative to ll. 63–6*   70 safe *inserted*

Since Prayers & entreaties with Myra is vain
Since her Bosom no pity bestows
Since she mocks with derision my sorows & pain
& makes but a jist of my woes
Grown hardend in croses no more Ill complain   95
Nor look with a languishing eye
—& this fond heart Ill burst it in spite of its pains
Ere it shall have vent for a Sigh

Ye oaks spreding round me so mournful & Green
What I feel now I traverse this spot   100
To think that I Wander unknown & Unseen
Neglected despisd & forgot
For theres not an object seems fair to the eye
(Unceasing Remembrance of pain)
But minds me of her & creates a fresh sigh   105
To think that I love her in vain
O was there a Leaf or a twig or a flower
Nay a blade of low Grass sprung in here
By the hand of false My[ra] presd under this bower
I would worship this blade with a tear   100
Ah me I will search for a smooth rined tree
& the name of dear Myra engrave
& there (as the best consolation for me)
Bow to the inscription—a slave
O Sensibility now Im alone   115
What thro thee am I doomd to endure
Fellow Clowns ah theyre happy with hearts of their own
In ignorance Resting secure

105 a fresh] atfresh

AUTOGRAPHS: Pet. MS A4, pp. 9–12: Nor. MS 1, pp. 158–61 (ll. 45–8, 69–72 omitted): Norris Museum SAVNM CL/6 (ll. 45–8 only).
TRANSCRIPTS: Pet. MS B1, pp. 148–50: Nor. MS 5, pp. 11–16 (ll. 73–6 omitted).
Printed in *RL*, pp. 73–9 (ll. 73–6 omitted).
Dated: '1815' (MS A4, p. 9, *RL* Introduction, p. xxii).

THE VILLAGE FUNERAL

To yon low church with solemn sounding knell
(Which 'tother day as rigid fate decreed
Mournfully knoll'd a widows passing bell)
The village funeral's warned to proceed

Mournfull indeed the orphans friends are fled   5
Their fathers tender care has long been past
The widows toil was all their hopes of bread
& now the grave awaits to seize the last

But that providing power forever high
The universal friend of all distress   10
Is sure to hear their supplicating cry
& prove a Father to the fatherless

Now from the low mud cottage on the more
By two & two sad bend the weeping train
The coffin ready near the propt-up door   15
Now slow proceeds along the wayward lane

THE VILLAGE FUNERAL *Title:* The Village Funeral *MS A4 MS 1 RL*
1 From *altered to* To: church *over* [spire] *MS A4*   Now tolls the Curfew from yon steeple tall *MS 1*   2 Yon taper steeple just across the mead *MS 1*   3 Tis the last sommons the last piercing call *MS 1*   4 To bid the mournful Funeral proceede *MS 1*   5 Mournful indeed; for lo! a Mother's dead!   6 Their fathers tender *through* Where the fathers fond *MS A4*   And left her babes (perhaps) without a friend *MS 1*   7 hope *RL*   Babes quite unable yet to get their bread *MS 1*   8 And o! if friend less what will be their End *MS 1*   9 But God allmercifull for ever nigh *MS 1*   10 That tender father to the father less *MS 1* 12 prove *through indecipherable MS A4*   And prove their friend in this their sad distress *MS 1*   13 Yon is the low-mud Cottage on the moor *MS 1* 14 By two & two] Where oer the corse *MS 1*   15 The . . . near] Lo now they issue from *MS 1*   16 slow proceeds *through* slowly wends *MS A4*   And now slow move along the way-ward lane *MS 1*

While as they nearer draw in solemn state
The Village neighbours are assembld round
& seem with fond anxiety to wait
The sad procession in the burial ground   20

Yet every face the face of sorrow wears
& now the solemn scene approaches nigh
Each to make way for the slow march prepares
& on the Coffin casts a serious eye

Now walks the Curate thro the silent crowd   25
In snowy surplis loosly banded round
Now meets the corse & now he reads aloud
In mournful tone along the burial ground

The church they enter & adown the isle
(Which more then usual wears a solemn hue)   30
They rest the Coffin on set firms awhile
Till the good priest performs the office due

& tho by duty aw'd to silence here
The orphans grief so piercing force a way
& O so moving do their griefs appear   35
The worthy pastor kneels in tears to pray

The funeral rites performd by custom thought
A tribute sacred & essential here
Now to the last, last place the bodys brought
Where all (dread fate) are summond to appear   40

17 sollemn *MS 1*   18 Neighbours: assembled *MS 1*   19 &] That
MS 1   20 The sad procession] For the sad funeral *MS 1*   in *through* to *MS A4*
22 And *MS 1*   24 And: coffin: serious] tender: eye *through* sigh *MS 1*
25 thro': r *in* crowd *inserted MS 1*   26 snowy] showy: r *in* surplis *inserted MS 1*
27 meets *through* met: Corse *MS 1*   28 Burial *MS 1*   29 Church: and
MS 1   30 than *MS 1*   31 forms *RL*   33 And: awd *MS 1*
34 The orphans] Yet still their *MS 1*   away *MS A4*   35 And o *MS 1*
36 prey *MS A4*   36/7 The funeral rites performd (which custom bears
/ (As tributes sacred and essetial here / Now to the last last place / The *MS 1*
37 Custom *MS 1*   38 Tribute *MS 1*   39 last, last *underlined MS A4*
40 Where] Whence *RL*, Whence *altered to* Where *Harvard proof copy*

The Churchyard round a mournfull view displays
Views where mortality is plainly pennd
Drear seems the object which the eye surveys
As objects pointing to our lat[t]er end

There the lank nettles sicken ere they seed   45
Where from old trees eves cordial vainly falls
To raise or comfort each dejected weed
While pattering drops decay the crumbling walls

Here stands far distant from the pomp of pride
Mean little stones thin scatterd here & there   50
By the scant means of poverty apply'd
The fond memorial of her friends to bear

O memory thou sweet enliv'ning power
Thou shadow of that fame all hope to find
The meanest soul exerts her utmost power   55
To leave some fragment of thy name behind

Now croud the sad spectators round to see
The deep sunk grave—whose heap of swelling moulds
Full of the fragments of mortality
Makes the heart shudder while the eye beholds   60

41 Mournful *through ?* weary *MS 1*   42 mortallity: pend *MS 1*   43 seem
RL   objects *MS 1 RL*   44 pointing *repeated*: latter *MS 1*
45–8

⟨There sic⟩kly nettles scarcly lives to seed
⟨Whe⟩r each old tree eves [burthen] cordial vainly falls
⟨There the⟩ wank nettle's dying while it seeds
⟨& each⟩ old trees Eves cordial vainly falls
⟨To raise⟩ or comfort the dgected weed   5
⟨While pa⟩ttering drops decay the crumbling walls *Norris*

(Torn; ll. 3–4 alternatives to ll. 1–2; l. 2 old through aged; l. 3 wank for 'wrank')

45 sicken *through* dye *MS A4*   46 While *through* Where *MS A4*   49 stand
RL   pomp *through* reach *MS A4*] reach *MS 1*   50 and *MS 1*   53 memory
underlined MS A4] Memory, *underlined MS 1*   sweet *through* fond *MS A4*   enliveing
altered to enliv'ning *MS A4*] enlivening *MS 1*   56 leave *inserted MS A4*   thy] a *RL*
57 croud *through ?* closd *MS A4*] crowd *MS 1*   58 mold *RL*   60 shudder
inserted MS A4   eyes behold *RL*

Aw'd is the mind by dreaded truths imprest
To think that dust which they before them see
Once livd like them!—chill concience tells the rest
That like that dust themselves must shortly be

The gaping grave now claims its destind prey   65
'Ashes to ashes dust to dust' is given
The parent earth recieves her kindred clay
& starts the soul to meet its home in heaven

Ah helpless babes now grief in horror shrieks
Now sorrow pauses dumb.—each looker on   70
Knows not the urging language which it speaks
'—A friend,—provider,—this worlds all is gone'

Such feeling grief lost Emigrants suround
When on some foreign land they seek redress
Hopeless they cast their wishful eyes around   75
& see no one to notice their distress

Envy & malice now have lost their aim
Slanders reproachful tongue can rail no more
Her foes now pity where they us'd to blame
The faults & foibles of this life are oer   80

The orphans grief & sorrows so severe
From every heart in pitys language speaks
Een the rough sexton can't withold the tear
That steals unnotic'd down his furrowd cheeks

63 them∧—Chill *MS 1*   conciense *altered to* consience *MS A4*] Concience *MS 1*
64 Dust *MS 1*   65 —The: destin'd *MS 1*   66 Dust *(fourth word) MS 1*
68: And: Soul: heaven— *MS 1*   the soul starts *RL*   70 dumb.— *through* ?silent
MS A4   72 is *over* [was] *MS A4*   73 feeling grief lost *over* [savageness
the lost]: s *in* Emigrants *inserted*: suround *over* [has found] *MS A4*   Such sorrows as
the emigrant has found *MS 1*   74 on] in *MS 1*   land *inserted*: they *through* he:
seek[s] *MS A4*   he seeks *MS 1*   75 Hopless *MS 1*   they cast their *through* he
casts his *MS A4*] he cast his *MS 1*   76 And *MS 1*   sees *MS A4 MS 1*   their
through his *MS A4*] his *MS 1*   78 can] need *over* [can] *MS 1*   79 blaim *MS 1*
80 this] vain *MS 1*   81 The orphans grief *through three indecipherable words MS A4*
sorrow *RL*   82 From] To: speak *RL*   83 Een *through* E'n *MS A4*] E'en *MS 1*
w[h]ithold *MS A4*   84 that: unnotis'd *MS 1*   cheek *RL*

Who is but grievd to see the fatherless 85
Stroll with their rags unnotisc'd thro the street
What eye but moistens at their sad distress
& sheds compassions tear where ere they meet

Yon Workhouse stands as their asylum now
The place where poverty demands to live 90
Where parish bounty scouls his scornful brow
& grudges the scant fare he's forc'd to give—

O may I dye before I'm doom'd to seek
That last resource of hope but ill suply'd
To claim the humble pittance once a week 95
Which justice forces from disdainful pride

Where the lost orphan lowly bending weeps
Unnotisc'd by the heedless as they pass
There the grave closes where a mother sleeps
With brambles platted on the tufted grass 100

85 but is *RL*   fatherless *MS A4*   What soul unpitying views the fatherless *MS 1*
86 The friendless orphan stroll about the street *MS 1*   87 sad distress *(pencil)*
MS 1   88 *Line in pencil MS 1*   compasions *MS 1*   89 Workhouse
underlined MS A4] parish house *MS 1*   stands as] is *MS 1*   90 The]
That: Poverty *MS 1*   91 scouls] shows *MS 1*   92 Grudges: hes: give∧
MS 1   93 —O: Im doomd *MS 1*   94 rescource: but ill suply'd] where
wants abide *MS 1*   95 the] that *over* [my] *MS 1*   96 Justice force's *MS 1*
—Where: Orphan *MS 1*   98 (Unnotisc'd: pass) *MS 1*   99 Grave closes—:
Mother *MS 1*   100 on] oer *MS 1*

AUTOGRAPH: Nor. MS 1, pp. 162–9.
TRANSCRIPTS: Nor. MS 4, pp. 60–4: Pet. MS C2, pp. 55–57a.
Dated: '1818' (MS 1, p. 162).

THE LAMENTATIONS OF ROUND-OAK WATERS

Oppress'd wi' grief a double share
   Where Round oak waters flow
I one day took a sitting there
   Recounting many a woe
My naked seat without a shade   5
   Did cold and blealy shine
Which fate was more agreable made
   As sympathising mine

The wind between the north and East
   Blow'd very chill and cold   10
Or coldly blow'd to me at least
   My cloa'hs were thin and old
The grass all dropping wet wi' dew
   Low bent their tiney spears
The lowly daise' bended too   15
   More lowly wi my tears

(For when my wretched state appears
   Hurt friendless poor and starv'd
I never can withold my tears
   To think how I am sarv'd   20
To think how money'd men delight
   More cutting then the storm
To make a sport and prove their might
   O' me a fellow worm)

With arms reclin'd upon my knee   25
   In mellancholly form
I bow'd my head to misery
   And yielded to the storm

THE LAMENTATIONS OF ROUND-OAK WATERS   *Title:* The Lamentations
of / Round-Oak Waters *MS 1*   2 flow[s] *MS 1*

And there I fancied uncontrould
　　My sorrows as they flew   30
Unnotic'd as the waters rowl'd
　　Where all unnoticd too

But soon I found I was deciev'd
　　For waken'd by my Woes
The naked stream of shade bereav'd   35
　　In grievous murmurs rose

'Ah luckless youth to sorrow born
　　'Shun'd Son of Poverty
'The worlds make gamely sport and scorn
　　'And grinning infamy   40
'Unequall'd tho thy sorrows seem
　　'And great indeed they are
'O hear my sorrows for my stream
　　'You'll find an equal there'

'I am the genius of the brook   45
　　'And like to thee I moan
'By Naiads and by all forsook
　　'Unheeded and alone
'Distress and sorrow quickly proves
　　'The friend sincere & true   50
'Soon as our happines removes
　　'Pretenders bids adieu'

'Here I have been for many a year
　　'And how My brook has been
'How pleasures lately flourish'd here   55
　　'Thy self has often seen
'The willows waving wi' the wind
　　'And here & there a thorn
'Did please thy Mellancholly mind
　　'And did My banks adorn'   60

31 the] they: waters *through* flew *MS 1*   36 *Space left for completion of stanza MS 1*
43 O *through* Ye *MS 1*   52 bids *MS 1*   54 My *through* thy *MS 1*

'And here the shepherd with his sheep
'And with his lovley maid
'Together where these waters creep
'In loitering dalliance play'd
'And here the Cowboy lov'd to sit   65
'And plate his rushy thongs
'And dabble in the fancied pit
'And chase the Minnow throngs'

'And when thou didst thy horses tend
'Or drive the ploughmans team   70
'Thy mind did natturally bend
'Towards my pleasing stream
'And different pleasures fill'd thy breast
'And different thy employ
'And different feelings thou possest   75
'From any other Boy'

'The sports which they so dearley lov'd
'Thou could's't not bear to see
'And joys which they as joys approv'd
'Ne'er seem'd as joys to thee   80
'The Joy was thine couldst thou but steal
'From all their Gambols rude
'In some lone thicket to consceal
'Thyself in Sollitude'

'There didst thou Joy & love to sit   85
'The briars and brakes among
'To exercise thy infant wit
'In fancied tale or song
'And there the inscect & the flower
'Would court thy curious eye   90
'To muse in wonder on that power
'Which dwells above the sky'

---

67 dabble in *through* scrabble oer *MS 1*   69 horeses *MS 1*   75 different
inserted MS 1

'But now alas my charms are done
    'For shepherds & for thee
'The Cow boy with his Green is gone   95
    'And every Bush & tree
'Dire nakedness oer all prevails
    'Yon fallows bare and brown
'Is all beset wi' post & rails
    'And turned upside down'   100

'The gentley curving darksom bawks
    'That stript the Cornfields o'er
'And prov'd the Shepherds daily walks
    'Now prove his walks no more
'The plough has had them under hand   105
    'And over turnd 'em all
'And now along the elting Land
    'Poor swains are forc'd to maul'

'And where yon furlong meets the lawn
    'To Ploughmen Oh! how sweet   110
'When they had their long furrow drawn
    'Its Eddings to their feet
'To rest 'em while they clan'd their plough
    'And light their Loaded Shoe
'But ah—there's ne'ery Edding now   115
    'For neither them nor you'

'The bawks and Eddings are no more
    'The pastures too are gone
'The greens the Meadows & the moors
    'Are all cut up & done   120
'There's scarce a greensward spot remains
    'And scarce a single tree
'All naked are thy native plains
    'And yet they're dear to thee'

101 l *in* gentley *inserted MS 1*   107 now *inserted MS 1*   115 ne'ery *through*
ne'er *MS 1*   *never any*   124 And *through* Tho *MS 1*

'But O! my brook my injur'd brook   125
  ' 'T'is that I most deplore
'To think how once it us'd to look
  'How it must look no more
'And hap'ly fate thy wanderings bent
  'To sorrow here wi' me   130
'For to none else could I lament
  'And mourn to none but thee'

'Thou art the whole of musing swains
  'That's now resideing here
'Tho one ere while did grace my plains   135
  'And he to thee was dear
'Ah—dear he was—for now I see
  'His Name grieves thee at heart
'Thy silence speaks that Misery
  'Which Language cant impart'   140

'O T[urnil]l T[urnil]l dear should thou
  'To this fond Mourner be
'By being so much troubl'd now
  'From just a Nameing thee
'Nay I as well as he am griev'd   145
  'For oh I hop'd of thee
'That hadst thou stay'd as I believd
  'Thou wouldst have griev'd for me'

'But ah he's gone the first o' swains
  'And left us both to moan   150
'And thou art all that now remains
  'With feelings like his own
'So while the thoughtles passes by
  'Of sence & feelings void
'Thine be the Fancy painting Eye   155
  'On by'gone scenes employ'd'

---

133 musings *MS 1*   140 impart.' *MS 1*   141 T———l T———l *MS 1*
154 void' *MS 1*

'Look backward on the days of yore
   'Upon my injur'd brook
'In fancy con its Beauties o'er
   'How it had us'd to look   160
'O then what trees my banks did crown
   'What Willows flourishd here
'Hard as the ax that Cut them down
   'The senceless wretches were'

'But sweating slaves I do not blame   165
   'Those slaves by wealth decreed
'No I should hurt their harmless name
   'To brand 'em wi' the deed
'Altho their aching hands did wield
   'The axe that gave the blow   170
'Yet 't'was not them that own'd the field
   'Nor plan'd its overthrow'

'No no the foes that hurt my field
   'Hurts these poor moilers too
'And thy own bosom knows & feels   175
   'Enough to prove it true
'And o poor souls they may complain
   'But their complainings all
'The injur'd worms that turn again
   'But turn again to fall'   180

'Their foes and mine are lawless foes
   'And L–ws thems——s they hold
'Which clipt-wing'd Justice cant oppose
   'But forced yields to G–d
'These are the f—s of mine & me   185
   'These all our Ru–n plan'd
'Altho they never felld a tree
   'Or took a tool in hand'

159 Beatuies *MS 1*   182 *Laws themselves*   hold' *MS 1*   185 *foes*
186 *Ruin*

'Ah cruel foes with plenty blest
  'So ankering after more   190
'To lay the greens & pastures waste
  'Which proffited before
'Poor greedy souls—what would they have
  'Beyond their plenty given?
'Will riches keep 'em from the grave?   195
  'Or buy them rest in heaven?'

AUTOGRAPH: Nor. MS 1, p. 165 (sideways in margin).
Dated: 1819 (Explanatory Notes).

ON DR TWOPENNY

Twopenny Wittle his nature is & Twopenny his name is
His task is not wort[h] Twopence & twopenny his fame is
Two pennys but a trifle one well may do wi out 'em
& as hes but a twopenny I dont care twopence about him

AUTOGRAPH: Pet. MS A32, p. 18.
Dated: 1819 (Explanatory Notes).

Towpenny his wisdom is & towpenny his fame is
Towpenny his merit is & towpenny his name is
& as twopence is a trifle I well may do without him
Ill sing in spite of twopenny & not care towpence about him

ON DR TWOPENNY   *Title:* On Dr T——y   2 & *repeated*
TOWPENNY HIS WISDOM IS & TOWPENNY HIS FAME IS   *Title: wanting*

AUTOGRAPHS: Pet. MS A4, pp. 1–4: Nor. MS 1, p. 169 (ll. 121–34 only, pencil beneath 'Old favourite tree art thou too fled the scene' in ink). TRANSCRIPT: Pet. MS B1, pp. 31–7 (pp. 32–3 blank). Dated: 1808–19 (MS 1).

ALPINS HARP NEW STRUNG

from A Piece of 'Ancient' Scottish 'Poetry'

Wild winds no longer rustle in the wood
The hasty rains cease bubbling on the flood
Like the noon day as silent & as calm
While scenes refresh'd present a sweeter charm
Each pearly drop Flowers burthen'd sweets renew   5
The clouds divide—the sky is cloth'd in blue
Oer the green hills the slopeing sun declines
Dash'd in the soil the hasty shower combines
The muddy streams flow rapid ting'd with red
& guggles furious oer their stony bed   10
& still ye murmur sweet—increasing streams
Tho not so sweet as yon far music seems—
Alpin the bard—his wild-strung-harp complains
While listening hills vibrate the mournful strains
The big tear starting reddens in his eye   15
Each wrinkl'd cheek swells smooth in many a sigh
By age deform'd—he bows his hoary head
& bent in mournful posture—wails the dead—
Now muses fire his dim eye rolls around
By fits—then sad—then strikes a solemn sound   20
Alpin thou aged bard what woes betide?
Son of sweet song thy wild harps native pride
What mournful cause can here thy woes regard
On these lone hills by echo only heard
As howls the tempest in regardless woods   25
As (wak'd in vain) waves fold the unfeeling floods

ALPINS HARP NEW STRUNG   *Title:* Alpins harp New Strung / From a piece of 'ancient' Scottish 'Poetry' *MS A4*   5 'Flowers *MS A4*   12 Tho not *through* Look ere *MS A4*

Alpin

My tears o Ryno are severe
They fall for him that slumbers here
My tears my song ah vainly gave
Mourns the still tenant of the grave   30
Tho tall thou art tho power is thine
As towering grows the mountain pine
Tho hills thy skill & strength declares
When chace is led or fight prepares
Tho beauty thine & strength & power   35
Of all the vallies flowers the flower
Sons of the plain the fairest pride
As flowers bedeck the streamlets side
Where health infusd on breezes team
& dips refreshing in the stream   40
But thou shalt fall! by fates decree
Morar is what thou shalt be
As on this grave I now recline
So mourning bards shall wail on thine
The day comes on—thy bow unstrung   45
Shall usless in the hall be hung
Then cease the hills thy voice to hear
Thy voice no more the hills shall cheer
Then even all—unknown unseen
Forgets that Ryno ere has been!   50

Soldiers grave

As swift as the roe leads the chase oer the mountains
Thy speed to the fight was O mighty Morar
Thy weapons glancd swift as the lightning—in battle
& horrid as meteors did shoot on the war
Thy wrath who could stand! like the wirl-windy tempest   55
Thy voice feard as thunder dread rumbling afar
What hundred & thousands o countless the numbers
That fell in the wrath of the mighty morar

---

33 declar'd *altered to* declares *MS A4*   34 chace *through* chaceing: prepar'd
altered to prepares *MS A4*   40 & dips *through* Dips do *MS A4*

But when welcome peace had compleated thy wishes
& Victorys crown haild thy toils from the war   60
As calm as the water curls over wi' breezes
Subsided the wrath of once dreadful Morar
After Rain as the Sun thro the water clouds gleaming
Thy face as serene—lost its frown in the war
As the moon in nights silence its horrid gloom chearing   65
Thy smiles cheerd thy foes—O victorious morar

Alas what avails it—the boast of the heroe
The pride of the victor—the honours of war
When victory triumphant has led from the conquest
What honours where thine thou brave fallen morar   70
The world once too bounded to tell of thy glory
When its shouts hail the heroe return'd from the war
Now silent has left the[e]—while I in three paces
Suround all thy glory! Once mighty morar

Vain vain are the shadows of greatness & Glory   75
& vain all their honours tho gaind in the war
Since perishd the victor his deeds all forgotten
Since low unrewarded lies fallen Morar
A leafless tree mourns the subduer of armies
& four mossy stones the reward—from the war   80
(Grass the while the winds wistling)—ah these & these only
Point out to the hunter the Grave of Morar

Brave shade ill requited thy low declin'd valour
& few be that mourns the sad tidings of war
All comfort was vain when thy mother recievd them   85
She languishd lamenting the fallen Morar
& Morglans fair daughter—O dearly bought conquest
How harden'd & cruel the bosom of war
Sick droop'd the fair lilly that lov'd thee sincerely
Broken hearted she dy'd for her wounded Morar   90

61 oever *MS A4*   63 Rain *through* as *MS A4*   64 frown[s] *MS A4*
83 ill *through* un: thy *inserted MS A4*   90 wounded *over* [fallen] *MS A4*

What tottering form approaches here?
Whose slow step tells his exit near
What bow bent sage my woe attends?
& oer his staff in sorrow bends
What shade whose locks are wooll'd in years   95
& eyes grown red wi briny tears
Lists to my sorrows mournfull strain
& weeps & looks & weeps again

O valiant heroe brave Morar
Thy father heard the noise of war   100
Of foes dispers'd of prisners ta'en
He heard alas but h[e]ard in vain
Thy valiant deeds the world proclaimd
He heard thy boastful conquest nam'd
But short the joy—thy fate remaind   105
Which lingering victorys pride detaind
Ah victorys battle dearly won
Here mourns the sire his fallen son
Morar thy fall thy deadly wound
His dampt soul sinketh to the ground   110

Ah weep away thy latest years
His worth well claims a parents tears
But deep in earth is laid his head
Sound, sound the slumbers of the dead
A parents cares the sons forgot   115
Thou weeps for him that heeds thee not
O when shall that morns mystery shine
That bids the grave its prey resign
All, all those mighty sons of war
& wake again the brave Morar   120

Adieu thou brave heroe—no more shall thou conquer
Nor foes to their terror distinguish afar
Thy armys spears glittering the dark woods emblazon
When led to the fight by the mighty Morar

91 r *through* o *in* approaches *MS A4*   96 grown] gownd *MS A4*   102 He
inserted MS A4   118/19 How sunden the change is o ill fated parent *(this line is
not part of the poem) MS A4*   121 heroe∧: shalt *MS 1*   124 ⟨   ⟩ to
⟨   ⟩ with mighty Morar *MS 1*

Tho no son is left in thy valour assuming   125
Valour once that increased the horrors of war
To distinguish in fight what distinguishd a father
Still still shalt thou live o brave fallen Morar

The Minstrelsys song shall swell high with thy story
Ever dear to the Minstrel the feats of the war   130
& Poets triumphant recording thy Glory
Shall warn future ages to notice Morar
Here while the turf swells near the scene of the Action
Where vengance once breath'd all the horrors of war
Cur[i]ositys Visits shall oft be exclaiming   135
'Thats the Grave of the Soldier—The Valiant Morar'.

AUTOGRAPH: Nor. MS 1, pp. 169–70.
TRANSCRIPTS: Nor. MS 4, p. 65: Pet. MS B1, p. 47: Pet. MS C2, pp. 57a–58.
Printed in *RL*, p. 200 (14-line sonnet).
Dated: 1808–19 (MS 1).

TO A FAVOURITE TREE

Old favourite tree art thou too fled the scene
Could not the ax thy clining age delay
& let thee stretch thy shadows oer the green
& let thee dye in picturesque decay

125 No son has been left for ⟨   ⟩ thy valour *MS 1*   126 increasd *MS 1*
127 distinguish in fight] tell future times *MS 1*   128 Still . . . live] But still thoult
? survive: Morar *omitted MS 1*   129 minstrelsys *MS 1*   130 Ever] For:
minstrel *MS 1*   131 & Poets triumphant] ⟨   ⟩: glory *MS 1*
132 Morar *omitted MS 1*   133 action *MS 1*   134 breathd *MS 1*
136 *Followed in MS A4 by:*

Title
Alpins harp new strung
An Imitative Versification
Of a piece of Ancient
Scottish Poetry

The Original may be seen by sending for

TO A FAVOURITE TREE *Title:* To a favourite Tree *RL, wanting MS 1*
2 thy 'clining age the axe delay *RL*

What hadst thou done to meet a tyrants frown   5
Be dragd a captive from thy native wood
What was the cause the raige that hewd thee down
Small value was the ground on which thou stood
So sweet in summer as thy branches spread
In such gay cloathing as thy boughs where drest   10
Where many a shepherd swain has laid his head
& on thy cooling fragrance sunk to rest
Adieu old friends ye trees & bushes dear
The flower refreshd by Morning dews
Hopeful blooms in asure skies   15
Anon the Noontide heat ensues
It hoples Withers droops & dies
O Cruel change of Love like mine
To bid me hope one only day
& ere that worst of days declind   20
To snatch that only hope away

AUTOGRAPH: Nor. MS 1, p. 171.
Dated: 1808–19 (MS 1).

The humble flowers that buds upon the plain
& only buds to blossom but in vain
By sensless rustics with unheeding eyes
Still troden down as they attempt to rise

So like the humble blossom of the Fields   5
Unculturd Genius humble life consceals

6 and 8 *Transposed RL*   6 Be dragd a] And dragg'd thee *RL*   7 But gain's
rude rage it was that cut thee down *RL*
9–21   So gay in summer as thy boughs were dress'd,
                            So soft, so cool, as then thy leaves did wave;
                        I knew thee then, and knowing am distress'd:
                            And like as Friendship leaning o'er the grave,
                        Loving ye all, ye trees, ye bushes, dear,   5
                        I wander where you stood, and shed my bosom-tear. *RL*

15 Its hopeful bloom unfolds to asure skies *altered to* Hopeful blooms in asure skies *MS 1*
    THE HUMBLE FLOWERS THAT BUDS UPON THE PLAIN   *Title: wanting*
4/5 *Space for five lines*

AUTOGRAPH: Nor. MS 1, p. 172.
Dated: 1808–19 (MS 1).

To meet the Breeze that fand the trees her snowy breast was
    bear
Sheethd on the Green he[r] Beauty seen to all advantage there
She meets his view sweet peace adieu & pleasures known before
He sighs—approves admires—& love[s] his hearts his own no
    more.

AUTOGRAPH: Nor. MS 1, p. 173.
Dated: 1808–19 (MS 1).

Young Damon long lovd charming Bess of the vale
Sweet Blooming & fair shes the maid to his mind
Still the shepherd was backward in telling his tale
Still doubting & fearing the maid to be kind
Little Birds in their courtship among the green trees   5
When they armor[ou]sly fix on a maid to their mind
They Reveal it in Fear & approach by degrees
Till some happy omen turns out to be kind
At length ventures [he] with low bended knee
And hopful addresses the maid to his mind   10
& just as he wishd so he found her to be
Politely good naturd condecending & kind

TO MEET THE BREEZE THAT FAND THE TREES HER SNOWY BREAST
WAS BEAR   *Title: wanting*
   YOUNG DAMON LONG LOVD CHARMING BESS OF THE VALE   *Title:
wanting*

AUTOGRAPH: Nor. MS 1, p. 173.
Dated: 1808–19 (MS 1).

DISSAPOINTMENT

Aslant the cottage ridge the sun
Sunk in the western skyes
& Evening had begun
To spread her tasty dyes

When milkmaid Kate prepard for home   5
Was sauntering down the road
Expecting sweetheart ned woud come
To help her with the load

She stopt to rest from stile to stile
& wisht & lookt around   10
& tinkling of her yokes the while
That he might know the sound

AUTOGRAPH: Nor. MS 1, pp. 174–5.
Dated: 1808–19 (MS 1).

The crowing coks the morns for told
The Sun begins to peep
And Shepherds Wistling to the Fold
Sets free the Captive Sheep
Oer pathless plains at early hours   5
The Sleepy Rustic goes
The dews brushd off from Gras & flowers
Bemoists his hardend Shoes

DISSAPOINTMENT   *Title:* Dissapointment
THE CROWING COKS THE MORNS FOR TOLD   *Title: wanting*

For every leaf that forms a shade
& flowrets silken top 10
& every shivering bent & blade
Bends with a pearly drop
But soon shall fly these pearly drops
The Sun advances higher
& stretching ocr the mountain tops 15
Sweet Gilds the Village spire
Again the Bustling maiden seeks
Her Cleanly pale & now
Rivals the morn her Rosy Cheeks
& hastes to milk her Cow 20
While Echo tells her Collin near
Blythe Wistling oer the Hills
The Powerful Magic charms her ear
& thro her Bosom thrills

Now Slow the hazy mist retires 25
A Wider Circle's seen
Thin Scatterd Huts & Neighbouring Spires
Augment the Bounded Scene
Brisk Winds the Lightnd Branches shake
By pattering Drops confest 30
& where Oaks Dripping shade the Lake
Prints Dimples on its Breast
The Larks now leave the tufted Corn
A Nightly Bed Supplies
& sweetly Singing hails the Morn 35
—A Minstrel in the Skies
On trembling Wings she leaves her home
& twitering Wistles loud
Now nearly lost a spot becomes
& mixes in a Cloud 40

12 with *repeated*   17 Bu *through* Bl *in* Bustling   18 C *through* n *in* Cleanly:
pale—   19 morn—   24/5 *Gap in the middle with extra lines to be added*
33 the[ir]
36/7

[O Memory now the Rustic pays
A Compliment to thee
Sweet painter of those by gone days
Those sports of infancy]

39 ne *through* los *in* nearly

O memory sweetner of my lays
What power belongs to thee
To paint the bliss of vanishd Days
& sweets of Infancy
When happy in our Golden hours   45
As free as air we range
When pleasure plucks her laughing flower
Unmindful of a change

AUTOGRAPH: Nor. MS 1, p. 176.
Dated: 1808–19 (MS 1).

My Native Village Native Fields
   Places by me so highly priz'd
That not one spot such pleasure yields
   No not in all the World besides
And this my cottage O so dear   5
   This place of my Nativity
Where I was 'bred and born' and where
   I still have livd from Infancy

48 *Followed by an asterisk which suggests further lines to follow, perhaps on the next leaf which has been torn from the MS*
  MY NATIVE VILLAGE NATIVE FIELDS   *Title: wanting*   5 cottage.

AUTOGRAPHS: Pet. MS A4, p. 8: Nor. MS 1, pp. 176–7: Pet. MS A40, p. 36.
TRANSCRIPTS: Pet. MS B1, p. 118 (deleted): Nor. MS 5, pp. 147–8 (ll. 29–32 omitted).
Dated: '? Old' (MS A4, p. 8).

ON THE DEATH OF A SCOLD

A scolding woman's worse then hell
Her tongue can never cease
She loves in quarrels to oppose
& hates the thoughts of peace
So hags delight to see the storm   5
Deform the smiling skye
& joys to hear the thunder roll
& see the light'ning flie
They know their tools is ready then
To prosper every spell   10
Which the black arts of malice plans
In journey work for hell
But that which seems as choise in those
Which bear the hellish mark
May be the effect of fear & dread   15
Hells mysterys are dark
Tis said their bodys when spells fail
Is like their souls condemn'd
& when they fail of Nickeys prey
He foxlike seizes them   20

ON THE DEATH OF A SCOLD   *Title:* On the Death of a Scold *MS A4 MS 1 MS A40*   *Note in MS A4:* This must either be in 8 Line verse or all together—(if 8s four will remain at last)   1 Womans *MS 1*] womans *MS A40*   than *MS 1*
3 Quarrels *MS 1*   6 Deform *through* Defile *MS A4*   sky *MS A40*   7 joy *MS A40*   Roll *or* Boll *MS 1*] roll *through* rout *MS A40*   8 lightning flye *MS 1 MS A40*   9 are *MS A40*   Ready *MS 1*   11 Black *MS 1*   12 journy *MS 1*] Journey *MS A40*   13 choice *MS A40*   14 Who *MS A40*   *Clare's footnote in MS A4:* For an account of these marks & mysterys see Mr Sinclairs 'Satans Invisible World discovered'   15 dred *MS 1*   16 misterys *MS 1*
17 'Tis *MS 1*   18 Are *MS A40*   an soul *MS 1*   condemnd *MS 1 MS A40*
19 And: of Nickeys] to bring him *MS 1*   20 fox like *MS A40*

So of old scolding nelly trix
The same thing may be said
Who after marrying husbands six
& scolding all to dead
She looking out for further work   25
A seventh still desir'd
But as Experience makes fools wise
Her customers grew tir'd
So when her tongue could find no more
To load with its abuse   30
It silencd not from being old
But only want of use
So Nicky seeing trade had faild
& no one car'd to come
He thought it time to shut up shop   35
& Instant took her home

AUTOGRAPHS: Nor. MS 1, p. 177: Pet. MS A3, p. 138.
Dated: 1808–19 (MS 1).

AN IMITATION OF BURNS

While Birdies wi their notes so sweet
Compeat for rival in their sang
Moping I gang wi weary feet
The dreary fields & wads amang

21 Nelly Trix *MS 1 MS A40*   26 Seventh *MS 1*   desird *MS 1*] desired *MS A40*
27 Expeirence *MS 1*] experience *MS A40*   made *MS 1*   28 customer
MS 1   tired *MS A40*   29 coud *MS A40*   31 silenced: from] with *MS A40*
33 Niky *MS 1*] nickey *MS A40*   failed *MS A40*   34 one] more *MS 1*   cared
MS A40   36 & [instant] took his darling home *(*her *altered to* his: darling *inserted)*
MS A4] & Instant took her home *(Clare's correction in MS A3, p. 142)*, & instant took her
home *MS 1*, & took his darling home *MS A40*

AN IMITATION OF BURNS   *Title:* An Imitation of Burns *MS A3, wanting MS 1,*
Followed in MS A3 by: (not to be publishd but only to let Mr D. see if I am qualified for
it—as he seemd to wish it (the scotch phrase was only a wanton thought that offerd it self
at the moment—   *Stanzas reversed in MS A3*   1 While little birdies lilting sweet
MS A3   2 fo' *MS A3*   raval *MS 1*   3 Moupin': wi' *MS A3*   4 fiel's
MS A3

O dreary fields are they to me   5
Sin she wha weel my heart esteems
Is absent all the live lang dee
An ony present in my dreams

O Fortun wiltu still unkind
Doom me to live & languish here   10
Say yif I war to spak my mind
Wad she be kind enou to hear
Or wad she treat me in disdain
And leave me still to pine & sigh
Ah me I see my fate too plain   15
I loo in fear and dare no try

AUTOGRAPH: Nor. MS 1, p. 178 (pencil).
Dated: 1808–19 (MS 1).

How oft (with hat pulld oer my eyes
To aid my aching sight)
Ive markd the little songster rise
& trac'd him out of sight

Delightful bird 'twas not thy song   5
Charmd my mischevous breast
Twas pleasing hopes that I ere long
Should find thy lowly nest

5 Oh: fiel's *MS A3*   6 Sin' *MS A3*   7 a' *MS A3*   8 An' on'y *MS A3*
9 Fortun' *MS A3*   10 lainguish *MS A3*   11 Saie gif: spak' *MS A3*
12 enou' *MS A3*   13 in] wi' *MS A3*   14 &: sigh— *MS A3*
16 &: na' *MS A3*   *Drury has pencilled: Wot do (i.e. won't do) following the poem MS A3*

HOW OFT (WITH HAT PULLD OER MY EYES   *Title: wanting*   1 how
3 markd *over* [watchd]   8 lowly *below* [curious]

AUTOGRAPHS: Pet. MS A3, pp. 53–6: Pet. MS A3, p. 92 (deleted): Nor.
MS 1, pp. 178–9 (ll. 1–40), p. 8 (ll. 41–8, pencil): Pet. MS A40, pp. 31–31a.
TRANSCRIPT: Pet. MS B1, pp. 109–10 (deleted).
Dated: 1815–:7 (MS A3, p. 53 '3 or 4 years ago').

DEATH OF THE BRAVE

A Song

1

In his countrys cause when his last breath is breathing
And maintaining her freedom the hero expires
In vain then may envy her snakes be unwreathing
She will near damp the fame which his valour aquires
No Ages to come shall grow warm at the story   5
To hear how a Briton in fight did behave
And courage & valour & honour & Glory
Tho vanquishd—shall triumph at the death of the brave

2

To his Country true to his king brave & loyal
No bribes the brave heart of the hero ensnares   10
True Courage—he proves it in hot bloody tryal
Hand and heart both together for battle prepares

DEATH OF THE BRAVE   *Title:* Death of the Brave / A Song *MS A3*, The Death
of the Brave / A Song *MS A3, p. 92 MS A40*, 'Death of the Brave' *MS 1   MS 1, p. 3
(by itself):* The Death of the Brave / A New Song / By / John Clare   *Stanzas numbered
1–6 in MS A3 and MS A3, p. 92*   1 country's: breath is *through* breathing *MS A3,
p. 92*   2 And *over* [While] *MS A3, p. 92*] [When fight] & *MS 1*, & *MS A40*
Maintaining *to* maintaining *(p.e.) MS A3*   his *MS A3 MS A40*   3 Envy *to* envy
(p.e.) MS A3   skakes *MS A3, p. 92*   unreathing *MS 1*   4 shall *below* ['ll] *MS
A3, p. 92*   ne'er *MS A3, p. 92*] neer *MS 1*   fame] flame *MS 1 MS A40*   [hero]
valour *(Valour to* valour *p.e.) MS A3*   acquires— *MS A3, p. 92*] acquires *MS A40*
5 No— *MS A40*   ages *MS A3, p. 92 MS 1 MS A40*   warm] vain *MS 1*   Story *MS
A3, p. 92*   6 britton *MS A40*   7 And] & *MS A40*   glory *MS 1 MS A40*
8 vanquish'd— *MS A3, p. 92*] vanquished‸ *MS A40*   Triumph: Death: Brave *MS
A3, p. 92*   9 country *MS A3, p. 92 MS 1 MS A40*   king] cause *MS A40*
11 courage— *MS A3, p. 92*] courage‸ *MS A40*   blooy *MS 1*   trial *MS A3, p. 92 MS
1 MS A40*   12 —Hand *MS A3, p. 92*   & *MS A3, p. 92 MS 1 MS A40*

To bribes and to fear all alike hes a stranger
While the warning to battle no terror ne'er gave
He smiles at its horrors & welcomes the danger   15
And feels no conscern but the death of the Brave

3

Where death with his horrors most horrible rages
Showers his Weapons so thick as to darken the skye
There look for the hero—tis there he engages
Undaunted—Resolving to conquer or dye   20
To live his brave heart by no hopes is attended
He falls over powred—& smiles at his Grave
Grim War e'en awhile holds her weapon suspended
And feels a concern at the Death of the Brave

4

His courage unbated—tho o'erpowred by Numbers   25
The hero falls bleeding to mix with the slain
Yet his eye ere it closes eternal to Slumbers
Still rolls on the foe with Exulting disdain
—Tho the hero's no more theres no mourning nor weeping
A tear for his death by a Soldier ere gave   30
Would hurt his brave Soul in its grave sweetly sleeping—
For honour remains at the Death of the Brave

13 & *MS A3, p. 92 MS 1 MS A40*   all *through* he *MS A3, p. 92*   he's *MS A3, p. 92*
MS A40   14 While the] The: teror *MS A3, p. 92 MS 1*   to] of *MS A40*   neer
MS 1] eer *MS A40*   15 & *through* a *MS A40*   16 & *MS A3, p. 92*
MS A40   conscern—*MS A3, p. 92*] concern *MS 1*, consern *MS A40*   brave *MS A3,*
p. 92 MS 1 MS A40   17 Were *MS A40*   with *over* [with]: [and] its *MS a3, p. 92*
18 her *MS A3, p. 92*   weapons: sky *MS A3, p. 92 MS 1 MS A40*   19 'tis *MS*
A3, p. 92   20 resolving *MS A3, p. 92 MS A40*   or] & *MS 1*   dye—*MS A3,*
p. 92   22 overpowrd— *MS 1*] over powered∧ *MS A40*   he smile *MS 1*   grave!
MS A3, p. 92] grave *MS 1 MS A40*   23 war *MS A40*   een *MS 1*
MS A40   weapons *MS 1 MS A40*   24 & *MS A40*   conscern *MS A3, p. 92*]
cosern *MS 1*, consern *MS A40*   death *MS A3, p. 92 MS 1 MS A40*   brave *MS 1*
MS A40   25 o'erpowered *MS A3, p. 92*] overpowerd *MS 1*, oer powered
MS A40   numbers *MS A3, p. 92 MS A40*   26 Bleeding *MS 1*   27 Yet]
But *MS A40*   e're *MS A3, p. 92*   it] at: close *MS 1*   slumbers *MS A3, p. 92 MS 1*
MS A40   28 [look] rolls *MS 1*   Still rolls on *below* [Rolls a look on]: with *below*
[of] *MS A3, p. 92*   exulting *MS A3, p. 92 MS 1 MS A40*   29 Tho: or
MS A40   heros *MS A3, p. 92 MS 1 MS A40*   more— *MS 1*   mourning] mouring
MS A3, p. 92   30 Tear *MS A3, p. 92*   soldier *MS A40*   e're *MS A3, p. 92*]
eer *MS 1*   31 Woud *MS A40*   brave *over* [proud] *MS 1*   soul: sleeping∧ *MS*
A3, p. 92 MS 1 MS A40   grave] dust *over* [grave] *MS A3, p. 92*   32 remains]
attends *MS A40*   at] to *MS 1*   death *MS A3, p. 92 MS A40*] last *MS 1*   brave *MS*
A3, p. 92 MS 1 MS A40

5

His Brothers his Soldiers who boast the proud Story
And Witness the last of their Leader and Friend
(Their Leader who often has lead them to Glory—)   35
And always stood loyal & true to the End
Still follow him now in the honours of battle
Muffl'd Drums beating up a dead march to the Grave
Where the last farewell three Vollies shall Rattle
To distinguish in thunder the death of the brave   40

6

No need of the Sculptor in marble be casting
To prolong the Fame which his actions acquire
In the hearts of true Britons he lives ever lasting
Till the World & their hero together expire
The ages to come shall grow warm at the story   45
And British youths fir'd by th' Examples gave
Shall hasten to Battle & hasten to Glory—
And Glory in Dying the death of the Brave

33 brothers: soldiers *MS A3, p. 92 MS A40*   story *MS 1 MS A40*   34 & *MS
A40*] To *MS A3, p. 92*, Shall *MS 1*   witness: & friend *MS A3, p. 92 MS 1 MS A40*
last *underlined MS A3, p. 92*   leader *MS A3, p. 92 MS A40*   35 ∧Their *MS 1
MS A40*   leader *MS A3, p. 92 MS A40*   often *inserted*: had *MS 1*   led *MS A3,
p. 92 MS 1 MS A40*   Glory—)] Glory ∧∧ *MS A3, p. 92*, glory ∧∧ *MS 1 MS A40*
36 And] & *MA40*   end—) *MS A3, p. 92*] end *MS 1 MS A40*   37 Still *through*
Shall *MS A3*] Shall *MS A40*   Shall leave for awhile the confusion of battle *MS A3,
p. 92*] Two & two shall they march—tho not as to Battle *MS 1*   38 Muffl'd *through*
Muffled *MS A3*] Muffld *MS 1*, Muffled *MS A40*   drums: grave *MS A40*   beating]
shall beat: March *MS 1*   & follow his honour'd remains to the grave *MS A3, p. 92*
39 Where [for]: farewell *over* [time they]: three] thier *MS A3*   Where as a last farewell
(last farewell *underlined*) *MS A3*] Where his Men Solemn Marching *MS 1*, Were
as a last far well *MS A40*   vollies *MS A3, p. 92 MS A40*   rattle *MS A3, p. 92 MS A40*
40 Distinguish: Thunder: Death: Brave *MS 1*   41 sulptor *MS 1*] sculptor
MS A40   becasting *MS A3, p. 92 MS 1*   42 fame *MS A40*   The fame his past
actions so nobly acquires *MS A3, p. 92*] The fame which his actions so nobly acquire
MS 1   43 true britons *underlined MS A3, p. 92*   britons *MS 1*] brittons
MS A40   he *through* it *MS 1*   everlasting *MS A3, p. 92 MS 1 MS A40*   44 Till]
& *MS 1*   world *MS 1 MS A40*   shall together *MS 1*   expires— *MS A3, p. 92*
45 Ages *MS A40*   46 & *MS A3, p. 92 MS 1 MS A40*   british *through* britons
MS A3, p. 92] britoish *MS 1*, british *MS A40*   fird *MS 1*] fired *MS A40*   th'
Examples] examples he *MS A3, p. 92 MS A40*, Examples he *MS 1*   47 battle *MS
A3, p. 92 MS A40*   glory∧ *MS A3, p. 92 MS A40*] Glory∧ *MS 1*   48 &: dying
MS A3, p. 92 MS 1 MS A40   glory: brave *MS A3, p. 92 MS A40*

AUTOGRAPHS: Pet. MS A3, pp. 41–8: Nor. MS 1, pp. 180–7 (ll. 1–192, ll. 193–206 and 229–58 pencil), p. 182 (ll. 85–90), p. 177 (ll. 259–64, pencil), p. 189 (ll. 207–13, 223–8, pencil), p. 193 (ll. 217–22, pencil).
TRANSCRIPTS: Pet. MS B1, pp. 101–7 (deleted): Nor. MS 5, pp. 81–95.
Dated: 1813–15 (MS A3, p. 41 '5 or 6 years ago').

THE TRAVELLERS

A Parody

A Tramper on a certain day
Met with another on his way
   An utter stranger he
But having many miles to go
They both familliar 'gan to grow   5
   & chatterd very free

One reason'd upon such & such
Then 't'other prais'd his judgment much
   & said he reasond well—
In short they talk'd of many things   10
(Of kingdoms, governments, & kings)
   Too numerous to tell

& so they talk'd whole hours away
& when one tale was ended they
   Did other tales begin   15
—Till suddenly in eager tone
One crys 'no halves its all my own
   'By jingos Peters in'

THE TRAVELLERS   *Title:* The Travellers / A Parody *MS A3*, The Travellers / a Tale. *MS 1*   1 Tramper] stranger *MS 1*   3 utter] other *MS 1*   4 But] Yet *MS 1*   5 familiar *MS 1*   6 And *MS 1*   7 and *MS 1* 8 t'other *MS 1*   9 And: reason'd well∧ *MS 1*   11 ∧Of Kingdoms∧ Governments∧ and Kings∧ *MS 1*   13 And *MS 1*   talkd [of] *MS A3* 14 And *MS 1*   16 ∧Till *MS 1*   17 Cryes 'No: own' *MS 1*   its *through* but *MS A3*] but *MS 1*

For (tho not often practis'd walking)
By using eyes as well as talking   20
   He saw a bundle lye
While tother not so sharp as he
Too busy in discourse to see
   Went gauming heedless bye

He shakes it round & somthing chinks!   25
His heart jumps up—he hopes—& thinks
   So a[n]xious to behold
& scarce could he contain himself
When wonderfull! he found his pelf
   Was nothing else but gold!   30

And's Comrade now too 'gan to stare
& instant claim'd an equal share
   As nothing but his due
& bolted up to plan the way
But sharper cries 'hold hard here—stay   35
   'I think theres none for you'

If I guess right when this appeard
(Which you no doubt on't plainly heard)
   I said no shares wi' me
Moreover too—your chance was full   40
As good as mine to get the whol'
   Had you but eyes to see

Therefore I cannot make it out
How you can bring your claims about
   To come at half my pelf   45
For if I rightly hit my aim
The only man that has a Claim
   Is one I call My self

22 t'other *MS 1*   24 Whent: heedles by *MS 1*   25 and something chinks⟨
MS 1   26 hearts *MS A3*   up⟨ : hopes⟨ and thinks[n] *MS 1*   27 S⟨
axious] All eager *MS 1*   28 And: contain his self *through* his self contain *MS*
29 wonderful! *MS 1*   30 Gold⟨ *MS 1*   31 comrade *MS 1*   32 An⟨
MS 1   34 And *MS 1*   35 'Hold: there⟨ : stay! *MS*
36 ⟨I: theres] heres: you⟨ *MS 1*   38 heard⟨ *MS A3*   39 says *MS*
40 More over too⟨ *MS 1*   41 whole *altered to* whol' *MS A3*   42 H *through*⟨
in Had *MS 1*   44 you *inserted MS 1*   47 claim *MS 1*   48 'My-self⟨
MS 1

He ended—& his mate begun
To say he cou'd'n't see no fun   50
   In such like hoggish jobs
Of one who so for fairness stuck
& now they lit o' this good luck
   To pocket all the dobs

& gave his reasons oer & oer   55
Which seem'd so natural heretofore
   But not so now they shine
To every reason he could show
Still cried the finder—'this I know
   'That every skerricks mine'   60

'For when' says he luck comes at last
The proverb tells you to hold fast
   & keep what you have got
So friend I'll never let you dip
But as you've been a brother chip   65
   I'll treat you with a pot

So now poor hopeless found for fact
That former reasons wou'd'n't act
   As half the prize to get
He work'd his nob again to make   70
A different plan he wishd would take
   To be a sharer yet

So now to gain his wish'd-for-ends
On lyes lapt-up-well he depends
   Drove to his P's & Q's   75
—'I tell you what old Chap' says he
Twas just before you lit O' me
   I heard some queerish news!

49 ended∧ and: Mate *MS 1*   50 cou'd'n't *through* didn't *MS A3*] could not *MS 1*
51 Hoggish *MS 1*   53 And: of *MS 1*   54 pockit *MS 1*   55 And: and
MS 1   56 smeem'd *MS A3*   natural *underlined MS A3*] pleasent *MS 1*   here
to fore *MS 1*   58 To every reason] For to all reasons *MS 1*   59 The finder
cried 'Well this I know' *MS 1*   60 ∧That: Skerrick's mine∧ *MS 1*   61 'luck
MS 1   63 And *MS 1*   65 brother-chip *MS 1*   67 hopeles *MS 1*
68 Thats: wou'dn't *MS 1*   69 prise *MS 1*   71 wishd *underlined MS A3*]
nop'd *MS 1*   73 wish'd-for-] wisht-for- *MS 1*   74 lapt-up-] lapt∧ up∧ *MS 1*
75 and *MS 1*   76 ∧∧I: Chap'] cock∧ *MS 1*   77 o' *MS 1*   78 heard]
ard: news∧ *MS 1*

But you may think I'm telling lyes—
'What is't?' the t'other eager cries   80
   I'll tell ye when I hear—
Well—you may take it as you will
T'is true depend upon't—but still
   You needn't see much fear

This 'needn't see much fear' was said   85
(So subtelty can work his head
   By wisdom scarce disern'd)
To make the tother (as he guest)
Or hop'd to make him think at least
   Self interest wa'n't concern'd!   90

Twas by the road but I've forgot
Th' name o' the place where it was at
   But does'n't matter where
Being rather faint for want o' drink
(Yet not so sadly off for chink)   95
   I went to ha' some beer

On entering in a house at hand
(As alehouses do mostly stand
   To catch all passers by)
I told my wants & sat me down   100
'Gen two near neighbours o' the town
   A talking very sly

At which so eager o' my beer
I first ga' little heed to hear
   Untill I 'gan to see   105

79 lyes∧ *MS 1*   80 ∧What is't∧∧ th 't'other: a *through* g *in* eager: cryes *MS 1*
81 hear∧ *MS 1*   82 Well∧ *MS 1*   83 upon't∧ *MS 1*   85–90 *Sideways
in margin MS 1*   85 This *through* But *MS A3*] But *MS 1*   neend'n't *MS A3*]
neednt *MS 1*   86 Sa Subtelty: head) *MS 1*   87 (By *MS 1*   88 other:
as] so *MS 1*   89 hopd *MS 1*   90 Self interest *underlined MS A3*   intrest:
consernd *MS 1*   91 T'was *MS 1*   i've *MS A3 MS 1*   92 th (*fourth word):*
was at] ot *MS 1*   94 of *MS 1*   96 whent *MS 1*   97 On *through* So *MS
A3*] So *MS 1*   98 ale houses *MS 1*   99 passers by∧ *MS 1*   100 and
MS 1   101 of *MS 1*   102 slye *MS 1*   103 which *through indecipherable
MS A3*   a *through* g *in* eager: of *MS 1*   104 ga'] took *MS 1*   105 gan
MS 1

Some queerish beckons come in vogue
& hear the name o' thief & rogue
   & then a look at me

At this queer comical affair
I silence broke & hitch'd my chair   110
   As neer em as I cou'd
To let 'em see I wa'n't asham'd
O' the suspicious things they nam'd
   Let them think as they wou'd

At first I gave a ham—& then   115
Began my speech wi gentlemen
   We've charming weather now
O yes Indeed sir—they reply'd
Tis rarley on the farmers side
   For land beneath the plough   120

& 'bout the farmers much was said
But thief & rogue still work'd my head
   'Twas that I wish'd to hear
& when by long discourse I found
A fitting time to bring it round   125
   I ask'd 'em how it where

Gentlemen I think says I
When first (if I'm not out be'guy)
   I call'd in here to drink
I heard you mention theif & rogue   130
Two names so very much in vogue
   Which made me apt to think

106 querish: vouge *MS 1*   107 And: of: and *MS 1*   thief *underlined MS A3*]
Thief *MS 1*   rogue *underlined MS A3*] Rogue *MS 1*   108 And *MS 1*
109 quere commical *MS 1*   110 and *MS 1*   111 near them *MS 1*
112 wa'nt *MS 1*   113 Of: thing *MS 1*   suspicious *underlined MS A3*] c *through*
in suspicious *MS 1*   115 ham∧ and *MS 1*   116 with *MS 1*   118 indeed
sir∧: replie'd *altered to* repliy'd *MS 1*   121 And *MS 1*   122 thief *underlined*
MS A3] Thief *MS 1*   and *MS 1*   rogue *underlined MS A3*] Rogue *MS 1*
124 And *MS 1*   126 them *MS 1*   128 i'm *MS A3*   be'guy *underlined MS*
A3] beguy *MS 1*   130 theif *and* rogue *underlined MS A3*   and *MS 1*
131 v *through* r *in* vouge *MS 1*

& as you seem both men o' sense
I think my freedom's no offence
   To neither one nor tother   135
For as I love my self to make
Free with all sorts for talkings sake
   I think so by another

So if—says I what you begun
Was any thing of robbery done   140
   I hope you'll not refuse
To tell the whole contents to me
For I am one you plainly see
   That loves a little news

This fetch'd a laugh & when twas done   145
'O to be sure Sir' they begun
   We can comply with ease
For we like you do love to be
With strangers as with neighbours free
   So drink sir if you please   150

Well so I did—I took the quart
Says I 'Your healths wi' all my heart'
   & fetch'd a charming pull
While by degrees the tale begun
'I guess'd says they somthing was done   155
   'The fellow look'd so dull'

—But this remark did only start
(While I was dipping i' the quart)
   Between themselves you see
& when they found me ready fix'd   160
They soon wi' no self talkings mixd
   Address'd the tale to me

133 And: of *MS 1*   134 think] hope *MS 1*   135 t'other *MS 1*
137 talking's *MS 1*   139 if‸ *MS 1*   140 robbery *underlined MS A3*
144 News *MS 1*   145 and when't was *MS 1*   146 ‸O *MS 1*   Sir‸ *MS*
A3] sir‸ *MS 1*   147 Comply *MS 1*   149 Neighbours *MS 1*   151 did‸
MS 1   152 ‸your: heart‸ *MS 1*   153 And *MS 1*   155 ‸I: something
MS 1   156 ‸The: dull‸ *MS 1*   157 ‸But: Remark *MS 1*   158 in
MS 1   160 &] But *MS 1*   161 soon[s] *MS A3*   talking-mix'd *MS 1*
162 the[ir] *MS 1*

'Well you must know Sir' they begun
The robbery we talk'd of being done
    Was in our village here   165
Last night about the hour of one
(An hour rogues mostly plans upon
    As theres the least to fear)

A neighbours house of ours was rob'd
Whose mony'd hurds the rascals fob'd   170
    & left him not a groat
Nor did they ever thank him for't
But worse then all when all they'd got
    They swore theyd cut his throat

Tho this to fright was only said   175
For him they left alive in bed
    Tho not so clean as found—
Yet if they'r catch'd (theres great reward)
That word will go agen 'em hard
    & hang 'em I'll be bound   180

Yes sure as ever they are hatch'd
They'll every one of 'em be catch'd
    —Aye—how comes that? says I
Why theres a man to London gone
To set the bow-street runners on   185
    & they you know will try

Well, well, says I—if thats the case
I'm sure I shou'dnt like their place
    Fex on't they'll quake i' fear

163 ∧Well: sir∧ *MS 1*   164 robbery *underlined MS A3*   talkt on
MS 1   167 rogues *underlined MS A3*] rouges *MS 1*   168 fear∧ *MS 1*
169 Neighbours *MS 1*   rob'd *underlined MS A3*   170 Whoses *MS 1*   mony'd
hurds *underlined MS A3*] monyd hurds *MS 1*   fob'd *underlined MS A3*] fobd *MS 1*
171 And *MS 1*   172 fo't *MS 1*   173 theyd *MS 1*   174 they'd *MS 1*
177 found∧ *MS 1*   178 theyr catcht— *MS 1*   theres great reward *underlined*
MS A3   179 This: em *MS 1*   180 And: em Ill *MS 1*   hang 'em *underlined*
MS A3   181 hatchd *MS 1*   182 Theyll: em *MS 1*   catch'd *underlined*
MS A3] catchd *MS 1*   183 ∧Aye∧: that∧ *MS 1*   184 Man *MS 1*
185 Bowstreet *MS 1*   186 And: they] them *MS 1*   187 I, I says I if...
MS 1   thats *and* case *underlined MS A3*   188 shouldnt *MS 1*   place *underlined*
MS A3   189 They'll make em quake for fear *MS 1*

Yes 'pend upon't says they theyre found   190
If any where above the ground
   As sure as we sit here

'& well'—(to know being fully bent)
Says I ist known which way they went
   —Yes—they returns—the ground   195
Confirms the truth that they'll be stopt
To day—(which in their haste they dropt)
   Theres several things been found

The tale being done welcome or not
Unbid I ventur'd to the pot   200
   As any christian wou'd
And being a dry I drank it up
& thank'd 'em for their friendly sup—
   E fex it did me good

They look'd askew well I could see   205
I'd made my self a bit too free—
   But faith I never care
For when chance offers I detest
That fellow that wornt do his best
   —At free cost never spare   210

---

190 they] he: they'r *MS 1*   193 ∧And well∧: bent∧ *MS 1*   194 says: wich
MS 1   known *underlined MS A3*   195 Yes *underlined MS A3*] ∧Yes∧
MS 1   Returns∧ *MS 1*   ground *underlined MS A3*] Ground *MS 1*   196 truth
and stopt *underlined MS A3*   theyll *MS 1*   197 Today— *MS 1*   dropt∧
underlined MS A3   198 several . . . found *underlined MS A3*   199 done—
MS 1   200 venturd *MS 1*
201/2   But at all this he made a Puff
                  & Calld it nought but Silly stuff
                  & Idle Childish Dreams
                  Then knapt his Eye—and fetchd a Laugh
                  —'You mus'n't catch old Birds wi' Chaff 5
                  'I'm up to all your Schemes.'   *MS 1, ink*

203 And thankd em: sup∧ *MS 1*   friendly *underlined MS A3*   205 lookd
askew— *MS 1*   206 Id: free∧ *MS 1*   207 But] I' *MS 1*   208 For
through When: when *inserted*: chance[s] *MS 1*   209 That] The: wort *MS 1*

For with excuses neer at loss
My saddle sits on every horse
   I've neer been wanting yet
Good friends says I—the freedoms ta'en
But word as bond when here again   215
   Mind I'm a treat in debt

Here I leave 'em & no doubt
You'll think my tale around about
   Tho sharpness quickly sees
'Bout what youve got this plainly tells   220
& as the hints to wish you well
   Excuse it if you please

Tother now star'd & cock'd his hat
Before he spoke—(but smelt the rat)
   —I hear ye friend—says he   225
Then stopt & fetch'd a hearty laugh—
But you mu'n't think your strowing chaff
   To catch such birds as me

Old scheemer finding all in vain
To be a sharer in the gain   230
   Now left his mate behind
When lo! all most beyond belief
He hears a noise 'stop thief—stop thief'
   Come echoing i' the wind

O! as you say the tother cries   235
This parcel which I thought a prize
   Is surely stolen goods!

211 For with] With *through* Ben: ne'er *MS 1*   212 My] 'The *through* Your: on *through* for: horse' *MS 1*   213 neer been wanting] al'a's found em *MS 1* 217 Here] There: left em *MS 1*   218 Youll: a round *MS 1*   219 quikly *MS 1*   220 youve got *underlined MS A3*   221 And: the[n] *MS 1* hints *underlined MS A3*   223 Tother now] The other: stard: cockd *MS 1* 224 but—(but smel *MS 1*   225 friend∧ *MS 1*   226 Then fetchd another hearty laugh *MS 1*   227 But you mu'n't *through* You mustn't *MS A3*] You musnt *MS 1*   228 sich *MS 1*   229 shcheemer *MS A3*] schemer *MS 1* 231 bhind *MS 1*   232 lo∧ almost *MS 1* belief] relief *MS A3*   233 ∧stop thief∧: thief∧ *MS 1*   234 Echoing in *MS 1*   235 O dear the other staring cries *MS 1*   237 goods∧ *MS 1*

What must we do they're found on us!
They'll put's in prison if no worse
   Lets run it to the woods   240

Poh—says the tother very cool
Whats we put in for now ye fool
   I'm free as e'er for ganging
For as yah said in past affairs
'Tis all my own & no half shares'   245
   So yah may say by hanging

When friends ha luck to rise above us
Spite how they once pretend to love us
   & all their flattering fuss
Reader observe—thoult find it true   250
They're strangers then to me & you
   & know no more of us

But when from—(fate ordains us crosses)
Neglect or overlooking losses
   Their former fate redoubles   255
Then like the man that dreads being taken
Poor we so long ago forsaken
   Are sought to share their troubles

From this we both may plainly see
The undermineing vanity   260
   Of Friendship vainly priz'd
Self interest 'rules the roast' below
& Friendships but a weigling show
   Of Treachery disguis'd

238 we *and* us *underlined MS A3*   *theyre: us*∧ *MS 1*   239 Prison *MS 1*
240 Shelter in *through* run it to: Woods *MS 1*   241 —*through* says
MS A3   other *MS 1*   242 you *MS 1*   243 Im: eer *MS 1*   245 ∧Tis:
shares∧ *MS 1*   246 hanging. *MS A3*   247 ha' *MS 1*   249 fuss]
stuff *MS 1*   250 thou'lt *MS 1*   251 There *MS A3*   255 Their]
They're *MS 1*   257 we *underlined MS A3 MS 1*   for saken *MS A3*
258 trouble *MS 1*   260 under minding *MS 1*   261 friendship: prizd *MS 1*
262 Self interest *underlined MS A3*   263 And frendships: a *omitted MS 1*
264 treachery disguisd *MS 1*

AUTOGRAPH: Nor. MS 1, p. 188 (pencil)
Dated: 1808–19 (MS 1).

O riches from thy cruel scorning
What divided hearts endure
Is worth enrichd by your adorning
Is worth the worse for being poor
Thou shade of merit los of thee   5
Is cause of all my pain
Fair Emas kind—but friends can see
No Worth were you disdain
Thus sighd poor Edwin—Hopes long vanishd
All alone to sorow left   10
His love discoverd he was banishd
Of Ema & his love bereft
Once lovly angel he resumd
Her smiles my hopes did warm
Then I had friends but now I'm doomd   15
To seek em in the storm
O was that tender Angel near me
My sorrows could but Ema see
Her heart O if her heart could hear me
If still unchang'd would pity me   20
Thus hoples Edwin sighd his pains
But short was his despair
For heaven that hears when worth complains
Directs his Ema there
Concious of his pains & grieving   25
Pearly tears bedewd her charms
& concious woes her bosom heaving
Sighd & sunk into his arms
O heaven Enrapturd Edwin c[r]ied
My angel keep from [h]arm   30
Love friends & all—My foes denyd
I've found eme in the storm

O RICHES FROM THY CRUEL SCORNING   *Title: wanting*   14 smiles]
simels   17 that *through* those   18 M *through* C *in* My   25/6 [Tears
bedewd each lovley charm]   32 eme *may be a diminutive for Emma*

AUTOGRAPHS: Pet. MS D4, p. 9: Nor. MS 1, p. 189 (pencil).
TRANSCRIPT: Pet. MS B1, pp. 24–5.
Printed in *RL*, pp. 114–15.
Dated: 1808–19 (MS 1).

ON THE DEATH OF A BEAUTIFUL YOUNG LADY

A Fragment

Ye meaner beauties cease your pride
  Where borrow'd Charms adorn
Here nature need of art defy'd
  & blossom'd all its own

The rose your paint but idly feigns   5
  Bloom'd natures brightest dyes
The gems your wealthy pride sustains
  Were natives of her eyes

But what avails superior charms
  To boast of when in power   10
Since subject to a thousand harms
  They perish like a flower

Alas we've nought to boast of here
  & less to make us proud
The brightest sun but rises clear   15
  To set behind a Cloud

Those charms which every heart subdues
  Must all their powers resign
—Those eyes like suns too bright to view
  Have now forgot to shine   20

ON THE DEATH OF A BEAUTIFUL YOUNG LADY   *Title:* [On the Death of
a Young Lady / A Fragment] / On the Death of a Beautiful Young Lady / A Fragment
MS D4, On the Death of a Young Lady *MS 1*, On the Death of a beautiful Young
Lady *RL*   *No stanza divisions in MS 1*   1 your] you *MS 1*   2 When borowd
plumes adorn *MS 1*   Charms *through* plumes *MS D4*   3 Here [The]
MS D4   need] aid *MS 1 RL*   defy'd] suplyd *MS 1*   4 blosomd: her *MS 1*
5 Rose: fains *MS 1*   6 Blooms *MS 1*   7 wealthy *through* richest *MS
D4*] richest *MS 1*   8 Are *MS 1*   13 weve *MS 1*   14 les *MS 1*
15 brightest *MS 1*   16 cloud *MS 1*   17 which] that: hart *MS 1*   subdue *RL*
19 — *through* Those *MS D4*   ∧Those: too] to *MS 1*

Such Beauties—so untimley fell
What mortal would be proud
The day return'd & found her well
But left her in her shroud

To day the blossom buds & blooms   25
But who a day can trust
Since the tomorrow when it comes
Condemns it to the dust

AUTOGRAPHS: Pet. MS A3, pp. 105–6: Nor. MS 1, p. 190 (ll. 1–8, 17–24
only): Pet. MS A40, pp. 33–33a (ll. 37–8 omitted, deleted).
TRANSCRIPT: Pet. MS B1, p. 162 (ll. 1–16 only, deleted).
Dated: 'Old' (MS A3, p. 105).

JEANNETTE

Near a grove of tall trees stretching far oer the pool
Whose broad shadows darken the stream as it flows
Where in summer the breeze from the waters so cool
Refreshes the flocks with a welcome repose
There nurs'd in a humble thatch'd cot that stands nigh   5
A sweet lovely blossom blooms lowly unseen
& call'd by the shepherds that wander hard bye
The lovley Jeannette the pride of the green

Cherish'd in solitude humble & warm
To the world & its vices unseen & unknown   10
No pride the sweet charms of the Angel deform
Adornd by the hand of sweet nature alone

21 Such] Her *RL*   beauty$_\wedge$: untimly *MS 1*   Beauties— *through* charms that *MS D4*
23 returnd *MS 1*   25 Today like flowers such charms may bloom *MS 1*
26 ⟨But who⟩ *smudged MS 1*   27 ⟨Since the⟩ *smudged MS 1*   28 em
MS 1

JEANNETTE   *Title:* Jeannette *MS A3*, Louisa a Ballad *MS A40*, *wanting MS 1*
1 Grove: trees] Oaks: Stretching: Pool *MS 1*   2 Broad Shadow darkens *MS 1*
3 Were *MS A40*   Summer: Breeze: Water *MS 1*   4 Welcome Repose *MS 1*
5 Ther *MS 1*   nursd *MS 1*] nursed *MS A40*   thatchd *MS 1*] thatched *MS A40*
6 Sweet lovley Blossom *MS 1*   lowley *MS A40*   7 calld *MS 1*] called *MS A40*
Shepherds: Wander: by *MS 1*   8 lovley *through* lovly *MS A3*   a *through* n *in*
Jeanette *MS 1*] Louisa *MS A40*   Green *MS 1*   9 Cherished *MS A40*
11 angel *MS A40*   12 Adorned *MS A40*

O charms so enchanting so winning to prove
Had I but ne'er seen her how happy I'd been
E'en ages chill blood would flow warm into love   15
At the sight of Jeanette the pride of the green

Nature lavish of charms steals the blush from the rose
& to give that cheek softness health rivals the morn
Despoil'd of its beauty the lorn lilly blows
Her lovley sweet bosom & neck to adorn   20
—O a curse on such villians so base to perswade
With hearts void of feeling so harden'd & mean
As to injure such beauties their lustre to fade
& hurt sweet Jeanette the pride of the Green

As list'ning the black bird I saunter'd along   25
Supris'd at such beauties ne'er witness'd before
She pass'd me—adieu—to the unfinish'd song
The music had power for to please me no more

---

13 to] do *MS A40*   14 neer: Id *MS A40*   15 Een: woud *MS A40*
16 Jeanette] Louisa *MS A40*   17 Blush: Rose *MS 1*   18 that] her
MS A40   Cheek: Rifles: Morn *MS 1*   19 Despoild *MS 1 MS A40*   Beauty:
Blows *MS 1*   Lilly *MS 1*] lily *MS A40*   20 Her] That: Bosom: Neck
MS 1   lovly *MS 1 MS A40*   21 —O a] & a *MS 1*, A *MS A40*   Curse: such]
those *MS 1*   Villians *MS 1*] villans *MS A40*   persuade *MS A40*   22 hardend
& *MS 1*] hard & so *MS A40*   23 Ingure: such] that: its *MS 1*   Beauty *MS 1*]
beautys *MS A40*   24 Jeanette] Louisa: green *MS A40*   Pride *MS 1*   *The poem
continues at this point in MS 1:*

> In the Cottage of Solitude humble & Warm
> To the World & its Vices unseen & unknown
> No Pride can the charms of the Angel deform
> Adornd by the hand of Sweet Nature alone
> O Charms so bewitching—what heart that can feel 5
> When ever such Exquisite Beauty is seen
> [But feels for Jeanette]
> But feels from his Bosom as sigh vainly steal
> For the Charming Jeanette the Pride of the Green
> Her Ways all so winning so endearing to Love 10
> So engaging her manners so timid & shy
> Simplicitys sweetness all her Beautys improve
> & Innocense Brightens the Blue of her eye

(l. 3 charms *over* [heart])

25 listning: saunterd *MS A40*   26 Suprised: beauty near witnessd *MS A40*
27 passd: adieu∧: unfinished *MS A40*

—The coy glance turn'd from me—the blushes—alone
On the bewitching cheek of Virginity seen   30
Made my heart from that moment—(no longer my own)
A Slave to Jeannette the pride of the green

So winning, so moving, who could but help loving?
So artless her manners so modest & shy
Simplicitys sweetness her charms still Improving   35
& Innocence bright'ning the blue of her eye
I've seen her,—I languish—O great is my anguish
—Ye chill pains that haunt me—O what can ye mean?
I've seen her—I sigh for—& seeing—must dye for
That angel Jeanette—the pride of the green   40

AUTOGRAPH: Nor. MS 1, p. 191.
Dated: 1808–19 (MS 1).

When from this vain World my spiri[t] is Reli[e]ved
& Chilling in my breast lifes ebbing tide
As like a Gest with da[i]ntes satisfi[e]d
Ill thank the fates for what I have recievd
& humbly wait what still they may provide   5

29 ∧The: turned: me∧: blushes∧ *MS A40*   30 virginity *MS A40*
31 moment∧ *MS A40*   32 slave: Jeanette] Louisa: of the green *MS A40*
33 winning∧: moving∧: coud: but] not: loving∧ *MS A40*   34 her[e] *MS A3*
shoy *altered to* shy *MS A40*   35 improving *MS A40*   36 innosence
MS A40   brightening *altered to* bright'ning *MS A3*] brightning *MS A40*   37 Ive:
her∧∧: O] & *MS A40*   38 ∧Ye: me∧: mean∧ *MS A40*   39 Ive: her∧: for∧
MS A40   seening— *MS A3*] seeing∧ *MS A40*   40 That angel Jeanette—] The
lovley Louisa∧ *MS A40*

WHEN FROM THIS VAIN WORLD MY SPIRIT IS RELIEVED *Title:*
wanting   1 from *inserted*: my . . . Relived *over* [essays to part]

AUTOGRAPH: Nor. MS 1, pp. 192–3.
Dated: 1808–19 (MS 1).

THE ROBBINS

The fading Autumn all resighn'd
   As consious of her dying state
Th' influence of the Sun declin'd
   And hopeless yielded to her fate

The Trees their faded colours mourn'd   5
   And shepherds with a tearfull eye
Review'd their changes as they turn'd
   And thought of winter with a sigh

No Blackbird sung to please his mate
   The Blackbirds songs was now no more   10
And all in silence mournd that fate
   Which songs where useless to restore

And while the Blackbirds still denied
   The trial of a single note
The Robins all their musick tried   15
   And anxious streatchd their little throats

Sweet little innocents alone
   In autumns sorrows they engage
And feel her sorrows as their own
   And comfort her declineing age   20

Twas in my native fields among
   Her woes two robins strove to share
Which are the subject of my song
   Perch'd in a little hovel there

THE ROBBINS   *Title:* The Robbins   9 his *through* her   10 The *through*
No   19 feel *through* sor

O lovely innofencive crew   25
  Most harmless of the featherd throng
Was but my Song as worthy you
  As you are worthy of my Song

Forever then my verse would live
  And you forever in my verse   30
And pleas'd I'll be so I can give
  Your songs for abler to rehearse

O then my Muse record the Lay
  Of Robin & his long-been Bride
Who love'd as at the Bridal day   35
  Was fondly nestl'd by his side

And tho the pretty Robin doats
  To pick and Clean his glossy wing
Low droop'd the wings & ruff the coats
  Of these two Robins which I sing   40

For they so griev'd at autumns fall
  No care upon themselves bestowd
She—pretty Loves requ[i]r'd it all
  And thus their dirge to Autumn flowd

AUTOGRAPH: Nor. MS 1, pp. 194–6.
Dated: 1808–19 (MS 1).

Now spring returns with all her wonted charms
And Winter leaves us conqu[e]rd & dismayd
Mild Nature bursting from his icy arms
Puts forth her buds & kindles into shade

38 and . . . wing *through* his wing & clean his coat
  NOW SPRING RETURNS WITH ALL HER WONTED CHARMS *Title: wanting*

And O what prospects! what delightful scenes   5
Attract the notice of each tactful eye
Farstretching Woods of many shading greens
& culturd fields & flowers of every dye

To day the Daisies silvers oer the green
& to the sun their starry leaves unfold   10
To morrow kin[g]cups varify the scene
Reflect the Sun & stud the plains wi' gold

O in this Season of delight & joy
Was it but mine thro natures charms to rove
How sweet would I my leisure hours employ   15
Strechd on the plain or nestld in the grove

Where the old ivyied Oaks rude mossy arms
Hangs oer the pond in Pictur[e]sque decay
Where full of life the flaggy water swarms
There would I sit and loiter life away   20

Or closly hid in some sequesterd nook
Where dead Grass rustles to the fanning gale
Pass the lone minutes with a storied Book
& read in rapture each deligh[tful] tale

Or else lone sitting by some Woods warm side   25
View the pale primrose in the hedgerow bloom
And Hare bells hang their heads in purple pride
And Creeping Vil'ets shedding sweet perfume

Or where the pasture spreads her rushy grounds
& scatterd Molehills make it wilder still   30
I'd thoughtless wander her bewilderd rounds
& rest when weary on some thymy hill

How oft ere twilight streakd the east with gray
Would I be musing oer the fallow fields
Where wistling Sky-larks hail aproaching day   35
While some brown Clot their lowly nest consceals

8/9 *Space for four lines*   17 arms *over* [grains]   24 & read in Read in
rapture   28 C *through* p *in* Creeping   32/3 *Space for another stanza*

And O ye Warblers dread no Rober nigh
Nor at my sighs be fearful or distrest
Nor oer my head in Wild disorder fly
I'll only peep to view your curious nest　　40

AUTOGRAPH: Nor. MS 1, p. 198.
Dated: 1808–19 (MS 1).

The dareing Bird that hardly shuns
　　The Fowlers open Net
That even dares the Pointed Guns
　　And flies in Safety Yet

And tho he's mist by every Gun　　5
　　And Every net that's cast
H[e] falls by Poltry Hawks when done
　　Most scandelous at last

To such a Birds may be compar'd
　　Poor lost Clarinda's fate　　10
And O how poor Clarinda's far'd
　　It grieves me to relate

AUTOGRAPH: Nor. MS 1, p. 199 (pencil).
Dated: 1808–19 (MS 1).

The beauties of Myra in it[s] lustre now dawning
As the spring is first seen to disclose
When the dew drop[p]ing silver of mays infant morning
Unfoldeth the blush of the Rose

37　dread] *successively (a)* [deem] *(b)* [fear] *(c)* dread
　　THE DAREING BIRD THAT HARDLY SHUNS　*Title: wanting*
　　THE BEAUTIES OF MYRA IN ITS LUSTRE NOW DAWNING　*Title: wanting*

While her charms O as varied as summers profusion   5
& Ripe as the autumn for love
In her blue Eyes sweet beaming the thrilling confusion
Near failing each bosom to move

While the snows of the Winter improvd on her bosom
No need of a Rival be told   10
—& O my sad pains—when I went to disclosem
I found it as killing & cold

AUTOGRAPHS: Pet. MS A3, pp. 34–40: Pet. MS A3, p. 94 (ll. 225–40 only, pencil, deleted): Nor. MS 1, p. 200 (ll. 1–32, pencil), p. 201 (ll. 33–44 pencil under ink, ll. 45–64 pencil), p. 204 (ll. 65–96 pencil, ll. 97–100 ink), p. 208 (ll. 101–48), p. 211 (ll. 149–76 ink, ll. 177–88 pencil), p. 213 (ll. 189–224, pencil), p. 216 (ll. 241–50, pencil): Nor. MS 1, p. 222 (ll. 65–72, 77–80 only, pencil): Nor. MS 1, pp. 21, 33, 34, 35, 86 (fragments in margins): Norris Museum SAVNM CL/9 (ll. 157–60 only).
TRANSCRIPTS: Pet. MS B1, pp. 168–70, 96–5, 99–100: Nor. MS 5, pp. 31–46 (ll. 241–8 omitted, ll. 121–4, 153–6, 209–28 deleted).
Printed in *RL*, pp. 16–29 (ll. 53–6, 121–4, 153–6, 209–28 omitted).
Dated: 1807–8 (MS A3, p. 34 'began 12 years ago', RL Introduction, p. xxii 'begun when he was fourteen').

THE FATE OF AMY

A Tale

Beneath a sheltering woods warm side
    Where many a tree expands
Their branches oer the neighbouring brook
    A ruind cottage stands

    THE FATE OF AMY *Title:* The Fate of Amy a Tale *MS A3 RL, wanting MS 1   Stanzas numbered 1–63 in MS A3   Pencil emendations in MS A3 are Taylor's*   1 Beside a lonly sheltering wood *MS 1*   2 tree] Oak *MS 1*
3 Its *MS 1 RL*   neibouring *MS 1*   4 Ruind *MS 1*

2

Tho now left desolate & lost
  Its origin & all
Owls hooting from the roofles walls
  Rejoicing in its fall

5

3

A time was come—(remembrance knows)
  Tho now that times gone bye
When that was seen to flourish gay
  & pleasing to the eye

10

4

On that same ground the brambles hide
  & stinking weeds oer run
A orchard bent its golden boughs
  & reddend in the sun

15

5

Yon nettles where they're left to spred
  There once a garden smild
& lovly was the spot to view
  Tho now so lost & wild

20

6

& where the sickly eldern loves
  To top the mouldering wall
& Ivys kind encroaching care
  Delays the tottering fall

---

5 Tho now decayd & desolate *MS 1* 6 & lost in Ruins all *MS 1* 7 roofles
to roofless *(p.e.) MS A3*] Roofles *MS 1* walls] shed *MS 1* 9 In by gone days
there was a time *MS 1* 10 that] the *RL* by *MS 1* 11 that] it *RL 4th edn.*
13 On *through* The: that same *inserted*: the] in *over* [in briars &]: hide] lost *MS 1*
14 oerrund *MS 1* 15 An *MS 1 RL* Orchard *MS 1* 16 Tho now
despisd & shund *MS 1* 17 Lo where the baleful nettle spreds *MS 1*
18 Garden *MS 1* 19 vie *MS 1* 21 the] that *MS 1* elder *MS 1*] alder
altered to elder *Harvard proof copy*, alder *RL* (elder *on errata slip*), elder *RL 2nd edn.*
22 tope *MS 1* 23 & darksom ivys creeping care *MS 1* 24 Illudeing still
the fall *MS 1*

7

There once a mothers only Joy   25
A daughter lovly fair
As ever bloomd beneath the sun
Was nursd & cherishd there

8

The cottage then was known around—
The neighbouring village swain[s]   30
Would often wander by to view
That charmer of the plains

9

Where softest blush of rosey wild
& awthorns fairest blow
But meanly serves to paint her cheek   35
& bosoms rival snow

10

The lovliest blossom of the plains
The charming Amy provd
In natures sweetest charms adornd
—Those charms by all belov'd   40

11

Sweet innoscence the charms are thine
That every bosom warms
Fair as she was she livd alone
A stranger to her charms

---

25 joy *MS 1*   26 lovly] sweet & *MS 1*   29 around∧ *MS 1*   30 [Aroun] The *MS 1*   swain *to* swains *(p.e.) MS A3*] swains *MS 1*   31 Would often pass in hopes to see *MS 1*   33–44 *In pencil beneath* I wish that I was but a gay blushing rose *MS 1 (see p. 291 below)*   33 Where] The: softest] softning *MS 1*   rosey *to* roses *(p.e.) MS A3*] rosys *MS 1*   34 The awthorns melting blow *MS 1*   awthorns *to* hawthorns *(p.e.) MS A3*   35 serve *over* [blush] *MS 1*] serve *RL*   36 Rival *MS 1*   37 lovilest *MS A3*   blosom *MS 1*   38 charming] artless *RL*   amy *MS 1*   39 Adornd in natures sweetest bloom *MS 1*   40 By health alone improvd *MS 1*   41 charms are] beauty's *RL*   & thou sweet Innocence was there *MS 1*   43 The sweet possesor livd alone *MS 1*   44 Stranger *MS 1*

12

Unmovd the praise of swains she heard 45
   Nor proud at their despair
But thought they scoft her when they praisd
   And knew not she was fair

13

Nor did she for the joys of youth
   Forget parental care 50
But to her aged mother provd
   As good as she was fair

14

Who then by age & pain infirmd
   On her for help relyd
& how to help her all she could 55
   Her every thought employd

15

No tenderer mother to a child
   Throughout the world could be
& in return no daughter provd
   More dutiful then she 60

16

The pains of age she sympathizd
   & soothd & wisht to share
In short the aged helples dame
   Was Amys only care

---

46 No pride colected there *MS 1*   47 when] while *MS 1*   48 & *MS 1*
50 parential *to* parental *(p.e.) MS A3*   Neglect her filial care *MS 1*   51 Who
then by age and pain infirm'd *RL*   52 On her for help relied *RL*   53 Infirmd
to infirmd *(p.e.) MS A3*   When she by age & palsy seizd *MS 1*   54 relyd *to* relied
(p.e.) MS A3   Was low & helples brought *MS 1*   55 To do for her the best she
could *MS 1*   56 Employd her every thought *MS 1*   57 Mother: Child
MS 1   58 r *through* o *in* Throueight *MS 1*   59 Return *MS 1*   provd *to*
prov'd *(p.e.) MS A3*   60 More *through indecipherable MS 1*   then *to* than *(p.e.)*
MS A3] than *MS 1*   61 age] alls *MS 1*   sympathizd *to* sympathiz'd *(p.e.) MS A3*]
sympathisd *MS 1*   62 soothd *to* sooth'd *(p.e.) MS A3*   wishd *MS 1*
63 helples *to* helpless *(p.e.) MS A3*   64 Amys *to* Amy's *(p.e.) MS A3*

17

But age had pains—& they was all   65
    Lifes cares they little knew
Its billows neer encompassd them
    —They waded smoothly thro

18

The tender father now no more
    Did for them both provide   70
The wealth by his Industry gaind
    All wants to come supplyd

19

Kind heaven upon their labours smild
    Industry gave increase
The cottage was contentments own   75
    Abode of health & peace

20

Alas the tongue of fate is seald
    & kept for ever dumb
To morrows met with blinded eyes
    We know not whats to come   80

65 pains∧ *MS 1*   were *RL*   But sorrows they where [but] little known *(they inserted)*
MS 1, p. 222   66 never *over* [little] *MS 1, p. 222*   67 neer *to* ne'er *(p.e.)*:
encompassd *to* encompass'd *(p.e.) MS A3*   His Billows neer encompasd them *MS 1*]
Cares billows . . . *MS 1, p. 222*   68 ∧They *MS 1*   waded] traveld *MS 1 MS 1,*
p. 222   thro *to* through *(p.e.) MS A3*   69 Father *MS 1*   71 Industry *to*
industry *(p.e.) MS A3*] industry *MS 1 MS 1, p. 222*   The wealth his industry had
gain'd *RL*   72 supplyd *to* supplied *(p.e.) MS A3*   The wants in them supplyd *MS*
1] The wants of life supplyd— *MS 1, p. 222*   73 [Heaven] Kind: Heaven *MS 1*
labours *to* labour's *(p.e.) MS A3*] labour *MS 1*   74 & Blest em with increase *MS 1*
75 The Cott contentment markd her own *MS 1*   76 Peace *MS 1*   77 *Preceded*
in pencil in MS 1, p. 222 by: But oh the dark decrees of fate / No human eye can see
77 Alas] But ah *MS 1 MS 1, p. 222*   the *through* some: Song *altered to* tongue *MS 1,*
p. 222   79 We blinded meet advacing time *MS 1*] advancing *MS 1, p. 222*
80 We] & *MS 1 MS 1, p. 222*

21

Blythe as the Lark as Crickets gay
That chyrup in the h[e]arth
This sun of beautys time was spent
In innofensive mirth

22

Meek as the lambs that throngd her door   85
As innoscent as they
Her hours passd on & charms improvd
With each succeeding day

23

So smiling on the sunny plain
The lovly daiseys blow   90
Unconsious of the carless foot
That lays their beauty low

24

So blooms the lilly of the vale
(Ye beauties o be wise)
Untimley blasts oertake its bloom   95
It withers & it dies

81 Blyth *MS 1*   Lark *to* lark *(p.e.) MS A3*] Lark— *MS 1*   'Crickets *to* crickets *(p.e.)*
MS A3] cricket *RL*   82 chyrupt *to* chirrupt *(p.e.) MS A3*] chirupt *MS 1*   in]
on *RL*   harth *to* hearth *(p.e.) MS A3*] hearth *MS 1*   83 beautys *to* beauty's *(p.e.)*
MS A3] beauty's *MS 1*   84 innofensive *to* innoffensive *(p.e.) MS A3*] innoscence &
MS 1   85–8 *Marginal note in MS A3:* The rest next Week or on Friday
85 throngd *to* throng'd *MS A3*   86 innoscent *to* innocent *(p.e.) MS A3*   As
harmles & as gay *MS 1*   87 hours *through* days: pasd *MS 1*   on— *to* on, *(p.e.)*
MS A3   88 With] By: suceeding *MS 1*   90 lovly] little *MS 1*   daiseys *to*
daisies *(p.e.) MS A3*] daisys *MS 1*   91 carless *to* careless *(p.e.) MS A3*] carles *MS 1*
92 lays] treds *MS 1*   theirs *to* their *(p.e.) MS A3*   93 vale] dale *MS 1*
94 Beauties *MS 1*   o *to* oh *(p.e.) MS A3*] O *MS 1*   bewise *to* be wise *(p.e.) MS A3*
95 Untimley *to* Untimely *(p.e.) MS A3*] Untimly *MS 1*   oertake *to* o'ertake *(p.e.)*
MS A3

25

The humble cot that lonly stood
  Far from the neighbouring Vill
Its church that topt the willow groves
  Lay far upon the hill   100

26

Which made all company desird
  & welcome to the dame
& oft to tell the village news
  The neighbouring gossips came

27

—Young Edward mingld with the rest   105
  An artful swain was he
Who laughd & told his merry jests
  For custom made him free

28

& oft with Amy toy'd & playd
  While harmless as the dove   110
Her artless unsuspecting heart
  But little thought of Love

29

But frequent visits gaind esteem
  Each time of Longer stay
& custom did his name endear   115
  —He stole her heart away

---

97 cot that] cottage *RL*   that] so: stood] lay *MS 1*   lonly *to* lonely *(p.e.) MS A3*
98 from[e]: Vill *to* vill *(p.e.) MS A3*   The nighest neighbouring hill *MS 1*
99 Its] Whose: that topt] oer lookd: Willow *MS 1*
101–4
                And oft the village swains & maids
                To the lone cottage came
                Their visits all as kindly took
                & welcome to the dame   *MS 1*

103 tell *over* [pass the boring] *MS A3*   105 Yound *to* Young *(p.e.) MS A3*] & *MS 1*
107 told] jokd *MS 1*   109 amy toyd *MS 1*   110 harmles *MS 1*
111 artles: heart] art *MS 1*   112 love *MS 1*   113 But ah he often sought
the cot *(often through* longer) *MS 1*   114 & made a longer stay *MS 1*
115 While use his presence more endeard *MS 1*

30

So fairest flower adorn the wild
  & most endangerd stand
The soonest seen—a certain prey
  To some destroying hand   120

31

& ah the hand their bloom destroys
  This truth too oft may show
That meaner charms superior shine
  & beauty but a foe

32

Her choise was fix'd on him alone   125
  The rest but vainly strove
& worse then all the rest is he
  But blind the eyes of love

33

Of him full many a maid complaind
  The lover of an hour   130
That like the ever changing bee
  Sipt sweets from every flower

34

Alas those slighted pains are small
  If all such maidens know
But she was fair & he designd   135
  To work her further woe

35

Her innoscence his bosom fir'd
  So long'd to be enjoy'd
& he to gain his wish'd for ends
  Each sub[t]le art employ'd   140

---

117 [On him] So: flowers *MS 1*   121 their *through* that: [Johnnies] bloom *(i in*
Johnnies *is elongated and resembles a 't') MS A3*   124 Beauty *MS 1*   125 choise
to choice *(p.e.) MS A3*   fixd *MS 1*   126 Rest *MS 1*   127 than: rest]
swains: was *MS 1*   128 Love *MS 1*   131 That] Who *MS 1*   133 Alas]
But ah *MS 1*   135 But she] The maid *MS 1*   137 innoscence *to* innocence
(p.e.) MS A3] innosence *MS 1*   fird *MS 1*   138 longd: enjoyd *MS 1*
139 wishd *MS 1*   140 [Each] His: arts employd *MS 1*   suble *to* subtle *(p.e.)*
MS A3] subtle *MS 1*

36
Ah he employd his subtle arts
Alas too sad to tell
The winning ways which he employ'd
Succeeded but too well

37
So artless Innosent & young   145
So ready to believe
A stranger to the world was she
& easy to decieve

38
Ah now fare well to beautys boast
Charms so admir'd before   150
Now innocence has lost its sweets
Her beauties bloom no more

39
Ye meaner beauties be advis'd
Let this as such remain
An hour of pleasure vainly spent   155
May leave an age of pain

40
The flowers the sultry summer kills
Springs milder suns restore
But innocence that fickle charm
Blooms once—& blooms no more   160

141 Ah] Yes *MS 1*   142 Alas too] & O to *MS 1*   143 employd *MS 1*
144 Suceeded: to *MS 1*   145 artles *MS 1*   Innosent *to* innocent *(p.e.) MS A3*]
inocent *MS 1*   147 Stranger: World *MS 1*   148 decieve *to* deceive *(p.e.)*
MS A3   149–52 *Marginal note in MS A3*: I think I left off at the 31 Ver: if I did
not you must tell me—   149 beautys *to* beauty's *(p.e.) MS A3*   & were was
now that beautys boast *MS 1*   150 That charmd so much before *MS 1*
151 innoscence *to* innocence *(p.e.)*: its *through* her MS A3   The sweets of innocence
was lost *MS 1*   152 & beauty was no more *MS 1*   153 advisd *MS 1*
156 leave] bring *MS 1*   157 sultry *inserted*: summers: kills *over* [heat destroys]
MS 1   159 innoscence *to* innocence *(p.e.) MS A3*] innosence *Norris*   charm!
Norris   But youth & beauty once destroyd *MS 1*   160 Blooms *through* Blosoms:
& *through* to *Norris*   Will never bloom no more *MS 1*

41

The swains who lov'd, no more admire
    Their hearts no beauty warms
& maidens triumph in her fall
    That envy'd once her charms

42

Lost was that sweet simplicity   165
    Her eyes bright lustre fled
& oer her cheeks where roses bloom'd
    A sickly paleness spread

43

So fade the flower before its time
    Where canker worms assail   170
So droops the bud upon its stem
    Beneath the sickly gale

44

The mother saw the sudden change
    Where health so latly smild
Too much—& O suspecting more   175
    Grew anxious for her child

45

& all the kindness in her power
    The tender mother shows
In hopes such kindly means would make
    Her fearless to disclose   180

161 no more admire *through* now ceasd their pains *MS A3*   The swains that lovd now
love no more *MS 1*   162 Their *through* The *MS A3*   163 Maidens
MS 1   triumphed *MS A3*] triumphd *MS 1*   164 That] Which: envied
MS 1   once envy'd *MS A3*] once envied *MS 1*, envied once *RL*   165 simplicity
MS 1   167 Rosys bloomd *MS 1*   168 palnes spred *MS 1*   169 [rosys]
fades: the flower] the Rose *inserted*: its *over* [their] *MS 1*   170 Where] When
through Who: Worms *MS 1*   171 bud . . . stem] lilly in its prime *MS 1*
173 mother] matron: sudden] sickly *MS 1*   175 o *MS 1*   177 Kindnes
MS 1   178 the *MS 1*   179 woud *MS 1*   180 fearles *MS 1*

46

& oft she hinted if a crime
  Thro ignorance beguild
Not to conceal the crime in fear
  For none should wrong her child

47

Or if the rose that left her cheek   185
  Was banish'd by disease
'Fear god my child' she oft would say
  & you may hope for ease

48

& still she pray'd—& still had hopes
  There was no injury done   190
& still advis'd the ruind girl
  The worlds deciet to shun

49

& many a Cautionary tale
  Of hapless maidens fate
(From trusting man) to warn her told   195
  But told alas too late

50

A tender mothers painful cares
  In vain the loss supply
The wide mouth'd world—its sport & scorn
  Then meet—she'd sooner dye   200

181 if a] at the *MS 1*   182 Thro *to* Through *(p.e.) MS A3*   183 Not to be
fearful to reveal *MS 1*   184 —For: wrong] hurt *MS 1*   186 banishd
MS 1   187 ∧Fear: Child∧ *through* god: woud *MS 1*   god *to* God *(p.e.) MS A3*
189 prayd∧ *MS 1*   191 advisd *MS 1*   192 world *to* world's *(p.e.) MS A3*
193 Cautionary *to* cautionary *(p.e.) MS A3*] cautonary *MS 1*   194 haples *MS 1*
195 (From trusting man) *to* From trusting man *(p.e.) MS A3*   (From] By: man∧ *MS 1*
196 to *MS 1*   197 mothers *to* mother's *(p.e.) MS A3*   care *MS 1*   198 los
suply *MS 1*   199 widemouthd world∧ *MS 1*   200 Than: shed *MS 1*

51

Advice but agravated woe
    & ease an empty sound
No one could ease the pains she felt
    But him that gave the wound

52

& he wild youth had left her now   205
    Unfeeling as the stone
—Fair maids beware lest careless ways
    Make amys fate your own

53

What hard'n'd brutes such villians are
    To wrong the artless maid   210
To stain the lillies virgin bloom
    & cause the rose to fade

54

O may the charms of Myra bloom
    Each bosom still to warm
& curse the Villian who would dare   215
    To do such beauties harm

55

To blight that rosebuds sweetest bloom
    That opens all divine
Those swelling hills of snow to stain
    & bid them cease to shine   220

---

201 Advise *MS 1*   agravated *to* aggravated *(p.e.) MS A3*   203 pain *MS 1*
204 him that] he who *RL*   205 &] But: yout: had] he *MS 1*   207 ∧Fair: be
ware: carles *MS 1*   208 amys *to* Amys *(p.e.) MS A3*   209 villians *to* villains
(p.e.) MS A3   O cruel men what brutes they are *MS 1*   210 artles *MS 1*
211 the *inserted MS A3*   lillies *to* lilly's *(p.e.) MS A3*] lilys *MS 1*   vergin *MS 1*
212 rose *inserted MS 1*   213 myra *MS 1*   214 Each] My *MS 1*
215 Villian *to* villain *(p.e.) MS A3*] vilain *MS 1*   216 such] thy: beauty *MS 1*
217 To fad that rose upon thy cheek *MS 1*   218 opens] blosoms *MS 1*
219 Thos sweling *MS 1*   220 em *MS 1*

56

O may that seat of Innosence
  As lovly still appear
& keep those eyes of heavenly blue
  Still strangers to a tear

57

Lov'd Myra if these artless strains   225
  Should meet your kind regard
Let amys fate a warning prove
  & I have my reward—

58

Ill fated girl too late she found
  As but too many find   230
False Edwards love as light as down
  & Vows as fleet as wind

59

But one hope left & that she sought
  To hide approaching shame
& Pity while she drops a tear   235
  Forbears the rest to name

60

The widow'd mother tho so old
  & ready to depart
Was not ordain'd to live her time
  The sad news broke her heart   240

221 Innosence *to* innosence *(p.e.) MS A3*] inocence *MS 1*   222 apear
MS 1   223 Eys: heavnly *MS 1*   225 lovd: artless] humbl *MS A3, p. 94*
226 Should] Can: meet *through* claim: Regard *MS A3, p. 94*   227 amys *to* Amys
(p.e.) MS A3   228 hav: reward₍ *MS A3, p. 94*   229 to *MS A3, p. 94*
231 Fals: lov: lite *MS A3, p. 94*   232 Vows *to* vows *(p.e.) MS A3*
233 hope's *RL*   234 aproaching *MS A3, p. 94*   235 &] But: pity *MS A3,*
p. 94   237 widowd *MS A3, p. 94*   tho *to* though *(p.e.) MS A3*   238 Ready
MS A3, p. 94   239 ordaind *MS A3, p. 94*

61

Born down beneath a weight of years
& all the pains they gave
But little added weights requir'd
To crush her in the grave

62

The strong oak braves the rudest wind   245
While to the breeze as well
The sickly aged willow falls
& so the mother fell

63

Beside the pool the Willow bends
The dew bent daisey weeps   250
& where the turfy hillock swells
The luckless amy sleeps

241–50 *Beneath* O native scenes for ever ever dear *MS 1 (see pp. 300–1 below)*
243 aded: requird *MS 1*   weights *to* weight's *(p.e.) MS A3*] weight *MS 1 RL*
245 A *MS 1*   249 Willow *to* willow *(p.e.) MS A3*] willow *MS 1*   250 dasy
MS 1   252 amy *to* Amy *(p.e.) MS A3*   *The following drafts in MS 1 may be
connected with this poem:*

Now day declines & morning shines again
& finds in marys heart a added pain
Thro all disguise her pains & sorrows break
& careless mantles on her sallowy cheek
Her hollow eys no longer awd by fears   5
Now moistens public in a shower of tears
Her sobbing heart no more her grief reveals
But still the tongue denies what it reveals
A ruind maid so timid so forlorn
Is basht to tell & dreads a meddlars scorn   10
The base bad world is so detested vain
& deaf to injurd innocences pain
Sooner then pity where such woes befall
They love to laugh & triumph in their fall

(l. 2 finds *through ?* resides; l. 14 h *written separately after* triumph)

Poor amy now found her last hope was gone
Whithout one friendly prop to lean upon
Her once best frien now turnd her worst of foes
Hardend in deep despair & hopless woes
That horrid fate that did erewhile ensue   5
Twas now that fate sat picturd on her view
A setteld glower [now] her hopless form retains
As looks the condemnd felon in his chains

Deep pondering oer the fate that is to come
His heart is hardend & his woes are dumb   *p. 21*

Her aching heart was ready to exclaim
& guilt & terror shook her trembling frame   *p. 33*

They often usd to chatter when

They stand no more to rest em oer their pales
To talk the village news & tattling tales
In shame & sorrow stung she sneakt along
& morns salute hung faltering on her tonge   5
Her horid fate hung clouding oer her view
Companions pleasures & to all adieu

The joys which early morn inspird are fled
The sun peept sweet—but she neer turnd her head
Tho woodlarks sung she heeded not the strain   10
& diasys opt their smiling charms in vain
The gazing cows in expectation stood
Whose bellowing calls disturbd the echoing ⟨wood⟩
Lashing their sleeky side with sweing tails
Full well they knew the rattles of her pails   15
& gatherd round the hoples girl the stand
Courting the stroakings of her milking hand   *p. 34*

(l. 13 ⟨wood⟩ *supplied*; l. 16 *second* the *for* 'they')

Saluting them as one salutes a friend
She pats their sides & hurries to her end
They rubd the creaking gate & bowd adieu
Seeming as tho they wishd to follow too

Distressing scene so moving it appears   5
She coudnt help it bursting in to tears
Poor things she sighd my milking days are oer
I then was what I neer must be no more
I then was happy & did then delight
To come & milk ye every morn & night   10
When oer my bucket neath ye as I hung
Ye bawld a timley chorus as I sung
Alas those days are past my doom comes on
She said & stroakt their forheads one by one   *p. 35*

(l. 11 bucknet)

The morning peepd & mary with her pail
Now seemd as usual hastening to the vale
Tho in her looks a solemn fate was fixd
Resolve & dread alternatively mixt
Her bonnet oer her eyes her head cast down   5
& passing many a partner of the town
Each gay enheeding bonny milking lass
The dewdrops bouncing from the grass
As grass & hay brushd along from sorrow free
As artless & as happy once was she   *p. 86*   10

(l. 3 fate *through* mixd; l. 4 m *through* f *in* mixt; l. 6 *first* r *in* partner *inserted*)

AUTOGRAPHS: Nor. MS 7, p. 43. A double folio sheet also containing
'Sonnet / Well have I . . .' (see p. 506 below): Nor. MS 11, pp. 58–9 (ll. 1–12,
15–19, 26–34 only, pencil): Nor. MS 1, p. 20 (ll. 131–40, 143–50, 156–64
only, margin) p. 26 (fragment).
Dated: 1807–8 (Explanatory Notes for 'The Fate of Amy').

HAUNTED POND

O superstition terryfying power
Thou dithering agent of Nights solemn hour
How (when pitch darkness glooms the awful night)
Thy dithering terrors rush upon the sight
Then the grim terrors of thy haunting train   5
Swim thro the gloom & stalk along the plain
Then all the horrid forms the eye can see
Which fancy moulds are realizd by thee
Here murder shudders on with giant stride
& heedless spirits cringes by his side   10
The calls of mercy—helpless wails of woe
Are still h[e]ard howling in the woods below
The bloody stainings undefacd by time
Still dyes the grass a witness to the crime

Now silent forms in musing mood suceeds   15
As mourning inly some unraveld deeds
The slowly solem step the drooping head
Such woes are plain depicted in their tread
Now usless mizers midnight hags forlorn
In shattered rags their saving deeds have worn   20

HAUNTED POND   *Title:* Haunted Pond *MS 7, wanting MS 11*   2 dithering]
quaking: Nights solemn] the mid night *MS 11*   Nights *through* things *MS 7*
3 When pitch black shades oer gloom the awful nite *MS 11*   5 the grim terrors]
waking demons: haunting] horrid *MS 11*   6 gloom] glowen *MS 11*   7 *First*
the] thy *MS 11*   9 shudders on] stalks along: stride] pride *MS 11*   10 cringing:
⟨side⟩ *worn MS 11*   11 mercy∧ helples *MS 11*   12 heard *MS 11*
15 Now silent forms] A silent form: ⟨suceeds⟩ *confused MS 11*   16 In anguish
pondering oer unraveld ⟨deeds⟩ *(deeds omitted) MS 11*   17 With solemn steps
& slow with hanging ⟨head⟩ *(head omitted) MS 11*   18 Such woes are] Her
sorrows: her *MS 11*   19 There restless mizers frown & boun⟨ce about⟩ *(ce
about omitted) MS 11*   *l. 19 turns into l. 25 in MS 11*

Pay their uneasy visits once again
To each devoted dwelling where in pain
They pind & starvd to hurd each mouldy heap
& left the spoil for thankless heirs to reap
Impatient urgd they frown & bounce about   25
& seem to wish to blab some secret out
To haunted man they every beckon make
To break the silence & to let them speak
Till vext & wearied with the quaking wight
They frown reproach & hurryd out of sight   30
Now rustling silks & sattins sweeps the ground
& antique spirits flirt the castles round
With pointed finger & with quizzing eyes
Marks out each monstrous stone that hides a prize!
& where yon pond with ash encircld round   35
Awthorns below above with ivy bound
Whose quaking leaves when night is glooming near
Rustles their terrors to the passing ear
Poor amys dripping spirit wanders round
For there the poor despairing maid was drown'd   40
& often there in superstitions eyes
Dithering & quaking from the pond shell rise
In the same cloaths then wore she wanders still
Wet as she draggles up the pond head hill
All wet & dripping from her watry bed   45
Echo seems startld with the gushing tread
As when our feet are wet squish squa[s]hing round
Folks knows it well & shudder at the sound
Thus superstition the weak mind decieves
Which village faith as stren[u]ously believes   50
So when a Boy my heart has 'chilld with dread
To hear what aged dames confirmd & said
& listning to the Haunted tales they told
My very blood within me curdld cold

---

22 To *through* The *MS 7*   24 spoul *MS 7*   26 & . . . wish] Impatient
urgd: some] the *MS 11*   28 spake *MS 11*   29 Grown vext & tird the timid
quaking ⟨wight⟩ *(wight omitted) MS 11*   wight] white *MS 7*   30 hurry *MS 11*
31 Now] While: sweep *MS 11*   32 sirpits *MS 11*   33 quizing *MS 11*
34 Marks out] Plain marks: prize∧ — *MS 11*   44 Wet as she *below* [Dripping
&]: draggling *altered to* draggles *MS 7*   46 startld *through* waknd *MS 7*

While from their Learning much ⟨   ⟩ & got   55
Throut the fields knew every haunted spot
When from their skill well stord with secret charms
I knew the art of passing free from harms
Which my wis[e] tutors by the setting sun
For safty Warnd me twas the best to shun   60
& oer the fields when late for home I hied
The days last shadow stauking by my side
How oft Ive turnd its giant length to View
& seemd as oftner watchd it faster grew
A monster larger still it stretchd from sight   65
Its head slow hiding in approaching night
& as dusk woods its outlines gan to trace
Fears flockd more fast & urgd a quicker pace
The haunted pond lay often in my road
Poor drownded amys comfortles abode   70
Whose restless soul denyd its rest above
Mourns the sad fate & falsities of Love
Oft fancy hears the sorrow breathing sound
& oft while passing have I squinted round
Keeping strickt watch upon the gloom of night   75
Lest unawares she stole upon my sight
My feet the while scarce touchd the 'chanted ground
Sliving Ive crept & wary lookd around
& even choakd my self to stop my breath
To cough that moment would be worse then death   80
A sleeping gost I knew was quickly woke
& amys catsleep might be quickly broke
E'en from the sigh when past one dares to make
To catch our puffing breath shes known to wake
& as the moon peeps thro her cloudy screen   85
The waking spirit may be plainly seen
Away I flew nor turnd a look no more
& scarcly felt the ground I rallied oer
& great the joy that told my village nigh
Each chim[n]ey smoking pleasure on my eye   90

55 *Hiatus MS 7*   57 charms *underlined MS 7*   58 free from *below* [hells]:
alarms *altered to* harms *MS 7*   59 [as] my . . . sun *below* [for more safer p] *MS 7*
66 approaching *below* [glooms of] *MS 7*   66/7 [Whose outlines 'gan each gloomy
wood to trace] *MS 7*   82 amys] marys *MS 7*   88 rallied *below* [wanderd]
MS 7

& sweet the noise which I then could hear
They raisd my spirits & dispelld my fear
The lifted latch with eagerness I prest
When in my cot I came a welcome guest
& in my corner mong my friends once more   95
I sat me down & talkt my terrors oer

The haunted pond still bears the maidens fate
& village legends still the tale relate
In that farm house which neighbours on the spot
She livd a servant but the times forgot   100
Tho many a day no doubt since thens gone bye
& amys dwelling claims a kindred sigh
Its fated ruin leans each mouldering wall
& gulshing eaves in rumbling horrors fall
The moping bats that haunt each gaping creek   105
Are oft unhousd some better place to seek
& ruins bird scard from their gloomy bed
Oft seek a Comfort in some safer shed
Here amy dwelt & of her dwelling fond
Still haunts the ruins as she haunts the pond   110
Here owls strike terror for old folks well know
Shes often took their form to shreik her woe
& even sparrows while theyre chelping here
Flings the same doubts in superstitions ear

A rosy bonny country lass was she   115
As ere a country girl was known to be
As good a servant village dames avow
As ever scourd a pail or milkd a cow
Gave good content where ere she went to dwell
& as her master likd her monstrous well   120
Tho what his meaning was they little knew
But they mistrusted as they often do
While many a thing which gossips quickly see
Serving for prattle oer their musing tea

95 & *through* Where *MS 7*   98 the *inserted MS 7*   99 which *through* that
MS 7   100 [&] but *MS 7*   102 amys] marys *MS 7*   104 earves *MS 7*
107 [of] scard *MS 7*   109 amy] mary *MS 7*   113 chelping *through* chirping
MS 7   124 musing *through* Newsing *MS 7*

Provd such suspicions more then groundless tales   125
Which in a Village commonly prevails
The passing neighbours often catchd a smile
Oft markt him take her milk pails oer the stile
& often while they passd each other bye
From amys bosom met the heavy sigh   130
& oft observd her while discoursing deep
As doubts might rise to give just cause to weep
In stifling notice with a wisht disguise
To slive her apron corner to her eyes
Remarks like these each each newser soon disernd   135
In such dark matters wondrous wise & learnd
Soon ravelld mysteries they unraveld all
Confirmd em proofs & prophesyd her fall
But still her griefs was to her self conceald
Griefs as none know but only them that feeld   140
In silent sorrow still did toils pursue
& made the best of all she felt & knew
Ah gay & artless once a maid was she
The birds that ranted on each neighbouring tree
With yok[e]s & buckets as she bouncd along   145
Was deafd to silence by her milking song
O fencless Innocence thy charms thy woes
As bees their honey tempt a world of foes
When beautys sweetest gem the eye beguiles
& opes its blossom in perfections smiles   150
The bud soon pluckt becomes a withering prize
& soon grows sickning in Lusts ravishd eyes
Loves chance is hazardous vain world in thee
With age encreasing grows each villany

---

130 amys] marys *MS 7*   131 her while] as in *MS 1*   132 might rise] arose
MS 1   133 In stifling] To stifle: with a] into *through* is a *MS 1*   134 To]
Shed: Apron *MS 1*   135 [Such proofs as] Remarks *(*[mar] *below* [proofs]*)*
MS 7   Such proofs as meddlers presently disernd *(proofs as *through *indecipherable)*
MS 1   136 dark] like: wonderous *MS 1*   138 Confirmd em] Markt each
as: prophecied *MS 1*   143 Ah] Tho: a maid] in youth *MS 1*   144 The . . .
ranted] & Blackbirds ranting *MS 1*   145 yokes *MS 1*   147 Inocence: Woes
MS 1   148 As *through* The: honny: tempt] draws: world] swarm *MS 1*
149–50 *Tranposed MS 1*   149 Beautys sweet gem perfections rosy smiles *MS 1*
150 Love true or false or cherish or beguiles *MS 1*   151 [smiles] prize *MS 7*
153 v *through* V *in* vain *MS 7*

What many jewels deckt in heavens charms   155
Have met with death in mans deluding arms
Those pleasing toys which heaven did ordain
To add a comfort to our toils & pain
Those gems how cruel they to meet their end
From man thats meant their guardian & their friend   160
Those beauties sent us for our comforts here
To please & be despisd is fate severe
& cruel man as hard a fate shall know
When ruind Innocence laments her woe
On that last day that brings their woes to light   165
Gods just revenge their baseness shall requite
Then injurd angels shall your woes be heard
& heavens blessings is the wisht reward
Then base seducers come your doom to view
& hell reserves her worst revenge for you   170
Ah dread ye villians just revenge then given
& beauty sleep thou are assurd of heaven

155/6 [Those beautys sent us for our comfort here / To please & be despisd—O fate
severe] *MS 7*   160 From] In: meant] sent *MS 1*   163 cruel] villain *MS 1*
166 Gods *through* Shall: just *through indecipherable MS 7*   169 come[s] *MS 7*
171 just *through* lest *MS 7*   *The following passage in MS 1, p. 26 is possibly connected with
this poem:*

> Hells dreaded horrors hunt the sutted gloom
> & terrors demons sile around the room
> Goblins flop oer
> As round her thorny bed the goblin flies
> Vengance seems ?reddings [by] in their saucer eyes   5
> They mock her griefs & urge her fate to come
> & seem rejoicd as she must share their doom
> Grim horid terrors on her fears encroach
> & jeer her weakness & her deeds reproach
> In all her deeds their quizing eyes detect   10
> And boastful hint what sinners may expect
> Shivering in dread as terrors more arise
> She shrinks beneath the Cloaths & hides her eyes
> On that dread night that brought its fated morn
> Poor mary wretched ruind & forlorn   15
> She dreamd a dream she oft before had dreampt
> But still till now had treated with contempt
> Tho dreams are faithful Omens provd by some
> That tell the victims of their fate to come
> & plain they told to her unending fate   20
> Which she near heeded till it came too late

(l. 2 aroung; l. 13 C *through* g *in* Cloaths; l. 17 till *inserted*; l. 19 victims *below*
[wretched])

AUTOGRAPH: Nor. MS 1, p. 201.
Dated: 1808–19 (MS 1).

I wish that I was but a gay blushing rose
    Pluckt from my loves favourite trees
That in my loves garden delightfully blows
    My loves fickle eye for to please

That when she in rapture pind me to her breast   5
    So white & so sweet to the eye
I might in that station of compact & rest
    Find the peace which I fre[quently] sigh

I wish I could be a woodbines gadding flower
    That in my loves garden appear   10
A twining so sweetly around my loves bower
    Whose sweets to my love are so dear

That when she delighted my fragran[c]e would sip
    & stooping my sweetness to gain
I might from the heaven that glows on her lip   15
    Snatch the blessing I long for in vain

AUTOGRAPH: Nor. MS 1, p. 202.
Dated: 1808–19 (MS 1).

Young Nanceys William for a Sailor press'd
    First bound on board the royal Charlotte lay
She like a widow'd bird alone distrest
    In mournful wailings sorrow'd night & day

I WISH THAT I WAS BUT A GAY BLUSHING ROSE   *Title: wanting*
8 Fond   9/10 [Whose perfumes to]   10 gardens appear[s]
11 bower[s]

YOUNG NANCEYS WILLIAM FOR A SAILOR PRESS'D   *Title: wanting*
2 [Charlotte]

But ⟨   ⟩ proves a friend & interferes   5
    In Loves behalf to tell her where he lyes
And soon as she the welcome tidings hears
    As swift as Lightning darting from the skies
Fearless of Dangers off the Charmer flies
    And soon the Fleet & soon the ship she spies   10

And soon the Royal Charlotte is adorn'd
    With charms unknown in Ship or fleet before
The sweetest Angel that was ever form'd
    Upon her Decks Lost William does implore
The Hardy Sailors round about her stands   15
    And all their hardness softens from her eyes
While she in sorrow wrung her Lilly hands
    And O you've press'd My William here she cries
O William William more than worlds to me
    I'll perish here if Im denied of thee   20

AUTOGRAPH: Nor. MS 1, p. 203.
Dated: 1808–19 (MS 1).

Young Damon for Delia Sighd
And Long he lovd the Beautious maid
But consious of the sexes pride
To tell his love was still affraid
—When lads and lasses pass'd him by   5
Opprest the swain would inly mourn
And often to him self would sigh
How sweet's the love that meets return

At length grown bolder by degrees
The swain resolves to tell his pain   10
Of doubts at once his heart to ease
And meet her pity or disdain

5 *Hiatus for the insertion of a name*   9 Charmers   11 [Charlotte]
20 im   *Followed by a row of asterisks*

YOUNG DAMON FOR DELIA SIGHD   *Title: wanting*

But O the Maid she lov'd her sell
And smiling bid him cease to mourn
And now the happy swain can tell   15
How sweets the love that meets return

But still the shepherd loves in Fear
And doubts of what he hopes to find
The Maiden proves his love sincere
And gies her hand to ease his mind   20
Undoubting now the shepherd loves
Both hearts with equal fondness burn
And to his joy he daily proves
How sweets the love that meet[s] return

AUTOGRAPH: Nor. MS 1, pp. 205–7.
Dated: 1808–19 (MS 1).

ELEGY TO PITY

O lovely Charming tender feeling maid
    Known by the Name of Pity hither haste
Be my Companion thro' the summer shade
    And stay my Partner in the wintry waste

I ask and long to view thy comley mien   5
    To press that Breast sweet heav'd wi' many a sigh
To kiss that cheek where tears are often seen
    And what I ask thy Nature can't deny

So come my Bride adornd with every grace
    And with thy power well stop the pointed gun   10
And when fell murder looks upon thy face
    His Heart will melt like Butter in the sun

20/1 [Now Hymen crowns their happy lov]

ELEGY TO PITY   *Title:* Elegy to Pity   2 haste *through* come
3 thro' *through* in   5 t *through* v *in* to   9 So *through* To   11 when
through if

For o more sweet then Indies spicey gales
   The Breeze from thee but scented with a sigh
And far more bright than Summers morning vales   15
   Shines that bright Pearl which falls from either eye

And first at home we'll search where mercy calls
   And baulk the mouth of many a gapeing grave
And drive the Spiders from our garden walls
   And weep for flies we came too late to save   20

And we will stop Grimmalkins murders too
   No more shall they for Sparrows Lurk & watch
Nor shall the schoolboys as they us'd to go
   In Murder bring a Ladder near my thatch

Nor shall my window by young chubs be made   25
   A slaughter shop to please his evil eye
And tho' they long & whine and make a trade
   While in our house they shall not touch a flie

And every trap my finger shall unlatch
   Which grissel sets with murder in her head   30
The poor unconsious little mice to catch
   Which forc'd by hunger nibble at the bread

And if we're nigh when granny shells the peas
   With joy I'll snatch the maggot from her sight
And slyley shakeing of her rotten cheese   35
   With equal joy I'll save the fellons mite

And blest with you I'll mourn for what you please
   And where you like I'll ne'er disdain to call
Upstairs I'll gang & mourn the scores of fleas
   Which Grissel kills & thinks no sin at all   40

Nor will I ere in Duty bound neglect
   To mourn with you the worst of Vermins Doom
To dying Lice I'll pay the same respect
   When ere we visit Chloes dressing room

15 vales *through* gales   27 song *altered to* long   37 mourn *through*
 indecipherable beginning with g

And now my Charmer we at home have done   45
    Wherever Mercey shall our aid require
Be it in Woods whose Briars resist the sun
    I'll go and do whatever you desire

And when we wander o'er the dewey vales
    From my Light tread the grass no bruise shall meet   50
And fear o' trampling on the worms & snails
    I'll always look before I set my feet

And without asking what I've got to do
    All I'll perform & never trouble thee
And this I hope will make my love seem true   55
    Which realley is as true as true can be

There while I tread as slow as foot can fall
    My conscious heart the dewey grass shall view
Thoughtfull of Inscets so uncommon small
    That would be drownded in a drop of dew   60

AUTOGRAPH: Nor. MS 1, p. 209.
Dated: 1808–19 (MS 1).

    'O Death were is thy victory! O grave were is thy sting'
    The inspird Bard & holy prophet sung
    His hands exulting swept the trembling string
    And all around with heavenly Music rung
    More loud & louder thrills the trembling chords   5
    His hands more Faster moves along the lyre
    The Bards strong faith triumphant joy affords
    And all his soul's enrapt in heavenly Fire
    The sounds vibrating still the Notes prolong
    And listning Seraphs throng the Bard around   10
    On Wings of Easter flocks to hear the song
    And smile in concert to the pleasing sound

50 i *in* bruise *inserted*   56 *Second* l *in* realley *inserted*
  'O DEATH WERE IS THY VICTORY! O GRAVE WERE IS THY STING'
Title: wanting   2 holy *over* [inspird]: phrophet   11 Easther

—'T'was thou O Jesus! Saviour of the World
'T'was thou that filld the Bards prophetic eye
He saw thy flag of 'Peace on Earth' unfurl'd   15
And heard 'Glad tidings' Melt along the Skye
But O! a Tear!—the Magic Scenes ensue
The Saviour dies—that sinners might be blest
—Dies!—Death & Hell's grim terrors to subdue
And make the grave a-wish'd-for-place of rest   20

AUTOGRAPH: Nor. MS 1, p. 210.
Dated: 1808–19 (MS 1).

SUPPOSD TO BE UTTERD BY WERTER AT THE CONCLUSION OF HIS LAST INTERVIEW WITH CHARLOTTE

O wretched Man—Now hopes are fled & past
Not one Word more—one look—& that the last?
O Charlotte Charlotte stay my Angel stay
Do hear the last your Werter begs to say
The last forever—Dying—I implore   5
One Word—and then—I'm gone to come no more
Then o for once anticipate the friend
Look back and pity if you cant commend
Bid one Adieu—& instant I'll depart
Your Werter craves it with a broken heart   10
O prayers intreaties—all are spent in vain
She hears me not or hears me in disdain
'Tis done—'tis Death—I go—my fates decreed
Sure now she hears—my inmost souls reveald
Yes Angel Yes Your Werters Vows are true   15
What Silent still? she Answers not—Adieu!

SUPPOSD TO BE UTTERD BY WERTER AT THE CONCLUSION OF HIS
LAST INTERVIEW WITH CHARLOTTE   *Title:* Supposd to be utterd by Werter at
the / Conclusion of his last Interview with / Charlotte   1 W *through* w *in* Word
2 last *underlined*   3 An[n]gel   4 last *underlined*   5 forever *and* Dying
underlined   8 [what] if   13 I['m]   16 Ans^rs

AUTOGRAPH: Nor. MS 1, p. 212.
Dated: 1808–19 (MS 1).

NIGHT

Once more o muse resume thy lowley flight
And tune thy oaten pipe to darksome night
Of darksome night in lowly numbers sing
When brooding darknes spreads his raven wing
Or when the moon illuminates the scene   5
And turns the forest to a silverey green
Alike is night when darkness reigns around
Or moon-light shadows mark the dewey ground
When Contemplation's sober silence reigns
And sleepy nature leaves the lonsome plains   10
When superstition bids the frighted hind
Leave hated night and all his plains behind

Sing rural muse & tune thy oaten reed
And in the silence of the night proceed
Walk down the meadows undistinguished green   15
And brush the dews from many a blade unseen
O sweetful time tho sweeter eve Retires
And all her beauties with herself expires
Tho the gold streaks which did adorn the west
And clothd fine evening in a golden vest   20
Are fled the scene in other worlds to shine
And left a darksome void in their decline
Tho all the feather'd songsters of the shade
And all the shepherds that so sweetly play'd
That sweetly sung when milder eve begun   25
And tun'd their dittys to the setting sun
Tho these are all to sleep & rest retir'd
Leaving the scene as soon as eve expir'd

NIGHT   *Title:* Night.   6 turns *inserted*   7 n *through* e *in* darkness
8 Or *through* And   17 eave   22 left *through* a   28 expir'd *through*
retir'd

And tho the beetle's buzzing drowzy lay
Delights no more the pilgrims homeward way   30
Tho all the beauties which at eve we see
Are fled & left the silent shade to me

AUTOGRAPHS: Nor. MS 1, pp. 214–15: Pet. MS A3, p. 104 (ll. 1–8 only).
Dated: 1808–19 (MS 1).

THE MILLERS DAUGHTER

A Miller lives a cante cheel
By W[ellan]ds bonny River O
And how tu use his toll dish Weel
Guid feth hes unco' cliver O
He keeps his Meel & sels his Bran   5
A trick O—Dirty Mil[l]ers O
Guid faith hes in a muckle plan
To come at gold & siller O

An' Blythe & strapping in her teens
He has a on'y Dauter O   10
An O to look upo her Een
It gars ones mou to Water O
Hur shape & size so paring Weel
Gars hur aboon em ony O
Her luiks wou melt a heart O steel   15
So sonsy & so bony O

Tho war she bad as dirty Meg
And cookd as Alsie Crowther O
Wi neer a Hosie to her leg
Crow toed & humpie shouther O   20

THE MILLERS DAUGHTER *Title:* 'The Millers Daughter' / First Verse
MS A3, wanting MS 1   Preceded in MS A3 by: I shall send you (some time) out of
Curosity a ballad in the scotch brogue   1 miller: chiel *MS A3*
2 W———ds *MS 1 MS A3*   river *MS A3*   3 An': weel *MS A3*   5 meel:
sells *MS A3*   6 O' Dirty millers *MS A3*   7 feth *MS A3*   8 Tu
cam: goud *MS A3*   12 mou[th]

Har titles muckle gear & gowd
An Acres one an twenty O
Bow shind hup backd or hou sho wou'd
Theyd fetch har sweet hearts plenty O

Sic skellums wine & mak a fuss   25
An cheat the dafty Miller O
Bu al they lang fo is his purs
That howds the gowd & siller O
They ony want his house An Lan
An lov her fo her Riches O   30
Ther ony scheme an Ony plan
'S to fill ther empty Breeches O

O wad she bad sic skelums gane
Spite o' her dirty daddie O
An turn to hear the sighs alane   35
O her artles looing laddie O
O wad she 'lieve him how he loos
Shed neve loo a nither O
Fo Hymen smiles to thred the Noos
When twa souls hang to gether O   40

To loo an to be lood again
O weres a bigger pleasure O
An woud she tak me fo her own
Shed soon find sic a treasure O
But ah thers naithing int I fear   45
Is naithing to befriend me O
I doubt the Millers muckle gear
Will surley gae agen me O

The Buited fop gars me sing dool
Sin finery gaes before me O   50
An tho there mowt bee taupie snool
Ther Riches will cam oer em O
—An tho Ise lovd the maid lang sine
An lovd her best o ony O
I neer need think she wad be mine   55
Sae adieu to the maid so bony O

25 Sic *looks more like* Skeek *but cf. l. 33*   33 bad *inserted*

AUTOGRAPH: Nor. MS 1, p. 216.
Dated: 1808–19 (MS 1).

> The Rose & lilly blooms again
> To our Greedy eyes
> But only bloom to show how vain
> Such short livd charms to prize
>
> Those Lilly Breasts—O Death to view   5
> Those Cheeks the Rosy warms
> Those Rolling Eyes of Heavenly Blue
> All Perishable Charms
>
> Yes—Myra tho Your Charms so Fair
> Admits no Rival nigh   10
> As Prizd as Boasted as they are
> They Blossom but to Dye

AUTOGRAPH: Nor. MS 1, p. 216.
TRANSCRIPT: Pet. MS B1, p. 46.
Printed in *RL*, p. 199.
Dated: 1808–19 (MS 1).

NATIVE SCENES

> O native scenes for ever ever dear
> So blest so happy where I long have been
> So charmd with nature in each varied scene
> To leave ye all is cutting & severe
> Ye hanging bushes that from winds woud screen   5
> Where oft Ive shelterd from an aprils shower
> In youths past bliss in Childhoods happy hour
> Ye Woods Ive wanderd searching out the nest
> Ye Meadows gay that reard me many a flower

THE ROSE & LILLY BLOOMS AGAIN   *Title: wanting*

NATIVE SCENES   *Title:* Native Scenes *RL*, Sonnet *MS 1*   2 where I long]
as I here *RL*   4 you *RL*   5 hanging] hawthorn *RL*   6 an aprils] a
threaten'd *RL*   8 searching] seeking *RL*   9 that *RL*

Culling my cow slips Ive been doubly blest   10
Huming gay fancies As I bound the prize
O Fate unkind beloved scenes adieu
Your vanishd pleasures crowd my swimming eyes
& makes this wounded heart to bleed anew

AUTOGRAPH: Nor. MS 1, pp. 217–18.
Dated: 1808–19 (MS 1).

DEATH OR VICTORY

Battle now is drawing near
Foes in sight of foes appear
Now the Heroes courage warms
Now the Cowards fears alarms
Heroes hottest fight defies   5
Cowards shrinking falls or flies
Frenchman Gallias Sons may fear
British Blood advancing near
But darken day & blush bright Sun
Shouldst thou see a briton run   10
Foes to flie or fight to shun
Till the battle's oer & won
In Glory! Glory! Glory!
For Britons still must Britons be
Away to Death or Victory!   15

10 Culling *through* Gathering *MS 1*   Culling my] Where, pulling *RL*   11 bound]
pluck'd *RL*   13 vanishd *below* [crowded] *MS 1*   14 makes this] make the *RL*

    DEATH OR VICTORY   *Title:* Death or Victory   11 *Line squeezed in*
15 Victory!!
15/16
                        ['Yes! Yes!' Proud victory smiling cries
                        As oer her favorite troops she flies
                        'The Day may darken in suprise
                        'The sun may blush & leave the skies
                        That ever sees a Briton run   5
                        Foes to flie or fight to shun
                        But while Brittanias isle remains
                        To boast a Briton on her plains
                        That day no foe shall never see
                        It never was and neer shall be]   10

(l. 9 s *through* n *in* shall)

Yes! Yes! proud Victory smileing cries
As oer the advancing troops she flies
'Be dark that day & blush that sun
'That ever sees a briton run'
But while Brittanias isle remains   20
To boast one Briton on her plains
Ye foes dispair that day to see
Which never was and neer shall be
A true bred Briton never flies
His very nature flight denies   25
His courage every fear defies
He either wins the day or dies
In glory! glory! glory!
For Britons still will Britons be
So on to Death or Victory   30

AUTOGRAPH: Nor. MS 1, p. 219.
Dated: 1808–19 (MS 1).

Ye spirits of the earth and air
Ye Naids of the Liquid plains
O will ye to my plaint repair
& allev[i]ate my restles pains
Ye Cherub Cupids of the skye   5
And all ye airy tribes unseen
Can ye with my request comply
To thaw the heart of Bonny Jean

AUTOGRAPH: Nor. MS 1, p. 219.
Dated: 1808–19 (MS 1).

Ive long been urgd friend for to write ye a Letter
To make it known to ye how much Im your debtor

24 [A Briton w] A
  YE SPIRITS OF THE EARTH AND AIR   *Title: wanting*
  IVE LONG BEEN URGD FRIEND FOR TO WRITE YE A LETTER   *Title: wanting*

For ye muses conpany so rare as chance might let her
I gingld her oer wi uncomon delight
'George bards from the ploughtail git better & better   5
By nature inspired from Nature they write

Tho fex friend to tell ye Im stung to the gristle
To hear how a lowland fen bardy can wistle
Whi nothing to charm him but bull Rush & thistle
I covet yer muse friend ye know how Im hinting   10
While here mong my highland shads dristly drizzle
I scarce make a song or a ballad worth printing

AUTOGRAPH: Nor. MS 1, p. 220.
Dated: 1808–19 (MS 1).

No Chilling fears nor trembling alarms
Are never witnes'd in no hackney'd charms
The throbbing bliss that heav'd her snowy breast
Full truly told what treasures I possest
And now uninterupted or reprovd   5
Love reghnd triumphant & her fears removd
In all the Charms endearing hopes could frame
Or heart desire or fondest wishes name
I freely revelld—freely then posses'd
And O such charms as not to be exprest   10
Such charms such softness O to feel & prove
My very soul was melted into love
Here rest fond Muse—they all thy powers excell
And if they did not—thou must cease to tell
Nor try nor venture secrets to reveal   15
Which she—sweet girl could wish thee to conseal
Near raise a Blush nor give that heart a pain
Which has been kind & will be kind again
To leave such charms as if not let alone
Would only make thy imperfections shown   20

3 let might   5 *By George*: bands
NO CHILLING FEARS NOR TREMBLING ALARMS *Title: wanting*
2 charms.   9 revelld.   10 r *in* exprest *inserted*   13 they all *through*
indecipherable   14 not.   20 *Followed by a row of asterisks*

AUTOGRAPHS: Pet. MS A3, p. 74: Nor. MS 1, p. 220.
TRANSCRIPTS: Pet. MS B1, p. 126: Nor. MS 5, p. 124.
Printed in *RL*, p. 44.
Dated: 1808–19 (MS 1).

EPIGRAM

For fools that would wish to seem learned & wise
   This Receipt a wise man did bequeath
'Let 'em have the free use of their ears & their Eyes
   'But their Tongue'—says he 'Tye to their teeth'

AUTOGRAPH: Nor. MS 1, pp. 221–2.
Dated: 1808–19 (MS 1).

STANZAS ADDRESS'D TO M.C.M.

   Tho fate & fortune both combines
   My Enemies to prove
   & Unrelenting sternly joins
   To force me from my love

   For ever constant ever true   5
   From thee it cannot part
   Or false or true the lots for you
   To hold your wanderers heart

EPIGRAM   *Title:* Epigram *MS A3 MS 1 RL*   *Headed* Altered *MS 1*
2 Receipt[e] *MS A3*] Reciepe *MS 1*   Man: Bequeath *MS 1*   3 eyes *MS 1*
4 tongues'∧: 'tie: teeth!' *MS 1*   *Preceded in MS 1 by:*

    A Fool that would wish to be thought a wise man
    May do it—nor blind—nor yet Deeth*
    Eyes and Ears may be free—to hear & see all they can
    But his tongue must be tied to his teeth
                         *Provincial.

(l. 1 *Second* o *through* l *in* Fool)

STANZAS ADDRESS'D TO M.C.M.   *Title:* Stanza's Address'd to M.C.M.
5–8 *In margin and preceded by:* Still in my P——ys breast remains / My

Should roaring seas as fate ordains
Divide my love from me   10
O Menie Menie still remains
My Constant heart with thee

Yes Menie dear my constant heart
For ever stays with you
Go where I will it cannot part   15
From her it loves so true

And when I'm doom'd no more to be
With Angel Menie here
In foreighn lands the thoughts of thee
Shall be to William dear   20

No weary miles that grow behind
Sad weary miles to me
Shall never change my constant mind
Nor wear my love from thee

The farther I am doom'd to steer   25
'More miles to wander oer
Shall only Menies name endear
And make me love the more

Yes love shall sweeten each remove
With an increasing flame   30
And hope my dearest friend shall prove
To wisper thine the same

And O when fixd in climes unknown
Should ought resemble thee
Should Love the faintest zembla[n]ce own   35
How great the bliss to me

The Clouds bound to my Menies sky
Or seeming so to be
Shall neer escape thy williams eye
Without his love to thee   40

11 Menei Menie   35/6 *In margin:* enemy / ennen *which may suggest the origin of*
the name Menie   36/7 [The winds that now so trifleing seem]

My hopes & all—while life remains
On Menie dear shall be
My Love its passion never feigns
But Centers all in thee

And hard as fortune now I find   45
My Constant hope shall be
That future fortune will be kind
And send me back to thee

But o my girl no tongue can tell
Nor fancys eye can view   50
At that (o cruel word) farewell
What I shall feel for you

And tho my Menie I'm distrest
O do not you repine
For the first sigh that.rends thy breast   55
Will break this heart of mine

AUTOGRAPH: Nor. MS 1, p. 223 (title and ll. 1–4 pencil).
Dated: 1808–19 (MS 1).

MYRA

O if the sorrows which true love inspires
In heavens eye could ere compasion find
O give ye gods my hearts supreme desire
& teach my angel myra to be kind
The lovly charmer she is all to me   5
My utmo[s]t hopes—the all my heart desires
& O beneath her scorn my pleasure flees
& all my wishes & my hopes expires

43 My *through* For   52 feel'd   53 my *inserted*: distrest [o d]
56 mine.
    MYRA *Title:* [To] Myra   3 gods—   7 scorn—: flees] flea

For her my Youth & vigour pines away
For her black sadnes turns my day to night   10
And by her Frown my chill soul shrinks away
And life itself grows hateful to my sight
Adieu the pleasures which I once posest
Those tastles charms that gave deligt & ease
The charms of her suplanted all the rest   15
& those posesd by her alone can please
In vain all pleasures art & nature yeilds
My sickning soul their sweetest pastimes shun
& like the blighted blossom of the fields
Sickens & dies beneath the brightest sun   20
Possesd of her the remedy is sure
All heaven is present when the charmers there
Denyd of her theres nought admits a cure
Absence is hell—I perish in despair

AUTOGRAPHS: Pet. MS A3, p. 109: Nor. MS 1, p. 224.
TRANSCRIPTS: Pet. MS B1, pp. 173–4: Nor. MS 5, pp. 135–7.
Printed in *RL*, pp. 176–8 (ll. 33–40 omitted).
Dated: 1813–15 (MS A3, p. 109 '5 or 6 years ago').

HER I LOVE—A SONG

Rose in full Blown blushes dy'd
Pink maturely spread
Carnations boasting all their pride
Of melting white and red
Are Charms confes'd by every eye   5
But ah how faint they prove
To paint superior charms—when nigh
The Cheek of her I love

10 her *inserted*   11 Frown—   20 Sicknens   24 Absence[s]
HER I LOVE—A SONG   *Title: Her I Love—a Song MS A3*, Her I Love *RL*,
wanting MS 1   No stanza division in MS 1   1 Blushes dyd *MS 1*
2 maturley *MS 1*   3 Boasting *MS 1*   4 Melting White & Red *MS 1*
5 confesd: Every Eye *MS 1*   7 charms‿ *MS 1*   8 Love *MS 1*

Ripe Cherrie on its parent Tree
With full perfection grac'd   10
Red corral in its native sea
To all advantage plac'd
What charms they boast the eye to please
And Beauty to improve
But ah alls lost when match'd with these   15
The Lips of her I love

When Pulpy Plums to ripeness swells
In down surrounding blue
When dews besprent on Heather Bells
Reflecting brighter hue   20
The Azure Skie when stars appear
Its Bluness to improve
Fades into dullest shades when near
The Eyes of her I love

Sweet is the blossom'd beans perfume   25
By morning breezes shed
And sweeter still the Jonquils bloom
When Evening moists its head
The Perfume sweet of pink and Rose
And Vi'let of the Grove   30
But ah how sweeter far then those
The kiss of her I love

9 tree *MS 1*   10 With] In: Perfection Gracd *MS 1*   11 Coral: Native Sea
MS 1   12 placd *MS 1*   13 charms] Glows: Boast—: Eye *MS 1*
14 &: to] een: Improve *MS 1*   15 Lost: matchd *MS 1*   16 Love *MS 1*
17 to] in: Ripeness swell *MS 1*   The pulpy plum, when ripeness swells *RL*
18 In] —The *MS 1*, Its *RL*   Downd Surounding Blue *MS 1*   19 When]
The *RL*   Dews Besprent *MS 1*   20 Refects a Brighter Hue *MS 1*
21 Sky: Stars *MS 1*   23 n *in* into *inserted*: Dullest *MS 1*   25 Blossomd
Beans *MS 1*   26 Morning Breezes *MS 1*   [spread] shed. *MS A3*] spread *MS 1*
27 &: Bloom *MS 1*   28 Evening moists] eve bedews *RL*, eve bedews *altered to*
Evening moists *Harvard proof copy*   29 perfume: Pink & *MS 1*   30 & Vi'lets
MS 1   31 ah] oh *MS 1*   32 kiss] lips *MS 1*   The kiss of her love *RL 2nd*
edn.] The kiss of her I love *RL 4th edn.*

How joy'd the Bard—when muse inclin'd
Sublimely treads the sky
How blest Ive been wi' fob well lin'd   35
And frothing tankard nigh
But was such pleasures hourly mine
As charming as they prove
All gladly now would I resign
To be with her I love   40

AUTOGRAPH: Nor. MS 1, p. 225.
Dated: 1808–19 (MS 1).

How blest is he—the happiest mortal known
With independant fortune of his own
With just as much as makes each wish compleat
& just as much as makes both ends to meet
& keeps that keen wolf hunger from the door   5
Tis quite enough contentment wants no more

AUTOGRAPH: Nor. MS 1, p. 226 (l. 18 pencil).
Dated: 1808–19 (MS 1).

Reader if undisguisd thou ownst a heart
That for thy countrys good woud act a part
& when her sorrows meets thy saddend eye
Sincerly heaves (the whole it durst) a sigh
Yet ready waits (if some woud bravly dare)   5
To save thy country or its fate to share
To join true Britons rous'd by Freedoms call
With them to triumph or with them to fall

33 joyd: Muse inclind *MS 1*   34 Sky *MS 1*   35 Blest: Ive been] am I: with
Fob: Lind *MS 1*   36 Frothing Tankard *MS 1*   37 Pleasures *MS 1*
38 Charming: Prove *MS 1*   39 Gladly: Resign *MS 1*   40 love. *MS A3*
HOW BLEST IS HE—THE HAPPIEST MORTAL KNOWN   *Title: wanting*
READER IF UNDISGUISD THOU OWNST A HEART   *Title: wanting*
3 eye[s]

Then oer this sacred spot impassiond bend
& mourn a heros Brother & a friend   10
But if self interest binding tyrants laws
Bribes the[e] a Villian to support their cause
O if thy heart an undermining foe
Dissembling plans thy countries over throw
O sham of Britain (Land of Liberty)   15
That brought to light thy villanies & thee
Go hence away thou poison & disgrace
Nor turn a look toward the sacred place

AUTOGRAPHS: Pet. MS A3, pp. 75–80 (torn words supplied from MS 1):
Nor. MS 1, p. 226 (ll. 1–34, deleted), p. 229 (ll. 225–46, 248, 250–88,
deleted), p. 232 (ll. 129–46, 149–222, deleted), p. 233 (ll. 35–78, deleted),
p. 234 (ll. 79–86, 89–128, deleted), p. 236 (ll. 289–352), p. 243 (ll. 353–74,
377–8).
TRANSCRIPTS: Pet. MS B1, pp. 126–36: Nor. MS 5, pp. 149–69.
Printed in *RL*, pp. 45–59 (ll. 19–22, 55–6, 71–2, 105–6, 117–22, 141–96,
201–2, 207–10, 215–16, 231–2, 239–40, 243–4, 275–82, 295–6, 311–12,
341–2, 347–80, 353–4, 356, 373–6, 386–95 omitted).
Dated: 'December 1817' (MS A3, p. 75, *RL* Introduction, p. xxii).

ADDRESS TO PLENTY IN WINTER

A Parody

O thou bliss to Riches known
(Stranger to the poor alone)
Giving most where none's requir'd
Leaving none where most desir'd

9 ore   13 underminding

ADDRESS TO PLENTY IN WINTER   *Title:* Address to Plenty / in Winter / a
Parody *(followed by* Written in December 1817*)* MS A3, Address to Plenty, in Winter
RL, wanting MS 1   MS A3, p. 233 *headed* Winter   1 blis *MS 1*   Riches *to* riches
(p.e.) MS A3] riches *MS 1*   2 (Stranger *to* Stranger *(p.e.) MS A3*] ∧Stranger *MS 1*
alone) *to* alone *(p.e.) MS A3*] alone∧ *MS 1*   3 giving *MS 1*   were nones requid
MS 1   4 none where] nonon when: desird *MS 1*   most's *RL*

Who sworn friend to mizers keeps   5
Adding to their usless heaps
Gifts on Gifts profusley stord
Till Thousands swell the mouldy hurd—
While poor Shatterd poverty
To advantage seen in me   10
With his rags his wants & pain
(Waking pity but in vain)
Bowing cringing at thy side
Begs his mite & is denied

—O thou blessing let not me   15
Tell as vain my wants to thee
Thou by name O' Plenty stil'd
Fortunes heir—her fav'rite child
All the powers of being blest
Ease & happiness & rest   20
And that heaven born Charity
Claim'd existence next to thee
—'Tis a maxim—hunger feed
Give the needy when they need
Him who all profess to serve   25
The same maxim did observe
—Their obedience here how well
Modern times will plainly tell—

5 mizers *to* miser *(p.e.) MS A3*] mizers *MS 1*   6 usless *to* useless *(p.e.) MS A3*]
usles *MS 1*   7 Gifts *to* gifts *(third word, p.e.):* profusley *to* profusly *(p.e.)*
MS A3   Thousands upon thousands stoods *MS 1*   8 Thousands *to* thousands,
(p.e.) MS A3] mountains *MS 1*   hurd *to* hoard *(p.e.) MS A3*] hurds∧ *MS 1*
9 Shatterd *to* shatterd *(p.e.) MS A3*] shatterd *MS 1*   poverty *underlined to* poverty *(p.e.)*
MS A3   10 ine *MS 1*   11 &] his: pains *MS 1*   12 (Waking *to* Waking
(p.e.) MS A3] ∧Waking *MS 1*   vain) *to* vain *(p.e.) MS A3*] vain∧ *MS 1*   pity—*MS 1*
13 cringin: her *MS 1*   15 blessing *underlined to* blessing *(p.e.) MS A3*] Blesing
MS 1   17 O' *to* Of *(p.e.) MS A3*] o *MS 1*   Plenty *underlined to* Plenty *(p.e.) MS*
A3] plenty *MS 1*   stild *MS 1*   18 heir∧ his: fav'rite] oldest *MS 1*
19 [While] All *(A through a):* the *inserted MS A3*   20 eas: hapines *MS 1*
21 &: heavn *MS 1*   Charity *to* charity *(p.e.) MS A3*] charity *MS 1*   22 Claimd
MS 1   23 ∧Tis *MS 1*   25 Him] One *MS 1*, He *RL*   whom *MS 1 RL*
profes *MS 1*   26 The] [Once] That *MS 1*   did *through* doth *MS A3*
27 ∧Their: obidience there *MS 1*   28 tell∧ *MS 1*

Hear my wants nor deem me bold
Not with out occasion told   30
Hear one wish—nor fail to give
Use me well—& bid me live
Tis not great what I solicit
Was it more thou woulds't not miss it
Now the cutting Winter's come   35
'Tis but just to find a home
In some shelter dry & warm
That will s[h]ield me from the storm—
Toiling in the naked fields
Where no bush a shelter yields   40
Needy labour dithering stands
Beats & blows his numbing hands
& upon the crumping snows
Stamps in vain to warm his toes
Leaves are fled that once had power   45
To resist a summer shower
& the wind so piercing blows
Winnowing small the drifting snows
The summer shade & loaded bough
Would vainly boast a shelter now   50
Piercing snows so searching fall
Sifts a passage thro 'em all—
Tho all's vain to keep 'em warm
Poverty must brave the storm
No dependance—(labour's all)   55
Sorry pittance mighty small

---

30 wiout: told] sold *MS 1*   32 Live *MS 1*   34 woudst *MS 1*] couldst
RL   mis *MS 1*   35 Now the] O now *MS 1*   Winter's *to* winter's *(p.e.) MS A3*]
Winters *MS 1*   36 'Tis but just] Fate be kind *MS 1*   37–8 *Transposed MS 1*
38 Shield me from the killing storm∧ *MS 1*   39 Toiling *over* [Pausing] *MS A3*
Toiling in] Snatch me from *MS 1*   40 Where no *over* [Where Nor]: a *over* [nor
tree no] *MS A3*   Where no bush] Nothing there: sheter *MS 1*   42 Beats
through Blows *MS A3*] Blows *MS 1*   blows] Pats *MS 1*   49 The summer] That
sumers *MS 1*   &] of *RL*   50 vainly boast] boast in vain *MS 1*   51 searching
over [sifting] *MS A3*   52 Sifts *to* Sift *(p.e.) MS A3*] Sifts *MS 1*, They sift *RL*   em
all∧ *MS 1*   53 Tho all's] Alls in *MS 1*   em *MS 1*] him *RL*   54 Poverty]
But Poverty: mut *MS 1*   54/5 Tho alls vain to keep em warm / Poverty must
stand the storm *MS 1*   55 ⟨No depen⟩dance torn *MS A3*   —Labours all∧
MS 1   56–8 *Last three lines of page worn away MS A3   Copy-text: MS 1*

Friendship none its aid to lend
Health alone his only friend
Granting leave to live in pain
Giving strength to toil in vain   60
To be while winters horrors last
The sport of every pelting blast

O sad sons of poverty
Victims doomd to misery
Who can paint what pain prevails   65
Oer that heart which want assails
—Modest shame their pain consceals
No one knows but him that feels
O thou charm which plenty crowns
Fortune smile now winter frowns   70
Thine the power by the[e] possest
To give sorrow ease & rest
Cast around a pitying eye
Feed the hungry ere they dye
Think o think upon the poor   75
Nor against 'em shut thy door
Freely let thy bounty flow
On the sons of want & woe—

Hills & dales no longer seen
In their dress of pleasing green   80
Summer robes are all thrown by
For the clothing of the sky
Snows on snows in heaps combine
Hillocks raisd as mountains shine

---

57 their *MS 1*   60 Giving] & giving: to *omitted MS 1*   61 las⟨t⟩ *torn
MS A3*   Fit thing designd—to loneger last *MS 1*   62 The ... every] A Mark to
stand the *MS 1*   b⟨last⟩ *torn MS A3*   65 pre⟨vails⟩ *torn MS A3*
66 ass⟨ails⟩ *torn MS A3*   67 their] the: pain] woe *MS 1*   cons⟨ceals⟩ *torn
MS A3*] conseals *MS 1*   68 him that] he who *RL*   fe⟨els⟩ *torn MS A3*
None can know but them that feels *MS 1*   69 charm] power *MS 1*
70 Winter *MS 1*   71 the *to* thee *(p.e.) MS A3*] thee *MS 1*   posest *MS 1*
74 eer *MS 1*   75 o *to* O *(p.e.) MS A3*   76 'em *to* them *(p.e.) MS A3*] em *MS 1*
77 bountys *MS 1*   78 woe∧ *MS 1*   79 hils *MS 1*   longer] more are *RL*
80 dres *MS 1*   81 Sumer *MS 1*] Summer's *RL*   Robes *MS 1*   83 'Snows
MS 1   84 Hiloks *MS 1*

& at distance rising proud   85
Shining seems a fleecy cloud

Plenty here thy gifts bestow
Exit bid to every woe
Take me in shut out the blast
Make the doors & windows fast   90
Place me in some corner where
Lolling in a Elbow chair
Haply blest to my desire
I may find a roozing fire
While in chimney corner nigh   95
Coal or wood a fresh supply
Ready stands for laying on
Soon as 't'other's burnt & gone
Now & then as taste decreed
In a Book a page to read   100
& inquirey to amuse
Peep at somthing in the News
Se[e] whos married & who's dead
& who through bankrupt beg their bread
Then to cock a pipe when tir'd   105
Changing just as I desir'd
While on nub or table nigh
(Just to drink before Im dry)
Pitcher at my elbow stands
& the Barrel nigh at hand   110
Always ready as I will'd
When 'twas empty to be fill'd
& to be posses'd of all
Corner cupboard in the Wall

85 rising] showing *MS 1*   86 Shining seems] Each appears *RL*   fleesy *MS 1*
87 here] now *RL*   89 Take] Close *MS 1*   90 Make] Shut *MS 1*
91 where] there *MS 1*   92 an *RL*   93 Hap'ly *MS 1*   94 I may find]
Sweating oer: roosing *MS 1*   95 (While *MS 1*   96 Coals: Wood *MS 1*
98 't'other's] thats: burnt out: gone) *MS 1*   100 to] I'd *RL*   101 inquiry
MS 1   102 Read a Column in the new *MS 1*   103 See: maried: whos *(fifth
word) MS 1*   104 through] by: their] for *MS 1*   beg[s] *MS A3*] begs *MS 1*
105 tird *MS 1*   106 desird *MS 1*   107 nub] hub *MS 1*, hob *RL*
108 ∧Just: dry∧ *MS 1*   109 Elbow *MS 1*   A pitcher at my side should
stand *RL*   110 &] With *RL*   111 willd *MS 1*   112 twas: filld *MS 1*
113 posesd *MS 1*   114 Corner] A corner *RL*   wall *MS 1*

Store o' victuals lin'd compleat   115
That when hungry I might eat
Till by plenty well supply'd
I became as satisfy'd
& ones Guts unusual eas'd
Stuft & cram'd becomes appeas'd   120
Painful croaking noises oer
Urging hunger calls no more

Then let me in plentys lap
For the first time take a nap
Falling back in easy lare   125
Sweetly slumbering in my chair
No Reflective thoughts awake
Pains to cause my heart to ache
Of contracted debts long made
In no prospect to be paid   130
& to want sad news severe
Of provisions getting dear
While the winter shocking sight
Constant freezes day & night
Deep & deeper falls the snow   135
Labour slack & wages low
These & more the poor can tell
(Known alas by them to[o] well)
Plenty O if blest by thee
Never more should trouble me   140
Peace & happiness & ease
All thy gay attendance these

115 Store] With store *RL*   o vitcuals lind *MS 1*   117 Till—: suplyd *MS 1*
118 satisfied *MS 1*   119 ones *through* m *MS A3*] my *MS 1*   guts unusal easd
MS 1   120 cramd: appeasd *MS 1*   121 Painful] Disturbing: noise *MS 1*
122 nomore *MS 1*   123 let me] would I *RL*   124 knap *MS 1*
125 Lare *MS 1*   126 Lost in sweetest slumbers there (Lost *through* Tost) *MS 1*
127 No] With no: awake] to wake *RL*   128 to] that *RL*   ⟨ache⟩ *torn MS A3*]
ache *MS 1*   129 mad⟨e⟩ *torn MS A3*   130 ⟨to be p⟩aid *torn MS A3*
131–4 *Lines worn away MS A3   Copy-text: MS 1*   131 want] poor: News *MS 1*
132 Provisions *MS 1*   133 Winter (schoking *MS 1*   135 ⟨Deep⟩ *torn*
MS A3   136 ⟨Lab⟩our *torn MS A3*   slack] scarce *MS 1*   137 ⟨The⟩se
torn MS A3   138 ⟨Kn⟩own *torn MS A3*] ∧Known *MS 1*   to well∧ *MS 1*
139 ⟨Plen⟩ty *torn MS A3*   140 ⟨Neve⟩r *torn MS A3*] These no *MS 1*
141 ⟨Peac⟩e *torn MS A3*   hapines *MS 1*   142 ⟨All⟩ *torn MS A3*
tendance *MS 1*

Should be my companions then
Fear'd no more the sight o' men
Shuddering as the door unlatch'd   145
Dreding fearing to be catch'd
By that monster seiz'd alone
By horrid name o' Bailiff known
Wi' all his plagues his debts & bills
The very thought my bosom chills   150
Cringing low at their comand
Creditors no more should stand
Dissapointed still unpaid
Hearing my excuses made
Carless quite to my affairs   155
Answering but wi' hums & ha's
When as soon as ere they see
How time's going on wi' me
Money none—old plaguing case
Anger redens in their face   160
Scowls his brow a dreadful frown
(I my nose strait looking down)
Finding alls no use to stay
Bangs the door too & away
Leaving me to think again   165
Fresh renewing every pain—

Now no more by these oprest
Wouldst thou give what I request
Free'd from Povertys chill north
That does bring these monsters forth   170

143 ⟨Shoul⟩d *torn MS A3*   144 ⟨F⟩ear'd *torn MS A3*] Feard *MS 1*
MS 1   145 Shudering: unlatchd *MS 1*   146 Dreading: catchd *MS*
147 [&] by *MS A3*   149 Thoughts of plagues wi lengthnd bill *MS*
150 Then no more should turn me chill *MS 1*   151 cammand *MS*
152 more should] longer *MS 1*   153 Disapointed *MS 1*   155 Carles
quite] all *MS 1*   156 wi: has *MS 1*   157 When] & *MS 1*   158 times
wi *MS 1*   159 Old *MS 1*   161 dredful *MS 1*   162 ∧I: strait] still
down∧ *MS 1*   163 ing *in* Finding *inserted MS A3*   Finding alls] While h
finds't *MS 1*   164 ⟨B⟩angs *torn MS A3*   to *MS 1*   165 ⟨Le⟩avin
torn MS A3   166 ⟨Fre⟩sh *torn MS A3*   pain∧ *MS 1*   167 ⟨Now
.*torn MS A3*   168 ⟨Wou⟩ldst *torn MS A3*   what I request] — & I am blest (
am *through* Im) *MS 1*   169 ⟨Fre⟩e'd *torn MS A3*] Freed *MS 1*   povetys ch
MS 1

Where the clouds of want prevade
& spread one continu'd shade
Hopes as soon as born destroy
Shuts out day & every joy
These tho they not cease to be   175
Now [no] more should trouble me
Tho existing they're not mine
Blest where pleasures sun can shine
Neath whose rays so deeply felt
Like to snow these monsters melt   180
Namless troubles causing grief
Want that begs in vain relief
Empty guts that pines & frets
Oer her poverty & debts
All as quick[l]y droops & dies   185
As the dew in summer dry's
Nought but plenty now & peace
Joy & pleasure health & ease—

Nothing wanting all possest
Blessings soon as wish'd for blest   190
No desire will fill my eye
But what thou canst satisfy
O so sweet the joys you give
Life may then desire to live
& no longer wish to die   195
Heaven below will satisfy
Hours & weeks will sweetly glide
Soft & smooth as flows the tide
Where no stones nor choaking [grass]
Force a curve ere it can pass   200

172 continued *MS 1*   176 no: shall *MS 1*   177 theyre *MS 1*
181 Namles *MS 1*   183 [Pining] guts: pines &] pining *MS 1*   185 quickly:
dies *through* flies *MS 1*   186 dries *MS 1*   188 ease ∧ *MS 1*
189 ⟨N⟩othing *torn MS A3*   posest *MS 1*   190 ⟨Bl⟩essings *torn MS A3*
wisht *MS 1*   191 ⟨No⟩ *torn MS A3*   desires *MS 1*   192 ⟨But⟩ *torn*
MS A3   wilt *MS 1*   192/3 [⟨   ⟩ (torn) will sweetly glide] *MS A3*
193 ⟨O so sweet the⟩ *torn MS A3*   194–8 *Last five lines of page worn away MS A3*
Copy-text: MS 5   194 will *MS 1*   197 will sweetly glide] as does the tide
MS 1   198 and: smoth: glide *over* [as floes the tide] *MS 1*   199 or *RL*
grass *MS 1*

Smoothing on meets no delay
So my Life would pass away
And as happy & as blest
As beast drop them down to rest
When in pastures at their will   205
They have roam'd & eat their fill
Every craving then supply'd
Every wish as satisfied
Not a pain nor want they feel
Rest o'er them as softly steals   210
Soft as nights in sumer creep
So should I then fall to sleep—
While sweet visions of delight
So enchanting to the sight
Such as pleasures fancy yield   215
To my sight should be reveal'd
Sweetly swimming o'er my eyes
Sinking me in extacys

Nor would pleasures dreams no more
As they oft have done before   220
Cause be to create a pain
When I woke to find 'em vain—
Bitter past the present sweet
Would my happiness compleat
O how easy should I lye   225
& the fire upblazing high
(Summers artificial bloom)
Like a oven keeps the room
Lovly may—as mild & warm
While without the raging storm   230

201 Smootheing *MS 1*   202 life woud pas *MS 1*   203 &: hapy *MS*
204 Beast *MS 1*   206 roamd: ther *MS 1*   207 suplyd *MS 1*   208 as
is *MS 1*   209 want nor pain *MS 1*   210 oer: softly] sweetly: steal *MS*
211 creep] sleeps *MS A3*   212 to sleep] asleep *RL*   sleep∧ *MS*
215 fancys *MS 1*   216 would: reveald *MS 1*   217 swiming oer *MS*
218 Would sink me into extacies *RL*   219 pleasure dream *MS 1*   no] once *R*
220 oft] of: had *MS 1*   222 wakd: em vain∧ *MS 1*   225 I should *R*
226 &] With *RL*   up blazing *MS 1*   226/7 [Kept the Room a stove as warm
MS 1   227 ∧Sumers: bloom∧ *MS 1*   228 Like a] That like an *R*
229 [May] Lovly *MS 1*] Or lovely *RL*   May∧: and *MS 1*

Still unwearied scorns to cease
Would my happiness increase
Roaring in the chimney top
In no likelihood to drop
& the whichen branches nigh   235
Oer my snug box towering high
That sweet shelterd stands beneath
In convulsive eddies wreath
& as in oppresion proud
Peals his howlings long & loud   240
& as tyrant like the storm
Takes delight in doing harm
To their uttermost extent
Gives his rage & fury vent
Down before him crushing all   245
Till his weapons usless fall
While the clouds with horrid sweep
Gives (as suits a tyrants trade)
The sun a minutes leave to peep
To smile upon the ruins made   250
& to make compleat the blast
Snow & hail comes hard & fast
Rattling loud agen the glass
While the snowy sleets that pass
Driving up in heaps remains   255

Close adhering to the pains
Stops the light & spreads a Gloom
Suiting sleep around the room

232 hapines *MS 1*   233 Roaring] Is roaring *RL*   chimny *MS 1*
235 wychen: nigh] high *MS 1*   236 [Towering] Oer *(through* oer*) MS A3*]
Towering oer *MS 1*   snug box *underlined:* towering *inserted MS A3*   [cottage] snug
box: high] nigh *MS 1*   238 Eddies *MS 1*   239–40 *Follow line 246 in RL*
240 Peal *RL*   his] is: and *MS 1*   241 & as] And *MS 1,* Then while *RL*
242 to harm *MS 1*   244 furys *MS 1*   245 chrushing *MS A3*
246 usles *MS 1*   *Followed in RL by:* And as in oppression proud, / Peal his howlings
long and loud,   246/7 [There as] *MS A3*   248 Gives] Then: ‸as: trade‸
MS 1   250 To smile] Smiles: ruins] havoc *MS 1*   251 & [While] *MS A3*]
—While *MS 1*   252 Snow] Sleet *MS 1*   Snow &] While the *RL*   hail *through*
sleet *MS A3*   253 glas *MS 1*   254 While] & *MS 1,* And *RL*   pas *MS 1*
255 remain *RL*   256 pane *RL*   257 Stop: spread *RL*   gloom *MS 1*
258 Room *MS 1*

O how blest mid winters storms
Shielded then in Fortunes arms   260
Who defying every frown
Hugs me on her downy breast
Bids my head lye easy down
& on winters ruins rest
So upon the troubld sea   265
Emblematic Simile
Birds are known to sit secure
While the billows roars & raves
Slumbering in their safty sure
Rock'd to sleep upon the waves   270
—So would I still slumber on
Till hour telling clocks had gone
& from the contracted day
One or more had clik'd away—
By her larum—slumbers broke   275
Then if felt when I awoke
Somthing like the wanting pain
Fall to eat & drink again
Then to smoke & then to read
Each the other to succeed   280
Just as taste should then require
Or as fancy would desire
Till wi' sitting wearied out
I for changes sake no doubt
Just might wish to leave my seat   285
& to exercise ones feet
Make a journey to the door
Put my nose out—but no more
There to village taste agree
Mark how times are like to be   290

259 —O: Winters *MS 1*   winters storms] these alarms *RL*   260 Shielded
then] I should bask *RL*   fortunes [h]arms *MS 1*   266 Emblematic] Sublimatic:
simile *MS 1*   267 sit] rest *MS 1*   268 bilows *MS 1*   roar and rave *RL*
269 saf[e]ty *MS A3*] safety *MS 1*   270 Rockd *MS 1*   wave *RL*   271 I;
MS A3   272 teling *MS 1*   274 clickd away $_\wedge$ *MS 1*   275 larum $_\wedge$ *MS 1*
280 suceed *MS 1*   283 wi siting weared *MS 1*   286 ones] my *MS 1*
RL   feet [make] *MS 1*   287 journy *MS 1*   289 vilage *MS 1*

How the weathers getting on
Peep in ruts where carts have gone
Or by stones a sturdy stroke
View the hole the boys have broke
Crizzling still inclin'd to freeze   295
& the ryhme upon the trees
Then to pause on ills to come
Just look upward on the gloom
See fresh storms approaching fast
View em busy in the air   300
Boiling up the brewing blast
Still fresh horrors schemeing there
Black & dismal rising high
From the north alarms the eye
Pregnant with a thousand storms   305
Huddld in her icy arms
Heavy hovering as they come
Some as mountains seem—& some
Jag'd as c[r]aggy rocks appear
Dismally advancing near   310
Earth unable seems to bear
The hughe mass thats moving there
Fancy at the cumberous sight
Chills & shudders with affright
Fearing lest the air—in vain   315
Strives her station to mentain
Wearied yields—& lets it fall
Wizzing horrid from the skys
World & nature, Life & all
Crush'd beneath its ruins lyes   320

291 How the] & how: gettin *MS 1*   292 Peep . . . carts] by a rut where Carts
MS 1   295 Crisling: inclind *MS 1*   297 pause] peep: Ills *MS 1*
298 looks *MS 1*   299 aproahing *MS 1*   302 horors scheming *MS 1*
303 black *MS 1*   304 from *MS 1*   alarms] they fright *RL*   306 Nuddeld
MS 1   their *RL*   307 hovering] heaving *MS 1*   308 seem∧ *MS 1*
309 Gag'd *MS A3*] Jagd *MS 1*   cragy *MS 1*   311 seems— *MS A3*
312 huge *MS 1*   314 shudders with affright] shuders at the sight *MS 1*
315 air∧ *MS 1*   316 mantain *MS 1*   317–20 And wearied, yielding to the
skies, / The world beneath in ruin lies. *RL*   317 yields∧ *MS 1*   318 Wizing:
skies *MS 1*   319 nature∧ life *MS 1*   320 Crushd: lies *MS 1*

—So may fancy think & fain
Fancy oft imagines vain
Natures laws by wisdom penn'd
Mortals cannot comprehend
Power almighty being gave   325
Endless mercy stoops to save
Causes hid from mortals sight
Proves 'what ever is is right'

—Then to look again below
Labours former life to view   330
Who still beating thro the snow
Spite of storms their toils pursue
Forc'd out by nessesity
(That sad fiend that forces me)
Troubles then no more my own   335
Which I but too long had known
Might create a care, a pain
Then I'd seek my joys again
Pile the fire up fetch a drink
Then sit down again & think   340
Which by seeing 'custom'd things
Fresh into my memory brings
Pause on all my sorrows past
Think how many a bitter blast
When it snow'd & hail'd & blew   345
I have toil'd & batter'd thro'
& how many a lengthn'd day
(Half the night as one may say)
Weary lowking in a barn
Humble twenty pence to earn   350

321 ∧So MS 1   322 imagine MS 1   323 pend MS 1   324 canot
MS 1   325 almigty MS 1   326 Endles MS 1   328 proves MS 1]
Prove RL   ∧what: wright∧ MS 1   329 ∧Then MS 1   330 to] I'd RL
332 his MS 1   333 ' through e in Forc'd MS 1   by sad RL   334 ∧That:
forced me∧ MS 1   fien'd to fiend (p.e.) MS A3   335 nomore MS 1
336 know MS 1   337 care∧ MS 1   338 Id MS 1   341 see'ng acustomd
MS 1   342 fresh MS 1   343 pause: sorows MS 1   344 biter MS 1
345 snowd: haild MS 1   346 toild: baterd thro MS 1   347 lengthend
MS 1   348 (half MS 1   349 lowking] luping MS 1

—Then to ease reflective pain
To my old sports fall again
Eat & drink till that would do
Then puff out a pipe or two
Till the clock had counted ten—   355
Then to fetch a nap agèn
I would seek my downy bed
Easy, happy, & well fed
Then might peep the morn in vain
Thro the rihmy misted pane   360
Then might bawl the restless cock
& the loud tong[u]'d village clock
& the frail might lump away
Waking soon the dreary day
They should never waken me   365
Independant blest & free
Nor as usual make me start
Yawning sighs wi' heavy heart
Loath to ope ones sleepy eyes
Weary still in pain to rise   370
Aching bones & heavy head
Worse then when one went to bed

O the trouble wants endure
O the pains of being poor
Independant plenty hail   375
May my hopes with thee prevail
Nothing then to raise a sigh
O how happy should I lye
Till the clock was eight or more
Then proceed as heretofore!   380
—Best o' blessings sweetest charm
Boon these wishes while they're warm

352 sport *MS 1*   To my sports I'd fall again *RL*   355 ten∧ *MS 1*   357 I
would] When I'd *RL*   358 Easy∧ happy∧ *MS 1*   359 peep] Call *through*
pee *MS 1*   360 ryhmy *MS 1*   361 restles *MS 1*   362 tong'd *MS 1*
363 flail *RL*   368 sigh *RL*   wi *MS 1*   369 ones] my *RL*   sleepy *below*
[weary] *MS 1*   370 stil: in pain] & loath *MS 1*   371 Aching] With aching
RL   372 one] I *MS 1 RL*

My fairy visions neer despise
As reason thinks—thou reallize
Depress'd i' want & poverty   385
I sink—I fall—deny'd o thee

Vain hope—thy Castles built in air
Could I but bid thee cease despair
Then, then adieu the vain extreams
The sad & mellancholly themes   390
As aid Encouragement essays
My strings to tune my songs to praise
In bolder flights—my muse begun
Should bask in plentys cheering sun
Nothing nothing then she sings   395
But laughing joys & pleasing things

—Hear me plenty—undeny'd
Bid my soul be satisfy'd
Grant the Boon—the happy hours
& thy return shall not be long   400
Ere my exerted utmost powers
Repay thy kindness with a song—

390 [dreams] themes *MS A3*   399 Boon *to* boon *(p.e.) MS A3*   400 & Thy
to And thy *(p.e.) MS A3*   402 Repay *to* Repays *(p.e.):* thy *to* the *(p.e.) MS A3*

AUTOGRAPHS: Pet. MS A3, pp. 49–51: Nor. MS 1, pp. 227–8 (ll. 49, 50, 66 pencil): Pet. MS A7, p. 34a (fragment).
TRANSCRIPTS: Pet. MS B1, pp. 107–8 (deleted): Nor. MS 5, pp. 131–4.
Dated: 1810–12 (MS A3, p. 49 '8 or 9 years ago').

THE RESIGNATION

(Supposed to be Written by the Unfortunate Chatterton Just Before he Took the Deadly Draught that Put a Period to his Existance)

Since dissapointment & dispair
The vainess of all hopes declare
Since toss'd upon this Restless main
I strive 'gainst wind & Waves in vain
The more I struggle for the shore   5
Misfortunes overwhelm the more
Then since I struggle to maintain
And strive alass—to live in vain
I'll hope no more—Since prov'd & try'd
The feeble light she once supply'd   10
Resembl'd but the tapers Ray
That only burns to dye away
—& leave me lost in endless night
(My follies but expos'd to sight)
—Then come misfortunes as ye will   15
Oppresions sink me lower still
Haste kind despair & urge my doom
And all that haunt the wretched come
Fate—from my heart all fears expunge
I stand resolv'd to take the plunge—   20

THE RESIGNATION *Title:* The Resignation *MS A3*, The Resignation (gn *through* n) *MS 1* Followed in *MS A3* by: (Supposed to be[)] Written by the / Unfortunate Chatterton / just before he took the deadly / Draught that put a Period / to his Existance) 1 Disappointment: despair *MS 1* 3 Since—tossd *MS 1* Restless *to* restless *(p.e.) MS A3* 4 strive *over* [struggle]: Wind *MS 1* Waves *to* waves *(p.e.) MS A3*] waves *MS 1* 6/7 [Then since I strive in vain to rise] *MS 1* 7 [alak] I strugle *MS 1* to maintain *over* [but in vain] *MS A3*] but in vain *MS 1* 8 alas∧: live *over* [Rise] *MS 1* 9 Since *through* Ive *MS 1* 10 supplyd *MS 1* 11 Resembld *altered to* Resembling *MS 1* tapers *to* taper's *(p.e.)*: Ray *to* ray *(p.e.) MS A3* 13 endles *MS 1* 14 exposd *MS 1* 17 kind] keen: &] to: my— *MS 1* 18 & *MS 1* 19 (—Fate—: expunge) *MS 1* 20 I stand resolv'd] Im ready now: plunge.—*MS 1*

—O thou Great being who resides
Far above where yon ether glides
Whose power almighty—'piercing eye
Marks all on Earth in Air & Sky
Who oft (such care we ought to praise)   25
The sand-grain call'd a World surveys
Nor deems unworthy of thy care
Vain Men as Worthless as we are
Who oft with liberal hands bestow
Thy guiding mercey here below   30
—& while our sins so multiply
Like Mountains heap'd before thee lye
—So loath—so tempted to chastize
And then to bless us in disguise
—To dissappoint our restless schemes   35
Our airy hopes and foolish dreams
Is but to prove the empty show
Of painted happiness below
—O thou that hears the wretched call
Thou Universal friend to all   40
I own thy goodness feel thy power
And humbl'd in this trying hour
Affecting as my troubles seem
I prove thy Mercy was extreem
But O thou Universal Lord   45
Some Shelter to the Wretch afford
Forgive the sin if sin it be
To sink beneath Adversity

21 Great *to* great *(p.e.) MS A3*] great *MS 1*   being *to* Being *(p.e.) MS A3*   22 Ether *MS 1*   23 Piercing *MS 1*   24 Earth *to* earth *(p.e.):* Sky *to* sky *(p.e.) MS A3*   Air *to* air *(p.e.) MS A3*] air *MS 1*   26 *Clare's correction MS A3, p. 120:* Instead of 'This Atom call'd a world &c' / Print This sand-grain call'd a world surveys / as it was at first / 'Sand-grain' instead of 'Atom' is all the diff^rn—   atom *MS A3 MS 1*   calld *MS A3*   World *to* world *(p.e.) MS A3*] world *MS 1*   27 unworthy] us worthless *(us through an) MS 1*   28 men *MS 1*   30 mercy *MS 1*   31 ∧& *MS 1*   32 Mountains *to* mountains *(p.e.) MS A3*] mountains *MS 1*   us *MS 1*   33 ∧So: chastise *MS 1*   34 & *MS 1*   35 ∧To: restles *MS 1*   dissapoint *to* disappoint *(p.e.) MS A3*] disapoint *MS 1*   36 & *MS 1*   38 happines *MS 1*   40 universal *MS 1*   41 goodnes *MS 1*   42 & humbled *MS 1*   43 Affecting] Afflicting *MS 1*   44 mercy: extreeme *MS 1*   45 univeral *MS 1*   46 Shelter *to* shelter *(p.e.) MS A3*] shelter *MS 1*   Wretch *to* wretch *(p.e.) MS A3*   48 Adversity *to* adversity *(p.e.) MS A3*] adversity— *MS 1*

—Prest down—O God—thou knowest all
I am but mortal & must fall—   50

Ye Grizly Ghosts that seem to rise
And swim before these frantic eyes
My blood runs chill—your hollow screams
But serve to terrify my dreams
And make this hopeless heart of mine   55
Desist & shrink from its design

—But hush ye fears ye lengthen pain
Here fancy may imagine vain
No terrors need the soul attend
When we are gone our sorrows end   60
Or why (my kindred fortunes hate
Those Victims sacrifis'd to fate)
Did they the self same road pursue
Unless they thought—& hop'd it true
And since that last resource is mine   65
Stern Fate resolve—& I resign

49 ∧Prest: god∧: knowst *MS 1*   50 fall∧ *MS 1*   51 Grizly *to* grizly *(p.e.)*
MS A3] grisly *MS 1*   Ghosts *to* ghosts *(p.e.) MS A3*] gosts *MS 1*   52 & *MS 1*
53 Blood: your] you *MS 1*   55 &: hoples *MS 1*   56 [its] from *MS A3*
57 ∧But: fears— *MS 1*   58 Fancy *MS 1*   62 victims sacrifisd *MS 1*
65 &: Resource *MS 1*   66 fate *MS 1*   resign. *MS A3 MS 1*   *MS A7, p. 34a*
contains a fragment of a poem on Chatterton (top of page is torn):

Youths more then ⟨   ⟩
Ah oer thy early da⟨   ⟩
To hear the droop neath wants un⟨   ⟩ sky
When hopes weak rushlight longer ⟨   ⟩ to burn
[& nights want around nor promisd days return]   5
& left black night around & promisd no return
On Chatterton

(l. 3 the *for* 'thee')

AUTOGRAPH: Nor. MS 1, p. 228.
Dated: 1808–19 (MS 1).

> Now spring returns with all the pleasing charms
> Which heart can wish or eye could hope to see
> And every vally with her bounty swarms
> But ah her bounty swarms in vain to me
>
> In [vain] for me she cloths the blooming fields   5
> And rears the flowers & beautifies the trees
> Fields flowers & trees to me no pleasure yields
> But all's in vain this aching heart to please

AUTOGRAPH: Nor. MS 1, pp. 230–1 (pencil).
Dated: 1808–19 (MS 1).

> O welcome to thy cheering light
> That smooths the raven down of night
> Fair moon I court thy peacful reign
> (Recourse to sleep with me is vain
> She seeks the Beds of healt[h] & ease   5
> But shuns the wretch devoid of these)
> Thy silence & thy peace I love
> The dim seen plain & darker grove
> & (balm for woe) an hours Reprieve
> I watch the sober close of eve   10
> To seek for the[e] & for the fair
> The maid of thy peculiar care
> That shuns the noisy & the rude
> & thou art nurse of Solitude

NOW SPRING RETURNS WITH ALL THE PLEASING CHARMS *Title:
wanting*

O WELCOME TO THY CHEERING LIGHT *Title: wanting*   1 *Preceded
by:* [O welcome moon thy cheering light / That shins to guide me thro the grove]
3/4 [A fond adoring dying swain]   6/7 [Awhile from woes to get reprieve]
10 watch *over* [seek]

When thou art present she is near   15
& thou & thine art ever dear
The gloomy haunt her taste approves
My coresponding genius love[s]
I always love & take delight
Be thine or not to rule the night   20
When suns set red & darknes lowers
Above my head in threatend showers
& when night spreads her sable shroud
Beneath one undivided cloud
—But more delighted love to seek   25
When thy light paints the maidens cheek
& softer shades the darksom folds
Which nights gloom in her mantle rolls
O then how sweet with her & you
& handmaid contemplation too   30
& sister silence lonly led
The solem scenes of night to tred
The pasture & the green to rove
Pacing neath the willow grove
Or oer brown fallows wher the sheep   35
For us a batterd pathway keep
Where strong voicd labours noises oer
Hollows at the plough no more
Ceasing to urge labour on
From the scene Industrys gone   40
Leaving her to breath awile
Strength Recruiting—farther toil

22 above   24 beneath   25 —but
34/5

       [Where to interupt our joys
       Cows & sheep have ceasd to noise
       Days companions all desird
       Night aproachd & they retird]

36/7

       [Where from the scene Industrys gone
       & ceases urging labour on
       Leaving him to breathe awhile
       Recruiting strength for farther toil]

38 hollows   39 ceasing   40 from   41 leaving   42 strength

—Short the sweets which I pursue
'Morrows dawn the toils renew
Dull the scenes I now survey   45
Blyth & jolly all the day
Kate has ceasd with idle bawl
Her Roving lowing cows to call
'Neath the awthorn by the spring
Collin ceases now to sing   50
& the ploughman as before
Rants his vulgar lays no more
All is still & desolate
Plains abandond to their fate
Save the lark that sweetly sleeps   55
Were the grasy bunches peeps
'Bove the clod that shields its nest
Moon sweet gilds its ruset breast

AUTOGRAPHS: Pet. MS A3, pp. 136–7: Nor. MS 1, pp. 235–6 (ll. 29–56 pencil, deleted).
TRANSCRIPTS: Pet. MS B1, pp. 8–9: Nor. MS 5, pp. 76–9.
Dated: 'Old' (MS A3, p. 137).

ON THE DEATH OF A QUACK

Here lyes Lifes Cobler who untimly fell
By name of Doctor Drug'em known to all
His frequent visits mad[e] him known full well
For where he'd business he ne'er faild to call
Fools praisd his power as great in saving Life   5
& for that purpose many a Journey made
To Village Lout & Tradesmans Wimsy Wife
But some there must be to incourage trade

43 (short   48 her   53 all   54 plains   57 'bove
   ON THE DEATH OF A QUACK   Title: On the Death of a [Docter] Quack MS
A3, wanting MS 1   1 lies 'Lifes Cobler' MS 1   2 'Docter Drug'em' MS 1
3 made: so well over [to all] MS 1   4 hed busines: neer MS 1   5 Fool's:
powers: life MS 1   6 journey MS 1   7 Farmers altered to Tradesmans MS
A3] Farmers MS 1   wimsy wife MS 1   8 encourage MS 1

For want of them full many a trade wou'd stop
& what wou'd docters do if't wa'n't for fools?   10
They then might keep at home & shut up shop
Their pills & mixtures would be usless tools
—The Doctors Drugs one certain Virtue claims
Which in his Wondorous Bills he never puts
E' faith why don't they?—'t'wou'd increase their fame   15
To empty Pockets well as scour the Guts
At this our Drug'em was Expert enough
The Art he practis'd knew it wondorous well
While money lasted he ne'er faild of Stuff
& Fools would buy 'em—he knew how to sell   20
& faith of Custom from his noted skill
He never faild—his fame the Village spred
Tho ignorant of the cause—too strong a Pill
Has workd a Paietent—now & then to dead
Yet still his fame & customers increas'd   25
Who he by Practise prov'd not over nice
& playd as good a part wi' them at least
For as they E'k'd his fame—he Ek'd his Price
His Drugs went off—(& Doctors will be paid)
So money tumbld in most wondorous free   30
But Fortunes Sun shine often finds a shade
The happiest crosses meet—& so did he
Death—who'd ta'en many a Patient off his hands
& wether want of Work—Or wether whim
What caus'd his coming—no one understands   35
But he was hunting & he hunted him

9 woud *MS 1*   10 woud Docters: fools∧ *MS 1*   12 Pills: Mixters: usles
MS 1   13 —The] ∧But: drugs: one *through* a: certain *over* [double]: virtue
claim *MS 1*   14 their wonderous: they: put *MS 1*   15 (E' Faith: do'n't
they∧—twould: fame) *MS 1*   16 To empty Pockets] That emptys pockets: scours:
guts *MS 1*   17 'Drug'em': expert *MS 1*   18 art: practisd—: wonderous
MS 1   19 neer: stuff *MS 1*   i *through* l *in* faild *MS A3*   20 fools: [&]
would: 'em∧ *MS 1*   21 Faith [his] of custom *MS 1*   22 village *MS 1*
23 ign'orant: pill *MS 1*   24 Has] Was: paitent∧ *MS 1*   25 increasd *MS 1*
26 who he by] & Who [he] by [his] (ˌ[he] *inserted*): practise: prov'd found *MS 1*
27 & *through* He *MS 1*   28 For] &: Ek'd his fame∧: price *MS 1*   29 drugs:
—& doctors: paid∧ *MS 1*   30 mony: wondrous *MS 1*   31 fortunes
sunshine *MS 1*   32 hapiest croses meet∧ *MS 1*   33 whod: patient *MS 1*
34 whethere *(second word)*: work— *MS 1*   35 causd: coming∧: under stand
MS 1

No Lingering–Illnes'd–Journy man—he sent
Himself at once—nor made one doubtful stop
Spite of his being a Doctor—Boldly went
& Seiz'd him in his Garrison—his Shop   40
Where all his Weapons dreadfully displayd
Bid bold Defiance on each hand Bill Read
& Pills & Powders desperate sallies made
Pelting like hail Round the Besiegers head
But Death feard nought—yet when the Phisic flew   45
The stink so nausious—made him turn about
& forcd him to Retreat awhile to spew
—But frequent Sallies wore the Doctor out
A Time to prove his Art was fairly bid
Patients Expected—(Fools have little wit)   50
That he would play his part—well so he did
But then it faild & then the fools were bit
They provd too well his Art of Getting Pelf
But tother Art was either Lost or past
If he sav'd them he cou'd not save him self   55
So here Poor Drug'em lies a Quack at Last?

AUTOGRAPH: Nor. MS 1, p. 237 (deleted).
Dated: 1808–19 (MS 1).

O thrice lucky town (the more lucky poor creatu'rs)
Who ere could have thought that such luck would be thine
Such a stranger as thou art to things o' like natur
But time bringeth all things to pass—so its sighn

37 No Lingering illns'd Journyman he sent *MS 1*   38 Him self *MS 1*
39 doctor—boldly *MS 1*   40 seizd: shop *MS 1*   41 weapons dreedfully
MS 1   42 defiance: bill read *MS 1*   43 pills: powders desprate *MS 1*
44 Pelting] & pelted: hail—round: besegers *MS 1*   45 he feared nout but when
the phisick flew *MS 1*   46 stink] smell *MS 1*   47 retreat *MS 1*
48 ∧But: sallies: doctor *MS 1*   49 A] &: time: art *MS 1*   50 expected∧
(fools: witt) *MS 1*   51 playd *MS 1*   — *through* (*MS A3*)   52 faild— *MS 1*
53 Art *through* rat *MS A3*] art *MS 1*   getting pelf *MS 1*   54 art: lost *MS 1*
55 savd: coudnt: himself *MS 1*   56 poor drugem: last∧ *MS 1*
    O THRICE LUCKY TOWN (THE MORE LUCKY POOR CREATU'RS) *Title:*
wanting

& O' what a blessing o' poor peoples sides   5
Who just before this wer' near pineing to dead
That his L—d——ps great goodnes condecends to provide
An odd sort of something that they may be fed
What a good christian heart must his honour posess
To 'mean him so l-w when so high riches rank him   10
In giving this h-ge p——dge—they cant do no less
Then down on their knappers & twenty times thank him

And benevolent charity sure such as this is
'll set others a going for the good o poor ce'turs
And warm squeezing Mizers to open their fis'es   15
And soften the wit-leather hearts of our betters

AUTOGRAPHS: Pet. MS A3, pp. 110 (ll. 1–44) and 107 (ll. 45–50): Nor.
MS 1, pp. 239 (ll. 1–32, deleted) and 238 (ll. 33–50, deleted), Nor. MS 1,
p. 238 (deleted variants of ll. 1–18, 23–32): Pet. MS A40, pp. 34a–35.
TRANSCRIPTS: Pet. MS B1, pp. 173–4: Nor. MS 5, pp. 73–5.
Dated: 'Old' (MS A3, p. 110).

A FEW HINTS TO A MAIDEN

*After Hearing Her Laughing & Diverting Herself
& Company With Railing at Anothers Misfortune*

To Laugh at others & their faults expose
To take a pleasure in anothers woes
Seems quite as bad by those it is exprest
As is the scandal by the wretch poses'd

7 *Lordships*   8 (odd sont   10 *low*   11 *huge porridge*: lese   15 *fists*
A FEW HINTS TO A MAIDEN   *Title:* A Few Hints to a Maiden / After hearing
her Laughing & Diverting Herself / & Company with Railing at anothers Misfortune
MS A3, Advise to a Maiden on hearing her diverting / herself & the Company in
Railling at anothers / Misfortune *MS 1, p. 238*, A Few hints to a Maiden / after hearing
her Laughing [Railing] and / Diverting herself and Company with / Railing at anothers
Misfortune *MS 1*, Hints to a Maiden / After hearing her laughing & diverting herself /
& company with railing at anothers misfortune *MS A40*   1 laugh: and *MS 1 MS
1, p. 238 MS A40*   2 Woes *MS 1*   To seem diverted at anothers Woes *MS 1,
p. 238*   3 expresd *MS 1, p. 238*] expressed *MS A40*   4 Wretch *MS 1 MS 1,
p. 238*   posess'd *MS 1 MS 1, p. 238*] possesd *MS A40*

Who jeers misfortunes laughs at their expence   5
Tis but a Witness of their want of Sense

Then lovley Girl resist so mean a vice
& pay attention to a friends advice
Nor frown offence on what he humbly moves
He loves the greater were he most reproves   10
He owns thy Beauty blossoms all divine
But Beautys frail & blossoms will decline
& while thy lustre blooms its brighter Ray
He only wishes those foul weeds away
That serve to poison while they're left to spred   15
With deep'ning shades that beautious white & Red
The fairest flowers will stain from lightest dyes
& faults less practis'd will the most supprise
Then charming creature from such vice Refrain
So fair thy beauty & so apt to stain   20
So free from failings of the slightest mould
How triumphs slander if he gets but hold

—Near think by making others faults your scorn
Those charms of thine to heighten & adorn
The victors valour is no more compleat   25
Then is the vanquish'd's lessen'd by defeat

---

5 Misfortunes: expense *MS 1*   The laugh & joke is raisd at thy expence *MS 1, p. 238*
6 'T'is *MS 1*   witness *MS A40*   sense *MS 1 MS A40*   They do but witness want
of common sense *MS 1, p. 238*   7 lovly *MS 1, p. 238*   girl *MS 1, p. 238*
MS A40   8 And *MS 1*   advise *MS 1, p. 238*   9 offence— *MS 1, p. 238*
10 He] His *MS 1 MS 1, p. 238*   where *MS 1 MS 1, p. 238 MS A40*   approves *MS
A3*] approves *altered to* reproves *MS 1*   11 beauty *MS A40*   12 Beauty's *MS 1*]
beautys *MS 1, p. 238 MS A40*   and *MS 1*   13 And *MS 1*   brightest *MS 1*
MS 1, p. 238] brightest *altered to* brighter *MS A40*   ray *MS 1, p. 238 MS A40*
14 wihes: fowl *MS 1, p. 238*   weeds] deeds *MS A40*   15 theyre *MS A40*   spread
MS 1, p. 238 MS A40   16 deepning *MS 1, p. 238*   Beautious *MS 1*   red *MS
1, p. 238 MS A40*   18 practisd: suprise *MS 1, p. 238*   19 refrain *MS 1*
MS A40   20 and *MS 1*   22 triumph's: hold! *MS 1*   it *MS A40*
23 ∧Neer *MS 1, p. 238*] ∧Near *MS A40*   thy *MS A40*   24 &] or *MS 1*
25 Victors *MS 1 MS 1, p. 238*   valour[s] *MS A40*   26 Then] As *MS 1 MS 1,
p. 238*   vanquishd's *MS 1 MS 1, p. 238*] vanquish'd *MS A40*   lessend *MS 1 MS 1,
p. 238 MS A40*

No Worth & honour takes a differ'nt range
& mercy spares where malice might revenge

—But when such meaness Beautys charms preceede
They only serve to magnify the deed   30
Superior talents trifles more demean
As smallest spots on snow are soonest seen
& more then this Defficiency of praise
In slanders ear some Jealousys may raise
The world from this may hint suspicious thoughts   35
Tho blind to worth she never winks at faults
Her chief delight exposes them to view
& ne'er fails adding somthing more than true

What others want—and we so quickly see
Betrays in us the like difficensy   40
Old sayings hint that 'Medlers are the Worst'
& Proverbs tell us 'Rotten stakes crack first'
Those faults which others do the most contemn
Are often prov'd the most belov'd by them
Maids rail at Whores—as whores would maidens blame   45
Only as each could like to be the same
Then from such meaness lovly Girl desist
If tis not fact tis common at the least
For folks to think—& mind if you pursue
They'll be as apt to think the same of You   50

27 No—worth: take: different *MS A40*   Real honours gaind by mercy thro exchange
MS 1] No honours worth admits a different change *MS 1, p. 238*   28 & mercy
spares] When ere she saves *MS 1*   &] Where *MS 1, p. 238*   mercey *MS A40*
where] when *MS 1, p. 238 MS A40*   Malice *MS 1*   revenge.— *MS 1*] Revenge *MS 1,
p. 238*   29 ∧But *MS A40*] And *MS 1*, No—*MS 1, p. 238*   beautys: precede
MS A40   31 Superiors tallent *MS A3*   bemean *MS A40*   32 Snow *MS 1,
p. 238*   33 &] As *MS 1*   deficiency *MS A40*   34 jealosys *MS 1*] jealousy
MS A40   35 World: g *through* t *in* thoughts *MS 1*   36 Worth: neve *MS 1*
38 neer *MS 1*] near *MS A40*   then *MS 1 MS A40*   39 want∧ & *MS A40*
Anothers faults which some so Greatly please *MS 1*   40 deficiency *MS A40*
Betray the like deficiency in these *(the through a) MS 1*   41 ∧meddlers: worst∧
MS A40   42 proverbs: 'rotten: first∧ *MS A40*   tell[s] *MS A3*   43 which
... the] & failings others *MS A40*   condemn *MS 1*   44 provd *MS 1*] proved
MS A40   beloved *MS A40*   45 Maids *through* Prudes *MS A3*] Prudes *MS 1*
at whores∧ *MS A40*   Whores *(sixth word) MS 1*   would *through* Whores *MS A3*]
woud *MS A40*   46 shoud *MS A40*   47 lovley *MS 1*   girl: desist *through*
for bear *MS A40*   48 —If 't'is *MS 1*   49 Folks *MS 1*   think∧ *MS A40*
50 Theyll *MS A40*   of] by *MS 1*   you *MS 1 MS A40*

AUTOGRAPH: Nor. MS 1, p. 240.
Dated: 1808–19 (MS 1).

> Now the Summers in its prime
> All in Youth & Beauty blest
> Myra mark the precious time
> Snatch the pleasure while posest

AUTOGRAPH: Nor. MS 1, p. 241.
Dated: 1808–19 (MS 1).

> Shakspear the Glory of the English stage
> Whose works shall only with the stage decay
> Who still Reaps Laurels from each rising age
> & still unrivald bears the palm away
>
> Such bold Descriptions all his lines adorn   5
> Such strong Resemblance he from nature drew
> So closly copied & so justly drawn
> They make the Reader a Spectator too
>
> No tagging notes to aid the sensless lines
> Are here requir'd————   10
> To every eye his natural beauty shines
> & Lifes near touches never fail to please
>
> But when the Poets Beauties to Recite
> The able actor all his power displays
> Astonishd wonder silencd at the sight   15
> At first beholds 'em in a mute amaze
>
> & as amazement gradualy subsides
> The Echoing clap each sounding period draws
> While bursting praises ring from side to side
> & all the play house thunders with applause   20

NOW THE SUMMERS IN ITS PRIME   *Title: wanting*
SHAKSPEAR THE GLORY OF THE ENGLISH STAGE   *Title: wanting*
3 Rieaps   9 lines] linen   17 & *through* But

So Comets light alarm with sudden flaze—
—So from the grace the able actor gives
The bards bold scenes alarm with sudden blaze
And all the Picture breaths & Walks & Lives

AUTOGRAPHS: Pet. MS D4, pp. 9a–10: Nor. MS 1, p. 242, Nor. MS 1,
p. 243 (variant of ll. 17–20).
TRANSCRIPT: Pet. MS B1, p. 25.
Printed in *RL*, pp. 116–18: *The Englishman's Fire-side* (*EF*), October 1820
(ll. 21–4 omitted).
Dated: 'Old' (MS D4, p. 10).

FALLING LEAVES

Hail falling leaves that patter round
   Admonishers & friends
Reflection wakens at the sound
   —So life thy pleasure ends

How frail the bloom how short the stay   5
   That terminates us all
To day we flourish green & gay
   Like leaves to morrow fall

Alas how short is fourscore years
   Lifes utmost stretch—a span   10
& shorter still when past apears
   The vain, vain life of man

21 flaze.—   23 scenes *over* [paintings]

FALLING LEAVES *Title:* Falling Leaves *MS D4 MS 1 RL EF* *No stanza
division in MS 1*   1 *Preceded in MS D4 by:*

> [Falling leaves
> Ye falling leaves that patter round
>   Admonishers & friends
> Reflection wakens at the sound
> 'Thus worldly   ]   5

Hail *through* Ye *MS D4*] Ye *MS 1*   Leaves: Round *MS 1*   4 All things must
have an end *MS 1*   5 Bloom *MS 1*   6 us *through* you *MS 1*   7 we
flourish] I see you *MS 1*   8 To morrow see you fall *MS 1*   9 Alas] & Ah
MS 1   9/10 [The farstrecthd life of man] *MS 1*   11 appears *MS 1*
12 & such the life of man *MS 1*

These falling leaves once flaunted high
   O pride how vain to trust
Now witherd on the ground they lye   15
   To mingle with the dust

So death serves all—& wealth & pride
   Must all their pomp resign
Een kings shall lay their crowns aside
   To mix their dust wi' mine!   20

—The leaves how once they cloath'd the trees
   Nones left behind to tell
The branch is naked to the breeze
   Nor known from whence they fell

A few more years as they—the same   25
   Are now I then shall be
With nothing left to tell my name
   Or answer—'who was he?'

Green turfs alow'd forgotten heaps
   Is all that I shall have   30
Save that the little daisy creeps
   To deck my humble Grave

13 These . . . once *through* Ere while in air you flaunted *MS D4*] Ere while in air you flaunted *MS 1*   14 (O *MS 1*   15 Ground you *MS 1*   16 To mingle] And mingled *RL EF*   17 Death levels all that dread of pride *MS 1*] Death levels all & wealth & pride *MS 1, p. 243*   18 & no distinction keeps *MS 1* 19 lay their *over* [powers &]: aside *over* [resign] *MS D4*   Kings lay their goldens crowns aside *MS 1*] & kings must lay their crowns aside *MS 1, p. 243*   20 wi mine∧ *MS 1, p. 243*   & with the beggar sleeps *MS 1*   21 The . . . trees] *successively (a)* [? Thus favour how they cloath the trees] *(b)* [How once they livd &] cloath'd the trees *(c)* The leaves how once they cloath'd the trees *MS D4*   Your favour how you clothd the trees *MS 1*   23 is *repeated MS D4*   branch is] branches *MS 1* 24 ye *MS 1*   We know not whence they fell *RL*   25 years—as you— *MS 1*   as they] and I *RL EF*   26 now— *MS 1*   As they are now, shall be *RL EF*   27 With] &: tell *inserted*: my *through* thy *MS 1*   28 —∧ who who: he?∧— *MS 1*   29 turfs—allowd— *MS 1*   forgotton *MS D4*   heap *MS 1 RL EF* 31 Creeps *MS 1*   daisies creep *RL EF*   32 grave *MS 1*

AUTOGRAPH: Nor. MS 1, p. 243 (pencil).
Dated: 1808–19 (MS 1).

Summer now its lustre shining
Like to Myra lovly maid
Youth & Beauty both combining
In their Richest suit arayd

Joys unnumberd without measure   5
In possesion of such charms
Myra grant thy swain the pleasure
Make him happy in thy arms

Take him to thy throbbing bosom
Make him happy while you may   10
Enjoy the flower while in its blossom
Time has wings & flies away

AUTOGRAPH: Nor. MS 1, p. 244.
Dated: 1808–19 (MS 1).

Yes Ra[l]ph Natures made you both clumbsy & stout
But ne'er think to crack on I prythe[e]
For the reasons she had for so doing chubby lout
Are not o' the least credit wi thee

When she'd fashiond you as the rest of us are   5
Save your head—it being empty—thats all
And as reason supplies the deficiency there
On her Mrs Nature must call

And where she had oft been she now whent again
To ask her opinion about it   10
The question was gave and the Answer was plain
And none o' the best never doubt it

SUMMER NOW ITS LUSTRE SHINING   *Title: wanting*   6 such *through*
like

YES RA[L]PH NATURES MADE YOU BOTH CLUMBSY & STOUT   *Title:*
wanting   4/5 *Space left for an additional stanza*   6 *First — through* it
8 M*rs*

No Ive been already says Reason too free
In giving fools Brains to abuse 'em
And this Chubby Lout I can plain enough see   15
Wornt a bit better know how to use em

Very well Mrs Reason said Nature & smil'd
Tho she seemd Rather quere when she said it
If thats your opinion of this Mothers Child
I own it's not much to my credit   20

But as he is—tho I hardly know whats to be said
He must make a shift tho a bad on'
And how to make up for the loss in his head
Your Opinion there Maum I'd be glad on

Why faith Replies Reason your Question's a hard case   25
But as he is as you say why he must do
Therefore knock up plenty of stuff in his carcass
As hes nought but his carcass to trust to

I take this the best scheme to ballance his nob
& Chub by your having recourse to't   30
Will then stand a chance to come in use for such Jobs
As Nobody'll do but whats forsd to't

14 Brains *over* [sence]   17 M^rs   18 he *altered to* she *twice*
23 up *through* out   26 *First* he *inserted*   28 *Second* to] too   29 *First* a
through 1 *in* ballance

AUTOGRAPHS: Pet. MS A3, p. 95: Nor. MS 1, p. 246 (ll. 21–32 omitted), p. 245 (first draft): Pet. MS A40, p. 34.
TRANSCRIPTS: Pet. MS B1, pp. 150–1: Nor. MS 5, pp. 113–15.
Dated: 'Old' (MS A3, p. 95).

EPITAPH ON MR C----LE WHO AFTER EXPERIENCING MISFORTUNES URG'D AT LAST BY DESPAIR PUT A PERIOD TO HIS EXISTENCE—

When honest worth born down beneath the weight
Of sad misfortunes yieldeth to his fate
Pity low bending where the sufferer sleeps
Recalls the past & reccolection weeps
—Beneath this humble stone (all fate would give   5
To better luck may every reader live)
Misfortune hides—& sorrow finds repose
The last resource adversity bestows
And while oblivion draws the vail between
& hides the present with the future scene   10
Let not ill judging jealousy distrust
Nor seek the fault forgotten in the dust
—But hold—ye hasty fears—ye jealous thoughts
The man's the man in spite of all the faults
The clouds of fate that blacken & oer cast   15
But vainly shade the present with the past
The former lustre merits sun displayd
Disperses clouds & lightens up the shade

EPITAPH ON MR C——LE WHO AFTER EXPERIENCING MISFORTUNES URG'D AT LAST BY DESPAIR PUT A PERIOD TO HIS EXISTENCE *Title:* Epitaph / On M^r C——le who after Experiencing many / Misfortunes Urg'd at last by despair put a period to / his Existence— *(by inserted)* MS A3, Epitaph / On M^r—C——le who after Experiencing many Misfortunes / Urg'd at last by despair put a period to his Existence *(after inserted)* MS 1, Lines on Mr C——e / Who after experiencing many misfortunes / put a period to his existance *MS A40*   1 Worth *MS 1*   2 yeildeth *MS 1*   3 — Pity *MS 1*   were *MS A40*   4 past—: Recollection *MS 1*   5 ∧all: woud *MS A40*   Give) *MS 1*   6 (To: Reader *MS 1*   live∧ *MS A40*   7 Misfortune[s] hides∧ *MS A40*   9 &*MS A40* Olivion: the] her *MS 1*   l *through* n *in* vail *MS 1*] veil∧ *MS A40*   10 & hides] Hiding *MS A40*   And: futer *MS 1*   11 jealosy *MS 1*   12 in] with: dust— *MS 1*   13 ∧But hold∧ *MS A40*   fears∧ *MS 1 MS A40*   fears ye jealous Fears—ye Jealous thoughts *MS 1*   14 mans: *second* the] his *MS A40*   man— *MS 1*   15 oercast *MS 1*   17 displayed *MS A40*

—His deeds he own'd em—wheres the man with none?
& those where his no man like him could shun   20
His dealings just his principals was good
He always strove (as far as ere he cou'd)
To keep an even ballance man with man
& tho he failed in this golden plan
Still slander may reproach—but cannot blame   25
(Here black designing malice lost her aim)
His puntual payments far as he was worth
Secur'd his honest fame while here on Earth
& the undoubted character he bore
Endears the memory now the mans no more   30
Such libral actions mark'd his honourd name
In life beloved & in death the same
Ye who succeed him do but act as well
Ye then may flourish where another fell
How vain the wreck to strive against the stream   35
Expierience prov'd it just the same with him
The more involv'd & vain the more he try'd
—Urg'd by despair—he prov'd it so—& dy'd
& contradict it malice if you can
Whats rarely found—he dy'd an honest man!   40

19 ∧His: them—weres *MS A40*   ownd *MS 1*] owned *MS A40*   none∧ *MS 1*
MS A40   20 And *MS 1*   were: coud *MS A40*   21 principles were
MS A40   22 ∧as *MS A40*   cou'd∧ *MS A3*] coud∧ *MS A40*   24 his *MS A40*
25 reproach∧ *MS A40*   27 punctual *MS A40*   28 Secured: earth *MS A40*
31 liberal: markd: honourd] honest *MS A40*   32 His *to* In *(p.e.)*: his *to* in *(p.e.)*
MS A3   33 *Preceded in MS 1 by:* [But dyd Sincere as would ye dy'd as well / That
rise & flourish where another fell]   —Ye: suceed *MS 1*   34 were *MS A40*
35 —How: Wreck *MS 1*   36 Experience *MS 1 MS A40.*   provd *MS 1*] proved
MS A40   37 ivolvd *MS 1*] envolved *MS A40*   tryd *MS 1*] tryed *MS A40*
38 —Urgd *MS 1*] ∧Urged *MS A40*   despair∧ *MS A40*] Despair *MS 1*   proved
MS A40] found *MS 1*   so∧: dyed *MS A40*   39 *Preceded in MS 1 by:* In spite of
all the present & the past / Just as he livd the same he dy'd at last   Contratict: Malice
MS 1   40 rarely] strangly *MS 1*   found∧ *MS 1 MS A40*   dyd *MS 1*] dyed
MS A40   man∧ *MS 1 MS A40*

                    And as he livd he dyd an honest man
                    & contradict it malice if you can
                    his dealings just his principles was good
                    he always strove as far as ere he could
                    To keep an even Ballance man with man   5
                    & tho he failed in this golden plan
                    let not ill judging jealousy distrust
                    nor seek the fault forgotten with the dust *cont.*

AUTOGRAPHS: Pet. MS A4, p. 16: Nor. MS 1, p. 247.
Dated: 1808–19 (MS 1).

CHUSING A FRIEND

As the old Proverb always prove true in the end
'All will cheat alike as cheat can'
Therefore let your judgment in chusing a friend
Be your self—as the properest man

AUTOGRAPH: Nor. MS 1, p. 247.
Dated: 1808–19 (MS 1).

EXPIRIENCE

Tho Expirienc's pupils pay dear to be wise
It's no Use a talking 'bout this that & to'ther
For we're all blind alike 'till she opens our eyes
And 'till then cant be made to be learnt by no other

cont.

all black designs of malice loose their aim
& slander may reproach but cannot blame   10
his puntual payments far as he was worth
secur'd his honest fame while here on hearth
& the undoubted character he bore
Endears the memory now the mans no more
—how vain the Wreck that strives agains the stream   15
& time has provd it quite as vain with him

—ah to much practisd & too often won
his friends were ready when he wanted none
—the more involvd he found the more he tryd
Urgd by despair he provd it so—& dyd   20

He had his failings wheres the man wi none
& those where his—no man like him could shun   *MS 1, p. 245*

(ll. 2/3 *Row of asterisks*; l. 12 hearth *for 'earth'*; l. 17 won *could be read as* gone;
l. 20 Urgd *through* Urging: provd *over* [found])

CHUSING A FRIEND   *Title:* Chusing a Friend *MS A4*, Chusing a friend *MS 1*
1 Old *MS 1*   3 let *over* let *through* leave *MS A4*   m *in* judgment *inserted MS A4*]
judgement *MS 1*   4 Be *over* Be *through* To *MS A4*] Chuse *MS 1*   as . . . man]
you're the only Man *MS 1*

EXPIRIENCE   *Title:* Expirience

AUTOGRAPHS: Pet. MS A3, pp. 102–3: Nor. MS 1, p. 247 (ll. 4, 21–32 omitted): Pet. MS A40, pp. 32a–33.
TRANSCRIPT: Pet. MS B1, pp. 161–2.
Dated: 'Old' (MS A3, p. 102).

MODERN LOVE

Occasioned by an Unequal Marriage

Modern love like to traffic turns all upon gain
& beautys shov'd out of the fashion
False curls paint & patches all labour in vain
    For ex[c]iting an amourous passion

Since wrinkld old shadows—wrong side o' four score   5
Where mouldy old coin is in plenty
Are prefer'd by our modern love jobbers before
    The plump rosey beautys o' Twenty

So now fusty maidens your sorrows lay by
Sin' your blest wi' a friend in your riches   10
Your hearts need no longer to dwindle & sigh
    Nor ache at the sight o' the breeches

MODERN LOVE   *Title:* Modern Love / Occasioned by an Unequal Marriage *MS
A3*, Modern Love Occasioned by an / Unequal Marriage— (A Young man to an old /
Woman on account of her Riches) *(*man *inserted) MS 1*, Modern Love a Ballad /
Occasoned by a young friend / marrying an old woman *MS A40   No stanza division in
MS 1*   1 turns] is *MS 1*   2 shov'd] quite *MS 1*, gone *MS A40*   fasion
MS 1   3 patches all] jewels are *MS 1*   all *through* are *MS A40*
4 exciting *MS A40*   5 wrikled *MS 1*] wrinkled *MS A40*   shadows∧ *MS A40*
0 *MS 1*] of *MS A40*   6 Were *MS A40*   If moneys possed in plenty *MS 1*
7 preferd *MS 1*] preferred *MS A40*   our . . . jobbers] the stock jobing lovers *MS 1*
8 rosy *MS 1*   of *altered to* o' *MS A3*] of *MS 1 MS A40*   20 *MS 1*] twenty *MS A40*
9 lay *over* [gone] *MS A3*   bye *MS 1 MS A40*   10 Since *altered to* Sin' *MS A3*]
Since *MS 1 MS A40*   youre *MS A40*   wi *MS 1*] with *MS A40*   Riches *MS 1*
11 heart *MS 1*   12 Nor] No: briches *MS 1*   ach: of *MS 1 MS A40*

Do but turn out your gold modern rakes to entice
Such a magical power there lies in it
Like a trap that is baited wi' bacon for mice   15
   The gilded snares seiz'd in a minute

So sport it about while by fortune your blest
Make use of the chance while you have it
For fortunes a fickle friend known at the best
   & you cant tell how long she has gave it   20

Friend R——— wi' a fourscore year fillies gone tether
Faith who could a thought that he meant it
But gold put the spring & the winter to gether
   & when the charms lost he'll repent it

Tis money alone modern fancies can tickle   25
& the language of love is mere jargon
The gold makes the marriage—the wifes an article
   Thats forcibly thrown in the bargain

Poor Cupids traid failing must stoop to low arts
Or he comes to a bankruptcy by em   30
In heaps of old coin he must look for his darts
   Myras eyes will no longer supply him

13 Rakes *MS 1*] rakes *through ?* loves *MS A40*   14 a *omitted MS A40*   lyes *MS 1*
15 with *MS 1 MS A40*   16 They'll swallow the charm *(charm over* [bait]*) to* The
gilded snares seiz'd *(p.e., Clare) MS A3*] Theyl swallow the bait in a minute *MS 1*
seized *MS A40*   17 a bout *MS 1*   by] with *MS A40*   20 cant tell] know
not *MS 1*   21 R.: with four score: fillys *MS A40*   y *through* f *in* year *MS A3*
22 coud: have *MS A40*   23 together *MS A40*   24 hell *MS A40*
25 fancys *MS A40*   27 make *MS A40*   — *through* & *MS A3*] & *MS A40*
29 trade *MS A40*   30 'em *MS A40*   32 Myras] Marys *MS A40*

AUTOGRAPH: Nor. MS 1, pp. 248–50.
Dated: 1808–19 (MS 1).

DICKS OPINION

A Simille after the Manner of Peter Pindar

One Morning in summer two Boys went a tenting
Three Calves and a Donk' that till then stood at tether
And none can immagine what they'll be inventing
When Boys so audacious assemble together

Tho their job even nothing as so't might be seeming 5
And their flock tho a motley collection so Small
Yet Lawrence bid Wages and they must be scheeming
An easier still to do nothing at all

'Do yah think' then says one 'We will stan' this D–md bustle
And be hamper'd & bother'd spoiling sport as we do 10
One can't play at ring-taw nor yet pick-&-hustle
Wi' out having somwere or other to go

'No no Bob we'll presently alter't' says Dick
And ne'er be plagu'd so wi' sich poor scrating devils
I'll soon fix a plan for their galloping tricks 15
And at once put an end to their progress & travels

I've just got a Method jump't into my nob
My Donkey yah know's pretty us'd to a tether
And them Calves o yah'n tho they seem the worst job
We'll pen 'em all up in a Corner to gether 20

The scheme was adopted and instant begun
Which the Calves little likeing—tried to shun it in vain
And poor Viscious who hop'd of his hardships being done
Went hanging his ears to his tethers again

DICKS OPINION   *Title:* Dicks Opinion a Simille / After the Manner of Peter
Pindar   4 W *through* B *in* When   5 m *through* b *in* might   6 Small
through pecu   23 his *inserted*

The pen of a shepherd batterd up like a pound   25
Just suited the Boys for their job ready done
And here soon as they had repaired it round
They drove in their Cattle & laughd at the fun

'What a stud!' one exclaims 'stud!' ah ah laughs the other
'Three calves & a donkey pin'd up in a pound'   30
'All my Life d–m m[e] if ever I see sich anuther
'Nor the oldest man living never did I'll be boun'

Yah may talk as yah please about this that & tother
& make what yah will of a donkey & calf
But I say they look squinting one at another   35
Like M—b—rs of P——y—nt sooner behalf

AUTOGRAPH: Pforzheimer Library, Misc. MS 197: Nor. MS 1, p. 249
(pencil beneath ink).
TRANSCRIPT: Pet. MS B1, p. 29.
Printed in *RL*, pp. 118–20.
Dated: '1819' (Pfz, *RL* Introduction, pp. xxii–xxiii 'In the last two years').

THE CONTRAST

Beauty & Virtue

'Beautys a transitory joy
'But virtues sweets shall never cloy'.

As oer the gay pasture went rocking a clown
A gay gaudy buttercups gold fringed gown
Engaged his attention as passing her bye
& rudly to gain her he stooped adown
　　Its beauty so dazzl'd his eye   5

33 talk . . . please *over* [say what yah what yah will]   36 *Members: Parlyment*
　　THE CONTRAST BEAUTY & VIRTUE   *Title:* The Contrast / Beauty & Virtue
Pfz, The Contrast of Beauty and Virtue *RL*   3 attention[s] *Pfz*

By outside appearence the sensless are caught
& beautys gay triumph is foolish & short
With nothing to gain the attention beside
Possession soon sickens—& fleet as a thought
 Beauty slips us forgotten aside   10

As snufting & snufting the clodhopper goes
& finding no sweetness for charming his nose
Frail beauties delusion soon wearied his eye
& away the gay flowret he heedlessly throws
 To wither unnotis'd & dye   15

Ye young giddy wenches gay buttercups mind
So tempting your dresses your nature so kind
Virgin beauty once tasted no longer endures
The charm that should please us fair virtues resignd
 & a *buttercups* fortune is yours   20

Let Modestys sweetness your blossoms adorn
Be virtue your guard as the rose has her thorn
Then as Chemists the sweets of the rosey secures
When beautys no more—still to please is your own
 & Virtues charm ever endures   25

7 &] But *RL* 11 snifting *(second word) RL* 12 nose] noes *Pfz* 19 Virtue *RL* 20 & a buttercups] A butter-cup's *RL* 23 roses secure *RL*
25 &] For: charms ever endure *RL* *MS 1 early draft reads:*

 As when oer the green a clown
 A buttercups gay gaudy gown
 & fringd wi golen cate
 As well he turnd his eyes adown
  Smiled on his fate   5

 By outside shows the mind is caught
 But beautys dazzling reign is short
 With naught to cheer beside
 Possesion palls & good for naught
  Its plopt aside   10

 When no perfume could charm his nose
 As snuft[ing] & snufting on he goes
 Delusion quickly tired his eye
 & on the ground the flower he throws
  To fade & die   15

cont

AUTOGRAPHS: Pet. MS A3, pp. 81–2: Pet. MS A3, p. R141 (ll. 23–36 only, deleted): Nor. MS 1, pp. 252 (ll. 1–12) and 127 (ll. 25–48, upside down, pencil).
TRANSCRIPT: Pet. MS B1, pp. 136–7: Nor. MS 5, pp. 48–50.
Printed in *RL*, pp. 59–62.
Dated: 1819 (MS A3, p. 81 '1819', 'fresh composed' preceded by 'New' deleted in margin; *RL* Introduction, p. xxii 'In the last two years').

THE FOUNTAIN

Her dusky mantle Eve had 'spread
The west sky glowr'd wi' copper red
'Sun bid 'good night' & slove to bed
   'Hind black clouds mimick'd mountain
When weary from my toil I sped   5
   To seek the purlin' fountain

Labour e'en 'gen it up fo' good
Save swains their folds that beetling stood
While Echo listning i' the wood
   Each knock kept 'stinctly counting   10
The moon just peep'd her horned hood
   Faint glimmering i' the fountain

cont.

   Ye giddy pated wenches mind
   A caution this for yere resignd
   Ye young giddy wenches gay buttercups mind
   So tempting your dresses your natur so kind
   Virgin beauty once tasted no longer endures   20
   Then the charm that should please us fair virtues resignd
     & a butter cups fortune is yours

   But let modest sweetness your blossoms adorn
   Be virtue your gard as the rosey its thorn
   Then as chemists roses sweets can secure   25

(l. 3 golen *for* 'golden')

THE FOUNTAIN   *Title:* The Fountain *MS A3 RL, wanting MS 1*   1 Ev'ning
her dusky mantle spred *MS 1*   2 sky *inserted*: wi *MS 1*   3 ∧Sun bad: ∧good
night∧ *MS 1*   slove *through* gangd *MS A3*] slove *through* ga *MS 1*   4 'Hind
altered to 'hind: black *through* a clouds: mimickd *MS 1*   7 E'en *to* e'en *(p.e.) MS*
A3] had *MS 1 RL*   gen *MS 1*] gi'en *RL*   8 Save swains] Sheperds: that] tho
MS 1   9 listning Echos: i'] from *MS 1*   10 nock *MS 1*   11 peep'd]
how'd *MS 1*   12 Faint glimmering i'] & glimmerd in *MS 1*   13 dimples,
MS A3   15 I'll par'd *to* Ill=paired *(p.e.) MS A3*   yours *RL*

Ye gently dimpled curling streams
Rilling as smooth as summer dreams
Ill-pair'd to thine lifes current seems   15
 When hope—rude cataracts mounting
Bursts cheated into vain extreems
 Far from thy peacefull fountain

I'd just streak'd down & wi' a swish
Wang'd off my hat (soak'd like a fish)   20
When 'bove what thought cou'd think or wish
 (Fo' chance theres no accounting)
A sweet lass came wi' wooden dish
 & dipt it i' the fountain

I've often found a rural charm   25
In pastoral song my heart to warm
But faith her beauties gave alarm
 'Bove all I'd seen surmounting
& when to th' spring she streach'd her arm
 My heart chill'd i' the fountain   30

Simple, 'witching, artless maid
So modestly she offer'd aid
'& will you please to drink?' she said
 —My pulse beat bye the counting
O Innocence such charms display'd   35
 I cant forget the Fountain

16 — *through* rude *MS A3*   18 thy] the *RL*   19 swish *underlined MS A3* *Clare's note in MS A3:* A provincial Expression signifying an anxious & eager manner of throwing anything aside that proves an hinderance in Obtaining the thing wish'd for—here we say '& it went wi' a <u>swish</u> to't— 20 hat—: fish)— *MS A3* 21 thought] heart *RL* 24 dipt *pencilled below* [dipt] *MS A3* 25 Ive *to* I've *(p.e.) MS A3*] Ive *MS 1* found] known *MS 1* 26 heart to warm *through* bosom *?* warm *MS A3* O pastoral song my bosom warm *MS 1* 27 gave ga *MS 1* 28 All other charms a mounting *MS 1* 29 to'th *MS A3*] to'th' *MS A3, p. R141*, toth' *MS 1* 'spring *MS A3, p. R141* strecht *MS A3, p. R141*] stretch *MS 1* 30 chilld i *MS 1* 31 Simple ∧ *MS A3* Bewitching simple artles maid *MS 1* 32 offerd *MS 1* 33 ∧&: pleas *MS 1* drink ∧∧ *MS 1*] drink ∧ *MS A3, p. R141* 34 ∧My *MS 1* by *to* bye *(p.e.) MS A3*] by *MS A3, p. R14 MS 1*, past *RL* 35 O' *MS A3, p. R141* innoscence: displayd *MS* 36 fountain *MS 1*

Ere lonely home she 'gan proceed
I said—whats secresy indeed!
& offer'd company as need
 The moon was highly mounting   40
& still her charms—(I'd scorn the deed)
 Wer' pure as was the fountain

Ye leaning palms that seem to look
Pleas'd oer your Image i' the brook
Ye ashes harbouring pye & nook   45
 Your shady boughs be mounting
Ye Muses leave Castalias nook
 & sacred make the fountain

AUTOGRAPH: Nor. MS 1, p. 252 (pencil).
Dated: 1808–19 (MS 1).

So Christianitys enlivening light
Dispersd the mistery with smiling ray
Of Ignorance & superstitions night
That gastly veild religions early day
Such light in Jesu's passion we 〈 〉   5
He died & sufferd that we might be blest
& death & hells grim terrors he subdues
He made the grave a wishd for place of rest

37 lonly: 'gan] made: proseed *MS 1* 38 said∧: indeed∧ *MS 1* 39 offerd
MS 1 41 &] But: ∧(Id sorn: deed∧ *MS 1* 42 Wor *MS 1* 43 leaning
palms] willows bowd *MS 1* *Clare's note in MS A3:* A species of Willow call'd 'English
Palm' instead of the more common name 'Sallow' 44 Pleasd: you image i *MS 1*
45 habouring ypye *MS 1* 47 muses: castalias *MS 1* 48 sacred make]
sacralize *MS 1*

SO CHRISTIANITYS ENLIVENING LIGHT *Title: wanting* 3 u *in*
superstitions *inserted* 8 he

AUTOGRAPH: Nor. MS 1, p. R252.
Dated: 1808–19 (MS 1).

>One monday morning sour & loath
>>To labour like a turk
>A tween the hour o' five & six
>>I took my corpse to work
>Deuce take a labourers life thought I 5
>>They talk o slaves els where
>I sees much choice in foreighn parts
>>As I do in Slavery here

AUTOGRAPH: Pet. MS A1, inside front cover (erased pencil).
Dated: 1819–20 (MS A1).

>⟨The maid who⟩ roams upon the plain
>Will no more trust your Songs
>For pride disguisd & love despisd
>Are bought with killing wrongs
>The swain that late beheld ⟨his Love⟩ 5
>While wandering by his side
>His ⟨maiden⟩ pain but told in vain
>Till life despaird & dyd

ONE MONDAY MORNING SOUR & LOATH   *Title: wanting*   1 morning *repeated*
THE MAID WHO ROAMS UPON THE PLAIN   *Title: wanting*

AUTOGRAPH: Pet. MS A1, f. 4ᵛ (erased pencil).
Dated: 1819–20 (MS A1).

O beneath such raptures in my forgetfull heart
That at that moment neath a oaks mossd bough
From all the world deberd world forgot
I sat as happy at that time as if
Id just recievd existence & as if   5
The world[s] sad troubles & the world[s] rude spite
   Had never never been

AUTOGRAPH: Pet. MS A1, ff. R6ʳ, R5ᵛ, 65ᵛ, 11ᵛ (erased pencil).
Printed in *RL*, p. 206.
Dated: 1819 (MS A1, *RL*).

EXPECTATION

When expectation in the bosom heaves
What longing anxious views disturb the mind
What fears what hopes distrust & then believes
That somthing which the heart expects to find
How the poor prisner ere hes doomd to die   5
Within his gloomy cell of dreary woe
How does he watch with expectations eye
The lingering long suspence of fate to know

O BENEATH SUCH RAPTURES IN MY FORGETFULL HEART   *Title:*
wanting   1 raptures *through* charms   7 had
 EXPECTATION   *Title:* Expectation *MS A1 RL*   3 distrust[s] *MS A1*   believe
RL   5 prisoner *RL*
The following variant of ll. 1–3 appears on MS A1, f. R5ᵛ:

   When Expectation does the bosom heave
   What lingering anxious views disturb the mind
   What fears what hopes distrust & then believe

Alas poor soul & so do I repine
The Walls his prison is the world is mine   10
So do I turn my weary eyes above
So do I look & sigh for peace to come
So do I long the graves dark end to prove
& anxious wait my long long journey home

AUTOGRAPH: Pet. MS A1, f. 8ᵛ (erased pencil, deleted).
Dated: 1819–20 (MS A1).

Crafty cats that were constantly fixt on the watch
As chances fell out they employd
& timley retreating as [he] lifted the latch
Unmolested their thieving enjoyd
Quite heedless to every domestic concerns   5
She hung her self over the fire

9 & . . . repine] though different bonds confine *RL*   confine *over* [do I repine] *MS A1*
The following appears on f. 65ᵛ:

As the poor prisner wishing to be free
Looks round his cell & sighs for liberty
So burthed down beneath a weight of woe
From this worlds care & pain below
So do I turn my weary eyes to home   5
& hope & sigh for better days to come

The following variant of ll. 11–14 appears on f. 11ᵛ:

So do I bend my weary eyes above
So now I wait & wish for peace to come
So do I long the graves dark end to prove
& anxious wait my long long journey home

CRAFTY CATS THAT WERE CONSTANTLY FIXT ON THE WATCH   *Title: wanting*   3 as *inserted*   5 [as] to: every *inserted*

AUTOGRAPH: Pet. MS A1, f. 8ᵛ (erased pencil, deleted).
Dated: 1819–20 (MS A1).

> Watching ⟨in that chill spot⟩ that wakend the gale
> ⟨Such fits⟩ to illness ⟨speak⟩ plainly
> The welcome voice of health & plenty
> Sweetly Reflected in toils ruddy cheek
> That health attends the labourers early hour   5

AUTOGRAPH: Pet. MS A1, f. 15ʳ⁻ᵛ (erased pencil).
Dated: 1819–20 (MS A1).

> Just as mornings rosy lass
> Unbeds from sleep & gins to dress
> Just as draws her curtains bye
> How sweet to watch her opening eye
> As her cheek is glowing warm   5
> & her finely turned arm
> First unfolding on the stretch
> Her⟨mantles⟩ crystal sheets to reach
> Sweet is then the graceful folds
> As round her lovly limbs it rolls   10
> Half revealing to the sight
> That seat of rapture & delight
> In beautys melting mingling hue
> Skin so white & veins so blue
> H[e]aveing on the ravishd eye   15
> Warming charms of extasy
> Till it fades in witching pale
> Neath a seeming swelling vale
> Of morning while it 'lopes away
> Mid the modest blush of day   20

WATCHING IN THAT CHILL SPOT THAT WAKEND THE GALE   *Title: wanting*

JUST AS MORNINGS ROSY LASS   *Title: wanting*

Then the sun with gentle creeps
Oer heavens surface softly peeps
To his toils again repairs
To [k]not in gold her spangld hairs
& as waiting in the skies   25
Till morn takes her exercise
High & brighter when shes drest
Hangs a locket at her breast
& to suit her softy tread
The sun this way to earth is led   30
& as proofs of gold esteem
Spreads around her ⟨   ⟩ gleam
When at first the while to wait
Like a watch man at the gate
Verdant on the morning sceen   35
Oer the carpets spreading green
Hies & summons every flower
To open at an early hour
Sweetly soon each flower unfurls
Capt within a crown of pearls   40
& each notty point of grass
⟨   ⟩
Or the brook ⟨   ⟩ as I pass
Witnessing ⟨   ⟩
To the wild wood shielded sweet   45
Where the branches branches meet
Where the ⟨   ⟩
& the morning songs are heard
& the holly branches spread
Spreads an arbour oer my head   50
As the woodland paths divide
Sweet to put the boughs aside

22 & surface   32 *hiatus*   50 harbour

AUTOGRAPH: Pet. MS A1, f. R19ʳ (erased pencil).
Dated: 1819–20 (MS A1).

PS: CL

Let churchs & chappels shrill your a[n]themns crye
Places ordaind for a sacred ⟨him⟩
Praise praise the Lord ye cherubs of the sky

AUTOGRAPHS: Nor. Item 175 (Clare's Library). In pencil on the back
flyleaf of John Cunningham's *The Poetical Works*, 1800: Pet. MS A1, f. 20ᵛ
(erased pencil, ll. 1–6 only).
TRANSCRIPTS: Nor. MS 4, pp. 44–5: Pet. MS C2, pp. 47–47a.
Dated: 1819–20 (MS A1).

JEAN BELL

A Ballad

In a fair town on the banks of the Wellan
For low vulgar fun noted well
There lives a fair maid which my song woud fain tell on
As known by the name o' Jean Bell
But to tell of her beauty its no use presuming   5
Its far yont my ballad to tell
We say the flowers fair in the spring morning blooming
& so we may say o Jean Bell

Her beauty shenes sweet on her cheeks & her bosom
Such sweetness as I canna tell   10
But look on the lilly & rose just in blossom
& then give a guess at Jean Bell

PS: CL   *Title:* Ps: CL *Psalm 150*   1 your *through* their

JEAN BELL   *Title:* Jean B—— / a Ballad *Item 175, wanting MS A1*   1 banks
of the Wellan] willow bound Welland *MS A1*   3 maid] lass *MS A1*   4 0
MS A1   B—— *Item 175*] Bell *MS A1*   5 But let others ⟨that⟩ flowers in the
garden wall blooming *MS A1*   6 In its self we its beauties can tell *MS A1*
7 e *through* h *in* We *Item 175*   8 B—— *Item 175*   12 B—— *Item 175*

Her voice is soft music when ere she is speaking
But the sounds Im not able to tell
Go when eves pencil the west sky is streaking   15
Hear the mavis & judge O Jean Bell

But her beauty is such—(if we ere so far fetch it)
As a simile never can tell
& as my low ballads unable to reach it
We'll sing little more o Jean Bell   20
Yet when ye see ane
Who has charms that can please ye
Ifs ye think yeve seen none to excell
While ye're heart in ye'r bosom gins ache & uneasy
Ye may give a nigh guess its Jean Bell   25

AUTOGRAPH: Pet. MS A1, f. 22ᵛ (erased pencil).
Dated: 1819–20 (MS A1).

Others in mixt alteration doubly blest
My woes unheeded leaves my heart at rest

AUTOGRAPH: Pet. MS A1 (erased pencil), f. 23ᵛ (ll. 1–11), f. 24ʳ (ll. 12–16), f. 59ᵛ (ll. 17–24).
Dated: 1819–20 (MS A1).

This hill on which I rest me now
Shaded by summers blooming bough
Where free the cowslips left to bow
& where the wild thymes printed now

15 when *repeated Item 175*   16 J.B. *Item 175*   20 J.B. *Item 175*
25 B—— *Item 175*
    OTHERS IN MIXT ALTERATION DOUBLY BLEST   *Title: wanting*
2 woes *over* [?]: leaves *over* [&]
    THIS HILL ON WHICH I REST ME NOW   *Title: wanting*

Waves from the zephers sigh 5
Upon this bare existing spot
As some day tho I heed it not
Might stand but castle hall or what
& when & how—why thats forgot
Or wether it was so or not 10
—— The Times gone bye
Where Sleep has dropt my weary head
To take its peace the weary bed
& closing sorrows nigh gone fled
Ive often thought & often said 15
As slumbering here I lye
Mynstrel of earliest aged days awake
Of thy wild Ignrance fain would I partake
Thy rusted wires thy old uncoothly make
& quaint expressions pleaseth much mine eye 20
As wandering aimlessly the wires among
Wild on the heaths on which thy harp has rung
Where druid mynstrel sung
   In days gone by

AUTOGRAPH: Pet. MS A1 (erased pencil), f. 27ᵛ (ll. 1–16), f. 28ᵛ (ll. 17–24), f. 60ʳ (ll. 25–41), f. 60ᵛ (ll. 42–9), f. 30ᵛ (ll. 25–9 variant). Dated: 1819–20 (MS A1).

    Spirit of the woods awake
    In thy wildest dress appear
    Trace with me the curdled brake
    Sound thy wildness in my ear
    Genius of the woods that dwells 5
    Sweeping boughs & grains among
    As I climb thy rough rude dells
    Breath thy roughness in my song

    While I brush the branches by
    & this woods still ways forsake 10
    Woodland spirit meet my eye
    Genius of the woods awake

SPIRIT OF THE WOODS AWAKE *Title: wanting*

Breath thy wildness in my ear
⟨   ⟩ I do belong
Genius of the woods appear   15
Sound thy roughness in my song

Who the woods delights can tell
For her many mixing greens
Old snub Oak & sleepy dell
All her wild romantic scenes   20
Who the woods delights can feel
⟨   ⟩ follys rude
In its ⟨peacful⟩ rest we steal
On the ⟨   ⟩ of Solitude

When the oakes huge branches spread   25
Waving in the breezes blow
& the hazels tassled head
Lights its humble leaves below
On a mos[s]y bed reclind
Then my reed to tune Id try   30
Mix my wild notes with the wind
Spirit of the Woods be nigh

Wild delights of natures ⟨shade⟩
Sings its songs of Infancy
Could my humble songs perswade   35
Neer an ax should injure thee
Many a line should thee recall
As its green head stoopd the ground
O to see my favrites fall
My soul shudders at the sound   40

Granduers groves my eye disdains
Uniformd to art & skill
Natures freedom suits my strains
Where thy branches spread

25–9

Where the huge oak over head
Shades the under wood below
Where the hazel branches spread
Oer the nursling flower that blow   *MS A1, f. 30ᵛ variant*

42 Uni[n]formd   44 spread *for 'spill'?*

O how I delight to be 45
Wandering in the wild wild wood
Pausing on Grey mossy tree
Oaks that have for ages stood

AUTOGRAPH: Pet. MS A1, f. R42ʳ⁻ᵛ (erased pencil).
TRANSCRIPT: Pet. MS C1, pp. 8a–9.
Dated: 1819–20 (MS A1).

I saw the girl just to my mind
I dreamd of joy & wakd in woe
She gaind my heart but she provd unkind
I hopd a friend & found a foe

The storm that rent the statly oak 5
I thought it was a trusty tree
But first it bowd & then it broke—
& so my love deceived me

My loves proud scorn my heart has rent
My love was fair my heart to win 10
But like the gilded monument
My love she provd corrupt within

I once lovd one that did love return
But love is changing like the sea
My love is crossd Im left to mourn 15
& now loves one that loves not me

Twas I that scornd my first fond maid
Disdaind her love & vows unbound
Twas I that smiles with frowns repaid
& gave to feel the latest wound 20

I SAW THE GIRL JUST TO MY MIND   *Title: wanting MS A1*, An Old Song
MS C1   1 the] a *MS C1*   2 My dream was joy but my waking woe *MS C1*
4 &] but *MS C1*   8 & so my] So my false *MS C1*   10 My love's fine charms
my heart did win *MS C1*   13 did love return] that love returned *MS C1*
14 like] as *MS C1*   15 That love's long cross'd & [now love one] long I've
mourn'd *MS C1* ·   16 love *MS C1*   19 frowns] vows *MS C1*

I could I meet her first fond love
No power on earth should part in twain
Could I once more her bosom move
Id never change my mind again

I stretchd my hand to a rose full blown   25
Thinking a sweeter rose to find
I prickt my finger to the bone
& left the sweetest rose behind

AUTOGRAPH: Pet. MS A1, f. 30ʳ (erased pencil).
Dated: 1819–20 (MS A1).

Hobbling to labour by some pasture side
While often stopping scenes to trace
The wonderous beauties in a flowers face
& often ⟨   ⟩ yet ⟨   ⟩
Tho be his sweet ⟨   ⟩   5
⟨   ⟩
⟨   ⟩
Captures the while his inward powers
& ⟨   ⟩ delight him which he ⟨   ⟩
Brings picture pleasing scenes to mind   10
For which his language can allegiance find
& other pleasures they portray
Till in each others love they now are gay

21 my *MS C1*
   HOBBLING TO LABOUR BY SOME PASTURE SIDE   *Title: wanting*

AUTOGRAPHS: Pet. MS A1, ff. 47ʳ–49ᵛ (erased pencil): Pet. MS A11, p. 10a (title and first line only).
TRANSCRIPTS: British Library, Eg. MS 2250, f. 157ʳ⁻ᵛ. In a letter from Drury to Clare, n.d.
Dated: 1819–20 (MS A1).

TO AN OAKEN STEM

& here I behold thee a young pliant tree
& in some far distant day
Can boast thy origin when talking of thee
When my head may be soberd in grey
But soon shall thy branches above me grow up   5
Their long shadows darken the spot
& when no more needing my watering cup
Soon soon shall my care be forgot

As others shall follow successors to me
To seek future shelter of thine   10
As little theyll think thee a large spreading tree
As once a small acorn of mine
& soft shall they listen the winds in thee sigh
When I shall be deaf to the sound
& gay shall the prime of thy ⟨youth⟩ flourish high   15
When mine moulders low in the ground

TO AN OAKEN STEM   *Title:* To an Oaken Stem *MS A1 BL*, To an oaken stem *MS A11*   *Readings are supplied when necessary from BL*   1 &here] Here *MS A11*   2 distant *through* distancd *with second* d *in* distancd *making the first letter of* day *MS A1*] distantce *BL*   3 of thy *BL*   4 heads *MS A1*   6 darenken *MS A1*   9–12 *MS A1, f. 47ʳ has the following variant:*

The curious to come predecessors to me
In seeking this shelter of thine
But little theyll think thee a magnifyd tree
As once a small acron of mine

9 As . . . follow] The curious to come *BL*   10 To] Shall *BL*   11 As . . . thee] And little shall think thou *BL*   12 As] Wast *BL*   13 listen to *BL*   15 youth *BL*] ⟨   ⟩ *over* [?] *MS A1*   16 *Replaces* When many shall lay in the ground *MS A1*   moulders] decays *BL*

How painful & pleasing reflection looks up
On the changes this life does endure
Last year a brown acorn thou shelld from thy cup
& now thou'rt a trees miniature   20
How anxious one lingers on what follows next
& the end of whats coming to learn
But here the dark scene in a misterys perplext
& conjectures but dimly discern

One fancys & sighs & one feareth it much   25
Some owner in gains rude abuse
As the blooms of thy boughs are but little to such
Should blight thy lifes prime for a use
& when to thy planting protector thourt lost
'Neath the ax thy complainings & all   30
To stand in some yard thy own trunk as a post
Recording thy foes & thy fall

Or doubtless a station more high thou shalt boast
In joining the crowns loyal trees
& mixing thy thunder with the wild warring host   35
Go to plough the salt brine of the seas
& when to thy birth place & owner forgot
In fresh foreign climates to range
The hand that once dropt thee in thy unshifted spot
Shall little be dreaming the change   40

O far better luck little promise to thee
Do I hope from this blossom of thine
Far far be the meddler to injure the tree
Or disturb this once acorn of mine
O may thy thin stem lift its branches on high   45
& waver their shadows around
& thus may thou live & thus may thou die
Till thy hollow trunk rots to the ground

24 conjecture: discerns *BL*   25 one *inserted MS A1*   27 bloom: thy]
the *BL*   35 & mixing] Mixing *BL*   39 once dropt thee] thee dropt *BL*

O would but some follow as tasteful as I
When age spreads this promise of thine   50
Or could some witchd bard with his wild rolling eye
Fall heir to this Acorn of mine
Long long should the wind in thy curly top sigh
& thy leaves evens wisperings wave
Long long should thy bloom lift into branches on high   55
When mine was decayd in the grave

AUTOGRAPH: Pet. MS A1, ff. 53ʳ–52ᵛ (erased pencil).
Printed in *RL*, pp. 155–6.
Dated: 1819 (MS A1, *RL*).

THE ADIEU

Lone lodge in the bend of the vally farwell
Thou spot ever dear to my view
My anguish my bosoms forbidden to tell
While wandering I bid thee adieu
Stained rose bud thou once of my ballads the pride   5
Till proof thy defilements could view
Though that thou heedlessly roamst from thy guide
I wish that thy foes may be few

My love thou hast never yet known to deceive
I vowed ever constant & true   10
& as faithfull returns as I fainly believe
Till proof furnishd failings in you
Thou'rt lovely I own it in many a sigh
But what has such beauty to win
The nightshade its blossom is fair to the eye   15
That harbours dead poison within

53 curly *could be read as* wily BL

THE ADIEU *Title:* The Adieu *RL, wanting MS A1*   4/5 [⟨Tho *hiatus*
adieu⟩] *MS A1*   5 ballad *RL*   6 thy defilements could] brought thy canker to *RL*
7 that . . . roamst] heedlessly now thou hast roam'd *RL*   thy *through* the *MS A1*
8 wish that] still wish *RL*   10 & true] to be *RL*   11 And thy faithful returns
did as firmly believe *RL*   12 Till proof found a failing in thee *RL*   15 its
blossom is] it blossoms as *RL*

O rose bud thou subject of many a song
Thy defilements so plain to a view
I love thee but cannot forgive thee this wrong
I hope but too vainly adieu   20
Resolvd never more to behold thee again
Or to visit the spot where ye dwell
My last look Im leaving on Walkerd[s] lovd plain
A last vow Im breathing—farwell

AUTOGRAPH: Pet. MS A1, f. 54ᵛ (erased pencil).
Dated: 1819–20 (MS A1).

Gee is thy name thou prating plodding creature
& at thy plough tail gee thy horses still
Twas all intented by thy mother nature
Tho ⟨framd⟩ it seems to thought of better skill

AUTOGRAPH: Pet. MS A1, f. 54ᵛ (erased pencil).
Dated: 1819–20 (MS A1).

O freedom freedom sacred name
Thy lands a land of slaves
Tho many a town thy right proclames
But trust me they are knaves
Theres many a slave shows in his notes   5
In freedoms intrest bawling
Woud sell his consciense for a groat
O freedom thou art fallen

17 many *through* my: a song *below* [? Well God has paid] *MS A1*   18 so] too: a]
my *RL*   19 this] the *RL*   20 [I] too *MS A1*] it's *RL*   21 you *RL*
22 you *RL*   24 A] My *RL*

    GEE IS THY NAME THOU PRATING PLODDING CREATURE   *Title: wanting*

    O FREEDOM FREEDOM SACRED NAME   *Title: wanting*   7 consciense
over [birthright]

AUTOGRAPH: Pet. MS A1, f. 62ʳ⁻ᵛ (erased pencil, alternative version of
ll. 17–24).
Printed in *RL*, pp. 152–3.
Dated: 1819 (MS A1, *RL*).

PATTY

>   Ye Swampy Falls of pasture ground
>   With rushy moors bestrewed
>   Ye moory swells with brambles crownd
>   Ye prospects wild & rude
>   Ive tracd ye oft & love ye dear   5
>   & kind was fate to let me
>   Tis you I found my all for here
>   Twas first my patty met me
>
>   Flow on thou gently plashing stream
>   Oer weed beds wild & rank   10
>   Delighted Ive enjoyd my dream
>   Upon thy mossy bank
>   Bemoistening many a weedy stem
>   Ive watchd thee wind so clearly
>   & on thy bank I found the gem   15
>   That makes me love thee dearly
>
>   ⟨Thou wilderness so rudely gay⟩
>   So wild as would love be
>   ⟨Oft as I wend my steps away⟩
>   Yere ever dear to me   20
>   Forever I your scenes admire
>   Your briars & thorns so matty
>   On you I met my hearts desire
>   On you I found my patty

PATTY   *Title:* Patty *RL*, *wanting MS A1*   2 And rushy spreading
greens *RL*   3 Ye rising swells in brambles bound *RL*   4 And freedom's
wilder'd scenes *RL*   5 tracd] trod *RL*   7 Tis] On *RL*   18 Oft as I seek
thy plain *MS A1 alternative version   RL*   20 & meet my joys again *MS A1 alternative
version   RL*   21 & brush thy weaving branches by *MS A1 alternative version*]
And brush the weaving branches by *RL*   22 Thy *MS A1 alternative version*]
Of *RL*   Briars *MS A1 alternative version*   23 As in my soul shall warm a sigh *MS
A1 alternative version*] So oft reflection warms a sigh *RL*   24 Here first I met my
Patty *MS A1 alternative version   RL*

AUTOGRAPH: Pet. MS A1, inside back cover (erased pencil, deleted).
Dated: 1819–20 (MS A1).

> O endless bright in life & light
> Thou mercys depths thou comforts height
> Triumphing faith acclaim
> Encouragd by his blest command
> As firm as lasting shall you stand   5
> Your heaven endures the same

AUTOGRAPH: Pet. MS A2, f. R1ʳ (erased pencil).
Dated: 1819–20 (MS A2).

> The ⟨   ⟩ has ⟨   ⟩
> He stopd ⟨   ⟩ loud
> Then kept his beaver up & bye & bye
> ⟨   ⟩ silly wench
> Ah hark ⟨   ⟩   5
> To urge ⟨   ⟩
> Galls up her starved ⟨   ⟩
> A poor loose good for nothing he was found
> So even had I heard his hogs noise round
> ⟨   ⟩ sure enough it was to guess as how   10
> That honest work kept not the racket life
> But veigling as he did twould be his delight
> To wench & drink & swear from morn to night
> & he was fane lie housed where one would
> Hed one was sure to seem boasting about   15

O ENDLESS BRIGHT IN LIFE & LIGHT   *Title: wanting*   2 comforts
below [transports]
    THE ⟨   ⟩ HAS ⟨   ⟩   *Title: wanting*

AUTOGRAPHS: Pet. MS A2, ff. 2ʳ–3ʳ (erased pencil): Pet. MS A50, p. R75.
Dated: 1819–20 (MS A2).

A SEAT AT NOON

Cool in the brook did stand the plashing cows
In depths & shallows that did softly creep
Sweet oer the water swung the maple boughs
That scarcly gave the sunbeams leave to peep

Upon a mol hill of wild creeping thyme   5
That found for rest a comfortable seat
While at my back the meadow sweet did climb
I sat me down to rest ones aching feet

Full in my view an old stone brig appeard
Green Ivy twining round its arches gay   10
Upon its top wood Rails had long been reard
& moss triumphant crowning its decay

How sweet the scene appeard the glaring sun
That on the warming water brightly shone
As throw the Ivied bending arch they run   15
Reflecting[s] twiterd on each smooth old stone

I love to stand upon an old archd brig
The sculpterd stone or glassy wave to view
Where willow grains & stones both small & big
Makes waves to mutter as they eddies thro   20

A SEAT AT NOON   *Title:* A Seat at Noon *MS A2,* The old Brig *MS A50*   *No
stanza division in MS A50*   4 scarcely *MS A50*   peep] creep *MS A2*
5 molehill *MS A50*   6 found] formed *MS A50*   6/7 [I sat me down] *MS A2*
8 my *MS A50*   9 appeared *MS A50*   11 rails: reared *MS A50*
13 appeared *MS A50*   15 Turned every thing to gold it shone upon *MS A50*
16 & rubies spangled oer each smoothened stone *MS A50*   17 arched *MS A50*
18 sculptured *MS A50*   19 Where pebbles stones & willows dipping twigs
MS A50   20 Make vext waves mutter as they eddie through *MS A50*

AUTOGRAPH: Pet. MS A2 (erased pencil), f. 4ʳ⁻ᵛ (ll. 1–18), f. 10ʳ (ll. 19–26), f. 51ᵛ.
Dated: Late 1819 (Explanatory Notes).

THE PAUSE BEFORE THE BATTLE

The[n] from the mist top of the far watched hill
The breath of the night came as softly & still
As it did any night in the working mans head
As quietly [he] slept on his flock pillow bed
Tho nothing seemd more than at other times past   5
Yet soldiers were thitherward marching em fast
The spot it was doubtfull where foe might meet foe
The fight it was certain that it would be so
Their horse on the pasture was freed from the plow
& wandering as usual where bullock & cow   10
To be sure there was noises the Watching dogs growls
The neighing of horses & whooping of owls
& gossips & nurses might quake in their beds
As the shriek of the owl was omen of dread
& the sheep they did bleat & the asses did roar   15
But the sheep & the asses did so before
Still the camps they was forming upon the wild Heath
& the bayonet waited for blood shed & death
The horses hoofs patter & waggons did jar
Just as the thunder clap mutters afar   20
& louder & louder it fell on the ear
As times counted moments advancd em near
& long the lines stretchd on the ⟨moon glazed⟩ heath
& silent the pause as one stopping his breath
Each soldier had fears but he mentiond them not   25
& each had a thought that to die was his lot

THE PAUSE BEFORE THE BATTLE   *Title:* The Pause Before the / Battle
3 the *repeated*   *The following lines appear on f. 51ᵛ (upside down):*

All silent is turnd as fixt on some sad omen[s]
Of coming fate determind to destroy
Nor beautys charms on the fair face of woman
Coud at that pause instill a moments joy
Nor warn off their attentions or their fear   5
Thats always felt when fight approaches near

AUTOGRAPH: Pet. MS A2, f. 7ʳ (erased pencil).
Dated: 1819–20 (MS A2).

The daises silver white
The king cups yellow bright
& shearing grasses green
That bloom so pure beneath
As when moonlight   5
Pald like consumptions cheek
Shall in a different dress be seen

I ⟨   ⟩ viewd ⟨sweet⟩ streaks
⟨   ⟩ to sight
But I may never see their ⟨strange brown⟩ stain   10
⟨   ⟩ of grass
& some ⟨   ⟩ growing an ⟨   ⟩
& ⟨   ⟩ where they was
What my life ⟨blood⟩ may ⟨   ⟩

AUTOGRAPH: Pet. MS A2, f. 7ʳ (erased pencil).
Dated: 1819–20 (MS A2).

& ⟨   ⟩ winding ⟨ways⟩ break
⟨   ⟩ to sight
But I may never see their strange mountains
The shining blade of grass
& some have moister growing on ⟨   grain⟩ where they was   5
& what my life leard may ⟨   again⟩

THE DAISES SILVER WHITE   *Title: wanting*
& ⟨   ⟩ WINDING ⟨WAYS⟩ BREAK   *Title: wanting*

AUTOGRAPH: Pet. MS A2, f. 7ʳ⁻ᵛ (erased pencil).
Dated: 1819–20 (MS A2).

Thou moon crazd man
Thy pale face like to mine
Seems chilld wi fear musing on Mystery
I now for the last time shall see thee shine
Fair moon good bye & thou shall drop & I shall dye   5
& I shall be [no] more thoult rise again
Fair moon good bye

Awful it is to the Eye
Now that its closing is near
How shocking it is for to know   10
We must die
—No way of 'scaping th
Vengance thats near

I saw the sun this morning rise
I watchd him to his bed   15
But ere agen he glads the skys
Hell shine upon me dead

AUTOGRAPH: Pet. MS A2, f. 8ʳ (erased pencil).
Dated: 1819–20 (MS A2).

Sweet sleep & peace good night
Ive oft had cause to bless thy soothing reign
& if Im blessd to live till Mornings light
& welcome thee again
Ill well know how to value thee   5
& prove the sweets of pleasure after rain

THOU MOON CRAZD MAN   *Title: wanting*   8 its   11 we
13 vengance
SWEET SLEEP & PEACE GOOD NIGHT   *Title: wanting*

Freed from the dread of war be thou my country
Blanketed in sleep from the Earths cold damp
Dreaming of her I love—Alas its vain
I fear my last repose is with the slain   10
Sweet sleep & peace good night

AUTOGRAPH: Pet. MS A2, f. R10ʳ (erased pencil).
Dated: 1819–20 (MS A2).

SONG

Canst thou ⟨buy⟩ my love so lightly
That I love thee to decieve
Prize my love ah not so slightly
As not a single sigh believe
Hark the[e] maid Ill leave thee never   5
Hark thee if thee love Ive given
When done loving here for ever
Thee Ill ever love in Heaven

AUTOGRAPH: Pet. MS A2 (erased pencil), ff. R11ʳ⁻ᵛ (ll. 1–22), R17ᵛ
(ll. 23–32), R18ʳ (ll. 33–40), R41ʳ (ll. 41–54), R 74ʳ–75ᵛ (ll. 55–64, 69–102):
Pet. MS A50, p. R78 (ll. 41–54), pp. R77–R76 (ll. 55–102).
Dated: Late 1819 (Explanatory Notes).

THE AUTUMNAL MORNING

O much I love thee autumn sere
When fragrant in the mellow year
While dropping leaves & blossoms dead
Makes pillows for thy sunny bed

SONG   *Title:* Song
   THE AUTUMNAL MORNING   *Title:* The Autumnal / Morning *MS A2, wanting*
MS A50

While faint short wirlwinds puffing bye   5
Breaths thy latest symphony
& much I love thy checkerd gloom
& dear I love thy waning moon
Or breaths the blue mist & the ⟨   ⟩
Or ⟨   ⟩   10
Or ⟨   ⟩
Or ⟨   ⟩ thy wintry bed
With hurkling stride & watchful tread
Let my ⟨   ⟩ be watching found
Let me as wont begin my wait   15
Inofensive keeping state
Where halfway bowd & neath the ground
Like a buble bright & round
The sun streams up till bove the wood
It meets the blue sky red as blood   20
& by degrees increasing high
It sticks a Gold stud in the sky
& view thy ripness growing up
Just as the acron leaves its cup
Just as the nut bunch ripnd brown   25
Leaves its shell & tumbles down
& the leams on every squall
Leaves the tree in softnd fall
⟨   ⟩
⟨   ⟩ blow   30
Nor doubts its dead nor wish to sigh
But as the autumn droops to dye
Now the Village calm & still
Droves its tenants up the hill
Gently lifts as tho it where   35
⟨   ⟩ shed proaching near
Tho far different be the cause
That the hinds attention draws
While oer wheat fields turning brown
Laughing flings its ⟨   ⟩ down   40
Emigrating swallows now
Sweep no more the green hills brow

31   doubts *over* [doubting] *MS A2*

Nor in circuits round the spring
Skim & dip their sutty wing
& no more their chimny nigh   45
Twitter round to catch their flye
But with more majestic rise
Practising their exercise
& their young brood to pursue
Autums weary journy through   50
Meditating travels long
Wher the freshing year is young
Leaving us our cold sojourn
'Turning more till springs return
Wild woods ring in echos round   55
Wi many a lusty rural sound
Thro the day the wooping call
Of ramping nutters ceasless brawl
Weaving branches tearing down
Plucking nuts now ripe & brown   60
Boys as soon as loosd from school
Run to get their pockets full
& many a village clown ⟨in extacys⟩
Rustling mong the faded trees
That bend beside her path is seen   65
Like the woodlands rural queen
Snatching hastes handfuls while she hies
To milking where her red cow lies
Venturing oer the woodland stile
Shepherds leave their sheep awhile   70
Dreading squalls & turning back
They snached a nut or 2 to crack
While the pindard quirking out
As the lawyer squints about

45 chimney *MS A50*   46 their] the *MS A50*   48 Practicing: excersise
MS A50   49 broods *MS A50*   50 journney *MS A50*   52 Try boldest
flights without a song *MS A50*   53 Leaving us our] To leave our winters *MS A50*
54 'Turning] & come no *MS A50*   55 ecchoes *MS A50*   56 With *MS A50*
57 Through: whooping *MS A50*   61 loosed *MS A50*   63 village clown]
maid: in extacys *MS A50*   64 mid *MS A50*   64/5 [Pull the yielding
branches] *MS A50*   65–8 *Copy-text: MS A50*   69 —Venturing *MS A50*
71 Dreading squalls &] & in haste of *MS A50*   72 They snached] Snatch *through*
Get: two *MS A50*   73 quirking *through* quirks: [about] out *MS A50*

Siezes on the chances found   75
& drives the straying sheep to pound
The Hedger who wi many a tap
Drives the stake down in the gap
Leaves his gaps & leaves his toil
& claims a share of autumns spoil   80
In short as full as it can snive
The hamlets dead & woods alive
The once so still & silent shade
Is now a scene of uproar made
& from her bowers of ash & oak   85
Where scarce a song besides crows have spoke
Till now the rolling seasons through
Scard Solitude now bids adieu
& from the thicket dark & deep
The fluttering pheasant scared from sleep   90
While nearly trampld on her lair
Bobbing jerks the startld hare
& the squirrels agilty
Sputters up the timber tree
There in safty on the grain   95
Wipes his face & peeps again
& the rabbits viving fears
Listning perks his taper ears
Bobbing round wi tail so white
He hurries from the gazers sight   100
& all the peacful things that flye
From meddling mans Accusing eye

---

75 Seizes *MS A50*   77 hedger: with *MS A50*   82 The thronging woods
are all alive *MS A50*   83 The once so] & each once *MS A50*   86 Where few
but birds the silence broke *MS A50*   87 rolling] changing *MS A50*
88 Scarred solitude *MS A50*   90 pheasants *MS A50*   91 trampld on] trod
on in *MS A50*   92 startled hair *MS A50*   95 safety: a *MS A50*
97 viving] restless *MS A50*   98 Listening *MS A50*   99 with *MS A50*
100 from the gazers] in his hole from *MS A50*   101 peacful: flie *MS A50*
102 Accusing eye *omitted MS A50*

AUTOGRAPH: Pet. MS A2 (erased pencil), ff. 14ʳ–16ᵛ, 38ʳ.
Dated: 1819–20 (MS A2).

When gentle even oer the wild scene creeping
Lays labour down free from his care
& the moons silver pencil nights landscape is sweeping
On the tree heads & thro mountains tops peeping
As fair as sweet woman is fair   5

When the lone night bird his love song is breathing
& his sorrow melts sweet on the ear
& the blew mist round the horison wreathing
On the moist cheek & the still bough is ⟨sweep⟩ing
As sweetly as kind warming tear   10

While the wild night wind his love tidings hushes
As a watch nurse oer her childs ⟨closing eye⟩
Whispering soft thro the trees & the bushes
While the brooke oer its ⟨mountain⟩ bed murmuring gushes
As soft as a sweet womans sigh   15

O blest at that hour when the ⟨doves tribes⟩ are snoozing
⟨As morn⟩ with sweet ⟨blushes o⟩ care
When the Nights fears in the moon light is loosing
& gilds sweet the snow of her soft heaving bosom
Sure never seems woman so fair   20

WHEN GENTLE EVEN OER THE WILD SCENE CREEPING   *Title: wanting*

1–5

       When oer the tall Firdales gentle Even is creeping
       While labour is sleeping from care
       [When the blue mist round the horisons sweeping]
       & the [full] moons silver pencil nights landscape is sweeping
       & in the tree top & the distant hills peeping   5
       As fair as sweet woman is fair   *MS A2, f. 38ʳ variant*

(l. 4 nights landscape *inserted*)

6–10

       The nights lonley bird his love laments breathing
       & his sorrow melts so sweet on the ear
       & the blue mist round the horison wreathing
       On the moist cheek & the still bough is ⟨sweep⟩ing
       As ⟨sweetly as kind⟩ warming ⟨tear⟩   5
                         MS A2, f. 38ʳ variant

But sad at that hour is fond lovers meeting
& fate frowning fate ⟨hovers⟩ near
Forcd from each other fond vows soft repeating
To part & perchance never more to be meeting
How dearer then life is sweet womans tear   25

When gentle eve in nights lap is desarting
& sinking moon dims in the eye
When modesty wispers its leave to be parting
When love seals a vow on their lips at departing
How sweet is the good womans sigh   30

AUTOGRAPH: Pet. MS A2, f. R18ʳ (erased pencil).
Dated: 1819–20 (MS A2).

⟨   ⟩
& if friendship ⟨   ⟩ you would win it
& should black guard fate leave us with ⟨   ⟩
I am yours to ⟨   ⟩ in it

AUTOGRAPH: Pet. MS A2, ff. R21ʳ–R22ʳ (erased pencil).
Dated: 1819–20 (MS A2).

SPORTS OF THE FIELD

Now the day break is the east sky adorning
Painting the clouds gleaming track
Forehand of sunrise hail sportsman the morning
& Break Echos sleep with thy pack

21 sad *over* [sweet]   22 *Appears to be deleted, but it is needed to make up the 5-line stanza*

Title: wanting

SPORTS OF THE FIELD   *Title:* Sports of the Field

Let beds not invite thee like veigling harlot   5
To sportsmen they no pleasures yield
Then mount on your saddle in doublet of scarlet
& bring in the hounds to the field

Some love to pause over chess & bag gammon
To sportsmen such pausings disgrace   10
Some deem persuasions of silver tongd woman
Bove break neck exploits of the chase
But careles of games playd ⟨& won⟩ upon ⟨table⟩
& softest charms love ever yields
The early horsd sportmans excursions will ⟨disable⟩   15
So away to the sports of the field

Then riders & horses with the horns hollo blowing
To Sports & to ⟨   ⟩ rise
& away helter skelter the high flyers going
⟨Amazd⟩ with the hark away noise   20
Now the white mist from the brook side is reeking
& breezes morns medicine yields
Sweet health & true pleasure the sportsman is seeking
So away to the sports of the field

AUTOGRAPH: Pet. MS A2, ff. R22ᵛ–R23ʳ (erased pencil).
Dated: 1819–20 (MS A2).

THE BIRTH OF CHARITY

A Beggar turnd up to [a] noblemans dwelling
Ere charity shone on our shore
The dogs kept on purpose gan barking & yelling
& drove him away from the door
His forhead was tore & his face deeply furrowd   5
& the Grave his last hope coming fast
& flying their fury Most deeply he sorrowd
When a maiden lookt out as he passt

THE BIRTH OF CHARITY   *Title:* The Birth of Charity   3 [&] kept

She heard his sad story of harms & of pining
& soon as his woes met her eye   10
In the half started tear Pitys Image was skining
& mercys loud mourn in the sigh

With the look of an angel Mixt beauty & feeling
She heerd the poor beggar forlorn
& when in her pocket her hand it was stealing   15
That moment was charity born

AUTOGRAPH: Pet. MS A2, f. R23ʳ (erased pencil).
Dated: 1819–20 (MS A2).

THE BIRTH OF EVE

How oft Ive noticed when the west sky blazed
At the sweet opening of the evenings birth
& often thought they gamb[o]ld as they glazed
The dying sunbeam on the cotters hearth
Red coal like clouds about the suns bed lying   5
First brightning up in many a burning track
⟨The   ⟩ & then like ⟨   ⟩ loosing cloud

AUTOGRAPH: Pet. MS A2, f. R23ᵛ (erased pencil).
Dated: 1819–20 (MS A2).

O CRUEL WAR

O cruel wars o bloody bloody wars
How long will you rage & burn
When begging on the road & oerladen with his cares
Ye set my Harry free to return

11 Pitys *over* [mercys]
   THE BIRTH OF EVE   *Title:* The Birth of Eve
   O CRUEL WAR   *Title:* O cruel war   2 bourne

O war in peaces mantle fold your bloody hand 5
& no longer urge me to mourn
Bring him safe back from your fighting frenzied hand
Tho nothing awaits his return

O cruel wars o bloody bloody wars
He vowd but 2 years I should mourn 10
But 3 times the cowslap summers bed prepares
& still hes for bid to return

AUTOGRAPH: Pet. MS A2, ff. R24ᵛ–R29ᵛ (erased pencil).
Dated: 1819–20 (MS A2).

OLD JOHNNY & DOROTHY CANNING

Many years in a cottage of mud
By the side of the wansford road stanning
Propt up wi a post of oak wood
Livd old John & his Dorothy Canning
Deed they livd an odd sort of life 5
& many odd ways they kept ⟨planning⟩
& deed an odd sort of a wife
Was old Johnnys Dorothy Canning

One shoulder stoopt under the other
Nose & chin threatnd battle above 10
This eye squinted this way & tother lookt tother
But John didnt marry for love
He recknd all beauty a whim
& the weak chap it trapt a poor ninney
That beauty shown charms unto him 15
& not Georges bright face on a Guinea

7 bring

OLD JOHNNY & DOROTHY CANNING *Title:* Old Johnny & Dorothy /
Canning   13–16 *f. R24ᶜ contains the following variant:*

> & old John called Beauty a whim
> '& the poor swain that lovd a mere ninney
> 'No beauty shewd charms unto him
> 'But Georges bright face in a Guinea

16 Ginuea   *Followed by a row of asterisks*

She was alus a stingy old toper
& ⟨   from⟩ a half pound of money
& these where the things John did like
& this & nought else tempted Johnny   20
When he used to go courting at night
There was neer a loving glass to keep merry
Twas her purse she pulled out to his sight
& such was the payments to Johnny

The very first hour that they met   25
They usd no fond words dear or darling
But just like a dog or a cat
Kept constantly yowling & snarling
Yet still the[y] savd money apace
& hurded up guineas by ⟨dozens⟩   30
& as often when this is the case
Their death prayd for by [neighbours &] cousins

One day a long journey John[s] taen
& twas very well known that when Johnny
Whent off in a prospect of gain   35
He woudnt loose bargains for money
So nickey a good for nought chap
Black designs on his life fell a planning
He went home & fetchd ⟨him a trap⟩
& layd schemes for Johnnys trepanning   40

His will he had made it before
& friends to his death began hurr[y]ing
They sorrowd as did many more
But all where mock tears at Johns burr[y]ing
Soon as they read Will oer at night   45
& to some not a /6ᵈ were stanning
Tho they sorrow before they said the[y] now sorrowd right
& D—d for a mizer Johnny Canning

So tho Johnny calld love a wim
& the poor fool it trapt a mere ninney   50
Fate as plainly brings out that in him
Love had to[o] strong a whim for a Guinea

Beautys a painted foot ball
Wirld up in the air for trepanning
& in one shape or other she weigles us all   55
& in this way she killd Johnny Canning

So a nother odd verse by the bye
In confirming the truth of the latter
This ninney too often can try
& when wealth woudnt make up the matter   60
Upon his poor uncle he fell
(The Devil he said was a planning)
Love of beauty brought him harrying o hell
Love of gold brought the end of John Canning

The sexton his moral was a giving   65
As he lapt up Johns bones wi his shovel
Saying Johnny I telld ⟨thee⟩ when living
We one day should come to one level
I never had gold upon me
⟨Or aught⟩ & friends may end ⟨by trepanning⟩   70
& now Johnnys dead do ye see
Im as rich as old rich Johnny Canning

AUTOGRAPH: Pet. MS A2, f. 35^{r-v} (erased pencil).
Dated: 1819–20 (MS A2).

OPENING OF THE MORNING
A Sketch

Tis the time just as morning is breaking
& the Colour arching blue skye
Just as the black clouds of the night are forsaking
Brightning up like as Marys blue eye

56/7

Tho Johnny neer hurded his Guineas
No one would have long for his penney
He then like to other loves ninneys
Might live to his means long as many
But beautys a painted &c &c &c   5

(ll. 49–53 variant)

OPENING OF THE MORNING   *Title:* Opening of the Morning / A Sketch

Where the red morns streaks was sweetly emerging   5
In the easts enlarging light
Just like the red corral beads of the Virgin
When hung on her neck so white

When the fresh springs of delight is beaming
& larks waken the labourers toils   10
When the first smile of the summer is gleaming
As sweet as when Mary smiles

Sweet when the dappeled sky is shrouded
In its milky water hue
Like as Mary her bosom's Clouded   15
Skin so white & veins so blue

AUTOGRAPH: Pet. MS A2, f. R41^{r-v} (erased pencil).
Dated: 1819–20 (MS A2).

JENNY BELL

In an old town of low livd fun
By wellands banks of meadow sward
Where groves of willows flourish well
To wants wild stream tho ill compard
For wellands waters muddy run   5
    There blossoms Jenny Bell

In that same town wher strangers come
& find their hearts too often gone
Where painted beauties dwell
But these are ill compard to some   10
Tho these are angels stild by some
    They are no Jenny Bells

JENNY BELL   *Title:* Jenny B–ll   6 B–ll   10 But *through ?* Ah
12 B–lls

In that same town I pass her bye
A finer girl I never passd
Her charms efeth I cannot tell   15
But shed such looks & such an eye
If maids wi angels may be classd
    Im sure its Jenny Bell

AUTOGRAPH: Pet. MS A3, p. 62.
TRANSCRIPTS: Pet. MS B1, pp. 114–15: Nor. MS 5, p. 117.
Printed in *RL*, p. 190.
Dated: '1818' (MS A3, p. 62).

THE MOON

How sweet the moon extends her cheering ray
To damp the terors of the darksome night
Guiding the lonley Trav'ller on his way
Pointing the path that leads his Journey right
Hail welcome blessing to thy silver light   5
That charms dull night & makes its horrors gay

So shines the Gospel to the christians soul
So by its light & Inspiration given
He (spite of sin & Satans black controul
Through all obstructions steers his course for heaven)   10
So did the Saviour his design pursue
That we unworthy sinners might be blest
So suffer'd death its terrors to subdue
& make the grave a wish'd for place of rest

18 B–ll   *Followed by:* Or / Tho not in list of angels classd / An angels charm had
Jenny B–ll

THE MOON   *Title:* The Moon *MS A3 RL*   9 controul *underlined MS A3*
10 for] to *RL*   14 made *RL*

AUTOGRAPHS: Pet. MS A3, p. 62: Pet. MS A4o, p. 36a.
TRANSCRIPT: Pet. MS B1, p. 114 (deleted).
Dated: '1818' (MS A3, p. 62).

TO OBSCURITY

Written in a Fit of Despondency

Hail dreaded fate of dark obscurity
Which lingering hopes so long delay'd to find
Now dissapointment reads my destiny
—Ah since Encouragement her aid declin'd
To thee for shelter from the world he flies   5
& oh that horrid blotch (fond Memory weeps)
Beneath whose buried shade of deep disguise
The sons of Merit unrewarded sleeps—
While Learning mourns & Ign'rance delights
To see worth perish in Eternal night   10
Thou last, last hope of Genius distrest
Redress the Wrongs which Envy joys to see
O bid my weak aspiring spirit rest
& bury all its hopes & pains in thee

TO OBSCURITY   *Title:* To Obscurity / Written in a fit of despondency *MS A3*, To
Obscurity *MS A4o*   1 dreaded fate *underlined MS A3*   2 delayed *MS A4o*
4 ∧Ah: encouragment: declined *MS A4o*   6 ah: horrid] vacant: memory
MS A4o   horrid blotch *underlined MS A3*   7 burying *MS A4o*   8 Full
many a hopeful bard unconsious sleeps *MS A4o*   9 learning *MS A4o*   Ignorance *to*
Ign'rance *(p.e.) MS A3*] ignorance *MS A4o*   10 eternal *MS A4o*   11 last∧:
genius *MS A4o*   12 wrongs *MS A4o*   Envy *underlined MS A3*] envy *MS A4o*

AUTOGRAPH: Pet. MS A3, p. 63.
TRANSCRIPTS: Pet. MS B1, p. 115: Nor. MS 5, p. 127.
Printed in *RL*, p. 189: *Gentleman's Magazine*, March 1820, p. 259 (reprinted from *RL*).
Dated: 'new 1818' (MS A3, p. 63).

CHRISTIAN FAITH

What Antidote or charm on Earth is found
To aliviate or soften fates decree?
To fearless enter on that dark profound
Where Life emerges in Eternity

Wisdom!—a rush light—vainly boasting power   5
To cheer the terror sin's first visit gave
Denies Existance at that dreadful hour
& shrinks in horror from a gaping grave

O Christianity thou charm devine
That firmness faith & last resource is thine   10
With thee the christian joys to loose his breath
Nor dreads to find his mortal strength decay
But dear in Friendship shakes the hand of death
& hugs the pain that knaws his life away

CHRISTIAN FAITH   *Title:* Christian Faith *MS A3 RL*   6 [gloom] terror *MS A3*] terrors *RL*   visit *underlined MS A3*   8 shrinks *through* thrusts: gaping *underlined MS A3*   11 lose *RL*   12 Nor *through* &: dreads *below* [pleasd]: find *through* feel *MS A3*   14 gnaws *RL*

AUTOGRAPH: Pet. MS A3, pp. 65–8 (ll. 69–76 deleted): Pet. MS A3, p. 90 (title and ll. 1–12 only, deleted): Pet. MS A5, p. 50 (ll. 37–40, 55–64 only). TRANSCRIPTS: Pet. MS B1, pp. 119–21: Nor. MS 5, pp. 52–7. Printed in *RL*, pp. 30–4 (ll. 77–96 omitted). Dated: 'Old' (MS A3, p. 65).

EVENING

Now grey ey'd hazy eve's begun
   To shed her balmy dew—
Insects no longer fear the sun
   But come in open view

Now buzzing with unwelcome din   5
   The heedles beetle bangs
Agen the cowboys dinner tin
   That oer his shoulder hangs

& on he keeps in heedless pat
   Till quite enrag'd the boy   10
Pulls off his weather-beaten hat
   Resolving to destroy

Yet thoughtless that he wrongs the Clown
   By blows he'll not be driven
But buzzes on till batter'd down   15
   For unmeant Injury given

Now from each hedgerow fearless peeps
   The slowly pacing snails
Betraying their meandering creeps
   In silver slimy trails   20

    EVENING   *Title:* Evening *MS A3 MS A3, p. 90 RL*   1 hazey Eve's *MS A3, p. 90*   begun *through* begins *MS A3*   2 balmey due ∧ *MS A3, p. 90* 3 Inscets *MS A3, p. 90*   7 Against: Cow-boys *MS A3, p. 90*   dinner tin *underlined MS A3*   9 And: keep: heedles *MS A3, p. 90*   11 of *MS A3, p. 90*   weather-beaten *underlined MS A3*   13 [Still] Yet *MS A3*   wrong'd *RL*] wrongs *RL 2nd edn.*   17 peep *RL*   19 creep *RL*

The dew worms too in couples start
 But leave their holes in fear
For in a moment they will part
 If aught approaches near

The owls mope out & scouting bats   25
 Begin their giddy rounds
While countless swarms of dancing gnats
 Each water pudge surrounds

& 'side yon pool as smooth as glass
 Reflecting every cloud   30
Securely hid among the grass
 The Crickets chirup loud—

That rural call—'Cum-mulls cum-mulls'
 From distant pasture grounds
All noises now to silence lulls   35
 In soft & ushering sounds

While Echo's weak from hill to hill
 Their dying sounds deplore
That wimper faint & fainter still
 Till they are heard no more   40

The breezes once so cool & brief
 At eves aproach all dy'd
None's left to make the aspin leaf
 Twirl up its hoary side

But breezes all are usless now   45
 The hazy dun that spreds
Her moist'ning dew on every bough
 Sufficient coolness sheds

25 sco *through* whis *in* scouting *MS A3*   26 round *RL*   27 While *through* &
MS A3   28 surround *RL*   32 Cricket *altered to* Crickets: chirup[s] *MS A3*
33 'Cum-mulls cum-mulls ∧ *underlined MS A3*   35 noises *through ?* others be I
MS A3   37 Echos *MS A5* w *through* fr *in* weak *MS A3*   39 whimper:
and *MS A5*   40 Till] While *MS A5*

The flowers reviving—from the ground
   Perk up again & peep   50
While many different tribes around
   Are shutting up to sleep

O lovliest time O sweetest hours
   The musing soul can find
Now meditations thinking powers   55
   At freedom fills the mind

Now let me hid in culterd plain
   Pursue my evening walk
Where each way beats the nodding grain
   Aside the narrow bau'k   60

While fairy visions intervene
   Creating dread suprise
From distant objects dimly seen
   That catch the doubtful eyes

& Fairy's now (no doubt) unseen   65
   In silent revel sups
With dew drop bumpers toast their queen
   From crowflowers golden cups

---

49 [? The] The *MS A3*   53–6 *Last stanza in RL*   53 [O lovlies] *over* O
lovliest *MS A3*   55 Now, Evening let thy soothing powers *RL*   meditation's
MS A5   57 cultur'd *MS A5*   60 bau'k *through* baulk *MS A3*] baulk *MS A5*
RL, balk *RL 2nd edn.*   62 a *in* dread *inserted*: suprise *MS A5*   63 dimley
MS A5
64/5

      [& peradventure while I roam

      & faireys now (no doubt) unseen
         In silent revel sups
      With dewdrops toasts their tiny Queen
         From cow flowers bumping cups]   5 *MS A3*

(l. 1 & *through* The; l.4 dewdrops *underlined*; l. 5 bumping *underlined*)

66 revels sup *RL*   67 dew drop bumpers *underlined MS A3*   68 cup *RL*

Altho about these tiny things
  Folks make so much ado   70
I never heed the darksome rings
  Where they are said to go

But Superstition still decieves
  & Fancys still prevails
While stooping Genius een believes   75
  Her Customary Tales

The plough man moiling all the day
  To addle needy pelf
Now homward plods & on his way
  Thus argues to himself   80

'Now I am left the fallow Clods
  'I'm happy & I'm free
'Then can I think there's ony odds
  'Between a king & me?'

'Why if there is the best I'se sure   85
  '(That I confess wi' pride)
'Tho kings ar' rich as I am poor
  'T'will fall to nathans side'

69–76 *Against these lines Clare has written in pencil:* the Author erases these verses *MS A3*
73–6 *Clare to Drury April 1819:* 'Please to take Notice that the following Verse in 'Evening' is a Plagarising

            'Nor do I earnestly believe
            'Such things could ever be
            'But superstition does decieve
            'Far wiser folks than me'

Alter it thus

            But Superstition still decieves
            & Fancys still prevails
            While stooping Genius een believes
            Her Customary Tales   *(Letters, p. 8)*

(*No quotation marks*; l. 1 do] can; l. 4 then me— *MS A3 cancelled verse*)

74 Fancys] fairies: prevail *RL*   76 Her] The: tale *RL*   85 [Why if there is the b] *over* Why . . . best *MS A3*

Thus Nat conceits as on he goes
   To seek his natal cot   90
Such fancies gives his soul repose
   & smooths his rugged lot

So welcome Evening since thy hours
   Brings happiness to all
& may nought cause thy soothing powers   95
   Contrary ways to fall

AUTOGRAPH: Pet. MS A3, pp. 69–70: Yale University Library Osborn
Collection 206/6 (four-line fragment).
TRANSCRIPTS: Pet. MS B1, pp. 121–2: Nor. MS 5, pp. 128–9.
Printed in *RL*, pp. 35–7: *The Englishman's Fire-side*, September 1820,
pp. 313–14 (*EF*).
Dated: 1818 (MS A3, p. 69 '1818', *RL* Introduction, p. xxii 'In the last two
years').

WHAT IS LIFE?

(a)

& what is Life?—an hour glass on the run
A mist retreating from the morning sun
A busy bustling still repeated dream
—Its Length?—A minutes pause—a moments thought
& happines?—A Bubble on the stream   5
That in the act of seizing shrinks to nought—

Vain hopes what are they?—Puffing gales of morn
That of its charms divests the dewy lawn
& robs each flowret of its gem—& dies
A Cobweb hiding dissapointments thorn   10
Which stings more keener thro the thin disguise

WHAT IS LIFE? *Title:* What is Life? *MS A3 RL EF*   7 morn[s]
MS A3   What are vain Hopes?—The puffing gale of morn *RL*   What is vain Hope?
. . . *RL 2nd edn. EF*   7/8 [That shakes the dew drops off the Lawn] *MS A3*
8 *Omitted RL 4th edn.*   9 *First* &] That *RL 4th edn.*   r *through* b *in* robs *MS A3*
11 keenly *RL EF*

—& thou o Trouble—nothing can suppose
(& sure the power of wisdom only knows)
   —What need requireth thee
So free & liberal as thy bounty flows 15
Some nessesary cause must surely be
—But dissapointments pains & every woe
   Adopted wretches feeld
The universal plagues of life below
Fate hides them all—& keeps their cause consceald 20

& what is death?—Is still the cause unfound
That dark mysterious name of horrid sound
—A long & lingering Sleep the weary crave—
& peace!—Where can its happines abound
No where at all But heaven & the—Grave 25
Then what is Life?—When stript of its disguise
A thing to be desir'd it cannot be
Since every thing that meets our foolish eye
Gives proof sufficient of its vanity—
Tis but a trial all must undergo 30
To learn unthankful mortals how to prize
That happiness vain mans deny'd to know
Untill he's call'd to claim it in the skyes

13 widom *EF*   17–20 *Against these lines in MS A3 Edward Drury has written:* unintelligible   18 Adopted] Devoted: feel *RL EF*   20 keeps *through* ? shuts *MS A3*   Are mysteries still 'neath Fate's unbroken seal *RL EF*   24 its *over* [thy]: abound *through* be found *MS A3*   25 But] save *RL EF*   28 eyes *RL EF*   31 learn] teach *RL EF*   *The following ll. at Yale may be connected with this poem:*

      & thou vain man in wisdoms eye may seem
      A thoughtles flye allowd lifes little day
      That heedless dances on this worlds wide streem
      To pride as pain & countless ills a prey—

(*Printed in A. J. V. Chapple, 'Some Unpublished Poetical Manuscripts of John Clare', Yale University Library Gazette, (1956), p. 35*)

AUTOGRAPHS: None known.
Printed in the *Stamford Mercury*, 26 June 1818.
Dated: Early 1818 (*SM*).

LIFE'S LIKENESSES

(b)

(Written in imitation of the Poetry of the 17th Century.)

LIFE is—what?
It is the shooting of a star,
That gleams along the trackless air,
And vanishes, almost ere seen, to nought.
And such is Man—   5
He shines and flutters for a span,
    And is forgot.

Life is—what?
It is the vermeil of the rose,
That blooms but till the bleak wind blows,   10
Then, all entomb'd in sweets, doth fade and rot.
And such is Man—
He struts in brav'ry for a span,
    And is forgot.

Life is—what?   15
It is a dew-drop of the morn,
That quiv'ring hangs upon the thorn,
Till quaff'd by sunbeams, 'tis no longer aught.
And such is Man—
He's steep'd in sorrow for a span,   20
    And melts—forgot.

Life is—what?
A stone, whose fall doth circles make
On the smooth surface of the lake,
Which spread till one and all forsake the spot.   25
And such is Man—
'Midst friends he revels for a span,
    And sinks—forgot.

LIFE'S LIKENESSES   *Title:* Life's Likenesses

Life is—what?
It is a bubble on the main,   30
Rais'd by a *little globe* of rain,
Whose heir destroys the fabric it hath wrought.
And such is Man—
Swell'd into being for a span,
And broke—forgot.   35

Life is—what?
A shadow on the mountain's side,
Of rack, that doth on aether ride,
Driv'n by the Northern gale, with tempests fraught.
And such is Man—   40
He hangs on greatness for a span,
And is forgot.

Life is—what?
It is the sound of cannon near,
Which strikes upon the startled ear,   45
And ceases ere we can distinguish aught.
And such is Man—
He frights and blusters for a span,
And is forgot.

Life is—what?   50
It is the swallow's sojournment,
Who, ere green Summer's robe is rent,
Flies to some distant bourne, by instinct taught.
And such is Man—
He rents his dwelling for a span,   55
And flits—forgot.

And is this—Life?
Oh yes! and had I time to tell,
A hundred shapes more transient still—
But, whilst I speak, Fate whets its slaughterous knife,   60
And such is Man—
While reck'ning o'er Life's little span,
Death ends the strife.

AUTOGRAPH: Pet. MS A3, p. 73.
TRANSCRIPTS: Pet. MS B1, pp. 124–5: Nor. MS 5, p. 120.
Printed in *RL*, p. 41.
Dated: 1807–10 (MS A3, p. 73 'Old 8 or 10', *RL* Introduction, p. xxii 'before
he was seventeen').

A REFLECTION IN AUTUMN

Now Autumn's come—adieu the pleasing greens
The charming Lanscape & the flowrey plain
All are deserted from these motley scenes
With blighted yellow ting'd & russet stain

Tho desolation seems to triumph here   5
Yet these are spring to what we still shall find
The trees must all in nakedness appear
'Reft of their foliage by the blustry wind

Just so 'twill fare with me in Autumns life
Just so I'd wish—but may the trunk & all   10
Die with the leaves—nor taste that wintry strife
Where Sorrows urge—& fear Impedes the fall!

A REFLECTION IN AUTUMN   *Title:* A Reflection / in Autumn *MS A3*, A
Reflection in Autumn *RL*   2 Lanscape *to* landscape *(p.e.) MS A3*   plain[s] *MS
A3*] plains *RL 4th edn.*   3 are] have *RL*   4 [Blighted with] With
MS A3   stains *RL 4th edn.*   5 Tho *to* Though *(p.e.) MS A3*   6 this
is *RL*   we *through* wh *MS A3*   12 Where] When *RL*   Sorrows *to* sorrows
(p.e.) : — *deleted (p.e.)* : Impedes *to* impedes *(p.e.) MS A3*

AUTOGRAPHS: Pet. MS A3, pp. 85–6: Norris Museum SAVNM CL/6
(ll. 29–40 omitted): Pet. MS A40, pp. 31a–32 (deleted).
TRANSCRIPTS: Pet. MS B1, pp. 139–40 (deleted): Nor. MS 5, pp. 69–72
(deleted).
Dated: April 1819 (Explanatory Notes, MS A3, p. 81 'fresh composed'
preceded by 'New' deleted).

THE SUPRISE

A maiden shuns the sultry day
   Oer powred with the heat
An hazel spreads its arching boughs
   & forms the wish'd retreat
The grass yields to her lovly charms   5
   Each dasie in suprise
Bends down delighted with the weight
   & sinks in Extasies

The breezes tremble round the maid
   (Their passion is confest)   10
& flaps the hankerchief in vain
   That shields her snowy breast

THE SUPRISE   *Title:* The Suprise *MS A3*, The Surprise *Norris*, The Surprise a
Ballad (Supprize *altered to* Surprise) *MS A40*   *Stanzas numbered 1–7 in Norris*
1 *Preceded in MS A3 by:*

          The Suprise
     [A maiden shuns the sultry day
        O'er powred with the heat
     An hazel spreads its arching boughs
        & forms the wishd retreat
     Each dasie in suprise   5
        Bends down delighted with the weight]

(l. 6 Bends *through* Bows)

2 O'erpowered *Norris*] Oerpowered *MS A40*   4 wished *MS A40*
6 daisey *Norris MS A40*   in *over* [with] *Norris*   supprise *Norris*] surprise *MS A40*
7 Bends *through* Bows *Norris*   8 extasies *Norris*] extacys *MS A40*
10 confessed *MS A40*   11 flaps] fans: in vain] aside *Norris*   the] her *MS A40*
12 shields] hides *Norris*   snowey *MS A40*

& fondling fans the wanton curls
　　& kisses sweet her lips
While amourous flies in rude delight   15
　　Their hony'd moisture sips

As chanc'd Hodge wistles by the spot
　　& gives by chance a peep
Her beauties meets his Vulgar eyes
　　Their fears are lost in sleep   20
Just so I've seen the marble stand
　　In figur'd man disguis'd
A statue there he gapes! & stares!
　　Astonish'd! & supris'd!

Her light robes past their modest bounds   25
　　For where the breezes faild
To gain their ravishing designs
　　The ruder winds prevail'd
Her bosom bare that throb'd & heav'd
　　With charms to cure or kill   30
Her leg—& swelling calf!—he sees
　　& charms more tempting still

O Love what art thou? whence thy power?
　　That feels for every heart
The fondling wish, the trembling sigh   35
　　The agravating smart—
He gazes, wishes, longs, & sighs
　　But cannot speak for shame
He warms & chills by turns & feels
　　A pain without a name   40

13 & playful shakes each wanton curl *Norris*   14 & kiss her ruby lips *Norris*
15 in] with *Norris*   16 honied *MS A40*   hony'd moisture] fragrant nectar
Norris   17 As chanc'd] By chance: hodge *altered to* Hodge *Norris*   chanced:
whistles *MS A40*   19 beautys meet *MS A40*   vulgar *Norris MS A40*
21 *Clare's correction MS A3, p. 132:* Instead of— 'Just so the marbles seen to stand'
Write thus—Just so I've seen the marble stand   *All texts have the uncorrected*
version   marble's *Norris*   22 figured: disguised *MS A40*   23 gapes∧:
stares∧ *Norris MS A40*   24 Astonishd! *Norris*] Astonished∧ *MS A40*   suprisd!
Norris] surprised∧ *MS A40*   25 bounds—*Norris*   26 For] Lo *Norris*   were
MS A40   fail'd *Norris*] failed *MS A40*   27 designs] desires *Norris*
28 prevaild *MS A40*   29 throbd: heaved *MS A40*   31 leg∧: calf∧∧
MS A40   33 love: thou∧: power∧ *MS A40*   34/5 [The trembling wish the
fondling sigh] *MS A3*   35 wish∧ *MS A40*   36 smart∧ *MS A40*
37 gazes∧ wishes∧ longs∧ *MS A40*   40 *Underlined MS A3*

As ventering nearer to the spot
   To feast his greedy eyes
His hobbling step disturbs her sleep
   She hears him in suprise
Instant her eyes their darts unsheath   45
   The vanquish'd hopes—& lives—
Love pops excuses in his mouth
   She hears them & forgives

'Gie me but leave' the rustic cries
   'My boldness ere you chide   50
'To tell you summats fix'd me here!'
   —Then paus'd a bit & sigh'd
'& might a kiss but ease mine pain'—
   The maiden heard & blush'd
Here he took courage—seiz'd the chance   55
   & found her as he wish'd

---

41 venturing *Norris MS A40*   43 her sleep] the maid *MS A40*   44 surprise *MS A40*   45 Her eyes unsheath their killing darts *(n through* e *in* unsheath*) Norris*   46 vanquished hopes∧: lives∧ *MS A40*   (Each lover hopes & lives) *Norris*   49 'Give *MS A40*   'Gie me but] 'O give me *Norris*   50 ('My: chide) *MS A40*   51 summats *underlined MS A3*] somthings *MS A40*   summats fix'd] —love directs *(directs through* ?here*) Norris*   fixed *MS A40*   here∧' *Norris*] here∧∧ *MS A40*   52 ∧'Then paused: a bit] awhile: sighed *MS A40*   (Here paus'd the Clown & sigh'd) *Norris*   53 '&] —O: but … pain'—] my pain relieve'— *Norris*   my pain'∧ *MS A40*   54 blush[t]d *Norris*] blushed *MS A40*   55 he *inserted*: courage∧siezed *MS A40*   The clown grew bold to sieze the chance *(clown inserted) Norris*   56 wisht *Norris*] wished *MS A40*

AUTOGRAPHS: Pet. MS A3, p. 91: British Library, Eg. MS 2245, f. 8ᵛ
(ll. 1–8, 24, 32, 40 omitted, pencil). On the back of a letter from J. B. Henson
to Clare, Deeping, 24 November 1818, saying he will come over to Stamford
on Tuesday, 1 December bringing the Prospectus 'for your "Collection of
Trifles"': Nor. MS 1, p. 199 (ll. 1–8, 16, 32–40 omitted, pencil): Nor. MS 17,
p. 23 (four-line fragment, deleted in pencil): Pet. MS B3, p. 6 (four-line
fragment, deleted).
TRANSCRIPT: Pet. MS B1, pp. 145–6.
Printed in *RL*, pp. 170–2.
Dated: 'new / 1818' (MS A3, p. 91).

TO DAY THE FOX MUST DYE

A Hunting Song

The cock awakes the rosey morn
& tells approaching day
While Reynold sneaks along the lawn
Belated with his prey
—O never think to find thy home   5
But for thy saftey fly
The Sportman's long proclaim'd thy doom—
'To day a Fox shall dye'

The bugle blows the sporting train
Swift mount the snorting steed   10
Each fence defiance bids in vain
Their pr[o]gress to impede—
The cover broke they drive along
& Raise a jovial cry
Each dog barks chorus to my song   15
To day a fox shall dye

TO DAY THE FOX MUST DYE   *Title:* A Hunting Song   *In margin:* **Print it with**
this title 'To Day the Fox must dye' / A Hunting Song (must *over* [shall]) *MS A3,*
wanting BL MS 1, To-day the Fox must Die. / A Hunting Song *RL*   1 cocks
inserted MS A3] cock *RL*   morn] dawn *RL*   3 Reynard *RL*   5 'O *MS A3*
9 bugle blows] horn no calls *BL*, horn awakes *MS 1*   sporting *over* [hunting] *BL*]
hunting *MS 1*   10 Swift] To *BL MS 1*   11 Vain *BL*   12 There
BL   progress: Impede ∧ *BL MS 1*   14 raise *MS 1*   Each hound with jovial
crye *BL*   15 each *MS 1*   Barks Corus to my sporting Song *BL*   16 This
day the fox must Die *BL*

Like lightning oer the hills they sweep
All readiest roads they go
The Five 'bar'd gate with ease they leap!
Hark forward tally ho   20
The mist hangs on & scents him strong
The moisture makes it lye
The Woods re echo to my song
'This day the Fox must dye'

Old Reynolds finding shifts in vain   25
While hounds & horns pursue
Now leaves the woods to try the plain
—The bugle sounds a View
Old Thread brake Gaily leads the throng
His bold unering cry   30
Confirms the burthen to my song
This day the fox shall dye

His Funereal knell the bugle blows
His end approaches near
He reals & staggers as he goes   35
& drops his brush wi' fear
More eager now they press along
& louder still the cry—
All join in Chorus to my song
To day the fox must dye   40

---

17 like *MS 1*   18 All *through* The *MS A3*] The *BL*, all *MS 1*   readiest]
nearest: they] the *MS 1*   19 five *MS 1*   bard *BL*] bards *MS 1*   leap∧ *BL MS 1*
20 Hark] highe *BL*, hie *MS 1*   Tally *BL*   21 & scents him] the Scent is *BL*, the
scent is *MS 1*   Strong *BL*   22 moisture *inserted MS A3*] moisteur *BL*
23

    The woods een echo to the noise
    As if they loved the race
    & all but Reynards self enjoys
    The tumults of the chase   *MS B3 MS 17*

(l. 1 een] they: eccho *MS 17*)

The woods bear chorus to my song *BL MS 1*   24 ∧This: a fox: dye∧ *MS 1*
25 reynolds *MS 1*] Reynard *RL*   finding shifts] shifts about *BL*, sculks & shifts *MS 1*
27 Now] He *BL*, he *MS 1*   wood *MS 1*   to try] & take *BL*, & takes *MS 1*
28 ∧The *MS 1*   Bugle *BL*   view *MS 1 BL*   29 break *BL*   Thread bake
underlined MS 1   Gaily *through* leads *and* Gaily *written below MS A3*] *omitted BL*
MS 1   throng] pack along *BL*, path along *MS 1*   30 his *BL MS 1*   unerring:
cry] way *BL*   31 confirms: to] of *MS 1*   32 a *RL*   33 Funeral *BL*]
funeral *RL*   36 &] He: wi'] in *BL*   38 & Raise a stronger cry *BL*

AUTOGRAPHS: Pet. MS A3, pp. 87–8: Pet. MS A3, p. 91 (ll. 1–28 only, erased pencil beneath 'A Hunting Song' in ink).
TRANSCRIPTS: Pet. MS B1, pp. 142–3: Nor. MS 5, pp. 63–6.
Printed in *RL*, pp. 65–8 (ll. 25–8 omitted 1st edn., but included in 2nd).
Dated: '1818' (MS A3, p. 87).

ELEGY
HASTILY COMPOSED & WRITTEN WITH A PENCIL
ON THE SPOT
IN THE RUINS OF PICKWORTH
RUTLAND

These buried Ruins now in dust forgot
These heaps of stone the only remnants seen
The 'Old Foundations' still they call the spot
Which plainly tells Enqu[i]rey what has been

A time was once—tho now the nettle grows   5
In triumph oer each heap that swells the ground
When they in buildings pil'd a village rose
With here a Cot & there a Garden crownd

& here while Grandeur with unequal share
Perhaps maintaind its idleness & pride   10
Industrys cottage rose contented there
With scarce as much as wants of life supplyd

Mysterious cause! Still more mysterious pland
(—Altho undoubtedly the will of heaven)
To think what carless & unequal hand   15
Met[e]s out each portion that to man is given

ELEGY HASTILY COMPOSED & WRITTEN WITH A PENCIL ON THE SPOT IN THE RUINS OF PICKWORTH RUTLAND *Title:* Elegy / Hastily composed & Written with a Pencil / on the Spot / In the Ruins of Pickworth / Rutland *MS A3,* Elegy / (Written with a Pencil) / in the Ruins of / Pickworth *MS A3, p. R 91,* Elegy on the Ruins of Pickworth, / Rutlandshire. / Hastily composed, and written with a Pencil on / the Spot. *RL*   1 ruins *MS A3, p. 91*   for got *MS A3*   2 remnants] fragments *MS A3, p. 91*   3 'The old foundations' *MS A3, p. 91*   4 Enquirey *MS A3, p. 91*   7 pild *MS A3, p. 91*   8 garden *MS A3, p. 91*   10 idleness] idle thought *MS A3, p. 91*   12 *First* as] so *RL*   13 cause‸ still *MS A3, p. 91*

While vain extravagance for me alone
Claims half the land their grandeur to mentain
What thousands—not a Rood to call their own
Like me but labour for support in vain   20

Here we see Luxury surfeit with excess
There want behol[d]ing beg from door to door
Still meeting sorrow where he meets sucess
By lengthening life that livd in vain before

Almighty power—but why should I repine   25
Or vainly live thy goodness to distrust
Since reason rules what providence designs
What ever is must certainly be just

Ye scenes of desolation spread around
Prosperity to you did once belong   30
& doubtless where these brambles claim the ground
The glass once flowd to hail the ranting song

The ale house here might stand—each hamlets boast
& here where elders rich from ruin grows
The tempting sign—but what was once is lost   35
Who would be proud of what this world bestows?

How contemplation mourns your lost decay
To view thy pride laid level with the ground
To see where labour clears the soil away
What fragments of mortality abound   40

17 me] one *MS A3, p. 91 RL*   18 his *RL*   19 What *through* There *MS A3*
22 beholding] bewailing *RL*   25 should] do *RL 2nd edn.*   26 [live *through*
leave] *before* live *MS A3*   27 what providence designs] each provident design *RL*
2nd edn.
33–6

        [The sent of Bowers here (each hamlets toast)
        Rich from the ruins where these elders grow
        Might be the spot that now its joys can boast
        Vain world how short the pleasures you bestow]   *MS A3, p. 132*

(l.3 the *inserted*)

33 (each *MS A3*   34 alder *altered to* elder *Harvard proof copy*] alder (*altered to* elder
on errata slip) *RL*, elder *RL 2nd edn.*   36 b *through* p *in* be *MS A3*   37 your
through their *MS A3*] their *RL*   38 their *RL*   ground *through* dust *MS A3*

Theres not a Rood of Land demands our toil
Theres not a foot of ground we daily tread
But gains increase from times devouring spoil
& holds some fragment of the human dead

The very food thats to support us gave   45
Claims for its share an equal portion too
The dust of many a long forgotten grave
Serves to manure the soil from whence it grew

—Since first these ruins fell—how chang'd the scene
What busy bustling mortals now unknown   50
Have com'd & gone as tho there nought had been
Since first oblivion call'd the spot her own

Ye busy bustling mortals known before
Of what you've done—where went—or what you see
Of what your hopes attaind to (now no more)   55
For everlasting lyes a mystery

Like yours awaits for me that 'common lot'
Tis mine to be of every hope bereft
—A few more years & I shall be forgot
& not a Vestige of my memory left   60

AUTOGRAPH: Pet. MS A3, pp. 89–90.
TRANSCRIPTS: Pet. MS B1, pp. 143–5: Nor. MS 5, pp. 7–10.
Printed in *RL*, pp. 69–72 (ll. 21–2 omitted).
Dated: 1809–10 (MS A3, p. 89 'Old 10 year ago', *RL* Introduction, p. xxii
'before he was seventeen').

NOON

All how silent and how still
Nothing heard but yonder mill
While the dazzel'd eye surveys
All around a liquid blaze

44 &] But *RL*   some *inserted MS A3*   45 thats . . . gave] which for support we
have *RL* (have] crave *RL 2nd edn.*)   51 come *RL*   52 first *over* [black] *MS A3*
54 went] gone *RL 4th edn.*   55 to *RL*   59 for got *MS A3*
   NOON   *Title:* Noon *MS A3 RL*   2 e *in* heard *inserted MS A3*

And amid the scorching gleams 5
If we earnest look it seems
As if crooked bits of glass
Seem'd repeatedley to pass
O! for a puffing breeze to blow
But breezes all are strangers now 10
Not a twig is seen to shake
Nor the smalest bent to quake
From the rivers muddy side
Not a curve is seen to glide
And no longer on the stream 15
Watching lies the silver bream
Forcing from repeated springs
'Verges in succesive rings'
Bees are faint and cease to hum
Birds are overpower'd and dumb 20
And no more loves oaten strains
Sweetley thro the air complains
Vocal voices all are mute
Tuneles[s] lies the pipe and flute
Shepherds with their panting sheep 25
In the swailiest corner creep
And from the tormenting heat
All are wishing to retreat
Huddel'd up in grass and flowers
Mowers wait for cooler hours 30
And the Cow-boy seeks the sedge
Ramping in the woodland hedge
While his cattle oer the vales
Scamper with uplifted tails
Others not so wild and mad 35
That can better bear the gad

---

9 *Second* e *in* breeze *inserted MS A3*   10 are all *RL*   18 *The quotation is from John Cunningham, 'Day', stanza xxv; but in MS D2, p. 8 Clare writes:* not my own alter the Couplet thus:

> Forcing from each vaunting spring
> Many a Curdling ring & * ring

* or in *as may suit best*

23 Vocal] Rural *RL*   24 lie *RL*   30 coolers *MS A3*

Underneath the hedgerow lunge
Or if nigh in waters plunge
—O to see how flowers are took
How It grieves me when I look   40
Ragged robins once so pink
Now are turnd as black a[s] ink
And the leaves being scorch'd so much
Even crumble at the touch
Drowking lies the Meadow sweet   45
Flopping down beneath ones feet
While to all the flowers that blow
If in open air they grow
The injurious deed alike is done
By the hot relentless sun   50
E'en the dew is parched up
From the teazle's jointed cup
O poor birds where must ye flye
Now your water pots are dry
If ye stay upon the heath   55
Ye'll be choak'd & clam'd to death
Therefore leave the shadeles goss
Seek the spring head lin'd with moss
There your little feet may stand
Safely on the printing sand   60
While in full poss[ess]ion where
Purling eddies ripple clear
You with ease and plenty blest
Sip the coolest and the best
Then away and wet your throats   65
Cheer me with your warbling notes
'T'will hot noon the more revive
While I wander to contrive
For my self a place as good
In the middle of a wood   70
There aside some mossy bank
Where the grass in bunshes rank

---

38 plunge. *MS A3*   49 Th' injurious *RL*   52 teasel's *RL 2nd edn.*
60 Safely printing on the sand *RL*   62 clear *through* clare *MS A3*   68 While
I [And still] *MS A3*   71 mossy] [creek or *through* hidden]: mossy bank *in margin*
MS A3

Lifts its Down on spindles high
Shall be where I'll chuse to lye
Fearless of the things that creep   75
There I'll think and there I'll sleep
Careing not to stir at all
Till the dew begins to fall

AUTOGRAPHS: Pet. MS A3, pp. 93–4: Pet. MS A40, pp. 32–32a
(ll. 17–24 omitted, deleted in pencil).
TRANSCRIPTS: Pet. MS B1, pp. 146–7: Nor. MS 5, pp. 141–3.
Dated: 1813–14 (MS A3, p. 93 'about 6 year').

'YOU'LL NEVER CATCH ME THERE'

A Ballad

Young Damon Wanton gay and wild
For Lucy feignd a Flame
The swain had many a maid beguild
And her he lovd the same
At first his love was urgd in vain   5
For she with scornful air
Would cry begone deluding swain
You'll never catch me there

But he more close his prayers apply
And binds em with a vow   10
And then would heave a tender sigh
Will you believe me now

78 fall [!] *MS A3*
    'YOU'LL NEVER CATCH ME THERE' *Title:* 'You'll never catch me there' / a
Ballad *MS A3*, A Ballad / In the fashionable style *MS A40*   1 wanton & *MS A40*
2 Lucey: flame *MS A40*   3 beguiled *MS A40*   4 &: loved *MS A40*
5 urged *MS A40*   7 Woud *MS A40*   8 Youll *MS A40*   9 applies
MS A40   10 &: them *MS A40*   11 &: woud *MS A40*   12 'Will:
now' *MS A40*

But still she scornful turnd aside
—And Foolish youth forbear
The haughty maid disdainful cried   15
You'll never catch me there

Unwearied still—he sobd & sighd
And told his breaking heart
—Tormenting is the sexes pride
She gloried in the smart   20
And still she scornful turnd aside
—And silly swain for bear
The frowning maid in triumph cried
You'll never catch me there

Convincd he bid his sighs remove   25
And wipd his tears away
And talkd of nought but Wedded love
And begd to set the Day
The Wedding gown the Nots & Rings
—What Maiden could for bear   30
O tempting and deluding things
He fairly catchd her there

Now lost to every Virgin sweet
That Won his heart before
The Shepherds conquest is compleat   35
He Wishes for no more
In vain the tear bedews her eye
To tell her jealous fear
To all he makes but this Reply
Your only catchd my Dear   40

---

13 turned *MS A40*   14 ∧& 'foolish *MS A40*   15 shaughty *MS A3 (Clare probably started to write a word beginning with 's', perhaps 'scornful', and then changed it to 'haughty')*   16 'Youll: there' *MS A40*   25 Convinced *MS A40*   [he] he *MS A3*   26 & whiped *MS A40*   27 & taulked: naught: wedded *MS A40*   28 & beged: day *MS A40*   29 wedding: knots: rings *MS A40*   30 ∧What maiden coud *MS A40*   31 & *MS A40*   32 caught *MS A40*   33 virgin *MS A40*   34 won *MS A40*   35 shepherds *MS A40*   36 wishes *MS A40*   39 reply *MS A40*   40 caught: dear *MS A40*

In vain she begs him to be true
& save her from her shame
In vain his former vows Renew
The Wedding Day to Name
For ah to all he turnd aside 45
& Foolish maid forbear
The Swain Retalliating cried
You'll never catch me there

AUTOGRAPHS: Pet. MS A3, p. 96: Nor. MS 41 (ll. 21–4 omitted, partly erased pencil).
TRANSCRIPTS: Pet. MS B1, pp. 151–2: Nor. MS 5, pp 106–8.
Printed in *RL*, pp. 79–82: *Boston Gazette*, 25 January 1820 (reprinted from *RL* with ll. 21–4 omitted).
Dated: '1817' (MS A3, p. 96).

EARLY RISING

Just at the early peep o' dawn
While brushing through the dewy lawn
& viewing of the sweets o' morn
   That shines at early rising

Ere the ploughman yokd his team 5
Or sun had power to gild the stream
Or woodlarks 'gan their morning hymn
   To hail its early rising

Wi' modest look & bashful eye
Artless Innosent & shy 10
A lovley maiden pass'd me bye
   & charmd my early rising

43 renew *MS A40*   44 wedding day: name *MS A40*   45 turned *MS A40*
46 foolish *MS A40*   47 swain retalliating *MS A40*   48 Youll *MS A40*

  EARLY RISING   *Title:* Early Rising *MS A3 RL, wanting MS 41*   2 thro:
Lawn *MS 41*   3 ⟨&⟩ *MS 41*   of] o' *MS 41,* all *RL*   of *(sixth word) altered to*
o' *MS A3*] o *MS 41*   4 shine *RL*   5 plough mans yok'd *MS 41*
6 ⟨to⟩ *MS 41*   7 wood larks *MS 41*   10 innoscent *MS 41*
11 ⟨me bye⟩ *MS 41*   12 ri⟨sing⟩ *MS 41*

Her looks had every power to wound
Her voice had music in the sound
When modestly she turn'd around   15
    To greet my early rising

Good nature forc'd the maid to speak
& good behaviour not to seek
Gave sweetness to her rosy cheek
    Improvd by early rising   20

—While brambles catch'd her passing bye
& her fine leg engag'd my eye
Oh who could paint confusions dye
    The blush of early rising

While offering help to climb the stile   25
A modest look & winning smile
(Love beaming in her eyes the while)
    Repay'd my early rising

Aside the green hills steepy brow
Where shades the oak its darksome bough   30
The maiden sat to milk her cow
    The cause of early rising

The wild rose mingling with the shade
Stung with envy clos'd to fade
To see the rose her cheeks display'd   35
    The fruits of early rising

The kiss desir'd—against he[r] will
To take the milk pail up the hill
Seem'd from resistance sweeter still
    Thrice happy early rising   40

---

14 ⟨in the⟩ *MS 41*   15 turnd *MS 41*   17 forcd *MS 41*
18 behaviour *to* behaviour, *(p.e.)* : seek *to* seek, *(p.e.) MS A3*   21 caught *RL*
24 *MS D1:* Hints & Corrections / 'Early Rising' / Instead of 'That blusht at early rising'
/ Print 'The blush of early rising *MS A3 has the corrected version*   28 Repayd *MS 41*
29 Green *MS 41*   30 shades] *? sheds or speds for 'spreads':* bough] brow *MS 41*
32 Rising *MS 41*   34 wi: closd ⟨to⟩ *MS 41*   35 displayd *MS 41*
37 arm in arm we scald the hill *(c through* k *in* scald) *MS 41*   38 The kiss that
seemd against her will *MS 41*   39 Seemd: Resistance *MS 41*   40 —O
happy early rising *MS 41*

& often since aside the grove
I've hie'd to meet the maid I love
Repeating truths that time shall prove
    Which past at early rising

May it be mine to spend my days   45
With her whose beauty claims my praise
Then Joy shall crown my rural lays
    & bless my early rising

AUTOGRAPHS: Pet. MS A3, p. 97: Yale University Osborn Collection 206/6.
TRANSCRIPTS: Pet. MS B1, pp. 156-7 (ll. 17-24 deleted): Nor. MS 5, pp. 109-11 (ll. 17-24 deleted).
Printed in *RL*, pp. 88-90 (ll. 17-24 omitted): *Worcester Journal* (ll. 17-24 omitted), 29 August 1844, in an account by 'J[ohn] N[oake]' (1816-94), journalist and antiquary, of his recent visit to Clare (*WJ*): *Northampton Herald* and *Northampton Mercury*, 7 September 1844 (reprinted from *WJ*).
Dated: 1811-20 (*RL* Introduction, p. xxii 'In the last two years'; in one corner of the Yale MS Clare has written what appears to be an elaborate '1820').

TO A ROSE BUD IN HUMBLE LIFE

Sweet uncultivated blossom
Reard in springs refreshing dews
Dear to every gazers bosom
Fair to every eye that views
Opening bud whose youth can charm us   5
Thine be many a happy hour
Spreading rose whos beauty warms us
Flourish long my lovley flower

42 Ive hied *MS 41*   maid] girl *RL*   43 truths] vows *MS 41*   that *over* [which]
MS A3] which *MS 41*   44 That passd *MS 41*   45 May it be] & was it *MS 41*
[to] my *MS A3*   46 with: whose beauty claims] who thus deserves *MS 41*
47 then joy should *MS 41*   48 ⟨& bless my⟩ *MS 41*

TO A ROSE BUD IN HUMBLE LIFE   *Title:* To a Rose bud in humble Life *MS*
A3, To a Rose Bud in humble Life *Yale,* To a Rose-bud in humble Life *RL WJ*
2 Reard *through* Blooming *MS A3*   Refreshing *Yale*   3 bossom *Yale*
7 whose *Yale*   beauties warm *WJ*

Tho pride looks disdainful on thee
Scorning scenes so mean as thine   10
Altho fortune frowns upon thee
Lovley blossom ne'er repine
Health unbought is ever wi' thee
—What their wealth can never gain
Innoscence her garments gie thee   15
Such as fashion apes in vain

Far be every evil from thee
Bud to blight or bloom decay
Still unborn the wretch to wrong thee
First beguile & then betray   20
—Who so destitute of feeling
Would such Innoscence beguile?
Who so base to be a villian
Would thy spotless sweets defile?—

When fit time & season grants thee   25
Leave to leave thy parent tree
May some happy hand transplant thee
To a station suiting thee
On some lovers worthy bosom
Mayest thou thy sweets resign   30
& may each unfolding blossom
Open charms as sweet as thine

Till that time may joys unceasing
Thy bards every wish fulfill
When thats come may joys increasing   35
Make thee blest & happier still

12 near *Yale*   13 o *in* unbought *inserted Yale*   14 ∧What *Yale*   15 her
doth *RL*   G *through* g *in* Garments: gi *Yale* give *WJ*   16 fashion[s] *Yale*
20 and *Yale*   21 ,∧Who *Yale*   22 Whould *MS A3*   such] thy: innoscence
beguile∧ *Yale*   23 Villian *Yale*   24 defile∧∧ *Yale*   25 When]
Till: and *Yale*   season] Reason *Yale*, reason *RL WJ*   Grant *Yale*] grant *RL WJ*
26 Leave] Time *Yale*   leave] quit *RL WJ*   28 Station *Yale*   29 worthy]
throbbing *Yale*, faithful *WJ*   bossom *Yale*   30 May'st thou then *RL WJ*
31 And *Yale*   32 [fair] sweet *MS A3*] fair *Yale*   34 Bards *Yale*
35 When thats come] Whan that time *Yale*   36 thee] the: and *Yale*

—Flourish fair thou artless Jessy
Pride of each admiring swain
Envy of despairing lasses
Queen of Walkherds lonly plain   40

AUTOGRAPH: Pet. MS A3, p. 98.
TRANSCRIPTS: Pet. MS B1, p. 158: Nor. MS 5, p. 51: Nor. MS 4, p. 91
(ll. 1–5 only, deleted).
Printed in *RL*, p. 192.
Dated: 'Old' (MS A3, p. 98).

A SCENE

The landscapes stretching view that opens wide
With dribbling brooks & rivers wider floods
& hills & vales & darksome lowering woods
With grains of varied hues & grasses pied
The low brown cottage in the shelter'd nook   5
The steeple peeping just above the trees
Whose dangling leaves keep rustling in the breeze
—& thoughtful shepherd bending oer his hook
& maidens stript haymaking too apear
& hodge a wistling at his fallow plough   10
& herdsman hallooing to intruding cow
All these with hundreds more far off & near
Approach my sight—& please to such excess
That Language fails the pleasure to express

37 ∧Flourish *Yale*   artless Jessy] flower of Jessys *RL WJ*   40 Walkherds *below*
Walkerds *underlined MS A3*   lonley *Yale*] lonely *altered to* lowly *on errata slip in RL 1st
edn., but* lonely *retained in 2nd edn.*

A SCENE   *Title:* A Scene *MS A3 RL*   4 grains] green *RL*   6 Correction—
In—'A Scene' A Sonnet   Instead of steeple peeping &c &c Print The Steeple strouting
just above the trees (strouting *through* sprouting) *MS D2, p. 8*   14 Tha⟨t⟩ *torn
MS A3*

AUTOGRAPHS: Pet. MS A3, p. 99: Norris Museum SAVNM CL/7.
TRANSCRIPTS: Pet. MS B1, p. 159: Nor. MS 5, p. 30.
Printed in *RL*, p. 193.
Dated: ? 1819 (MS A3, p. 99 '1819', Norris 'Old').

TO THE GLOW-WORM

Tastefull Illuminations of the night
Bright scatter'd twinkling stars o' spangl'd earth
Hail to the nameless colour'd dark-&-light
The watching nurse o' thy illumin'd birth
In thy still hour how dearly I delight   5
To rest my weary bones—from labour free
In lone spots out o' hearing & o' sight
To sigh days smother'd pains & pause on thee
Bedecking dangling brier & ivied tree
Or diamonds tipping on the grassy spear   10
Thy pale fac'd glimmering light I love to see
Gilding & glistering i' the dew drop near—
O still hours mate—my easing heart sobs free
While tiny bents low bend wi' many a added tear

TO THE GLOW-WORM   *Title:* To the Glow-worm *MS A3 Norris RL*
1 Illumination *RL*   2 star[s] *Norris*] star *RL*   3 colourd: and *Norris*
4 watching] witching *RL*   5 dearly *through indecipherable Norris*   6 bones∧
Norris   7 lone-spot[s] *Norris*   &] out *RL*   8 To] &: d *through* s *in* days:
smotherd *Norris*   9 brier] leaf: &] or *through* o' *later alteration*: ivied] mossy *Norris*
10 Or diamonds tipping] On tipping diamonds: spear,— *Norris*   11 pale . . .
light] tiny glimmering face *Norris*   12 in: near∧ *Norris*   13 still-hours-
mate∧ *Norris*   13/14 [& bents oer burthen'd bend wi' many a added tear] *(many a*
inserted) Norris   14 an *RL*   *Norris also contains the following lines in pencil which*
are torn at the top:

                                                  conceals

The rose & ruby beautys boast & pride
But vainly please the wise ? devoid of thine
A dazzleing toy by fools & childern ey'd
A brazen lure that daubs inviting sign   5

(l. 3 But *through* And)

AUTOGRAPHS: Pet. MS A3, p. 100: Pet. MS A40, pp. 34–34a.
TRANSCRIPTS: Pet. MS B1, pp. 159–60: Nor. MS 5, p. 171.
Dated: '1819' (MS A3, p. 100).

TO INNOSCENCE

O Innoscence thou captivating charm
Thou beauty's gem pure, heavenly, & divine
The Virgins cheek—when thy soft flushes warm
What 'witching sweetness & what powers are thine

Coy bashfull looks turn'd from admiring eyes   5
Chill'd trembling paleness aw'd by fancied fear
Short timid Answers blushing sweet suprise
When Loves soft sighs are wisper'd in her ear

These charms! The very soul's recesses thrills
These sweet confusions every bosom feels   10
In every heart the magic sweet Instills
Which each coy lover painfully consceals—

The rose & rubys charms—frail beautys pride
But vainly please the wise—devoid of thine
A dazzling toy by fools & younkers ey'd   15
Like brazen lure that daubs inviting sign

Tho tempted Eve thy sweet origin lost
A 'zembling shade the virtues still retain—
Still Emmas Face thy sweetest charm can boast
& heaven it self more sweetness boasts in vain   20

TO INNOSCENCE *Title:* To Innoscence *MS A3*, To Innocence *MS A40*
1 Innocence *MS A40*   2 beautys: pure, heavenly, &] of origin *MS A40*
3 virgins cheek∧which: flushes] blushes *MS A40*   4 witching *MS A40*
5 bashful: turned *MS A40*   6 Chill: awed *MS A40*   7 answers: suprise
MS A40   8 loves: whisperd *MS A40*   9 charms∧ the: souls: thrill[s]
MS A40   11 sweet *altered to* sweets: instill[s] *MS A40*   12 conceals∧
MS A40   13 rubeys charms∧ *MS A40*   14 wise∧ *MS A40*   15 childern
altered to younkers *MS A3*   eyed *MS A40*   17 Though: eve *MS A40*
18 retain∧ *MS A40*   19 Emmas] Marys: face *MS A40*   20 itself *MS A40*

AUTOGRAPHS: Pet. MS A3, p. 104: Pet. MS A40, p. 33.
TRANSCRIPT: Pet. MS B1, p. 162.
Dated: '1818' (MS A3, p. 104).

SONG

The beauties o' youth lovley Emma adorning
  As the spring is first seen to disclose
When the dew dropping silver o' mays infant morning
  Unfolds the sweet blush o' the rose
While her charms—O as varied as summers profusion   5
  & ripe as the autumn for love
In her blue eyes sweet beaming the thrilling confusion
  Near failing each bosom to move
While the snows o' the winter improvd on her bosom
  No need o' a rival be told   10
—& O my sad pains—when I 'gan to disclose em
  I found it as killing & cold

AUTOGRAPH: Pet. MS A3, p. 107.
TRANSCRIPTS: Pet. MS B1, p. 172: Nor. MS 5, p. 125.
Printed in *RL*, p. 195.
Dated: '1817' (MS A3, p. 107).

TO HOPE

Ah smiling cherub cheating hope adieu
No more I'll listen to your pleasing themes
No more your flattering scenes with joy review
For ah I've found em all delusive dreams

SONG   *Title:* Song *MS A3 MS A40*   *Three four-line stanzas in MS A40*
1 beautys of: Emma] Mary *MS A40*   3 of Mays *MS A40*   4 of *MS A40*
5 charms∧oh: Summers *MS A40*   9 o' *through* of *MS A3*] of *MS A40*   improved
MS A40   10 of *MS A40*   11 ∧& oh: pains∧: them *MS A40*   'gan *through*
went *MS A3*   12 killing] chilling *MS A40*

TO HOPE   *Title:* To Hope—a Sonnet *MS A3*, To Hope *RL*   3 review] renew
RL

Yes mere delusions all—therefore adieu   5
No more shall you this aching heart beguile
No more your fleeting joys will I pursue
That mock'd my sorrows when they seem'd to smile
And flatterd tales that never would be true
Tales only told to aggravate distress   10
& make me at my fate the more repine
By wispering joys I never can posess
& painting scenes that never must be mine

AUTOGRAPH: Pet. MS A3, p. 107 (deleted in pencil).
TRANSCRIPTS: Pet. MS B1, p. 172: Nor. MS 5, p. 123.
Printed in *RL*, p. 196: *Stamford Mercury*, 21 January 1820 (reprinted from *RL*).
Dated: '1817' (MS A3, p. 107).

TO A WINTER SCENE

Hail scenes of Desolation & despair
Keen Winters over bearing sport & scorn
Torn by his Rage in ruins as you are
To me more pleasing then a summers morn
Your shatter'd scenes appear—despoild & bare   5
Stript of your clothing naked & forlorn
—Yes Winters havoc wretched as you shine
Dismal to others as your fate may seem
Your fate is pleasing to this heart of mine
Your wildest horrors I the most esteem.—   10
The ice-bound floods that still with rigour freeze
The snow clothd valley & the naked tree
These sympathising scenes my heart can please
Distress is theirs—& they resemble me

9 will *RL*   13 must] can *RL*

TO A WINTER SCENE   *Title:* To a Winter Scene *MS A3*, A Winter Scene *RL*
1 Hail *through* Ye *MS A3*   5 scenes appear] state appears *RL*

AUTOGRAPH: Pet. MS A3, p. 108 (deleted in pencil).
TRANSCRIPTS: Pet. MS B1, p. 172: Nor. MS 5, p. 111.
Printed in *RL*, p. 91.
Dated: 1809–12 (MS A3, p. 108 '8 or 10 years ago', *RL* Introduction, p. xxii
'before he was seventeen').

THE UNIVERSAL EPITAPH

No flattering praises daub my stone
My Frailties & my faults to hide
My faults & failings all are known
—I livd in sin—in sin I dy'd
& O condemn me not I pray   5
All who my sad confession see—
But ask your soul if it can say
That your a Better man then me

THE UNIVERSAL EPITAPH   *Title:* The Universal Epitaph *(preceded by* Title
through An Epitaph*) MS A3*, The Universal Epitaph *RL   Two four-line stanzas RL
2nd edn.*   6 All] You: see] view *RL*   8 your *altered to* you're *probably not by
Clare MS A3*   That I'm a viler man than you *RL*

AUTOGRAPHS: Pet. MS A3, pp. 111–16: Pet. MS A3, pp. 134–5 (ll. 1–34, 37–52, 55–8, 61–94, deleted).
TRANSCRIPT: Pet. MS B1, pp. 175–80.
Dated: 'old' (MS A3, p. 111).

THE LOVERS MEETING

An Imitation
of the Fifth Elegy of the First Book of Ovid
'*Who can but love the sex? Whoever hates them is a stranger to virtue,*
grace, & humanity'.
Agrippa. Europ: Mag:

Hot was the noon in summers sultry hour
The sun then raging with meridian power
When I more burning with the scorching heat
Of hot desire—lay hid in close retreat
Beneath the covert of a secret shade   5
Flush'd 'with expectance of the lovley maid'
Sweet was the spot no one throughout the grove
Was better suited to the sports of Love
Thick twin'd the shade above my thoughtfull head
& all around me close embowering spread   10
So closely wove—the leaves that fan'd the air
Defy'd the sunbeams from intruding there
As when dull twilight streaks the east with grey
& only serves to tell approaching day
So shone the light in this my close retreat   15
The more endearing as the more discreet
For light like this to modest maids is dear
As shame in secret has the least to fear

THE LOVERS MEETING *Title:* The Lovers Meeting / An Imitation / Of the Fifth Elegy of the First Book of Ovid *MS A3*, The Meeting an / Imitation / Of the Fifth Elegy of the First Book / of Ovid. *MS A3, p. 134   Quotation omitted in MS A3, p. 134*   1 Summers *MS A3, p. 134*   3 Burning *MS A3, p. 134*   4 Desire— *MS A3, p. 134*   6 Flushd ∧with: maid∧ *MS A3, p. 134*   8 sports] joys: love *MS A3, p. 134*   9 thoughtful *MS A3, p. 134*   10 And: C *through* h *in* Close *MS A3, p. 134*   11 Closley: Leaves *MS A3, p. 134*   fan'd *over* [play'd] *MS A3*] playd in *MS A3, p. 134*   12 Defied: Intruding *MS A3, p. 134*   13 Dull *MS A3, p. 134*   14 And: Day *MS A3, p. 134*

And now before a doubt disturb'd my mind
Of ere distrusting she would prove unkind   20
True to her time & to her love the same
My lovley charmer to a moment came
O then what joys my happy bosom fir'd
I view'd her charms & viewing more admir'd
Charms form'd by nature pleasing to excess   25
Delightfull heighten'd by the charms of dress
Adorning tortoise crown'd her lovley head
Her snowy neck with little curls bespread
While wilder ringlets did her forhead grace
Readding beauties to her beautious face   30
Around her shoulders negligently flung
Rich silks of Indias produce loosly hung
That kindly carless of loves glances there
Left the sweet beauties of her bosom bare
Those swelling charms such throbbing bosoms prove   35
All blooming beauties ripn'd into love
Her gown short-sleeved to set off her charms
Display'd the fineness of her well turnd arms
Her careless robes loose floating in the air
(As negligence in dress becomes the fair)   40
For scorching summer suited—light & thin
Improvd the beauties they conceald within
No dress compleater throughout fashions sphere
Could set her charms off better then they were
Queens (tho more costly) in a dress neer mov'd   45
Half so enticeing as my charmers prov'd

19 disturbd *MS A3, p. 134*   20 mistrusting *MS A3, p. 134*   21 and *MS A3, p. 134*   22 lovely *MS A3, p. 134*   23 fird *MS A3, p. 134*   24 viewd: and *MS A3, p. 134*   25 formd *MS A3, p. 134*   26 Delightful heightn'd *MS A3, p. 134*   27 crownd *MS A3, p. 134*   29 for head *MS A3*   30 beutious *MS A3, p. 134*   31 shoulders] neck all *MS A3, p. 134*   32 silk: s *through* n *in* Indias: loosley *MS A3, p. 134*   33 careless: Loves *MS A3, p. 134*   34 Bosom *MS A3, p. 134*   36 into *through* beauties *MS A3*   37 short sleaved *MS A3, p. 134*   38 finess: well-turn'd *MS A3, p. 134*   39 Carless *MS A3, p. 134*   looss *MS A3*   40 Dress *MS A3, p. 134*   41 suited,— *MS A3, p. 134*   42 beauties] heaven: they *through* of: conseald *MS A3, p. 134*   43 compleator through out Fashions *MS A3, p. 134*   45 ∧tho: costley∧: ne'er *MS A3, p. 134*

Soon as she enter'd—'O my lovley bride
'Welcome thrice welcome to my arms' I cry'd
'My charmer come for thee I love & live
'To taste those charms which thou alone canst give   50
'Charms (happy fate) reserv'd for me alone
'Charms kings & princes would be proud to own
'O come my angel take that earnest kiss
'& now convey me to the realms of bliss!'
She blushing turn'd & turning hung her head   55
So stands the Virgin at the nuptial bed
Tho fond—still fearing—bashfull to comply
At joys untasted—still asham'd to try
Alternate changes in her face prevaild
Now roses blush'd & now the lilly pal'd   60
Trembling she stood & silent mus'd awhile
Then fondly look'd & answer'd with a smile—
I saw her fondness—O delightfull charms!
& instant snatch'd her to my longing arms
Her lilly hand I prest which fondly burn'd   65
& soon the fondling token was return'd
O with what softness heav'd each swelling breast
'Courting the hand & sueing to be prest'
Eager I travers'd all their snowy charms
& gaz'd with rapture on their fond alarms   70
Her rosey cheeks whose blooms eternal shine
I sweetly kiss'd & press'd em close to mine
Then with more freedom than I'd ever shown
I try'd to traverse beauties still unknown

47 enter'd∧: Lovley Bride *MS A3, p. 135*   48 arms∧: cried *MS A3,
p. 135*   48/9 [To give those charms which thou alone canst give] *MS A3, p. 135*
51 ∧happy fate∧ *MS A3, p. 135*   52 king: own' *MS A3, p. 135*   55 turnd
MS A3, p. 135   56 virgin *MS A3, p. 135*   57 fond∧: fearing∧ Bashfull *MS
A3, p. 135*   58 untasted∧ *MS A3, p. 135*   62 answerd: smile∧ *MS A3,
p. 135*   63 fondness∧: delightful charms∧ *MS A3, p. 135*   64 And:
snatchd *MS A3, p. 135*   66 And *MS A3, p. 135*   fondling *over* [pressing] *MS A3*]
tender *MS A3, p. 135*   67 wat: h *through* w *in* heav'd *MS A3, p. 135*
68 ∧Ripn'd in Love & sueing to be prest∧ *MS A3, p. 135*   69 traversd *MS A3,
p. 135*   70 And *MS A3, p. 135*   71 rosy Cheeks who's *MS A3, p. 135*
72 kissd: 'em *MS A3, p. 135*   73 than] then *MS A3, p. 135*

'Her envious gown to pull away I try'd   75
'But she resisted still & still deny'd—
'O L—d' she sigh'd 'what is he going to do?
'I know his meaning—& must love him too
'O would he bless me with the name of wife
'I should be happy to the end of Life   80
'But thats not mine—offended powers above
'Do what he will I cannot cease to love!'
She sigh'd & said no more but gaz'd on me
& as fond Ivy clasps around the tree
So round my neck her lilly arms she flung   85
& on my breast in fondest raptures hung
O heaven of Love! O paradise of bliss!
'What love' sigh'd I 'can equal love like this?'
To clasp such yielding sweetness in my arms
& be in full possesion of her charms   90
Oer all her virgin sweets to wander free
Charms safley virgin—know to none but me!
For well the lover may such truths declare
Their timid fears are truths sufficient there
No chilling fears, no trembling alarms   95
Are never witnessed in hackny'd charms
The t[h]robbing bliss that heav'd her snowy breast
Full truly told the treasure I possest
& now uninterrupted or reprov'd
Love reign'd triumphant—& her fears remov'd   100
In all the charms endearing hopes could frame
Or heart desire, or fondest wishes name
I revell'd freely; freely then possest
(Charms so endearing not to be exprest)

75–6 *Note in MS A3, p. 135*: This Couplet is from Duke as modesty forbid inserting a thouhght of my own to answer purpose as well—   75 en *through* ha *in* envious *MS A3*] Hated *MS A3, p. 135*   tried *MS A3, p. 135*   76 denied'∧ *MS A3, p. 135* 77 do∧' *MS A3, p. 135*   78 must] to: too!! *MS A3, p. 135*   82 love∧' *MS A3, p. 135*   83 sighd *MS A3, p. 135*   84 And *MS A3, p. 135*   86 And *MS A3, p. 135*   87 love∧: bliss∧ *MS A3, p. 135*   88 sigh'd I *through* I sigh'd *MS A3*   What love∧: sigh'd] thought: ∧can: this∧∧ *MS A3, p. 135*   *Clare's note in MS A3, p. 142:* Instead of 'What love sighd I &c' Print What love thought I' as at first This difference is left to you preference   89 Clasp *MS A3, p. 135*   90 And: Charms *MS A3, p. 135*   91 sweets] Charms *MS A3, p. 135*   92 virgins— *MS A3*] virgin∧: me∧ *MS A3, p. 135*   96 witness'd in no *Clare's correction note on a slip of paper facing MS A3, p. 139*

Such warmth such softness—O to feel & prove   105
My very soul was melted into love—
Here rest fond muse—For these thy powers exce⟨ll⟩
& if thou hadst not thou must cease to tell
Nor try nor venture secrets to reveal
Which she sweet girl could wish thee to consceal   110
Nor raise a blush nor give that heart a pain
Which has been kind & may be kind again
So rest & let such matchless charms alone
That would but make thy imperfections known
For they're as far above thy power to tell   115
As her sweet charms inferior charms excell
As the sweet roseys blush & lillys snow
Out shines the blossoms that around her blow
Then let the sequel of the scene be guest
Let fancy paint—& silence think the rest.   120

When day declining usher'd to a Close
& evening silence bid the world repose
& deep'ning darkness hover'd oer the grove
Compell'd (not weary with the joys of love)
We fearless ventur'd from the blissfull seat   125
& blest the night that kept us still discreet
Unheeded home ward down the dusky plain
I led my charmer to her home again
& as weak troubles discompos'd her breast
I vow'd to love & kiss'd its fears to rest—   130
'O do you love me? sighs the timerous maid
'Will you still come?—I really am afraid
'—O am I not Or am I to complain?—
'When will you come?—O will you come again?

107 exce⟨ll⟩ *binding MS A3*   111 Nor *through indecipherable MS A3*
119–20

                              I think in this couplet Viz

                              'Then let the Sequel of the <u>Scene</u> be guest
                              'Let fancy paint & silence think the rest'
That <u>Scene</u> was left out—if it was that defect is remedied—*MS A3, p. 142, correction*
119 scene] [tale] *through a gap MS A3*

'—Stay Strephon stay—I cannot let you go   135
'Promise me truly—will to morrow do?'
'It will' I cry'd—'O Strep[h]en prove it true!—
'I will sweet girl—& till its prov'd adieu'

Thus was our parting interview exprest
& these the fears that discompos'd her breast   140
I kiss'd her lips—& then resolv'd to part—
& O I left her with an aching heart
For in their abscence love redoubl'd burns
& aching fondness painfully returns
Anxious I wish'd the tedious night away   145
& eager waited for approaching day—
With careless step—(as musing lovers roam)
I stroll'd unwilling to my dreary home
& there in pleasing pain past joys review'd
& wisht in dreams to have them still renew'd.   150

AUTOGRAPHS: Pet. MS A3, pp. 121–6: Nor. MS 7, p. 45 (ll. 47–50,
57–60, 95–6, 112–15, 135–42, 153–4, 166, 179–200 omitted, pencil
beneath ink).
TRANSCRIPT: Pet. MS B1, pp. 1–5.
Dated: '1819' (MS A3, p. 121).

THE AUTHORS ADDRESS TO HIS BOOK

Now little book the time is come
That thou must leave thy dad & home
To seek for friends—(the L—d knows wither)
The very thoughts o't makes me dither

136 me *inserted:* truly *through* me *MS A3*   146 r *through* o *in* approaching *MS A3*
147 musing *through* the *MS A3*   150 wisht *over* [hop'd] *MS A3*   In the Last line
'& hop'd in dreams to have them still renew'd'   So it was at first—but thinking <u>wish'd</u>
more proper I inserted it—So this is left to your Judgement Like wise—J.C. *MS A3,
p. 142, correction*

    THE AUTHORS ADDRESS TO HIS BOOK: *Title:* The Authors Address to his
Book *MS A3*, Authors Address to his Book *MS 7*   2 That thou'rt of years to leave
thy home *MS 7*   3 r *through* o *in* friends: k *through* w *in* knows *MS A3*   friends∧:
Lord *MS 7*

But thou art young the world is wide 5
& tho for travel ill supply'd
I'll gie thee what shall do thee good
(As every loving parent shou'd)
Some good advice before ye go
The utmost kindness I can show 10
Full well thou knows't my little book
What pains in rearing thee I took
To bring thee up as I ha' brought thee
To teach thee things as I ha' taught thee
What moping days—nay weeks—I've led 15
Wi' nought but empty wishes fed
What sleepless nights been doom'd to see
To study & contrive for thee
Then whilst thou hears thy fathers blessing
—Some kindness for the past expressing 20
Wi' strict attention listen to't
& what I say observe & do't
For from my rules thou'lt plainly know
How to distinguish friend from foe—
Without this caution mind my book 25
Thou ne'er need's for Preferment look
The world's a dangerous Ocean found
Where daring dangers threaten round
& if thou takes the head long tide
With out some Reason for thy guide 30
The perils of a 'whelming sea
Is safe enough to ruin thee
On some foul Rock or craggy shore
Thy Bark will sink to rise no more—

9 advise: you *MS 7*   10 & thats the utmost you can do *MS 7*   11 knowst:
Book *MS 7*   12 rearing] raising *MS 7*   13 have *MS 7*   14 the *(third
word)*: have *MS 7*   15 weeks‿Ive *MS 7*   16 Wi *MS 7*   17 doomd
MS 7   18 *In ink through pencil* & all to think & strive for thee *MS 7*
19 while: hearst: Fathers *MS 7*   20 ‿Some *MS 7*   21 Wi strickt *MS 7*
22 & *through* Take: what … & *through indecipherable MS 7*   23 For] &: thoult
MS 7   24 foe‿ *MS 7*   26 neer needs: preferment *MS 7*   27 worlds:
ocean *MS 7*   28 dareing … round *(ink) through* shoalls & rocks & shelves abound
(pencil) MS 7   29 &] Where *MS 7*   30 reason *MS 7*
31 'whelming] danger⟨ou⟩s *torn MS 7*   33 On some foul *through* Some
craggy: rock: craggy *through* shallow *MS 7*   34 Thy *through* Will: bark: more‿
MS 7

Then mind—pursue the safest plan   35
And be as wary as you can
Mark first—for Friendship never go
Mong (like thy self) the mean & low
But pass thou by the peasants door
Who's quite as ign'rant as their poor   40
A sensless laugh & silly stare
With humming here & hahing there—
'Why's!—now't b't nonscence now its cem'
Thats all that thou mayst hope from them
For what can thou expect to find   45
Where Ignorance continues blind—
The ploughboy when behind his heels
The restless hogs tormenting squeals
Near seems supris'd about their bother
They're hogs & he expects no other   50
Such silly dunces pass 'em by
& ne'er so much as turn thy eye

& mind thee Bookey what I say
There's others quite as bad as they
That boast their learning & their knowledge   55
As tho' they'd ta'en degrees from Colledge
Despisers of Establish'd laws
The Churches old protestant cause
(Where Eloquence & learning preaches
Where Wisdom Sense & reason teaches)   60
Those mushrooms plentiously abound
To day from dung hills starting found

---

35 mind∧ *MS 7*   36 & *MS 7*   37 friendship *MS 7*   38 Mo *in* Mong
in ink: (like thy self) *ink*: the *inserted in ink*: *dash after* low *in ink MS 7*   *Through pencil*
Among the vulgar mean & low *MS 7*   39 pheasants *MS A3 MS 7*
40 Ign'rant: their] his *MS 7*   41 sensless *and* silly *underlined MS A3*
43 *Underlined MS A3*   —Why's—nou't *(*Why *through* Where*)*: nonscence: cem∧
MS 7   'Why its nought but nonsense now its kem' *over* ['Why's! nou't but nonsense
now't cem'] *in Clare's hand MS B1*   45–6 *Ink insertion MS 7*   45 For
through But *MS A3*   canst: f⟨ind⟩ *torn MS 7*   46 bl⟨ind⟩ *torn MS 7*
49 about *through* to *MS A3*   50 hogs *underlined MS A3*   51 dunces
underlined MS A3   em *MS 7*   52 neer: thine *MS 7*   53 Booky *MS 7*
54 Theres *MS 7*   56 tho: colledge *MS 7*   61 mushrooms *underlined MS
A3*] Mushrooms *MS 7*

To morrow in a pulpit drest
A Learned lecturer shines confest
Where Ignorance around him stands   65
Groaning applause wi' lifted hands
Admiring with astonish'd wonder
Each thoughtless pause—& helpless blunder
'And sure' they cry 'the mans uncommon
'He never cou'd be born o' woman   70
'He either comes or has from heaven
'The Gift to give us what he's given!'
So Ignorance & conseit will swell 'em
For they'll know more then thou canst tell 'em
Besides the dress that thou art in   75
It rather smells too much o' sin
Their sacred touch it wou'd defile
Nor would they think it worth their while
Poor outcast ere to notice thee
Thourt none o' their comunity   80
'Blind as a beetle' they wou'd call thee
& safe as death to over haul thee
Say every page wants rerevising
& every ballad spir'tualizing
Call thee old Nickeys choise observant   85
& stile thy dad his humble servant
Then mind my book—I wish well to thee
I tell thou shun 'em—see & do thee

The next thing mind thee's neer to stop
To peep in to a grocers shop   90

63 Morrow *MS 7*   pulpit *underlined MS A3*   *In margin in Clare's hand in MS B1*:
'Among a number one is reckoned none'   64 Learned *underlined MS A3*] learned
MS 7   shines *over* [stands] *MS A3*] stands *MS 7*   65 [is rang'd] around *MS 7*
67 wi astonishd *MS 7*   68 Each thoughtless]? They wispring *MS 7*
69 & *MS 7*   70 could: woman' *MS 7*   m *through* a *in* woman *MS A3*
71 ⟨Hes⟩ either *faded*: come: has] sent *MS 7*   72 ⟨To give⟩ poor mortals
what he's given' *faded MS 7*   73 ⟨So⟩ *faded*: ignorance: consceit: will] may: em
MS 7   74 know m⟨   ⟩ *torn MS A3*   ⟨em⟩ *in fold of paper MS 7*
76 smells] stinks *MS 7*   77 would *MS 7*   78 think *through* they *MS A3*
79 Poor outcast ere *over* [My hopful book] *MS A3*] My godly book *MS 7*   n⟨oti⟩ce
torn MS 7   80 of *MS 7*   81 would *MS 7*   82 f *through* v *in* safe:
overhaul *MS 7*   83 w[h]ants *MS A3*   84 spiritualizing *MS 7*   85 Call
through Say: thee] the *MS 7*   87 book ∧ *MS 7*   88 em *MS 7*
89 mind—: thee's neer to] & never *MS 7*   90 into *MS 7*

For if thou dost—'as sure's a Gun'
Thy travels end & I'm undone
Thee for his use he'll quickly handle
As rapper for some farthing candle
(His Customers politley pleasing   95
By Keeping Misses hands from greasing)
Or binding more disgracful stuff
Help goody to her ounce o' snuff
I tell thee plain enough—observe me
This & no better way he'll serve thee   100
No more thou need expect from him
Then being shatterd limb from limb
I can but tell thee for the best
Then shun him as thou shun'd the rest

Next—when you happen on the road   105
To find [out] Industrys abode
Known 'mong the vulgar by a farm
Be cautious how you meet wi' harm
Tho with a caution little doubt it
(Theres nothing can be done without it)   110
You needn't see much fear in speeding
Tho few such folks delight in Reading—
However be it as it will
If here we're dissapointed still
Thou'rt none the worse for't—take but heed   115
So hark thee Book—& I'll proceed
Thou in a kitchen (dreadful place)
Must ne'er attempt to show thy face

91 you do: —∧ as: Gun∧ MS 7   92 Thy travels] Thou meets thy: Im MS 7
93 Thee] The MS 7   95 His inserted MS A3   96 By inserted MS A3
97 disgraceful MS 7   99 ye: enough∧ MS 7   101 Nomore MS A3
103 for through as its MS A3   104 Then through To MS A3   shund MS 7
106 To ⟨chance on⟩ Industrys MS 7   out inserted in Clare's hand MS Bl   108 There
you may venture wi out harm MS 7   109 ⟨& wi a⟩ caution (a over
[may]): little] never MS 7   110 wi'out MS 7   111 Your very like enough to
speed MS 7   115 none through the MS A3   116 Then listen tot & I'll
proceede MS 7   116/17 [A Farmers kitchen is the place / Where thou must never
show thy face] MS 7

For there each sensless wench will be
The worst of enemys to thee   120
They'll know no more 'bout what y' mean
Then thou 'bout them thoust never seen
But think thourt for no other use
(So ignorance wi' us plays the deuce)
Then just to rap their greazy heads   125
In curls each night they go to bed
Which every morning when they rise
Fresh kindling for the fire supplies
& pot & kettle holders serving
As if no better fate deserving   130
Till (like old News or almnacks)
Every page has gone to rack
This is the use they'll make of thee
Such is their taste for Poetry!

Nay—thy superiors & betters   135
Which fashion decks in golden Letters
'Spite o' their fine 'morocco backs
(A dress which thou must ever lack)
Are all tore up! disgracful shame
For jobs the muses blush to name   140
(Which often I've in sorrow seen)
Some booby's sh–tt–n clouts to Clean
To wish thee well in friendship trust me
If thats thy fate—why—so it must be

Now Bookey mind—(while I am wi' thee)   145
The last advice I'm going to gie thee
Hardships past to this are small
Here both must rise or both must fall

---

121 She'll: ye *MS 7*   122 s *through* r *in* thou'st *MS 7*   123 for *inserted*
MS A3   124 Ignrance wi *MS 7*   125 rap *through* bind: greazy *through*
wreathed: head *MS 7*   their *through* theyre *MS A3*] her *MS 7*   126 she goes
MS 7   127 Which *through* &: when *through* as *MS 7*   128 F *through* W *in*
Fresh *MS A3*] With *MS 7*   131 & as when other papers scarce *MS 7*
132 To wipe some boobys sh–tt–n ar–e *MS 7*   143 Friendship *MS 7*
144 Fate: —why—so it] what lotted *MS 7*   145 Booky mind∧∧: wi thee∧ *MS 7*
146 Im *MS 7*   147 Hardships *underlined MS A3*   Hardships past] The strings
MS 7   148 [we] *inserted before* both: rise *over* [sink]: both must *over* [both must]
MS A3   Here both must either stand or fall *MS 7*

(Oh dear I shudder while I think
On expectations doubtful brink)   150
Tis thine to meet the learned now
Wi' scraping boot & bending bow
& tho in manners little read
Simple, shanny, lowly bred
Yet never mind push forward book   155
Worth will excuse thy clownish look
Thy vulgar faults wi' them's but small
Good breeding over looks it all
& as to merit ne'er despair
If merits thine—thoult find it there   160
Worth tho drest mean they'll still regard it
& if its thine they'll sure reward it
Then trace the City & the town
Look up in hopes to meet —renown!
Exalted stations never mind   165
When chances fall ne'er sneak behind
But if they'll condesend to hear
Do thou brush on & never fear
And prythee book I beg the[e] mind
When its thy luck a friend to find   170
When worth & learning comes to own thee
As thy best friend thourt al'a's known me
Dont let thy pride thy dad forsaking
Forget the trouble he's been taking
To get thee what thy luck has gotten   175
& then to leave me here forgotten

---

149 O *MS 7*   150 Expectations *MS 7*   152 Wi *MS 7*   ⟨bending bow⟩
torn MS A3   *Pencil note in margin:* Rest part / next week. *MS A3*   153 *Preceded in
MS A3 by:* Authors Address to his Book / Continued   155 Yet] But: mind] fear
MS 7   158 Good *through* Gla *MS A3*   over looks it] will oer look em *MS 7*
159 As to merit ⟨   ⟩ *hiatus MS 7*   160 Never in the least despair *MS 7*
161 Thy weakness they will neer regard thee *MS 7*   162 Mean as thou art they
besure reward thee *MS 7*   164 meet—renown! *(*renown! *underlined) MS A3*] find
renown *MS 7*   164/5 [Go never heed their occupation / Mind no degree nor]
MS A3   Never heed their occupation *MS 7*   165 Or of what exalted stations
MS 7   167 If they will but stoop to hear *MS 7*   they'll *through* thou will *MS A3*
168 Do thou brush] Brush thou *MS 7*   169 &: thee *MS 7*   beg *through* prey
MS A3   171–2 *Transposed MS 7*   174 trouble[s] *MS A3*   hes *MS 7*

—I'll trust thee Book—to friends petition
Nor make the best o' my condition

No never be asham'd to own it
Far better folks then I have known it   180
But tell em how thou left him moping
Thro oblivions darkness grouping
Still in its dark corner ryhmeing
& as usual ballad chyming
Wi' few ha'pence left to speed wi'   185
Poor & rag'd as beggars need be
—Money would be useful stuff
To the wise a hints enough
Then might we face every weather
Gogging hand in hand together   190
Tow'rds our Journeys end & aim
That fine place ycleped fame
May this be thine wi' all my heart
A Sigh still doubts it but depart
I've ga'e thee all as I can gie thee   195
So go & may good luck go wi' thee

Seek for the learned rich & great
They'll never mind thy Vulgar dress
& while I tremble for thy fate
I'll still have hopes of thy success   200

177 ∧Ill: book ∧ *MS 7*   178 Nor] Dont: o *MS 7*   180 Far *through* As: folks
through far: I *through* us *MS A3*   181 m *through* g *in* moping *MS A3*   185 to
inserted MS A3   187 Money *and* useful *underlined MS A3*   192 fine place
underlined MS A3   200 success. *underlined MS A3*   Followed *in pencil in MS A3*
by: Finished *and in ink by:* [Revd C. Mossop wishes you to send / him a few prospectuses
as soon as printed]

AUTOGRAPH: Pet. MS A3, pp. 127–8.
TRANSCRIPT: Pet. MS B1, pp. 163–4 (deleted).
Dated: '1819' (MS A3, p. 127).

HOME

Muses no more what ere ye be
   In fancys pleasures roam
But sing (by truth inspir'd) wi' me
   The pleasures of a home

Nor vain extreems I sigh for here   5
   No Lordlings costly dome
'Be thine the choice' says reason 'where
   'Contentment crowns a home'

O! fate to give my bosom peace
   Unsettl'd as I roam   10
To bid my restless wanderings cease
   & fix me in a home

A evening cot days toils to cheer
   When tir'd I ceas'd to roam
& lovley Ema smileing near   15
   O happy happy home

How oft the tramping Vagrant sighs
   (By fate ordain'd to roam)
For labours best & happiest joys
   The comforts of a home   20

& O when labour night descries
   When ceas'd to toil & roam
What joys will in his bosom rise
   To think he owns a home

HOME   *Title:* Home *MS A3*

How anxiously he leaves behind   25
   His labour & his care
His childern, wife, his home to find
   Their happiness to share

So when the Lark declines his flight
   Nor higher wills to flye   30
Grown faint & weary with the height
   & glad to leave the sky

How eager does he Eddy round
   To seek his peace & rest
& blest to know where peace is found   35
   Drops happy in his nest

Ah pleasures but in vain display'd
   My lot to discommode
Where hope but checkers up the shade
   To show my gloomy road   40

Alas to me no home belongs
   But what my dreams create
Vain Cuckoo like I sing my songs
   & leave the rest to fate

27 home *underlined MS A3*   35 [abounds] is found *MS A3*   44 fate.
MS A3   Followed in MS A3 by: [Last line] / [or this] / ['The rest is left to fate'] / [Just
as you think properest] *and* The last verse may be thus if you think it best you have your
choise

      Alas to me no home belongs
         But what my dreams create—
      So cuckoos sing their summer songs
         & leave the rest to fate

AUTOGRAPHS: Pet. MS A3, pp. 129–30: Nor. MS 7, p. 41 (ll. 1–16, 18–25 only).
TRANSCRIPTS: Pet. MS B1, pp. 6–7: Nor. MS 5, pp. 26–9 (ll. 29–37 omitted).
Printed in *RL*, pp. 98–102 (l. 27 omitted).
Dated: '1819' (MS A3, p. 129, *RL* Introduction, pp. xxii–xxiii 'In the last two years').

THE HARVEST MORNING

Cocks wake the early morn wi' many a Crow
Loud ticking village clock has counted four
The labouring rustic hears his restless foe
& weary bones & pains complaining sore
Hobbles to fetch his horses from the moor   5
Some busy 'gin to team the loaded corn
Which night throng'd round the barns becrouded door
Such plentious scenes the farmers yards adorn
Such busy bustling toils now mark the harvest morn

The birdboy's pealing horn is loudly blow'd   10
The waggons jostle on wi' rattling sound
& hogs & geese now throng the dusty road
Grunting & gabbling in contension round
The barley ears that litter on the ground—
What printing traces mark the waggons way   15
What busy bustling wakens echo round
How drives the suns warm beams the mist away
How labour sweats & toils & dreads the sultry day

THE HARVEST MORNING   *Title:* The Harvest Morning *MS A3 RL*, Harvest Morn *MS 7*   1 wi: crow *MS 7*   2 ticking] striking *RL*   4 complainning *MS 7*   And weary, of his pains . . . *RL*   6 Some busy 'gin] While some are left *MS 7*   7 Which night unfinishd left agen the door *MS 7*   8 yard *RL*   & bird boy scaring sounds his hollow horn *MS 7*   9 Such] What: toils] labouring scene *MS 7*   busy bustling] noisy, busy *RL*   10 Swift hies the waggon in the field to load *MS 7*   11 & wakes the early morn wi rattling sound *MS 7*   14 ear: litters: ground∧ *MS 7*   16 busy] dusty *RL*   What rural noises waken Echo round *MS 7*   17 drive *RL*   18 Poor labour sweating dread the sultry day *MS 7*

His scythe the mower oer his shoulder leans
& wetting jars wi' sharp & tinkling sound   20
Then sweeps again 'mong corn & crackling beans
& swath by swath flops lengthening oer the ground
While 'neath some friendly heap snug shelterd round
From spoiling sun lies hid their hearts delight
& hearty soaks oft hand the bottle round   25
Their toils pursuing with redoubl'd might
Refreshments cordial hail—
Great praise to him be due that brought thy birth to light

Upon the waggon now with eager bound
The lusty picker wirls the rustling sheaves   30
Or ponderous resting creaking fork aground
Boastful at once whole shocks o' barley heaves
The loading boy revengefull inly greaves
To find his unmatch'd strength & power decay
Tormenting horns his garments inter weaves   35
Smarting & sweating 'neath the sultry day
Wi' muttering curses stung he mauls the heaps away

A Motley group the Clearing field surounds
Sons of Humanity O neer deny
The humble gleaner entrance in your grounds   40
Winters sad cold & poverty is nigh
O grudge not providence her scant suply
You'll never miss it from your ample store—
Who gives denial harden'd hungry hound
May never blessings crow'd his hated door   45
But he shall never lack that giveth to the poor

---

19 His . . . mower] The mower scythe now *MS 7*   20 wettings *MS A3*   wi']
a: *second* &] shill *MS 7*   21 sweep: mong: crackling] rustling *MS 7*   23 &
neath some friendly heap the bottles found *MS 7*   24 their] the *RL*   Shelterd
securely from the spoiling sun *MS 7*   25 hands *MS A3*   & oft theyll take a
hearty soak around *MS 7*   28 be *through* is *MS A3*   thy] its *RL*   31 resting
ponderous *RL*   35 Tormenting horns] The barley horn *RL*   38 field[s]
MS A3   surrounds *altered to* surround *Harvard proof copy*] surround *RL 2nd edn.*
40 grounds *altered to* ground *Harvard proof copy*] ground *RL 2nd edn.*   41 are *RL*
42 Grudge not from Providence the scant supply *RL*   46 *Note:* Proverbs !!
MS A3

Ah lovley Ema mingling wi' the rest
Thy beauties blooming in low life unseen
Thy rosey cheeks thy sweetly swelling breast
But ill it suits thee in the stubs to glean   50
O poverty! how basely you demean
The imprison'd worth your rigid fates confine
Not fancied charms of an arcadian queen
So sweet as Emas real beauties shine
Had fortune blest sweet girl this lot had neer been thine   55

The suns increasing heat now mounted high
Refreshment must recruit exausted power
The waggon stops the busy tools thrown bye
& 'neath a shock's enjoy'd the beavering hour
The bashful maid—sweet healths engaging flower   60
Lingering behind—oer rake still blushing bends
& when to take the horn fond swains implore
With feign'd excuses its dislike pretends
So pass the beavering hours—So harvest morning ends

O rural life what charms thy meaness hide   65
What sweet descriptions bards disdain to sing
What Loves what Graces on thy plains abide
O could I soar me on the muses wing
What riffel'd charms should my researches bring
Pleas'd would I wander where these charms reside   70
Of rural sports & beauties would I sing
Those beauties wealth which you but vain deride
Beauties of richest bloom superior to your pride

59 beavering *underlined MS A3*   65 hide[s] *MS A3*   67 abide *through*
resides *MS A3*   72 but] in *RL*   73 pride. *MS A3*

AUTOGRAPHS: Pet. MS A3, p. 131: Pet. MS A40, p. 35.
TRANSCRIPTS: Pet. MS B1, p. 164: Nor. MS 5, pp. 169–70.
Dated: 'Old' (MS A3, p. 131).

IMPROMTU ON WINTER

O Winter what a deadly foe
Art thou unto the mean & low
What thousands now half-pind & bare
Are forcd to stand thy piercing air
All day neer numb'd to death wi' cold   5
Some petty Gentry to uphold
Paltry proudlings hard as thee
Dead to all humanity—
O the weathers cold & snow
Cutting winds that round me blow   10
But much more the killing scorn
—O the day that I was born
Friendless,—poor as I can be
Struck wi' death o' poverty
But why need I the winter blame   15
To me all seasons come the same
Now winter bares each field & tree
She finds that trouble sav'd in me
Stript already—pennyless!
Nothing boasting but distress   20
& when spring chill'd nature cheers
Still my old complaint she hears
Summer too in plenty blest
Finds me poor & still distrest
Kind Autumn too so liberal & so free   25
Brings my old well known present—'Poverty'

IMPROMTU ON WINTER   *Title:* Impromtu on Winter *(on through* in*) MS A3,*
Impromptu on Winter *MS A40*   1 winter *MS A40*   3 half-pind *underlined
and through* half starvd *MS A3*] half pined *MS A40*
5 near: with *MS A40*   6 gentry *MS A40*   7 the *to* thee *(p.e.) MS A40*
8 humanity∧ *MS A40*   12 ∧O *MS A40*   13 Friendless∧∧ *MS A40*
14 with: of *MS A40*   15 the *omitted MS A40*   16 To me *through*
Now *MS A3*   18 saved *MS A40*   19 already∧penny less∧ *MS A40*
21 chilled *MS A40*   25 autumn: so liberal &] of gifts *MS A40*   26 gift & *to*
well known *(p.e.) MS A3*] omitted *MS A40*   ∧∧poverty∧ *MS A40*

AUTOGRAPH: Pet. MS A4, pp. 6–7.
TRANSCRIPTS: Pet. MS B1, p. 117: Nor. MS 5, pp. 118–19.
Printed in *RL*, pp. 165–7.
Dated: '1818' (MS A4, p. 6, last figure altered from '7' to '8').

PATTY OF THE VALE

Where lonesome woodlands close surrounding
Marks the spot a solitude
& natures uncheck'd scenes abounding
Forms a prospect wild & rude
A cottage cheers the spot so glooming   5
Hid in the hollow of the dale
Where in youth & beauty blooming
Lives sweet Patty of the Vale

Gay as Lambs her cot surrounding
Sporting wild the shades among   10
Oer thy hill & bushes bounding
Artless inoscent & young
Fresh as blush of morning roses
Ere the mid day suns prevail
Fair—as lilly bud uncloses   15
Blooms sweet Patty of the Vale

Low & humble tho her station
Dress tho mean she's doom'd to wear
Few superiors in the nation
With her beauty can compare   20
What is Riches?—not worth naming
Tho with some they may prevail
Theirs be choise of wealth proclaiming
Mine is—Patty of the Vale

PATTY OF THE VALE   *Title:* Patty of the Vale *MS A4 RL*   2 Mark *RL*
4 Form *RL*   9 the lambs *RL*   11 thy hill] the hills *RL*   15 bud[s]
MS A4   16 vale *MS A4*   21 are *RL*

Fools may fancy wealth & fortune   25
Join to make a happy pair
& for such the God Importune
With full many a fruitless prayer
—I their pride & wealth disdaining
Should my humble hopes prevail   30
Happy then without complaining
Blest wi' Patty of the Vale

AUTOGRAPHS: Pet. MS A4, p. 21: Pet. MS A1, ff. 42^r–43^v (erased pencil, ll. 13–20 omitted, alternative version of ll. 29–32).
TRANSCRIPT: Pet. MS B1, pp. 68–9 (deleted).
Dated: '1819' (MS A4, p. 21).

SUPRESSION OF A SIGH

Why do I tread my wilds around
Where peace its silence wispers here
& not one comfort to be found
To wipe aside the falling tear

Why thus to mourn my fate severe   5
Why hope alas to hope in vain
I am no worse then erst I were
I was but poor & so remain

While others more distrest then I
Severer urg'd to mourn then me   10
Look up beyond the tear the sigh
& deem them foolish vanity

31 without] would cease *RL*

SUPRESSION OF A SIGH   *Title:* Supression of a Sigh *MS A4, wanting MS A1*
1 tread] trace *MS A1*   2 its . . . here *below* [might blos] *MS A4*   Where
Comforts blooming so wild so dear *MS A1*   5 thus to] do I: sever *MS A1*
7 where *MS A1*   8 was *through* were *MS A4*   10 urgd *MS A1*

Yon wreck of many a famish'd week
That only begs to be deny'd
A smile still prints this beggars cheek   15
& sorrows tear is wip'd aside

There tied to family & wife
Does labour bear wants chilling frown
Still the rough edge of Irksome life
Contentment smoothly evens down   20

Yon pair of birds that weary roam
Have far more cause to grieve then I
Their rest is gone—their peaceful home
Could not escape the schoolboys eye

Their sorrow still its toil resumes   25
& of their loss they make the best
They chirp again & smooth their plumes
& painful build another nest

No nest have they from night to hide
Then fool to think that I alone   30
The killing frowns of fate abide
While Ive a cot to call my own

Poor bee that labours hard the hour
In hopes to find some honied store
Vainly peeps in each rifl'd flower   35
To prove its sweets was robd before

---

15 this *through* that *MS A4*   18 Does *through* Where *MS A4*   23 Their egs
are gone & peaceful home *MS A1*   rest is *over* [eggs are] *MS A4*   24 Coud:
schoolboys] ploughmans *MS A1*   28/9 [This bee that] *MS A4*
29–32   Then fool to think that I alone
                          Of all that lives have cares to sigh
                          That 〈   〉 but 〈   〉 to my own
                          & noone so distrest as I   *MS A1 alternative*
                                                                       version, f. 43ʳ

32 a cot *to* that peace *(p.e., not Clare's) MS A4*   33 [That] Poor *MS A4*] That
MS A1   34 some] hs: honyd *MS A1*   35 each] the *MS A1*   rif[f]l'd
MS A4] rifld *MS A1*   36 sweet is as *altered to* sweets was *MS A4*   & finds his
sweets was won before *MS A1*

Yet still his toil his hopes recruits
& on he hums till setting sun—
O god thou knowst my station suits
& as thou wilt—thy will be done   40

Toil on poor bee companion sweet
Live on vain world thy joys are small
Compar'd to those I hope to meet
From God my peace, my hope, my all!

AUTOGRAPHS: Pet. MS A11, p. 11a: Pet. MS A4, p. 21.
TRANSCRIPT: Pet. MS B1, pp. 69–70.
Dated: '1819' (MS A4, p. 21).

THE RECANTATION

Tho false virtue disaproves thee—
Whats the harm the world wont raise
Nor conscerns it him who loves thee
Thus believing all she says
Now that ruins foes infest thee   5
Now thourt most in need of friends
Who so right as now to help thee
Who but him who thus pretends

Coud their lies urge me to slight thee
Seeming worth to dissaprove   10
Coud thy sorrow then delight me
Thus to hurt the maid I love

37 Another stay his hopes recruits *MS A1*   38 As on he works & hopes the best
MS A1   40 So Ill betake me to my rest *MS A1*   43 Compard *MS A1*
44 From god my hope my peace my all *MS A1*

   THE RECANTATION *Title:* The Recantation *MS A11,* The Recantation /
To Myra Scandilizd / After crediting the Report *MS A4   Stanzas numbered Ver 1–4
in MS A4*   1 dissaproves thee∧ *MS A4*   2 wi'n't *through* wont *MS A4*
3 concerns: it *inserted*: who] that *MS A4*   4 T' believe all slander says *MS A4*
5 Now that] While thus: infect *MS A4*   6 Now *inserted*: [While] thou'rt *MS A4*
8 Who—: thus] so *MS A4*   9 Could *MS A4*   10 Seeming] Such provd
MS A4   11 Would: sorrows: then] thus *MS A4*   12 hurt] wrong *MS A4*

Listning them O coud I leave thee
Nearest friend & foulest foe
So pretend & then decieve thee   15
Coud I do it—never—no

Fains the base that joy to blame thee
Wish thou bad as them shoud seem
First are such who woud defame thee
Glad to undermine esteem   20
Why shoud I then—but defy it
Why let slanders tongue deceive
When no proof can justify it
Who so foolish to believe

While rose sweets the canker draws on't   25
While we see the poisonous power
Little gardners doubt the cause ont
They but wish to save the flower
Bud while cankerworms surround thee
Joyd to wait thy overthrow   30
Ere my added scorn coud wound thee
My repentance shares thy woe

---

13 could *MS A4*   14 Join'd with them become thy foe *MS A4*   15 So
pretend] Vow so true *MS A4*   16 Can *MS A4*   17 Fain *MS A4*   joy *over*
[wish] *MS A11*] hope *MS A4*   18 should *MS A4*   19 who] to *MS
A11*   Such are these that would defame thee *MS A4*   20 under mine *MS A4*
20/1 [What should I do but def] *MS A4*   21 should *MS A4*   then—but] but
what? *MS A11*   22 Nor let slander thus decieve *MS A4*   23 When]
Where: proofs: i *through* y in justify *MS A4*   24 to] as *MS A4*   25 While]
When: rose': ont *MS A4*   26 While] When: pois'nous *MS A4*   see *over* [prove]
MS A11   27 gardners *below* [need we] *MS A11*] need we *MS A4*   28 [While
we] *over* They *MS A11*] While we *MS A4*   but wish] hope *MS A4*   29 Bud—:
canker worms *MS A4*   30 Joy'd: over throw *MS A4*   31 could *MS A4*
32 Repentance: woe. *MS A4*   share's *MS A11*

AUTOGRAPH: Pet. MS A5, p. 1 (pencil).
Dated: 1819–20 (MS A5, p. 43 inscribed 'John Clare / Helpstone / 1820').

O gentle star so placidly
That brings the news of pearly even
The first of all the arching sky
To whom the glinting light is given

O gentle star I hope to view   5
Thy bright eye smile the lonly lee
Reflecting in a globe of dew
Thy silver light is dear to me

O gentle herald thee I hail
Thou tellst the glaring day is gone   10
O coudst thou bring a better tale
From one sweet cot thourt shining on

AUTOGRAPH: Pet. MS A5, p. 5.
Dated: 1819–20 (MS A5).

Closly confind among humdruming wheels
Wi surly old mother & grumping old gran
If I tek a step out why theyr close at one[s] heels
For fear I shoud stan in the way of a man

Where are ye going now high the winds blowing   5
& night creeps apase on yer dark gloomy road
What do ye seek for I long to be knowing
Taent fit sich a young thing shoud wander abroad
Confind all the day to my humdruming wheel
Not even alowd to peep ater a man   10
I put on my bonnet & out I did steal
From sour scolding mamy & old grumping gran

O GENTLE STAR SO PLACIDLY   *Title: wanting*   1 placid ly
4/5 *No stanza division*   9 thee I hail *through* even star
CLOSLY CONFIND AMONG HUMDRUMING WHEELS   *Title: wanting*
8 fi[s]t   10 [dar] even

& what do ye mean then my young roving lilly
& who do ye seek then my dew dropping rose
If yell take a walk wi yer wife wanting billy 15
Ill near do a harm to yer person or clo'hs

AUTOGRAPH: Pet. MS A5, p. 6.
Dated: 1819–20 (MS A5).

Ye promisd me mary last michaelmas fair
As how yed be mine—that ye woud
& to buy ye a wreath Id but sixpence to spare

AUTOGRAPHS: Pet. MS A5, p. 7: Pet. MS A1, f. 45ʳ⁻ᵛ (erased pencil, deleted).
TRANSCRIPTS: Nor. MS 4, pp. 37–8: Pet. MS C2, p. 44.
Printed in *RL*, p. 204.
Dated: 1819 (MS A5, *RL*).

TO RELIGION

Thou sacred light that right from wrong discerns
Thou safe guard of the soul—thou heaven on Earth
Thou under valluer of the worlds concerns
Thou disreguard of all its joys & mirth

16 Aye *below* Ill

YE PROMISD ME MARY LAST MICHAELMAS FAIR   *Title: wanting*

TO RELIGION   *Title:* To Religion MS A5 RL   *Preceded in MS A5 by:*

To Religion

[Thou safe guard of the soul—thou heaven on Earth
Thou sacred light that right from wrong discerns
Thou undervaluer of this mortal birth
Thou disregard to all this worlds concerns]

1–2 *Transposed MS A1*   1 descerns *MS A1*   2 thou ... Earth] of heavenl⸱
birth *MS A1*   3 Neglect & undervaluer of the earth *MS A1*   4 disregar⸱
MS A1   disregard of all *to* disregarder of *(p.e., Clare) MS C2*] disregarder of *R⸱*
joys & mirth] vain conscerns *MS A1*

Thou only home the housless wanderers have   5
Thou prop by which the pilgrims woes are born
Thou peace thou comfort of the hermits cave
That beds him down to rest on fates rude thorn
Thou only hope to sorrows bosom given
Thou voice of mercy when the weary call   10
Thou faith extending to thy home in heaven
Thou peace thou rest thou comfort all in all
My end & aim & guidance must thou be
My crutch to prop me to Eternity

AUTOGRAPHS: Pet. MS A5, pp. R9–R8 (l. 53 omitted, ll. 65–70 pencil):
Pet. MS A1, ff. 34ᵛ–37ᵛ (ll. 1–5, 16–25, 31–65 only, erased pencil), f. 1ʳ
(fragment, erased pencil).
TRANSCRIPTS: Nor. MS 4, pp. 36–7: Pet MS C2, pp. 43–4.
Dated: 1819–20 (MS A5, MS A1).

MIDNIGHT

(a)

The day has clos'd its weary toils in bed
The clouds gloom sleeping on the mountains head
Nor noise nor sound is heard as hushd as dead
Silence most awful pause as on I tread
    The wild wood Silently   5

6 Thou propt up burthen of the Pilgrims woes *MS A1*   7 Thou solace of the
lonely hermit's cave *RL*   8 That makes its bed upon the thorn *MS A1*   rude]
sharp *RL*   11 Thou faith that reaches to the ⟨promisd⟩ heaven *MS A1*
12 *Second* thou] & *MS A1*   13 & *through* my *twice*: guidance . . . be *below*
[substance must thou be] *MS A5*   guidance] substance *MS A1*   O sovereign good!
on thee all hopes depend *RL*   14 To hold the promise of Eternity *MS A1*] Till thy
grand source unfolds its realizing end *RL   Followed in pencil in MS A5 by:* Return
the Paper when done with as it is a scarce Article with me / Or thus 'O propping crutch
on thee all hopes depend / Till thy grand sounding ⟨mo⟩ralizing end' *torn*

    MIDNIGHT   *Title:* Midnight *MS A5, wanting MS A1   Preceded upside down in
MS A1 by:* Bridge Casterton / Rutland   1 closd *MS A1*   2 glooms sleepy
MS A1   4 pauses *MS A1*   5 *Deleted in pencil by Clare in MS C2*   silently
MS A1

Awful indeed it is to wander now
As not a sound is heard but save as how
Silence is ruffl'd by the parting bough
Stilling agen more dread as past it now
    It rests most silently   10

Awful indeed it is in lonliest place
The forming dew drops melted birth to trace
As sauntering doubtful oer a fearful pace
Its misty moisture chillys on my face
    Falling so silently   15

Midnight is deep indeed awfully deep
The world so busy once all lost asleep
Nor flies a bird nor inscet cares to creep
Ones thoughts their drowsy sabbath even keep
    Musing so silently   20

Awful indeed it is to think that I
In these deep woods & dark black dismal skye
Of all the world am left with unclosd eye
To tread the lonly wood & think & sigh
    Creeping most silently   25

Awful indeed it is to hear as now
A sudden rustle from the oaks dark bough
& night hawks shriek most terrible as how
It stills again & solemn longer now
    I pause most silently   30

Awful indeed it is to catch the sight
Of trav'lling glow worms with their lanthorn light
Twinkling its circling rings of glimmering light
Peeping upon the solemn gloom of night
    Fearful & silently   35

15 *Deleted in pencil by Clare in MS C2*   so *over* [most] *MS A5*   18 Inscet *MS A1*
19 their: drowsy] slumbering *MS A1*   even *to* Even *(p.e., Clare) MS C2*
20 Museing: silently] etc. *MS A1*   25 *Deleted in pencil by Clare in MS C2*
silently] etc *MS A1*   29 longer *could be read as* langor *for 'langour' MS A5*
31 sight] sighs *MS A5*   33 Circling in glimmering 〈   〉 twinkling bright
MS A1   34 Upon the awful gloom of deep midnight *MS A1*

& awful ah most awfully it seems
As when the horrid owl deaths token screams
Stooping beneath some abby[s] massy beams
As thro the grated tower the moonshine gleams
    On bones heapd silently   40

Solemn it is the castles Tower to climb
Winding its stony steps around sublime
Clocks soloquising oer their ticking time
Swords rusting oer with many a hidden crime
    Hung pondering silently   45

How hushd the pause nights stopping breath detains
This night peace who can miniature that reigns
The stops that dozes in the forest grains
Then stills their qualms a night song ill explains
    So rapt so silently   50

How deep the shades that cringes to the hill
The church bell strikes fear counts & shudders chill
& terrors highest pitch his fears instill
Listening he drops the twelve more loudly shrill
    & gen stops silently   55

Midnight! dread thing & can a word unfold
The glooms & shades the fearful eyes behold
We say 'as nature sleeps' & have we told
That dead suspence in nights black robes enroll'd
    Hovering so silently   60

36 & awful ah] Awful it is: it seems *below* [indeed] *MS A1*   37 when] while
MS A1   38 Stooping] Swooping: abbeys mossy *MS A1*   39 moon shine
MS A1   42/3 [When clocks on watch tick] *MS A1*   44 with *over* [in] *MS A5*]
wi *MS A1*   45 Lye Pondering Silently *MS A1*   *Followed upside down in MS A1*
by: While distant clocks sololoquise the hours / While midnights deepest   46 How
hushd the] Awful that: detaines *MS A1*   47 piece *MS A5 MS A1*   minature
MS A1   48 doses: forrest *MS A1*   50 Musing so Silently *MS A1*
51 hill[s] *MS A1*   52 chill *MS A1*] still *MS A5*   53 *Copy-text: MS A1*
54 Listening he] & listning: twelve more loudly] twelfth stroke loud & *MS A1*
56 *Preceded in MS A1 by:*

    As likest will it be to midnight dread
    When grey beard sextons scooping earthly bed
    & dust to dust resigns thy aching head
    Midnight its long long glooms have fled
      In musing silently   5

Midnight∧ *MS A1*   58 as] all *MS A1*   59 suspense: enrold *MS A1*

How solemn doubly solemn is the scene
Nights twelve when counted off—its intervene
Dead hour that dozes twelve & one between
No blank in chaos ere the world had been
    Was lost more silently   65

While deepest night upon the ruins glower
& fear counts trembling on the midnight hour
That distant clocks soloquises oer
O terrors highest pitch who feels thy power
    Of midnight Silently   70

AUTOGRAPH: Pet. MS A40, pp. 41a–42.
Dated: 1819–1820 or subsequently (MS A5, MS A1).

VERSES ON MIDNIGHT MADE DURING A JOURNEY

(b)

The day hath closed its weary toils abed
The clouds gloom deep on natures sleeping head
Nor noise nor sound is heard all hushd and dead
Silence most awful pauses as I tread
    This wild woods dismal gloom   5

63 one] 1 *MS A1*   64 [th] in *MS A5*   67 on *through* out *MS A5*   *Followed*
in *MS A5 by:*

    Where swords & spears the remnants of old time
    Perchance all rusted by some hidden crime

(l. 1 swords *over* [?belts]: the *inserted*; ll. 1/2 [Rusted] swords (Rusted *through* ?Old))

The following lines in MS A1, f. 1ʳ may be connected with this poem:

    The clouds slow mounting
    The slanting sun its solemn
    & on the
    Now silently
    The curving   5

    VERSES ON MIDNIGHT MADE DURING A JOURNEY   *Title:* Verses on
Midnight made during a Journey

Midnight is deep indeed awfully deep
The world so busy once all lost asleep
Nor flies a bird nor insect cares to creep
Even ones thoughts a drowsy sabbath keep
    And makes the heart their tomb   10

Awful the darkness thro the wild woods spread
A drowsy stillness oer their leaves prevade
Just stirring their dull mass of horrid shade
As if they trembled at the noise they made
    And dare not stir again   15

Awful indeed it is to hear it now
That sudden rustle from the oaks dark bough
As shrieks the night hawk loud—but hushed and low
It stills again and midnights musings now
    In their still fears remain   20

How dismal seems the thought to think that I
In this deep wood and dark black dismal sky
Of all the world am left with unclosed eye
Treading the lonly wood to think and sigh
    In startling fears alarm   25

Yet soothing now it is in this lone place
The forming dewdrops melting birth to trace
As sauntering doubtful on in fearful pace
Its misty moisture chilleth on my face
    A soft refreshing calm   30

And soothing woud it be to catch the sight
Of traveling glow worms with their lanthorns bright
Twinkling their circling rays of glimmering light
Like dewdrops filled with fire to cheer the night
    But all is dark as death   35

9 drowsy *through* dismal   12 their leaves *through* my eye   32 light *altered to* bright

And e'en to eke the terror fancy dreams
Of stooping neath some abbys massy beams
Down Isles in ruins while the white owl screams
And some dim dying lamp above head gleams
    To show the tombs beneath   40

Or up some rugged castles towers sublime
Winding along its stoney steps to climb
Were swords and speers the remnants of old time
Perchance all rusted by some hidden crime
    Each dismal corner fills   45

While deepest night upon the ruins glower
And fear seems counting oer the midnight hour
Told by the old clock in its rifted tower
O highest pitch of terror fancys power
    At her own picture chills   50

Midnight dread thing and can a word unfold
The gloom and shades the fearful eyes behold
Thoughts say 'all nature sleeps' but have they told
That dread suspence in nights black robe enrolled
    And fears dread history   55

That solemn deadly solemn awful scene
Nights twelve just counted off its intervene
Dead hour that slumbers twelve and one between
No blank in chaos ere the world had been
    Was lost more silently   60

38 Isles *through* ruind   55 history[s]

AUTOGRAPH: Pet. MS A5, p. 10 (ll. 29–36 pencil), p. 7 (ll. 29–36 only).
TRANSCRIPT: Nor. MS 4, p. 38 (ll. 1–10 only, deleted).
Printed in *RL*, pp. 147–50 (ll. 13–14 omitted).
Dated: 1817–19 (*RL* Introduction, pp. xxii–xxiii 'In the last two years').

DAWNING OF GENIUS

Genius a pleasing rapture of the mind
A kindling warmth to Learning unconfin'd
Glows in each breast & flutters every vein
From arts Refinements to th'unculter'd swain
Such is that warmth the lowly shepherd proves   5
Pacing his native fields & willow Groves
Such is that joy which every scene unfolds
Which taste endeareth & fond memory holds
Such is that sympathy his heart attends
Makes bush & tree companions seem & friends   10
Such is that fondness from his soul sincere
That makes his native place so doubly dear
The sparks of genius Ignorance conceals
Gleams forth to relish what his Bosom feels
In those low paths which poverty surounds   15
The rough rude ploughman of his fallow grounds
Those nessascery tools of wealth & pride
While moild & sweating by some pasture side
How oft he'll stoop inquisitive to trace
The opening beauties of a daiseys face   20
& often witness with admiring eyes
The brooks sweet dimples oer the pebbles rise
& often bent as oer some magic spell
Hell pause & pick his shaped stone & shell

DAWNING OF GENIUS *Title:* Dawning of Genius *MS A5*, Dawnings of Genius *RL* 3 & flutters] flutters in *RL* 4 refinement *RL* 5 Such] Hence *RL* 7 Such] Hence: which] when *RL* scene unfolds] *successively (a)* [scene can give unfolds] *(b)* [prospect moves] *(c)* scene unfolds *MS A5* 8 endears: fond] latest *RL* holds *through* loves *MS A5* 9 Such] Hence *RL* 10 Makes] When *RL* 11 Such] Hence *RL* 14 Bosom *through* age *MS A5* 16 off *RL* 17 Those] That: tool *RL* 18 pasture's *RL* 19 How oft he'll] Will often *RL* 21 & often] Oft will he *RL*

Raptures the while his inward powers inflame   25
& joys delight him which he cannot name
Ideas picture pleasing views to mind
For which his language can no utterance find
Increasing beauties fresh'ning on his sight
Unfold new charms & witness more delight   30
So while the present please the last decay
& in each [other] loosing melt away
Thus pausing wild on all he saunters by
He feels enrapturd tho he knows not why
& hums & mutters oer his joys in vain   35
& dwells on somthing which he cant explain
The bu[r]sts of thought with which his souls perplext
Are bred one moment & are gone the next
Yet still the heart will kindling sparks retain
& thoughts will rise & fancy strive again   40
(So have I markt the dying embers light
When on the hearth it fainted from my sight
A Glimmering glow oft redens up again
& sparks crack bright'ning into light in vain)
Still lingering out its kindling hopes to rise   45
Till faint & fainter the last twinkle dies
Vain burns the soul & throbs the fluttering heart
Their painfull pleasing feelings to impart
Till by successless sallies wearied quite
The memory fails & fancy takes her flight   50
The wickett nipt within its socket dies
Born down & smother'd in a thousand sighs

29 freshning MS A5, p. 7   30 Unfolds MS A5, p. 7   31 last] past RL
32 And: Melt MS A5, p. 7   each losing MS A5, p. 7] each other losing RL
34 enraptur'd tho' MS A5, p. 7   35 And: o'er MS A5, p. 7   36 & dwells
below [Fallen] MS A5   And: something: can't MS A5, p. 7
36/7   As others please anew the last decay
              So in each other lost they melt away
              [What the heart feels the tongue cannot explain]
              Humming & muttering namless joys in vain
              What warms the heart his songs but ill explain   5   MS A5

37 thought below [bliss]: whith MS A5   41 flight altered to light MS A5
43 A] With RL   redens through readnd MS A5] redden RL   44 crack[t] MS A5]
crack'd RL   light] life RL   45 hope RL   46 fainter] fainting RL
47 Vain] Dim RL   48 Its RL   painffull MS A5   51 wickett nipt] wick
confin'd RL

AUTOGRAPH: Pet. MS A5, p. 12.
TRANSCRIPTS: Nor. MS 4, p. 52: Pet. MS C2, p. 51.
Dated: 1819–20 (MS A5).

THE ANCIENT HEROE

Not with the nodding feathers modern pride
Or gilded swordcase dangling by his side
Or fringed shoulder nott or blazing star
Was bravery born the triumph of the war
But naked to the winds & dreary plain   5
Save wrapt in Skins his infant hands had slain
The hard young hero first appeard in sight
When David met the giants in the fight
With all the war armd soldiers vengance stung
The spear like thrust was dealt & stone he flung   10
& were the unskilful war the hottest came
His young unpractisd valour made its aim
While victory haild him not by thousands slain
But dauntless valour which the brave mentain
As beetling rocks wears the waves vengance out   15
His steady stands no shocks coud put to rout
The onset of the fight the last retir'd
The bright example which his followers fir'd
& each young Hero his rude weapon plied
With all a Soldiers valour by his side   20
& when beat down beneath a stronger foe
His feeble hands still turnd its vengful blow
Lookd up on braverys face for vengance sighd
& strove to rise & graspd his stick & dy'd

THE ANCIENT HEROE   *Title:* The Ancient Heroe *MS A5*   8 moses *MS*
A5] Moses *to* David *(p.e., Clare) MS C2*   10 was dealt *through* has made *MS A5*
11 i *in* unskilful *inserted MS A5*   15 wear[s] *(p.e., Clare) MS C2*   21 stronger
foe *over* [thrust or blow] *MS A5*

AUTOGRAPH: Pet. MS A5, p. 12 (deleted).
Dated: 1819–20 (MS A5).

> Lost on the wild to the Storms biting breath
> That thro her rags winnow so chill
> All torn by the brambles & furze on the heath
> & beat by the storm on the naked blea hill
> A shade of the human form daily appears   5
> The wild ecchos oft with her yell

AUTOGRAPH: Pet. MS A5, p. R12.
TRANSCRIPT: Nor. MS 4, p. 53: Pet. MS C2, p. 51a.
Dated: 1819–20 (MS A5).

> Wants yet on every side as deep suround me
> & still deny life bettering sun to shine
> & thou sweet bud wears sharpest thorns to wound me
> Since every beauty every witcheries thine
> To bind in triple ties this heart for ever   5
> & every want & woe & sorrow mine
> With contradicting force that tie to sever
> Lifes storms may wreck but hope shall leave thee never
> Towering far oer what bars my bliss from me
> Where wants foul hinderance owns no worldly power   10
> But freedom opening on equallity
> Gives fre[e] acess to crop thy Virgin flower
> Ah then like werter tho lifes joys we miss
> Our wreckt desires shall meet in heavens eternal bliss

LOST ON THE WILD TO THE STORMS BITING BREATH   *Title: wanting*
WANTS YET ON EVERY SIDE AS DEEP SUROUND ME   *Title: wanting MS A5*
6 w *though* y *in* woe *MS A5*   11 d *through* m *in* freedom *MS A5*   12 fre *inserted*
MS A5   14 m⟨ee⟩t *torn MS A5*

AUTOGRAPH: Pet. MS A5, p. 20.
Dated: 1819–20 (MS A5).

Violet—thou art a lovly blossom
In early spring time purpling on my eye
Most snugly seated in the woods warm bosom
Neath budding brambles sheltering canophy
Untoucht by frowning tempest howling high   5
Their terrors thro the oak twigs melting green
That bows the daisey down upon the green
& threatens much the cowslaps trembling flow[er]s
Thou ere dwelst peacful in thy lonly scene
Thy oaks high towering & thy hazel bowers   10
Thou lowly hermit flower of Solitude
Thou plainly tellst a lesson unto me
The naked hill bears all the tempest rude
That wind decends to touch such thing as thee

AUTOGRAPH: Pet. MS A5, p. 32.
Dated: 1819–20 (MS A5).

Tis sweet to view as on we pass
Foot pads bending thro the grass
Leading to a thatched cot
In a sweet sequesterd spot
Side a wood or side a brook   5
Or pend snugly in a nook
Or left carless on a lea
Where the drooping willow tree
Friendly backs the roof behind
Keeping off the northern wind   10
There we think that peace abounds
Tracking sweet the cotters rounds
Rising as the mornings rise
Soon as dawn streaks red the skyes

VIOLET—THOU ART A LOVLY BLOSSOM *Title: wanting*

TIS SWEET TO VIEW AS ON WE PASS *Title: wanting*   14 *Followed by:*
[In his own small fields]

AUTOGRAPH: Pet. MS A5, p. 49.
Dated: 1819–20 (MS A5).

TO THE NIGHTINGALE

Ah eve lov'd bird how sweet thy music floats
E'en hodge fine musics vulgar tasteles foe
Entirely thoughtless where's he's got to go
Stands struck with wonder at thy varied notes
Untill a pause ensuing brings to mind   5
His work at which he starts but touch'd so strong
Rememb'rance makes him as he plods along
Sing 'Sweet jug, jug,' and often look behind
To where they first begun—then such as these
O bird again repeat and let me know   10
If they (which do so much with others please)
Can sooth in me this anguish more than woe
For sure no anguish more tormenting stings
Then that which vexing dissapointment brings

AUTOGRAPH: Pet. MS A6, pp. 9–10.
Dated: 1819–20 (MS A6).

TO THE MEMORY OF JAMES MERRISHAW
A VILLAGE SCHOOLMASTER

What no plain stone? to court the strangers eye
No mournful strain to heave the tender sigh
Is not one record left? to mark the spot
Where thou art laid; or is thy name forgot
All! All! are lost, All perish'd in the tomb   5
And black oblivion triumphs oer thy doom
Ah! tho no careless muse one tribute gave
Nor cast one flowret on thy injur'd grave

TO THE NIGHTINGALE   *Title:* To the nightingale   6 work.
TO THE MEMORY OF JAMES MERRISHAW A VILLAGE SCHOOLMASTER
Title: To the Memory of James Merrishaw A Village Schoolmaster

Thy worth shall never die; while life remains
And health and memory their course sustains   10
While the blest vissitants attend my frame
I'll never cease to tell, thy worthy name
Tho weak my genius which would fain attone
To make thy memory and thy virtues known
Tho mean the lay to what thy worth requires   15
'Yet naught is vain which gratitude inspires'
'Tis she that bids my artless muse pursue
Her lowly flight & give the tribute due
Due to thy worth thy memory and thy grave
For thou it was dear injur'd Man that gave   20
This little Learning which I now enjoy
A Gift so dear that nothing can destroy
T'was thou that taught my infant years to scan
The various evils that encompas man
Twas thou that taught my eager breast to shun   25
Those vain pursuits where thousands are undone
And if such choise Examples I decline
Then Shame belongs to me:—the praise is thine
This he has done for me:—Then rise my soul
Above the littlenes of lifes controul   30
Mind not what Booklearnt men or Critics say
Thine is the debt—and be it thine to pay

AUTOGRAPH: Pet. MS A6, pp. 18–19.
Dated: 1819–20 (MS A6).

AN ACT OF CHARITY!!!

At H[elpsto]n town O rariety
What mighty acts of charity
Performing are—but chiefly one
The which we mean to treat upon
Bestow'd by that—but halt awhile   5
Such gifts require a loftier stile

AN ACT OF CHARITY!!!   *Title:* An act of Charity!!!   1 H————n: O *through* o
15 too

In these uncommon things I trow
'Bestow'd' will sound a note too low
Then haste ye muse's haste away
And all your lofty sounds convey   10
Ransack your far-fam'd temple's oer
Bring musick never heard before
For sure such noble deeds require
Immortal hands to sound the lyre
But now a lucky thought pops in   15
Which makes high metaphors run thin
Methinks while thus invokins flow
My anxious reader longs to know
The Gift I sing 'Bless us' quoth he
'Who can the great donator be'   20
'For sure it must if I can read'
'Be more than charity indeed'
'If so; why need he sue for aid'
'For "lofty sounds" or rich brocade'
'Blest Charity!! her self illumnes'   25
'Nor wants high "sounds" nor borrow'd plumes'
'She is a subject so divine'
'That nought on earth can brighter shine'

AUTOGRAPH: Pet. MS A6, p. 21.
Dated: 1819–20 (MS A6).

EPIGRAM ON LONDON

Ocasioned by Reading Mr Rolts Translation of
Sannazario's (Famous) Epigram
on Venice

Sannazar was a fool when he exclaim'd
That only men built Rome, and Gods fine Venice fram'd
For surely if we give old rome her due
She must be call'd the grandest of the two

16 thin.   28 hearth
   EPIGRAM ON LONDON   *Title:* Epigram on London / Ocasioned by reading (Mr Rolts Translation of) / Sannazario's (Famous) Epigram / On Venice

Or why does History yield to her the praise?   5
In Architecture, Arts, and Laureat Bays
And must this be lookt oer in modern days?
That would be wrong indeed intirely wrong
To loose Vitruvious or a Virgil's song
But we may stop,—with Venice &c   10
For had he took Excursions further North
He'd found a City grander then 'em both
More skilld in Architectural Arts to build
More skilld in Arms to conquor in the field
Nay if Venice was fram'd so:—the only odds!   15
Is:—that London was fram'd by better men than gods!!

AUTOGRAPH: Pet. MS A6, pp. 22–3.
Dated: 1819–20 (MS A6).

LUBIN & COLLIN

A Pastoral

Collin

Come Lubin let us leave this maple tree
Or we shall soon be dripping wet I see
E'en now (so thin the straggling branches spread)
The rain begins to patter on my head

Lubin

With all my heart for I could wish to gain   5
Our poor old hut that stands beside the plain
For see yon black'ning cloud begins to lower
And that loud hissing speaks a heavier shower
The sooner the better we get there I know
Then no more parley I'lle this instant go   10

LUBIN & COLLIN   *Title:* Lubin & Collin / A Pastoral   2 dropping *altered to*
dripping   5 with *altered to* wish

Collin

Running so hard has put me out of breath
But I dont care so long as I'm beneath
This welcome hut once more—for now beguy
Rain e're so hard my shelter keeps me dry
Bring that shift tray & place it for a door   15
And strew that bunche of rushes on the floor
I'll sit me down and con my lesson well
For I have got a pleasant tale to tell
And something on your side ——

Lubin

———————— why have you tho?   20
Then I dont care how soon you let me know

Collin

I mean to tell you all I've heard & seen
Since I've been keeping sheep upon the green
Whether by chance or how I cannot tell
Before I never speeded half so well   25
When going along one day to shift my penn
Some time last week but now I can't say when

Lubin

Well never mind the day nor when nor where
Tell me the tale that's all I whant to hear

Collin

Then you must know as I was going along   30
List'ning attentive to the woodlarks song
I heard or thought I h[e]ard a cheering sound
Come sweetly breathing oer the fallow ground
So soft so graceful did the tones combine
Young Thenot's piping ne'er was half so fine   35
Away I brush't inquisitive to know
From whence & where such Melody could flow
But when on coming near about the spot
The sounds where vanish'd & the song was not

11 heard

Lubin

Aye how was that—it should be something quere   40
To hear far off and lose the sound when near
Twas fancy sure—but never mind what past
The heads give now and tell the substance last

AUTOGRAPH: Pet. MS A6, p. 39.
Dated: 1819–20 (MS A6).

IMPROMTU ON THE BATTLE OF ALEXANDRIA IN EGYPT

In one accord they shout with anxious breath
We fight! We fight! for Victory or death
Their halloo rends the vaulted skies
Their thundering Cannons sound
Away the frighted fre[n]chmen flies   5
By britons Courage drownd

AUTOGRAPH: Pet. MS A6, p. 40.
Dated: 1819–20 (MS A6).

SONG

I

Come lovley Jenny haste away
Quickly come make no delay
Come & view these sweetful flowers
Nurs'd by Aprils softest showers
Haste & greet their happy shade   5
Soon they'l wither soon they'l fade
Then haste my dearest haste away
Come & taste the sweets of May

IMPROMTU ON THE BATTLE OF ALEXANDRIA IN EGYPT *Title:*
Impromtu on the Battle of Alexandria in Egypt

SONG   *Title:* Song   1–8 *Against the first stanza Clare has written:* s & last. v——

2

Lovley sweets that never cloy
Happiest hours that yield to joy   10
Hedgerows dappl'd green & white
Look so graceful to the sight
Meadows cloth'd in yellow hue
Banks streak'd oer with vi'lets hue
Yet their charms will soon decay   15
Soon they'l fade & dye away

3

Then lovley Jenny haste away
Quickly come make no delay
Come & view these sweetful flowers
Nurs'd by Aprils softest showers   20
Haste & greet their happy shade
Soon they'l wither soon they'l fade
Then haste my dearest haste away
Come & taste the sweets of May

14 n *in* Banks *inserted*   15 these *altered to* their: [sweet] charms   16 *Through*
Then haste my dearest haste away   19 sweetful *through* pre *(for ? 'pretty')*

AUTOGRAPHS: Yale University Library Osborn Collection 206/6. In a letter to ? Drury dated in Taylor's hand 'About 20 Decr 1819': Pet. MS A8, pp. R32–R31 (deleted, ll. 9–16 omitted, pencil): Pet. MS A8, p. R33 (deleted): Pet. MS A8, pp. R42–R40 (deleted, pencil): Pet. MS A8, p. 1 (ll. 13–16 only).
Printed in *RL*, Introduction, pp. xxiii–xxiv: *Stamford Mercury*, 21 January 1820 (reprinted from *RL*): Catnach broadside, n.d., facsimile in *Deacon*, p. 65 (*C*). Dated: mid-1819 (Yale).

THE MEETING

Here we meet too soon to part
Here to leave will raise a smart
Here I'll press thee to my heart
   Where nones a place above thee
Here I vow to love thee well   5
& coud words unseal the spell
Had but language strength to tell
   Id tell too how I love thee

THE MEETING   *Title:* The Meeting *Yale MS A8, p. R32 RL*, Song *MS 8, p. R33 MS A8, p. R42,* Here We meet too soon to part *C*   2 to leave will] will absence raise *MS A8, p. R32,* will absence raise *(*abscence *over* [language]*) MS A8, p. R33,* will abscense rais *MS A8, p. R42*   Smart *MS A8, p. R32*   3 Ill *MS A8, p. R32 MS A8, p. R33 MS A8, p. R42*   4 nones a] none have *RL C*   5–8 *In pencil in MS A8, p. R34:*

> Here I vow to love thee well
> & cou'd words conseal the spell
> Had but language strength to tell
> Id prove too how I love thee
> or tell   5

(l. 2 conseal *over* [divine]; l. 4 prove too *below* [tell thee] (prove *underlined*); l. 5 tell *underlined*)

5 I vow to] I'll vow to *MS A8, p. R32,* to say I *MS A8, p. R33,* Id prove I *MS A8, p. R42* 6 & coud] Could but *C*   Words tho weak to break the spell *MS A8, p. R32*] Had but words the power to spell *MS A8, p. R33 MS A8, p. R42*   7 Had but language] Language has not *MS A8, p. R32*   I but *C*   Language *MS A8, p. R42*   8 Id . . . how] How dotingly *MS A8, p. R32,* I wou'd say how *MS A8, p. R33,* Id say how much *MS A8, p. R42,* I might tell how *Yale variant (not Clare's),* I'd say how much *RL C*

Here the rose that decks thy door
Here the thorn that spreads thy bower   10
Here the willow on the moor
  The birds at rest above thee
Had they light of life to see
Sense of soul like thee & me
Soon might each a witness be   15
  How dotingly I love [thee]

& by the night skys purple ether
& by the evens sweeter wether
That oft has blest us both together
  The moon that shines above thee   20
& shows thy beauty cheek so blooming
& by pale ages winter coming
The charms & casualties of woman
  I will for ever love thee

---

9 Heres: decks] hangs *over* [decks] *MS A8, p. R41*   10 Heres: spread *MS A8,*
p. R41   11 Heres: Willow *MS A8, p. R41*   12 at] that *Yale variant*
(not Clare's) MS A8 p. R33   The . . . rest] Heres the birds *MS A8, p. R41*
13–16 *In MS A8, p. 1:*

> Had they lip to hear & see
> Souls & feeling like to me
> Soon woud each as witness be
> How doting I love

13 light of life] thoughts & eyes: *MS A8, p. R33 MS A8, p. R41*   14 Sence *MS*
A8, p. R41   of soul] & looks *MS A8, p. R33 MS A8, p. R41*   15 Quickly
woud they prove to thee *MS A8, p. R33*] Quickly woud they tell to thee *MS A8,*
p. R41   16 thee *MS A8, p. R33 MS A8, p. R41*   17 [The] *over* & *MS A8,*
p. R40   & by] By *RL*   the night skys] this night skies *MS A8, p. R32*, the nights skys
MS A8, p. R40   18 the] Each *MS A8, p. R32, omitted RL*   even's *MS*
A8, p. R40   sweetest weather *MS A8, p. R32 MS A8, p. R33 MS A8, p. R40 RL*
19 to gether *MS A8, p. R40*   20 The] &: Moon *MS A8, p. R40*   21 beauty
altered to beauties *MS A8, p. R40*] beauteous *RL*   cheek] face *MS A8, p. R31 MS A8,*
p. R33 MS A8, p. R40   23 Casual'ties *through* Cass *MS A8, p. R31*] casual'ties *MS*
A8, p. R33   Woman *MS A8, p. R31*   24 I . . . ever] Ill never cease to *MS A8,*
p. R31   *Followed in MS A8, p. R40 by:* [Or / I near can ceas to love thee]
17–24

There's the church upon the hill,	No longer happiness delay,
Here the pure and murm'ring rill,	But make me blest for ever.
Where oft I've vow'd to love thee still,	For then my love no more we'd part,
'Till death our love shall sever;	No more by leaving raise a smart, 10
Then to the altar let's away, 5	I'd fondly press thee to my heart,
Make this my love our bridal day,	And still for ever love thee. C

AUTOGRAPH: Pet. MS D1: Pet. MS A2, ff. R1ʳ–R2ʳ (erased pencil).
TRANSCRIPT: Pet. MS B1, pp. 26–8.
Printed in *RL*, pp. 208–15.
Dated: '1819' (MS D1, *RL* Introduction, pp. xxii–xxiii 'In the last two years').

CRAZY NELL

The Maniac

The sun lowly sinking behind the far trees
& crossing the path humming home were the bees
& darker & darker it grew by degrees
   & Crows they flock'd quawking to rest
When unknown to her parents nell slove on her hat   5
& oer the fields hurried—scarce knew she for what
But her sweetheart in taking advantage & that
   Had kiss'd & had promis'd the best

Poor maidens so much of a husband conciet
The daisy scarce touch'd rose unhurt from her feet   10
—So eager she hasten'd her lover to meet
   As to make him to wait was unjust
On the wood dim discover'd she fixed her eyes—
Such a quere spot to meet in—suspisions might rise
But the fond word a sweetheart! such goodness implies   15
   Ah who would a lover distrust

More darker & gloomy—black clouds hung the wind
Far objects diminish'd before & behind
More narrow & narrow the circle declin'd
   & silence reign'd awfully round   20
When nelly within the wood riding sat down
She listen'd & lapt up her arms in her gown
Far far from her cottage & far from the town
   & her sweet heart not yet to be found

CRAZY NELL   *Title:* Crazy Nell / The Maniac / a Fragment *MS D1*, Crazy Nell. A
true Story *RL*   1 low *RL 2nd edn.*   9 so . . . husband] of husbands so much
they *RL*   10 touch'd; *MS D1*   12 As] For *RL 4th edn.*   16 lover *below*
[sweetheart] *MS D1*   17 gloomy and darker *RL*   23 the[s] *MS D1*
24 not yet] no where *RL 4th edn.*

The minutes seem'd hours—with impatience she heard   25
The flap of a Leaf & the twit of a bird
The least little trifle that wisper'd or stird
   Hope picter'd her lover as nigh
When wearied with sitting she'd wander about
& open the wood gate & give a look out   30
& feign would have halloo'd but fear had a doubt
   That theives might be lurking hard bye

Far clocks counts eleven—'he wornt be long now'
Her anxious hopes wisper'd—hoarse wav'd the wood bough
—'He heeds not my fears or hes false to his Vow'   35
   Poor Nelly sat doubtful & sigh'd
The fellow whod promis'd her husband to be
& wed on the morrow—her friends that could see
(As a good for nought sort of a fellow was he)
   Hop'd nothing more worse might betide   40

At length as in fear slowly tapt the wood gate
Twas Ben!—she complain'd so long painful to wait
Deep design hung his looks he but mumbl'd 'tis late'
   & pass'd her & bid her come on
The mind plainly pictures that night hour of dread   45
In the midst of a wood! where the trees over head
The darkness increaseth—a dungeon they spread
   & the clock at the moment tolls one

& fain would she forc'd as she follow'd some chat
& trifl'd on purpose with this thing & that   50
& complain'd of the dew droppings spoiling her hat
   But nothing Bens silence would break
Extensive the forest the road too & fro
& this way & that way above & below
As crosses the ridings as winding they go   55
   —Ah what road or way can he seek

29 she wander'd *RI*.   30 open'd: gave *RL*   31 i *through* y *in* feign *MS D1*
32 That] Lest *RL 4th edn.*   33 count: won't *RL*   37 fellow whod] man who
had *RL*   38 to wed: that] all *RL*   39 As] That *RL*   40 Hop'd
nothing more] And they hop'd nothing *RL*   41 in *inserted MS D1*   45 night
hour *underlined and* nigh *altered to* night *MS D1*   47 increased *RL*   48 toll'd *RL*
49 &] Nell: she] have *RL*   51 dew-dropping *RL*] dew-droppings *RL 4th edn.*
53 to *RL*   55 crossing *RL*

Her eye ever watchful now caught an alarm
Lights gleam! & tools tinkle! as if nigh a Farm
'O, dont walk so fast Ben—I'm fearful of harm'
   She said & shrug'd closer behind   60
'That lights from my house!'—twas the first word she caught
From his Lips since he through the dark wood had her brought
A house in a Wood! O good god what a thought
   What sensations then rush'd on her mind

The things which her friends & her neighbours had said   65
Afresh at that moment all jumpt in her head
& mistrust for the first time now fill'd her wi' dread
   & as she approach'd—she could see
How better for her their advice to have taen
& wish'd to her self then she had—but in vain   70
—A heap of fresh moulds! & a spade she saw plain
   & a Lanthorn ty'd up to a tree!

'Here they come!' a voice wispers—'haste put out the light'
'—No dig the grave deeper'—'Very dark is the night'
Slow mutterings mingled—O dismal the sight   75
   —The fate of poor Nelly was plain
Fear chill'd thro her heart—but hope wisper'd her 'flye'
Chance seiz'd on the moment—A wind gust blew high
She slipt in the thicket—he turn'd not his eye
   & the grave diggers waited in vain   80

Ah at that dread moment so dredfully dark
How welcome the song of the shepherd or lark
How cheary to harken & hear the dog bark
   As thro the dark wood she fled fast
But horror of horrors all nature was hush   85
Not a sound was there heard—save a blackbird or thrush
That started from sleep flusker'd out of a bush
   Which her brushing cloaths shook as they past

65 *Second* her *inserted MS D1*   66 all *inserted MS D1*   70 wish'd *through* &
MS D1   she wish'd *RL*   71 mould *RL*   72 lantern *RL*   74 *First
dash through* No *MS D1*   75 Slow mutterings mingled *over* [Still mingled
her murmurs] *MS D1*   78 A *through* The: gust *through* it *MS D1*
79 —he *through* he turnd *MS D1*   81 Ah . . . dread *(*Ah *through* T*) MS D1*] At
that fearful *RL*   dredful *altered to* dredfully: [&] dark *MS D1*   83 harken] listen
RL 2nd edn.   87 a *through* the *D1*] the *RL*   88 clothes *RL*

Fear now truly pictur'd near turned her head
Nor this way nor that way—strait forward she fled   90
& fancy still hearing the horrors with dread
 On faster & fearfuller stole
—The matted leaves rustle—the boughs swiftly part
Her hands & her face thro the brambles did smart
But ah the worst anguish was felt at her heart   95
 Bens unkindness struck death to her soul

Now glimering lighter the forest appears
& hope thou sweet comforter soften'd her fears
Light & liberty—Darkness thy horrors endears
 Great bliss did the Omen impart   100
The Forest its end & its horrors was by
She breath'd the free air & she saw the blue sky
Her own fields she knew—to her home did she flye
 & great was the joy of her heart

O prospect endearing the Village to view   105
The morn sweet appearing & gay the cock crew
& mangl'd by brambles & dabbl'd in dew
 She fetch'd a loud rap at the door
The parents in raptures wept over their child—
She mutterd her terrors—her eyes rolled wild   110
'They dig the grave deeper!'—your Nellys beguil'd'
 She said & she sil'd on the floor

Poor Nell soon recover'd but ah to her cost
Her sense & her reason forever was lost
& scorch'd by the summer & chill'd by the frost   115
 A Maniac restless & wild

89 she ne'er *RL* 90 Nor] Either: or *RL* 94 thro] with *RL* 95 oh! *RL*
98 thou] the *RL* 99 horror *RL* 101 The . . . its *through* The forest its end
did *MS D1* horrors was] terrors gone *RL* 103 *First* she *inserted MS D1*
107 *First* & *to* When *(p.e.) MS D1*] When *RL* 107/8 [She anxiously waited for
day] *MS D1* 108 fetch'd] gave *RL* 108/9 [—Soon rose the Enquirey O
heavens my child] *MS D1* 109 wept *through* went *MS D1* 111 They
through The: dig *through* dug: —your Nellys beguil'd' *below* [then utterd these words]
MS D1 114 were *RL*

Now Crazy Nell rambles & still she will weep
& fearless at night into hovels she'll creep
Fond Parents alas their affliction is deep
   & vainly they comfort their child   120

AUTOGRAPH: Pet. MS D2, p. 3.
Dated: 1819–20 (MS D2).

TO THE FOX FERN

Haunter of woods lone wilds & solitudes
Were none but feet of birds & things as wild
Doth print a foot track near were summers light
Buried in boughs forgets its glare & round thy crimped leaves
Feints in a quiet dimness fit for musings   5
& mellancholy moods with ere & there
A golden thread of sunshine stealing through
The evening shadowy leaves that seem to creep
Like leisure in the shade

118 she'll] will *RL*   119/20 [Since comforts are vain to their child] *MS D1*
Possibly part of an early version of this poem:

    With ⟨pen⟩ & paper bring such as folks could read
    A black scoundrels ⟨burthen⟩ of bad schemes
    But kept still tongues about ⟨every thing⟩ hed said
    His ⟨   ⟩ all ⟨   ⟩ now only
    & if himself knew ⟨how⟩ the rogues deciet   5
    Did if he coud her ⟨   ⟩ &
    He fussd her up wi mariage ⟨all⟩ the day
    & strange to sayt the plot was ⟨   ⟩ as nought
    In a dark wood miles distant from the town
    He ⟨did recall⟩ hed plotted Nellys death   10
    The Grave was Ready as her bridal bed   *MS A2, f. R1ʳ*

    O god I sighd restore her to her reason ⟨   ⟩
    The ⟨   ⟩ it to its promisd home
    Where ⟨Wretches⟩ shall have rest   *MS A2, f. R2ʳ*
TO THE FOX FERN   *Title:* To the Fox Fern

AUTOGRAPH: Pet. MS D2, p. 6 (deleted).
Dated: 1819–20 (MS D2).

Mary I dare not call thee dear
Ive lost that sound so long
Once more I teaze thy careless ear
With memorys idle song
Ah seasons change hath blotted out   5
With this worlds cheating ways
Thou wert the last that I shoud doubt
Of pleasing with my praise

I hopd that we shoud be as one
& felt it soon woud be   10
But hopes of every kind are gone
Nor left a dream of thee
& hopes that all have met their end
Close linkd with many a vow
Nor left one een to call thee friend   15
How wide the difference now

How loath to part how fond to meet
Had we two used to be
When abscence past what eager feet
Did haste me back to thee   20
Three days scarce past before we met
In spring or winter weather
Now years thrice three have rose & set
Nor found us once together

MARY I DARE NOT CALL THEE DEAR   *Title: wanting*   1 *Preceded by:*
Why Mary do I teaze thy ear / With many an idle song   5 Ah *through* In: change
(change *through indecipherable*) . . . out *below* [far away from cause] (cause *through* there)
6 With this worlds *through* In memory *and one indecipherable word*   9 we[e] . . . one
below [I shoud win the once]   10 it . . . be *below* [that hope as true]
11 h *through* tr *in* hopes   13 [Loves] &: that *through* &   13/14 seemd truths
14 Close *through?* Now   17 How *through* So: loath to part *over* [fond to
meet]: how *through* so: fond to meet *over* [loath to part]   18 Had we two *through*
How warm we use   21 days *over* [suns]: past *through* set   22 spring *through*
?summer   23 have *through* has

What honied tokens did each tongue 25
Tell how we warmly lovd
How a[rdent] to thy lips I clung
Were noght but smiles reprovd
But now methinks if but a word
Was utterd in thy ear 30
Thoudst startle like an untamd bird
& blush with stranger fear

The vainest hope I had for thee
Did ease its foolish will
With coming days that were to be 35
Its wishes to fulfill
But now what is my name to thee
Jests for an idle ear
From one who made me down trod be
Than nought on earth more dear 40
Like counterfited coin thy loves
Impression lingers on
When all the gilt is washd away
& all the worth is gone

Thy face was so familiar grown 45
Thy self so often bye
A moments memory when alone
Woud bring thee in my eye
But now my very dreams forget
That witching look to trace 50
Tho there thy memorys often met
It wears a strangers face

---

25 tokens *over* [words]: each *over* [our]: tongue[s] 26 Tell in the warmth of love
altered to Tell how we warmly lovd 26/7 [What raptures round thy bosom hung]
27 *Hiatus* 28 noght but *inserted*: [did but] reprovd (reprove *altered to* reprovd)
33 vainest *through ?* highest 36/7 But [weakest hopes that common hearts] /
common hopes / When 37 is my] *successively (a)* [& I] *(b)* [am I] *(c)* is my
38 A jest for idle ears *altered to* Jests for an idle ear 40 Than] Perhaps That
(Perhaps *inserted*: That *through two indeciperable words*) 45 face] *successively (a)*
[voice] *(b)* [face] *(c)* [voice] *(d)* [love] *(e)* face 46 Thy self *through* How often: o
through d *in* often

AUTOGRAPH: Pet. MS D2, p. 8.
Dated: 1819–20 (MS D2).

'Pink pink' the bunting sings & picks its feather
I love the note it speaks of winter weather
The blue cap seeks the mossy apple tree
& pecks the buds & flutters merrily
The sparrow noises in the cottage eaves   5
& hides from cats among the opening leaves

AUTOGRAPHS: Pet. MS D3, pp. 1–3: Pet. MS D4, p. 2 (ll. 1–40, 81–8 only, deleted): Pet. MS A4, p. 22 (ll. 1–25, 41–56 only, deleted): Pet. MS A1 (erased pencil), inside front cover (ll. 5–8), f. 1ʳ (ll. 41–8), f. 1ᵛ (ll. 49–56), f. 5ʳ (upside down, ll. 33–40, 81–4), f. 5ᵛ (ll. 57–64), f. 6ᵛ (ll. 65–72), f. 8ʳ (ll. 73–80), f. 65ʳ (ll. 85–8), f. 67ʳ (ll. 1–8), f. 70ᵛ (ll. 9–16, 25–32), inside back cover (ll. 17–24).
Dated: 1820 (Explanatory Notes).

THE FAREWELL

Ah adieu to the scene pastorallity yields
& adieu my dear village to thee
No one when we're parted will notice thy fields
Thoult then be as wretched as me
Sweet magic that holdeth my bosom in thrall   5
Thou parent of many a sigh
That makes that lovd siren the 'Jewel of all'
True love & sweet Patty—Good bye

'PINK PINK' THE BUNTING SINGS & PICKS ITS FEATHER *Title:* *wanting*   2 its

THE FAREWELL *Title:* The Farewell / Written after being appris'd / Of the Intention of Sending him to London / For Improvment *MS D3*, The Farewell *MS D4 MS A4*, *wanting MS A1*   1 Ah] Now: scenes *MS A4 MS A1*   pastorallity] rurallity *MS A1*   1/2 [& adieu my dear village to thee / Rural muse a] *MS D3* [Ah my dear native village adieu unto thee] *MS D4*   2 & *through* Ah *MS A1*   3 No] Nor: were *MS A1*   5 majic *MS A1*   (O love so lingering forgets not to call *MS D4*] & Love O so . . . *MS A4*, O the while lingering love we'll forget not to call *MS A1, p. 67ʳ*   6 While the startld tear dims in my eye) *MS D4*] (While the startld dims in my eye) *MS A4*, While the startle dims in the eye *MS A1, f. 67ʳ*   7 ∧jewel: all∧ *MS A1*   In her the best lovd dearest treasure of all *MS D4*] On her . . . *MS A4 MS A1*   8 Sweet 'Patt of the Vally' Good bye *MS D4 MS A4*] First love and fond patty good bye *MS A1*, My darling sweet patty good bye *MS A1, f. 67ʳ*

Ah why can I sweetest of blessings exchanging
Ere sigh for the charms of the town   10
Ah why do I hope to be happy in ranging
Ah [why] wou'd I seek for renown
In vainly pursuing the shadow of pleasure
I bid to the substance adieu
Alas thou cant think it my hearts dearest treasure   15
The pain of departing from you

Where spread the wild roses in blushes oerladen
Where droops the buds burthen of dew
There in the wild pasture I met the sweet maiden
Provd since so endearing & true   20
While chance found the worth which remembrance endeareth
Ah in vain City beauties may shine
When beauties superior to others appeareth
The[y]ll be but advancments to thine

I vowd not to leave thee I vowd & I broke it   25
& left my best blessing forlorn
Its value thy tear at our parting bespoke it
O the stamp of that worth is a thorn

9 Ah . . . sweetest *through four indecipherable words MS A1*   can] did *MS A1*
sweetest . . . exchanging *below* [think it my hearts dearest treasure] *MS D3*
10 Eer: charms] sweets *MS A1*   11 do I hope] did I think: hapy: rangeing
MS A1   hope] think *MS D4 MS A4*   12 why *MS D4 MS A4 MS A1*   wou'd]
did *MS A1*   13 shadows *MS A1*   14 I bid] & biding *MS A1*   16 [That]
The *MS D4*   What I feel now Im severd from you *MS A1*   17 spead *MS D4*]
spreads *MS A4*   rosey *MS D4 MS A4*   oerlading *MS A4*   Where the wild rose
spreads in bushes oerladen *MS A1*   18 Where . . . buds] & the wild bud
droops its *MS A1*   19 Thier *MS D3*] There *through ?* Where *MS A1*
20 so endearing] the best blossom kind hearted *MS A1*   endearing] engaging *MS A4*
21 Remembrance that worth endeareth *MS A1*   found *through* paid *MS D3*
rembrance *MS D4*   22 city *MS D4 MS A4*   beautys *MS A4*   In vain the city
beauties shine *MS A1*   23 beauty *MS D4 MS A4*   sperior *MS A4*   & when
superior charms apeareth *MS A1*   24 Theyll *MS A4*   They'll serve but to
magnify thine *MS D4*] They only serve to equal thine *MS A1*   25 ⟨I⟩ vowd not
binding *MS D4*   vow *(second word)*: vow'd *(eighth word) MS A4*   Followed in *MS A4*
by:
                    [O the stamp of thy worth is a throne
                    But boom on sweet 'Rose Bud' thy sweetness still wear it
                    & let not grief blight thee for me
                    Whatever my fortune my angel shall share it
                    I'll stoop to be equal to thee]   5
27 ⟨Its⟩ *binding MS D4*   thy] the *MS D4 MS A1*   28⟨O⟩ *binding MS D4*]
Ah *MS A1*   that] her *MS D4*   to my heart is *MS A1*

But bloom on sweet 'rose bud' thy beauty still wear it
& let not grief blight it for me   30
What evers my fortune my angel shall share it
Ill stoop to be equal to thee

The rivers with held from their scources the ocean
Which commerces Intrest[s] detain
When once freedom rolls its curld waves into motion   35
Retreats to the Ocean again
So when on the road my fond hopes are sojourning
From the noise of the city set free
Ah then best of blessings to speed my returning
I'll retreat my dear patty to thee   40

The coach as soon rumbling along the hard road
Shall stifle the heart swelling sigh
I soon must be missing from comforts abode
& biding my kindred good bye
Adieu my dear village lovd cottage adieu   45
No language my feeling can tell
Departing from comforts departing from you
All, all I love dearly—farewell

O the wildness the warmth in my heart that did melt
A ranging field meadow & moor   50
O blisses enjoy'd o the raptures I felt
I wander to feel ye no more

29 ⟨But⟩ *binding MS D4*   ‸rosebud‸ *MS A1*   beauty *below* [sweetness] *MS D4*]
sweetness *MS A1*   30 ⟨&⟩ *binding MS D4*   it] thee *MS A1*
31 ⟨W⟩hat *binding*: shear *MS D4*   angel] *hiatus MS A1*   32 ⟨Ill⟩
binding MS D4] & Ill *MS A1*   33 ⟨The⟩ *binding MS D4*   witheld
MS D4 MS A1   river: its source: wide Ocean *MS A1*   34 ⟨W⟩hich *binding
MS D4*] — Which *MS A1*   intrests *MS D4*] intrest *MS A1*   detains *MS A1*
35 ⟨When⟩ *binding MS D4*   its *to* their *(p.e.) MS D3*   curld] white: wave *MS A1*
36 ⟨Re⟩treats *binding MS D4*   the] its *MS A1*   ocean *MS D4 MS A1*
37 ⟨So⟩ *binding MS D4*   on] in *MS A1*   39 ⟨Ah⟩ *binding MS
D4*   speed] urge *MS A1*   40 ⟨I'l⟩l *binding*: retreat *below* [fly]: Patty
MS D4   Ill fly my dear—to thee *MS A1*   41 as soon rumbling] soon shall
rumble *MS A4*   42 Shall] & [deaf] *MS A4*   the] thy *MS A1*   43 soon[s]
MS D3   44 [adieu] good bye *MS D3*] adieu *MS A4*   45 adieu *through* good
bye *MS D3*   46 langauage *MS D3 MS A4*   feeling *over* [sorrowings] *MS D3*]
sorrows *MS A4 MS A1*   48 All,] Ah *MS A4*, & to *MS A1*   dearly‸ *MS A4*
MS A1   49 the] of: heart] bosom: did melt] melts *MS A1*   50 While
rambling the meadow & more *MS A1*   51 blisses enjoy'd o] the bliss I enjoyd O
MS A1   enjoyd: the] ye *MS A4*

Once more adieu village lovd cottage & plain
Long long Ive been happy in you
How I love you & mourn you I cannot Explain   55
So all I love dearly—adieu

Ye swains of the teams & ye swains of the fold
Ye ploughmen & shepherds adieu
You rural enchanters—ye angels! of old
Sweet milkmaids Good bye unto you   60
So warm in your praise as Ive often times been
The fields & the meadows among
As happy ye maids as Ive strolld oer the Green
To picture your charms in my song

Ah maidens & swains & all blessings beside   65
I leave higher means to pursue
Ah blessings unknown to politness & pride
That made me your equal adieu
Ah foolish allurements that bids ye adieu
The citys defilements a stain   70
Its taste & its fashion will deem such as you
Unworthy of notice again

Rural muse sweet inspirer so oft on whose arm
Ive been led her sweet scenes to behold
To notice domestic conscerns of the farm   75
& rural delights of the fold
From all thy endearments I forcibly part
False taste has no being with you
O the sigh that unfoldeth my anguish of heart
Now I bid ye a final adieu   80

---

53 Thou dear native village sweet meadow & plain *MS A1*   55 explain *MS A4*
MS A1   56 dearly∧ *MS A4 MS A1*   57 team *MS A1*   58 shepherd &
ploughmen *MS A1*   59 enchanters∧: Angels∧ *MS A1*   60 Good . . . you] I
bid you adieu *MS A1*   61 praises: as *omitted MS A1*   62 amoung *MS A1*
63 As] So: green *MS A1*   65 Ah . . . swains] The swains & the maids *MS A1*
66 persue *MS A1*   67 politeness *MS A1*   69 The citys inticements soon
bids all adieu *MS A1*   71 fashions *MS A1*   74 behold *through* unfold
MS D3   79 Sigh *MS A1*

The coach now is ready to rattle & start
Muse throw down thy pastoral pen
I leave thee to learn the refinements of art
& never shall meet thee agen
Thou low simple somthing so ready to please   85
To nature so vulgar & true
Thou sweetness perfuming such simples as these
Thou last rural rapture—adieu

AUTOGRAPHS: Pet. MS D4, p. 1: Pet. MS A1, f. 21ʳ (erased pencil): Pet.
MS A1, f. 22ʳ (erased pencil, deleted, ll. 7, 13, 14 omitted).
TRANSCRIPT: Pet. MS B1, p. 73.
Printed in *RL*, p. 203.
Dated: 1818–19 (MS D4).

SONNET ON THE RIVER GASH

Where winding gash wirls round its wildest scene
On this romantic bend I sit me down
On that side view the meads their smoothing green
Edg'd with the peeping hamlets checkering brown
Here the steep hill as dripping headlong down   5
While glides the stream a silver streak between
As glides the shaded clouds along the sky
Brightning & deep'ning loosing as they're seen

82 throw] lay *MS D4 MS A1*   83 ⟨I leave⟩ *binding:* learn *through* find
MS D4   84 ⟨& n⟩ever *binding MS D4*   agen *through* again *MS D3 MS D4*
85 ⟨Thou⟩ *binding MS D4*   86 ⟨To⟩ *binding MS D4*   so] tho: &] so *MS*
D4 MS A1   87 simples] ballads *MS D4*   Thou simple that shines in such
ballads as these *MS A1*   88 rapture_∧ *MS D4*] comfort *MS A1*

    SONNET ON THE RIVER GASH   *Title:* Sonnet on the River Gash *MS D4 MS*
A1, ff. 21ʳ and 22ʳ, The River Gwash *RL*   1 winding] sweeping: wirls] winds:
scenes *MS A1, f. 21ʳ*   Gash *MS A1, f. 22ʳ*] Gwash *RL*   3 view the meads their]
viewing meadows *MS A1, ff. 21ʳ and 22ʳ*   meads their] meadow's *RL*   smoothing]
waving: greens *MS A1, f. 21ʳ*   4 Edgd *MS A1, ff. 21ʳ and 22ʳ*   peeping *over*
[checkering] *MS D4*] checkerd *MS A1, ff. 21ʳ and 22ʳ*   5 hill] bank: dropping
RL   as dripping] dark droping *MS A1, f. 21ʳ*   7 glide *RL*   8 & *through* or
MS D4   deep'ning . . . they're] loosing as they are often *MS A1, f. 21ʳ*, deepning
⟨loosing⟩ as theyre often *MS A1, f. 22ʳ*   losing *RL*

In light & shade—so when old willows lean
Thus their broad shadow—runs the river bye   10
With tree & bush repleat a wilderd scene
& mossd & Ivyd sparkling on my eye—
O thus wild musing am I doubly blest
My woes unheeding—& my heart at rest

AUTOGRAPHS: Pet. MS D4, p. 1: Pet. MS A1, f. 17ʳ (erased pencil): Pet.
MS A1, f. 16ʳ (erased pencil).
TRANSCRIPT: Pet. MS B1, p. 73.
Printed in *RL*, p. 207.
Dated: 1818–19 (MS D4).

TO MY OATEN REED

Thou warble wild of rough rude melody
How oft Ive wood thee—Often thrown thee bye
In many a doubtful rapture touching thee
Waking thy rural notes in many a sigh
Fearing the wise the wealthy proud & high   5
Would scorn as Vain thy lowly extacy
Deeming presumptious thy uncultur'd themes
Thus vainly courting taste's unblemish'd eye

9 In] This *MS A1, ff. 21ʳ and 22ʳ*   [?] light *MS A1, f. 22ʳ*   shade∧ *MS A1, f. 21ʳ*   so when] to where *RL*   10 its: shadow∧ *MS A1, f. 21ʳ*   11 wildering *MS A1, f. 21ʳ*   12 moss'd *MS A1, f. 22ʳ*] moss *RL*   Ivied *MS A1 f. 22ʳ*] ragged *MS A1, f. 21ʳ*, ivy *RL*   sparkling *through* speck'ling *MS D4*] speckling *RL*   sparkling . . . eye—] meets my wildered eye *MS A1, f. 21ʳ*, mingling meets my eye *MS A1, f. 22ʳ*   13 wild] while: am I] wild, I'm *RL*   Autumnal music ? spare such things as these *MS A1, f. 21ʳ*   14 rest. *MS D4*   Forgetful grief subside & leave a moments ease *MS A1, f. 21ʳ*   *Followed in MS A1, f. 21ʳ by:* This is an obscure Water but some parts of it are very Picturesque Casterton Rutland

TO MY OATEN REED   *Title:* To my Oaten Reed *MS D4 MS A1, f.17ʳ RL, wanting MS A1, f. 16ʳ*   1 warble . . . rude] string of rough & modest *MS A1, f. 16ʳ*   2 Often] oft have *MS A1, f. 17ʳ*   thee∧: Often . . . bye] oft have thrummd the lyre *MS A1, f. 16ʳ*   3 In *through* With *MS D4*] With *MS A1, f. 17ʳ*   doubtful rapture] fearful feaver *MS A1, f. 17ʳ*, fearful finger *MS A1, f. 16ʳ*   4 notes *over* [sounds] *MS D4*] sounds *MS A1, f. 17ʳ*, sound *MS A1, f. 16ʳ*   6 vain *MS A1, ff. 7ʳ and 16ʳ*   lowly *through* him *in* humble *MS D4*] humble *MS A1, ff. 17ʳ and 16ʳ*   7 Deeming presumptious] & deem presumtious: theme *MS A1, f. 16ʳ* unculturd *MS A1, f. 17ʳ*] unculterd *MS A1, f. 16ʳ*   8 tastes unblemished *MS A1, f. 7ʳ*] taste a lowering *MS A1, f. 16ʳ*

To list a simple labourers artless dreams
—Erst may I wander into wide extreams—   10
But O thou sweet wild winding Rapsody
Thou gurgling charm that sooths my hearts controul
I take thee up—to smoothen many a sigh
& lull the throbbings of a woe worn soul

AUTOGRAPHS: Pet. MS D4, pp. 4–6: Pforzheimer Library, Misc. MS 197
(ll. 45–60 only, deleted).
TRANSCRIPT: Pet. MS B1, pp. 20–2 (deleted).
Printed in *RL*, pp. 111–13 (ll. 57–92, 97–100 only).
Dated: '1818' (MS D4, p. 4).

THE WAGTAILS DEATH
&
PITYS FEELINGS ON BABARITY

A Scene from Nature

The wise & good shall not deride
    The tear in pitys eye
Tho laugh'd to scorn by sensless pride
    From them it meets a sigh

Compassion sees & feels & weeps   5
    Ah feels for every pain
& pitys eye in sorrow steeps
    & Mercy loves the strain

9 a[s]: simple *below* [vulgar] *MS D4*   A artless simple ploughboys humble dreams
(dreams *over* [?lies]) *MS A1, f. 17*ʳ, & humble ploughboys simple dreams *MS A1, f. 16*ʳ
10 —Erst may] —So may *MS A1, f. 17*ʳ, Erst may *MS A1, f. 16*ʳ, Haply *RL*
extreams∧ *MS A1, f. 16*ʳ   11 0 *MS A1, ff. 17*ʳ *and 16*ʳ   wild winding Rapsody] of
wildest melody *MS A1, f. 16*ʳ   12 gurgling] gingling *MS A1, f. 17*ʳ, jingling *RL*
sooths my hearts] dost my heart *RL*   Led on by Ignorance prest by controul *MS A1,*
*f. 16*ʳ   13 take . . . smoothen] touch thy string to stifle *MS A1, f. 16*ʳ   smoothen]
smooth full (smooth *over* [full]) *MS A1, f. 17*ʳ, smother *RL*, smother *altered to* smoother
Harvard proof copy   14 a *over* [my]: woe-worn *MS A1, f. 17*ʳ   So thou my harp
art comfort to my soul (my harp *below* art *over* [art]) *MS A1, f. 16*ʳ

   THE WAGTAILS DEATH & PITYS FEELINGS ON BABARITY   *Title:* Pity
Feelings on Barbarity / —A Scene from Nature *and (in margin)* The Wagtails Death / &
/ Pitys feelings on babarity / A Scene from Nature *MS D4*, On Cruelty *RL, wanting Pfz*

A wagtails toil with dabbl'd breast
   By far fetch'd bit & bit   10
Within a rock had form'd her nest
   & just prepar'd to sit

But—fate thou surely art unkind
   Such Innocence to wrong
—Such painful toil each hair to find   15
   To warm & hatch her young

A cruel hawk O sad to tell
   The hawks act to their kind
Found (& when rob'd) her little cell
   Left her own egg behind   20

Poor bird—so friendship from deciet
   Courts daggers to her breast
Affection blind to every cheat
   It still endear'd her nest

The robbers charge she deems her own   25
   How strong parental ties
The loss discovery would bemoan
   This evil pledge suplies

When tenderest care had hatchd the fiend
   —As Friends for wicked heirs   30
Its comforts how she toild & glean'd
   Forgetfull of her cares

Its gluttony with age increas'd
   More savage was the cry
Nor night nor day she scarsly ceas'd   35
   To seek the vain supply

The worms & flies how would she look
   Load home & off again
How—draggling pace along the brook
   To give content in vain   40

9 dabbl'd *through* draggling *MS D4*   16 [Such sun] & *(& through to) MS D4*
26 parential *MS D4*   30 A *altered to* As: Friends *through* hier *MS D4*

The shocking scene approaches nigh
  The feeling bosom bleeds
The tender soul has dropt a tear
  Oer less inhuman deeds

Fatig'd the little sufferer came   45
  I think I see her still
Slav'd past her strength weak maul'd & lame
  The worm was in her bill

Hunger had made his nature known
  The wagtail stood the prize   50
A step dames love no more he'll own
  He pounces! & she dies

O sad inhuman fratraside
  She struggling 'neath his claws
Look'd up a mothers love & dy'd   55
  —Hard; nature are thy laws

Compassion reads & feels & weeps
  Ah feels the every pain
& tho a wagtails sorrows sleeps
  Still mercy loves the strain   60

47 Slavd: mauld *Pfz*   50 The wagtail stood] His parent flies *Pfz*   51 step-dams:
hell *Pfz*   52 pounces∧ *Pfz*   54 She struggling 'neath (struggling
through indecipherable) MS D4] Patient beneath *Pfz*   55 Look'd . . . mothers] She
lookd a parents *Pfz*   56 ∧Hard∧ *Pfz*
57–60

Ah pitys eyes in sorrow steep
Her bosom feels the wrong
Compasion bids her feeling weep
& Mercy loves the song   *Pfz*

(l. 2 feels *altered to* feeling)

If the Wagtail's Death, though truth, is thought a mere conceit, a piece called
'Compassion—written on viewing a dead bird' may be collected by beginning at the 15th
verse, altered thus.

'Compassions sighs, & feels, & weeps,
Retracing every pain,
Inhuman man in vengeance wreakes
On all the lower train.

*** Omit the 24th verse *(Margin note in MS B1)*

Compassion sighs, and feels, and weeps;
Retracing every pain
Inhuman man, in vengeance, heaps
On all the lower train.   *RL*

& pity oft thy heart has bled
　　As gauling now it bleeds
& tender tears thy eyes have shed
　　To witness cruel deeds

The lash that weald poor dobins hide　　65
　　The strokes that cracking fall
On dogs dumb cringing by thy side
　　Ah thou hast felt them all

The burthen'd asses mid the laugh
　　To see them wipt & drove　　70
How breath'd thy soul in their behalf
　　Humanity & love

E'en 'plaining flies to thee have spoke
　　Poor trifles as they be
& oft the spiders web thoust broke　　75
　　To set the captive free

The pilfering mouse entrapt & cag'd
　　Within the wirey grate
Thy pleading powers has oft engag'd
　　To mourn its rigid fate　　80

How beat thy breast its conscious woes
　　To see the sparrow die
Poor little thieves of many foes
　　Their food they dearly buy

Where nature groans where nature cries　　85
　　Beneath the butchers knife
How vain how many where thy sighs
　　To save such guiltless life

And ah that most inhuman plan
　　Where reasons name ador'd　　90
Unfriendly treatment man to man
　　Thy wrongs have oft deplor'd

61 & *through* Ah *MS D4*] Ah *RL*　　　62 galling *RL*　　　65 side *altered to* hide
MS D4　　　70 & drove] would move *RL*　　　71 How . . . soul] Thy soul
to breathe *RL*　　　81 its] with *RL*　　　82 sparrows *RL*　　　87 were *RL*
90 name's *RL*　　　92 wrongs] tears *RL*

& thousands more compassion weeps
& sees & weeps again
& tho a wagtails sorrow sleeps 95
Still Mercy loves the strain

Nor wise nor good shall neer deride
The tear in pitys eye
T[h]o laugh'd to scorn by sensless pride
From them it meet a sigh 100

AUTOGRAPHS: Pet. MS D4, p. 7: Pet. MS A40, p. 35a (ll. 25–30 omitted).
TRANSCRIPT: Pet. MS B1, pp. 22–3 (ll. 25–30 deleted).
Dated: 1818–19 (MS D4).

THE DISCOVERY

or
Song of Truth

While fancy thrums the prinking strings
A stranger to the heart she sings
Her Emmas Myras fancied things
Till truth inspires the tale
—Then heart & soul in raptures springs 5
To Patty of the Vale

A Cheek to praise or Lips or Eyes
Each Fair my simple song supplies
But here the heart the tongue denies
When truth inspires my tale 10
Ah then the only maid I prize
Is patty of the Vale

97 e'er *RL*　　　100 meets *RL*

THE DISCOVERY *Title:* The Discovery / or / Song of Truth *MS D4*, The
Confession / Or Song of Truth *MS A40*　　　4 [But alas when] Till *(*Will *altered to*
Till*) MS D4*　　　5 ∧Then: rapture *MS A40*　　　6 vale *MS A40*　　　7 cheek:
lips: eyes *MS A40*　　　8 fair: supplys *MS A40*　　　9 But *through* While: e *in*
heart *inserted MS D4*　　　12 vale *MS A40*

The guiless smile that dints the cheek
Eyes thro whose looks the heart will speak
That truest love the wise would seek   15
   How strongly these prevail
To bind the Vow I ne'er can break
   With Patty of the Vale

Tis not the zemblers wiles can prove
This purest gem—the truth of Love   20
Its tipe exists in heaven above
   Ah where such charms prevail—
A heaven below my soul can prove
   In patty of the Vale

True as the needle to the pole   25
My fixed fond unwavering soul
(But only mov'd as forc'd controul
   Or rigid fates prevail)
To be at rest must north ward roll
   To patty of the Vale   30

Tho fate may change & want depart
As fortune wills—(with all my heart!)
But never will I worth desert
   Or flourish hopes or fail
Still near & dearest to my heart   35
   Is Patty of the Vale

13 guiltless *MS A40*   15 woud *MS A40*   17 vow: near *MS A40*
18 patty: vale *MS A40*   19 'zemblers *MS A40*   20 gem∧: love *MS A40*
the truth of Love *underlined MS D4*   21 type *MS A40*   22 were: prevail∧
MS A40   24 vale *MS A40*   25 pole[s] *MS D4*   27 as *through* by
MS D4   28 prevail *through* ? propose *and* prevail *written again in margin MS D4*
32 wills∧: heart∧) *MS A40*   36 patty *MS A40*   Vale. *MS D4*] vale *MS A40*

AUTOGRAPHS: Norris Museum SAVNM CL/13: Pet. MS A52, p. 2: Pet.
MS D4, p. 11 (ll. 1–8 only, deleted).
TRANSCRIPT: Pet. MS B1, p. 39.
Printed in *RL*, pp. 178–9.
Dated: 1819 (Explanatory Notes).

'MY LOVE THOU ART A NOSEGAY SWEET'

A Song

My love thou art a Nosegay sweet
  My sweetest flower I prove thee
& pleasd Ill pin thee to my breast
  & dearly will I love thee

& when my nosegay thou shalt fade   5
  As sweet a flower I'll prove thee
& as thou witherst on my breast
  For beautys past I'll love thee

& when my nosegay thou shalt dye
  & heavens flower I prove thee   10
My hopes shall hail thee in the sky
  & Everlasting love thee

'MY LOVE THOU ART A NOSEGAY SWEET'   *Title:* 'My love thou art a
Nosegay sweet' / A song *Norris,* 'My Love thou art a Nosegay Sweet' / A Song *MS A52,*
'My Love thou art a Nosgay sweet' / A song *MS D4,* My Love, thou art a Nosegay
Sweet *RL*   1 Love *MS A52*   thou[s]: nosgay *MS D4*   3 pleas'd *MS A52*
MS D4   I *MS A52 MS D4 RL*   4 will] do *MS A52 MS D4 RL*   thee *omitted*
MS D4   5 fade *through* spye *Norris*   6 a] my *MS D4*   Ill *MS D4*]
thou'lt *RL*   7 & hug thee withering to my heart (& *through* Ill) *MS D4*   witherest
RL   8 beauty *RL*   beautys past *below* [better change] *MS A52*   & ever ever
love thee *MS D4*   10 Flower *MS A52*   I] shalt *RL*   11 hail thee in] follow
to *MS A52 RL*   12 Ever lasting *MS A52*

AUTOGRAPH: Pet. MS D4, p. 11 (deleted).
TRANSCRIPT: Pet. MS B1, p. 43.
Printed in *RL*, pp. 179–80.
Dated: '1819' (MS D4, p. 11).

A BALLAD

My loves like a lily my loves like a rose
My loves like a smile the spring mornings disclose
And sweet as the rose on her cheek—her love glows
   When sweetly she smileth on me
& as cold as the snow of the lilly—my rose   5
Behaves to pretenders who ever they be
In vain higher stations their passions disclose
   To win her affections from me

My loves like the lilly my loves like the rose
My loves like the smile the spring mornings disclose   10
& fine as the lilly & sweet as the rose
   My loves beauty bloometh to me
& smiles of more pleasure my heart only knows
To think that pretenders who ever they be
But vainly their love & their passions disclose   15
   My love remains constant to me

A BALLAD   *Title:* A Ballad *MS D4*, My Love's like a Lily *RL*   1 lily *through*
rose *MS D4*   5 &] But *RL*   9 the] a *twice RL*   11 fine] fair *RL*

AUTOGRAPH: Pet. MS D4, p. 11.
TRANSCRIPT: Pet. MS B1, p. 44.
Printed in *RL*, p. 181.
Dated: 1818–19 (MS D4).

SONG

True love the virgins first fond passion
   How blest the swain to prove it
Should hymen snatch the lucky hour
   No power on earth can move it

When death such loving hearts divide   5
   & love on earth is blasting
Firm fixd the hope in heaven remains
   Where love is ever lasting

SONG   *Title:* Song *MS D4*, True Love *RL*   *Preceded in MS D4 by:*

[*Song*

True love the virgins first fond passion
  How blest the swain to prove it
Should hymen snatch the lucky hour
  No power on hearth can move it

& when grim death such hearts divide   5
  & every hope is blasting]

4 move *through indecipherable MS D4*   5 divides *RL*   6 hearth *MS D4*

AUTOGRAPHS: Fitzwilliam Museum: Pet. MS D4, p. 12 (ll. 25–32 omitted, ll. 33–40 pencil, deleted).
TRANSCRIPT: Pet. MS B1, p. 58.
Dated: April 1819 (Fitz).

BETTY SELL

When woodbine blossoms twining high
   Comingld with the thorn
& busy bees wewed bumming bye
   To sip the sweets of morn
A stranger lass with rake afield   5
   Blyth stepping thro the dell
As wisht a swain her name reveald
   'Good morning betty Sell'

She gave me room to climb the stile
   I lingerd soodling bye   10
My jumping heart beheld the smile
   & vanishd in a sigh
As bird lime daubs the linnets nest
   By her enchantments fell
I pausd me trembling at her feet   15
   A slave to betty sell

Her ringlets black as gloss rind sloes
   The hazel melts her eye
As flusht as the dayrosey blows
   Who coud gang safly bye   20

BETTY SELL   *Title:* Betty Sell *Fitz*, Betty Sell / A Ballad *MS D4*   1 Where *MS D4*   2 Comingld] Comingling mix *MS D4*   3 wewed *to* whewed *(p.e.) Fitz*] wued *MS D4* buming *MS D4*   4 To sip] A sipping: the morn *MS D4* 5 Stranger *MS D4*   6 Blythe: bushy dell *MS D4*   7 As *through* I: wisht] wist *MS D4*   8 ∧Good morning to ye betty sell∧ *MS D4*   10 & as I lingering soodld by *MS D4*   12 & Vanishd captive in a Sigh *MS D4* 13 nest] seat *MS D4*   14 By] So by *MS D4* By her *through* So by *Fitz* 15 I stood still fixd at her feet *(*still *through* me at her: fixd *through* feet*) MS D4* 16 A Slave to the sweet betty Sell *MS D4*   18 Hazle shades melting soft in her eye *MS D4*   19 flusht *through* fair: & as fair as *MS D4* dayrosey *to* dayroses *(p.e.) Fitz*] hedge roeses *MS D4*   20 Who on wonder coud pass her safe bye *MS D4*

Love unmasked wi a sigh
I gan my story tell
While new charms shone in curls wip'd bye
O charming betty Sell

Ye busy bees intruding round   25
Some meaner blossom seek
Think not your welcom tho your found
A rose upon her cheek
Your medling insults here decline
To hunt the ether bell   30
The honey of the flower is mine
While courting betty Sell

While woodbine flowers in wanton twine
Weave round the matted thorn
While bees their humming musick join   35
To rob the sweets of morn
When ere I wipe the boughs away
To tread the bushy dell
Or be't a year or be't a day
I'll think of Betty Sell   40

21 Love instant unmaskd with a sigh *MS D4*   22 When I gan my fond story to tell
MS D4   23 Kinder charms still appearing from curls she wipt by *MS D4*
24 O will you be mine betty sell *MS D4*   27 *Second* your *to* youve *(p.e.) Fitz*
35 their] in: music *MS D4*   36 Morn *MS D4*   38 tred *MS D4*   39 a
year] ten years *MS D4*   40 I: betty *MS D4*

AUTOGRAPH: Pet. MS D4, pp. 13–14: Nor. MS 7, p. 41 (except for a few indecipherable lines at the beginning ll. 17–47, 53–60, 71–84 only, faint pencil, ll. 17–34, 53–60, 71–84 pencil beneath ink).
TRANSCRIPT: Pet. MS B1, pp. 44–6.
Printed in *RL*, pp. 125–9.
Dated: '1818' (MS D4, p. 13, *RL* Introduction, pp. xxii–xxiii 'In the last two years').

THE POETS WISH

A wish will rise in every breast
For somthing more then whats possest
Some trifle still or more or less
To make compleat ones happiness
& feth a wish will oft incline   5
To harbour in this breast of mine
& oft old fortune hears my case
Told's plain's the nose upon her face
But vainly do we beggars plead
Altho not askd before we need   10
Old fortune like sly farmer dapple
Where theres an orchard flings her apple
But where theres no return to make ye
She turns her nose up 'deuce may take ye'
So riches get their wealth at will   15
& beggars why the'yre beggars still—
But tis not thoughts of being rich
That makes my wishing spirit itch
Tis just an independant fate
Betwixt the little & the great   20
No out oth' way nor random wish
No ladle crav'd for silver dish

THE POETS WISH   *Title:* The Poets wish *MS D4*, The Poet's Wish *RL*, *wanting*
MS 7   4 happaness *altered to* happiness *MS D4*   5 faith *RL*   8 Told's
plain's the] Told plain as *RL*   15 riches] rich men *RL*   17 But tis] Tis *MS 7*
18 make *RL*   my *omitted MS 7*   19 Tis just] O tis *MS 7*   20/1 Then land
were powr & powr distrest / We'll wish—& let what be to rest *MS 7*   21 Nor
muse frame now a random wish *MS 7*   out-o'-the-way *RL*   22 No[e] *MS D4*]
Nor *MS 7*   [beg] crav'd *MS D4*] usd *MS 7*

Tis but a comfortable seat
While without work both ends would meet
To just get hand to mouth with ease   25
& read & study as I please
A little garret warm & high
As loves the muse sublime to flye
With all my Friends encircl'd round
In golden letters richly bound   30
Dear English poets luckless fellows
As born to such—so fate will tell us
Might I their flowrey themes peruse
& be as happy in my muse
Like them sublimly high to soar   35
Without their fate—so cursed poor

While one snug room not over small
Containd my ness[ess]ary all
& night & day left me secure
'Mong books my chiefest furniture   40
With littering papers many a bit
Scrawld by the muse in fancied fit—
& curse upon that routing jade
My territorys to invade
That found me out in evil hour   45
To brush & clean & scrub & scour
& with a dreaded brush & broom
Disturbd my learned lumber room
Such Busy things I hate to see
Such troublers neer should trouble me   50
Let dust keep gathering on the ground
& roaping cobwebs dangle round

23 Tis but] But just *MS 7*   24 While] Where: with out: woud *MS 7*
25 To] & *MS 7*, 'Tis *RL*   26 as *through* I *MS D4*   29 friends encircld *MS 7*
32 such$_\wedge$ *MS 7*   33 Might *through* May *MS D4*   Might I] Let me *MS 7*
35 Like *through* Let m *MS D4*] Let me *MS 7*   them . . . to] as sweet sublimly *MS 7*
36 With out: fate$_\wedge$: cursed] very *MS 7*   37 Wile: wroom *MS 7*   38 nessary
MS 7   39 left me] I woud *MS 7*   40 Mong *MS 7*   42 Scrawld]
Scrigd: fancied] happy: fit$_\wedge$ *MS 7*   43 rousting *MS 7*   44 teritorys *MS 7*
45 That found] & find *MS 7*, Who finds *RL*   47 a] her: ⟨& broom⟩ *torn*
MS 7   *Second* & *through* or *MS D4*] or *RL*   48 Disturbs *RL*   50 shall *RL*

—Let spiders weave their webs at will
Would cash when wanted pockets fill
To pint it just at my desire   55
& drooping muse with ale inspire
& fetch at least a roll of bread
Without a debt to run or dread
Such Comforts wou'd they were but mine
To somthing more I'd neer Incline   60
But happiest then of happy Clowns
Id sing all cares away
& pitying heads thats capt with crowns
Id see more joys then they

Thus wishd a bard—whom fortune scorns   65
To find a Rose among the thorns
& musing oer each heavy care
His pen stuck usless in his hair
His muse was dampt—nor fir'd his soul
& still unearn'd his penny roll   70
Th'unfinish'd labours of his head
Was listless on the table spread
When lo!—to bid him hope no more
A rap—an Earthquake! jars the door
His heart drops in his shoes with doubt   75
'What fiend has found my lodging out?'
Poor trembling tenants of the quill
—'Here sir I bring my masters bill—
He heavd a sigh & scratchd his head
& Credits mouth wi' promise fed   80

53 ∧Let: Webs *MS 7*   54 Woud *MS 7*   55 To] &: at my desire] as i
require *MS 7*   56 & *through* My *MS D4*] My *MS 7 RL*   muse with ale] spirits to
MS 7   57 a roll of] some a penny *MS 7*   58 Without] & neer *MS 7*
59 Comf *through* frolics *in* Comforts *MS D4*   woud *MS 7*   60 Id: incline *MS 7*
63 heads thats] monarchs *RL*   67 [humming] musing *MS D4*   71 The
unfinishd *MS 7*   72 Were *RL*   table[s] *MS D4*   74 Earthquake! *underlined*
MS D4 A gentle rap assaild the door *MS 7*   75 drops . . . with] bran full of fear
& *MS 7*   76 *Underlined MS D4*   ∧What: my lodging] me dwelling: out∧∧ *MS 7*
78 bill *underlined MS D4*] bill∧∧ *MS 7*   78/9 ['He says you owd it yesterday / He
wants the cash & bid me stay] *MS 7*   80 credits: wi⟨th⟩ *torn MS 7*

Then Set in terror down again
Invok'd the muse & scrig'd a strain
A trifling somthing glad to get
To earn a dinner & discharge the debt

AUTOGRAPH: Pet. MS D4, p. 14.
TRANSCRIPT: Pet. MS B1, p. 46 (deleted).
Dated: 1818–19 (MS D4).

SONG

Women still are cold & jealous
    When our loves sincerly
Still they doubt us weigling fellows
    Love we ere so dearly

Patty hear my hearts confession   5
    That neer did yet decieve thee
Heart & soul shall prove their passion
    Wou'd ye but believe me

Heart & soul revenge deserted
    Patty but believe me   10
Love disembl'd when we parted
    They cou'd never leave thee

AUTOGRAPH: Nor. MS 2, p. 28 (pencil).
Dated: 1819–20 (MS 2).

Fair grows the tree by the side of the fountain
Green green grows the grass in the falls of the plain
Sweet smells the thyme on the caps of the mountains
& sweet from the woods thrill[s] the Mavis [h]is strains

81 Set] *successively (a)* [met] *(b)* [yet] *(c)* Set *MS D4*] set *MS 7*, sat *RL*   in terror down] at
his desk *MS 7*   82 Invokd: scrigd *MS 7*   83 A trifling *through* & scrigd *MS 7*
84 a] the: defer *through* discharge *(or vice-versa) MS 7*
    SONG   *Title:* Song *MS D4*   5 my *through* thy *MS D4*
    FAIR GROWS THE TREE BY THE SIDE OF THE FOUNTAIN   *Title: wanting*

The fair dripping branches & grasses green blooming   5
Adorn the cool fountain & carpet the plain
& molehills of thyme the wild mountains perfuming
Still do they bloom but to please me in vain

AUTOGRAPH: Nor. MS 2 (erased pencil), p. 29 (ll. 1–9), pp. R49–R48
(ll. 10–17).
Dated: 1819–20 (MS 2).

Lost to all pleasures when pl[e]asure can please [me]
Lost to all comfort when comfort I need
Balm of despair when misfortune did tease me
Suceeder of hope when my wishes prove vain
All that could ⟨content⟩ me or ⟨delight me⟩ again   5
All that of Joy or of comfort imparted
All that could make me a ⟨fortune⟩ again
All that I Valued or lovd is departed
Adieu to all pleasure Since Patty's away

O sad was the farwell of many a prayer   10
Arose from the heart on the wings of a sigh
When I clasped her hand so speechless with ⟨care⟩
& uttered heart brouken my darling good bye
Bright as the day shone the heavens beam starting
Thro swift morning showers that stain the fair sky   15
Bright was the look that she gave me at parting
Soft was the tear that shown love in her eye

LOST TO ALL PLEASURES WHEN PLEASURES CAN PLEASE [ME]   *Title:*
wanting   12 [?] speechless

AUTOGRAPH: Nor. MS 2, pp. R46–R45 (pencil).
Dated: 1819–20 (MS 2).

SUMMER

Ere the sun the east reddens or yellows the hill
The morning breeze naturally warms
& doll where she urges her cows to stand still
The flies waken round em in swarms

The sun is all bustl[e] the meadows among   5
The waggons keep bowling away
Down wheel rifted rampers they jolter along
'& while the sun shines they make hay'

Hodge stript in his shirt is the first in the fray
& his driving a furlong we hear   10
& gaily he wistles & sings i the may
When he hives afield dinner & beer

The mowers labour toughly wears
As archd to tugging suns they strain

MSS: None known.
TRANSCRIPTS: Nor. MS 4, pp. 66–8: Pet. MS C2, pp. 58–9.
Dated: 1819–20 (MS 4, MS C2).

MORNING WALK

Come lovely Lucy lets away
Sweet morning calls and we'll obey
Look yonder see the rising sun
His daily course has just begun
Lets lightly beat the dewy grass   5
And mark each object as we pass

SUMMER   *Title:* Summer   8 hay$_\wedge$

MORNING WALK   *Title:* Morning Walk, a Fragment *MS 4*, Morning Walk: a
Fragment *MS C2*   2 obey *through* away *MS 4*

There the unheeded daisy grows
There the golden kingcup blows
There the stinking briony weaves
Round the hazel her scollopt leaves   10
Here the woodbine and the rose
All their blushing sweets disclose
Ah lovely Lucy to describe
The different flowrets tribe by tribe
Would be too much for me or you   15
Or any shepherd lad to do
Nay had I Darwins prying thought
Or all the learing Ray has taught
How soon description would exaust
And in sweet floras lap be lost   20
Then let us leave this flowry nook
And hasten down to yonder brook
Behold how clear the dimpling stream
(Illuminated by the beam
Of glare-ey'd sol whose piercing rays   25
Along the babbling water plays)
Murmuring winds along the mead
O'er grown with sedgy rush and reed
O Lucy see how swift it flows
Continually—nor stillness knows   30
Just so is mortal man I ween
Toss'd along from scene to scene
He does no rest nor pleasure know
Untill hes' laid at rest below
Aye! Lucy why so wan and pale   35
Dost thou dislike my moral tale
Or does some wrankling thought molest
The peaceful harbour of thy breast
If so the lurking fiend disarm
Drive away this magic charm   40
All thy meek beauties reasume
Let the soft flush thy face illume

14 flow'rets *MS C2*   15 too *inserted*: m *through* y *in* me *MS 4*   18 learning
MS C2   20 Floras *MS C2*   21 flowery *MS C2*   25 glare eyed *MS C2*
28 O'ergrown *MS C2*   34 Until *MS C2*   37 rankling *MS C2*   41 reassume
MS C2

Let all be gentle all be gay
Like yon skipping lambs at play
See how they chase along the rill   45
Now they scale the thymy hill
Now sporting backwards now advance
Now they join in merry dance
There they frisk it round and round
Till weariness their limbs confound   50
Contented then they sink to rest
In tranquil ease and plenty blest
Learn then from these thy mind to form
And no weak thought or passion storm
Thy tender breast—let all be calm   55
None but the foolish dream of harm
These trifles which thy mind surprise
Are counted blessings by the wise
Hark how the birds in yonder lawn
Ply forth their notes to hail the morn   60
Then let us haste their songs to hear
Melodious sweet divinely clear
First I list the woodlarks song
Now the linnet joins the throng
Next the cuckoo's well known tale   65
Echo's responsive through the vale
Now the thrush and black birds sing
While the air with music rings
Now the Hedge-chat on the spray
Warbles forth her feeble lay   70
Nay e'en the meanest birds that fly
The rook the jay and chattering pie
Join their harsh notes intent to praise
The god who all their wants repays
What thankful songs these creatures give   75
For the small morsels they receive
While we who all his bounties share
Scarce offer up a single prayr
Now we'll thro' the coppice stray
Behold this riding points the way   80

69 hedge chat *MS C2*   72 jay] day *MS 4*, may *to* jay *(p.e.) MS C2*   74 God
MS C2   80 way. *MS 4*

Delightful walk enchanting shade
For nymphs and dryades only made
Here the albion muses dwell
In oaken bower and primrose cell
Here heartfelt peace is only found   85
Sitting on the leaf strew'd ground
And every nymph and goddes slim
Lives here unseen in gaily trim
Hail rural shades retirement sweet
We once more tread with willing feet   90
Thy briery wood-bound paths among
(Where nature dwells in ample throng)
Intent on every charm to gaze
And pry along thy leafy maze
How pleasant . . .   95

MSS: None known.
TRANSCRIPT: Nor. MS 5, p. 172.
Dated: 1818–19 (MS 5).

EMMA—SONG

The fresh beauties of youth, lovely Emma adorning,
  Like the Spring's are first seen to disclose,
When the dew-dropping silver of May's infant morning,
  Unfolds the sweet blush of the rose.

While her charms, oh as varied as Summer's profusion,   5
  And ripe as the Autumn for love,
In her blue eyes sweet beaming the thrilling confusion
  Neer failing each bosom to move.

And the snows o' the Winter, improv'd on her bosom,
  No need as a rival be told.   10
And oh! my sad pains when I 'gan to disclose them
  I found it as chilling and cold.

82 dryads *MS C2*   83 Albion *MS C2*   91 woodbound *MS C2*   94 pry
could be read as prey *MS 4*
  EMMA—SONG   *Title:* Emma—Song

AUTOGRAPH: Nor. MS 5, pp. 175–6 (pencil). Clare's autograph in an MS
which is otherwise a transcript.
Printed in the *London Magazine*, January 1820, p. 11 (*LM*): *Drakard's Stamford
News*, 7 January 1820 (*reprinted from LM*).
Dated: November 1819 (Explanatory Notes).

THE INVITATION

A Witch or wizard g–d knows what
Rally'd i' D[rur]ys sh–p like thunder
Or riding besom sticks or not
Her message struck a lout wi' wonder

She 'quired for J[ohnn]y—aye! for what   5
His muse had made him known g–d speed her
He hobbl'd up put on his hat
& hung like ass behind its leader

The door was shown—he gave a tap
His fingers neath the knocker trembld   10
A Lady! hastn'd to the rap
She welcom'd in he bowd & mumbl'd

The finery dazzld on his sight
Rooms far too fine for clowns to bide in
He blinkt like owls at candlelight   15
& glad woud wisht a hole to hide in

He sat him down most spruce the night
His head might itch—he dare not scrat it
Each flea had liberty to bite
He dare not wave a finger at it   20

THE INVITATION   *Title:* The Invitation *LM, wanting MS 5*   1 God *LM*
2 i' D——ys sh–p] at Drury's door *LM*   3 beesom—stick *LM*   5 'quired]
ask'd *LM*   J——y *MS 5*] Johnny *LM*   6 His *through* The *MS 5*   God *LM*
8 his *LM*   10 trembld neath the knocker (knocker *below* [knocker *through* latch])
altered to neath the knocker trembld *MS 5*   11 hasten'd *LM*   13 dazzld *over*
[round hung] *MS 5*   on] a'e *LM*   14 R *through* F *in* Rooms *MS 5*   16 glad
woud wisht] vainly wish'd *LM*   17 spruce] prim *LM*   18 scratch *LM*
20 dare] could *LM*

But soon he provd his notions wrong
Each good friend tho most finly 'pearing
Did put clowns language on his tongue
That suited to his clownish hearing

He feels the gentrys kindness much   25
The muse she mutterd pen a sonnet
Ye cant gie less returns for such
So he that moment fixt upon it

& much he star'd & gausd about
& mutterd oer his undertaking   30
& glad was he to shamble out
Wi little Ceremony making

AUTOGRAPH: Nor. MS 7, p. 13. Signed 'John Clare'.
Printed in *RL*, p. 205.
Dated: ?1818–19 (MS 7).

ANXIETY

One oer heaths wandering in a pitch dark night
Making to sounds that hope some village near
Hermit retreating to a chinky light
Long lost in winding caverns dark & drear
A slave long banish'd from his country dear   5
By freedom left to seek his native plains
A soldier absent many a long long year

22 Each] For each: most *omitted LM*   24 As suited well the Rustic's hearing *LM*
25 felt *LM*   26 mutterd] whisper'd *LM*   27 return *LM*   28 he *through* I
MS 5   he . . . fixt] instantly begin *LM*   29 & *through* So *MS 5*   So, after gazing
round about *LM*   30 mutterd] musing *LM*   31 &] Right *LM*

   ANXIETY   *Title*: Anxiety *MS 7 RL*   *The initial letters in each line in MS 7 have been cut
away. The text has been supplied from RL*   1 ⟨One⟩ *MS 7*   2 ⟨Mak⟩ing:
near *through* nigh *MS 7*   3 ⟨Herm⟩it *MS 7*   4 ⟨Long⟩ *MS 7*
cavern *RL*   5 ⟨A sla⟩ve *MS 7*   6 ⟨By free⟩dom *MS 7*
7 ⟨A sold⟩ier *MS 7*

In sight of home ere he that confort gains
A thirsty labourer wight that wistful strains
O'er the steep hanging bank to reach the stream   10
A hope delay so lingeringly detains
We still in point of its disclosure seems
These pictures weakly 'zemble to the eye
A faint Existance of Anxiety

AUTOGRAPHS: Nor. MS 7, p. 13 (ll. 1–52 only). On the back of the
previous poem 'Anxiety': Pet. MS A1 (erased pencil), ff. 2ʳ (ll. 1–11, 17, 19),
70ʳ (ll. 20–3, 33–48, 50), 70ᵛ (ll. 51–2), 11ʳ (ll. 53–66), 13ʳ (ll. 67–80): Nor.
MS 2, pp. 3–4 (pencil, ll. 81–98).
Dated: 1818–20 (MS 7, MS A1, MS 2).

A RAMBLE

How sweet & dear
To tastes warm bosom & to healths flusht cheek
Morns flushing face peeps out her first fond smile
Crimsoning the east in many tinted hue
The horison round as edgd with brooding mist   5
Penc'ling its seeming circle round so uniform
In ting[e] of faintly blue—how lovly then
The streak which matchless nature skirting sweet
Flushes the edges of the arching sky
& melting draws the hangings of the morn   10
O who that lives as free to mark the charms
Of natures earliest dress far from the smoak
& cheerless bustle of the citys strife
To breathe the cool sweet air mark the blue skye

8 ⟨In sig⟩ht *MS 7*   9 ⟨A thirs⟩ty: white *MS 7*   labouring *RL*
10 ⟨O'er the⟩: hanging *inserted MS 7*   11 ⟨A ho⟩pe delay[s] *MS 7*
12 ⟨We sti⟩ll *MS 7*   in] on: seem *RL*   13 ⟨These⟩ *MS 7*   14 ⟨A⟩
MS 7

A RAMBLE   *Title:* [Solitude] / A Ramble *MS 7, wanting MS A1*   1 rosy sweet
MS A1   3 flushing] peeping: peeps] puts *MS A1*   5 The] & while the: as
omitted MS A1   6 Pencils *MS A1*   7 tinge: blew∧ *MS A1*   8 skirting]
skirts so charming: sweet *omitted MS A1*   9 Flushing: skye *MS A1*   11 as . . .
the] to cherish nature & her varied *MS A1*   14 breathes *MS 7*

& all the namless beauties limning morn   15
So beautifully touches who when free
By drowsy slumbers ere would be detain'd
Snoaring supinley oer their idle dreams
Would lie to loose a charm so charming now
As is the early morn—come now well start   20
Arise my dog & shake thy curdled coat
& bark thy friendly symptoms by my side
Tracing the dewy plains well muse along
Behind us left our nooked track wild wound
From bush to bush as rambling in we tread   25
Peeping on dew gilt branch moist grassy tuft
& natures every trifle ere so mean
Her every trifle pleases much mine eye
So on we hie to witness what she wears
How beautiful een seems   30
This simple twig that steals it from the hedge
& wavering dipples down to taste the stream
I cannot think it how the reason is
That every trifle natures bosom wears
Should seem so lovly & appear so sweet   35
& charm so much my soul while heedless passenger
Soodles me bye an animated post
& neer so much as turns his head to look
But staulks along as tho his eyes were blinded
& as if the witching face of nature   40
Held but now a dark unmeaning blank
        O Taste thou charm
That so endears & nature makes so lovly
Namless enthuseastic ardour thine

---

17 Who coud drows in sleep & curtaind round ⟨   ⟩ snoar *MS A1*   19 And
lie to loose a bliss as sweet as this *MS A1*   20 As . . . start] Now let us start *MS A1*
21 My dog arise: curled *MS A1*   22 symptons *MS A1*   23 As on we muse the
charms of early morn *MS A1*   *Followed in MS A1 by:* While each dewdropping branch
bend down so beautiful / & every where so cloathd so charming at this early hour
25 in *through* on *MS 7*   31 [steals] that *MS 7*   35 Shoud *MS A1*   36 my
soul so much *MS A1*   37 by *MS A1*   39 but *MS A1*   40–1 & as if
natures sweet face a dark unmeaning blank *MS A1*   41 [as] *inserted before* now *MS 7*
42 ⟨   ⟩ taste tis thou *MS A1*   43 [O thou] That *MS 7*   so . . . nature]
natures charms endears &: lovley *MS A1*

That wilderd witching rapture 'quisitive   45
Stooping bent genius oer each object—thine
That longing pausing wish that cannot pass
Uncomprehended things withou[t] a sigh
For wisdom to unseal the hidden cause
That ankering gaze as thine that fainly would   50
Turn the blue blinders of the heavens aside
To see what gods are doing

What ist wi breaking thro the hedge
& in the dyke pit pattering rustles in
Through moss & witherd leaves uncoothly ⟨born⟩   55
Tis that poor hedgehog every bristles up
A thousand spears in the defensive winds
Protects these timid creatures & preserves
For combat or for flight
Ah quiet disconcerted timid friend   60
Thy claw is rough as ⟨   ⟩ through
A trifle such as nature musters up
To wind her way compleatly round
& make a graceful finish
A trifle such as every bosom loves   65
Which honest taste of nature does Inspire

How sweet to wind the lane confined as now
In a lovd prison of oer hanging boughs
As loosd & wirls each turning round & round
Some new variety keeps d[r]op[p]ing in   70
Fresh flowr or scene speckt cot or steeples point
Just sprouting oer the horizon still changing sweet
⟨Flowering⟩ lovley & for ever new
As on proceeding to the lanes last end
⟨Pastor[a]lls⟩ gently on a hill whose rise commands   75
A bursting view apprising on the eye

45 wilderd . . . 'quisitive] tempting charm *MS A1*   46 Stooping] That stoop: object∧
MS A1   47–8 That longing pause on things uncomprehended thine *MS A1*
47 [lingering] longing: wish *inserted MS 7*   50 [Then] that *(first word) MS 7*   That
restless ankering searching that woud fain *MS A1*   51 blinder *MS A1*
53–66 *Copy-text: MS A1*   58–9 *Deleted MS A1*   67–80 *Copy-text: MS A1*
74 [lane] lanes *MS A1*

Brooks silver shined & wood shades greening deep
Meadow & culterd field of varied hue
& Hierogliphs of art dropt here & there
& mingling patchd with cottages & spires   80

As rugged & as barren as it seems
This heath too has its beauties
Brush we on Unheeding rude assaults
Of Brambles' pertinent & catching finger
So sweetly wild & perminant of hue   85
& heaths low creeping in their pinky bloom
& here beside the dead bents rustling tuft
A blossom hides its beauties from the world
& such a one as natures happiest hand
Neer took a tool to scoop & hollow out   90
One of more curious interesting form
Its speckld petals c[a]lyx burnishd gold
Inmixd with somber hues exactly forms
A living ins cot for Industry famd
& hence this natures solitary gem   95
That numbers in her calender of curosities
⟨Gains⟩ its distinguishment tho neer unknown
The 'Bee flower' apt characteristic name

---

77 [cottage] wood *MS A1*   81–98 *Copy-text: MS 2*   89 hand *through* thought
MS 2   90 [in hand] to *MS 2*
95
              & hence [its apt characeristic name]
              This [almost lost curosity of nature]
              This [solitary plant]
                  natures solitary gem   *MS 2*

97 *?* Gains *through ?* Meets *MS 2*

AUTOGRAPH: Nor. MS 7, p. 41.
Dated: ? 1818–20 (MS 7).

To stand the brunts of toil & stormy weather
What many gewgaws of the softer sex
What simpring charms to tempt us & perplex
Some with a killing dart from ⟨   ⟩ eye
Our heart receives em as we pass em bye   5
Some with a rosy cheek have hearts at will
A smile relieves us or a frown must kill
A ruby lip shapd hand or swelling breast
Forbids the aching heart to be at rest
Needless to mention every zembling art   10
Curls paint & patches but a minutes smart
Deception charms while ignorance befriends
But hate atends the cheat expeirence ends
Charms purly nature beautys still remain
Charms patchd by Art are sickning & vain   15
Some with a voice bewitch our ravishd ears
As tho they stole the music of [the] spheres
& many a heart has been deserted found
Smit with the eden that appears in sound
& here sweet D[amo]n thy pleasing power excels   20
Where many a captive heart enrapturd dwells
Here where thy charms an easy conquest makes
Here heaven breaks silence while the angel speaks
But when she sings then charms before unknown
Make all that hear her wish such charms unknown   25
Blest is the authors toil her voice displays
For what she sings can never fail of praise
No longer in despair he lives unknown
But meets applause for merits not his own
& woudst thou d–m the ⟨   ⟩   30

TO STAND THE BRUNTS OF TOIL & STORMY WEATHER   *Title:*
wanting   This fragment starts in mid-poem, the previous line ending in lump together
1 To] The: stormy *confused and followed by* to *through* ye *both deleted*   2 gugaws
3 sinpring   4 *Hiatus*   8 chapd hann   13 th⟨e⟩ *torn*   20 D——n
30 *Possibly* hu⟨mble   ⟩ *cut away together with another line of verse*

AUTOGRAPH: Nor. MS 7, p. 41.
Dated: ? 1818–20 (MS 7).

Thy eye can witness more then others
   Thy feelings are thy own
& labours anguish & her sorrows
   To thee has long been known
Luxurys wealth & pride uphold my 〈   〉   5
   Poor labours slav'd to dead
While they die gorg'd like beast in clover
   We die for wants of bread

& what is worse—our little earnings
   For which we toil & sweat   10
To uphold em [a]nd urge their coaches
   They tax back half we get
We wear no rags but they ha part ont
   They tax yer sho & shoetye
Yer barly bannock—theyle ha share   15
   Like robber oer a booty

They run so eager arter wealth
   Such upstarts & contrivers
Im made a very slave among em
   Curst witling negroe drivers   20
Our p——s talk of hardships bless em
   Well hells doom they unravel
But labour here in luxury proves
   The devils very devil

& thou thought right their ans[we]rs matey   25
   Tho plain to all thy kind
Thy feelings only coud disern it
   Poor ignorance is blind
Im Labour friend & thats what I am
   & that fat podgy knave   30
Is Luxury ye know 'nough on him
   & I am Luxurys slave

THY EYE CAN WITNESS MORE THEN OTHERS   *Title: wanting*
5 *Word missing*   11 —nd: urge *could be read as* crye   15 Yer *through* Ther
21 *?princes*   25 ans^{rs}

AUTOGRAPHS: Pet. MS A40, p. 37: Pforzheimer Library, Misc. MS 197:
Nor. MS 7, p. 43: Norris Museum SAVNM CL/14.
TRANSCRIPT: Pet. MS B1, p. 38 (deleted).
Dated: '1815' (Pfz).

SONNET

Well have I learnd the value of vain life
Long have I stood the worlds reproach & scorn
& braved fates sea full many a cloudy morn
Long bristling many a waves contending strife
Long curs'd the luckless day that saw me born   5
& brought to light my miserys & me
But now vain life & use me how ye will
Ill kiss the rod & smile at every ill
Ive learnd thy value & I've learnd thy end
A mad braind wanderer & without a friend   10
Age learnd me little & experience much
& as a beggar leans upon his crutch
On my last hope a pilgrim here I bend
For peace beyond the grave were all my woes shall end

SONNET   *Title:* Sonnet *MS A40 Pfz MS 7 Norris*   1 learnt: Value: Vain
Norris   Life *MS 7 Norris*   2 Scorn *Norris*   3 *Replaced by* ————— Oer
whelming sea *Pfz*] ————— Oer whelming sea —— *MS 7,* ————— Oer
whelming Sea *Norris*   4   brustled *Pfz*] brustld *MS 7*, brustl'd *Norris*   Waves
Norris   5 curst *Pfz MS 7 Norris*   luck less *MS 7 Norris*   saw me *through* I was
MS A40   6 mesiries *Pfz*] miseries *MS 7 Norris*   me— *Norris*   7 —But *Pfz*
MS 7   Life *MS 7*] Life—*Norris*   (&: will) *Pfz MS 7 Norris*   8 the] thy
Norris   at] on *Pfz MS 7 Norris*   9 learnt *twice*: Ive *(sixth word) Pfz MS 7*
Norris   end, *Pfz*   10 Friend *Norris*   11 learnt *Pfz MS 7*] tells *Norris*
Expierence *MS 7*] Expierience *Norris*   12 —& *MS 7*   Beggar *MS 7 Norris*
leans upon] leaning oer *Norris*   13 Pilgrim *MS 7 Norris*   14 Grave *MS 7*]
Grave— *Norris*   where *Pfz MS 7*] when *Norris*   woes shall] sorrows *MS 7*   End
Norris

AUTOGRAPH: Nor. MS 7, p. 45 (ink through pencil).
Dated: ?1818–20 (MS 7).

So now says he weegling how matters went wi im
As Ive begd food & clothing & nobody gi em
The next plan to take is—hard fortune a curs ont
As beging wornt speed I mun rob & make wors ont
Tho the case stans wi that as it stood wi the tother   5
I may as well dy by one death as dye by another
The hemp fevers dreadful—as terrors can mak it
But still reasons plain if as plain I can take it
Where force puts no choise we mun put up wi pinches
Hemp mays well end at once ont what hunger but inches   10
So now for their desent behaviour Ill comb em
What they wornt gie fairly Ill foul take from em
So said on the high road he took up his station
Wi trifles he first gan his new occupation
But in practise grown bolder—succeses still speeding   15
Tempted actions more dareing to crown the preceeding
Till hardend in robbing—O horror forbidding
He dard to do murder—which shall not be hidden
Young readers take warning ye ha the Example
O the 'fruits of Idleness' this is a sample   20
Friendship is but Vanity hope not there giving
Let your hands be your trust for the honestest living
He was taen & condemnd in the hopes o' his glory
& a Gallows deservd serves to finis the story

SO NOW SAYS HE WEEGLING HOW MATTERS WENT WI IM   *Title:*
wanting   1 weeghing   2 *Second &`through* there   11 comb *could be read*
as courb   12 wornt] wound   17 hardend *through* ? cunning   19 ha
inserted   21–2 *Inserted*

AUTOGRAPH: Nor. MS 7, p. 53 (sideways in margin, pencil).
Dated: ?1818–20 (MS 7).

      Had they but got a haunch of bread
         & silver george to spare
      The labours pay without the work
         I shoudnt may be care
      Till pitch dark night the light een shows   5
         & cheerfulness on monday

AUTOGRAPH: Nor. MS 7, p. 53 (sideways in margin, pencil).
Dated: ?1818–20 (MS 7).

      Full many troubles vext my hate
         & many silly wims
      & fain upon the sunny bank
         Id stretchd my lazy limbs
      The fleering witches nigh at hand   5
         Kep ⟨   ⟩ me forsooth
      Muses I ⟨   echo agen⟩ are vain
         Ive ⟨   ⟩ uncooth

AUTOGRAPH: Nor. MS 7, p. 53 (ll. 1–68 pencil).
Dated: ?1818–20 (MS 7).

      Shepherd why is this complaining
      So I askd a langu[i]d swain
      Bending oer his hook in sorrow
      As I wanderd oer the plain

HAD THEY BUT GOT A HAUNCH OF BREAD   *Title: wanting*
FULL MANY TROUBLES VEXT MY HATE   *Title: wanting*   6–8 *Partly*
discoloured   6 forsooth *through indecipherable*
SHEPHERD WHY IS THIS COMPLAINING   *Title: wanting*

Great he answrd is my anguish 5
  My poor dog a slave to me
Brutish as I usd him left me
  Cruel cruel should I be

Had I said some word of comfort
  As he limpt across the plain 10
Had I said come back my rover
  Twoud have comforted his pain

Cruel how the blow sup[r]isd him
  Little did he think to see
Such usage from his once kind master 15
  Kind as he once usd to be

O the Pitying looks he left me
  As he limpt across the plain
Whats my fault he turnd to ask me
  Wreathing in the greatest pain 20

O the howl that told his anguish
  From the blow he had from me
Master thy hot anger cruel
  Cruel cruel shoud I be

But I struck him in my passion 25
  While a worthless fellow sed
He killd his lambs a nights—morover
  If I should [k]no[w] hed shoot him dead

Cruel was the blow I gave him
  Vengance when the fellow spoke 30
Wangd my hook at my poor rover
  O it was a cruel stroke

A broken leg he traild behind him
  As he limpt across the plain
Still my evil eyes behold him 35
  Still he turns & howls again

10 lipmpt   17 Pitying *through* the   21 houl   23 angere

Had my rover but been guilty
   Then I should not sorrowd long
But my dog was good & harmless
   Never known to do a wrong   40

Tother night the trap was fixed
   This morning did the snare suceed
A crafty fox had done the murder
   Here afresh my bosom bleeds

Rover why did I believe it   45
   Guilty thou wast never known
O to be of crimes suspected
   Caus thou pickt the ofal bone

Thus the shepherd told his anguish
   Verily my bosom bled   50
Th[r]ee days have I hunted vainly
   For my dog he sighing said

Childern oer the green came running
   Shepherd stop the childern said
In yon wood your dog is dying   55
   Now abouts your rovers dead

When we calld him rover rover
   Wistfuly he lookd around
Strove to stir then wimperd loudly
   Then again he lick his wound   60

Ah we dearly lovd poor rover
   Fain woud we have gen him bread
He lickt our hands & woud not eat it
   Lookd & howld & hung his head

Others came wi news more piercing   65
   Shep[h]erd rovers dead they cryd
Oer & oer he rolld him howling
   Then he lickt his wound & dy'd

---

42 morning *through* murder   48 f *through* v *in* ofal   62 Fain] Fair
64 g *through* d *in* hung

O the shepherds grief & anguish
   Verrily my bosom bled   70
Pity left him to his sorrow
   Mourning oer his rover dead

AUTOGRAPHS: Pet. MS A40, p. 37 (deleted): Nor. MS 7, p. 69 (reduced to
11 lines).
TRANSCRIPT: Pet. MS B1, p. 47.
Dated: 1819 (Explanatory Notes).

TO REVD MR HOLLAND

When trembling genius makes her first essay
By ignorance & poverty opprest
Nipt struggling in oppressions cloudy day
Ah who can tell the anguish of the breast
The doubts & fears that throng her thorny way   5
That fill the eye & rob the Soul of rest
Hail Holland hail thou friend to worth distrest
Thou man of taste from thy discerning eye
My artless strains have found a ready friend
The muse by thee a loftier flight will try   10
Tho thou alone her artless strains commend
& feign some token in return she'd send
Though rough the strain great will thy praise appear
Canst thou believe it that she sings sincere

69–72 *Sideways in margin*   70 'Verrily

TO REVD MR HOLLAND   *Title:* To Rev^d Mr Holland *MS A40*, To the Rev^d M^r
Holland *MS 7*   2 Ignorance: oprest *MS 7*   5 her] the *MS 7*   6 soul
MS 7   7 worth] the *MS 7*   8 'man: taste': from thy] in whose *MS 7*
11 art less *MS A40*
9–14   My artless strains art ready to commend
            The muse encouragd lofteir flight will try
            & great the pleasure where she meets a friend   *MS 7*

AUTOGRAPH: Nor. MS 7, p. 69.
Dated: 1819 (MS 7).

> Not booted foplings when their cloaths misfit
> Not cleanly nurs maids when the babes be——t
> Not the old toper his most dreadful curse
> That slinks the last sad sixpence from his purse
> Not the young wench that coxcombs lies believd   5
> Not wrinkld dames a second time decievd
> Not doubtful bard that first appears in print
> Dreading the evils the vain World has int
> Not all the plagues that haunt this world below
> Nor each sad Victim with his several woe   10

AUTOGRAPH: Nor. MS 7, p. 69.
Dated: 1819 (MS 7).

> The driving clouds in dark condension hung
> The village bell its warning summons rung
> & every witch that doubtful forcd to roam
> Was by the welcom call conducted home
> The roads bemird with hasty showers of rain   5
> & Evenings cautions hung her lamps in vain
> The sweeping moonbeams momentary peep
> Behind the racking clouds was ushd to sleep
> The fare moon neath many a lulling sweep
> Of bright rack riding clouds had sunk in sleep   10
> Or only winking thro thin folded shrouds
> & only wakend thro disparted clouds

NOT BOOTED FOPLINGS WHEN THEIR CLOATHS MISFIT *Title:*
wanting   2 *beshit*   3 curse *repeated*

THE DRIVING CLOUDS IN DARK CONDENSION HUNG *Title: wanting*
6 Evenings *through* warnings   9 *First* l *through* f *in* lulling   10 bright
through rack   11 winking *through* blinking *through indecipherable*

AUTOGRAPH: Nor. MS 11, p. 109.
Dated: 1804–6 (MS 11).

Twas but a wild bramble that catchd at her gown
While the bramble of doubt stung her breast
Uneasy she saunterd again to the town
& in bed waited vainly for rest

AUTOGRAPH: Nor. MS 11, p. 230.
Dated: 1804–6 (MS 11).

Man in that Age no rule but Reason knew
And with a native bent did good pursue,
Unawd by punishment, and void of fear,
His words were simple and his soul sincere
By no forced laws his passions were confin'd   5
For conscience kept his heart, and calm'd his mind,
Peace o'er the world, her blessed sway maintain'd
And e'en in Desarts smiling Plenty reign'd—

AUTOGRAPH: Nor. MS 11, p.247.
Dated: ?1804 (MS 11).

I Saw a Tree with Cheries Red,
Whole Height was 40 Foot,
A Moat against it hinder'd me
That I could not get to't,

TWAS BUT A WILD BRAMBLE THAT CATCHD AT HER GOWN *Title:*
wanting   2 of doubt *repeated*

MAN IN THAT AGE NO RULE BUT REASON KNEW *Title: wanting*

I SAW A TREE WITH CHERIES RED *Title: wanting*   3 it *inserted over* [it]
squeezed in

The Moat was 30 Feet all Wet   5
The Question now must be
How Long a Ladder I must Set
To reach the Top o' the Tree.

AUTOGRAPH: Nor. MS 11, pp. 251–2.
Printed in the *Northampton Herald*, 26 August 1893 (from MS 11).
Dated: ?1804 (MS 11).

As I was walking out one Day,
Which happened on the first of May;
As luck would have it, I did spy,
A May Pole raised up on high;
The which at first me much surpriz'd,   5
Not being before hand advertiz'd;
Of such a strange uncommon sight,
I said I would not stir that Night;
Nor rest content, until I'd found,
Its height exact from off the Ground;   10
But when these Words, I just had spoke,
A blast of Wind the May-Pole broke;
Whose broken Piece I found to be,
Exact in length, yards sixty three,
Which by its fall broke up a hole,   15
Twice fifteen Yards from off the Pole;
But this being all that I can do,
The May-Pole now being broken in two
Unequal Parts, to aid a Friend,
Ye Youths pray then an answer send.   20

Clare gives 50 *as the answer to the problem*

AS I WAS WALKING OUT ONE DAY   *Title: wanting MS 11 NH*   4 raised
up on] resting upon *NH*   5 at first] does make *NH*   *Clare gives* 118 yards 1'
2.04" *as the answer to this problem*

AUTOGRAPHS: Nor. MS 11, facing p. 447 (inside back cover): Nor. MS 11, p. 409 (ll. 1–10 only, pencil).
Dated: 1804–6 (MS 11).

Thrice Welcome to thy song sweet warbling thrush
May you be happy as you still have been
The present sunshine warms your covert bush
The future clouds you know not what they mean
Vain foolish thought & why should ye be [sad]   5
Why be like me with ills to come oprest
To pass the present bliss that may be had
& wait on sorrow as a welcome guest
No sing thou on & let me sorrow still
I cant be happy be it as it will   10
In vain the sun gleams thro the prison grate
To cheer the felon thats condemnd to dye
[H]is soul in anguish mourns impending fate
Such pains are his & such a one am I

AUTOGRAPH: Nor. MS 13, inside back cover.
Dated: ?1818–20 (MS 13).

Beneath thies hedge how happy have I felt
As I have hummed oer my rustic songs
Upon this bank how often have I knelt
& wi the cow boy plated rushy thongs

THRICE WELCOME TO THY SONG SWEET WARBLING THRUSH   *Title:*
wanting MS 11, facing p. 447 MS 11, p. 409   1 Good morning to ye ballad
singing thrush *MS 11, p. 409*   1/2 [May good success your early songs attend]
MS 11, p. 409   2 hapy *MS 11, p. 409*   3 C *through* p *in* Covert *MS 11,*
p. 409   5 shoud: sad *MS 11, p. 409*   6 ills . . . oprest] fancy'd ills distrest
MS 11, p. 409   7 bliss] ill *MS 11, p. 409*   8 on] for: sorrows: welcome]
wanted *MS 11, p. 409*   9 let me sorrow] be thou foolish *MS 11, p. 409*
10 as] how *MS 11, p. 409*   13 Is soul *MS 11, facing p. 447*
BENEATH THIES HEDGE HOW HAPPY HAVE I FELT   *Title: wanting*
2 rus⟨tic⟩ *torn*   4 rus⟨hy⟩ *torn*

AUTOGRAPH: Nor. MS 22–6. A letter to the Editor of the 'Morning Post' in the Strand, 'I send you these for your kindness to me and my poetry.' Dated: 1818–19 (Paper watermarked 1818).

TO SUSAN ETHINNINGTON

1

& We have been so very blest
In undisturb'd domestic rest
Each word with love light softly drest
    Each thought in silence blending
I could not wish our life to be   5
Framed of a rarer quality
All moments kind so worthy thee
    And thou wast so befriending

2

Ah Why am I so wan & low
So pitched by nature to the snow   10
Of this wild winters life to know
    The pains of proud enduring
Is the sun made too rich & grand
To shed its gold light on my hand
And must I yield thee to a band   15
    More gay & more alluring?

3

I kiss'd thy lip but could not speak
Thy full lip kissd my trembling cheek
Our eyes with passions dim & weak
    In mingled lustre fainted   20
We parted—so the world decreed,
But still we have been blest indeed
To thee come wealth to me come need
    I' both I am contented

TO SUSAN ETHINNINGTON   *Title:* To Susan Ethinnington (*or* Ethinningtier)
Additional punctuation is not Clare's   1 blest,   2 rest,   4 blending;
6 quality,—   7 thee,—   8 was't: befriending!   9 Ah!: low,
10 snow,   12 enduring,—   13 grand,   14 hand,—   17 lip: speak,
18 kiss'd: cheek,   19 weak,   20 fainted;—   22 indeed,
23 need,   24 I both: contented.

MSS: None known.
Printed in *RL*, pp. 150–2.
Dated: 1819 (Explanatory Notes).

TO A COLD BEAUTY, INSENSIBLE OF LOVE

Eliza, farewel! ah, most lovely Eliza,
  So much as thy beauties excel;
So much as I love thee, so much as I prize thee,
  Unfeeling Eliza, farewel!
The heart without feeling, the beauty's but small,   5
  Though tempting it be to the view;
The warmth of a soul crowns the beauty of all,
  Without it thou'rt nothing—adieu!

Thou Image of Beauty, endeavour is vain,
  To warm thee to life and to love,   10
Could I but the skill of the artist attain,
  And steal thee a soul from above;
Though as fair as the statue he finish'd art thou,
  'Twere folly his plan to pursue;
I would give thee feeling, but cannot tell how;   15
  I would love thee, dear—but, adieu!

To all that life sweetens eternally lost,
  Where love makes a heaven below,
Thy bosom's congealed in apathy's frost,
  As white and as cold as the snow: 20
Since no spark of soul its dead tenant can warm,
  Thou Icicle hung on Spring's brow,
I'll turn my sighs from thee to mix with the storm;
  The storm's full as tender as thou.

That heart where no feelings or raptures can dwell,   25
  Be its owner in person most fair,
Were beauty a bargain to buy or to sell,
  I never would purchase it there:

TO A COLD BEAUTY, INSENSIBLE OF LOVE   *Title:* To a cold Beauty,
insensible of Love   11 but] e'en *RL 4th edn.*   27 Where *RL 2nd edn.*

So cold to the joys that in sympathy burn,
  Joys none but true love ever knew,   30
How lost should I be could I prove no return:
  I wish to be happy—adieu!

MSS: None known.
Printed in *RL*, p. 154.
TRANSCRIPT: Pet. MS B1, p. 48.
Dated: ?1818–19 (*RL*).

ON YOUTH

Ah, youth's sweet joys! why are ye gone astray?
  Fain would I follow could I find a plan:
To my great loss are ye exchang'd away,
  For that sad sorrow-ripening name—a man.
Far distant joys! the prospect gives me pain: 5
  Ah, happiness! and hast thou no return?
No kind concern to call thee back again,
  And bid this aching bosom cease to mourn?
The daisies' hopes have met another Spring,
  Poor standard tenants on a stormy plain;   10
The lark confirms it on his russet wing;
  And why alone am I denied? in vain:
Ah, youth is fled!
  A second blossom I but vainly crave:
The flower, that opes with peace to come,   15
  Is budding in the grave.

ON YOUTH   *Title:* On Youth *RL*   12 why *through* while *MS B1*

MSS: None known.
Printed in *RL*, pp. 182–4.
TRANSCRIPT: Pet. MS B1, pp. 53–4.
Dated: 1817–19 (*RL* Introduction, p. xxii 'In the last two years').

THE FIRST OF MAY   A BALLAD

Fair blooms the rose upon the green,
  Pretending to excel;
But who another rose has seen,
  A different tale can tell.
The morning smiles, the lark's begun   5
  To welcome in the May:
Be cloudless, skies! look out, bright sun!
  And haste my love away.

Though graceful round the maidens move,
  That join the rural ball,   10
Soon shall they own my absent love
  The rival of them all.
Go, wake your shepherdess, ye lambs!
  And murmur her delay:
Chide her neglect, ye hoarser dams!   15
  And call my love away.

Ye happy swains, with each a bride,
  Were but the angel there,
While slighted maids despair'd and sigh'd,
  You'd court th' unequall'd fair.   20
Dry up, ye dews! nor threat'ning hing,
  To soil her best array:
Ye birds! with double vigour sing,
  And urge my love away.

  THE FIRST OF MAY   A BALLAD   *Title:* The First of May. / a Ballad.
RL   *Stanzas numbered 1–5 in MS B1*   18 Were *to* Was *(p.e.) over* [Wh] *MS B1*
20 th' unequall'd] the absent *MS B1*

Welcome, sun! the dews are fled,   25
    The lark has rais'd his song;
The daisy nauntles up its head,—
    Why waits my love so long?
As flowrets fade, the pleasures bloom,
    All hastening to decay: 30
The day steals on, and showers may come:
    This instant haste away.

What now, ye fearful cringing sheep!
    Who meets your wondering eyes?
What makes you 'neath the maples creep,   35
    In homaging surprise?
No ladies tread our humble green:
    Ah! welcome wonders, hail!
I witness your mistaken queen
    Is Patty of the Vale.   40

MSS: None known.
Printed in *RL*, p. 201: Hone's *Every-day Book*, 1827, col. 318.
TRANSCRIPT: Pet. MS B1, p. 59.
Dated: ?1818–19 (*RL*).

APPROACH OF SPRING

Sweet are the omens of approaching Spring,
    When gay the elder sprouts her winged leaves;
When tootling robins carol-welcomes sing,
    And sparrows chelp glad tidings from the eaves.
What lovely prospects wait each wakening hour,   5
    When each new day some novelty displays;
How sweet the sun-beam melts the crocus flower,
    Whose borrow'd pride shines dizen'd in his rays:

27 d *through* D *in* daisy: nauntles *underlined MS B1*   38 [hail] hail *MS B1*

APPROACH OF SPRING   *Title:* Approach of Spring *RL Hone   Ink and pencil
alterations in MS B1 are Taylor's*   2 elder] *(a)* elden *(b)* Elden *(c)* Eldern *(p.e.)*
MS B1*   3 Robins carol∧: bring *in pencil in margin MS B1*   8 borrowed *over*
[border'd] *MS B1*

Sweet, new-laid hedges flush their tender greens;
Sweet peep the arum-leaves their shelter screens;   10
    Ah! sweet are all which I'm denied to share:
Want's painful hindrance sticks me to her stall;—
    But still Hope's smiles unpoint the thorns of Care,
Since Heaven's eternal Spring is free for all.

MSS: None known.
Printed in *RL*, p. 202.
TRANSCRIPT: Pet. MS B1, p. 60.
Dated: ?1818–19 (*RL*).

SUMMER

The oak's slow-opening leaf, of deepening hue,
    Bespeaks the power of Summer once again;
While many a flower unfolds its charms to view,
    To glad the entrance of his sultry reign.
Where peep the gaping, speckled cuckoo-flowers,   5
    Sweet is each rural scene she brings to pass;
Prizes to rambling school-boys' vacant hours,
    Tracking wild searches through the meadow grass:
The meadow-sweet taunts high its showy wreath,
And sweet the quaking grasses hide beneath.   10
    Ah, 'barr'd from all that sweetens life below,
Another Summer still my eyes can see
    Freed from this scorn and pilgrimage of woe,
To share the Seasons of Eternity.

9 flush their] flush'd with *altered to* blush their *Harvard proof copy*, blush with *MS B1*
10 peep[s]: aron *to* arum *(p.e.)*: it's *MS B1*   arum-leaves; *altered to* arum-leaves
Harvard proof copy   Marginal note in MS B1: Aron flower is the 'Lords-&-lady' flowers
11 is *Hone*   12 hinderance *MS B1*   13 hope *to* hope's *(p.e.)*: unpaints *to*
unpaint *(p.e.)*: care *MS B1*   14 Heaven's *over* [leaves]: spring *MS B1*   for]
from *Hone*

   SUMMER   *Title:* Summer *RL*   5 peeps: flower *to* flowers *(p.e.) MS B1*
8 meadows *to* meadow *(p.e.) MS B1*   11 bard *altered to* 'bar'd *MS B1*
12 still] seen *altered to* still: can] shall *altered to* can *Harvard proof copy*   14 seasons
MS B1

MSS: None known.
TRANSCRIPT: Pet. MS B1, pp. 54–7 (deleted).
Dated: ?1818–19 (MS B1).

Ah doubtful bard perhaps in vain
You scribble your expected gain
Fortunes a hazard all would wait
As hopeful of some better fate
Trembling victims want wears down   5
Chance deals not worth her smile or frown
A Southey hears the whispering strain
The bards own'd great but sings in vain
A Southey hears his numbers roll
Of poetry the very soul   10
Go witness his inspired strains
And ask the poet what's the gains
A suffocating shower of praise
A treetops mighty crown of bays
And the same time ah who'd believe   15
As crawls the louse the beggars sleave
May hopeless faint and poor as thee
Sing those fine strains to Poverty
The scribbler next behold him shine
⟨Keen⟩ to correct the poets line   20
In many a wise unmeaning slare
And many a consequential stare
And sits him down and hums along
And finds where he fancies must be wrong
And insect dry discoursing gammer   25
Tells what's not rhyme and what's not grammar
Leering and pleas'd at faults the while
To help the lame dog o'er the stile
And was this Critic known forsooth
(Twould be ill manners speaking truth)   30
Spite of his learning glean'd at colledge
His outward titles inward knowledge

AH DOUBTFUL BARD PERHAPS IN VAIN   *Title: wanting   Pencil heading*:
Unhatcht (*Clare's*)   6 (not worth)   15 ah *through* the: ah who'd *through*
who'd b   20 *Hiatus*

His learning which he brags so much
To act Longinus or as such
A Critic brag who learning pothers   35
So great himself to judge for others
Is just as fit if I discern
As whopstraw lowking in a barn
Who B fro' bulls foot couldn't tell ye
Nor yet the deep hid difference tell ye   40
Or fitless as with less a farce on
The parish clerk to act the parson
Then smiling at me o'er the table
And told a corresponding fable
'Mong the wood minstrels years ago   45
'There always join'd a scoundrel crow
'Pretending much to critics learning
'In singing wonderous deep discerning
'Such taste such baseness (neer doubt him)
'Twas vain to sing aught without him   50
'Of so much consequence was he
'Such insolence and poetry
'As neither blackbird thrust or linnett
'Could meet in peace to sing a minute
'Without the jabbering beggars bother   55
'In finding fault with one or other
'Once on a time the croaking devil
'As fate ordaind bad luck to cavil
'The birds all met no way to quarrel
'But just to talk about the laurel   60
'Each one to give as was the thesis
'Of his abilities a species
'Extempore ode or song to be
'Or any choice of poetry
'To's worth and judgment might bequeath   65
'The then left vacant laurel wreath
'Which lay as crowns off left bargaring
'Till heads were found as worth the wearing
'The crow still first in each affair
'As chief decider took the chair   70

34 or *through* on   40 difference[s]   43 o'er] on   66 wreath *through*
leaf

'With great pretensions (ham) and spirit
'To see who had and had not merit
'In his eye merits fex were small
'None earnd a praise faults due to all
'To some he bid them hold their tongues   75
'And never more pretend to songs
'Best for your selves I'd have ye know it
'Ye'll never match to be the poet
'So ne'er be hurt at my refusal
'But follow your calling 'gain as usual   80
'To others he was more a friend
'And said by practise they might mend
'Gave hopeful hints when faults confuted
'As corresponding genius suited
'And though he said the prize is vain   85
'Each competition strove to gain
'They might in time wi' careful pushes
'At such a meeting meet their wishes
'Each bird had sung his ode or sonnet
'And heard the critics 'pinions on it   90
'Some nettld their revenges mutter'd
'And all disliking inly flutter'd
'At last a mavis from the bush
'Or if ye like a mavis thrush
'Bespoke the criticiser thus   95
'Old friend you make a monstrous fuss
'And find says he uncommon fault
'More doubtless far than what you ought
'Sure you must be so vers'd in taste and learning
'So deep and witty in discerning   100
'To judge of others as you do
'What might we not expect from you
'You've prov'd us all we've all a fault
'And no one sings so well's we ought
'Your singings chance 'bove ours is double   105
'The wreath is yours without the trouble

74 a *through* in   87 *Did Clare write 'pishes'?*

MSS: None known.
TRANSCRIPT: Pet. MS B1, pp. 60–1.
Dated: ?1818–19 (MS B1).

ADDRESS TO THE SLUGGARD

Awake thou sluggard cou'd thy drowzy soul
Lay sloth aside—be resolute enough
To trace the fields and silver studded woods
While each grass point and velvet knobbed flower
Bends arching with a gem—O couldst thou but   5
Meet the first breath, which morning zephyrs breath
Pilfering and culling, skimming woods and fields
Who like a robber lingers for the chance
When wakening nature opens all her stores
Molests her entrance and unbid intrudes   10
With forcing rape—to sip her sweetest charms
Then in a heedless and make gamely fit
Scatter their beauties o'er a thankless world
  O wouldst thou but
List to the hymn of day break when the woods   15
Echo in harmony where lark and thrush
And blackbirds music thrilling low and loud
  Ah didst thou witness
What the morning is when sun beams sweet
As curdling through the dewy misted panes   20
Checkers the wall and urges thee to rise
  Couldst thou but tell
What charms which Ign'rance passes unconcernd
At that same hour enraptur'd genius sees
And with enchanted ravishment admires   25
With natures charms intoxicated—how
Trace wood and field
Pause on each flower and varied leaf 'cognise
Lost in the bliss which nature yields & none
But natures children know   30

ADDRESS TO THE SLUGGARD   *Title:* Address to the Sluggard
13 Scatter[s]   17 music *over* [strong counter and tenor voices]   20 panes
over [plains]

O couldst thou feel
The thrilling burning extacy of soul
The throbbing beat that heaves the bosoms charm
While musing on the work of power divine
When in each meanest mite on earth or sea   35
Its makers Image wonderfully shines
When genius left in wonders void to pause
Thrills into adoration's silent praise
And bent enraptur'd hails the Lord of all
Didst thou know this thy shocky bed   40
Which seems to thee so comfortable now
Lost in its drowsy apathy and ease
Would like a dungeon seem and please no more
But when nights curtain lap't thee up to sleep
And shut in darkness natures weary eye   45
As sickness bed is to the fated wretch
To thee its necessary rest would seem
A forc'd releif as loath'd to be enjoy'd

AUTOGRAPHS: Pet. MS B7, p. 18: Pforzheimer Library, Misc. MS 197 (four-line fragment).
Dated: ?1818–20 (Pfz).

On Saturday night she was strewing her sand
I gently went up & caught hold of her hand
Catched hold of hand kisses I gave her three
But the cunning oxford stole her from me

The saturday after while milking her cow   5
I stept up & muttered love how do you now
She gave me cross answers & bid me be gone
& said Id been dandling & loving too long

40 this,   41 [Thy shocky bed] Which
ON SATURDAY NIGHT SHE WAS STREWING HER SAND *Title: wanting*
MS B7 Pfz   4 *Hiatus between* oxford *and* stole *MS B7*   8/9 *Space for two lines*
MS B7
On saturday her sand she strews
& cleans her floor & mops & stews
The cat & dog commend the news
& from the house get   *Pfz*

(l.1 [?] her; l.4 *final word missing*)

You must kiss them & court them & often times go
For I lost my Jenny for being too slow   10

AUTOGRAPHS: Pet. MS B7, pp. 19–20: Nor. MS 25 (ll. 26–30, 41–55
omitted): Pet. MS A1, f. 28ʳ (ll. 1–10, 32–5 only, erased pencil).
TRANSCRIPT: Pet. MS C1, pp. 8–8a.
Dated: ?1818–20 (MS B7, MS 25).

SONG TAKEN FROM MY MOTHERS & FATHERS RECITATION & COMPLEATED BY AN OLD SHEPHERD

He   Fare you well my own true love
     & fare you well for a while
     I will be sure to return back again
     If I go ten thousand mile my dear
     If I go ten thousand mile   5

She   Ten thousand mile is a long way
     When from me you are gone
     Youll leave me here to lament & sigh
     But you never will hear me mourn my dear
     But you never will hear me moan   10

He   To hear you mourn I cannot bear
     Nor cure you of your disease
     But I shall be sure to return back again
     When all your friends is pleased my dear
     When all your friends is pleased   15

SONG TAKEN FROM MY MOTHERS & FATHERS RECITATION &
COMPLEATED BY AN OLD SHEPHERD *Title:* Song taken from my Mothers &
Fathers recitation & compleated / by an old shepherd *MS B7*, The Origin of Burn's Red
Red Rose— *MS 25, wanting MS A1* *The two initial 'He's and the 'She' are omitted in*
MS 25 and MS A1   2 & fare] Fare *MS 25*   3 And I *MS 25*   4 mile,
MS 25   5 mile. *MS 25*   6 mile's *MS 25*   long *repeated MS 25*
8 You'll *MS 25*] You *MS A1*   sigh & lament *MS A1*   9 neer *MS A1*   shall
MS 25 MS A1   mourn] moan, *MS 25,* moan *MS A1*   10 neer *MS A1*   shall
MS 25 MS A1   moan. *MS 25*   11 mourn] moan *MS 25*   12 Or *MS 25*
13 But *omitted MS 25*   14 frieends be pleas'd,: dear, *MS 25*   15 be
pleas'd. *MS 25*

Suppose my friends should never be pleased
Theyre grown so lofty & high
I never will prove false to the girl I love
Till all the seas gang dry my dear
Till all the seas gang dry   20

The stars they shall fall from the sky
The rocks melt in the sun
If ever I prove false to the girl I love
Till all these things be done my dear
Till all these things be done   25

Suppose that the stars never fall from the sky
The rocks never melts in the sun
I never will prove false to the girl I love
Till all these things be done my dear
Till all these things be done   30

O dont you see yon turtle dove
That sits on yonder tree
Shes making a moan for the loss of her love
As I shall do for thee my dear
As I shall do for thee   35

The blackest crow that ever flyes
Shall change her color white
If ever I prove false to the girl I love
Bright day shall turn to night my dear
Bright day shall turn to night   40

16 Suppose] If *MS 25*   17 They're: and high— *MS 25*   19 Till the stars fall from the sky, my dear *(stars through ? seas) MS 25*   20 Till the stars fall from the sky. *MS 25*   21 The . . . shall] O if the stars never *MS 25*   22 The rocks melt] Nor the rocks never *MS 25*   23 If ever I] I never will *MS 25*   24 are done,: dear, *MS 25*   25 are done. *MS 25*   31 O dont] Don't: little turtle *MS 25*   32 The dove sits in yonder tree *MS A1*   33 Shes making] Making *MS 25*   Shes . . . moan] A making her moans *MS A1*   34 will: thee,: dear, *MS 25*   35 will: thee. *MS 25*   36 flies *MS 25*   37 his *MS 25*   37/8 [The day shall turn to night, my dear] *(* [night] *over* [white] *) MS 25*   38 If] And if: the . . . love] thee *MS 25*   39 Bright] The: night,: dear, *MS 25*   40 Bright] The: night. *MS 25*

Till the red cocks back turns woolley grey
& the ravens silver white
Ill never prove false to the girl I love
Till day shall change to night [my dear]
[Till day shall change to night]   45

O keep your peace at home my dear
Nor wear it out for me
Ill never prove false to the girl I love
Till the fish drown in the sea [my dear]
[Till the fish drown in the sea]   50

Till the fish drown in the sea my dear
& the birds forget to flye
& I will love thee on my dear
Till the moment I shall dye [my dear]
[Till the moment I shall dye]   55

Supposing these things shoud never come to pass
So long as you & I should live
I never will prove false to the girl I love
Till we both lye in one grave my dear
Till we both lye in one grave   60

---

54 Till . . . I *through* Too the hour that *MS B7*   56 Supposing] But if: shoud
never] ne'er *MS 25*   57 you . . . should] we both do *MS 25*   58 ne'er: to . . .
love] my love to thee *MS 25*   59 we both lye] we're both laid: grave, *MS 25*
60 we both lye] we're both laid *MS 25*

AUTOGRAPH: Norris Museum SAVNM CL/11 (pencil).
Printed in the *Literary Gazette*, 20 November 1819, p. 748 (*LG*).
Dated: 1819 (*LG*).

THE FOUNTAIN

Sweet fountain neeth thy pendant boughs
　　May cool thy waters run
While flocks of sheep & herds of cows
　　Seek shelter from the sun
Unhead[ed] be thy willow ranks　　　　　　　　5
　　Thy waters pure & clear
For her I meet upon thy banks
　　Thou fountain thou art dear

Still shingling on thy silty bed
　　Wi gurgling windings play　　　　　　　　10
While musing on thy banks I tread
　　On memory[s] happy day
When mary milkd her brinded cow
　　While sky larks did sing clear
& for her sake thats absent now　　　　　　　15
　　Thou fountain thou art dear

The poesy last I her did make
　　Speckt cowslaps gilt wi dew
She hurded for the gatherers sake
　　& on thy banks they grew　　　　　　　20

THE FOUNTAIN　　*Title:* The Fountain *LG, wanting Norris　　Norris sheet cut off on the right and the readings are supplied from LG*　　　1 ⟨pendant boughs⟩ *Norris*　　2 Cool may *LG*　　　3 h⟨erds of cows⟩ *Norris*　　　4 t⟨he sun⟩ *Norris*　　5 Unheaded: be] by *LG*　　⟨ranks⟩ *Norris*　　　6 cle⟨ar⟩ *Norris*　　　7 met *LG*　　⟨banks⟩ *Norris*　　　8 fountain[s]: ⟨art dear⟩ *Norris*　　　9 Still *through* While: ⟨silty bed⟩ *Norris*　　on] o'er *LG*　　　10 Wi *through* In *Norris*] In *LG*　　p⟨lay⟩ *Norris*　　11 ⟨banks I tread⟩ *Norris*　　　12 On memory] And bless that *LG*　　⟨day⟩ *Norris*　　　13 mil⟨kd her brinded cow⟩ *(possibly* was mil⟨king . . . ⟩*)* *Norris*　　　14 And sky-larks sang so clear *LG*　　⟨? sing clear⟩ *Norris*　　15 that⟨s absent now⟩ *Norris*　　　16 ⟨art dear⟩ *Norris*　　　17 The . . . her] Her posy here I then *LG*　　d⟨id make⟩ *Norris*　　　18 cowslips *LG*　　⟨wi dew⟩ *Norris*　　　19 hurded] kept them *LG*　　⟨gatherers sake⟩ *Norris*　　　20 g⟨rew⟩ *Norris*

The Sigh so true the kiss so free
All past & witnessd here
& as my love is dear to me
Thou fountain thou art dear

AUTOGRAPHS: Norris Museum SAVNM CL/13: Pet. MS A52, p. 2.
TRANSCRIPT: Pet. MS B1, p. 39 (deleted).
Printed in *RL*, p. 122.
Dated: Mid 1819 or earlier (Explanatory Notes).

TO HOPE

(In a Melancholy Hour)

Come flattering hope now woes distress me
　Thy Syren themes I crave again
Again rely on thee to bless me
　To prove thy vainess doubly vain

Now dissapointments vex & fetter   5
　& jeering wispers thou art vain
Still must I rest on thee for better
　Still hope—to be deciev'd again

I cant but listen to thy prattle
　I still must hug thee to my breast   10
Like weaning child without its rattle
　Without my toy I cannot rest

21 tru⟨e the kiss so free⟩ *Norris*   22 pass'd *LG*   wi⟨tnessd here⟩ *Norris*
23 ⟨dear to me⟩ *Norris*   24 ⟨thou art dear⟩ *Norris*

TO HOPE *Title:* To Hope / (In a Melancholy hour) *Norris*, To Hope / (In a
Melancholly hour) *MS A52*, To Hope *RL*   2 Sy *through* fl *in* Syren *Norris*   Thy
flattery I desire again *MS A52 RL*   4 [& try] *over* To *through* By *MS A52*   prove]
find *MS A52 RL*   5 Now] Though *RL*   6 jeering *through* moving
MS A52   whisper *RL*   8 hope] live *MS A52*   to] & *MS A52*, and *RL*
11 without *over* [thats lost] *Norris*] thats lost *MS A52*, that's lost *RL*

AUTOGRAPHS: Pforzheimer Library, Misc. MS 197 (ll. 17–40 omitted): Pet. MS A2, ff. R8ᵛ–R9ᵛ (erased pencil, ll. 17–40 only), f. R61ʳ (fragment). TRANSCRIPTS: Pet. MS B1, pp. 18–19 (ll. 17–40 omitted): Nor. MS 43. Printed in *RL*, pp. 105–10 (ll. 17–24 omitted, moved to later in the volume in 2nd edn. and omitted in 3rd edn.).
Dated: '1819' (Pfz, *RL* Introduction, pp. xxii–xxiii 'In the last two years').

DOLLYS MISTAKE OR WAYS OF THE WAKE

Ere the sun oer the hills round & red 'gan a peeping
    To beckon the chaps to their ploughs
Too thinking & restless all night to be sleeping
    I brusht off to milking my Cows
To get my jobs forward—& eager preparing   5
    To be off in times to the Wake
Where yielding so freely—a kiss for a fairing
    I kickt up a shocking mistake

Young Ralph met me early & off we wer' steering
    I cuddl'd me close to his side   10
& neighbours while passing my fondness kept jeering
    'Young ralphs timely suited' they cried
But he bid me mind not their evil pretentions
    'Fools mun' says he 'talk for talks sake'
'&'—(kissing me)—'Doll if youve ony 'prehensions   15
    'Let me tell ye my wench you mistake'

The Eve fore the fair when he met me to parley
    & help find my buckets & yokes
I well do remember while crossing the barley
    Tother night fore titheing the shokes   20
That as clouds hung the sun like to heavens blue curtain
    Ah hadnt he grievd for my sake
But alas while he peard beforehand so heartfully certain
    I little smelt out the mistake

DOLLYS MISTAKE OR WAYS OF THE WAKE   *Title:* Dollys Mistake / Or Ways of the Wake *Pfz*, Dolly's Mistake; or, the Ways of the Wake *RL, wanting MS A2*
1 round *through* rosey: & *inserted Pfz*   6 time *RL*   8 kickt up a] made a most *RL*   11 & *through* The *Pfz*] The *RL*   my *through* his *Pfz*
14 mun∧: ∧talk *Pfz*   15 'prehensions *underlined Pfz*   16 e *through* o *in* ye *Pfz*] you *RL*   17–40 *Copy-text: MS A2*

My cows when we passd em kept tooing & froeing 25
  Indeed & truth ont they made me be ware
As much as to say well I should now be agoing
  Mind how you get on at the fair
Claimd farwel Good Speed from each gazing beholder
  Good journey away to the wake 30
The mowers stopd whetting to look oer their shoulder
  Saying Dolly dont make a mistake

I couldnt but mind it the morn was so charming
  The dewdrops they glittered like glass
& all oer the lawns where the butter cups swarming 35
  Like so many suns in the grass
I thought as we passd them how such things coud be
  What a fine string of beads they would make
But when I was thinking how such beauties shoud be
  I was Innocent of the mistake 40

So on his arm huging wi' storys beguiling
  Of what he wou'd buy me when there,
(The road cutting short wi' his kissing & smiling)
  He weigl'd me off to the fair
Sich presents he proffer'd before I could claim 'em 45
  To keep while I liv'd for his sake
& what I lik'd best oer & oer beg'd me name it
  As he mightn't go make a Mistake

& lud what a crushing & crouding wer' wi' them
  What noisies is heard at a fair 50
Heres some sells so cheap as they'd even go gi' them
  If consience wou'd take they declare

---

25 tooing & froeing] booing and mooing *RL*   26 In truth, but they made me to stare *RL*   27 I . . . agoing] now, Dolly, you're going *RL*   28 you yet *MS A2* 29 Claimd farwel] While bidden *RL*   33 it . . . was] the fine morning *RL* 35 lawns] meads *RL*   37 them *inserted*: them *altered to* how *MS A2*   how such things] if such a thing *RL*   39 But when I could think of such nonsense, it would be *RL*   40 Because I had made no mistake *RL*   41 huging] hanging *RL* 44 'veigl'd *RL*   45 Such *RL*   47 it] 'em *RL*   48 As] that *RL* 50 are *RL*   51 Here: sell *RL*

Somes so good tis een worth more then money to buy 'em
  Fine ginger bread nuts & plumb cakes
For truth they bid Ralph ere he treated me try 'em   55
  & then there could be no mistakes

& sly merry Andrew wer' making his speeches
  Wi chaps & girls round him a swarm
'& mind' said he fleering 'ye chubby fac'd bitches
  Your fairing dont do you no harm   60
The hay cocks he nam'd in the meads passing by 'em
  When weary we came from the Wake
So soft so inviting for rest we mun try 'em
  What a fool shou'd I be to mistake

But promis'd so faith full—behaviour so cleaver   65
  Sich gifts as he cram'bd i' me' hand
How cou'd one distrust of his goodness o never
  & who could his goodness wi' stand
His Ribbons his fairings past counting or nearly
  Some return when he prest me to make—   70
Good manners mun give—while he lov'd me so dearly
  Ah where cou'd I see the mistake

Till dark night he kept me wi fussing & lying
  How he'd see me safe home to my cot
Poor maidens so easy & free in complying   75
  I the show mans good caution forgot
All bye ways he led me twas vain to dispute it
  The moon blusht for shame nasty rake
Behind a cloud sneaking—but darkness well suited
  His baseness to cause the mistake   80

& vain do I beg him to wed & adone wi' t
  So fair as he promis'd we shou'd
We coudnt do worse then how we begun wi' t
  Let matters turn out as they wou'd

53 Some *RL*   'em *through* them *Pfz*   54 plum-cake *RL*   56 mistake *RL*
57 &] A: was *RL*   59 [chubby] *Pfz*   bitches] witches *RL*   60 fairings:
no] some *RL*   66 i *through* u *in* Sich *Pfz*] Such *RL*   he] Ralph: cramm'd: me']
my *RL*   67 one] I *RL*   73 Till dark *over* [He kept] *Pfz*   75 maiden:
&] so *RL*   78 nasty] naughty *RL*   80 to cause] who caus'd *RL*   81 *First*
&] In: have done *RL*   *Second* & *through* have *Pfz*   83 worse than as how we've
begun wi't *RL*

But he's al'as talking 'bout wedding expences   85
   & the wages he gotten to take
Too plain can I see in his Evil pretences
   Too late I find out the mistake

O what mun I do wi' m' mothers reprovin'
   Sin' she will do nothing but chide   90
For when old transgressers ha' bin i' the oven
   They know where the young on's may hide
In vain I seek pity wi' 'plaints & despairings
   Al'ays dung o' th' nose wi' the Wake
Young maidens be cautious who gi's ye y'r fairings   95
   Ye see what attends a Mistake

85 always a talking *RL*   86 he's *RL*   87 in] through *RL*   89 my *RL*
reprovin' *underlined Pfz*   90 Since *RL*   91 have been in *RL*   94 Al'ays
[I'm]: Wake *underlined Pfz* *Footnote in Pfz:* Al'ays / Vulgarism of always ding'd *RL*
95 give you your *RL*   96 Mistake. *Pfz*   98 *Followed by a footnote in Pfz:*
'Came' where ever you wish to preserve the provincial stile must be writ <u>Cam</u>

Possibly a first attempt at this poem:

     O while the west sky the crimson streak traces
     & the night hides us from rumours foul eye
     While meeting with heaven in Dollys embraces
     & nourishing hopes & ⟨   ⟩ sighs
     How sweet now to listen loves tender confession   5
     (Coward addressing in honey his part)
     & O how far sweeter is Dollys expression
     When I know their origin comes from the heart

                                       MS A2, f. R61ʳ

Drury to Taylor 8 Aug. 1819: The following verses he would wish to be the 3ᵈ 4th & 5th in
'Dolly's Mistake or Ways of the Wake'; provided you do not think it wd be driveling.

                                3ᵈ

     My cows when we pass'd them kept boo-ing & mooing,
     Indeed & truth! they made me to stare;
     As much as to say, 'Well', now, Dolly, youre going,
     Mind how you get on at the fair!
     While bidden 'good speed' from each gazing beholder,   5
     'Good journey away to the wake,
     The mowers stopt whetting to look oer their shoulder,
     Saying, 'Dolly, don't make a mistake.'

                           4 Verse

     I couldnt but mind the fine morning so charming,
     The dew-drops they glitter'd like glass;   10
     And all o'er the meads where the buttercups swarming,
     Like so many suns in the [glass] grass.

                                       over.

AUTOGRAPHS: Pet. MS A40, pp. 41–41a: Pforzheimer Library, Misc.
MS 197 (ll. 1–8, 13–16, 29–40 only): Pet. MS A31, p. R49 (ll. 9–12, 17–28
only). In a letter to H. S. Van Dyk dated September 1825.
TRANSCRIPT: Pet. MS B1, p. 65 (ll. 1–8, 13–16, 29–44 only).
Dated: ?1818–20 (Pfz).

VERSES WRITTEN ON THE BANKS OF THE RIVER GWASH AT BRIDGE CASTERTON

While swift the mail coach rattles up the hill
Nearly unseen beneath a cloud of dust
& the poor beggar pined & weary still
Drops on the bank to rest or eat his crust

cont.

I thought as we pass'd them, if such a thing could be,
What a fine string of beads would they make;
But when I could think of such nonsense it would be   15
Because I had made no mistake

5th Verse

[The eve 'fore the fair when he met me to parly
And help home my buckets & yoke
I well do remember while crossing the barley
Taking in all for truth that he spoke,   20
That a cloud hung the south like a great huge blue curtain
Oh had it but rain'd for mysake
But alas when the token appeared so hurting
I little thought on a mistake.]

(l. 10 The *through* They; l. 15 how *to* of *(p.e.)*: should be *to* it would be *(p.e.)*; l. 16 I
was innocent of a *to* Because I had made no *(p.e.)*)
I copy out the above to oblige Clare, and because I think you may wish to keep one or
two of them, which are pretty & applicable. *MS 43*

VERSES WRITTEN ON THE BANKS OF THE RIVER GWASH AT BRIDGE
CASTERTON   *Title:* Verses written on the banks of the River Gwash / at Bridge
Casterton *MS A40*, Written on the banks of the River gash Rutland *(pencil) Pfz*
1 Mail Coach Rattles: Hill *Pfz*   1/2 [Forever followd by a Cloud of D] *Pfz*
2 Cloud: Dust *Pfz*   3 Poor: pine *altered to* pin'd: weary] hoples *Pfz*
4 Drops wearied down to eat his mouldy crust *Pfz*   on *through* down *MS A40*

Upon thy winding side wild gwash I lie   5
Viewing with curious eye the silver bream
Taking vaunting springs to trap the thoughtless flye
That heedless dances on thy gentle stream

The black snail wakens from the swoons of day
& from the boughs that nestle by thy side   10
The light wing'd moths steal out again to play
Crossing with hasty wing thy rippling tide

How sweet the blackbird chaunts her evening song
While the shrill larks in twittering chorus join
& O sad deed while boys thy shades among   15
With hardnd hearts her unfledg'd young purloin

The cows stand loitering by thy flaggy brink
Free from noons sultry flies & in delight
The weary cart horse hastens in to drink
Then knaps the moist grass with a keener bite   20

The singing milk maid journeying from the town
Skips oer the stones that stride the meadow slough
& on thy banks she sets her bucket down
To reach a wild rose ere she calls her cow

---

5 side *through* gwash *MS A40*   side . . . lie] banks o Gash I lye *Pfz*   7 Take:
thoughtles *Pfz*   8 danses *Pfz*   *Followed in Pfz by:*

> [& thou vain man in wisdoms eye may seem
> A thoughtles flie alowd lifes little day
> That heedless dances on the worlds wide stream
> To pride a stain & countless ills a prey]

9 *Through an indecipherable line beginning:* & snail *MS A40*   10 & from the *through*
Thro the thin *MS A40*   boughs] trees *MS A31*   11 *Through an indecipherable line*
MS A40   wingd: agen *MS A31*   12 Crossing . . . wing *through three or*
four indecipherable words possibly ending in spangles *MS A40*   wing] flight *MS A31*
13 Blackbird Chaunts: Evening *Pfz*   14 Lark: joins *Pfz*   15 Boys *Pfz*
16 unfledgd: purloins *Pfz*   17 thy *through* the *MS A31*   19 hastens in]
stoops its full *through* thy stream *MS A31*   21 *Preceded in MS A31 by:* Light footed
maids come tripping from the town *(*Light footed *through* & loitring*)*   milkmaid
journeys *MS A31*   22 Skips oer] Stepping *MS A31*   23 bucket[s] *MS A31*
24 a] the: ere] while *MS A31*   calls *through* milks *MS A40*

With heedless step the homward journeying boys   25
Climb the rude plank that totters oer thy deeps
& pelt the fish while startled at the noise
From hollow tree the plunging otter leaps

Cooling & pleasant to the river side
The skipping breezes on the waters run   30
That sweetly curl along the gentle tide
& swell in spangles to the setting sun

Which now as clouds brood round & breezes drop
In reddning lustre siles & slinks from view
& on the village steeples peeping top   35
Hangs feint & weary in a last adieu

The slender rush in idle motion bows
With meek obedience to the floods below
Were jostling reeds & willows dangling boughs
Impede their gurgling progress as they flow   40

On the thorn bush that overhangs the streams
The morehen slumbers in her nest of sedge
While the shrill dormouse in its summer dreams
Chitters unceasing from the waters edge

Sheep seek their folds in many a hurried troop   45
Frit by the dogs that bark them to their rest
Who with their noises often startle up
The partridge coveys from their grassy nest

---

25 *Preceded in MS A31 by:* [The herd boys heedless laugh]   With heedless homward
step the herding boys *MS A31*   26 Climb *through* The: the *over* [rude]: rude]
oak: the *altered to* thy: s *inserted in* deeps *MS A31*   27 While startled by the stones
thrown in the stream *MS A31*   28 From his old tree the otter fearful leaps
MS A31   29 Cooling] How cool: pleasent *Pfz*   river *through* water *MS A40*]
River *Pfz*   30 breases: on] oer *through* on *Pfz*   31 sweetly *over* [wave in
gentle]: curl[s]: gentle *inserted Pfz*   32 swell[s] *Pfz*   33 Which] Who: brood]
gloom *Pfz*   34 reddening *Pfz*   35 peeping] taper *Pfz*   36 Hangs ...
weary] Now fainting glimers *to* Hangs faint & weary *(p.e.) Pfz*   37 The Taper
Rush in Idle Motion bows *Pfz*   39 Were *altered to* Where: jossling Reeds *Pfz*
40 thier *Pfz*   *Followed in Pfz by:*

> The morehen slumbers in her flggy nest
> & in the hanging branch enjoys her peace
> While I alone of all denyd of rest
> Desert from sorrows which shall never cease

The weary mower on the meadow path
With wallets oer his shoulder rocks along   50
Leaving the cricket in the moistning swath
To brood in quiet oer its evening song

And pleased to watch the summer evenings birth
I linger here wild gwash thy quiet guest
And from reposing natures sober mirth   55
Catch these soft sounds that lull my carcs to rest

AUTOGRAPH: Pforzheimer Library, Misc. MS 197.
TRANSCRIPT: Pet. MS B1, pp. 41–2.
Dated: '1818' (Pfz).

THE BATTLE

an A Air Intended for a Dramatic Entertainment
'The Man of my Chusing'

Centinels proclaim the morning
Cowards dread the daylight daw[n]ing
Trumpets sound—the battles warning
    Foe his fellow foe can see
Heroes every peril scorning   5
Watch impatient Foes & morning
Now my boys the day is dawning
    Now for death or Victory

Trumpets sounding—colours flying
Cowards in their fears are dying   10
Heroes every fear defying
    Fight & fall for Liberty!
Trumpets sounding—colours flying
Now my boys it comes for trying
Whos for fighting whos for flying   15
    Now its shame or Victory

THE BATTLE *Title:* The Battle / an A air / Intended for A Dramatic
Entertainment / 'The Man of My Chusing' *Pfz*   14 its *Pfz*

Cannons thunder—Battle rages
Heroes Lion like engages
Now for fame that lives for ages
   Who would now a coward be   20
Cannons thunder—Battle rages
Soldiers soldier like engages
Now my boys the fame for ages
   Now for death or Victory

Blood & Groans—wars dead to sorrow   25
Cowards wish for peace & 'morrow
Heroes kindle at the horror
   Now will Brittons brittons be
Wounded Lions—Vengance!—horror!
Foemen now begins your sorrow   30
Weep your Leigons slain to morrow
   Now its death or Victory

Trumpets sound—the battles ended
War her Weapon holds suspended
Heroes still for fight defended   35
   Britons stand & foemen flee
Britons rage like hell descended
Foemen but in vain contended
Trumpets sound—the battles ended
   England thines the victory   40

Foemen threaten foemen thunder
Foemen fight for spoil & plunder
Britons never will knock under
   Brittons fight for liberty
Foe but vainly dream of plunder   45
Vain their threat'ning vain their thunder
Britons never shall knock under
   Death is theirs or Victory

21/2 [Britons heroes all engages] *(*Britons *through* Soldiers*) Pfz*   22 like[s] *Pfz*
25 ⟨Bl⟩ood *seal*: a *through* d *in* dead   34 W *through* f *in* Weapon *Pfz*
41 *Preceded in Pfz by:* Stanza added

AUTOGRAPHS: Pforzheimer Library, Misc. MS 197 (deleted): Pet. MS
A50, p. R59.
Dated: ?1818–20 (Pfz).

A pleasant path a little path
Goes thro the meadow hay
Where in the summer many a swath
Fresh mown stops up the way

AUTOGRAPH: Pforzheimer Library, Misc. MS 197 (ll. 1–8 pencil gone
over in ink, ll. 17–20 in pencil at foot of page, added later and marked for
insertion).
Dated: ?1818–20 (Pfz).

As hopes fair sun breaks fates desponding gloom
Then flusht with fancied tales my bosom warms
Of better times & better days to come
& I made happy in my Pattys arms

But short the reign when reason takes her seat 5
& weighs the present with the future scene
With anguish then I view the cobweb cheat
That stang in dissapointment doubly keen

Ye horrid powers the hellish fates mentain
To haunt adopted victims such as me 10
With dissapointed hopes & vexing pains
Crush me at once or set your prisoner free

—Where carless shores in view no succour lends
To sinking wrecks that on the oceans reels
While lingering waves their horrid fate suspends 15
Cant feel more horrors then my bosom feels

A PLEASANT PATH A LITTLE PATH *Title: wanting*   2 through *MS A50*
AS HOPES FAIR SUN BREAKS FATES DESPONDING GLOOM *Title:
wanting*   1 glooms *in pencil altered to* gloom *in ink*   8 stang[s]
9 p *through* h *in* powers   10 victims *below* [wretches]   16 [anguish] horrors

I view the past O horrid scenes gone by
What hopes & fears have mingld & distrest
I look on whats to come—all hopes & sighs
& O I tremble when I hope the best   20

O Resolution whither art thou fled
Away ye cheating hope that linger near
When laid within the grave—my aching head
Shall find that peace it seeks but vainly here

AUTOGRAPH: Pforzheimer Library, Misc. MS 197.
TRANSCRIPT: Pet. MS B1, p. 43 (deleted).
Dated: 'old' (Pfz).

SONG

Slighted love I little heeded
  Slighted love I little fear
Ever love (tho vainly) speeded
  Ever Emma loves sincere

Ever kind & ever tender   5
  Still my lay is fond & Vain
Nothing boasting to befriend her
  Poverty is all the pain

Here the glooms of fate surround me
  Every sorrow there impart   10
There oppressions thorn can wound me
  Theres the anguish of my heart

SONG   *Title:* Song *Pfz*   4 Emma[s] *Pfz*   6 lay *through* love *Pfz*

AUTOGRAPH: Pforzheimer Library, Misc. MS 197.
TRANSCRIPT: Pet. MS B1, pp. 42–3 (deleted).
Dated: 'Old' (Pfz).

SONG

In a bonny black wench & the best I set eyes on
A love at first sight I have found
But shame dare not name it—ah there lies the poison
That serves to keep open the wound

Then what must I do for the best I set eyes on   5
For the love at first sight I have found
The wench is a stranger—ah there lies the poison
That hoplesly burns in the wound

Come muse gi' me hopes of the best I set ey[e]s on
Sing the Love at first sight I have found   10
The praise of the stranger—O Curse the foul poison
Will serve but to deepen the wound

AUTOGRAPH: Pforzheimer Library, Misc. MS 197 (pencil, deleted).
Dated: ?1818–20 (Pfz).

The hind that were chopping them up for his fire
Een stood like a poet awhile to admire
& when I last sat here to listen the thrush
I lookd on yon knowll at our favourite bush
Were gipseys campd round it in freedom did dwell   5
& a swain told its history that knew it so well
About a court yearly being kept neath its boughs
In its youth—when his forefathers herded the cows

SONG *Title:* Song *Pfz*   1 *Second* e *inserted in* eyes *Pfz*   11 t *through* T *in
first the Pfz*

THE HIND THAT WERE CHOPPING THEM UP FOR HIS FIRE *Title:
wanting*

While the bush oer our heads blooming feeble & old
Seemd listning in sorrow the story he told   10
& sighd as the winds summer breath flutterd bye
Its few scatterd leaves as one ready to dye
Tho the gipseys haunt still the lovd spot as before
& the swain calls it still by the name it once bore
Langley bush with its scard trunk & grey mossy bough   15
Is fled & the scene is left desolate now
A storm that made shepherds in dread for an hour
& boild oer the hills with its thunder & shower
Struck it down to the earth were it withering lay
Till the gipseys sought firing & hauld it away   20
When the shepherd returnd as the tempest was bye
From his hut of thatchd brakes that had sheltered him dry
He lookd with supprise & a fearful anoy
On the fall of his favourite known from a boy
& I thus to witness its sorrowful end   25
Feel a loss for its fate as I do for a friend

AUTOGRAPHS: Pforzheimer Library, Misc. MS 197: Norris Museum
SAVNM CL/14.
TRANSCRIPT: Pet. MS B1, p. 41.
Dated: Mid-1819 or earlier (Explanatory Notes).

A SIMPLE EFFUSION ADDRESS'D
TO MY LAME FATHER

Yes my father pains distress thee
Help & succor dost thou need
Tis not in my power to help thee
Here my heart will often bleed

12 one . . . dye *below* [its end it was nigh]   14 [that] it: once *inserted*   15 with
. . . bough *below* [the wild spots mossy tenant is gone]   22 his hut *through* the hant
26 Felt *altered to* Feel

  A SIMPLE EFFUSION ADDRESS'D TO MY LAME FATHER   *Title:* A Simple
Effusion / Address'd to my Lame Father *Pfz*, A Simple Effusion / Addressd to my Lame
Fathe *Norris*   1 Father *Norris*

Parish bounty fate alows thee   5
Sad suport in time of need
Could I keep thee from their frowning
Here I should be blest indeed

Father while I thus adress thee
Fames vain praise I little heed   10
Tis for thee my hopes are shining
Here my Prayer is 'Hopes succeed'

Friends believe your poets wishes
Vain as poet to intrude
Tho you cant commend his tallents   15
Here you may his Gratitude

Yes my father pains distress thee
Help & succor dost thou need
Tis not in my power to help thee
Here my heart must vainly bleed   20

AUTOGRAPH: Pforzheimer Library, Misc. MS 197.
TRANSCRIPT: Pet. MS B1, p. 40.
Printed in *RL*, pp. 123–5.
Dated: '1819' (Pfz, *RL* Introduction, p. xxii 'In the last two years').

AN EFFUSION TO POETRY

*Written after recieving a damp from a genteel opinionist in poetry & of
some sway (as I am told) in the literary world*

Despis'd, unskill'd or how I Will
Sweet poetry I love thee still
Vain, (cheering comfort) tho I be
I still must love thee poetry

9 address *Norris*   12 Prayer[s] *Pfz*] prayers *Norris*   are 'hopes *Norris*
13 Friend: Poets *Norris*   14 Poet *Norris*   15 talents *Norris*   19 help]
bless *Norris*

AN EFFUSION TO POETRY *Title:* An Effusion to Poetry / Written after
recieving a Damp from a Genteel Opinionist / in Poetry & of some sway (as I am told) in
the Literary World *Pfz*, An Effusion to Poesy, on receiving a Damp from a genteel
Opinionist in Poetry, of some sway, as I am told, in the Literary World *RL*
1 W *through* w *in* Will *Pfz*   2 Poesy! I'll *RL*   3 cheering comfort
underlined Pfz   4 Poesy *RL*

A poor rude clown & what of that   5
I cannot help the will of fate
A lowly clown altho I be
Nor can I help it loving thee
Still must I love thee sweetest charm
Still must my soul in raptures warm   10
Still must my rudeness pluck the flower
Thats plucked in an evil hour
While learning scowls her scornful brow
& damps my soul—I know not how—
Labour 'cause thourt mean & poor   15
Learning spurns thee from her door
But despise thee how she will
Poetry I love thee still
When on pillowd thorns I weep
Vain when stretc[h]'d me down to sleep   20
Then thou charm from heaven above
Comforts cordial dost thou prove
Then engaging poesy
Then how sweet to talk with thee
& be despisd or how I will   25
I cannot help but love thee still
Endearing charm vain tho I be
I still must love the[e] poetry
Still must I—aye I cant refrain
Dampt despisd or scorn'd again   30
With vain unhallow'd liberty
Still must I sing thee poetry
& poor & vain & prest beneath
Oppressions scorn altho I be
Still will I bind my simple wreath   35
Still must I love thee Poetry

5 [vain] rude *Pfz*   17 thee how] me as *RL*   18 Poesy! *RL*
19 thorns— *Pfz*   20 Vain when stretc'd] And vainly stretch *Rl.*   28 Poesy *RL*
32 Poesy *RL*   35 will *over* [must] *(deleted in pencil) Pfz*   35/6 [Still must I
love thee Poetry] *Pfz*   36 Poesy *RL*   *Followed in Pfz by the alternative line:* Still
will I love thee Poetry

AUTOGRAPH: Pforzheimer Library, Misc. MS 197.
TRANSCRIPT: Pet. MS B1, pp. 29–31 (deleted).
Dated: ?1818–20 (Pfz).

'HOW D'YE DO & GOOD BYE'

Come muse brush up to try thy skill
When patrons bid thee try
Be thine the pride to sing the theme
Of 'how' do' & 'good bye'

—This vain worlds manners, trust, & hope,　　　5
By each diserning eye
Is plain enough observ'd to be
A how do & good bye

When thou & I (as who can tell?)
Have gaind the point in view　　　10
Thou may'st from flatterys tongue expect
The 'Sir—& how d' ye do?'

But should we still keep 'as we were'
(My doubtfulness excuse)
Then hark ye Muse I prophecy　　　15
Good bye to how d' ye do's

To Madam wealth how do belongs
She's neither you nor I
Content then wispers 'sing thou on
'& put up wi' good bye　　　20

As simple as my ballad seems
Their may in wisdoms eye
Be somthing more then what there seems
In how do & good bye

'HOW D'YE DO & GOOD BYE'   *Title:* 'How d' ye do & Good bye / The hint
given & requested / By a Literary Gentleman *Pfz*　　　8 A *over* [Our]: & *over*
[ye do] *Pfz*　　　9 as . . . tell? *over* [who knows whats what] *Pfz*　　　11 s *added to*
flattery: tongue *below* [first] *Pfz*　　　12 do?∧ *Pfz*　　　13 we *through* she *Pfz*
15 prophecy *through* phecy *Pfz*　　　19 wispers *over* [he'll mutter] *Pfz*

Tis 'money makes the mare to go'   25
(For money's all the cry)
& fortunes weels & turns at will
Then how do & good bye

Wealth's a maschine & load stone like
To one point ever true   30
She cogs self interest's hopfull wheel
That turns wi' how d' ye do

'How do' says quack today & smil'd
His hopes was in his eye
But soon as provd my wants the same   35
His skill prescrib'd good bye

Those evil spirits o' the pen
While Clients find employ
Will how d' ye do' 'em out of all
& then y' f[oo]l good bye   40

& where each sign post tells its tale
(So tempting to the view)
Youll find as ready as elswhere
Th' inviting how do' ye do

They'll howd' ye do & treat & fuss   45
While you with cash supply
But soon as fill'd mugs need the chaulk
Your welcome to good bye

So (suiting fashion) cupid's darts
(Success atends em too)   50
Each amorous passion to ex[c]ite
Are tipt wi' how d' ye do

29 & *below* [that] *Pfz*   33 [&] today *Pfz*   34 was *below* [shone] *Pfz*
35 But *through* &: my *over* [our]: [alike] the *Pfz*   38 While *through* When *Pfz*
40 f—l *Pfz*   40/1 *Row of asterisks Pfz*   45 [talk & fuss] treat: & fuss *over*
[to stay] *Pfz*   45/6 [Your pocket drowning dry] *Pfz*

Then now rich virgins old & stale
Neglect tho's made you sigh
Spun out you[r] tempting how d ye do's   55
& sorrow bids good bye

Een 'ill star'd' ragamuffin bards
(Poor poets flatter too)
As season suits or hopes appear
Will find their how d' ye do   60

But beggar like that chaunts the streets
(A unsuccesfull cry)
Their how d ye do's to come at gain
Is but a mere good bye

& thus all hope & 'how do' on   65
Till death has cast the dye
& pops pat in my ballads end
A 'how d'o' & 'good bye'

AUTOGRAPHS: Pet. MS A40, p. 37a: Fitzwilliam Museum.
TRANSCRIPT: Pet. MS B1, p. 59.
Dated: 1819 (Fitz).

AUTUMN

Now autumns sorrows meet the faded leaf
& sick & faint resumes her hopless care
No flower or minstrel bird consoles her grief
Silent & wan as beauty in despair
Still autumn do I love thy faded face   5
Thy sad still musings on the dying year
Thy downcast eye thy solemn suited pace
Holds each a charm as beauty with her tear

58 ∧Poor *Pfz*   59 *Second* p *in* appear *inserted Pfz*   67 ⟨& p⟩ops *torn Pfz*
68 ⟨A⟩ *torn*: o' *in* do' *inserted*: [ye do] & *Pfz*

  AUTUMN   *Title:* Autumn *MS A40 Fitz*   1 Autumns Sorrows meets *Fitz*
2 sick *through* sicken *MS A40*   their *Fitz*   3 Minstrel *Fitz*   5 Autumn:
faded] sober *Fitz*   8 Charm *Fitz*

Thy mournful sighs that wake the woods despair
Thy fading dress that leaves thy bosom bare   10
All all exulting while they seem to sigh
Another spring & seasons bloom is given
& man frail flower hope glads his tearful eye
That tho he dies on earth he blooms again in heaven

AUTOGRAPHS: British Library, Add. MS 37538, f. 39^{r-v} (ll. 61–136 only):
Fitzwilliam Museum (ll. 49–56, 61–8 only, deleted): Pet. MS A1, f. 1^r
(ll. 69–72, 81–4 only, erased pencil).
TRANSCRIPT: Pet. MS B1, pp. 61–4.
Printed in *RL*, pp. 139–47 (ll. 125–32 omitted): *Pledge of Friendship* (*PF*),
1827, pp. 198–9 (ll. 1–16, 25–40 only): Hone's *Every-day Book*, 1826, col. 962
(ll. 1–16, 25–40 only).
Dated: 1819–19 (*RL* Introduction, p. xxii 'In the last two years', BL paper
watermarked 1818).

SUMMER MORNING

The cocks have now the morn foretold,
    The sun again begins to peep;
The shepherd, whistling to his fold,
    Unpens and frees the captive sheep.

O'er pathless plains, at early hours,   5
    The sleepy rustic sloomy goes;
The dews, brush'd off from grass and flowers,
    Bemoistening sop his harden'd shoes;

For every leaf that forms a shade,
    And every flowret's silken top,   10
And every shivering bent and blade,
    Stoops, bowing with a diamond drop.

9 that wakes ... despair *below* [that wake each dying squall] *Fitz*   11/12 [That
for] *Fitz*   12 Spring: seasons] second *Fitz*   13 Man Frail: tearfull *Fitz*
flower *to* flower, *(p.e.) MS A40*   14 Earth *Fitz*

SUMMER MORNING *Title:* Summer Morning *RL Hone,* The Summer Morning
PF, wanting BL Fitz   1–48, 57–60 *Copy-text: RL*   49–56 *Copy-text: Fitz*
6 sloomy] gloomy *PF*   9 For] While *PF Hone*   12 drop] top *PF*

But soon shall fly those pearly drops,
    The red, round sun advances higher;
And stretching o'er the mountain tops,   15
    Is gilding sweet the village spire.

Again the bustling maiden seeks
    Her cleanly pail, and eager now,
Rivals the morn with rosy cheeks,
    And hastens off to milk her cow;   20

While echo tells of Colin near,
    Blithe, whistling o'er the misty hills:
The powerful magic fills her ear,
    And through her beating bosom thrills.

'Tis sweet to meet the morning breeze,   25
    Or list the giggling of the brook;
Or stretch'd beneath the shade of trees
    Peruse and pause on nature's book;

When nature every sweet prepares
    To entertain our wish'd delay,—   30
The images which morning wears,
    The wakening charms of early day!

Now let me tread the meadow paths,
    While glittering dew the ground illumes,
As, sprinkled o'er the withering swaths,   35
    Their moisture shrinks in sweet perfumes;

And hear the beetle sound his horn;
    And hear the skylark whistling nigh,
Sprung from his bed of tufted corn,
    A hailing minstrel in the sky.   40

First sunbeam, calling night away,
    To see how sweet thy summons seems,
Split by the willow's wavy grey,
    And sweetly dancing on the streams:

13 those pearly] their diamond *PF*   pearly] diamond *Hone*   26 giggling] gurgling
PF Hone   40 in] of *PF*

How fine the spider's web is spun,   45
    Unnoticed to vulgar eyes;
Its silk thread glittering in the sun,
    Art's bungling vanity defies.

Roaming where the dewey field
Neath its morning burthen leans   50
While its crops my searches shield
Sweet I scent the blossomd beans

Making oft remarking stops
Watching tiny nameless things
Climb the grasses spiry tops   55
As they try their silken wings

So emerging into light,
    From the ignorant and vain,
Fearful Genius takes her flight,
    Skimming o'er the lowly plain,   60

While in gay green glossy coat
On the shivering benty baulk
The grass hopper chirps his note
Bounding on from stalk to stalk

While the bee at early hours   65
Sips the bowing beans perfumes
Butter flys infest the flowers
Just to show their Glossy plumes

As oft industry seeks the sweet[s]
Which weary labour ought to gain   70
As oft the bliss the idle meets
& heaven bestows the bliss in vain

46 to] by *RL 4th edn.*   49 *Preceded in Fitz by:* [While embrowning wheaten fields /
Neath their dewey burthen leans]   where] while: fields *RL*   50 their: lean *RL*
51 crop: shields *RL*   52 bean *RL*   55 Climb[ing] *Fitz*   56 As] Ere:
silken] gauzy *RL*   61 While] Now *RL*   While in] In their: coats *Fitz*
62 bauk *Fitz*   63 free grasshopper *RL*   Grasshoper *Fitz*   64 [Hopping]
Bounding] Bouncing *Fitz*   65 While] And *RL*   Early *Fitz*   66 bowing]
tawny *Fitz RL*   67 While butterflies *RL*   Butterflys *Fitz*   68 Glossy]
spangld *Fitz*   69 As oft industry] So industry oft *RL*   Industry *MS A1*   sweets
RL 2nd edn.   71 As] And *RL*   meets *MS A1*   72 bestows the bliss] bliss
bestows *MS A1*

Pleasd I list the rural themes
Heartning up the ploughmans toil
Urging on the gingling teams   75
As they turn the mellow soil

Industrys care abounds again
As now the peace of night is gone
Many a murmur wakes the plain
Many a waggon rumbles on   80

The swallow wheels his circling flight
& oer the waters surface skims
Then on the cottage chimney lights
& twittering chaunts his morning hymns

Stationd high a towering height   85
On the sun gilt weather cock
Now the jack daw takes his flight
Frighted by the striking clock

Snug the wary watching thrush
Sits to prune her speckled breast   90
Where the wood bine round the bush
Weaving hides her mortard nest

Till the cows with hungry low
Pick the rank grass from her bower
Startld then—dead leaves below   95
Quick recieve the pattering shower

Now the sythe the morn salutes
In the meadow tinkling soon
While on mellow tutling flutes
Sweetly breathes the shepherds tune   100

Where the bank the stream oerlooks
& the wreathing worms are found
Anglers sit to bait their hooks
On the hill with wild tyhme crownd

74 Heartening *RL*   78 [fled] gone *BL*   81 swallows *MS A1*   fliight *BL*
82 & *through* As *RL*   water: surface *omitted MS A1*   84 twittering chaunts]
twits his *MS A1*   89 wary] weary *RL*   99 tootling *RL*

While the treach'rous watching stork   105
Nigh the heedless gudgeon flies
Bobbing sinks the vanishd cork
& the roach becomes a prize

Neath the black thorns stunted bush
Cropt by wanton oxen down   110
Wistling oer each culling rush
Cowboys plats a rural crown

As slow the hazy mist retires
Crampt circle more distinctly seen
Thin scatterd huts & neighbouring spires   115
Drops in to stretch the bounded scene

Brisk winds the Lightnd Branches shake
By pattering plashing drops confest
& where oaks dripping shade the lake
Prints crimpling dimples on its' breast   120

The misted brook its edges reek
Sultry noon is drawing on
The east has lost its ruddy streak
& proves that mornings sweets are gone

In torturd haste retreating cows   125
Plunge head long in the spangld flood
Or sweeping by the oaken boughs
Brusing trace the tangld wood

In all directions buzzing by
Wakend by the sultry heat   130
Once again the tiresome flye
Bold intruding plagues repeat

Now as morning takes her leave
& while swelterd nature mourns
Let me waiting soothing eve   135
Seek my cot till she returns

105 c *through* h *in* treach'rous *BL*   106 Nigh] With *RL*   112 plat *RL*
113 mists retire *RL*   114 circle's *RL*   115 spire *RL*   116 Drop *RL*
117 the *repeated BL*   120 Print *RL*   124 And Morning sweets are almost
gone *RL*

AUTOGRAPH: British Library, Add. MS 54224, f. 144^r.
TRANSCRIPT: Pet. MS B1, p. 57.
Dated: 1819 April (BL).

THE DYING SNOWDROP

Snow drop I mourn thee oer thy early tomb
Thy witherd fragrance so autumly shed
Killd by the pride that gave thy spotless bloom
Upon the Snow low droops thy witherd head

So artless beauty oftentimes undone   5
Unconsious sleeping on Seductions breast
Like the poor Lark the fowlers wiles have won
Falls on the spot when profferd of his rest

AUTOGRAPHS: Pet. MS A40, p. 37: British Library, Add. MS 54224,
f. 144^r.
TRANSCRIPT: Pet. MS B1, p. 57.
Dated: 1819 April (BL).

TO THE VIOLET

Hail to the[e] violet sweet carless spread
Neath each warm bush & covert budding hedge
In many a pleasing walk have I been led
To seek thee—promise of springs earliest pledge
In modest coyness hanging down its head   5
Unconsious hiding beautys from the eye
& sweetly brooding oer its gracful form
Shunning each vulgar gaze that saunters by

THE DYING SNOWDROP   *Title:* The Dying Snowdrop *BL*

TO THE VIOLET   *Title:* To the Violet *MS A40*, Sonnet *BL*   1 thee
Violet: Carless *BL*   2 Covert *BL*   3 Walk *BL*   4 thee$_\wedge$: Springs *BL*
5 Coyness *BL*   6 beauties *BL*   7 &] So: Graceful *BL*   8 Vulgar:
gaze] pause: bye *BL*

& timly stooping from an april storm
As virtue startled by approaching harm   10
Shrinks from delusions false betraying hand[s]
With bashful look that more the bosom warms
So sweetest blossom the coy violet stands
Tempting the plunderer with a double charm

AUTOGRAPH: British Library, Add. MS 54224, f. 143ᵛ (pencil): Pet.
MS B3, p. 75 (ll. 1–2 only).
Dated: 1817 or later (BL paper watermarked 1817).

There was three ravens sat upon a tree
  High down high derry down
There was three ravens sat upon a tree
  Down O
There was three raven[s] sat upon a tree   5
  As black as black as they could be
(As deep in love as he & she)
  High down derry O

Said the middlemost raven to her mate
  Where shall we go our fill to take   10
Down in yonder grass green fields
(There we may go & take our fill
  There runs a river clear [&] chill)

There lies a man on a grass green hill
Where we may go & take our fill   15

With a greyhound standing at his feet
Licking the wounds that was so deep

9 April: shower *to* storm *(p.e.) BL*   10 Virtue startld *BL*   11 hands *BL*
12 Each bashfull look that still endears her form *BL*   13 Violet *BL*
14 plunderer *to* gazer *(p.e.) MS A40*

  THERE WAS THREE RAVENS SAT UPON A TREE   *Title: wanting BL MS B3*
1 three] 3 *MS B3*   2 Heigh down derry ho *MS B3*   high down *BL*
4 down *BL*   7 love I as *BL*   8 high *BL*

pp. 17–18 LINES WRITTEN WHILE VIEWING SOME REMAINS OF
AN HUMAN BODY IN LOLHAM LANE   1 hand,: low;   2 club,:
knife,   3 weapon,: blow;   4 body,: life.   5 Nay!: not,
6 bones;   7 life,: ago,   8 musick,: tones.   9 genious,:
powerful,: strong,   10 all,: majesty,: song,   11 dust: : wish,
12 spot: 13 thought: : grave?   14 forgot,   15 reward,?
16 eloquence,   17 bard,?   18 recompence.   19 be:–
howe're,: shown,   20 congecterings,: vain;   21 fate,: fame,:
unknown,   22 searching,: obtain.   23 he,: all,   24 earth,:
air,: sky,   25 death,: end; : fall,   26 when,: where,: nigh.
27 ruffian,: low,   28 he,: they,: was,: blow,   29 appear,: day!!
30 redeemer,: land,   31 all,: crimes,: display,   32 disguise: :
hand,   33 fate,: prepar'd,   34 this,: offence,   35 get,:
reward,   36 thou,: recompence.

p. 18 LINES TO BATH   1 waters,: life,: heal,   2 son,: Father,
3 He,: out,: pain;   4 relief,: alas!: vain.   5 repairing,: wave,
6 hopes,: means,: save,   7 now,: retain,   8 now,: shore,   9 now,:
pain,   10 back:

p. 19 THE FLOWER POTT   1 morning,: clean;   2 pot: : plac'd,
3 branches,: green,   4 blue-bells,: grac'd,   5 colors,: inclin'd,
6 wall,   7 morality,: mind,   8 thus,: fall;   9 tempting,: flowers;
10 stranger,: on,   11 here,: hours,   12 whither'd,   13 thinking,:
said,   14 Reflection,: sigh,   15 reviewing,: shade,   16 suppos'd,:
flowers,: reply,   17 mortal,: prone,   18 date,: flowers,   19 morals;
: own!   20 it,: our's;   21 us,: ground,   22 us,: before!
23 moralizer,: round,   24 blossom,

p. 20 FAREWELL TO A THICKETT   1 wild,: shades,   2 grown,
3 rapture,: call,   4 scenes,   5 love:- : part;   6 shades,
7 leave,: heart;   8 But,   9 bower's,: twine,   10 wove,
11 breast,   12 settle,   13 shades,: love,   14 love,: subdue,
15 love,: heart,   16 me,   17 boast,: bower,   18 shrubs,:
drest,   19 single,: branch,: flower,   20 By,: prest,   21 then,:
thoughts,   22 love,: true;   23 sit,: day,: day,   24 never,:
adieu!.

pp. 21–9 ROBIN AND SUKE   1 loud: : nine,   2 come;   3 suke,:
whine,   4 Robin,: home.   5 moon,: light,   6 crost,   7 think,:
night,   8 lost.   9 chair,: sobs,: cries,   10 plight: 11 fire,:

lies,   12 sight.   13 street,   14 profound,   15 thinks,:
feet,   16 ground.   17 thoughts,: vain,   18 robin,: nigh:
19 shuts,: again,   20 heaves,: sigh;   21 lost,   23 nasty,
24 settled,: pate.   25 hope,: enough,   26 park,   27 footpads,:
rough,   28 so,: dark? !   29 fishponds,   30 road,   31 peep,
32 bestow'd: 33 doubts,: fears,   34 breast,   35 conduct,:
appears,   36 distrest.   37 hope,: invokes,   38 free;   39 cries,
40 About,: he.   41 despair: 42 hopes,   43 chair,   44 rest.
45 when,   46 trifles,   47 owl,   48 flew!   49 shriek't,:
tone,   50 her,   51 sigh'd,: cried,: this,: shown;   52 things,
53 doubts,: fears,   54 breast.   55 park!: appears,   56 mantle,:
drest.   57 wood,: stand,   58 strife,   59 hears,: demand,
60 money,: life? !   61 death,   62 threw,   63 where,: appease,
64 true.   65 fire,: tinder,   66 mourn'd,: troubles,   67 struck,:
stamp!!   68 something,   69 strict,: anew!   70 then,: cough,
71 sighn,: well,   72 man!: off.   73 joy,: think,   74 blood,
75 fishponds,: drink,   76 Perplex'd,: brains.   77 him,   78 again,:
late;   79 now,   80 pate!   81 stopt,: door,: clench!   82 sight,
83 in,: well,   84 lost!   85 soft,: greeting,: tone,   86 civil,:
blame;   87 Yet,: joan,   88 same.   89 lost,: indeed,   90 that,
91 so,: free'd,   92 lot!   93 heard,   94 refer,   95 boy,:
thought,   96 stood,   97 lost,: us,   98 odd,   99 'And':
lot,: be?,   100 nodd'!   101 he,: himself,   102 still,: seek,
103 lost,: lot,   104 appeard,: greek!   105 thus: : show,   106 suke,:
wrong: 107 time,   108 shepherds,   109 left: : loth,
110 employ!   111 both.   112 boy.   113 delight,   114 con;
115 whent,: way,   116 on.   117 round,   118 night,
119 change,   120 sight!!   121 quick,: away,   122 awhile,
123 call'd,: trey,   124 Boy,: out.   125 hill,: dale,: went,: night,
126 ground.   127 shepherd,: right,   128 pointed,: pound.
129 oer,   130 Joy,: breast,   131 fears,: doubts,   132 All,:
thoughts,   133 lost!: see,   134 griefs,   135 rouge's,   136 pin.
137 cause,: late,   138 plump,: plainly,   139 tale,: fate: 140 visit,:
joan.   141 much,: head,   142 But,: Fox,: sly,   143 patiently,:
said;   144 never,: reply.   146 down,   147 hat,   148 scarce,:
Crown.   149 dad,: taste,   150 barge,   152 buckles,: large.
153 coat,: hat,   154 still,: home,   155 ballad,: pat,   156 come.
157 things,   158 future,   160 hum.   161 Suke,: all,
162 scolding,   163 Bob,   164 Vic'try,   165 Turn'd,: tone,
166 seek,   167 torment,: stone,   168 dumb,   169 sight,
170 Disgraceful,: men!   171 would,: tight,   172 labour,: vain.
173 mend,: sen,   174 ive,   175 been,   176 too.   177 coat,
179 since,   180 out.   181 vain: : stroy,   182 hose,: will,

183 young,: boy!   184 always,: still.   185 ruff,   186 conduct,
187 determin'd,: enough;   188 rap,: rend,: more.   189 Thus,:
on,: wad,   190 too!   191 For,: mad,   192 He,: do.
193 spake,: mute,   194 try,   195 coats,: suit,   196 him,:
reply.   197 Ya,: fool,   198 me,   199 boy,: school,   200 power,:
show!   201 coats,: this,: that,   202 duke,   203 hear,: chat,
204 Money,: suke!?   205 point: : ya,: I,?   206 that,: else,: oer,
207 finder,: beguy,   208 never,: more!   209 This,: deep: : said,
210 striving,: o'er,   211 Wang,: platter,: head,   212 candle,:
floor,   213 him,: could,   214 other,: blind,   215 For,:
thought,: would,   216 way,: find!   217 deciev'd,: time!   218 lark,
219 He,: climb,   220 dark!.   221 spot,   222 he,: lain;
223 got,   224 "point,": again!   225 judie,: joint,   226 conceit,:
way!   227 say,: "points,": "point,"   228 money,: day!   229 will,:
care,   230 quite,   231 there,   232 match,: night!   233 drunk,:
think,   234 be,   235 drink,   236 not,   237 drunk,:
will,   238 fools,: suke!   239 once,: still,   240 duke.
241 "points,": "point;": song!   242 love,: play,   243 suke,: it,:
long,   244 morning,: day!   245 words,: triumph,: led!!!   246 quite
247 Muse,: head,   248 Victor,: fight.!

pp. 30–2 THE INVOCATION   1 glides,: streem,   2 oaks,: lonley,:
seem: 3 grove.   4 cause,?: near,   5 dear,   6 love.
7 loves,: trees,   8 loves,: breeze,   9 loves,: grove.   10 absent,
11 sighs,   12 love.   13 breeze's,: oak's,: streem,   14 thought,:
form,: dream,   15 herald,: prove?.   16 'yes,': scenes,   17 shades,:
greens,   18 Go,: love.   19 first,: addrest,   20 Perhaps,:
prest,   21 hither,: rove.   22 flower,: she,   23 press,: me,
24 fail,: love.   25 softer,: sweeter,: strain,   26 sweets,: complain,
27 move.   28 know,: fickle,: fair,   29 flower,: there,   30 quickly,:
love.   31 you,: breezes,: bland,: cool,   32 reed,: pool,   33 shake,:
grove.   34 waft,: lies,   35 nothing,: suprise,   36 truly,: love.
37 clouds,: flie,   38 Beneath,: skie,   39 And,: move.   40 fall,:
rain,   41 ear,: strain,   42 truly,: love.   43 night,: wear,
44 form: : there;   45 pillow,   46 shade,: eye,   47 name,:
sigh,   48 truly,   49 still,   50 else,: found,   51 Succesfully,
52 take: : alas!,   53 absent,: pass,   54 never,   55 bird,:
gain,   56 Reception,: pain,   57 thee,   58 ear,: fate,
59 soft,: mate,   60 truly,: love.   61 fancy,: lend,   62 assistance,:
friend,   63 might,: prove.   64 Go,: stream,   65 mood,:
dream,   66 truly,: love.   67 Then,: ask,: powers,   68 Enough,:
breezes,: birds,: showers,   69 flowrets,: grove.   70 O!,: way,
71 one,: convey,   72 truly,: love!.

p. 33 THE GIPSIES EVENING BLAZE   1 me,: scene,   2 present,:

hour;   3 Gipsies,: green,   4 nook,: power,   5 starts,
6 bushes,   7 keep:-   8 lost,: shines,: wind,   9 sybil,: reclin'd,
10 stick,: blaze,   11 sparks,: flaze.   12 view,: mind,   13 exclaim:
: prevades,   14 shades !.

pp. 34–5 TO MRS ANNA ADCOCK AUTHOR OF 'COTTAGE POEMS'
1 Sweet,: Songstres,: grove,   2 me,: strain;   3 faults,: deem,:
lays,: love,   4 trifles,: vain.   5 child,   6 roam,: dew,
7 'Poems,': me,: wild,   8 lustre,: view: 9 There,: rose,
10 wildness,: Simplicity;   11 sting,: knows,   12 bosom,: thee.
13 know,: impart,   14 lays,: court,: bestow,   15 breast;: heart,
16 pity,: woe.   17 fate,: alas,!: vain,   18 more,: doom,   19 ease,
20 hill,: bloom.   21 Thompson,: grief,   22 charms,: gaind,
23 Goldsmith,: relief,   24 Labour,: maintain'd.   25 Epithet,:
Child,   26 stores,: weave,   27 beauties,: wild,   28 kindred,:
grieve!

p. 36 SUN-RISING IN SEPTEMBER   1 pleasent,: air,   2 september,:
globe: 3 morning,: hedges,: bushes,   4 green,   5 rise,:
wood,   6 mantle,: lovley,: red,   7 spirits,: good,   8 stubbles,
9 beams,: scene,   10 Landscape,   11 is,: seen,   12 hours,:
warm!   13 poet,: world,   14 sence,: comply,   15 view,:
unfurl'd,   16 only: high!.

pp. 36–7 SONG   1 me: : swain,   2 Forever,: adore: 3 Tray,:
crook,: plain,   5 charming,: gay,   6 she;: despise,   7 me,:
far-away,   8 Quik,: valley,   9 contempt,: maiden,
10 Resolution,: vain;   11 kindness,: fuel,   12 serves,
13 reason,! : unknown,   14 fortnight,: change: 15 call,:
shepherd,   16 pleasd,   17 then,: fair,   18 meadow,: grove,
19 culled: : wove,: wreaths,: hair,   20 falsely,: love!   21 illusions,:
ease,   22 folly,: blind,   23 pleasures,: please,   24 erase,:
maid,: mind!.

p. 40 THE PISMIRE   1 insect,: small,   2 texture,: frame,   3 foresight,:
withall,   4 tallents,: fame!   5 raise,: hills,: plain,   6 mountains,:
thee!   7 crumb,: swain,   8 self,: strange,: me.   9 instinct,: cold,
10 gard,: winters,: power,   11 mite,: hold,   12 labours,: hour.
13 power,: Misery,   14 Pilghrim,: Eternity!!

p. 41 SONG   1 Brook, beneath,: willow: 2 shrubs,: glade.   3 cups,:
pillow;   4 retirement;!! blest,   5 heat,: came,   6 harm,: bring,
7 down,: flame,   8 slumber,   9 crook,: lay,   10 Rover,
11 things,: betray,   12 Collin,: flew!.   13 fear,: charms,   14 robe,:
breast,   15 Eager,: arms,   16 longing,: wickedness,   17 unconscious,:
fate,   18 Startled,: suppris'd,: feelings,: begun,   19 girl,: slumbers,:
late,   20 sweetnes,: Beautys,   21 Caution,: then,: maids,   22 boast,:

maidenheads,   23 trust,: florimel,: shades,   24 seeming,: lonley,: secure!.

pp. 42–3 SONG   1 Kittys,: now,   2 chance,: sight!   3 oft,: vow, 4 witness,: delight,   5 church,: spire,   6 bosom,: desire!   7 kitt,: delay,   8 Time,   9 sung,   10 along,   11 Echo,: viebriating,: strain,   12 back,: song.   13 rocks,: plains,   14 sound,: strains,   15 all,: roundelay,   16 Join,

pp. 43–50 THE WISH   1 gaind,   2 things,: crave,   3 Such,: strife,   4 happy,: life.   5 this,   6 contentment, 8 house,   9 hill,   10 south,   11 plan,: long,   2 roughly,: durable,   13 door,: suffice,   14 trifles,   15 oak,: roofing,: made,   16 slate,   17 slate,: thatch,: desire,   18 roofs, 19 wall,: roof,   20 convienience,   21 cellar;: found, 22 Wholesome,: cool,   23 fabrics,: load,   24 harbour, 25 Therefore,: rest;   26 ale,: oldest,: best,   27 strength, 28 welcome,: friend!   29 drone,: friendship,   30 stranger,: heart! 31 next,: pantry,   32 nourishment,   33 dairy,: joining,: pale, 34 situation,   35 window,: northward,: made,   36 elder,   37 far,: things,: compleat,   38 fair,: seat!.   39 parlour,: desire, 40 convinient,: fire,   41 season,: cold,   42 snuger, 43 pictures,   44 trifles,   45 fireside,: wall,   46 cubboard,: small,   47 breadth,: pland,   48 eightvo,: size,: more,   49 use,: made,   50 none,: authors,   51 Dermody,: Scott,: Macniel,: Burn, 52 Bloomfield,: Templeman,: Hurn,   53 authors,: power,   54 raptures, 55 them,   56 songs,: fail,   57 Bed,: prove,   58 appendage,: stove.!   59 in't,: air,   60 warm,: dry,   61 compleat; 62 kitchen,   63 this,: have,: coppers,   64 oven,: arch'd,: strong, 65 things,: nescesity,: plan,   66 shelves,: dishes,   67 trifles,   68 now, 69 these,: two,   70 quite,   71 one,: summer,   72 should,: orchards,   73 bed,: be,   74 those,   75 this,: shown; 76 friends,: kin,: own,   77 self,   78 lasted,   79 window,: east,   80 views,: eyes,   81 crimson,: sun,   82 trees,: journey, 83 moment,: higher,   84 increases,: fire,   85 times,: mist, 86 quuite,   87 shine,: dews,   88 time,: views!   89 Tree,: Wood,: Cot,: Spire,   90 after,   91 too,   92 production,: muse;   93 eves,: throng,   94 fail,   95 house,: excuse, 96 else,   97 preserve,: along,   98 roughly,: descent,: durable,: strong!   99 Pomfret,; endure,   100 pomp,   101 want,: explain,   102 useful,: nesessary,: plain,   103 more,: choise, 104 cot,   105 garden,   106 attention,   107 soil,   108 small,: great,   109 extreems,   110 throughout,   11 wall,: fence, 112 suns,   113 Walltrees,: row: 114 Peach,: Pear,   115 bed,: wall,   116 compleat,: trees,   117 seeds,: sallading,   118 Parsley,

119 Garden,: quarters,   120 taste,   121 walk,   122 exposed,
123 southend,: made,   124 summer,   125 rose,: jessamine,
126 virginbower,   127 these,   128 harbour,: smell!.   129 sit,:
agree,   130 pride,: scenery,   131 productions,: spade,
132 liberty!!: shade!!   133 spot,: flowers,   134 me,
135 books,: study,: bring,   136 Fancy,   137 time,: eye,
138 stragglers,   139 clean,: care,   140 weed,   141 thus,:
know,   142 trifles,   143 spot,: place,   144 plan'd,
145 plat,: eye,   146 week,   147 this,   148 level!,: green!!.
149 they,: flue;   150 flowers,: dew,   151 blush,: snow,
152 uniform,   153 ranuncullus,: fair,   154 perfumer,: air.
155 too,: dusk,   156 seen;: musk.   157 tree,   158 door,
159 wall,: place.   160 roses,   161 walk,   162 Exactly,
163 footsteps,: bower,   164 leisure,   165 again,
166 ornament,   167 pond,: laid,   168 nice,   169 side,:
freestone,   170 same,   171 Nymphea,   172 pool,
173 steps,: hour, 174 high,: power;   175 leaves,: lie,
176 Pleasure,: flye!.   177 happy,: controul,   178 prospects,
179 bright,   180 flight;: eyes!   181 vain: 182 mind;:
slave!   183 will,   184 wishing,: still!   185 For!: mind,
186 expect,: true,   188 wishing,   189 I: 190 Acres,
192 woods,   193 plains,: cow.   194 foot,   195 toiiling,
196 slave!   197 spring,   199 health: 200 torments,
201 will,   202 rises,   205 do,   206 morning,   207 right,
208 garden,   209 employment,   210 day,: renew;   212 spend,
213 read,: study,   214 life,   215 Unmaried,: Happy,   216 he,
217 enjoy,   218 belong: 219 torch,   220 needs,   221 assistance:
222 mistres,: conscern.   223 do,   224 seek,   225 made,:
proud,: meek;   226 fond,: witty,: books,   227 mind,: modest,
228 she,   229 fail,   231 desent,   232 me: 233 descency,
234 plus,   235 Beggar,: friend;   236 left,: spare,   237 always,
238 all,   239 these,   240 Save,: numbers,   241 standard,
242 wish,   243 Exit,!: grave!.

p. 50–1 EDWARD'S GRAVE   6 heard;   7 above.   11 pale.
13 winds,   15 rage;: Yew: 16 maid!   17 mind,   21 urgh'd,
31 up;   32 God!.

p. 52–3 MY LAST SHILLING   1 lot;   2 got.   3 willing;
4 sore,   5 shore;   6 shilling,: shilling,   7 shilling.
8 reflection,: store,   9 wore,   10 chilling;   13 shilling,:
shilling,   14 shilling.   15 corner,: pate,   16 shilling,: fate,
17 world,: sporting,: billing,   20 shilling, : shilling,   21 shilling.
22 answer,: store,   23 Question,:. : poor: 24 me,
27 shilling,: shilling,   28 call'd,: shilling.   29 reflection,: friend,:

all,   30 friendles,: stall,   31 trouble,: cheary,: willing,
32 Thee,: contrive,   34 shilling, : shilling,   35 shilling.
36 companion,   37 pockett,: sticthes,   38 thee,: willing;
39 now!   40 shilling!: shilling!   41 shilling!.

pp. 54–5 LINES ON WELLINGTON   1 cease: : doom,   2 cries!
3 he,   4 rise!   5 rather,: bewail,   6 choise: 7 hail,
9 cause,: mantain,   10 triumphant,   11 crave,   12 Land,:
Sea,   13 Element,   14 skilful,: brave!   15 dy'd,
16 more,   17 Nelsons:. : Name!   18 shore!   19 Nap,:
fight,   20 done.   21 thought,: night,   22 bring,: Sun!
23 knew,   24 boast,: more!   25 surely,   26 Nelson,
27 arise,   28 Clay!.

p. 55–8 TO THE MEMORY OF JAMES MERRISHAW A VILLAGE
SCHOOLMASTER   1 Remem'brance,: days,   2 Mem'ry,   3 pause!: :
grieve,   4 sadness,   6 Clown;   7 churchyard,   8 grave,
9 dust,: alone,   10 walnut,   11 branches,   12 sod,: muse,
13 kindred;   14 learning,   15 friendless,   16 this: 18 right:
22 grave,   24 vain:.   25 lay,: made,   26 attempts,: seem'd,
27 weakness:.   28 attempt;   29 language,: way!   30 boast,:
part;   31 origin,: heart!!   32 tempt,   33 reward,   34 succeed,
35 memory,   36 point,   37 reward,   38 without,: stone,
39 left,: know,   40 muse;   41 bier;   42 worth,   43 remains,
44 shade,: lay,   45 kindnes,   46 genious,   47 memory,
48 lay,: worth,   49 vain,: inspires;   50 she,: pursue,   51 flight,
52 worth,: memory,   53 was,   54 learning,   55 dear,:
destroy!!   56 taught,   57 evils,   58 taught,   59 pursuits,:
undone!!   60 Examples,   61 me:.   62 me:.   63 littlenes,
64 men;   65 debt;   66 arise:.   67 grave,: stone!   68 Learning,:
fame,   69 toils,   70 wreck,: regards,   71 rewards!   72 pursue'd,
73 shoots,: blossom,: bear.   74 labour,   75 man,   76 arts,:
none!   77 him,: son.   78 shore,: land,   79 notes,   80 depths,
81 windings,   82 Geometry,   83 figure,   84 Figures,:
symbols,   85 answer,   86 sing,: plan,: write,: read,   87 genius,
88 he,   89 grave,: stone!   90 this,: dear,   91 fate,
92 rich,: power,   93 scene,   94 way:.   95 praises,   97 Lines,:
odes,   98 now,   99 carry,   100 grave,   101 features,
102 muse,   103 adieu,: live!   104 verse,   105 deed,
106 perhaps,   107 basenes,   108 rich,   109 poor,: own!
110 Genius,: stage,   111 labours,   112 this,   113 fate,
114 poverty,   115 Grave,: stone!.

p. 59 ON BEAUTY   1 changhing,: frail,   2 skies,: showers: 3 Or,:
gales;   4 Or,   5 skies;: shades,   6 gales;: flies.   7 flowers,:
fades,   8 dies!.

p. 59–60 A CHARACTER   1 tortoise,: flowing;   2 show,   3 jet,: glowing,   4 sloe!   5 blushes,: morning,   6 lustre,: gay. 7 neck,   9 bosom,   10 make,   11 eyes,: lips,   13 height,: propotion,   14 defective,   15 conceal'd,   17 form,: fine,: tall,: slender,   19 Modest,: Obliging,: Tender,   21 Witty,   23 proficient, 24 Draw,: Write,   25 thou,: pursuing,   26 heart: 27 Maid, 28 aim,: dart!.

p. 60–1 THE POWERFUL SMILE   1 Collin,: frown!   2 Shot,: tower,   3 dart,   4 heart,   6 deigns,   7 emerging, 8 death,: life,: spring!!.

p. 61 TO HOPE   1 bestow,   3 clown,   4 Fit,   7 hope, 8 penitence,   9 proof,: hour,   13 far,   14 (Of: is;   15 chear'd, 19 balmy,: bland,   20 false,: true,

p. 62 AUTUMN   1 come: 3 All! all!   10 wish: 11 leaves: 12 fall!!.

pp. 119–21 ELEGY   1 death,: foe,   2 power,   3 instant,   6 clan, 7 band,   8 fit,: Angel,   13 toments,   14 anguish,   15 him, 17 sure,   19 begun,   20 more,   21 scenes,   24 companion,: dead!   25 green,   26 bank,   28 snailhorn,   30 surface, 31 bush,   32 hovel,   33 name,: life!   34 bridge,   35 rudley, 36 remains!   37 dints,: eventide,   38 scene,: woe: 39 rays, 41 scenes,   42 wheat-field,   43 corn-flowers,   45 days, 46 sports,   47 serve,   48 renew'd!   60 pain!

pp. 125–7 THE DISABLED SOLDIER   1 Neighbours,: men,   2 distress; 3 lie,: believe,   4 confess.   5 years,   6 mentain;   7 whereof, 8 brav'd,: main.   9 Battle,   10 stood,   11 flie: 12 Death,: Victory,: blood!   13 myself,   14 Briton,: name!   15 Limb,: gave,   16 turn,: same.   17 shine,   18 stumps!: side!   19 so,: mine,   20 pride.   21 loss,: abate,   22 was.: remains,   23 firm,: fierce,   24 Victory,: plains!   25 country,   26 again,: mentain; 28 field,: main.   29 mark,   31 once,: know,   32 Valour,: isle!   33 rage,   34 around,   35 exit,   36 Britton,: death! 37 death,   39 Field,   40 shouts,: Victory'!.   41 heart: 42 distress,   43 lie,   44 soon,: confess!?

pp. 127–9 THE DEATH OF MYRTILLA   1 plight,   3 relief,   5 roar, 7 nigh,   9 near,: chear,   11 brought,   13 crying,   15 morning,: dawning,   17 rain,   19 fate,   21 plain,: swain,   23 rain,: amain,   25 floods,: woods,   27 hear,: near,   29 lad,: clad, 31 wind,: designd,   35 sounds,   47 woe,   49 nigh,   55 grief, 57 severe,: hear,   59 love,: prove,   61 dead,   63 isles, 65 grave,: have,   67 here,: revere,

EXPLANATORY NOTES

p. 16 ON MR—LOCKING UP THE PUBLIC PUMP Cf. 'The Parish', ll. 436–46, in our volume for 'The Village Minstrel', where Clare expresses similar sentiments.

pp. 17–18 LINES WRITTEN WHILE VIEWING SOME REMAINS OF AN HUMAN BODY IN LOLHAM LANE Lolham Road which leads to Lolham Bridges.

p. 18 LINES TO BATH Taylor, in his Introduction to *RL*, describes a visit by Clare's father to the 'Sea-bathing Infirmary' at Scarborough where he found great relief from his rheumatism, but this is the only reference we have to a visit to Bath.

pp. 30–2 THE INVOCATION l. 5: Elizabeth Newbon. For Clare's account of his relationship with Elizabeth Newbon of Ashton see *Autobiographical Writings*, pp. 73–4. He still remembered her in early 1845 (*Later Poems*, I. p. 169) and in 1851 'remember me to . . . Betsey Newbon' (*Letters*, p. 681).

p. 34 EPIGRAM ON ROME Jacopo Sannazaro (?1458–1530) Renaissance humanist and pastoralist in Italian and neo-Latin. Cf. 'Epigram on London' pp. 458–9 above. We have not identified Mr Rolt.

pp. 34–5 TO MRS ANNA ADCOCK AUTHOR OF 'COTTAGE POEMS' Anna Adcock, *Cottage Poems* (1808). Clare, in a letter to Taylor, 19 June 1825, considered that, for his *Shepherd's Calendar* volume, ' "Cottage Stories" woud certainly have been a fair title & I think a better title then the Calender but it has been made use of by a Poetess here (at Oakham) name Anna Adcock who a little while back published a Volumn of very middling poems under that Title' (*Letters*, p. 333). L. 9: Cf. *Cottage Poems*, p. 10 'The Wild Rose', l. 2: 'The wild, the straggling rose'. Ll. 21–4: Thomson's *The Seasons* (1726–30) and Goldsmith's *The Deserted Village* (1770) were two of the main literary influences on Clare's earlier work. L. 25: Cf. *Cottage Poems*, p. 9 'Reflections at the Foot of a Hill', l. 28: 'Great God, thy child of nature hear'.

pp. 43–50 THE WISH Clare to Taylor, 2 Jan. 1821: 'The wish is earlyish I think about 15 [*i.e. 1808–9*] when I had got the knack of writing smoothly with little sense the line from Pomfret I got from a second hand vol of Miscellanies by "Werge" a man then (when his book was printed) residing at Stamford the authors I mention I had never seen them further then the title page—Hurn & Templman is bad bad stuff as I have since heard' (*Letters*, p. 131). L. 51: Thomas Dermody (1771–1803), *Poems* (Dublin, 1789), *Poems, Moral, and Descriptive* (London, 1800). Sir Walter Scott

(1771–1832). Hector Macneill (1746–1818), *The Poetical Works of Hector Macneill*, 2 vols. (1801). Robert Burns (1759–96). L. 52: Robert Bloomfield (1766–1823), *The Farmer's Boy* (1800), *Rural Tales, Ballads, and Songs* (1802). James Templeman, *Gilbert; or, The Young Carrier. An Amatory Rural Poem in Four Books* (1808). David Hurn, *Rural Rhymes* (Spalding, 1813). L. 99: John Pomfret (1667–1702), *The Choice or Wish: A Poem Written by a Person of Quality* (1700), *Poems on Several Occasions* (London, 1699). L. 100: Cf. ll. 11–12 of *The Choice*: '. . . and I'd ne'er endure / The needless pomp of gaudy furniture'.

pp. 54–5 LINES ON WELLINGTON 'I send the Sonnet to Wellinton for fear you sh^d have lost the other—if it is not like it (As I copy it from memory) you print it like the other—I could wish to hear of this Trifle being in M^r· Newcombs "Mercury" next week—this would be taken a Great favour—' (MS A3, p. 132). Drury responded that the Sonnet to Wellington was 'too ungrammatical' to appear in the *Stamford Mercury*, and Clare replied April 1819: 'Your Omission of the Sonnet in the above is not forgotten' (*Letters*, p. 9).

pp. 55–8 TO THE MEMORY OF JAMES MERRISHAW A VILLAGE SCHOOL MASTER By 1803 James Merrishaw was the schoolmaster at Glinton and Clare attended his classes in the church vestry. His burial is recorded in the Glinton Parish Register 26 Nov. 1809 and internal evidence points to a considerably later date of composition. C. Carr to Clare, 29 June 1822: 'His place of rest is a quiet and retire corner of the church-yard, at the greatest possible distance from the school room. I have directed his grave to be covered with verdant turf' (MS Eg. 2246, f. 66^r). There is another poem of the same title pp. 456–7 above.

p. 62 AUTUMN 'Autumn' appears among a list of titles of poems either 'Written or now Writing' included in a letter from Clare to Holland, Oct.? 1819 (*Letters*, p. 16), but as Clare used this title for several poems we cannot be sure that this is the one referred to here. There is a poem called 'Autumn' in our volume for 'The Village Minstrel' pp. 73–80.

pp. 62–4 O WHO CAN PAINT THE ANGUISH OF THE HEART In an undated letter to Holland (not included in *Letters*): 'You Hinted the Loss in "The Fate of Amy" of the Omission in that Dreadful Castrophy where the Victim take the plunge from this mortal Scene to *unknown* Eternity—I here send the scene from the tale now Composing—But as you say Kirk White has done it before me I am in great Diffidence as to its merit—. . . The period dont end harmonious enough to end happy but the whole is in its rough state & will undergo an entire Alteration' (Norris SAVNM CL/14).

pp. 64–7 LOVE EPISTLES BETWEEN RICHARD AND KATE L. 84: The *Helpstone Inclosure Award*, 1820, refers to Ley Close, a small plot of land adjacent to Rice Wood (Royce Wood).

p. 68 AN ANSWER TO M.L.A. M.L.A. is unidentified.

pp. 68–9 AN ACROUSTIC See note to pp. 30–2, l. 5 for Elizabeth Newbon.

pp. 69–70 SONG l. 9: See note to pp. 30–2, l. 5 for Elizabeth Newbon.

pp. 70–8 A HUNT FOR DOBIN OR THE FORCE OF LOVE ll. 212–15 also appear as ll. 49–52 in 'Dawning of Genius' pp. 451–2 above.

pp. 78–82 MY MARY Omitted from later editions of *RL* under pressure from some of Clare's patrons. It was not everybody's idea of a love poem and doubtless offended because of the crude vigour of its language, but it makes an interesting contrast with Cowper's sad lament in his 'My Mary', otherwise identical in stanza-form, rhythm, and refrain.

pp. 84–90 THE DEATH OF DOBBIN Cf. 'Death of Dobbin' in our volume for 'The Village Minstrel'.

pp. 97–8 SONG See note to pp. 30–2, l. 5 for Elizabeth Newbon.

pp. 99–101 ADRESS TO A LARK SINGING IN WINTER 'the address to a Lark was made one cold winters morning on returning home from raking stubble as the ground was so froze that I coud not work   I frit the lark up while raking & it began to sing which suggested the poem that was written in a mellancholy feeling' (*Autobiographical Writings*, p. 102).

pp. 102–3 TO THE WELLAND l. 22: David Hurn, *Rural Rhymes* (Spalding, 1813). L. 30: The birthplaces of Hurn and Bloomfield respectively.

p. 104 TO MR J. TURNILL For Clare's account of his friendship with the Turnill brothers, John and Richard, see *Autobiographical Writings*, pp. 39–41. John, born in 1789, was the elder and shared with Clare his intellectual interests, especially after the death of Richard, Clare's schoolfellow and first close friend. They were the sons of a well-to-do local farmer. John Turnill later became an exciseman and left the district.

pp. 105–6 THE DISSAPOINTED MILKMAID l. 35: Cf. 'To count one's chickens before they are hatched'. L. 36: Cf. 'Golden dreams make men awake hungry'.

p. 110 A MOMENTS RAPTURE WHILE BEARING THE LOVLEY WEIGHT OF A. S——R——S Anna S——r——s is unidentified.

pp. 113–14 A BEGGING ORPHANS ADDRESS TO A LADY l. 11: 'Overseer of the parish—& unfeeling wretches most of them are' (Clare's note in MS D4, p. 8).

pp. 119–21 ELEGY Clare to Taylor, 3 Sept. 1821: 'he was one of the earliest friends I ever had being intimate from childern & the first whose loss accostomd me to the lorn sorrows & feelings expierencd in departed friendship that comes with increasing substance of pleasures till it passes away in a lingering shadow of lonliness & misery' (*Letters*, p. 212). Richard Turnill was baptised 7 July 1795. See also note to p. 104.

pp. 127–9 THE DEATH OF MYRTILLA H.... B... is unidentified.

p. 130 WRITTEN IN WESLEYS PHILOSOPHY Clare's library at Northampton contains three editions of Bacon's *Essays* as well as Southey's *The Life of Wesley* (1820). 'Read in Southeys Wesley   he has made a very entertaining book of it but considering the subject I think he might have made more of it   the character of Wesley is one of the finest I have read of   they may speak of him as they please but they cannot diminish his simplicity of genius as an author & his piety as a christian   I sincerely wish that the present day coud find such a man' (*Natural History Prose Writings*, p. 204).

pp. 130–1 THE ROSE See note to pp. 30–2, l. 5 for Elizabeth Newbon.

l. 5: Proteus, a sea-god, who resided in the Carpathian Sea and had the power of changing his form at will.

pp. 135–6 TO AN APRIL DAISY One of the poems sent by Clare to Holland, mid-1819 (*Letters*, p. 11) which confirms the 1819 date.

pp. 137–8 LOBIN CLOUTS SATIRICAL SOLILOUQUY ON THE TIMES Lobbin Clout is a shepherd in love with Blonzelinda in Gay's *The Shepherd's Week, Pastoral* 1 (1714).

p. 141 ON LABOUR l. 1: Cf. l. 15 of 'Dawning of Genius' pp. 451–2 above.

pp. 142–7 A FAMILLIAR EPISTLE TO A FRIEND The quotation is ll. 1–4 and 17–20 of 'An Ode to Friendship'. See David Nichol Smith and Edward L. McAdam, *The Poems of Samuel Johnson*, 2nd edn. (Clarendon Press, 1974), pp. 36–9. Clare to Holland, early 1819: 'I return "Burns" . . . I have sent an Imitation (at least in the Measure no other ways I know of) of his familiar Epistles—I was charm'd with the Manner of Expressing his home spun thoughts & have attempted accordin[g]ly' (*Letters*, p. 5). Preceding the Postscript in Norris is a deleted note to Drury:

Mr Drury
This piece is sent for Insertion in the "trifles"—& in the Authors opinion crowns the whole—He cou'd wish its perusal by some Literary Gent:—who has read "Ramsay" & "Burns" if theres any Imita^tns they might be notic'd to him—but he is partly assured there is not the shade of an Imita^n to be found in it
So you do as you please

pp. 148–9 TO JANE — OF — IN THE MANNER O' BURNS The young lady is unidentified.

p. 150 THE SETTING SUN One of the poems which 'were begun when I was 14 or 15 & finishd & in some cases alterd throughout' (*Autobiographical Writings*, pp. 102–3), one of 'the earliest I ever wrote' (*Autobiographical Writings*, p. 98). This suggests 1807 as the year of composition. However, Clare was using MS A3 in 1819 and p. 57 gives '3 or 4 years ago' suggesting 1815. Perhaps it was first written about 1807 and reworked about 1815. Drury to Taylor, postmark 20 Apr. 1819: 'The first piece I saw was the

Setting Sun, which fell into my hands in the following manner. Thompson, of Stamford, whom I succeeded, was in altercation with a man about some books that he had bound for Clare; and during the wrangling I observed a piece of dirty paper, that had enveloped the letter brought by the man, had writing like verse on it; and picking it up found the Sonnet of the Setting Sun signed J.C.—Learning that it was most probably written by Clare, as his love of '*song writing*' was common talk and fun to the village, I paid the 18/- in dispute & sent home the books' (MS 43). '. . . his [*Drury's*] account of first meeting with the Sonnet to the Setting Sun in MSS is all a hoax, and of no other foundation then his own fancy: but wether a mistake or intended falsity I cant justly assert, but I am apt to imagine, what I am loth to discover' (*Autobiographical Writings*, p. 21). Clare included this poem in his 'Proposals / For Publishing, by Subscription, / A Collection of / Original / Trifles, / On Miscellaneous Subjects, / Religious and Moral, / In Verse,' printed by Henson in 1818. Few copies survive, but there is one in the Beinecke Library, Yale University.

pp. 156–61 HELPSTONE Clare may have started 'Helpstone' in 1809, when he was sixteen, and before the effects of the Helpstone Enclosure Act of that year were being felt; a certain reader 'H.B.', from London, however, pointed out the inconsistency of this date with ll. 51–2 which refers to 'twenty lingering years' and suggests that Clare was still working on the poem as late as 1813, when he was twenty. Barrell (p. 228) comments that 'If in fact the poem was begun earlier, this may explain the confusion in the poem's theme: the poem began in one convention, but after the enclosure was moved into the other.'

Clare comments on this poem in his MSS as follows:

Sir
I did not think of compleating "helpstone" but as I have I send it   I hinted to you that I had seen the "Deserted Village"   you may think I imitated it (I saw it as I have seen a many dipping in it here & there   I perhaps may have read a hundred lines   the "Parish priest" was what struck me) therefore to clear this & let you see I am not a plagarist I beg of you to compare them together & then the difference will be seen— my Imitations I may be proud of—I have never took a single line or Sentence from any but What I ownd too—' (MS A3, p. 32).

'The smile of the vainess of hope in the corister birds is best out with the rest that appertain to it' (MS D4, p. 11).

'I had great hopes in my fragment of "Helpstone" my native Village—that spot so belovd in my Infancy & as dear to me at this moment—I fancied it my Master piece (it may be) but my hopes are vanishd since I am told that Nat Bloomfield has far outdone me in a piece of a Similar subject— "Honington Green"   Your Information would be thankfully Rec'd' (Norris SAVNM CL/13).

ll. 177–8: Cf. ll. 95–6 of Goldsmith's 'The Deserted Village': 'I still had hopes, my long vexations past' / Here to return—and die at home at last.'

pp. 164–70 THE QUACK & THE COBLER Followed in Pfz by: 'The plan of these are my first performances—above is a true tale—but they have under gone an Entire alteration—In pieces like these they cant call me an Imitator as they are drawn from the Life—The "cobler" once was an Inhabitant of this place & the bungling descriptions found in the "Tale" are exact Portraits of his manners & Character'.

pp. 172–80 DOBSON AND JUDIE l. 92: See Leslie Shepard, *The History of Street Literature* (Newton Abbot, 1973), p. 111, quoting Thomas Holcroft: 'Even the walls of cottages and little alehouses would do something; for many of them had old English ballads, such as Death and the Lady, and Margaret's Ghost, with lamentable tragedies, or King Charles's golden rules, occasionally pasted on them.'

l. 200: 'then there was eastwell spring famous in those days for its spaws & its trough at the fountain were we usd to meet of a sunday & have sugard drink' (*Autobiographical Writings*, p. 30). Eastwell Spring never went dry and supplied the whole village in dry times. It had another purpose as the waters were said to have medicinal value, especially for eye troubles. At the different seasons the villagers came to drink the waters and hold some kind of seasonal festival there. They sweetened the water with honey and the place of foregathering became known as Golden Drop after the pale gold tint of the sweetener.

p. 182 THE PRIMROSE One of the poems which 'were begun when I was 14 or 15 and finishd and in some cases alterd throughout' (*Autobiographical Writings*, pp. 102–3). As with 'The Setting Sun' this suggests 1807 as the year of composition. MS A3, p. 58 gives '2 year ago' suggesting 1817. Perhaps it was first written about 1807 and reworked about 1817.

p. 184 CRAZY JANE This title is included in James Catnach, *Catalogue of Songs and Song-books* (1832) (see Leslie Shepard, *The History of Street Literature*, p. 218).

pp. 197–9 LINES ON THE DEATH OF MRS BULLIMORE Mrs Bullimore ran the local dame-school at Helpston which Clare attended from the age of five. He remembered her with affection in a letter to his son Charles, 1 June 1849 (*Letters*, pp. 663–4). The burial of an Alice Bullimore, widow, is recorded in the Woodnewton Parish Register, 27 Sept. 1798. Ll. 22–4: These tales would be among the '6py Pamphlets that are in the possesion of every door calling hawker & found on every book stall at fairs & markets whose titles are as familiar with every one as his own name' (*Autobiographical Writings*, p. 56).

pp. 202–4 ON SEEING A LOST GREYHOUND 'the Lost Greyhound was made while going & returning from Ashton one Winters day' (*Autobio-*

graphical Writings, p. 102). This poem would probably have been written between 1807 and 1809 when Clare was making frequent visits to Ashton to see either his friend Thomas Porter or Elizabeth Newbon.

p. 211 A PLOUGHMANS SKILL Linnaeus (1707–78), the Swiss naturalist and founder of the internationally recognized binomial system for scientifically naming animals and plants.

pp. 216–18 ADDRESS TO AN INSIGNIFICANT FLOWER OBSCURELY BLOOMING IN A LONELY WILD 'I love all wild flowers (none are weeds with me) affectionatly   there is a little white starry flower with pale green grassy leaves grows by woodsides & among bushes   I know not its name but it is a boyish favourite & the same that those stanzas address as "a namless flower obscurly blooming in a lonly wild" ' (*Natural History Prose Writings*, p. 23). Followed in MS A4 by pencil notes: 'You have the Liberty to make the Book as Large as you like print just what suits you—& in any form whatever—You seem to be fearful of Henson an Ignorant fellow like that is not worth notice—I care nothing about him'.

pp. 223–7 THE VILLAGE FUNERAL 'when he [*Revd Isaiah Holland*] first came to see me I was copying out the "Village funeral" to send to Drury & as he leand over my shoulder to read it he said "these are the things that will do & if they do not succeed the world deserves a worse opinion then I am inclined to give it but go on & be not cast down by the doubts or surmises of any one" ' (*Autobiographical Writings*, pp. 44–5). Followed in MS A4 by: '(Such pieces as these I hope will please you they are copied exactly from nature & Village manners—the pieces you mention as masterpieces where In my opinion reckoned as nothing & I even hesitated to send them—had I known my talent lay that way I would have made more use of it then what I have done—) (All I can send this Week) but I will make amends for it next—)'

pp. 228–34 THE LAMENTATIONS OF ROUND-OAK WATERS Round Oak Waters is the stream fed by Round Oak Spring, a natural spring in the south-west corner of Royce Wood.

l. 141: Richard Turnill, Clare's childhood companion who died of typhus. See also notes to pp. 104 and 119–21.

p. 234 ON DR TWOPENNY Revd Richard Twopenny (1757–1843), who was Vicar of Little Casterton in Rutland from 1783 till his death. In MS A32 Clare writes that Drury showed his poems 'to the Revd Mr Towpenny of Little Casterton who sent them back with a cold note stating that he had no objection to assist in raising the poor man a small subscription tho the poems appeard to him to posses no merit to be worthy of publication   Drury read this presious thing to me & as I fancyd all men in a station superior to me as learned & wise especialy parsons I felt my fortune as lost & my hopes gone & tho he tryd to cheer me I felt degected a long time & almost carried it too

far　after prosperity shone out upon me I rememberd it keenly & wrote the
following lines on his name & a letter which I never sent' (*Autobiographical
Writings*, pp. 101–2). Drury reported to Taylor, 5 May 1819, that he had
shown Clare's poems to Twopenny (MS 43). Drury to Clare, 26 July 1820:
'N.B. I have given old Dr Twopenny a little fillip just now, & I hope he will
be affronted by it, & then your epigram shall issue slap-dash on his poor
weak crown' (MS Eg. 2245, f. 189^r).

pp. 235–9 ALPINS HARP NEW STRUNG Alpin, Morar, and Ryno also
figure in an anonymous poem entitled 'Alpin's Lamentation for Morar' in
the *Boston Gazette*, 11 Dec. 1821, but this is unlikely to be Clare's.

pp. 245–6 ON THE DEATH OF A SCOLD 'the following was written on an
old woman with a terrible share of tongue who was actually married to a
sixth husband & survivd them' (*Autobiographical Writings*, p. 51).

p. 247 HOW OFT (WITH HAT PULLD OER MY EYES) Part of an unidentified
poem on the skylark.

pp. 248–50 DEATH OF THE BRAVE 'There is some difference in the Copys
but that you have got is the best' (MS A3, p. 92).

pp. 251–60 THE TRAVELLERS Followed in MS A3 by:

Sir
You may think I finish the story in an abrupt manner but in doing this I have no worse
a poet then Homer for my pattern his pieces I am told are left (as it were) unfinish'd'

pp. 262–3 ON THE DEATH OF A BEAUTIFUL YOUNG LADY Followed in
MS D4, p. 9a by: 'Let it pass under this title / On the sudden (& much
lamented) death / of a beautiful young Lady　If you think this fragment
worthy continuation (dont print it) but send me word & I w[i]ll compleat it
ready for another time'.

pp. 270–84 THE FATE OF AMY 'the fate of Amy was begun when I was a
boy　I usd to be very fond of hearing my friend J Turn[ill] read the Ballad
of Edwin & Emma in weeding time & as Amys 'story was popular in the
village I thought it might make a poem so tryd it & imitated the other as far
as the ideas of it floated on my memory' (*Autobiographical Writings*, p. 102).
Clare to Holland, mid-1819:

Sir
I have sent you the tale as promisd　I would have corrected it but repet[it]ions are
irksome & tireing & I could not set my self to it—you will excuse it
　　The verse you hinted—I have corrected in this manner [*i.e. ll. 157–60*]
　　As trifling Anecdotes are ever pleasing to Literary Curosity—I send you the Origin
of the tale—
　　I heard it related (some years ago) by an old Woman in this manner—"The poor
Girls name was Amy" said she "& as fine a Girl as ever was seen　she liv'd at
"Garners Farm" (now call'd) & at this time belonging to Mr Clark
　　But she was ruind by a base young man & went early one morning from the house

(half drest) (Curosity remarks her red petty coat which she had on when found) to the Pond below in the Close—which" says the simple Narrator "was call'd when I was a Child "Amys pond" & she lovd the fellow so much that she could not rest afterwards but was often seen walking round the pond in her red petty coat even in the day time!—till latley"—here the old lady ended [thu]mping her stick several times to the ground [to] confirm its reality & boasted her remembrance as witness You will see by this that I have deviated widely from the Original—I once (when a boy) had the tale in another manner as near to the truth as possible—under the title of the "Haunted pond" [*see next poem*]—it is now lost or I would have sent it—but this crampt the Imagination (truth in my opinion in poetry always does)—I therefore wrote it in the manner you see & gave my imagination free scope' (*Letters*, p. 13).

We suggest that Amy can be identified with Amy Levit, who in the Helpston Parish Register is described as 'Felo de See' and was buried without Christian burial 15 July 1722.

l. 121: The alteration in MS A3 suggests that Clare was drawing a comparison between his seduction of Patty and the seduction of Amy.

pp. 291–2 YOUNG NANCEYS WILLIAM FOR A SAILOR PRESS'D l. 2: The Royal Charlotte is unidentified and may be no more than a poetic convenience as in 'The Ship Charlotte' (*Later Poems*, II. p. 757).

pp. 295–6 'O DEATH WERE IS THY VICTORY!' l. 1: 'O death, where is thy sting? O grave, where is thy victory?' (1 Cor. 15:55).

p. 296 SUPPOSD TO BE UTTERD BY WERTER AT THE CONCLUSION OF HIS LAST INTERVIEW WITH CHARLOTTE Goethe, *The Sorrows of Young Werther* (1774), a semi-autobiographical novel, the story of Werther, a sensitive artist, ill at ease in society and hopelessly in love with Charlotte, who is promised to another. This novel, with the eventual suicide of the hero, caused a sensation throughout Europe.

pp. 298–9 THE MILLERS DAUGHTER This is finisishd you may have it when you please by sending fort—my glossary of the Scotch Lan^{ge} is too narrow—& I may be wrong in some o' the words (MS A3, p. 104).

l. 18: Alsie Crowther is unidentified.

pp. 302–3 IVE LONG BEEN URGD FRIEND FOR TO WRITE YE A LETTER l. 8: Presumably a reference to David Hurn (see notes to pp. 102–3). See also 'After Hearing Rural Ryhmes of W.H. praisd by a Lady' in our volume for 'The Village Minstrel'.

pp. 304–6 STANZAS ADDRESS'D TO M.C.M. M.C.M. is unidentified.

pp. 325–7 THE RESIGNATION Thomas Chatterton (1752–70) who tried to pass off his poems as old manuscripts and took his life at the age of seventeen. See 'Resignation. A Poem', Donald S. Taylor and Benjamin B. Hoover, *The Complete Works of Thomas Chatterton* (Clarendon Press, 1971), pp. 468–93.
'My mother brought me a picturd pocket hankerchief from Deeping may

fair as a fairing on which was a picture of Chatterton & his Verses on Resignation   chance had the choice of it . . . I was fond of imatating every thing I met with & therefore it was impossible to resist the oppertunity which this beautiful poem gave me' (*Autobiographical Writings*, p. 83).

Henson approved of 'a poem on the death of Chatterton which he wanted to print in a penny book to sell to hawkers but I was doubtful of its merits & not covetous of such fame so I declind it' (*Autobiographical Writings*, p. 98).

pp. 330–2 ON THE DEATH OF A QUACK 'the "Elegy on the Death of a quack" was written on a quack Docter who came to Deeping & whom the dupd people calld Docter Touch as it was rumourd about on his first appear[en]ce there that he curd all diseases by touching the patient with his hand which made the Villages round all anxious to know the truth of it   lame & blind & such felt a vain hope that he might be inspird & sent on purpose for their relief & Deeping was threatend to be as crowded with cripples as the Pool of Bethsheba   my Father & Will Farrow the shoemaker mentiond awhile back went over to Deeping directly on his arival there to assertain the truth & leave their infirmitys behind them if possible but experience put a new face on the story   the fellow did not cure them by touch but by blisters which he laid on in unmercifull sizes at half a guinea a blister & the money was to be paid down before he did his work   this last demand compleatly shook my fathers faith as to his mission for he understood that [the] prophets of old curd for nothing & he expected to see modern miracles performd in the same manner but when he found it was no such thing he & his companion refusd to have any thing to do with the medical prophet who was very importunate & even abusive at their credulity   when they returnd home & told their tale I sat down & wrote the following Epitaph . . . the fellow stopt at Deeping a good while for he found plenty of believers to mentain his hoaxing pretensions   in his bills he made a great parade against all knowledge & the faculty & made a boast of his ignorance by starting what he thought a better plea in making his patients believe he was born a docter by being the seventh son of a parent who was himself a seventh son & the seventh son of a seventh son is reckond among the lower orders of people as [a] prodigy in medicine who is born to perform miracles so he readily got into fame amongst them till 2 or 3 patients dyd under his hands & then on the turning of the tide he decampd in the night' (*Autobiographical Writings*, pp. 49–51).

pp. 333–5 A FEW HINTS TO A MAIDEN l. 41: Cf. 'Medlars are never good till they are rotten'.

pp. 341–2 EPITAPH ON MR C——LE WHO AFTER EXPERIENCING MISFORTUNES URG'D AT LAST BY DESPAIR PUT A PERIOD TO HIS EXISTENCE— The name in the title is a disguise for James Eastwell. Clare's margin note in MS A3, p. 95: 'If this Title is thought to alude too plain to the Late   Mr. D. may alter it as he thinks proper' [*the missing name has not been inserted*].

'in the bankrupt list of last september the Name of James Eastwell Bookbinder & stationer appeared & the world passed the name over in the common occurances of the day as a common matter   yet those who knew him never met with a deeper history of sorrow   he did not retire to a splendid mansion to live upon his means for he was left without a shilling with a wife & 2 lovely daughters (last september *over* [Saturday fortnight]) perished in gaol of a broken heart' (MS A42, p. 17).

pp. 346–7 DICKS OPINION Peter Pindar was the pseudonym of John Wolcot (1738–1819), author of *The Lousiad* (1785) in which he ridiculed King George III, Pitt, and others.

pp. 347–8 THE CONTRAST The prefatory quotation is untraced.

pp. 349–51 THE FOUNTAIN Margin note in MS A3, p. 81: 'This to be copied et literatum' 'the one on the Fountain was written one sunday evening while sitting bye a brook in Casterton cowpasture with patty' (*Autobiographical Writings*, p. 102).

p. 351 SO CHRISTIANITYS ENLIVENING LIGHT Note similarities between this rough draft and parts of such poems as 'The Setting Sun', 'The Moon', and 'O Death were is thy victory! O grave were is thy sting'.

pp. 357–8 JEAN BELL Jean Bell of Stamford is unidentified.

pp. 361–2 I SAW THE GIRL JUST TO MY MIND See *Deacon*, pp. 206–7, who does not use the MS A1 text. This ballad is connected with another beginning 'Dream not of love to think it like' which appears at Pet. MS A40, pp. 98a–99, Pet. MS B4, p. 32, and Nor. MS 18, pp. 19–20. Ll. 27–8 in the poem printed here correspond to ll. 11–12 in the later poem.

pp. 365–6 THE ADIEU l. 23: Walcot, near Barnack.

p. 366 GEE IS THY NAME THOU PRATING PLODDING CREATURE 'old Mr Gee who had been a farmer & who lived in a part of our house which once was his own' (*Autobiographical Writings*, p. 46).

p. 370 THE PAUSE BEFORE THE BATTLE 'Pause before the battle' appears in a list of titles under the heading 'Written in the Winter 1819' (MS A2, f. 11ʳ). 'Pause before the Battle' appears in a list of titles 'either Written or now Writing' in a letter to Holland, Oct. ? 1819 (*letters*, p. 16).

pp. 373–6 THE AUTUMNAL MORNING 'Autumnal Day' appears in a list of titles under the heading 'Written in the Winter 1819' (MS A2, f. 11ʳ) and in a list of titles 'either Written or now Writing' in a letter to Holland, Oct. ? 1819 (*Letters*, p. 16). We assume this is an alternative title.

pp. 381–3 OLD JOHNNY & DOROTHY CANNING Johnny and Dorothy Canning are unidentified.

pp. 388–92 EVENING 'Evening was alterd from a very early one of a great length made one evening after I had been cowtending on the common' (*Autobiographical Writings*, p. 102). See *Letters*, p. 8 for further details of Clare's 'Plagarising'.

pp. 392–3 WHAT IS LIFE? '. . . in one of these musings, my prosing thoughts lost them selves in rhyme, in taking a view, as I sat neath the shelter of a woodland hedge, of my parents distresses at home, & of my laboring so hard, & so vainly to get out of debt, & of my still added perplexitys of ill timed love,—striving to remedy all, & all to no purpose, I burst out in an exclamation of distress, "What is Life", and instantly reccolecting, such a subject woud be a good one for a poem, I hastily scratted down the 2 first Verses of it as it stands, as the begining of the plan which I intended to adopt and continued my jorney to work' (*Autobiographical Writings*, p. 19).

pp. 394–5 LIFE'S LIKENESSES We have already stated in the Introduction (p. xvi) that this poem appears anonymously in the *Stamford Mercury* and that it may not be by Clare. Arguments in favour, however, are fairly strong—resemblance in theme, wording, and stanza-form to 'What is Life?'; Clare is known to have imitated seventeenth-century poetry; the imagery is typical Clare (dew-drop of the morn, stone falling into the lake, bubble on the main); it is an unusually accomplished poem of roughly the same date as 'What is Life?' when Clare himself was in a depressed state and contemplating suicide. The words 'vermeil' and 'sojournment' may seem foreign to Clare, but they could be explained as a conscious attempt to imitate a former poetic idiom.

pp. 397–9 THE SUPRISE Clare to Drury, Apr.? 1819: 'This morning I have got the "Suprise" in a rough dress it shall be ready Friday Week' (*Letters*, p. 10).

'A Gent: hinted that a Scene neatly painted from the "Suprise" in the Simile of the Statue & given as a Frontispiece—would be striking & pretty & an advantage to the sale—the hint was for your Notice—I give it accordingly' (MS D1).

'This "ballad" has gaind the approbation of a Learned Gent:—in this sort he tells me I equal (if not excell) the several poets he has seen—& in the Rural Line he advises me to Continue—he Cautions me not to exert myself in proposd Subjects but follow the bent of my Inclination be what it will—I shewd him the *Crambo*—it was very well he said but Mr. M— was very much to blame to propose it—yours & J.C. (this Ballad popt in my head one night & down with it the next morning)' (MS Λ3, p. 86).

pp. 402–4 ELEGY HASTILY COMPOSED & WRITTEN WITH A PENCIL ON THE SPOT IN THE RUINS OF PICKWORTH RUTLAND It is tempting to believe that the pencil version on MS A3, p. 91 is the one referred to in the title. Clare's note: 'written on Sunday morning, after I had been helping to dig the hole for lime-kiln, where the many fragments of mortality and perished ruins inspired me with thoughts of other times, and warmed me into song' (*RL* Introduction, p. xxii). The kiln at Pickworth, one of Rutland's lost villages, was close to the 'Old Foundations' of a buried church.

pp. 405–7 NOON 'Noon which I wrote very early & composed on a hot day in summer while I went to fill my fathers bottle with water at round oak spring' (*Autobiographical Writings*, p. 102).

pp. 411–13 TO A ROSE BUD IN HUMBLE LIFE 'Under the Conscealment of the "Rose bud in humble Life" the author takes an oppertunity of paying a Complimentary Address to his favourite "Pa[tty o]f the Vale"' (MS A3, p. 97). However, the 'Queen of Walkerd' of l.40 may not in fact refer to Patty (from Walk Farm, near Casterton), but to an 'artless Jessy' (l. 37) from Walcot, near Barnack (see *Natural History Prose Writings*, p. 302, n. 8).

p. 415 TO INNOSCENCE 'Curosity led me to Peterbro' Sessions on Wednesday I had never been there before—nor am I now the wiser—I could not crush into the hall—Here while I mix'd among the gapeing crowd of Vulgar Spectators A young beauty of about 17 struck me with admiration—"O the charms of Innosence" wisper'd I "what A Captivating power!"—she was not daub'd with the roses & rubies of common beauties but her sweetness & simplicity of Countenance so charm'd me that a Few Verses "To Innocence" became the fruits of the Journey' (MS A3, p. 82).

Despite the information Clare provides, it is difficult to date this poem closer than 1819. Peterborough Quarter Sessions were held in 1819 on the following Wednesdays: 13 Jan., 21 Apr., 14 July, 20 Oct. The least likely date of the incident described by Clare seems to be 14 July when according to the *Stamford Mercury*, 16 July 1819, there was 'Not a single prisoner for trial', and perhaps the most likely 20 Oct. when John Clarke, William Ward, John Billings, and John Crowson, all of Helpston, were on the Grand Inquest.

pp. 419–24 THE LOVERS MEETING We have been unable to trace the *European Magazine* reference after the title.

'The Author (as the Learned reader will presently observe) being no ways acquainted with the Original is nescessarily obliged to Mr Dukes translation for his Imitation of whom he has borrow'd a few lines which are inserted in double inverted Commas this he hopes will in no ways disgust the reader or undervalue his humble attempt—J.C. This note may be printed if mr Drury thinks it of Consequence—for my part I think it might—& as such could almost desire it (tho in such matters I am always ready to agree with the opinion of my superiors' (MS A3, p. 116).

l. 68: The quotation is from Ovid's *Amores*, I, v. 29, p. 152 of Clare's copy of *The Art of Love* (1813), Item 323 of the Northampton Collection. See

Later Poems, I. 196 where Clare again makes use of this quotation.

pp. 424–31 THE AUTHORS ADDRESS TO HIS BOOK Clare to Drury, Apr. 1819: 'I am Likewise Composing the "Travels of the Book" In Three Cantos to be Pub: Seperate in Answer to the "Authors Address to his Book"' (*Letters*, p. 9). We have not traced 'Travels of the Book'.

ll. 61 ff.: 'This only will do—This only alludes to that Illetirate sect Called Methodists
Note printed in "Address to Book" Speaking of Religious opinions say— "Those Mushrooms &c" This only aludes to that Illetirate sect Methodists Where deciet & Hypocrisy wears the mask of Religion to advantage' (MS D2, p. 10, last three lines begining 'Speaking' deleted).

pp. 434–6 THE HARVEST MORNING l. 46: 'He that giveth unto the poor shall not lack' (Prov. 28: 27).

pp. 439–41 SUPRESSION OF A SIGH On the same page in MS A4 Clare has written, upside down: 1819 presumably working out his age. This date 26 could well refer to this poem and to 'The —— Recantation' (see pp. 441–2 below) written 1793 sideways on the same page, with a note ' "The Dissapointment" ready soon'.

pp. 441–2 THE RECANTATION See note to pp. 439–41.

pp. 443–4 CLOSLY CONFIND AMONG HUMDRUMING WHEELS Part of an unidentified poem.

p. 444 YE PROMISD ME MARY LAST MICHAELMAS FAIR Feast of St Michael: 29 Sept.

pp. 445–8 MIDNIGHT Drury to Taylor, 3 June 1819: 'Two pieces that I now send you are the best proof that his powers are as yet only *young*, "Midnight" was written one Sunday afternoon on his walk homeward. He had been dining with me, and as I bear in mind Pope's line "men must be taught as though you taught them not" whatever subject I wish him to write on I strive to impress it on his mind, by comparing my observations with his; Midnight, its solemnity, stillness, horrors, occupied our conversation that Sunday; the walk in the wood, the chill dew, scream of the hawk, Abbey ruins, Clock at distance striking midnight, were pointed out to each other as increments to the picture, and still further to raise his imagination to the brooding pitch I concluded our conversation by reading Penrose's Two Helmets which you must have read—it begins "Tw'as midnight!" &c. On his walk home he pencilled down on paper the piece I send you, & gave it me on the following morning: there were not more corrections than a cross through one or two syllables and two verses transposed, when it was copied from his book as you have it . . .' (MS 43). See also note to pp. 517–18.

pp. 451–2 DAWNING OF GENIUS ll. 49–52 also appear as ll. 212–15 in 'A Hunt for Dobin', pp. 70–8 above.

p. 454 WANTS YET ON EVERY SIDE AS DEEP SUROUND ME l. 13: Goethe's hero Werther whose name in nineteenth-century Europe became synonymous with self-indulgent melancholy.

pp. 456–7 TO THE MEMORY OF JAMES MERRISHAW A VILLAGE SCHOOLMASTER See the other poem of the same title pp. 55–8 above and note.

pp. 458–9 EPIGRAM ON LONDON Cf. 'Epigram on Rome' p. 34 above and note.

l. 9: Vitruvius Pollio, Marcus (first century BC) Roman architect and military engineer, author of *De Architectura* the only Roman treatise on architecture to have survived.

l. 10: Was Clare looking for a rhyme with 'North' since this and the next two lines are bracketed in the margin?

p. 461 IMPROMPTU ON THE BATTLE OF ALEXANDRIA IN EGYPT The Battle of Alexandria, also known as the battle of Aboukir, took place 21 Mar. 1801 and resulted in a British victory over the French.

pp. 463–4 THE MEETING The Yale letter reads: 'The Meeting is several months old & the one in the Book varies a great deal from my improved one, which I here send you, which is very little different however from what it was when first Written' (*Letters*, pp. 20–1). The Yale variants are probably Drury's.

'on the night we got into London it was announcd in the Play Bills that a song of mine was to be sung at Covent garden by Madam Vestris & we was to have gone but it was too late' (*Autobiographical Writings*, p. 130). 'The Meeting', set to music by Haydn Corri, was sung by Madame Vestris and was published as a broadsheet (see *Deacon*, pp. 64–7).

Drury to Clare, 4 Feb. 1820: ' "The Meeting" is most beautifully set to music by Haydn Corri, and will be sung at Covent garden by the first singer there, Madame Vestris. You shall hear the air played by Mr. Atter whenever you come over, for Haydn Corri has obliged Dubois with a manuscript copy' (MS Eg. 2245, f. 35ᵛ).

pp. 465–9 CRAZY NELL 'Crazy Nell was taken from a narative in the Stamford Mercury nearly in the same manner it was related I was very pleasd with it & thought it one of the best I had written & I think so still' (*Autobiographical Writings*, p. 103). 'Abounding in Scenes rather terific & the mind held so long in suspence before it comes to the cause will undoubtely suit most novel readers As their favorite books are in the same Class & as the End of the scene contains nothing—like them it is not worth finishing but better as it is—the End of Novels & Romances being but just comparison of Esops "Mountain in Labour"

The hint of "Crazy Nell" was taken from an Account (Some time since) printed in the "Mercury" or "Stamford News" I dont know which' (MS D4, p. 6, pencil). 'As you wishd somthing more engaging for the first Eds: readier Sale—I have done my utmost both in terrific & pathetic Scenery— in the two Trifles "Wagtails Death" & "Crazy Nell"   They are the extent of my abilities & I can do nothing better—' (MS D1).

Drury to Taylor, 8 Aug. 1819: ' "The Maniac" or "Crazy Nell" is so much in the style you recommend that I am greatly surprised it is overlooked; the story is founded on fact, & appeared in all the newspapers about 2 years ago—the descriptions are taken from nature—and the piece was written in the wood it attempts to describe. The wood-ridings, the anxiety of Nelly, the clap-to of the gate, the conversation between Nelly & Ben, the suspicions that there's mischief intended—tinkle of the tools— light, escape, & derangement from fear, are so truly natural, (and are all mentioned in the [story] that appeared in the newspapers) that I think you will change your determination & admit it in the book, if you again read it over with fairness' (MS 43). Searches through the files of the *Stamford Mercury*, *Drakard's Stamford News*, *Boston Gazette*, and *Northampton Mercury* 1814–19 have failed to identify the original newspaper story as referred to in the above passages.

pp. 470–1 MARY I DARE NOT CALL THEE DEAR Clare's relationship with Mary Joyce ended about 1815 so if 'years thrice three' of l. 23 is accurate the date of this poem would be about 1824. However, its autograph context suggests a date as early as 1819.

pp. 472–6 THE FAREWELL Mrs Emmerson to Clare, 7 Aug. 1820: 'In your proposed "Farewel" I hope you will "speak most feelingly"—it were indeed a subject, that, would prove "affecting" ' (MS Eg. 2245, f. 197ᵛ). 'The Farewell Written after being appris'd Of the Intention of Sending him to London For Improvment' (MS D3).

'If I go to London as I heartily wish I may I intend to treat you at my departure with "The Farewell" ' (Fitz). Clare's visits to London took place in Mar. 1820, May 1822, May 1824, and Feb. 1828. MS D3 suggests that his visit on this occasion was for health reasons and this would point to the 1824 visit, but its place in the Clare MSS makes the first date more likely.

p. 484 'MY LOVE THOU ART A NOSEGAY SWEET' Sent to Holland, mid-1819 (*Letters*, p. 11).

pp. 487–8 BETTY SELL Betty Sell was the daughter of a labourer at Southorp, near Barnack. '& while I was at home in the winter I renewd my acquaintance with a former love & had made a foolish confidence with a young girl at Southorpe & tho it began in a heedless [flirtation] at Stamford fair from accompanying her home it grew up in to an affection that made my heart ach to think it must be broken for patty was then in a situation that marriage coud only remedy' (*Autobiographical Writings*, p. 104).

p. 494 SUMMER l. 8: Cf. 'Make haste while the sun shines.'

pp. 494–7 MORNING WALK l. 17: Erasmus Darwin (1731–1802); Clare was later to possess copies of *The Botanic Garden* (1825) and the *Temple of Nature* (1824), and was an admirer of his poetry. L. 18: John Ray (1627–1705), *Wisdom of God Manifested in the Works of Creation* (1691), *Historia Plantarum*, 3 vols. (1686–1704).

pp. 498–9 THE INVITATION Recalling Clare's visit in Nov. 1819 to his house in Stamford where Taylor was staying at the time, Gilchrist writes in the *LM* for January 1820: 'he had not parted from us more than ten minutes, when his sensations were thrown into verse, and sent to us in the shape of a poem which he called—THE INVITATION.'

p. 506 SONNET Sent to Holland, mid-1819 (*Letters*, p. 11).

p. 507 SO NOW SAYS HE WEEGLING HOW MATTERS WENT WI IM l. 20: Cf. the proverb 'Love is the fruit of idleness'. Drury to Taylor, 8 Aug. 1819: 'John Clare has no objection against the piece called Betty Sell being added, but as Betty Sell is not a very reputable damsel, you will think with him that the name had be better "Patty Bell" or "*Fanny Bell*". Mistress Betty Sell it appears is a Cyprian, although that was not known to Clare when he saw her "jump the style" . . .' (MS 43). Clare's notes: 'Not to be printed in the vol' and in pencil: 'This is not to be in this vol.', and following the poem: 'I dont wish you to print this in the Vol: as it will offend my favourite "Patty of the Vale" There is plenty without it   you said I shoud have my humour by marking them not to be printed' (Fitz).

p. 511 TO REVD MR HOLLAND Revd Isaiah Knowles Holland (d. 1873), Congregational minister at Market Deeping from 1815 and then at St. Ives, Huntingdon, from 1820. Clare dedicated 'The Woodman' to him. See *Autobiographical Writings*, pp. 44–5 for Clare's account of their friendship.

Clare to Holland, Oct. 1819: 'I have a Sonnet adress'd to you but dont know whether it will come out in the Book this time   I have not a Copy or would Send it' (*Letters*, p. 17).

p. 513 MAN IN THAT AGE NO RULE BUT REASON KNEW This may be a quotation and not Clare.

pp. 513–14 I SAW A TREE WITH CHERIES RED, AS I WAS WALKING OUT ONE DAY As Clare was using this cypher-book from the age of ten these two arithmetical poems may be his earliest attempts at rhyme.

p. 515 THRICE WELCOME TO THY SONG SWEET WARBLING THRUSH ll. 11–14: MS D20 is an old Copy Book of William Clare's, Apr. 1841, with a woodcut of a chained felon with the sun gleaming through the prison grate and titled 'The Felon'.

p. 516 TO SUSAN ETHINNINGTON Susan Ethinnington is unidentified.

pp. 517–18 TO A COLD BEAUTY, INSENSIBLE OF LOVE Drury to Taylor, 3 June 1819: '. . . The other piece "To a Cold Beauty" was as hastily written:—indeed, I own it, that I thought Clare was not unassisted although I had received proofs enow to the contrary, & therefore once begged him to write on a set subject; describing a character whose conduct he was to imagine and dilate upon: he seemed to catch the pinch of the character almost at first word from me; I received in two days his composition which he formed complete as he lay sleepless in bed; in the morning he wrote it down & brought it early, so that the ink was pale: "thou *Image* of Beauty" is a beautiful expression indeed' (MS 43). See also note to pp. 445–8.

pp. 522–4 AH DOUBTFUL BARD PERHAPS IN VAIN l. 34: Longinus the name bestowed by a scribe's error on the author of the first-century Greek critical treatise *On the Sublime* which locates the sources of poetic excellence in the profundity of the writer's emotions and the seriousness of his thought.

pp. 527–9 SONG TAKEN FROM MY MOTHERS & FATHERS RECITATION & COMPLEATED BY AN OLD SHEPHERD Following the title in MS 25: 'This is an old Ballad which my father sings, he learnt it when a child of his mother who knew it when a lass, therefore it cannot be much less than 100 years old—John Clare.' See *Deacon*, pp. 83–90.

pp. 530–1 THE FOUNTAIN Drury to Taylor, n.d.: 'Clare desired me to send anonymously a little piece called "The Fountain" (not the one in the book) to the Literary Gazette; which request in my desire to oblige him, I complied with.' (MS 43). In *LG* the title is followed by: 'By a Northamptonshire Rustic.*' and the poem is followed by: '*So described by our anonymous correspondent, but too refinedly pastoral (we think) to be what "it seems"—ED.'

p. 531 TO HOPE Sent to Holland, mid-1819 (*Letters*, p. 11).

pp. 532–5 DOLLY'S MISTAKE See *Letters*, pp. 83–4 for Clare fulminating against 'false delicasy' occasioned by the omission of 'Dolly's Mistake' and 'My Mary' from the third edition of *RL*.

pp. 539–40 THE BATTLE 'The Man of My Chusing' has not been identified.

pp. 543–4 THE HIND THAT WERE CHOPPING THEM UP FOR HIS FIRE Part of a poem that has not been identified.

pp. 544–5 A SIMPLE EFFUSION ADDRESS'D TO MY LAME FATHER Sent to Holland, mid-1819 (*Letters*, p. 11). See *Autobiographical Writings*, pp. 15–16 for an account of Parker Clare's lameness and its effect on Clare.

pp. 547–9 'HOW D'YE DO & GOOD BYE' l. 25: This proverb is among a list of 'Old Proverbs' which Clare made in Bodleian Montagu MS Dc 64, ff. 23^r–24^v.

pp. 550–4 SUMMER MORNING In reverse BL, f. 39ᵛ Clare has written: 'most of the following Pieces are Juvenile written at 11. 12. 13. 14. 15 & none later   these are not intended for Publication'

p. 556 THERE WAS THREE RAVENS SAT UPON A TREE See *Martin*, p. 9 and *Deacon*, pp. 24 and 211. Unfortunately the BL text, written on the back of a note to Drury, was overlooked by *Deacon*.

INDEX OF TITLES FOR VOLUME I

Poems with no title other than *Song*, *Ballad*, or *Sonnet* are not included in this index.

INDEX OF FIRST LINES FOR VOLUME I